COMPLEX KNO

'*Complex Knowledge* is a thought-provoking, insightful, and deeply engaging exploration of the nature of knowledge in and about organizations. Not only does it offer a compelling critique of contemporary ways of understanding organizational knowledge, but it articulates a powerful alternative vocabulary grounded in such notions as situated practice, enactment, mutual constitution, improvisation, temporality, and creativity. Most importantly, it forces us – as researchers and practitioners – to take seriously the inherent reflexivity of our ongoing actions in the world.'

Wanda J. Orlikowski, Eaton-Peabody Chair of Communication Sciences and Professor of Information Technologies & Organization Studies, Massachusetts Institute of Technology

'*Complex Knowledge* shows just how important and rich is the emerging insight that organizations are systems of knowledge. Hari Tsoukas' deep, accessible probing of ways in which organizations construct, process, and justify their knowledge is a defining moment in organizational scholarship. It vaults the idea of organizational knowing to the top of the stack of explanations that work. An extraordinary mind is at work in this marvellous volume!'

Karl Weick, Rensis Likert Distinguished University Professor of Organizational Behavior and Psychology, University of Michigan

'Providing a comprehensive collection of Prof. Tsoukas' work, this book is an eye-opener for anyone who studies knowledge in organizations. Prof. Tsoukas demonstrates with clarity and brilliance, that knowledge is a complex construct that gives rise to new ways of understanding the very phenomenon of organizing. Highly recommended!'

Georg von krogh, Professor of Management, University of St.Gallen

'The long conceptual journey undertaken in the organizational sciences from a simple robotized view of man – a cog in a machine – to something more intelligent, more complex, and altogether more human, has been a long one. The studies described in Hari Tsoukas' exciting new book shows us that we may at last be nearing the end of the journey. The new world of organizations is one of complexity and change rather than one of order and stability – one that pays homage to Heraclitus rather than to Parmenides. In this dynamic and evolving setting knowledge is at a premium as never before. But what kind of knowledge? Tsoukas' exploration of this question leads him to link issues of organizational epistemology to the new theories of complexity. In doing so, he develops an ecological approach to the nonlinearities that characterize most of organizational life and that have been so neglected by more traditional treatments of organization. Tsoukas' book will be essential reading for those wishing to understand where the new science of organizations is heading for in the twenty-first century.'

Max Boisot, Professor of Strategic Management, Open University of Catalunya

'Not all of us can grasp the what and the why of the philosophical bits of the emerging knowledge management conversation – even though we know 'knowledge' is a profoundly obscure term. Hari Tsoukas is one of a small handful capable of illuminating how whatever we might mean by knowledge and its management hangs from our epistemological assumptions. The chapters in this book are clear-cut jewels, accessible and practical, grounded in deep philosophical study, and wide reading of the new literature on knowledge in organizations. We are fortunate to have Tsoukas to guide us – his incisive thinking and impish style shine brightly through the gloom and confusions of our theorizing about knowledge.'

J. C. Spender, Visiting Professor of Management, Open University Business School, UK

Complex Knowledge

Studies in Organizational
Epistemology

Haridimos Tsoukas

OXFORD
UNIVERSITY PRESS

OXFORD
UNIVERSITY PRESS

Great Clarendon Street, Oxford OX2 6DP

Oxford University Press is a department of the University of Oxford.
It furthers the University's objective of excellence in research, scholarship,
and education by publishing worldwide in

Oxford New York

Auckland   Cape Town   Dar es Salaam   Hong Kong   Karachi
Kuala Lumpur   Madrid   Melbourne   Mexico City   Nairobi
New Delhi   Shanghai   Taipei   Toronto
With offices in
Argentina   Austria   Brazil   Chile   Czech Republic   France   Greece
Guatemala   Hungary   Italy   Japan   South Korea   Poland   Portugal
Singapore   Switzerland   Thailand   Turkey   Ukraine   Vietnam

Oxford is a registered trade mark of Oxford University Press
in the UK and in certain other countries

Published in the United States
by Oxford University Press Inc., New York

ISBN 978-0-19-927558-8

Printed in the United Kingdom by
Lightning Source UK Ltd., Milton Keynes

In memory of Tom Lupton and Stafford Beer, and for
Alan B. Thomas and Richard Whitley, all of whom
were my teachers at the Manchester Business
School, University of Manchester, in the late
1980s—Thank you, gentlemen

ACKNOWLEDGEMENTS

THIS book would not have come into existence had it not been for OUP editor David Musson's support and encouragement. I cannot thank him enough. I would like to acknowledge publishers' permission to reprint or draw on papers of mine that first appeared in other sources (the original source of the papers is indicated at the start of each chapter). Thanks also to the co-authors of the jointly written papers, who gave me permission to include or draw upon material jointly published: Robert Chia, Mary Jo Hatch, Christian Knudsen, Demetrios B. Papoulias, and Efi Vladimirou. I would like to acknowledge the help of Jane Wheare, who did a splendid job in meticulously editing the manuscript and saving me some embarrassing errors. Thanks to Sophia Tzagaraki for her assistance with the preparation of the manuscript and her unfailing willingness to help, and to my wife Efi for tolerating my antisocial retreat into my cave when I needed it.

CONTENTS

FIGURES

TABLES

Introduction: Professor Bleent, the Floon Beetle, and Organizational Epistemology

It is the mark of an educated man to seek in each inquiry the sort of precision which the nature of the subject permits

(Aristotle, *Nicomachean Ethics*)

Science *probes*; it does not prove

(Gregory Bateson, *Mind and Nature*)

Life is a *process*, not a justification

(Stafford Beer, *The Heart of Enterprise*)

The *ethical* imperative: Act always so as to increase the number of choices. The *aesthetic* imperative. If you desire to see, learn how to act

(Heinz von Foerster, 'On Constructing a Reality')

[W]e are actually at the beginning of a new scientific era. We are observing the birth of a science that is no longer limited to idealized and simplified situations but reflects the complexity of the real world, a science that views us and our creativity as part of a fundamental trend present at all levels of nature

(Ilya Prigogine, *The End of Certainty*)

Our first intellectual obligation is to abandon the Myth of Stability that played so large a part in the Modern age: only thus can we heal the wounds inflicted on Reason by the seventeenth-century obsession with Rationality, and give back to Reasonableness the equal treatment of which it was for so long deprived [...] The ideals of practical thinkers are more realistic than the optimistic daydreams of simple-minded calculators, who ignore the complexities of real life, or the pessimistic nightmares of their critics, who find these complexities a source of despair

(Stephen Toulmin, *Return to Reason*)

Alongside [...] the experience of repetition, humans have a second experience, that of creativity. These two experiences are not incompatible, nor a matter of choice. We have both experiences, and both experiences are part of reality. Science, in its most universal form, has to be the search for 'the narrow passage' between the determined and the arbitrary

(Immanuel Wallerstein, *The End of the World as we Know It*)

THERE is a cartoon by Don Martin in Karl Weick's classic *The Social Psychology of Organizing* (1979) that I find myself often thinking about. Professor Bleent, an entomologist, sets out, along with his assistant, Miss Fonebone, to search for a rare insect, the Floon Beetle, which lives in the desert. This is a very rare insect: only one Floon Beetle lives at a time, and it comes out from the sand every 1300 years to lay just one egg! Having spotted this valuable beetle in the desert, Professor Bleent runs expectantly towards it, waving his magnifying glass, full of joy at being so unbelievably lucky as to have the chance to study this rare insect. As soon as he approaches the Floon Beetle he kneels in the sand, eyes wide open with excitement and curiosity, and puts his magnifying glass over the beetle. Alas, as soon as he starts examining it with his magnifying glass, under the scorching desert sun, the Floon Beetle is burnt. Professor Bleent's investigation has come to a sad end. His very object of study, the extremely rare Floon Beetle, disappears with a sizzling sound. The method of his investigation destroyed what he had long been looking forward to studying with such enthusiasm.

This is an insightful cartoon. Weick (1979: 27–9) refers to it to argue that it helps to 'know what you are doing'. He makes this point in the context of his critique of those obsessive quantitative investigators who, being so fixated on counting, are determined to get the organization into a countable form and, consequently, strip it 'of what made it worth counting in the first place' (ibid. 29). The broader issue, I think, is the extent to which our forms of knowledge and methods of investigation respect the complexity of the phenomenon at hand (Wallerstein 1999: chs. 10, 14). To put it differently, what are the forms of understanding and modes of knowing that will do justice to the object of study? How can organizational researchers avoid ending up in the position of Professor Bleent, whereby they oversimplify, caricature, and even destroy the phenomena they wish to know about? How can researchers' and practitioners' thinking ac-*knowledge* the complexity of a phenomenon without being paralysed by it? What are the complex forms of thinking and acting in organizations?

These epistemological questions have always been important, in one way or another, in organization and management studies (and the policy sciences at large), but they are particularly so today since, thanks to a number of technological, economic, and cultural changes in the last couple of decades, the idea that organizations can be usefully seen as *knowledge systems* has gained credence (Boisot 1998; Choo and Bontis 2002; Easterby-Smith and Lyles 2003;

Grant and Spender 1996; Newell et al. 2002; Tsoukas and Mylonopoulos 2004*a*). It is not only organizational and management researchers who, as professional enquirers, are concerned with knowledge, but organizational members too, at least if we take a knowledge-based view of organizations. Epistemology is the domain of all those concerned with knowledge, in all its forms.

Viewing organizations as systems of knowledge highlights the crucial role of human interpretation, communication, and skills in generating effective organizational action. Moreover, it enables us to move beyond the individual to explore the broader social basis—the social practices, forms of interaction, values, routines, power structures, and the organization of work—upon which individual knowledge and action in organizations draw. Seen from a knowledge-based perspective, the locus of individual understanding is not so much in the head as in *situated practice*. Accordingly, such a view opens up possibilities to explore how individuals, in concrete contexts of work, make use of tools, communicate with others in authoritative systems of coordination, and draw on institutionalized beliefs and cognitive schemata to carry out their tasks.

From a knowledge-based perspective, questions of epistemology—What is knowledge, how can it be obtained, and how can knowledge claims be justified?—are no longer the prerogative of philosophers and social scientists alone but of organizations too. If we see epistemology in Bateson's sense (1979: 246), namely as a branch of science concerned with 'the study of how particular organisms or aggregates of organisms *know*, *think*, and *decide*' (emphasis in the original), it makes good sense to want to study how organizations construct, process, and justify knowledge (Churchman 1971; Daft and Weick 1984; Krogh and Roos 1995; Mitroff 1990). An enquiry into organizational epistemology would be concerned, *inter alia*, with the following questions: What is organizational knowledge and what forms does it take? What are the forms of life within which different kinds of knowledge are embedded? How is new knowledge created? How do individuals draw on different forms of organizational knowledge, with what effects? What are the representational and social practices through which organizations construct and communicate their forms of knowledge? How are knowledge claims justified and legitimated within organizations?

An enquiry into organizational epistemology would, however, be incomplete without looking at organizations not only as users of knowledge but also as makers of knowledge claims put forward in the public arena. While it is important that we look at organizations from 'within' to examine how they construct different forms of knowledge and how they draw on them, with what effects (Tsoukas and Mylonopoulos 2004*b*), it is also important to look at organizations from 'outside' to explore how the knowledge claims they make are justified to external audiences, with what effects. This is especially important in the 'semiotic' (or 'digital') economy (Brynjolfsson and Kahin 2000; Lash and Urry 1994) and the 'risk' and 'network' society (Beck 1992; Castells 1996), since, in such a sign-rich, high-connectivity environment, organizations not only produce knowledge-intensive products and services, or draw on sophisticated forms of knowledge and expertise along their value chain, but put forward explicitly knowledge claims for public adoption. A company, for example, that claims its products or waste do no harm to the environment or, even stronger, that its products conform to certain standards of excellence, values, and ethical work practices, or that its policies are informed by certain conceptions of human rights and the common good is in the business of, among other things, putting forward certain knowledge claims, which, like all knowledge claims, invite further questions of justifiability. How are organizational knowledge claims justified to outside stakeholders? What conceptions of the public good do they assume? How are they rhetorically articulated and organizationally supported? How are competing organizational knowledge claims decided upon?

Epistemological questions may not always have as dramatic a quality as in the case of Professor Bleent's expedition, but they certainly involve questions related to requisite variety: Are our methods of knowing adequate for the task at hand? This applies both to practitioners and organizational researchers. Epistemological questions are not only social-scientific ones—namely, how organizations use, create, and justify knowledge—but also philosophical: whether methods of knowing employed by organizational members and organizational researchers are good enough. From a knowledge-based perspective, a focus on organizational knowledge is a focus on two levels: on the one hand, how practitioners in organizations use forms of knowledge to carry out their tasks and, on the other, how individuals, be they practitioners or researchers, think about organizational phenomena. At the first level the main question is: How do individuals in organizations know and act? At the second level—the meta-level—the main question is: How do individuals know what they know? How do researchers know what they know?

For Bateson, epistemology is not only a branch of science but also a branch of philosophy. 'As philosophy', says Bateson 'epistemology is the study of the necessary limits and other characteristics of the processes of knowing, thinking, and deciding' (1979: 246). As the study of necessary limits, epistemology involves exploring the limits to dominant forms of knowing—those forms I call, in several places in the book, 'representational' or 'intellectualist'—and how such limits might be overcome. Hence my concern here with investigating what may be called 'complex' forms of knowing.

An object of study is complex when it is capable of surprising an observer, and its behaviour cannot be reduced to the behaviour of its constituent parts (Axelrod and Cohen 2000; Stacey 1996; Taylor 2001). Complex social systems require complex forms of knowing; namely, forms of understanding that are sensitive to context, time, change, events, beliefs and desires, power, feedback loops, and circularity (Tsoukas 1994). Complex understanding is grounded on an open-world (as opposed to a closed-world) ontology, an enactivist (as opposed to representational) epistemology, and a poetic[1] (as opposed to instrumental) praxeology. A complex form of understanding sees the world as being full of possibilities, which are enacted by purposeful agents embedded in power-full social practices. As Winograd and Flores (1987: 33) point out, aptly summarizing the Heideggerian perspective, 'a person is not an individual subject or ego, but a manifestation of *Dasein* within a space of possibilities, situated within a world and within a tradition' (see also Spinosa, Flores, and Dreyfus 1997).

An open-world ontology assumes that the world is always in a process of becoming, of turning into something different. Flow, flux, and change are the fundamental processes of the world. The future is open, unknowable in principle, and it always holds the possibility of surprise. An enactivist epistemology assumes that knowing is action. We bring the world forward by making distinctions and giving form to an unarticulated background of understanding. Knowledge is the outcome of an active knower who has a certain biological structure, follows certain historically shaped cognitive practices, and is rooted within a consensual domain and sociocultural practice. A poetic praxeology sees the practitioner as an active being who, while inevitably shaped by the sociocultural practices in which he/she is rooted, necessarily shapes them in turn by undertaking action that is relatively opaque in its consequences and unclear in its motives and desires, unreflective and situated in its mode of operation, but inherently capable of self-observation and reflexivity, thus susceptible to chronic change. According to this view, a human agent is similar to a poet, who gives distinctive form to linguistic raw materials in often unexpected ways, but under the influence of past genres and current literary norms and the *Zeitgeist*, without being fully conscious of the process of creation and without controlling how his/her work will be interpreted by others and incorporated into further cycles of poetic creation and language change. A poetic praxeology acknowledges the complicated motives of human action, makes room for the influence of the past and its transmutation into new forms in the present, understands the relatively opaque nature of human intentionality, allows for chance events, influences, and feedback loops, and accepts the inescapable contextuality and temporality of all human action.

The studies published in this book focus on knowledge in Bateson's double sense of epistemology: as social-scientific explorations they address questions of how knowledge is used in and by organizations, and as meta-theoretical enquiries they address questions of how practitioners and researchers know what they know and how they may attain complex forms of understanding. The first sense is epistemology as a social-scientific enquiry, while the latter is epistemology as a philosophical enquiry.

What I find so attractive in the knowledge-based view of organizations is that it enables researchers to raise important questions related to knowledge in precisely the double sense mentioned above. The benefit is that, by so doing, researchers can show the recursive loop between ways of knowing and knowledge produced—epistemology-as-a-branch-philosophy is connected with epistemology-as-a-science. Moreover, practitioners' use of organizational knowledge can be recursively connected with researchers' modes of knowing. If practitioners are to cope with organizational complexity—how people in organizations interactively know, think, act, create, and change—they must be prepared to complexify their modes of enquiry (that is, complexify organizational epistemology). And if researchers are to acknowledge the complexity of organizational epistemology, they must try to complexify their formal theoretical explorations too. *What* we know and *how* we know are recursively linked. Researchers will not be able to understand and theorize how effective and creative action in organizations arises unless they obtain a nuanced understanding of organizational knowledge. And vice versa: a subtle understanding of organizational knowledge is possible if an open-world ontology, an enactivist epistemology, and a poetic praxeology are adopted. Like the Floon Beetle, the study of how practitioners know, think, and act requires a non-traditional mode of enquiry that embraces creative human agency, and acknowledges its inevitable historicity and its fundamental embeddedness in social practices.

Although the studies published here were written as independent papers, published in journals, as chapters in books, or conference presentations, there are recurring themes throughout them. These are: creative action, incessant change, process, novelty, the complexity of organizational life, the unknowability of the future, complex management, requisite variety, theory development in organization and management studies, complex forms of understanding and theorizing, *phronesis* and practical reason, and the relationship between thinking and acting, theory and practice, reason and praxis in organizations and in organizational research. If you see more than a fair share of references to Bergson, Dewey, Gadamer, Heidegger, James, Lakoff, MacIntyre, Polanyi, Toulmin, Taylor, Rorty, Whitehead, and Wittgenstein, it is because I find the work of these philosophers not only useful but highly inspiring. In pointing out the limits of Cartesian reason, they have helped us obtain, each in his own way, a more reasonable view of reason—reason as *orthos logos*—a view that avoids hubris, is aware of the inescapably social as well as embodied basis of all knowing, is reflexive, accepts agency and novelty, and takes account of the arrow of time.

If you see several references to the work of Bateson, Beer, Foerster, Maturana, and Varela, that is not only because these cyberneticians have provided a holistic account of human knowledge that resonates with interpretativism, but also because, in their search for wisdom, they have endowed us with an ecological understanding of the world. I am neither a philosopher nor a cybernetician but ever since I had the good fortune, at the Manchester Business School, to have Richard Whitley teach me epistemology, Alan B. Thomas methodology of social-scientific research, Stafford Beer cybernetics, and Tom Lupton socio-technical systems, I can't help thinking about organizations (and social life in general) in philosophical and cybernetic terms.

And if you find Konl Weick popping up on nearly every other page of this book, that is because I regard Weick's work as the epitome of thoughtful scholarship in organization studies, an enviable pursuit of creative explorations into organizations broad-mindedly informed by American pragmatists, European phenomenologists, social and cognitive psychologists, sociological constructivists, and systemic and evolutionary thinkers. It is the ecological, interpretive, process-driven orientation to organizations and organizational research that I find so stimulating in Weick's work and, in so far as I could, I have tried to incorporate it in my own work.

What Toulmin (1990: 193–4) has aptly called the 'ecological style' of thinking is how I would describe the underlying concern of the studies included in this book, and how I would invite readers to judge them. The ecological style seeks to embrace complexity rather than reduce it; it is sensitive to process, context, and time; makes links between abstract analysis and lived experience; is aware of the reality-constituting role of language; accepts chance, feedback loops, and human agency as fundamental features of social life; outlines the social basis of all human knowing and thinking, and the constructed character of knowledge; and highlights the inherently creative nature of human action. In pursuing an ecological style of thinking I have drawn eclectically on strands of ethnomethodology and sociological analyses of modernity, discursive psychology, Austrian economics, post-rationalist and process philosophy, and organizational ethnography. Although I find the pursuit of an ecological understanding of organizational and social behaviour exhilarating, it is for the reader to judge how well this eclectic mix hangs together.

Since this is a collection of papers, most of which were originally published in other sources,[2] there is inevitably some redundancy and several overlaps, although I would like to think this is not necessarily a bad thing, provided new insights are obtained. The extent to which this is the case is, of course, for others to judge. As far as I am concerned, I am not building a theoretical system in this book—I never consciously embarked on such a project in the first place. In retrospect, I realize that what I have spent time doing in the last ten years is to have explored a number of the above-mentioned themes, and now, looking back, I am noticing, and drawing readers' attention to, what has been my main preoccupation all along—complex knowledge.

Part I, 'Towards a Knowledge-based View of Organizations and their Environments', focuses on understanding the different forms of organizational knowledge and the forms of life within which they are embedded, the nature of tacit knowledge, the limitations of a purely information-based understanding of knowledge, and the implications for organizations if the latter are seen as makers of knowledge claims put forward for public adoption. In this part,

I explore the problems associated with a Cartesian understanding of know-ledge, which is predicated on individualist, asocial, and objectivist notions of cognition, and develop a perspective that highlights the inherently social nature of knowledge while, at the same time, allowing for the exercise of individual interpretation and judgement.

In Part II, 'Organization as *Chaosmos*: Coping with Organizational Complexity', I explore how we can think of organizational complexity in complex terms. By organizational complexity I mean those features of organizations that give the latter patterns but also unpredictability, order and disorder, stability and change, regularity and creativity—in short, *cosmos* and *chaos*. To think about *chaosmos* in complex terms implies the ability to maintain multiple inequivalent descriptions about the world, which is achieved, I argue, through narrative forms of knowledge.

In Part III, 'Meta-knowledge: Towards a Complex Epistemology of Management Research', I explore some meta-theoretical issues in organizational and management research; notably, the different ways of developing formal theories in management studies, focusing on strategic management research in particular; how the paradigm war in organization studies is pointless if theory development is seen as a knowledge-based practice; and I outline the way I would like to see organization theory develop as a field, following a largely Wittgensteinian analysis. Most of the chapters in this part aim at outlining what a complex meta-theoretical understanding of organizational research and theory development should look like, and the sort of issues organizational and management researchers should take into account when developing theory that seeks to embrace meaning, agency, novelty, and change, and intends to inform practice.

In conclusion, the challenge in organization and management studies (and in social science at large), it seems to me, is how to acknowledge the complexity of organizations without being overpowered by it. We are lucky today to have at our disposal insights from different disciplines that help us realize the 'ecological style' more fully than ever before. We need further work to refine our conceptual distinctions and build ever more synthetic theoretical frameworks by drawing on hitherto separate disciplines and theories. While intelligent practice should seek to avoid doing what Professor Bleent did to the Floon Beetle, smart thinking should take heed of Weick's wise advice (1979: 261): 'Complicate yourself!'.

Notes

1. Poetic is from the Greek verb *poiein*, which means 'to make'. Poetic praxeology is a form of action that is concerned with making and creating.
2. The original source of each of the papers included here is indicated at the start of each chapter.

References

Axelrod, R., and Cohen, M. D. (2000), *Harnessing Complexity* (New York: Basic).

Bateson, G. (1979), *Mind and Nature* (Toronto: Bantam).

Beck, U. (1992), *Risk Society*, trans. M. A. Ritter (London: Sage).

Boisot, M. (1998), *Knowledge Assets* (Oxford: Oxford University Press).

Brynjolfsson, E., and Kahin, B. (2000), *Understanding the Digital Economy* (Cambridge, Mass.: MIT Press).

Castells, M. (1996), *The Rise of the Network Society* (Malden, Mass.: Blackwell).

Choo, C. W., and Bontis, N. (2002) (eds.), *The Strategic Management of Intellectual Capital and Organizational Knowledge* (Oxford: Oxford University Press).

Churchman, C. W. (1971), *The Design of Inquiring Systems* (New York: Basic).

Daft, R., and Weick, K. (1984), 'Toward a Model of Organizations as Interpretation Systems', *Academy of Management Review*, 9, 284–95.

Easterby-Smith, M., and Lyles, M. A. (2003) (eds.), *Handbook of Organizational Learning and Knowledge* (Oxford: Blackwell).

Grant, R. M., and Spender, J.-C. (1996) (eds.), 'Knowledge and the Firm', *Strategic Management Journal*, 17, (special winter issue).

Krogh, G., and Roos, J. (1995), *Organizational Epistemology* (Houndmills: Macmillan).

Lash, S., and Urry, J. (1994), *Economies of Signs and Space* (London: Sage).

Leebaert, D. (1998) (ed.), *The Future of the Electronic Marketplace* (Cambridge, Mass.: MIT Press).

Mitroff, I. (1990), 'The Idea of the Corporation as an Idea System: Commerce in the Systems Age', *Technological Forecasting and Social Change*, 38: 1–14.

Newell, S., Robertson, M., Scarbrough, H., and Swan, J. (2002), *Managing Knowledge Work* (Houndmills: Palgrave Macmillan).

Spinosa, C., Flores, F., and Dreyfus, H. L. (1997), *Disclosing New Worlds* (Cambridge, Mass.: MIT Press).

Stacey, R. (1996), *Complexity and Creativity in Organizations* (San Francisco, Calif.: Berrett-Koehler).

Taylor, M. (2001), *The Moment of Complexity* (Chicago, Ill.: University of Chicago Press).

Toulmin, S. (1990), *Cosmopolis* (Chicago, Ill.: University of Chicago Press).

Tsoukas, H. (1994), 'Introduction: From Social Engineering to Reflective Action in Organizational Behavior', in H. Tsoukas (ed.), *New Thinking in Organizational Behavior*. (Oxford: Butterworth-Heinemann), 1–22.

—— and Mylonopoulos, N. (2004*a*), *Organizations as Knowledge Systems* (Houndmills: Palgrave Macmillan).

—— and Mylonopoulos, N. (2004*b*), 'Introduction: Knowledge Construction and Creation in Organizations', *British Journal of Management*, 15, (special issue), pp.S1–S8.

Wallerstein, I. (1999), *The End of the World as We Know It* (Minneapolis, Minn.: University of Minnesota Press).

Weick, K. E. (1979), *The Social Psychology of Organizing*, 2nd edn. (Reading, Mass.: Addison-Wesley).

Winograd, T., and Flores, F. (1987), *Understanding Computers and Cognition* (Reading, Mass.: Addison-Wesley).

I

TOWARDS A KNOWLEDGE-BASED VIEW OF ORGANIZATIONS AND THEIR ENVIRONMENTS

ONE

The Tyranny of Light: The Temptations and the Paradoxes of the Information Society

> In these dark rooms where I live out empty days,
> I wander round and round
> trying to find the windows.
> It will be a great relief when a window opens.
> But the windows aren't there to be found—
> or at least I can't find them. And perhaps
> it's better if I don't find them.
> Perhaps the light will prove another tyranny.
> Who knows what new things it will expose?
>
> (Constantine Cavafy)

THE advent of the 'information society' (or 'knowledge society') has been enthusiastically hailed by several authors (Bell 1999; Drucker 1993; Naisbitt 1982; Thurow 2000; Toffler 1971). A society in which a wealth of information is immediately available for use by anyone concerned seems to fulfil the modern dream of the knowledgeable individual who, freed from the shackles of ignorance, can think for himself/herself and can undertake informed, responsible action. Indeed, a society in which information has become the most valuable resource holds out the promise, or so it seems, of the realization of one of the most cherished values in the western tradition: the making of a transparent, self-regulated society (Brin 1998; cf. Vattimo 1992).

The assumption has been irresistibly powerful since the first days of the Enlightenment: the more human beings know, the more able they will be to control their destiny. Not too long ago, in *The Coming of the Post-industrial*

An earlier version of this chapter was first published, under the same title, in *Futures*, 29(9) (1997), 827–43. Parts of the original paper are reprinted by permission of Elsevier, Copyright (1997).

Society, Bell captured the optimism about a new society based on knowledge by asserting that the 'development of new forecasting and "mapping" techniques makes possible a novel phase in economic history—the conscious, planned advance of technological change, and therefore the reduction of indeterminacy about the economic future' (Bell, 1999: 26; see also Castells 1996, 2000; Kenney 1996; Makridakis 1995).

Of course, alongside the optimists there have always been the pessimists (Roszak 1994; Virilio 1997, 2000): those who, looking at the impressive technological developments of modernity, would prophesy a world dominated by machines and, increasingly these days, a world populated by *intelligent* machines, displacing ever larger numbers of people from work (Rifkin 1995), leading to the surrender of culture to technology (Postman 1985), and subjecting the population to Big-Brotherly surveillance (Dandeker 1990; Lyon 1994; Norris and Armstrong 1999; Rosen 2001; Webster and Robins 1989). The image of the ingenious inventor being ultimately haunted by his own artefacts has been a corrective to the unqualified technological optimism of the modern age.

Yet in this debate, rich and illuminating though it has been, elements of a more nuanced approach have been missing. It is not so much a question of hope versus despair as of an understanding of the simultaneously seductive and paradoxical character of the information society. As I will argue in this chapter, the information society is a society full of temptations: it tempts us into thinking that our characteristically modern desires of transparency and societal regulation will be realized through greater knowledge. But not any kind of knowledge will do; only knowledge conceived as *information* (to be precise, as objectified, abstract, decontextualized representations) is seen as useful.[1] This tantalizing dream, however, I will argue, is bound to remain unfulfilled. Like Tantalus, the members of the information society, much as they desire it, will not be able to taste the fruits of higher transparency: society will remain as opaque as it has always been, and in some ways it will become more unfathomable as well as unmanageable. The information society spawns paradoxes that prevent it from satisfying the temptations it creates. The light that the information society promises to cast upon itself may well constitute a new tyranny: the tyranny of radical doubt, of disorientation, and of heightened uncertainty.

The Temptations of the Information Society

Late modern (or postmodern) societies are marked by generalized communication. Indeed, the impact of Information and Communication Technologies (ICTs) on modern societies has been beyond anything imagined. The main feature of that impact is that ICTs have brought about 'the dissolution of centralized perspectives' (Vattimo 1992: 5), and the consequent proliferation of local rationalities. In a society where communication proliferates, diversity thrives; the hitherto marginalized cultures and subcultures of all kinds step into the limelight of public opinion—they become widely visible and audible.

To get a feel for the enormous proliferation of communication possibilities in late modernity it may be useful to take a very brief historical look at the effects of the development of communication technologies. Printing technology was developed around 1440. It is estimated that by the end of the fifteenth century something between 15 and 20 million copies of books and pamphlets were in circulation in Europe—an astonishing number compared with the 100 million people which was the population at that time of the central European countries where printing had developed (Thompson 1995: 55). In 1517 Luther's *Ninety-Five Theses* were distributed in a printed form throughout Germany in a fortnight, and throughout Europe in a month (ibid. 57). Although printing significantly enhanced the capability for generalized communication, the real impetus came only with the use of electrical energy. As Thompson (ibid. 154) notes:

the contrast with earlier forms of transport-based communication was dramatic. Up to the 1830s, a letter posted in England took five to eight months to reach India; and due to monsoon in the Indian Ocean, it could take two years for a reply to be received. In the 1870s, a telegram could reach Bombay in five hours, and the answer could be back on the same day. And in 1924, at the British Empire Exhibition, King George V sent himself a telegram which circulated the globe on all-British lines in 80 seconds. Rapid communication on a global scale—albeit along routes that reflected the organization of economic and political power—was a reality.

The advent of telecommunications has brought about the uncoupling of space and time and led to what Thompson (ibid. 32) calls 'despatialized simultaneity': it is now possible for one to experience events as simultaneous without being close to where they happen. In a society of generalized communication the world tends to be experienced as *information*; namely, as a collection of codified, abstract, decontextualized representations (Lash 2002). For example, one learns that there is war in Iraq, chronic unrest in Palestine, famine in Africa: the events reported are necessarily detached from their contexts in order for them to be processed and electronically transmitted to far-away audiences. To use Ryle's terms (1949), the 'knowing how' of those participating in the events reported is transformed into the 'knowing that' of those who, through the media, come to know about the same events. The experiential knowledge of the participant (or the participant observer) is turned into information for the curious spectator (Rosen 2001).

The temptation to view all knowledge in terms of information is considerably enhanced by the impressive development of electronic storage, processing, retrieval, and communication of information. Computerized databases allow both access to comprehensive information and instant retrieval of it—'information at your fingertips'.[2] The richness and interactivity of the Internet is perhaps the best example of the easy access to vast amounts of information. Having today such sophisticated technologies of information and communication, it is tempting for one to engage in *information reductionism*. It is possible for everything to be viewed as information (especially digitized information); namely, as some-*thing* (an object) that can be processed, stored, sent over, retrieved. Thus, in a modern hospital the sick person is turned into an information-rich patient. Information about his or her illness can be systematically gathered: the information speaks for—describes, represents—the patient. And ever since the British NHS computerized its files, a patient can be e-mailed, so to speak, from one part of the country to another (see *The Independent*, 5 June 1996). Likewise, something as complex as the quality of university education and research can be reduced to a set of 'objective' measurements and audits thought to represent it. In short, a set of indices is thought to adequately describe—to represent—the phenomenon at hand: this is the essence of information reductionism.

A society obsessed with information tends to conceive of communication in terms of what Reddy (1979) calls 'the conduit metaphor': ideas are thought to be like objects that can be sent through a channel of distribution (a conduit) to a recipient, who recovers them in their original form. As Lakoff (1995: 116) observes:

one entailment of the conduit metaphor is that the meaning, the ideas, can he extracted and can exist independently of people. Moreover [...] when communication occurs, what happens is that somebody extracts the same object, the same idea, from the language that the speaker put into it. So the conduit metaphor suggests that meaning is a thing and that the hearer pulls out the same meaning from the words and that it can exist independently of beings who understand words.

According to the conduit view of knowledge, the latter is thought to be identical with information and is viewed as a manual: if you want to learn about something, all you have to do is look up the appropriate entry. For us moderns information is conceived to be a collection of free-standing items; it is objective; it is 'out there'. Information-technology researchers push the modernist objectification of knowledge to the extreme and identify information with numbers. The late Dertouzos, former Director of the MIT Laboratory for Computer Science says :

[The Information Marketplace] rests on five essential pillars:
1. Numbers are used to represent all information.
2. These numbers are expressed with 1s and 0s.
3. Computers transform information by doing arithmetic on these numbers.
4. Communications systems move information around by moving these numbers.

5. Computers and communications systems combine to form computer networks—the basis of tomorrow's information infrastructures—which in turn are the basis of the Information Marketplace. (Dertouzos 1997: 317)

Notice the conduit image of communication underlying Dertouzos's view: all information is numbers, and numbers are moved around through modern communication systems. By decoding those numbers one (anyone) gets to see what they represent.

Since a particular phenomenon is thought to be the sum of the information gathered about it, the phenomenon acquires a shadowy presence that is defined by the chosen representations. Thus, for a credit-card company, Mr Jones is the sum of his transactions. To the police, the file held on him. To the shopping-mall security manager, what the closed-circuit camera has recorded about him. At the end of the day, who is Mr Jones? Answer: in a society turning everything into information, Mr Jones is the sum total of his interactions with, and behaviours in, certain institutions. As Poster (1995: 91) aptly observes:

to the database, Joe Jones is the sum of the information in the fields of the record that applies to that name. So the person Joe Jones now has a new form of presence, a new subject position that defines him for all those agencies and individuals who have access to the database. The representation in the discourse of the database constitutes the subject, Joe Jones, in highly caricatured yet immediately available form.

In the information society Mr Jones is a dismembered subject. Portions of himself, as manifested in his several activities, are scattered around in multiple databases.

What, however, the conduit metaphor of communication and knowledge ignores is precisely what makes human communication a distinctly *human* activity; namely, the presence of an information item presupposes an act of *human will and interpretation*. Information cannot be as neutral as, say, a planet or a stone: it is there because *someone* put it there. In short: information presupposes a purposeful subject (Lakoff 1995). Ordinarily, perhaps you would not necessarily be curious to find out how many acts of sexual intercourse take place every day all over the world. But if you headed a multinational company producing condoms, that information would be valuable to you, and you would be looking for it. Just as there is no database without a designer, so there is no particular information without a particular actor requesting or producing it.

Moreover, the purpose of the actor looking for certain kinds of information is not (it *cannot* be) made manifest in the information per se—it needs to be inferred. Thus, to reduce something to allegedly objective information and then treat that information as if it were an adequate description of the phenomenon at hand is to obscure the *purpose* behind the information, a purpose that is not made explicit in the information as such. For example, a credit-card company keeps a file with all the transactions in which Mr Jones has used his credit card. That information, of course, has a purpose. One such purpose may be to help the company decide whether Mr Jones is a trustworthy individual in the event that he asks for a loan or higher credit. However, as Lakoff (ibid. 119) remarks, 'that is not an objective matter. [Mr Jones's] trustworthiness is not information that can be in a computer. The only information that can be in a computer is whether a certain bill got paid in time, and things of that sort'. In a society of generalized communication, in which information is obsessively created and sought, there is the temptation to view information as having the status of an objective, thing-like entity, and as existing independently of human agents (Lakoff 1995; Rosen 2001).

If all knowledge is reduced to information—if, in other words, 'to know' means having information on the variation of certain indicators thought to capture the phenomenon at hand, our knowledge of the phenomenon itself risks becoming problematic. The quality of a social practice, for example, such as teaching, belongs to a dimension different from that of its manifestations in the form of certain indicators. Just as a cube belongs to a dimension different from that of its sides and the angle from which each side is seen at any point in time, so the quality of teaching is not the sum of its appearances. It is something that is presented through them all and through other possible appearances as well. We recognize quality when we see it—we *infer* it—but quality itself is not contained in any of the formal statements describing it, usually in the form of procedures and indicators.

Not only is the identity of a phenomenon different from its manifold representations—for example, the quality of teaching differs from indicators of quality; trustworthiness differs from the payment of debts—but the representations themselves are only a part of all the representations that could be brought into existence. Our information about a phenomenon is clearly constrained by the measurement and observation instruments (both human and technological) available. A bank statement is a particular description of some of one's actions, but it is by no means the only one available. There are many other aspects of one's life that are not captured through a bank statement. Even those aspects that *are* captured could be presented differently— who knows, one day our names and addresses may not be enough for a bank and our DNA profiles might also be printed. Our descriptions of the world are inherently incomplete. There always are more ways of thinking about the world than those in use at any point in time.

More generally, the presence of a phenomenon is surrounded by *absence*— what we know about it at any point in time, what is available, is a subset of what *could* be. Any phenomenon can be represented through other forms that may not yet have been stated or invented—indeed this is what is assumed by, say, efforts to continuously improve quality. In other words, phenomena are surrounded by the horizon of the potential and the absent. What we have available is a finite representation of something, never a complete one. As Solokowski (2000: 28) observes: 'The horizon of the potential and the absent surrounds the actual presences of things. The thing can always be presented in more ways than we already know; the thing will always hold more appearances in reserve'.

The information representing a phenomenon and the phenomenon itself are not identical—the map is not the territory (Weick 1990). Any phenomenon is given in a mixture of presence and absence—what is and what might be—and is thus inherently richer than information, which focuses on presence by revealing what is or has been. Notice that if all knowledge is reduced to information, the distinction between presence and absence is lost. Our notion of knowledge is impoverished, since to have knowledge of something is, among other things, to be aware of its *potential*—to have a sense of what it may become—whereas to have information is to be confined to the past, to what *has* been (Tsoukas and Mylonopoulos 2004: 4). The need to focus on potential—on how things could be different—is well understood by Argyris (2004), who criticizes organizational scholars for excessively focusing on the status quo: describing organizations as they are, instead of discussing how they might be.

This is not to say that the 'absent' is somehow objectively available 'out there', waiting to be discovered by the persistent researcher. There may be certain objective properties that simply escape our current information set but, importantly, since social phenomena are continuously reconstituted by human interpretation and action, their potential informational properties are indeterminate. Thus, the information regarding the number of, say, acts of sexual intercourse per year would not exist without government planners, condom manufacturers, and some voluntary organizations, in the first instance. What information is generated depends on who is looking for it and why.

A world that is seen as consisting of pools of information makes *social engineering* a very tempting way of thinking and acting. Foucault (1991) dubbed the kind of systematic action associated with social engineering 'governmentality' (see also Poster 1990). The latter, a distinctly modern mentality, is based on the conception of society as a malleable entity that can be rationally administered and steered, provided the authorities have the necessary knowledge to do so. What kind of knowledge might this be? Information, of course—census data, surveys, records, any decontextualized representation which, in a printed or electronic form, will allow control at a distance (Cooper 1992; Kallinikos 1996). Thus, the relatively recent proliferation of audits and league tables in many countries (especially in the Anglo-Saxon ones) is a testimony to the emergence of a distinct managerial rationality centred on the notion that institutional behaviour can be shaped if the right kind of reinforcement is combined with the generation of appropriate information (Power 1994). At any rate, the assumption is that if those in charge know what is going on, they can manage a social system better. 'To know' in this context means having information on the variation of certain indicators that are thought to capture the essence of the phenomenon at hand.

For example, we read in *The Times* (25 March 1992) that 'prison officers and psychologists are working on a computer database that will carry data on the populations of individual prisons including details of prisoners' behaviour, their records of assault against staff and fellow inmates, and any escape attempts. Prison staff will be trained to observe inmates more systematically'. What is the use of such a database? As a psychologist involved in the project explains, in the same article, 'it will give us a measure of an individual's badness, if you like. If you have a certain number of individuals with a high score, what we would say is "don't be surprised if you have trouble"' (ibid.). Likewise, data showing that about a quarter of the offences in the UK are committed by people under seventeen prompted the Home Office to launch a project whereby it will be possible for children as young as five and six years old to be identified as potential criminals, depending on the presence of certain factors that Home Office research has uncovered (e.g. criminal history in the family, truancy patterns, family break-up, etc.) (*Sunday Times*, 15 September 1991). It is worth stressing again the kind of reductionism that is presupposed by the mentality of social engineering: that which is measurable, standardizable, auditable, is measured and is thought to stand for—to represent—the phenomenon at hand (McSweeney 1994; Power 1994: 308). Thus, with reference to higher education in the UK, the quality of teaching (an inherently ambiguous notion) tends to be formally ascertained by the quality of the *procedures* that are thought to lead to good teaching. Procedural ideals of performance represent (and thus reconstruct) our understanding of quality. Notice, however, that, like 'trustworthiness', 'quality in teaching' is nowhere to be seen in the information gathered—it rather needs to be inferred from it.

To sum up, the information society tempts us into thinking in an objectivist manner about the world. First, the world, social and natural alike, is thought of as consisting of items of information—decontextualized representations—and we get to know the world through layers of abstract representations about the world. This is what I have called here 'information reductionism'. Second, information is seen through the lenses of the conduit metaphor: information is supposed to be objective and exist independently of human agents. And third, in an information-rich society social engineering tends to be the dominant form of policy-making: the world is thought to be rationally governable primarily through the collection, processing, and manipulation of the necessary information about it. In the next section I will argue that, contrary to the hope of achieving the ideals of societal transparency and regulation through the use of ever greater amounts of information, the information society is permeated by paradoxes that put off the fulfilment of those very ideals driving it. To simplify somewhat, the more tempted we are to see the world as transparent and tinker with it, the less likely we are to succeed.

The Paradoxes of the Information Society

More information, less understanding

The primary mode of human communication has historically been face-to-face interaction. In the information society the development of ICTs has ushered in new forms of social interaction, the main feature of which is their *mediated* nature (Giddens 1991: 23–7; Thompson 1995: 81–118). Two types of mediated human communication can be distinguished: *mediated interaction* and *mediated quasi-interaction* (Thompson 1995: 82–5). Mediated interaction involves the extended transmission of information in space and time through the use of a technical medium (e.g. telephone). Mediated quasi-interaction involves the production and transmission of symbolic forms for an indefinite range of potential recipients across space and time (e.g. television). The chief characteristic of experience gained through both types of mediated communication is its systematically *fabricated* nature. To understand why and how this happens, it is necessary to make use of some relevant sociological concepts.

As Goffman (1969: 109–40) argued, an act of human communication takes place within a particular interactive framework that involves certain assumptions, conventions, and physical features. Individuals acting within an interactive framework adapt themselves to its requirements and seek to project the kind of image they think is appropriate. This is what Goffman calls the 'front region'. Whatever interferes with the image sought to be projected is relegated to the 'back region'. In back regions individuals often knowingly act in ways that contradict the images they project in the front regions. As Thompson (1995: 88) remarks, 'in back regions [individuals] relax and allow themselves to lower their guard—that is, they no longer require themselves to monitor their own actions with the same high level of reflexivity generally deployed while acting in front regions'.

Although the distinction between a front and a back region is not always empirically clear, it is analytically useful. In restaurants the kitchens (back region) are kept physically separate from the dining areas (front region). In a typical telephone conversation the exchange between the two interlocutors is the front region, while the likely background noises and the body language of the two individuals are in the back region. Each interlocutor seeks to manage the boundary between these two regions. What happens in mediated interaction is the establishment of an interactive framework between agents whose front regions are separated in space (and probably in time), with each agent having his/her own separate back region (think, for example, of a telephone conversation). In mediated interaction the separation of front regions and the accompanying narrowing of symbolic clues available to participants, involves, in principle, the *fabrication* of experience, at least to a degree that is greater than in face-to-face interaction. As admissions tutors know all too well, it is easier to project the image you wish to convey over the phone than in a face-to-face meeting.

In the case of mediated quasi-interaction (e.g. television) the fabrication of experience is even more acute. As Thompson (ibid. 89) argues:

> symbolic forms are produced in one context (what I shall call the 'interactive framework of production') and received in a multiplicity of other contexts (the 'interactive frameworks of reception'). Each one of these contexts is characterized by its own regions and regional demarcations. Since the flow of communication is predominantly one-way, the front region of the framework of production is typically available to the recipients and is therefore a front region relative to the frameworks of reception. But the reverse does not hold.

In tele-vision, the separation of the interactive framework of production from the interactive frameworks of reception entails the absence of the reflexive monitoring of recipients' responses, which is a routine feature of the face-to-face interaction and, to a more limited extent, of mediated interaction (ibid. 97) This is quite important, for it means, among other things, that the traits of what is tele-vised are largely defined within the interactive framework (i.e. the front region) of production. Thus, in mediated quasi-interaction tele-presence becomes systematically fabricated at a distance (although it conveys the feeling of immediacy): persons become personalities (e.g. politicians, TV presenters); personalities become persons (witness, for example, the presentation, in popular magazines, of well-known soap-opera characters who are talked about as if they were real-life persons); events are turned into spectacles (e.g. the televisation of trials); spectacles become events (as, for example, when forms of social protest or unrest take place because of their potential to be televised) (Bauman 1992: 33; Thompson, 1995: 109–18).

Mediated experience is not only fabricated, but also *self-referential* (Luhmann 2000:16–17; Thompson 1995:110; Woolley 1992: 189–210). Media messages refer to other media messages, in an ever lengthening chain of mediated references. For example, Alan Langlands, Chief Executive of the NHS, remarked as follows: 'When I go round the country I am not just interested to know what the length of stay is—I am interested in infection rates, readmission rates, and just what life is actually like out there' (*Independent*, 19 June 1995). Notice that his interview (a media message) makes references to certain relevant indicators (which are representations; that is to say, mediated information items) and will probably be commented upon by other people in further mediated (quasi-) interactions.

The self-referential character of mediated experience entails that, in an information-rich environment, there is always a danger that one may lose one's sense of sense (i.e. the meaning of the information at hand) and *reference* (i.e. the phenomenon information refers to) (Baudrillard 1983; Kallinikos 1996: 42–5). The distancing from the tangible world that is effected through extended 'mediazation' tends to empty the world of its meaning and to weaken its referential function (i.e. its about-ness), to the extent that the question 'What for?' is often neglected or cannot he easily answered. As Zuboff (1985: 11) remarks, 'the central problem that confronts the person who must accomplish a significant portion of his or her work through the information interface is that of reference. People find themselves asking, "To what do these data refer? What is their meaning?"'.

In the information society the abundance of information tends to over-shadow the phenomena to which information refers: the discussion about crime easily slips into debating crime rates and spending on police; the debate about quality in education more often than not leads to arguing about league tables; the concern with the performance of hospitals leads to debating re-admission rates and other indicators. In short, the more information we have about the world, the more we tend to distance ourselves from what is going on in the world and the less able we become to comprehend its full complexity. Information becomes a surrogate for the world (Beer 1973); what is actually going on tends to be equated with what the relevant indicators (or images) say is going on.

Furthermore, in a society of generalized communication, as Baudrillard (1983) and Vattimo (1992) have aptly noted, reality is 'weakened'. The distinction between the real and the simulacrum is increasingly more difficult to sustain. The paradox is that, in such a society, the more information we have, the less able we are to understand what is going on. Since the world appears to consist of an array of images and is reduced to a repository of information items that are not systematically connected, it is exceedingly difficult for one to form an in-depth understanding of it. For understanding is based on the existence of a relatively stable hermeneutic horizon from which an agent may attempt to make sense of the world. As Gadamer (1975: 328) remarked, 'one of the conditions of understanding in the human sciences is belonging to trad-ition'; namely, viewing the world from a relatively stable standpoint (see also MacIntyre 1985: 204–25; Taylor 1985: 23–8).

To put it differently, understanding presupposes an Archimedean point, a perspective (undoubtedly an irremediably open-ended and evolving perspec-tive, but a perspective nonetheless) from which the world may be viewed, accounted for, and interpreted. Yet in the information society the sense of perspective is precisely what is eroded. When every 'fact' and every opinion is equally available and accessible, 'the nifty Web page of the Holocaust-denier can seem just as convincing as the rerun of "Schindler's List"' (*Newsweek*, 27 January 1997, 28). Just as a tourist's knowledge of a foreign culture is normally more superficial than that of an anthropologist who has studied the culture, so individuals, through mediated communication, find it extremely easy to satisfy fragments of their curiosity but difficult to form a coherent understanding of the issues they have been informed about. Ironically, abundantly available in-formation leads to form-lessness and, thus, to a diminished capacity for understanding.

More Information, Less Trust

As has often been noted by sociologists (Bell 1999; Giddens, 1990), a distinguishing feature of modern societies is the development of what Giddens calls 'expert systems' (Giddens 1990: 27–8; 1991: 18); namely, the significant growth of specialized, codified, abstract knowledge. Expert systems, remarks Giddens (1991: 18), 'bracket time and space through deploying modes of technical knowledge which have validity independent of the practitioners and clients who make use of them'. Expert systems permeate all aspects of modern life and are best exemplified by the work of professionals such as doctors, engineers, therapists, and lawyers. For expert systems to be used effectively, they depend on trust; namely, on those who benefit from expert systems to be able to place blind confidence in them. 'Trust', remarks Giddens (ibid. 19), 'presumes a leap to commitment, a quality of "faith" which is irreducible. It is specifically related to *absence in time and space,* as well as to *ignorance'* (emphasis added).

Expert systems develop their own esoteric languages, distinctive values, and particular practices that can be neither fully articulated (Polanyi 1962; Tsoukas 2003) nor completely appreciated or understood by those who do not practice them (MacIntyre 1985: 189). The practices of, say, treating patients, doing scientific research, teaching students, or providing legal advice cannot be adequately made sense of but by those who have been engaged in the respective practices. Just as the experience of driving through a place cannot be captured by reading a map, there is bound to be a knowledge gap separating those *participating* in an expert system from those *observing* it. A practitioner and an observer do not normally share the same form of life and, thus, neither do they draw the same distinctions nor do they attach the same meanings to what their statements refer to (Winch 1958: 40–65).

In other words, an expert system cannot be made fully transparent for all to see its workings; there is no detached Olympian high ground from which it may be inspected. Transparency inevitably presupposes a subject: transparent to whom? If this question is raised, one realizes that what the outsiders see (and the significance they attach to what they see) is not the same as what the insiders see (and the significance they attach to their experiences). There is an important knowledge asymmetry between a participant and an observer that cannot be removed by generating more information, for the particular shape of information reflects a subject's priorities, interests, and cognitive categories, all of which may be contested. However, the knowledge asymmetry may be overcome by creating trust between a practitioner and an observer (O'Neil 2002).

Yet it is the ideal of transparency that the information society promises to deliver. What, however, is not often realized is not only that such 'transparency' is illusory (as mentioned above), but that the very process for allegedly reaching it undermines the trust that is necessary for an expert system to function effectively. Making more information on an expert system publicly available entails creating more opportunities for conflicting interpretations, and so it is less likely for trust to be achieved. This happens because, as argued earlier, the decontextualized nature of information requires that it be placed in a context in order for the information to be made intelligible. Since, however, the context of the observer is different from the context of the practitioner, it is most likely that different, even conflicting, interpretations will be offered. To put it differently, the paradox is that the more information on the inner workings of an expert system observers seek to have, the less they will be inclined to trust its practitioners; the less practitioners are trusted, the less likely it is for the benefits of specialized expertise to be realized.

To illustrate this paradox, consider the proposal to allow closed-circuit cameras to be installed in operating theatres to monitor and record surgeons' likely mistakes. We read in *Sunday Times* (19 March 1995): 'The spy-in-the-theatre cameras have been proposed by Roy Lilley, chairman of the Federation of NHS Trusts resources committee, as a way to make operations safer, hold surgeons more accountable for their performance and provide documentary evidence if patients sue'. What is interesting is the language Lilley uses in order to justify his proposal. He says: 'Closed-circuit TV has made the world safer for pedestrians, passengers and shoppers, but not NHS patients' (ibid.). Notice the assumptions behind the analogies used: operating on a patient is like an individual crossing the street, taking the bus, or doing his/her shopping. What is missing from this account, however, is an understanding of medical practice as a complex social practice that cannot be recorded in the same way that the act of, say, a passenger validating his/her ticket can. A surgeon draws on a set of skills that are *collectively* sustained and applied; he/she takes part in a form of life that cannot be fully accounted for through an externalist perspective (Taylor 1993: 45–59). A camera records only what can be articulated, not what is tacit; it conveys only what can be seen, not what is taken for granted. A camera installed in an operating theatre does indeed inform an observer about some of what is visibly going on in there, but at the expense of trust, which is a *sine qua non* condition for an expert practice to be effective.

Indeed, as was reported in the same article in *Sunday Times* (19 March 1995), some doctors fear that faith in their work would be undermined if people discovered operating theatres were in reality relaxed places, often full of laughter and joking—some of it at the expense of the patient—and that intricate life-threatening surgery is being performed to the accompaniment of heavy rock music or streams of oaths at every unexpected gush of blood.

In other words, by being part of a form of life, a surgeon engages in practices that may not make much sense from the perspective of an observer, but they may be perfectly reasonable from the perspective of the practitioner. The patient sees the surgeon as primarily an expert, being normally ignorant of the context within which the surgeon's expertise is applied. The patient's trust in the surgeon's expertise is maintained, at least to some extent, in so far as several aspects of that context remain *opaque* to the patient. The practice of the surgeon listening to music while operating may be associated with carelessness by the patient, but it may be rather helpful for a surgeon spending eight or more hours per day in the operating theatre. The perspective of the patient (the observer) is different from that of the surgeon (the participant), and the two can be reconciled only when there is trust between them, which, alas, is undermined by the monitoring of the surgeon by cameras (O'Neil, 2002).

More Social Engineering, More Problems

A fundamental assumption upon which the conduit metaphor of communication and knowledge rests is that information is merely the mirror in which the world is reflected; or, as some philosophers put it, that language merely represents an objectively given state of affairs (MacIntyre 1985; Rorty 1991; Taylor 1985). The representational view of language is one of the pillars upon which the current notion of the information society is based (Tsoukas 1998). The idea is that since information reflects what is going on 'out there' in the world, if policy makers are to actively shape the world according to their desires and beliefs, they need to be collecting relevant information on an ongoing basis. The more (refined) information policy makers collect and the faster they collect it, the more informed decisions they will be able to take and, thus, the more effective the management of social problems will be—or so the argument goes. As mentioned earlier, this is the social-engineering model of policy-making and management (Tsoukas 1994).

While the representational model of language has its attractions, it is flawed in one crucial respect. The language we use to refer to the world does not merely represent it, but also helps constitute it (Gergen and Thatchnenkery, 1996; Tsoukas 1998). I alluded to this earlier when I remarked that information is produced by someone for a purpose and, in so far as this is the case, the information chosen to describe a state of affairs is bound to reflect the purpose, values, and priorities of its creator. Put simply: Tell me what questions you have asked, to tell you what information you have gathered.

As Wheatley (1994: 108–9) elegantly remarks, 'we do not exist at the whim of random information; that is not the fearsome prospect which greets us in conscious organizations. Our own consciousness plays a crucial role. We, alone and in groups, serve as gatekeepers, deciding which fluctuations to pay attention to, which to suppress.'[3] In other words, far from information representing a pure world 'out there', it is already implicated in its constitution.

What, however, is not often appreciated is the paradoxical implications of the social-engineering model of policy-making: instead of more information enabling policy makers to manage a social system more effectively, the reverse may occur. For example, the constant canvassing of public opinion may lead (particularly on occasions in which strong sentiments are held) to the impulsive passing of ill-thought-out legislation, as well as to factionalism. Also, the temptation of social engineering may lead to oscillatory management. In short, to put it somewhat crudely, the more information we have, the more ineffective we may become in managing important social problems. Let me try below to illustrate this claim with two examples, one drawn from the USA, the other from the UK.

(1) In an illuminating article in *Time*, Wright (1995) argued that in a 'hyperdemocracy'—the political system in which information about the mood of public opinion is constantly sought and fed back to policy makers—as many (or even more) problems are spawned as are solved. As Wright shows, the passing of the 'three strikes and you're out' law is a good example of how a poorly conceived law, widely criticized by both sides of the political spectrum, was hastily enacted after a hideous crime took place in California. That criminal incident was widely reported in the media, and extensive public reactions to it were swiftly organized mostly via phone-in radio talk shows.

If the impulsive passing of dubious laws is a relatively limited side effect of the pervasive use of ICTs, the weakening of the notion of 'public interest' is a more subtle and, potentially, more pernicious problem. The information society makes instant communication widely available, thus allowing ever increasing numbers of people to organize themselves, overcoming the constraints of space and time. The phenomenal growth of organizations lobbying policy makers in order to secure benefits for their members owes a lot to the development of ICTs. Whether in the form of subsidies for farmers, tax breaks for shopkeepers, or new taxes for the environment, the American government (which means the American public) is asked to pay more for the benefit of the few. Thus, as Wright (ibid. 41) illustrates,

when in February 1993 President Clinton proposed an energy tax that was hailed by economists and environmentalists, something called the Energy Tax Policy Alliance paid for a fatal multimedia campaign. When he suggested in the same budget plan cutting the business-lunch deduction from 80% to 50%, it was the National Restaurant Association that stirred to action, sending local TV stations satellite feeds of busboys and waitresses fretting about their imperiled jobs.

The paradox is that information, rationally processed, leads to the hijacking of public interest by special interests. Notice that this is a perfectly rational way of thinking: it is in the interest of a particular group to try to spread the cost of its demands across all taxpayers, while capturing all the benefits. This is a classic case of the Prisoner's Dilemma (see Hargreaves Heap et al. 1992: 244): 'though every group might prosper in the long run if all groups surrendered just enough to balance the budget, it makes no sense for any of them to surrender unilaterally' (Wright 1995: 41). Instantly available information facilitates factional political mobilization and obscures the public good which, as a regulative principle, underlies the governance of a liberal democratic society. Instead of abundant information helping to sustain the idea of the 'public interest', it often helps dissolve it into a sea of private interests.

Another side effect of hyperdemocracy is that it turns leaders into followers: find out what the population thinks and play to that tune. As Wright (ibid. 42) pithily notes, 'politics is pandering in a hyperdemocracy; to lead is to follow'. Of course, the electorate knows this, and this is one reason it thinks politicians are spineless and have no convictions. Hence another paradox: 'the voters demand slavish obedience, but the more they receive it, the less they respect it' (ibid. 42). By merely following public opinion, leaders may be missing opportunities to shape and educate it—the leader ceases to be a role model and a pedagogue, a special person for the followers to look up to, thus becoming the impoverished figure of a mere administrator. Paradoxically, although in the Babylonian confusion of the information society the population expects leadership, in a hyperdemocracy it receives, instead, followership.

(2) Since 1993 each local authority in England and Wales has had to publish in the local press 152 performance indicators covering a variety of issues of local concern, from how accessible public buildings are to people in wheelchairs to the number of potholes in their area. The Audit Commission collates the information nationally and produces a national league table. Allowing citizens to compare the indicators over time and across the country, the objective of this exercise is to make councils' performance transparent and, thus, offer them an incentive to improve their services. The idea is that an informed electorate would be able to use their votes to reprimand underperforming councils (see *The Economist*, 19 September 1992).

What, however, is underestimated in exercises of this kind is the constitutive (as opposed to merely representational) character of language (and thus of information). Indicators are supposed to represent a true and objective reality (i.e. councils' performance). But what is often ignored is that the very same reality is crucially shaped by the indicators. The reason is simple. Councils are bound to want to look good in the league table, for numbers matter a lot in politics. Wanting to look good in the league table, councils may thus choose to abandon sensible policies if they think that they do not give councils a high enough profile, opting instead for policies that will enhance a council's standing in the league table.

Although I am not aware of empirical research on the extent to and the ways in which league tables have influenced the behaviour of councils in the UK, there has been rigorous empirical research with regard to the impact of health-care report cards on resources use and health outcomes in the USA. Health-care report cards publicly provide information about the performance of hospitals, physicians, and patient health outcomes. The idea is that in a health-care market the public disclosure of information on health outcomes relating to physicians and hospitals would enable patients to make better-informed hospital choices and to give medical-care providers the incentive to make appropriate investments in delivering better care.

Using national data on Medicare patients at risk for cardiac surgery, Dranove et al. (2002) found that the introduction of cardiac-surgery report cards in New York and Pennsylvania led to increased sorting of patients to providers and increased selection of patients by providers. Specifically, report cards led to an improved matching of patients with hospitals—the proportion of iller cardiac patients who were treated at teaching hospitals, arguably better equipped to handle such complex cases, increased. At the same time, however, report cards led medical-care providers to shift surgical treatment for cardiac illness toward healthier patients.

The net effect of the disclosure of information through cardiac-surgery report cards was that the latter led to higher levels of Medicare hospital expenditures and worse health outcomes, especially for iller patients. The benefit of increased sorting of patients to providers on the basis of the severity of their illness was offset by providers engaging in increased selection. As the authors remark, 'mandatory reporting mechanisms inevitably give providers the incentive to decline to treat more difficult and complicated cases' (ibid. 17). Moreover, distinguishing between, on the one hand, the *medical* problem of caring for ill cardiac patients on the basis of the complex knowledge possessed by medical practitioners, and, on the other, the *managerial* problem of scoring high on report cards on the basis of the less complex knowledge possessed by the developers of report cards, Dranove et al. (ibid. 2) remark as follows:

It is essential for the analysts who create report cards to adjust health outcomes for differences in patient characteristics ('risk adjustment'), for otherwise providers who treat the most serious cases necessarily appear to have low quality. But analysts can only adjust for characteristics that they can observe. Unfortunately, because of the complexity of patient care, providers are likely to have better information on patients' conditions than even the most clinically detailed database. For this reason, providers may be able to improve their ranking by selecting patients on the basis of characteristics that are unobservable to the analysts but predictive of good outcomes.

In other words, the public disclosure of information per se does not necessarily lead to better outcomes. The abundance of information risks converting real complex problems (namely problems about, say, improving health care or teaching, or treating homelessness, all of which involve the effective organization of collective practices) into informational-cum-managerial ones that encourage 'gaming' behaviour.

To see why this may happen, let us return to the earlier example of the performance indicators used in local authorities. Imagine the case of a council in which elderly residents would rather have a deep freeze and a microwave than have their food delivered to them daily by home helps. As Margaret Hodge, at that time Vice-Chairman of the Association of Metropolitan Authorities noted, 'If the authority responds to what people want and cuts down on home helps it will look terrible in the league table, which merely asks how many home helps there are per thousand of population. It could be tempted to abandon its policy and hire more home helps simply for the sake of appearances' (*Independent*, 11 September 1992).

The paradox here is that a system invented to make councils more responsive to their citizens may actually achieve the reverse. The more elderly residents demand a bespoke solution to their demands for daily food, the more a council is likely to respond by using home helps (that is, by not meeting their demands). In other words, if the elderly residents' demands are met, then they are not 'met'; if they are 'met', then they are not met—the paradox turns into an oscillation.

This paradox is created because of a confusion of logical levels (Watzlawick et al. 1974: 62–73). One logical level is that of the elderly residents' *real* demands (that is, what they want: a deep-freeze and a microwave). A logically higher level is that of elderly residents' demands as these are *represented* by (or reduced to) a standardized indicator: home helps per thousand of population. Collapsing one level into the other, that is to say by conflating meeting elderly residents' demands with 'meeting' their demands as the league table prescribes (which is what the social-engineering model of policy-making does), creates paradoxes and makes the management of a system oscillatory (Bateson 1979: 61–3; Tsoukas 1994: 7).

A system that is in oscillation cannot be managed effectively, it is never quite right: it tends to sway between extreme positions. What is even more important is that such a social system leads eventually to the management of problematic 'solutions' (i.e. managing league tables, namely 'gaming') instead of the management of the *original* problems that the system was set up to deal with in the first place (i.e. managing the problem of helping elderly residents). Pushing the logic of social engineering to the extreme, management becomes tantamount to keeping up appearances and fighting shadows: managing via league tables leads to managing the league tables themselves!

Discussion and Conclusions

> Where is the life we have lost in living?
> Where is the wisdom we have lost in knowledge?
> Where is the knowledge we have lost in information?
>
> (T. S. Eliot)

The phenomenal development of information and communication technologies in late modernity has brought about a type of society that is fundamentally dependent on knowledge for its functioning. Knowledge now is, as Giddens (1991: 20) has noted, 'not incidental to modern institutions, but constitutive of them'. Nowhere is the knowledge-dependent character of late modernity more dramatically manifested than in the new types of risks societies now face. Whereas at earlier times of human history the risks human societies confronted came primarily from nature, today they are mostly derived from the all-pervasive scope of technical systems; that is, from abstract knowledge and its material embodiments (Beck 1992).

The knowledge that late modern societies so much depend on is different from the kind of knowledge pre-modern societies made use of. A modern individual understands knowledge rather differently from how a classical Greek or a medieval European craftsman did. Philosophers such as Feyerabend (1999), MacIntyre (1985), and Toulmin (1990), among others, have described how the meaning of knowledge has radically changed in the last three centuries. Until the Middle Ages, knowledge was conceived of in essentially classical Greek (particularly Aristotelian) terms: knowledge was primarily self-knowledge and the search for the virtuous life; it did not so much imply the exercise of the individual cognitive faculty as the ability to participate effectively in a larger collective; it was context-dependent and infused with values. By contrast, with the mechanization and secularization of the world during the modern age, knowledge acquired a strongly utilitarian meaning. It gradually became identified with abstraction and the ability to obtain results; it no longer incorporated ultimate values but acquired descriptive neutrality.

Whereas in Aristotelian thinking individuals and objects were defined in terms of characteristic purposes, or roles they were expected to fulfil, in modern thinking they are described in abstract terms, dissociated from any evaluative criteria. Modern thinking has split apart evaluative and factual statements, which for the pre-moderns formed a unity (MacIntyre 1985; Tsoukas and Cummings 1997). For example, in Aristotelian thinking the concept of a 'knife' cannot be defined independently of the concept of a *good* knife. Because we know that a knife is a tool for cutting things (that is to say, we know what it is *for*) we can draw the conclusion that a sharp knife is a good knife. A factual statement ('sharp knife') is also an evaluative statement ('a good knife').

Similarly, from such factual statements as 'He has more customers than any other carpenter in town', and 'He repeatedly wins prizes for his artefacts', we can draw the evaluative conclusion that 'He is a good carpenter'. We can do this because to think of people as carpenters (or teachers, farmers, managers, and so on) is to think of them as having certain purposes by virtue of their roles (MacIntyre 1985). In such a mode of thinking, individuals and objects are not defined merely 'factually' (that is, as abstract entities), but socially—as being embedded in particular social practices and contexts—and this is what enables evaluative and factual statements to merge. From the Greek classical period until the late Middle Ages knowledge was seen, in what is now the western world anyway, not as the exercise of an individual cognitive ability (i.e. information processing) but as a category of being.

Drucker (1993) has remarked that one of the key events that reflected the changing meaning of knowledge in the eighteenth century was the publication of the *Encyclopédie* in France (edited by Diderot and d'Alembert between 1751 and 1772). For the first time knowledge ceased to reside in the heads of certain authoritative individuals. It was extracted from social practices and contexts, taking instead the form of a manual, which contained generic statements—information—describing how the world works. In Drucker's words, '[the *Encyclopédie*] converted experience into knowledge, apprenticeship into textbook, secrecy into methodology, doing into applied knowledge' (ibid. 26). On the basis of such abstract, objective, codified, results-oriented, publicly available knowledge, modern individuals would be able to control their destiny in a way that was never possible before. More than anything else, knowledge was power to change the world.

This conception of knowledge is reflected in the current use of the term 'information'. In late modern societies 'information' denotes a set of abstract, value-free, decontextualized items, subject to human manipulation, allegedly representing the world as it is. As Drucker (ibid. 42) put it, 'the knowledge we *now* consider knowledge proves itself in action. What we now mean by knowledge is information effective in *action*, information focused on results'. When terms like 'knowledge society' or 'information society' are used, it is this conception of knowledge they normally presuppose.

Since the Enlightenment, knowledge has been viewed through the metaphor of light. More knowledge has been taken to mean a stronger human ability to see and thus an enhanced capability for action or, to be precise, for control. This assumption underlies the functioning of the information society, although for the first time we have now begun to recognize its limits. The abundance of information in conditions of late modernity as well as the amazing ease with which information is now collected, processed, stored, retrieved, and communicated across the globe make the information society full of temptations. It tempts us into thinking that knowledge-as-information is objective and exists independently of human beings; that everything can be reduced to information; and that the information available can assist in the rational management of social problems.

That more knowledge could cause problems, that light might prove another tyranny, that knowledge might bring suffering, were not thoughts the philosophers of the Enlightenment were prepared to entertain. Perhaps we needed the mixed experience of the twentieth century to realize how paradoxical knowledge is (particularly abstract, decontextualized knowledge), although throughout human history, from the Presocratics, through the Bible, to the Romantics, there had been warnings. The information society, being the apotheosis of the modern trend towards publicly and abundantly available information, is riddled with paradoxes that make it look like Tantalus striving to reach, but always failing to grasp, the fruit tree.

The information society delivers more information but, ironically, undermines the human capacity for understanding. The self-referential world of information combined with the ocean of instantly available, evanescent images and information items weaken the human ability to form a coherent understanding of the issues at hand. More subtly, the information society, through making information about complex social practices potentially available to all, tends to erode the trust that underlies the increasingly more sophisticated systems of expertise upon which the information society depends for its effective functioning. Enhancing the speed and increasing the amount of feedback between policy makers and the results of their actions, instead of improving the quality of decisions and making the management of social problems more effective, may lead to the opposite results.[4]

The reflexivity of modernity, that is the 'susceptibility of most respects of social activity, and material relations with nature, to chronic revision in the light of new information or knowledge' (Giddens 1991: 20), infuses the information society with unprecedented dynamism and endemic change. Although the philosophers of the Enlightenment and the progenitors of modern science hoped that reason would provide securely founded knowledge, the reflexivity of modernity has confounded such hopes: more information has led to more doubt, enhanced uncertainty, higher unpredictability (Giddens 1990: 139; 1991: 21; Stehr 1994: 222–60). 'The integral relation between modernity and radical doubt', notes Giddens (1991: 21), 'is an issue which, once exposed to view, is not only disturbing to philosophers but is *existentially troubling* for ordinary individuals'.

The dissolution of perspective in the information society brings about not just doubt but also disorientation (Vattimo 1992: 8). In such a society individuals need constantly to make choices about the most fundamental aspects of their lives—to reflexively (re)construct themselves on an ongoing basis. In a society of mediated experience, as the information society is, the world becomes a fable; image and reality are difficult to disentangle and, thus, social problems become more difficult to tackle rationally. The weakening of the notion of the public interest, fuelled by the easy political mobilization the information society facilitates, exacerbates the problems of societal governability.

In conclusion, it needs to be said that what I have argued in this chapter has not been intended to convey a feeling of pessimism about the prospects of the information society—'optimism' and 'pessimism' are too simplistic categories that hinder reflective action. It has rather been an attempt to take a critical view of the naive and, at times, soteriological optimism often associated with the increasingly pervasive use of information in late modernity.[5] Knowledge is—it has always been—dangerous for those professing it. Prometheus was punished for stealing it from the gods; Adam and Eve were expelled from the Garden of Eden for eating from the tree of knowledge. The unlimited euphoria surrounding the current hype about the information society tends to obscure the paradoxes that are inherent in human knowledge. Being aware of those paradoxes may refine our ability to reflect on them and—who knows?—may enable us to find more sophisticated ways of coping with them. Perhaps the greatest insight to derive from such an awareness would be the realization that light and darkness are two sides of the same coin; that, in the words of Ecclesiastes, 'in much wisdom is much vexation'; that knowledge and hubris are—always have been—intimately linked.

Notes

1. Throughout this paper I have adopted an interpretive sociological approach to 'information': the latter is thought to derive its meaning from the way it tends to be used within a specific form of life. Thus, in late modern societies information tends to be a commodity, that is a set of objectified, abstract, decontextualized representations, and it is in this sense I will be using the term here. (See Stehr (1994), Webster (1995), Giddens (1991), Kallinikos (1996).) I am not trying in this chapter to suggest new ways of conceptualizing 'information'. For such attempts see Bateson (1979), Mingers (1995), Simms (1996), and Brier (1992).
2. Within the last two decades the global network of computers, telephones, and televisions has increased its information-carrying capacity over one million times. Computer power doubles every eighteen years (see *The Economist*, 'A survey of the World Economy', 28 September 1996,   4–5). Every year since 1988 the Internet has doubled in size. In the late 1990s, it had over fifty million users worldwide. Since the Web was created it has grown nearly twenty times. As *The Economist* remarks, 'no communications medium or consumer electronics technology has ever grown as quickly; not the fax machine, not even the PC. At this rate within two years the citizens of cyberspace will number all but the largest nations' (*The Economist*, 'A survey of the Internet', 1 July 1995, 3).
3. At another point Wheatley draws on quantum physics to support her constructivist argument concerning information. She says: 'Think of organizational

data for a metaphoric moment as a wave function, moving through space, developing more and more potential explanations. If this wave of potentialities meets up with only one observer, it will collapse, into one interpretation, responding to the expectations of that particular observer' (Wheatley 1994: 63–4)
4. As Wright aptly notes: 'if there are "arrangements" that would indeed bring stability to a cyberdemocratic society, they might be found by first dispelling all residues of election-year rhetoric and acknowledging that Washington, far from being out of touch, is too plugged in, and that if history is any guide, the problem will only grow as technology advances. The challenge, thus conceived, is to buffer the legislature from the pressure of feedback'.
5. An example of such naive optimism is the adoption by *Wired* of the seminal Enlightenment thinker Thomas Paine as the patron saint of the information revolution. The new media have only benefits to bring about, according to J. Katz ('The Age of Paine', *Wired*, April 1995, 64–9): they 'advance human rights, spread democracy, ease suffering, pester government'. Echoing Paine, Katz argues that through the new media human beings have it in their power to begin the world all over again.

References

Argyris, C. (2004), 'Double-loop Learning and Implementable Validity', in H. Tsoukas and Mylonopoulos N. (2004) (eds.), *Organizations as Knowledge Systems* (Houndmills; Palgrave Macmillan), 29–45.
Bateson, G. (1979), *Mind and Nature* (Toronto: Bantam).
Baudrillard, J. (1983), *Simulations* (New York: Semiotext(e)).
Bauman, Z. (1992), *Intimations of Postmodernity*, (London: Routledge).
Beck, U. (1992), *Risk Society: Towards a New Modernity*, trans. M. Ritter (London: Sage).
Beer, S. (1973), 'The Surrogate World We Manage', *Behavioral Science*, 18: 198–209.
Bell, D. (1999), *The Coming of Post-industrial Society* (New York: Basic).
Brier, S. (1992), 'Information and Consciousness: A Critique of the Mechanistic Concept of Information', *Cybernetics and Human Knowing*, 1: 71–94.
Brin, D. (1998), *The Transparent Society* (Reading, Mass.: Perseus).
Castells, M. (1996), *The Rise of the Network Society* (Oxford: Blackwell).
—— (2000), 'Materials for an Explanatory Theory of the Network Society', *British Journal of Sociology*, 51: 5–24.
Cooper, R. (1992), 'Formal Organization as Representation: Remote Control, Displacement, and Abbreviation', in M. Reed and M. Hughes (eds.), *Rethinking Organization* (London: Sage), 254–72.
Dandeker, C. (1990), *Surveillance, Power and Modernity* (Cambridge: Polity).
Dertouzos, M. (1997), *What Will Be: How the New World of Information Will Change our Lives* (New York: Harper-Collins).
Dranove, D., Kessler, D., McClellan, M., and Satterthwaite, M. (2002), 'Is More Information Better? The Effects of 'Report Cards' on Health Care Providers', National Bureau of Economic Research, working paper no. 8697.
Drucker, P. (1993), *Post-capitalist Society* (Oxford: Butterworth/Heinemann).

Feyerabend, P. (1999), *Conquest of Abundance* (Chicago, Ill.: University of Chicago Press).

Foucault, M. (1991), 'Governmentality', in G. Burchell, C. Gordon, and P. Miller (eds.), *The Foucault Effect: Studies in Governmentality* (London: Harvester), 87–104.

Gadamer. H.-G. (1975), *Truth and Method* (London: Sheed and Ward).

Gergen, K. J., and Thatchnenkery, T. J. (1996), 'Organization Science as Social Construction: Postmodern Potentials', *Journal of Applied Behavioral Science*, 32: 356–77.

Giddens, A. (1990), *The Consequences of Modernity* (Cambridge: Polity).

—— (1991), *Modernity and Self-Identity* (Cambridge: Polity).

Goffman, E. (1969), *The Presentation of Self in Everyday Life* (Harmondsworth: Penguin).

Hargreaves Heap, S., Holis, M., Lyons, B., Sugden, R. and Weale, A. (1992), *The Theory of Choice: A Critical Guide* (Oxford: Blackwell).

Kallinikos, J. (1996), *Technology and Society* (Munich: Accedo).

Kenney, M. (1996), The Role of Information, Knowledge and Value in the Late Twentieth Century, *Futures*, 28(8): 695–707.

Lakoff, G. (1995) (interviewed by I. A. Boal), 'Body, Brain, and Communication', in J. Brook and I. A. Boal (eds.), *Resisting the Virtual Life: The Culture and Politics of Information*, (San Francisco, Calif.: City Lights), 115–30.

Lash, S. (2002), *Critique of Information* (London: Sage).

Luhmann, N. (2000), *The Reality of the Mass Media* (Cambridge: Polity).

Lyon, D. (1994), *The Electronic Eye: The Rise of Surveillance Society* (Cambridge: Polity).

MacIntyre, A. (1985), *After Virtue*, 2nd edn. (London: Duckworth).

McSweeney, B. (1994), 'Management by Accounting', in A. Hopwood and P. Miller (eds.), *Accounting as Social and Institutional Practice* (Cambridge: Cambridge University Press), 237–69.

Makridakis, S. (1995), 'The Forthcoming Information Revolution: Its Impact on Society and Firms', *Futures*, 27(8): 799–821.

Mingers, J. (1995), 'Information and Meaning: Foundations for an Intersubjective Account', *Information Systems Journal*, 5: 285–306.

Naisbitt, J. (1982), *Megatrends: The New Directions Transforming our Lives* (New York: Warner).

Norris, C., and Armstrong, G. (1999), *The Maximum Surveillance Society*, (Oxford: Berg).

O'Neil, O. (2002), *A Question of Trust* (Cambridge: Cambridge University Press).

Polanyi, M. (1962), *Personal Knowledge* (Chicago, Ill.: University of Chicago Press).

—— (1990), *The Mode of Information* (Cambridge: Polity).

Poster, M. (1995), 'Databases as Discourse, or Electronic Interpellations', in M. Poster, *The Second Media Age* (Cambridge: Polity), 78–94.

Postman, N. (1985), *Amusing Ourselves to Death* (London: Methuen).

Power, M. (1994), 'The Audit Society', in A. Hopwood and P. Miller (eds.), *Accounting as Social and Institutional Practice*, (Cambridge: Cambridge University Press), 299–316.

Reddy, M. J. (1979), 'The Conduit Metaphor—A Case of Frame Conflict in our Language about Language', in A. Ortony, (ed.), *Metaphor and Thought* (Cambridge: Cambridge University Press). 284–324.

Rifkin, J. (1995), *The End of Work* (New York: J. P. Tarcher/Putnam).

Rorty, R. (1991), *Objectivity, Relativism, and Truth* (Cambridge: Cambridge University Press).

Rosen, J. (2001), *The Unwanted Gaze* (New York: Vintage).

Roszak, T. (1994), *The Cult of Information* 2nd edn. (Berkeley, Calif.: University of California Press).

Ryle, G. (1949), *The Concept of Mind* (Chicago, Ill.: University of Chicago Press).

Simms, J. R. (1996), 'Information: Its Nature, Measurement, and Measurement Units', *Behavioral Science*, 41: 89–103.

Solokowski, R. (2000), *Introduction to Phenomenology* (Cambridge: Cambridge University Press).

Stehr, N. (1994), *Knowledge Societies* (London: Sage).

Taylor, C. (1985), *Philosophy and the Human Sciences: Philosophical Papers, ii* (Cambridge: Cambridge University Press).

—— (1993), 'To Follow a Rule . . .', in C. Calhoun, E. LiPuma, and M. Postone (eds.), *Bourdieu: Critical Perspectives* (Cambridge: Polity) 45–59.

Thompson, J. B. (1995), *The Media and Modernity: A Social Theory of the Media* (Cambridge: Polity).

Thurow, L. (2000), *Creating Wealth* (London: Nicholas Brealey).

Toffler, A. (1971), *Future Shock* (New York: Bantam).

Toulmin, S. (1990), *Cosmopolis: The Hidden Agenda of Modernity*, (Chicago, Ill.: University of Chicago Press).

Tsoukas, H. (1998), 'The Word and the World: A Critique of Representationalism in Management Research', *International Review of Public Administration*, 21: 781–817.

—— (1994), 'Introduction: From Social Engineering to Reflective Action in Organizational Behaviour', in H. Tsoukas (ed.), *New Thinking in Organizational Behaviour*, (Oxford: Butterworth/Heinemann), 1–22.

—— (2003), 'Do We Really Understand Tacit Knowledge?', in M. Easterby-Smith and M. A. Lyles (eds.), *Handbook of Organizational Learning and Knowledge* (Oxford: Blackwell), 410–27.

—— and Cummings, S. (1997), 'Marginalization and Recovery: The Emergence of Aristotelian Themes in Organization Studies', *Organization Studies*, 18: 655–83.

—— and Mylonopoulos, N. (2004), 'Introduction: What Does It Mean to View Organizations as Knowledge Systems?', in H. Tsoukas and N. Mylonopoulos (eds.), *Organizations as Knowledge Systems* (Houndmills: Palgrave Macmillan), 1–26.

Vattimo, G. (1992), *The Transparent Society* (Cambridge: Polity).

Virilio, P. (1997), *Open Sky*, trans. Julie Rose (London: Verso).

—— (2000), *The Information Bomb*, trans. Chris Turner (London: Verso).

Watzlawick, P., Weaklans, J. , and Fisch, R. (1974), *Change: Principles of Problem Formulation and Problem Resolution* (New York: Norton).

Webster, F. (1995), *Theories of the Information Society* (London: Routledge).

—— and Robins, K. (1989), 'Plan and Control: Towards a Cultural History of the Information Society', *Theory and Society*, 18: 323–51.

Weick, K. (1990), 'Introduction: Cartographic Myths in Organizations', in A. S. Huff (ed.), *Mapping Strategic Thought* (Chichester: Wiley), 1–10.

Wheatley, M. J. (1994), *Leadership and the New Science* (San Fransisco, Calif.: Berret-Koehler).

Winch, P. (1958), *The Idea of a Social Science and its Relation to Philosophy* (London: Routledge and Kegan Paul).

Woolley, B. (1992), *Virtual Worlds* (London: Penguin).

Wright, P. (1995), Hyperdemocracy: Washington Isn't Dangerously Disconnected from the People; The Trouble is It's Too Plugged In', *Time*, 23 January 1995, 63–4.
Zuboff, S. (1985), 'Automate/Informate: The Two Faces of Intelligent Technology', *Organizational Dynamics*, 14: 5–18.

TWO

David and Goliath in the Risk Society: Making Sense of the Conflict between Shell and Greenpeace in the North Sea

Lilliputian organizations cannot compel immoral rulers to apologize on their knees, as Henry II had to do; but they do subject rulers who refuse to mend their ways to damaging embarrassment in the eyes of the world. [...] [In late modernity] the name of the game will be *influence*, not *force*; and, in playing on that field, the Lilliputians hold certain advantages

(Stephen Toulmin 1990: 198, 208)

IN June 1995 Shell and Greenpeace locked horns in the North Sea, over the offshore disposal of Brent Spar, a defunct oil platform which had been decommissioned after nearly twenty years of service. The Brent Spar controversy, which originally started as a local incident involving Greenpeace, Shell UK, and the British government, escalated rapidly and, mainly through intense media-generated publicity, quickly assumed wider significance, involving European governments and consumer boycotts in several Western European countries. In the end, Shell was forced to reverse its decision.

The purpose of this chapter is to understand how the victory of a small organization such as Greenpeace over a large organization such as Shell was made possible. To do this we need to reconceptualize both the environment in which organizations operate and the texture of organizational action in late

An earlier version of this chapter was first published in *Organization*, 6(3) (1999), 499–528. Reprinted by permission of Sage, Copyright (1999).

modernity. Indeed, the Brent Spar controversy raises certain issues which have not been adequately tackled in organization studies. For example, it has often been suggested that organizations in late modernity are increasingly dependent on knowledge (Drucker 1991; Nonaka and Takeuchi 1995; Quinn 1992) for their functioning, and the indicator of how knowledge-intensive a firm is normally taken to be the share of R&D expenditure in the unit cost of its products. However, it has rarely been asked, if at all, what happens when organizations do not just compete in a market of *knowledge-intensive products* but put forward competing *knowledge claims* in the public arena, as is the case with environmental disputes.

Similarly, while institutional analyses of organizational environments have been particularly illuminating in underscoring the significance of institutionalized values and beliefs underlying the social context in which firms operate (Powell and DiMaggio 1991; Scott 1995), they have tended to leave out the very *texture* of organizational environments. Rarely, for example, has it been pointed out that, in late modernity, the organizational environment increasingly consists of *signs*, namely mediated images, symbols, and knowledge claims. A company like Shell, for example, does not deal only in resources (economic and institutional), but also in risks: its productive activities generate environmental hazards the impact of which comes under focus and debate. Moreover, in a semiotic environment organizational action tends to be reflexively shaped: organizations act in the knowledge that they are under public scrutiny.

The thesis put forward here argues that in late modernity risk production increasingly becomes at least as important as wealth production. In late modern societies symbolic power assumes great significance which, in certain circumstances, may turn out to be even more significant than economic power; social reflexivity is an increasingly integral part of societal functioning; and the role of mediated communication occupies a central place. In a largely de-materialized environment the traditional competitive advantage afforded by superior size, industry positioning, and resources does not have the same value as before: power differentials in terms of economic capital may not be always translatable into successful strategies. In a society in which risk production is so central as to feature prominently in social debate and policy-making, business organizations not only compete in the market place but (increasingly so) in a discursive space in which winning the argument is just as important. These claims will be illustrated with reference to the Brent Spar controversy.

My analysis in this chapter draws heavily on the recent work of Giddens (1990, 1991, 1994) and Beck (1992, 1994, 1995, 1996, 1997), as well as on the work of sociologists such as Friedland and Boden (1994), Lash and Urry (1994), and Thompson (1995), who, broadly, share Giddens's and Beck's neo-modernist perspective. The chapter is organized as follows. In the next section a conceptual framework concerning organizations and their environments in late modernity is set out. This is followed by a discussion of the events that took place in the Brent Spar controversy. And, finally, the conflict between Shell and Greenpeace is analysed in terms of the concepts set out in the proposed conceptual framework.

Organizing in Late Modernity: A Conceptual Framework

Action at a Distance

The abstraction of time and space.   Identifying the distinguishing features of modernity has always been a major sociological concern. From Durkheim and Simmel to Giddens and Beck, an important recognition stands out in sociological analyses: modernization is thought to be a process of disembedding—of emptying out of social systems. To put it differently, modernization is a process of abstraction. To appreciate this, perhaps it is best if one starts the other way around: in traditional societies to be is to be embedded in a concrete spatio-temporal context, defined by the presence of others; human interaction is limited by conditions of co-presence. People communicate when they are physically together. Time and space are intimately linked through place: 'when' is connected with 'where', or with natural or religious occurrences. The emptying out (abstraction) of time took a decisive boost with the invention of the mechanical clock and, later, with the standardization of calendars (Kallinikos 1996: ch. 1). It was now possible for time to be treated as a uniform, quantifiable, abstract category. The process of the emptying out of time has reached an extreme point today with the creation of a 'global present' (Adam 1996: 86–9; Friedland and Boden 1994: 15): economic activities are carried out around the globe, around the clock (Cairncross 1997; Sproull and Kiesler 1991).

The lifting out of time from local contexts of interaction has enabled the emptying of place and, thus, made possible action at a distance (Cooper 1992; Kallinikos 1996: 34–42). Whereas in traditional societies place is identical with space, in modernity this is no longer the case. It is not difficult to see why. In pre-modern societies social interaction occurs in physical settings which are situated geographically—space *is* place. When, however, social interaction no longer presupposes a single, geographically situated setting, as is the case for example in a telephone conversation or in communication through the Internet, then space becomes separated from place. Since we can now interact without being physically co-present, our interaction occurs in abstract space, not in a locally situated place. ZOOM/TEAMS/OTHER COMMS

What is the significance of the abstraction of time and space? Abstract time STUFF and abstract space can be separated and recombined at will. Organizations, HAS

Really filled this gap since Covid 19

being the carriers of modernity par excellence, both exemplify and contribute to the disembedding of social systems: social relations are lifted out from their local contexts of interaction and are recombined across indefinite spans of time-space (Giddens 1990: 21; 1991: 18; 1994: 4). It is the ability for systematic coordination of 'absent' others and, therefore, for action at a distance, that is the most enduring feature of modern organizations. The dialectic of presence and absence becomes the central principle of modern organization—human interaction is no longer limited by the context of co-presence (Tsoukas 2001).

The phenomenon whereby abstract time and abstract space are recombined so as to connect presence and absence is called by Giddens (1990: 14) 'time-space distanciation' (see also Friedland and Boden 1994: 15; Thompson 1995: 32). Through the latter, social systems can extend their activities beyond the here and now. One is not hard pressed for examples in the late modern world. From the systematic use of automatic teller machines (ATMs), through tele-banking, to electronic commerce, we are witnessing the gradual substitution of cyber-economy for conventional economic exchange (Cairncross 1997; Lash and Urry 1994). Late modernity makes the possibilities latent in modern institutions a fully-fledged reality.

Disembedding mechanisms.   Giddens (1990: 21–9; 1991:18) distinguishes two types of disembedding mechanisms: 'symbolic tokens' and 'expert systems', both of which make the recombination of abstract time and abstract space possible. *Symbolic tokens* are standardized media of exchange, such as, for example, money, which are interchangeable across different contexts. A monetary economy is a prime example of time-space distanciation: economic transactions between individuals who never physically meet each other are rendered possible. *Expert systems* are impersonal systems of knowledge and expertise whose validity is independent of those drawing on them. In modern societies such systems are ubiquitous and are exemplified by the work of scientists, engineers, physicians, accountants, lawyers, and therapists, or, more generally, what Reich (1991: 177–80) calls 'symbolic analysts' (see also Drucker 1991).

In what way are expert systems disembedding mechanisms? 'An expert system', says Giddens (1990: 28), 'disembeds in the same way as symbolic tokens, by providing "guarantees" of expectations across distanciated time-space. This "stretching" of social systems is achieved via the impersonal nature of tests applied to evaluate technical knowledge and by public critique (upon which the production of technical knowledge is based), used to control its form'. Drawing on expert systems implies an attitude of *trust* in the expectations provided by them: a belief that such systems do work as they are supposed to. Trust in expert systems is related to absence in time and space as well as to ignorance. I have no idea how my computer functions, but I do rely upon those who have made it, who are physically absent from me, to guarantee that it does function as it is meant to.

The Economy of Signs (Especially Risks)

In late modernity it is not only time and space that have been emptied out; the objects produced and exchanged are being increasingly emptied of material content. As Lash and Urry (1994: 15) remark, 'what is increasingly being produced are not material objects, but signs' (see also Stehr 1994: 121–59). The semiotization of late modern economies has not only to do with their gradual transformation into service economies (Makridakis 1995; Stehr 1994), or with the growing 'technization' of work (Barley 1996), but also with 'the increasing component of sign value or *image* in material objects' (Lash and Urry 1994: 15). For Lash and Urry this process is manifested in the growing importance of design and of R&D for the value of goods, to the effect that the labour process has lost the centrality it once had in the value-added chain.

A particular type of signs that are systematically produced in late modern societies are *risks*. The sign value of risks is not, of course, aesthetic (as is the case with various goods and services) but informational (ibid. 15). Why are risks thought to be signs? Because, as will be shown below, modern risks become perceptible largely through evidence supplied by scientific models. Thus, a distinguishing feature of modern risks (as opposed to traditional ones) is that they exist only in so far as they can be pointed out in scientific theorizing and experimentation (Gephart 1996: 212–16).

Risks-as-signs are far from being marginal or mere side effects in late modern societies. For some analysts, like Beck (1992: 19), risks now define so heavily the nature of late modernity that he attributes 'the logic of risk distribution' to late modernity, in contrast to 'the logic of wealth distribution' which characterized industrial society (Shrivastava 1995: 119–21). In industrial society the logic of wealth production dominated the logic of risk production, according to Beck. Partly because risks then were less hazardous and less global than today, as well as because it was easier for risks to be rationalized and be seen as mere externalities or unintended consequences to be corrected through the further development of technology, they were not taken seriously; productivism ruled. In late modernity the relationship is reversed: the systematic production and the potentially catastrophic effects of various contemporary risks mean that the latter are no longer thought to be mere externalities, but an extremely important issue around which politics, policy-making, and social debate are increasingly organized (Beck et al., 1994: vii; Shrivastava 1995: 119–21). It is the centrality of risk production in late modern societies that Beck (1992) wants to capture by calling them 'risk societies'.

Are risks in late modernity really different from risks in other epochs? Are risks not part and parcel of the human condition? While it is certainly true that human beings have always been exposed to hazards and dangers of all kinds, there are also some crucial discontinuities between pre-modern and modern risks which need to be analysed.

First, in pre-modern times risks were largely localized, not *global* as they are today. The risks associated with, for example, Columbus' trip to America were exclusively born by Columbus and his crew. However, today, the effects of acid rain, or the consequences of global warming, are borne by all, even by those who have contributed very little to the genesis of acid rain or global warming (Jamieson 1992).

Second, contemporary risks stem not so much from nature *per se* (although extreme phenomena such as floods and earthquakes keep reminding us of the fundamental human vulnerability to nature's whims) but from human arte-facts. As Giddens (1990: 60, 124–34) and Beck (1992: 22–3) point out, the great risks facing late modernity are no longer natural but *manufactured*: they are the results of human intervention in nature and society (Jamieson 1996; Freuden-burg 1996). In Giddens's words (1994: 4):

Life has always been a risky business. The intrusion of manufactured uncertainty into our lives doesn't mean that our existence, on an individual or collective level, is more risky than it used to be. Rather, the sources, and the scope, of risk have altered. Manufactured risk is a result of human intervention into the conditions of social life and into nature [...] The advance of manufactured uncertainty is the outcome of the long-term maturation of modern institutions.

Third, risks in the past were usually directly perceptible, whereas now, by and large, they are not. The terrible pollution of the Thames in the early nine-teenth century was there for all to see and smell; the contamination, however, induced by radioactivity and toxic substances is not. As Beck (1992: 21) comments, 'hazards in those days assaulted the nose or the eyes and were thus perceptible to the senses, while the risks of civilization today typically *escape perception* and are localized in the sphere of *physical and chemical formu-las* (e.g. toxins in foodstuffs or the nuclear threat)'. The knowledge-depend-ence of modern risks is extremely important, for it means that such risks can only be identified through causal interpretations by expert-systems specialists. Since contemporary risks become perceptible through the sensory organs of science, their nature as well as their effects are primarily *mediated* through interpretation and argument (Gephart 1984, 1988). Thus, modern risks 'can be changed, magnified, or minimized within knowledge, and to that extent they are particularly *open to social definition and construction*' (Beck 1992: 23).

Several studies have shown that how risks are defined, measured, and as-sessed depends on the values, interests, priorities, and epistemologies of those who have been charged with the task of risk assessment (Wynne 1992, 1996), in the context of broader organizational factors such as established cultures, power games, and professional practices (Clarke 1993; Clarke and Short 1993; Kasperson and Kasperson 1996; Perrow 1984; Turner 1976; Vaughan 1996). Even apparently simple and technical matters, such as how to measure human fatalities, have been shown to be complex and judgemental (Kunreuther and Slovic 1996: 119–20).

Fourth, the very notion of risk implies *normative* criteria, defining what is and is not acceptable; a set of values in terms of which a particular activity is considered risky. Rappaport (1996: 69) put it nicely, noting that 'risk assessment cannot be value free because values define what is at risk, and what is at risk may be values themselves'. Similarly, Beck (1992: 28) asks: 'Behind all the objectifications, sooner or later the question of *acceptance* arises and with it anew the old question: *how do we wish to live?* What is the human quality of mankind, the natural quality of nature which is to be preserved?' It is questions of this kind that lead Beck to think that although risk assessment crucially depends on scientific knowledge, nevertheless, in so far as risks presuppose values, the scientific monopoly on rationality cannot be sustained (Hellstrom and Jacob 1996; Jamieson 1992; Martin 1996; Welsh 1996). The interweaving of scientific and social rationalities is for several researchers a welcome return of ethics inside one of the bastions of modernity—business organizations.

Fifth, there is something *unreal* in modern risks. Although damage to the environment is all around us, there is a sense in which the most harmful risks are not-yet-events: counterfactuals which cannot be subjected to empirical testing; possibilities which, should they ever happen, would have extremely harmful consequences (Beck 1992: 33–4; Giddens 1990: 134). Thus, several modern risks exist as apocalyptic scenarios which must forever remain fictional, anticipations which ought to remain only in the sphere of possibility.

The strongly counterfactual nature of modern risks draws the future into the present: human action is motivated not so much by the desire to effect positive changes as by the urgency to prevent certain events from ever happening (Giddens 1994: 219–23). As Beck (1992: 34) remarks,

the center of risk consciousness lies not in the present, but *in the future*. In the risk society, the past loses the power to determine the present. Its place is taken by the future, thus, something non-existent, invented, fictive as the 'cause' of current experience and action. We become active today in order to prevent, alleviate or take precautions against the problems and crises of tomorrow and the day after tomorrow—or not to do so.

Thus, scientific arguments concerning large-scale risks often cannot be brought to a close, since conducting the necessary experiments or waiting to collect the requisite data may be self-destructive. Disputes, therefore, over the  environmental impact of certain policies, say the dumping of radioactive waste or the cultivation of genetically modified plants, tend to be open-ended and difficult to settle conclusively. Ironically, instead of scientific knowledge creating more certainty, as was once triumphantly presumed, it generates ever more uncertainty (Giddens 1990: 36–45; 1994: 3–4).

If Beck's and Giddens's thesis about the centrality of risks in late modern societies is accepted, it follows that organizations, which have been hitherto thought of only in terms of wealth production, need to be reconceptualized.

Thus, for example, a business organization like Shell should no longer be seen as being engaged only in the production of wealth but, also, in the production of signs, especially risks. (The fact that the production of risks is an unintended activity does not diminish its importance in the least). A non-governmental organization (NGO) like Greenpeace should be seen as being primarily engaged in the production and diffusion of symbolic forms pertaining to the environment (Eyerman and Jamison 1989). In the risk society the contest for the definition of symbolic forms assumes great importance.

Symbolic power.   Drawing on Thompson's typology of power (1995: 12–18), business organizations can be seen in terms of both economic power and symbolic power. As Thompson (ibid. 14) observes, economic power stems from human productive activity involving the use of certain material resources and their transformation into goods to be sold in a market. Economic power is essentially the capacity to transform resources into products efficiently and effectively, and sell them in a market.

Symbolic power 'stems from the activity of producing, transmitting and receiving meaningful symbolic forms' (ibid. 16). The resources upon which actors draw when they engage in symbolic activity are the following. First, the technical means of transmission of symbolic forms. The role of media here becomes crucial. Second, the cultural capital; that is, the skills and knowledge forms employed in the process of symbolic exchange (Bourdieu 1991: 230). And third, the symbolic capital; that is, the accumulated prestige and recognition (legitimacy) that has been afforded to an actor (ibid. 72–6, 230). Symbolic power is, as Thompson (1995: 17) remarks, 'the capacity to intervene in the course of events, to influence the actions of others and indeed to create events, by means of the production and transmission of symbolic forms' (see also Bourdieu 1991: 163–70).

From the above it follows that business organizations are simultaneously engaged in two 'fields of interaction' (ibid. 230–1): in the economic field and in the symbolic field. And if it is accepted that, in late modernity, the production of risks (as well as signs, more generally) increasingly becomes as important as the production of wealth, it seems that competition between organizations should not be thought of in economic terms alone but, increasingly, in symbolic terms. Indeed, as institutionalists have cogently shown, a firm may seriously disadvantage itself if its symbolic capital is wasted—legitimacy matters (Elsbach 1994; Grolin 1997; Suchman 1995). In the increasingly reflexive risk society the quest for legitimacy (i.e. the quest for the accumulation of symbolic capital) becomes extremely important and, as a result, it is possible for economically powerful organizations to become symbolically weak, with potentially serious performance implications. This is what Toulmin (1990: 208) means when he points out that, in late modernity, 'the name of the game will be *influence*, not *force*; and, in playing on that field, the Lilliputians hold certain advantages'. The more the contest between organizations is carried out in the symbolic field of interaction, the less important conventional competitive advantages, such as size, market share, industry positioning, etc., are, and the more important symbolic capital is.

Mediated Communication

It was mentioned earlier that a key feature of late modernity is the uncoupling of time and space it effects and, thus, the distanciation of time and space it entails. In this way, action at a distance is made possible. Nowhere is this more clearly illustrated than in the case of telecommunication. Through the latter, the uncoupling of time and space has led to what Thompson (1995: 32) calls 'despatialized simultaneity'—the experience of events occurring at distant locales as simultaneous. Whereas in the past simultaneity presupposed locality (that is, 'the same time' presupposed 'the same place'), with the uncoupling of time and space this is no longer necessary. As Thompson (ibid. 32) remarks, 'in contrast to the concreteness of the here and now, there emerged a sense of "now" which was no longer bound to a particular locale. Simultaneity was extended in space and became ultimately global in scope'.

Telecommunication extends the traditional mode of interaction which was confined to contexts of co-presence, to include new forms of *mediated interaction*, such as a telephone conversation, and *mediated quasi-interaction*, such as the transmission of symbolic forms through the television (ibid. 82–118). The distinguishing feature of both types of non-physical interaction is that they enable the extended availability of symbolic forms in space-time. There is no need to examine here in detail each type of interaction; it would be more useful, for the purpose of this chapter, to focus our attention on mediated quasi-interaction, especially television, since the latter has become the most influential medium of communication in late modernity.

Television involves the separation of the context of production from the contexts of reception. There is a multiplicity of contexts of reception, since symbolic forms are produced for an indefinite range of recipients. Television is monological in character: there is a one-way flow of messages from the producer to the recipients. The separation of the context of production from the contexts of reception, and the monological character of television mean that, 'televisual quasi-interaction [...] is severed from the reflexive monitoring of others' responses which is a routine and constant feature of face-to-face interaction' (ibid. 96). This is significant, for it gives rise to *mediated indeterminacy*, since the recipients can interpret what they see in their own ways, and their responsive actions can evolve in ways which cannot be predicted or controlled (ibid. 29, 109).

Thompson (ibid. 100–18) distinguishes two types of action at a distance: 'acting for distant others' and 'responsive action in distant contexts'. 'Acting for distant others' is a form of action in which the producer addresses recipients who are not physically present in the context of production (e.g. the news broadcast). A particular kind of acting for distant others is the media events which are exceptional occasions, planned in advance and broadcast live. Examples range from a presidential oath, through the Olympic Games, to Greenpeace happenings. Such events are 'reflexively shaped by the orientation towards an absent audience' (ibid. 108–9)—participants know that their actions have wider significance and are managed accordingly.

'Responsive action in distant contexts' is a form of action by the recipients in response to broadcast distant events. Although recipients cannot respond directly to producers, they do respond indirectly; namely, as a contribution to other interactions of which recipients are part (e.g. comments between viewers on what they watch on the TV). Thompson (ibid. 110) calls this process 'discursive elaboration', whereby media messages 'are elaborated, refined, criticized, praised and commented on by recipients who take the messages received as the subject matter of discussions with one another and with others' (see Fig. 2.1). Notice that discursive elaboration need not be limited to primary recipients, that is to individuals who have watched a particular programme, but may include others, secondary recipients, who assimilate parts of the media message through face-to-face interactions with the primary recipients (ibid. 110).

It is also important to point out that in late modern societies, along with the process of discursive elaboration, there is the process of 'extended mediazation' (ibid. 110): most of the media messages individuals receive refer to other media messages and are incorporated into new media messages, in an ongoing process of communication and debate. A dispute, for example, over an envir-

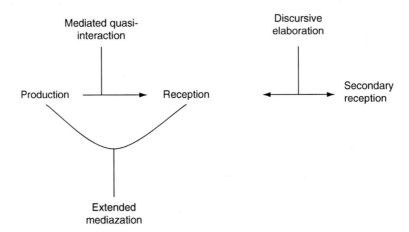

Fig. 2.1: Action at a distance in mediated communication: televisual quasi-interaction.
Source: Thompson (1995: 111)

onmental issue normally involves references to scientific reports which are summarized by the media; media reports then become an object of discussion for media commentators, whose comments are further commented upon by other commentators, and so on. It is the crucial role of media in the processes of discursive elaboration and extended mediazation that has led certain researchers to argue for the centrality of mass media in the social amplification and attenuation of risks in late modern societies (Kasperson and Kasperson 1996).

The reception and discursive elaboration of media messages may lead recipients to undertake responsive action to events relayed via the television, a phenomenon which Thompson (1995: 112) calls 'concerted forms of responsive action'. The extent to which such action is explicitly coordinated may vary. When it is coordinated within the contexts of reception, it becomes an articulated form of collective action, seeking to influence a remote course of events. It is mainly in this sense that the media in late modernity do not merely report what is going on, but actively shape what is going on—media presence is conducive to creating events which would not have taken place otherwise. The opposition to the Vietnam War in the 1960s, the revolutions of 1989 in Eastern Europe, and the management of both the Gulf Wars by the American military are clear examples of the reflexivity induced by television in late modernity: actors undertake forms of action while watching the whole world watching them (Friedland and Boden 1994: 19; Thompson 1995: 114–18).

Social Reflexivity

Knowledge and information are not only central to the constitution of late modern societies, they are also deeply implicated in the endemic change and instability that characterize modernity. Indeed, for analysts like Beck, (1992; Beck et al., 1994), Giddens (1990: 36–43; 1991: 14–21; 1994: 78–97), and Lash and Urry (1994) a distinguishing feature of late modernity is its thoroughgoing reflexivity. 'The reflexivity of modern social life', notes Giddens (1990: 38), 'consists in the fact that social practices are constantly examined and reformed in the light of incoming information about those very practices, thus constitutively altering their character'.

Of course, as Giddens (ibid. 36–7) is quick to point out, reflexivity is, in a sense, an intrinsic feature of human action. The reflexive monitoring of action is a necessary and ongoing process implicated in every act of human behaviour: human beings normally keep in touch with what they do and incorporate the results of their actions to modify their behaviour. However, it is only in late modernity that the loop between thought and action extends so widely as to cover all aspects of individual behaviour and institutional action. Examples abound: from the decision to get married, through the choice of what food to eat, to the social policies of nation states, actors' behaviour is reflexively organized in the light of available pertinent information and knowledge. The reflexive organization of social practices is particularly evident in the risk society, since risk estimates and, thus, the necessary policies, are chronically revisable in the light of new information about risks and, crucially, the change of normative horizons and the emergence of new sets of values. The risk society cannot help but be an intensely reflexive and, therefore, politicized society (Beck 1994; Friedman 1996).

Giddens is so impressed with the reflexivity of modernity that he takes reflexivity to be the distinguishing feature of modern organization. As he remarks, 'what distinguishes modern organisations is not so much their size, or their bureaucratic character, as the concentrated reflexive monitoring they both permit and entail' (Giddens 1991: 16). Organizational reflexivity is not confined to traditional business concerns, such as how to increase productivity, competitiveness, and so on, but permeates several other aspects of organizational life, hitherto unavailable to public debate. As *The Economist* (24 June 1995, 15) notes in its leader, in the aftermath of Shell's decision to abandon the offshore dumping of the Brent Spar, 'the universe of behaviour to which standards of correctness are being applied is growing. The hiring, firing, pay and promotion policies of a firm were once its own business. Nowadays there is a trend [. . .] to treat such policies as a legitimate area of public scrutiny'. In other words, in late modernity organizations are under increasing pressure to explain their policies to the rest of society and, thus, to revise more and more aspects of their activities in the light of both new information and changing values (Friedman 1996; Pilisuk et al. 1996). Debate, accountability, and reflexivity—in a word: politics—are key features of a social order in which tradition has lost its taken-for-granted status.

Lash and Urry (1994: 60–110) take the theme of modern reflexivity further by arguing for the 'reflexive accumulation' encountered in late modern economies. Knowledge and information, they suggest, are not only sought as a way of tackling complex problems but, in so far as contemporary economies are increasingly dematerialized, knowledge and information constitute, in large part, the products in a reflexive economy. It is not only reflexive production that is taking place in such an economy but also reflexive consumption. What is actually going on, note Lash and Urry (ibid. 61), is a wider process of 'detraditionalization', whereby individuals are increasingly freed from traditional social structures, such as the family, corporations, and social classes, and make their own choices and decisions (see also Beck 1992, 1994, 1996; Beck et al. 1994; Giddens, 1990, 1991, 1994; Heelas et al. 1996). A similar thesis is echoed in Beck's argument (1992: 10, 14) concerning the reflexive modernization involved in risk societies: having interrogated the principles of feudal society, modernization now interrogates its own principles.

The dematerialization of economic activities needs to be seen in conjunction with detraditionalization, and the emergence of post-materialist values in late modern societies (Beck 1992; Inglehart 1987; Stehr 1994: 242–3). High

growth rates and rising incomes, the globalization of communication, and the
dramatic proliferation of risks have given rise to a post-materialist outlook in
which environmental concerns occupy a central place. Indeed, for certain
researchers environmentalism has become the new ideology in public discourse (Eder 1996; Jamison 1996). As Eder (1996: 204–5) argues, 'the master-
frame constituting this new ideology is "ecology", and "ecological discourse"
is becoming the common ground on which collective actors meet in today's
public discourse and public place'. Moreover, the twentieth century has seen a
noticeable emergence of a global civil society through, mainly, the huge
increase, both in terms of numbers and influence, of international NGOs
(INGOs) (Mathews 1997: 52–4). In their study of INGOs between 1875 and
1973 Boli and Thomas (1997) have shown not only the increase in the number
of INGOS (for example, by 1947 over ninety INGOs per year were being
founded), but also their contribution towards building a set of cosmopolitan
values centred on universalism, individualism, progress, and world citizenship
(Beck 2000).

To sum up, the setting within which organizations in late modernity operate
is marked by four interconnected features (see Fig. 2.2). The first feature is
action at a distance (distanciation). Late modernity, through the abstraction of
time and space and their subsequent recombination, makes possible the
stretching of social activities beyond contexts of co-presence. Social systems
are, thus, disembedded, and a crucial disembedding mechanism is expert
systems.

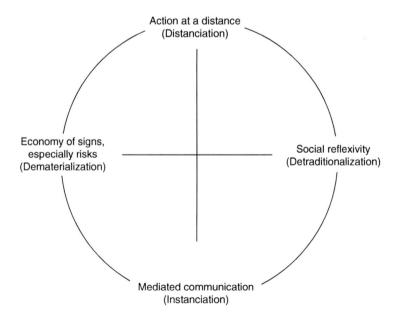

Fig. 2.2: The texture of organizing in late modernity.

The second feature is instantly mediated communication (instanciation). Action at a distance is significantly enhanced through the uncoupling of time and space effected by the media. In particular, mediated quasi-interaction through the television extends the availability of symbolic forms across space and time. It thus facilitates acting for distant others, mainly through staging media events to be relayed to an indefinite range of recipients. Moreover, televisual interaction creates mediated indeterminacy in so far as the separation of the context of production from the contexts of reception enables recipients to put their own interpretations to, and discursively elaborate on, what they see, and undertake concerted forms of responsive action.

The third feature is the production of risks, in the broader context of the dematerialization of economic activities, whereby the economy of wealth is increasingly transformed into an economy of signs. Modern risks tend to be global; they are produced by human intervention in nature rather than caused by nature itself; they are perceptible largely through scientific theorizing and, thus, are socially constructed as well as open-ended in terms of their acknowledged consequences; they presuppose normative criteria of acceptance; and they are unreal and counterfactual. In the economy of signs the superiority of economic power over symbolic power is weakened: organizations compete not only for economic resources but also for legitimacy and public approval.

Finally, the fourth feature of late-modern organizational environments is social reflexivity (detraditionalization). Organizational practices are endemically unstable in so far as they tend to be revised in the light of both new information about those very practices, and the emergence of new values. Traditional structures tend to lose their taken-for-granted status, resulting in the reflexive organization of individual and organizational projects. Environmental values possess a central place in the emerging set of post-materialist values and, as the action of several INGOs demonstrates, are a key concern of a gradually growing global civil society.

Below I will first describe the controversy between Shell and Greenpeace over the offshore disposal of the Brent Spar, which I will later analyse in the light of the concepts set out in this section.

The Brent Spar Controversy[1]

The Brent Spar oil-storage buoy had been in operation since 1976. Owned by Shell Expro (a subsidiary of Shell UK, which is a member of the Royal Dutch/Shell group, one of the largest oil companies in the world), Brent Spar was designed to hold 300,000 barrels of oil. In September 1991 it was decommissioned and, following the recommendation of a three-year scientific study sponsored by Shell, and a subsequent permission by the UK government, it was decided that the buoy would be disposed of in the North Atlantic, at a depth of 2,300 metres. The UK government had given Shell the licence for deep-sea disposal as the 'best practicable environmental option' (BPEO). The BPEO study was based on reports by consultants employed by Shell, and its recommendation for deep-sea disposal was suggested 'on the grounds of reduced technical risk; the reduced safety risk to the workforce; the insignificant environmental impact; and the total cost' (Shell UK 1994: 9). It was estimated that the cost of offshore disposal would be £11.8 million against the £46 million cost of onshore disposal.

Given the cost difference between the two options, the fact that disposal costs would be tax deductible in the UK, and that fifty other platforms were waiting to be similarly disposed in the near future, the offshore disposal appeared a more attractive, financially speaking, option to the UK government, as evidenced in public statements by the then Energy Minister Tim Eggar (Grolin 1997: 8). However, Shell's decision was severely criticized by, among others, the Scottish Association for Marine Science for containing important errors. This criticism, along with a leaked report by a government scientist in which he supported the case against shallow-water disposal, were taken up by Greenpeace in its campaign to prevent the sinking of the Brent Spar.

Brent Spar is a big cylindrical structure weighing 14,500 tonnes, made up of 7,700 tonnes of steel and 6,800 tonnes of haematite ballast embedded in concrete. The platform is 140 metres high, of which 30 metres are above water, and 29 meters in maximum diameter. According to Shell the buoy contains a few dozen tonnes of toxic metals, several dozen tonnes of oily sludge, and some mildly radioactive salts which have built up on its pipework and tank linings.

The bone of contention was the likely impact of the sinking of the Spar on the marine environment and, indirectly, through the food chain, on human life. The prevailing scientific view (reflected in the BPEO study) was that the environmental impact would be negligible and, at any rate, sinking the buoy in the Atlantic would indeed be the 'best *practicable* environmental option'. What would have been the likely effect of deep-sea disposal? *The Economist* (24 June 1995, 110–11) summarized the mainstream scientific view as follows:

[in the deep ocean] animal life is sparse, and only loosely connected to the main food chain. True, the buoy would have crushed some deep-sea inhabitants when it hit the bottom; the cloud of sediment raised by the impact would have smothered others. Yet having been stripped of most of its contents (including lightbulbs) by Shell, the Brent Spar contains only small quantities of pollutants: a residue of oil; perhaps 100 tonnes of sludge; some heavy metals; and some radioactive salts.

In the still depths the pollutants might well have leaked out only slowly, perhaps too slowly to kill many more animals. The level of radioactivity would have been 'equivalent to what you're exposed to in any city with granite buildings', says Alasdair McIntyre of Aberdeen University.

By contrast, Greenpeace, the most vociferous as well as active critic of offshore disposal, took a sceptical view. Quoting from various scientific publications, its main argument was that not enough was known about the ocean to be able to predict with some measure of certainty the impact of the Spar's disposal. In her reply to Anthony Rice, a senior biologist at the Institute of Oceanographic Sciences who had written in the *Times Higher Education Supplement* (hereafter *THES*) on 11 August 1995 arguing for the deep-sea disposal, Sue Mayer, the Director of Science at Greenpeace, remarked:

No one, Mr Rice or Greenpeace, knows exactly what would happen if the Spar was dumped. Other scientists at the Scottish Association for Marine Science, for example, are much less sanguine about the dangers than Mr Rice. They have expressed 'broad agreement' with the arguments Greenpeace used to justify its action, and pointed to a series of deficiencies in Shell's scientific documents. They have pointed out that Rice's assumption that the deep seas will not be used for commercial fisheries is already incorrect in practice and that there are links in the food chain between deep water and shallow water organisms. They have also pointed to inadequacies in our knowledge of 'benthic storms' and how any dumped material will be dispersed.

Greenpeace was not only concerned about the Brent Spar *per se*, but also about the likely offshore disposal of 440 platforms in the North Sea, several of which were due for decommissioning in the near future. Brent Spar was, for Greenpeace, a crucial test. Writing a few months after Shell's climbdown, Sue Mayer observed:

The whole of the oil industry was watching and waiting. The Brent Spar was going to set a precedent for how other oil installations and possibly other waste could be disposed of. The real debate was about whether companies like Shell would have to take responsibility for their waste [...] To look at the impact of the Brent Spar in isolation makes no sense, scientific or otherwise (*THES*, 25 August 1995)

In February 1995 the UK government granted Shell the permit to dispose of the Brent Spar in the North Atlantic. True to its tradition of spectacular happenings, Greenpeace decided, in April 1995, to oppose actively the offshore disposal of Brent Spar by occupying it. Greenpeace activists from the UK, Germany, and the Netherlands began planning the occupation, which took place on 30 April. It was the start of an escalating, Europe-wide campaign which attracted considerable media attention. On 23 May police and security men stormed Brent Spar and Shell regained control of it. A hide-and-seek game followed. On 7 June five Greenpeace activists briefly reboarded the platform after it had been rigged with explosives for deep-sea sinking. Three days later, on 10 June, activists chained themselves to the platform's sea anchors in a last attempt to obstruct the Spar's removal, but were thrown into the sea. As the platform was being towed from the North Sea to the Atlantic dumping site, followed somewhat spectacularly by Greenpeace ships and helicopters, Greenpeace managed, on 16 June, to land two activists on the platform. Three days later two more activists were dropped on board.

The timing of these events was ideal for Greenpeace's campaign: the occupation of the Brent Spar coincided with the 4th North Sea Conference, 8–9 June, attended by the environment ministers of North Sea countries. In that conference not only was Brent Spar on the agenda but the majority of participant countries adopted a recommendation against the offshore disposal of Brent Spar and other decommissioned platforms. Prior to that, on 18 May, the European Parliament had adopted a similar resolution.

Meanwhile, the extensive media coverage had begun drawing attention to the controversy in other European countries. In Germany a 10-day boycott of Shell's 1,700 petrol stations was organized, cutting sales by up to 50 per cent; two petrol stations were firebombed and at another shots were fired. Consumer boycott spread in other countries such as Denmark and the Netherlands. Moreover, in addition to individual consumers, companies and public authorities entered the fray by either cancelling their contracts with Shell or threatening to do so (Grolin 1997: 4–5). As the case attracted more publicity, governments and church groups joined the debate, taking Greenpeace's side. Chancellor Kohl told Prime Minister Major that stopping the dumping was 'not the looniness of a few Greens but a Europe-wide trend for the protection of our seas' (*THES*, 11 August 1995). Likewise, Anna Lindh, the Swedish Minister of the Environment, commented: 'The sea must not be used as a rubbish dump' (ibid.).

In the face of such strong opposition Royal Dutch/Shell announced, on 20 June, after a meeting between the company's four top executives and the CEOs of the Shell subsidiaries in the EU countries whose governments had criticized Shell, that plans for the disposal of the Brent Spar in the North Atlantic would be called off. Dr Chris Fay, Chairman of Shell UK, announcing on 20 June the parent company's decision to climb down, acknowledged that strong public reactions throughout Northern Europe against the dumping had created an 'untenable position' (*Independent*, 21 June 1995) for European subsidiaries of Shell. Similarly, Peter Duncan, CEO of Shell Germany, said that the group's decision reflected the fact that 'the planned deep-sea disposal could not be forced through against the resistance of the population, and especially the customers' (*Independent*, 22 June 1995).

Shell was puzzled at the ferocity of public reaction to its policy, given that what the company had done was, in the words of Peter Duncan, 'fully in accord with the British and in particular the international conventions' (*Independent*, 22 June 1995). As Dr Fay said: '[this is] the first example where governments have openly protested against an option which has been carried out in a lawful and proper manner' (*Independent*, 21 June 1995). The conflict was thought by Shell to be, in the words of John Wybrew, Shell UK's director of public affairs, 'an unusual clash between the head and the heart—a conflict in which scientific reason and careful judgement were set against the power of emotion, fear and even myth' (quoted in Grolin, 1997: 11).

The victory of Greenpeace over Shell was widely depicted in the UK and German press as a modern-day victory of David over Goliath. In an extensive article entitled 'David's great Victory over Goliath', (*Independent* 21 June 1995) underscored the unevenness between the two organizations: 'On the face of it', it wrote, 'it seemed a massively uneven contest. The Royal Dutch/Shell Group had global sales of £84.3 bn last year. It employs 106,000 people in more than 100 countries. Greenpeace had a global income of $131 m last year, some 0.001 percent of Shell's. It employs about 1,000 people, and has offices in 30 countries'.

Following Shell's climbdown, the same newspaper praised Greenpeace in its leading article and drew attention to the fact that 'neither governments nor big business are strong enough to withstand a new phenomenon: an alliance of direct action with public opinion' (*Independent*, 21 June 1995). Even *The Economist*, not particularly sympathetic to Greenpeace's campaign, pointed out that, 'after Shell's climbdown' (the title of its leader) 'companies that choose to defy their consumers' political demands are placing their businesses in jeopardy. [...] Tomorrow's successful company [...] will have to present itself more as if it were a person—as an intelligent actor, of upright character, that brings explicit moral judgments to bear on its dealings with its own employees and with the wider world' (*The Economist*, 24 June 1995, 15, 16).

But it was not only praise and admiration that Greenpeace attracted from the Brent Spar affair. Its campaign for deep-sea disposal was thought by some to have been 'emotional' (*The Economist*, 24 June 1995, 110), 'a defeat for rational decision-making' (*The Economist*, 24 June 1995, 110), 'kneejerk populism' (*The Economist*, 24 June 1995, 16), 'irresponsible' (Anthony Rice, writing in the *THES*, 11 August 1995), and 'a pyrrhic victory' (Roger Hayes, Director-General of the British Nuclear Industry Forum, writing in the *THES*, 23 June 1995). Even the *Independent*, which throughout the Brent Spar conflict took a sympathetic stance towards Greenpeace, acknowledged in its leading article that Shell was right in wanting to dispose of the Brent Spar in deep sea (*Independent*, 21 June 1995). Eventually, after Shell's policy reversal, it was Greenpeace's turn to modify its stance, although it did not change its mind over the whole matter. A few months after the events of June 1995 Greenpeace admitted that its estimate that the Brent Spar contained 5,000 tonnes of toxic sludge was based on flawed samplings (Grolin 1997: 11).

Discussion

The Brent Spar controversy displays in an exemplary manner the contours of the postmodern setting[2] within which inter-organizational conflict now takes place. In this particular case Shell was not competing with Greenpeace in the market place but in the global *agora*. It was not, in other words, a competition as to who would sell more, but a contest as to who would be more convincing. Influence was more important than competitiveness.

The object of dispute was a particular company decision with environmental implications, which might become policy for handling other similar matters in the future. The risks of a policy of dumping defunct oil platforms in the deep sea were not directly perceptible. It was the knowledge of expert systems which was drawn upon by both supporters and critics of offshore dumping. The risks were largely artefacts of the particular assumptions and arguments of the scientific models used. Different assumptions made by the conflicting parties led to different probabilistic risk assessments. The conflict was, right from the beginning, mediated through interpretation and argument. However, whatever the conclusions drawn by each party, the uncertainty surrounding the dumping of Brent Spar was far from being dispelled. To the following questions the answers were not very clear: What exactly will the effects be on marine life? How certain is it that the sea pollution effected by the dumping will not pass into the food chain? At the end of the day, how will the ocean behave? Even more, what will be the effect of the offshore dumping of fifty other defunct oil platforms likely to be decommissioned in the near future?

Of course, it may be argued that risk assessments cannot but be probabilistic, and that one will never be able to be absolutely certain about the environmental impact of any policy pursued. While this is true, the built-in contestability of Environmental Impact Assessments (EIAs) also needs to be acknowledged. The modelling of an environmental problem, the assumptions upon which such modelling is based, and even the statistical measures used, are all judgemental (Freudenburg 1996: 49; Kunreuther and Slovic 1996: 119). The reason is that, as Freudenburg (1996: 48–9) argues, in an environmental controversy the following three questions need to be answered. First: How safe is the solution adopted? (a question about facts); second: Is it safe enough? (a question about values); and third; Are we overlooking something? (a question of blind spots).

Whereas conflicting claims exchanged between scientists over the sinking of Brent Spar aimed at settling the first question, there was a noticeable absence of social mechanisms for deliberating on the other two questions. In fact, one can safely assume that the strength of public reaction to Shell sprang not so much from the fact that consumers-cum-citizens had an informed view on the technicalities of the case, as from consumers' desire to uphold the *value*, best expressed by the Swedish Minister of the Environment, that 'the sea must not be used as a rubbish dump' (*THES*, 11 August 1995). John Vidal echoed a similar sentiment in the *Guardian* (22 June 1995) when he wrote: 'How can you tell 90 million Germans religiously to sort their rubbish and not expect them to cry foul when they see a global company fly-tipping its rubbish into the sea' (see also Grolin 1997: 9).

By defining the terms of the debate in narrowly techno-scientific terms, Shell and the UK government did not raise the question: Are we overlooking something here? The question about blind spots—acknowledging and debating the limitations of one's perspective—is a particularly interesting one, for it can be answered only in a reflexive manner by drawing into the debate those organizations whose *raison d'être* leads them to take environmental positions radically different from one's own. Shell had not realized before the dispute broke out what it did realize after it reversed its decision: the significance of extensive consultations with interested parties. Admittedly, prior to submitting its proposal for deep-sea disposal to the UK government in October 1994 Shell consulted those explicitly required by the British Petroleum Act of 1987, namely Scottish fishery organizations and British Telecom, but it made no effort to elicit the views of organizations such as the Scottish Association for Marine Science and Greenpeace, which had expressed grave concerns about Shell's plans. It was only after the events of June 1995 that Shell initiated the 'Brent Spar Dialogue Process' and, in its attempt to review its disposal options, it made it one of its prime concerns to 'ensure that the proposed BPEO carries the wide support of stakeholders in general' (Shell UK, quoted ibid. 14).

As argued earlier, the centrality of risks in late modern societies turns the latter from economies of material production to economies of signs. Shell is not only in the oil business; it is also involved in the systematic production of risks associated with its productive activities. When the production of risks comes to dominate wealth production, as it did with the decision to dispose of the Brent Spar in the sea, the field in which an organization like Shell operates is no longer conventionally economic, but symbolic.

In a symbolic field scientific rationality does not reign supreme: given the inherently value-laden character of modern risks, several other interested parties may be drawn into the debate. It is in this sense that 'the invasion of ecology into the economy opens it to politics' (Beck 1997: 59), and fundamental questions about substantive rationality—about what constitutes 'the good life'—gain a fresh impetus (Wallerstein 1999: 14). The systematic production of risk brings home the point that corporate decisions are not as value-free or apolitical as was once thought, but rather society, being seriously affected by such decisions, ought to have a say in what is being decided. Hence the perennial questions, long suppressed in the business world, come to the fore, more pressingly than ever: How should we live? How should we relate to one another (born and unborn), and to nature? (Jamieson 1992; Wallerstein 1999). Consequently, politics, understood in its original meaning, namely as the handling of uncertainty through collective deliberation (Castoriadis 1991: 104; Giddens 1994: 15–16, 104–33), becomes an intrinsic feature of the reflexive, risk society (Beck 1992, 1994, 1996).

In a symbolic field of interaction symbolic capital is, by definition, extremely important. Like several others INGOs, Greenpeace, in contrast with

Shell, has had plenty of it (Eder 1996; Eyerman and Jamison 1989; Toulmin 1990: 197). In its twenty-odd years of operation Greenpeace has been defending the cause of the environment consistently and, often, victoriously, against 'greedy' corporations and governments. A few spectacular feats, such as sailing into the atomic-fallout zone off Muroroa and the sinking of the *Rainbow Warrior*, have helped it consolidate its reputation (Eyerman and Jamison 1989: 107). Its no-companies, no-governments funding policy has further increased its image as an independent (and therefore morally authoritative) defender of mother earth. The spread of its influence is indexed by the significant increase of its membership, to include in 1994 around three million people, in thirty countries. Considering also the centrality of environmental values in late-modern public discourse, it is not surprising that Greenpeace's campaign was able to convince so many people in Northern Europe, a region traditionally more sensitive than others to environmental issues.

By contrast, Shell, being an oil company, was tainted with the image of greed and exploitation, which has tended to accompany oil multinationals (Sampson 1975). Although it is credited with being a far-sighted organization (*The Economist*, 24 June 1995; Ketola 1993), it has not been easy for Shell to forsake the environmental stigma that has historically been attached to the 'Seven Sisters'. Several well-publicized cases of oil leakage in the sea, including the particularly nasty damage caused by *Exxon Valdez*, and the stigma associated with certain technologies and products such as hazardous waste (Gregory et al. 1995; Kasperson and Kasperson 1996: 99–100), have made oil companies not particularly trusted when it comes to their environmental credentials; hence, their symbolic capital tends to be low.

Yet, as mentioned earlier, the issue of trust assumes great significance in late modernity. Drawing on expert systems implies an attitude of trust in the knowledge claims incorporated in them; such trust is related to both ignorance and absence in time and space. The disembedded knowledge of expert systems, especially knowledge as technical and remote from daily life as that associated with modern risks, cannot be drawn upon unless it is also expected to be credible. It is perhaps considerations like these that prompted Freudenburg (1996: 53) to argue that 'we [scientists] are in effect trustees for something more important than money. We are trustees for the credibility of science and technology'. Likewise, any business organization is a trustee for something more important than wealth: it is a trustee for the credibility of its industry and even of business as a whole. When it comes to risks, trust is even more important, for the stakes are especially high (Leiss 1996: 89–90; Slovic 1993). The not-so-brilliant environmental record of the oil industry, in combination with the stigma associated with its products and its waste, have tended to compromise the credibility of its environmental messages. This is not only a matter of good communication practices. It has been found that even when risk communication is good, its effectiveness may be limited due to lack of trust by the public in the message source (Slovic and MacGregor, quoted in Leiss 1996: 89).

It is interesting, however, that the issue of trust hardly ever came up in the Brent Spar debate. Influential printed media in Britain praised Shell's technical analyses and condemned Greenpeace's 'irresponsibility', without ever considering how credibility and trust could have been better elicited by Shell. The uncertainty surrounding the sinking of Brent Spar was seen as a 'management problem'—a technical problem to be fixed via more information and better scientific argument (Jamieson 1992: 142–6). However, as Jamieson (1996: 37–9; Herrick and Jamieson 1995) convincingly argues, uncertainty is not a merely technical matter but a socially constructed phenomenon (Stallings 1995): uncertainty arises when the parties involved in a debate or transaction no longer take its context for granted. For every interaction to be carried out in a reasonably certain manner it presupposes a background knowledge which is tacitly accepted by the interactants. It is only when such background knowledge is contested (no longer trusted) that uncertainty increases. Reducing uncertainty, therefore, in an environmental dispute is not a narrowly scientific matter, but a broadly social issue (Hellstrom and Jacob 1996). As Jamieson (1996: 43) concludes, 'many of our problems about risk are deeply cultural and cannot be overcome simply by the application of more and better science'.

What, however, turned the Brent Spar controversy into something of a real-life drama, witnessed by millions of people around the world, was its extensive media coverage. Whereas Shell was quietly planning the disposal of the defunct oil platform in close cooperation with the UK government, Greenpeace's intervention turned what hitherto was Shell's private matter into a public affair, through making it a public spectacle. Through its successive occupations of Brent Spar, its real-life theatre in which Greenpeace helicopters and ships were pursuing the Brent Spar on its final journey to the dump site in the North Atlantic, and its successful efforts to make the dumping of Brent Spar an issue for Northern European governments and consumers, Greenpeace ensured that Brent Spar remained in the news all over Europe.

In other words, taking advantage of the media coverage, Greenpeace was staging media events for the distant public—it was action at a distance par excellence. Through its actions the public was kept in touch with what 'was going on'; the television cameras were the public's 'eyes' in the North Sea. Notice, however, the inverted commas: that what 'was going on' was reflexively being shaped by Greenpeace. The latter's media events were staged with the knowledge that the entire world had its eyes on them—Greenpeace was watching itself being watched, and acted accordingly. The confrontation in the North Sea did not follow its own 'independent' course, but developed the way it did as a result of the fact that it was under the public gaze. In that sense one might argue, echoing Baudrillard's (1991) provocative argument about the first Gulf War, that the whole conflict was a staged event in which the stage was not so much in the North Sea as on the television screen (Woolley 1992: 197). The representation of events overtook the events; images of conflict became the conflict (Virilio 1989: 1).

However, all Greenpeace's efforts might have been wasted had its action at a distance not been reciprocated by the public's own action at a distance. This is what Thompson (1995: 109) calls 'responsive action in distant contexts', discussed earlier. Mediated quasi-interaction effected through the television gives rise to discursive elaboration: it enables recipients to talk about and comment upon media messages, and draw into the debate even people who did not themselves watch the messages broadcast. This is an important feature of televisual quasi-interaction, for it highlights the reception of symbolic forms as an essentially hermeneutic act: '[it] involves the contextualized and creative process of interpretation in which individuals draw on the resources available to them in order to make sense of the messages they receive' (ibid. 8). As mentioned earlier, one such resource in late modernity is the ideology of environmentalism (Eder 1996); another is the symbolic capital organizations have—high in Greenpeace's case, low in the case of Shell. Discursive elaboration, in turn, may lead recipients to undertake concerted forms of responsive action.

Indeed, this is what happened in the Brent Spar controversy. The North Sea events relayed via (as well as shaped by) the television were widely interpreted as yet another instance of a greedy oil multinational behaving as though the world was its oyster. A leading article in the *Independent* (21 June 1995, the day after Shell reversed its decision) captured the public mood: 'Popular opinion has ruled that, whatever destruction may be wrought elsewhere, the oceans cannot simply be regarded as waste disposal sinks'. The concerted responsive action took the form of consumer boycott against Shell's petrol station in Germany and elsewhere in Northern Europe. Shell started feeling the pinch through a steep reduction in sales. More importantly, its image was being severely tainted. In Germany the boycott was supported by the majority of the population; gradually, not only politicians from all the main political parties but even the Church supported the boycott (*Independent*, 22 June 1995). The momentum of the public reaction reached its peak when the governments of Germany, the Netherlands, Sweden, and Denmark made clear their support for Greenpeace's stance.

Thus, by providing individuals with images of reflexively shaped events taking place in distant locales, the media create a public space in which the actions and reactions of a multitude of actors, albeit located in different places, are linked together in time, constituting concerted forms of responsive action. Such action transcends the boundaries of nation states and, as the dramatic events of 1989 have shown, may constitute a formidable force for change. In a reflexive social order, in which institutional accountability is highly valued, and in an economy increasingly dominated by signs (especially risks), whose interpretation is bound to be open-ended and contested, instant mediated communication makes possible action at a distance, with large-scale as well as unpredictable consequences.

Of course, nobody could have foreseen the unfolding of the controversy in the North Sea—disputes of that kind are inevitably shaped by unforeseeable contingencies. Since the risk society is rich in arguments and direct political action (what Beck calls 'subpolitics'—politics from below), a widening of the debate to include multiple rationalities, and the politicization of the issues at hand are to be expected. However, the process of reception, appropriation and discursive elaboration of symbolic forms is bound to be indeterminate. As Beck et al. (1994), Giddens (1991, 1994) and Stehr (1994: 236), have noted, uncertainty, fragility, and unpredictability are inherent features of knowledge-based societies in a way in which they never were for industrial societies. In such a context, influence, symbolic power, and political mobilization assume great importance.

Conclusions

My purpose in this chapter has been to explain what made the victory of Greenpeace over Shell in the North Sea in June 1995 possible. I have not dealt here with how Shell's decision to sink Brent Spar in the deep sea came about, nor have I sought to explore the implications of the conflict for corporate management. I have rather taken the conflict between these two organizations as exemplifying a broader theme; namely, the advantage potentially enjoyed by certain small organizations in late modernity. Although one cannot, of course, predict the outcome of similar conflicts in the future, our understanding of power differences and the way they are brought to bear upon a course of events needs revising, to take into account the conditions of late modernity. I have argued here that organizations increasingly operate in a new environment whose main features are the following four (see Fig. 2.2 p. 51).

First, accentuating the modern trend towards the abstraction and subsequent recombination of time and space, late modernity amplifies the uniquely modern capacity for action at a distance to an unprecedented degree. Moreover, absence in time and space, as well as ignorance, highlights the importance of trust in the activities of social systems.

Second, this tendency is further enhanced via the mass media, especially television. Mediated communication extends the availability of symbolic forms across time and place, thus creating a public space in which actors situated in distant locales are linked. Televisual quasi-interaction, in particular, makes possible acting for distant others (through creating media events), and facilitates concerted responsive action by distant recipients.

Third, economies in late modernity are increasingly economies of signs, especially risks. Modern risks are perceived through scientific theorizing and are mediated through argument. In an economy of signs interpretation is clearly important and, therefore, the quest for symbolic power (legitimacy) is extremely significant.

And fourth, risks presuppose normative criteria for their assessment, thus drawing multiple social rationalities and actors into the debate, and making possible the politicization of seemingly technical issues. The economy of signs is an intensely reflexive economy in which tradition loses its taken-for-granted status, while actors' behaviour is continuously revised in the light of new information and the emergence of new values. Such a value in late modernity is environmentalism, aggressively championed by, among others, certain INGOs. Within a semiotic environment it is possible for an INGO David to be victorious over a multinational Goliath. When risks are the focus of inter-organizational conflict (as is often the case in the risk society), the symbolic capital held by the actors involved is important. This is particularly so at a time when environmentalism is part of the public discourse in late modern societies. Tainted with the largely negative image of being a greedy oil multinational, Shell's symbolic capital was low. Perceived as a small but morally authoritative defender of the environment, Greenpeace's symbolic capital was high.

Moreover, given that risk assessment is an inherently ambiguous and subjective process, mediated through argument, the debate over risk consequences tends to be open-ended and inconclusive (scientific arguments by themselves are of limited effectiveness). Acceptance of risks by the public implies the acceptance of certain values, thus turning the question of risks into a wider social-cum-political issue; as a result, the public may be drawn into the debate. The perceptibility of modern risks through, mainly, the claims of expert-systems specialists implies that public trust needs to be won by those advancing such claims. In this case there was a notable lack of sensitivity by Shell and the UK government concerning the establishment of mechanisms for eliciting trust for the proposed solution. Shell insisted on a narrowly technical definition of the problem, while those opposing its decision were implicitly pointing at the values underlying it. Sticking to its technical definition, Shell made sense of the conflict in terms of 'reason' against 'emotion', and 'head' versus 'heart', failing to see the conflict as the clash of two rationalities; namely, the instrumental, techno-scientific rationality espoused by Shell versus the value-driven rationality espoused by the public (Grolin 1997: 11).

Modern risks are deeply political issues in so far as they transcend a merely technical perspective to include values and ethics. By virtue of being political issues, modern risks are a source of concern and a subject of debate for the informed public (Beck 1994). The extended availability of symbolic forms made possible by the mass media, especially television, is capable of drawing large portions of the public into an environmental dispute, circumventing the traditional institutions of representative democracy; direct political intervention by individuals and the civil society at large, as well as the political use of consumer power are not only possible but occasionally decisive. Formal political institutions tend to lose their quasi-exclusive right to define what is 'in the public interest' and, instead, the latter may be defined by 'a global nexus of responsibility' (Beck 1997: 64), including NGOs, citizens' groups, and individual consumers.

Greenpeace turned out to be a crucial node in such a nexus, challenging the decision made by the old 'progress coalition' (i.e. corporations and governments). Greenpeace successfully assumed the role of being the public's eyes, mind, and heart in the North Sea, and staged spectacular media events to that effect. At the same time the public reciprocated: the discursive elaboration of televisual images relayed from the North Sea made possible a concerted public response, which took the form of a consumer boycott and political pressure on North European governments to condemn Shell's dumping policy. A global-action network proved stronger than a state–corporate alliance.

To conclude, late modernity gives rise to a semiotic business environment in which traditionally defined concepts of size and power do not always give their possessors an advantage. On the television screen Shell does not necessarily appear more powerful than Greenpeace; on the contrary, it may well appear less persuasive and, therefore, less influential. In the risk societies of late modernity the market place coexists side-by-side with a global political *agora*: a reflexive public space of debate, conflict, and deliberation in which symbolic capital and persuasive arguments may count as much as market share, and sometimes even more. In such a type of society winning the argument can be as important as securing a competitive advantage; influence can be more important than force; moral authority can be more significant than financial strength. Notice, however, the caveat: late modernity does not entail the developments just mentioned, but it makes them *possible*. I hope that the preceding analysis of the victory of Greenpeace over Shell in the North Sea has demonstrated the plausibility of my thesis.

Notes

1. The following printed and electronic sources were drawn upon in writing this case study: *Independent*, 21 June 1995, 22 June 1995, 23 June 1995, 4 July 1995, 11 July 1995, 29 August 1995; *The Economist*, 24 June 1995, 15–16, 79–80, 110–11); 19 August 1995, 65–6; 20 July 1996, 17–18, 63–4; the *Times Higher Education Supplement*, 11 August 1995, 25 August 1995, 31 May 1996; <http://www.shell.com/brentspar>, accessed June 2004; <http://www.archive.greenpeace.org/comms/brent/>, accessed June 2004.

2. The terms 'late modernity' and 'postmodernity', as well as 'late modern' and 'postmodern', are used interchangeably here (see Giddens, 1990: 43–54, 163–73; Lash and Urry 1994).

References

Adam, B. (1996), 'The Centrality of Time for an Ecological Social Science Perspective', in S. Lash, B. Szerszynski, and B. Wynne (eds.), *Risk, Environment and Modernity* (London: Sage), 84–103.

Barley, S. (1996), *The New World of Work* (London: British-North American Committee).

Baudrillard, J. (1991), 'The Reality Gulf', *The Guardian*, 11 January 1991, 25.

Beck, U. (1992), *Risk Society*, trans. M. A. Ritter (London: Sage).

—— (1994), 'The Reinvention of Politics: Towards a Theory of Reflexive Modernization', in U. Beck, A. Giddens, and S. Lash, *Reflexive Modernization* (Cambridge: Polity), 1–55.

—— (1995), *Ecological Enlightenment*, trans. M. A. Ritter (New Jersey: Humanities).

—— (1996), 'Risk Society and the Provident State', in S. Lash, B. Szerszynski, and B. Wynne (eds.), *Risk, Environment and Modernity* (London: Sage), 27–43.

—— (1997), 'Subpolitics: Ecology and the Disintegration of Institutional Power', *Organization and Environment*, 10: 52–65.

—— (2000), 'The Cosmopolitan Perspective: Sociology of the Second Age of Modernity', *British Journal of Sociology*, 51: 79–105.

—— Giddens, A., and Lash, S. (1994), preface to U. Beck, A. Giddens, and S. Lash, *Reflexive Modernization* (Cambridge: Polity), pp. vi–viii.

Boli, J., and Thomas, G. (1997), 'World Culture in the World Polity: A Century of International Non-governmental Organization', *American Sociological Review*, 62: 171–90.

Bourdieu, P. (1991), *Language and Symbolic Power*, trans. G. Raymond and M. Adamson (Cambridge: Polity).

Cairncross, F. (1997), *The Death of Distance* (Boston, Mass.: Harvard Business School Press).

Castells, M. (1996), *The Rise of the Network Society* (Malden, Mass.: Blackwell).

Castoriadis, C. (1991), *Philosophy, Politics, Autonomy*, ed. D. A. Curtis (New York: Oxford University Press).

Clarke, L. (1993), 'The Disqualification Heuristic: When Do Organizations Misperceive Risk?', *Research in Social Problems and Public Policy*, 5: 289–312.

—— and Short, J. F., Jr. (1993), 'Social Organization and Risk: Some Current Controversies', *Annual Review of Sociology*, 19: 375–99.

Cooper, R. (1992), 'Formal Organization as Representation: Remote Control, Displacement, and Abbreviation', in M. Reed and M. Hughes (eds.), *Rethinking Organization* (London: Sage), 254–72.

Drucker, P. (1991), *Post-capitalist Society* (Oxford: Butterworth/Heinemann).

Eder, K. (1996), 'The Institutionalization of Environmentalism: Ecological Discourse and the Second Transformation of the Public Sphere', in S. Lash, B. Szerszynski, and B. Wynne (eds.), *Risk, Environment and Modernity* (London: Sage), 203–23.

Elsbach, K. (1994), 'Managing Organizational Legitimacy in the California Cattle Industry', *Administrative Science Quarterly*, 39: 57–88.

Eyerman, R., and Jamison, A. (1989), 'Environmental Knowledge as an Organizational Weapon: The Case of Greenpeace', *Social Science Information*, 28: 99–119.

Freudenburg, W. (1996), 'Risky Thinking: Irrational Fears about Risk and Society', *The Annals of the American Academy of Political and Social Science*, 545: 44–53.

Friedland, R., and Boden, D. (1994), 'NowHere: An Introduction to Space, Time and Modernity', in R. Friedland and D. Boden (eds.), *NowHere: Space, Time and Modernity* (Berkeley, Calif.: University of California Press), 1–60.

Friedman, M. (1996), 'Grassroots Groups Confront the Corporation: Contemporary Strategies in Historical Perspective', *Journal of Social Issues*, 52: 153–67.

Gephart, R. P., Jr. (1984), 'Making Sense of Organizationally Based Environmental Disasters', *Journal of Management*, 10: 205–25.

—— (1988), 'Managing the Meaning of a Sour Gas Well Blowout: The Public Culture of Organizational Disasters', *Industrial Crisis Quarterly*, 2: 17–32.

—— (1996), 'Simulacral Environments: Reflexivity and the Natural Ecology of Organizations', in D. M. Boje, R. P. Gephart, and T. J. Thatchenkery (eds.) *Postmodern Management and Organization Theory* (Thousand Oaks, Calif.: Sage), 202–22.

Giddens, A. (1990), *The Consequences of Modernity* (Cambridge: Polity).

—— (1991), *Modernity and Self-Identity* (Cambridge: Polity).

—— (1994), *Beyond Left and Right* (Cambridge: Polity).

Gregory, R., Flynn, J., and Slovic, P. (1995), 'Technological Stigma', *American Scientist*, 83: 220–3.

Grolin, J. (1997), 'Corporate Legitimacy and Public Discourse: Shell, Greenpeace and the Dumping of Brent Spar', paper presented at the 6th International Conference of the Greening of Industry Network, Santa Barbara, Calif., 16–19, November 1997.

Heelas, P., Lash, S., and Morris, P. (1996), *Detraditionalization* (Oxford: Blackwell).

Hellstrom, T., and Jacob, M. (1996), 'Uncertainty and Values: The Case of Environmental Impact Assessment', *Knowledge and Policy*, 9: 70–84.

Herrick, C., and Jamieson, D. (1995), 'The Social Construction of Acid Rain', *Global Environmental Change*, 5: 105–12.

Inglehart, R. (1987), 'Value Change in Industrial Society', *American Political Science Review*, 81: 1289–1303.

Jamieson, D. (1992), 'Ethics, Public Policy, and Global Warming', *Science, Technology, and Human Values*, 17: 139–53.

—— (1996), 'Scientific Uncertainty and the Political Process', *The Annals of the American Academy of Political and Social Science*, 545: 35–43.

Jamison, A. (1996), 'The Shaping of the Global Environmental Agenda: The Role of Non-governmental Organisations', in S. Lash, B. Szerszynski, and B. Wynne (eds.), *Risk, Environment and Modernity* (London: Sage), 224–45.

Kallinikos, J. (1996), *Technology and Society* (Munich: Accedo).

Kasperson, R., and Kasperson, J. (1996), 'The Social Amplification and Attenuation of Risk', *The Annals of the American Academy of Political and Social Science*, 545: 95–105.

Ketola, T. (1993), 'The Seven Sisters: Snow Whites, Dwarfs or Evil Queens? A Comparison of the Official Environmental Policies of the Largest Oil Corporations in the World', *Business Strategy and the Environment*, 2: 22–33.

Kunreuther, H., and Slovic, P. (1996), 'Science, Values, and Risk', *The Annals of the American Academy of Political and Social Science*, 545: 116–25.

Lash, S., and Urry, J. (1994), *Economies of Signs and Space* (London: Sage).

Leiss, W. (1996), 'Three Phases in the Evolution of Risk Communication Practice', *The Annals of the American Academy of Political and Social Science*, 545: 85–94.

Makridakis, S. (1995), 'The Forthcoming Information Revolution', *Futures*, 27: 799–821.

Martin, B. (1996), 'Introduction: Experts and Establishments', in B. Martin (ed.), *Confronting the Experts* (New York: State University of New York), 1–12.

Mathews, J. (1997), 'Power Shift', *Foreign Affairs*, 76: 50–66.

Nonaka, I., and Takeuchi, H. (1995), *The Knowledge-Creating Company* (New York: Oxford University Press).

Perrow, C. (1984), *Normal Accidents* (New York: Basic).

Pilisuk, M., McAllister, J., and Rothman, J. (1996), 'Coming Together for Action: The Challenge of Contemporary Grassroots Community Organizing', *Journal of Social Issues*, 52: 15–37.

Powell, W., and DiMaggio, P. (1991), *The New Institutionalism in Organizational Analysis* (Chicago Ill.: University of Chicago Press).

Quinn, J. B. (1992), *The Intelligent Enterprise* (New York: Free Press).

Rappaport, R. (1996), 'Risk and the Human Environment', *The Annals of the American Academy of Political and Social Science*, 545: 64–74.

Reich, R. (1991), *The Work of Nations* (London: Simon & Schuster).

Sampson, A. (1975), *The Seven Sisters* (New York: Viking).

Scott, W. R. (1995), *Institutions and Organizations* (Thousand Oaks, Calif.: Sage).

Shell UK (1994), *Brent Spar BPEO Assessment*, paper prepared for Shell UK Exploration and Production by Rudall Blanchard Associates Ltd.

Shrivastava, P. (1995), 'Ecocentric Management for a Risk Society', *Academy of Management Review*, 20: 118–37.

Slovic, P. (1993), 'Perceived Risk, Trust, and Democracy', *Risk Analysis*, 13: 675–82.

Sproull, L., and Kiesler, S. (1991), *Connections: New Ways of Working in the Networked Organization* (Cambridge, Mass.: MIT Press).

Stallings, R. A. (1995), *Promoting Risk: Constructing the Earthquake Threat* (New York: de Gruyter).

Stehr, N. (1994), *Knowledge Societies* (London: Sage).

Suchman, M. (1995), 'Managing Legitimacy: Strategic and Institutional Approaches', *Academy of Management Review*, 20: 571–610.

Thompson, J. B. (1995), *The Media and Modernity* (Cambridge: Polity).

Toulmin, S. (1990), *Cosmopolis: The Hidden Agenda of Modernity* (Chicago, Ill.: University of Chicago Press).

Tsoukas, H. (2001), 'Re-viewing Organization', *Human Relations*, 54: 7–12.

Turner, B. A. (1976), 'The Organizational and Interorganizational Development of Disasters', *Administrative Science Quarterly*, 21: 378–96.

Vaughan, D. (1996), *The Challenger Launch Decision* (Chicago, Ill.: University of Chicago Press).

Virilio, P. (1989), *War and Cinema*, trans. P. Camiller (London: Verso).

Wallerstein, I. (1999), 'Ecology and Capitalist Costs of Production: No Exit', in Wallerstein, *The End of the World as We Know It* (Minneapolis, Minn.: University of Minnesota Press), 76–86.

Welsh, I. (1996), 'Risk, Global Governance and Environmental Politics', *Innovation*, 9: 407–20.

Woolley, B. (1992), *Virtual Worlds* (London: Penguin).

Wynne, B. (1992), 'Misunderstood Misunderstanding: Social Identities and Public Uptake of Science', *Public Understanding of Science*, 1: 281–304.

—— (1996), 'May the Sheep Safely Graze? A Reflexive View of the Expert–Lay Knowledge Divide', in S. Lash, B. Szerszynski, and B. Wynne (eds.), *Risk, Environment and Modernity* (London: Sage), 44–83.

THREE

Forms of Knowledge and Forms of Life in Organized Contexts

M AINSTREAM organization and management studies (OMS) has historically been antagonistic towards the lay knowledge organizational members possess. One of OMS's foundational assumptions has been that the management of people in organizations will be more effective the more lay knowledge is displaced by social scientific precepts. It has also been assumed that the body of formal knowledge necessary to enable this is increasingly becoming available from OMS, as the discipline of the social sciences dealing with the human aspects of organizing and managing (see Donaldson 1985; Lupton 1983; Pinder and Bourgeois 1982; Simon 1957 [1976]; Thompson 1956–7). A unified science of man in organizations, Pugh, Mansfield, and Warner have characteristically argued, would generate the sort of knowledge that would bring 'increasing benefits if man is to control the social institutions he has established, and hence the nature of the society in which he lives' (1975: 1).

Such an unqualified optimism has been a distinguishing feature of several OMS textbooks as well as of more esoteric mainstream OMS research. For example, addressing the readers of his organizational behaviour textbook, Robbins remarked in unequivocal terms: '[O]ne of the objectives of this text is to encourage you to *move away from your intuitive views of behavior* towards a systematic analysis, in the belief that the latter will enhance your effectiveness in accurately *explaining* and *predicting* behavior' (Robbins, 1989: 4, emphasis added). Similarly, the efforts to formalize organization theory through the

An earlier version of this chapter was first published in R. Chia (ed.), *In the Realm of Organization: Essays for Robert Cooper* (London: Routledge, 1998), 43–66. Reprinted by permission of Routledge, Copyright (1998).

I have benefited greatly from several discussions with Alan B. Thomas, whose ideas, criticism, and suggestions were invaluable in improving an earlier draft. I would also like to thank Gibson Burrell, Robert Cooper, Kenneth Gergen, Jannis Kallinikos, Steen Sorensen, Richard Whitley, and Arndt Sorge for their very useful comments on earlier drafts. The responsibility for any mistakes or omissions is obviously mine.

design of expert systems have been explicitly motivated by the view that intuitive reasoning is inherently 'flawed' and 'prejudiced' (Baligh, Burton, and Obel 1990: 35; Glorie, Mvlasuch, and Marx 1990: 80) and, thus, it ought to be replaced by scientifically derived knowledge.

It is partly my aim here to explore the presuppositions and limitations of such a view of organizational knowledge.[1] More generally, the purpose of this chapter is twofold: first, to delineate the different types of organizational knowledge and the way they relate to one another; and second, and more importantly, to ground the different types of organizational knowledge in particular dimensions of organized contexts. My thesis is that the propositional structure of knowledge produced by mainstream (or classical) OMS stems from, and is fully realized within, highly institutionalized social contexts (that is to say, in formal organizations or organized contexts—the two terms will be used interchangeably here). However, as will be shown later, even in such contexts propositional knowledge on its own is of limited utility. It will be further argued that as well as being *institutions*, organized contexts are *practices* (or communal traditions—these two terms will be used interchangeably) in which organizational members live their working lives. Practices are intrinsically related to narrative knowledge; namely, to knowledge organized in the form of stories, anecdotes, and examples.

Thus, in the argument put forward here, propositional organizational knowledge is intrinsically related to the institutional dimension of organized contexts, while narrative organizational knowledge is intrinsically related to the latter's practice dimension. The two pairs, however, are in conflict: for practices to endure they need to be sustained by institutions to whose corrosive influence they are inescapably exposed. At the same time, institutions cannot function unless they are supported by communal traditions. The implications of this conflict are explored later in this chapter.

The chapter is organized as follows. In the next section the scope of propositional knowledge will be outlined, underlining its necessary relationship with highly institutionalized forms of social action. Subsequently, the limits of propositional knowledge will be discussed, followed by an outline of the narrative form of organizational knowledge, which will be shown to be grounded on communities of tradition.

Organized Contexts as Institutions: The Case for Propositional Knowledge

The basic characteristic of propositional knowledge is the formulation of conditional 'if, then' statements relating a set of empirical conditions ('If X ...'—the factual predicate) to a set of consequences that follow when the conditions specified in the factual predicate obtain (' ... then Y'—the consequent) (Johannessen 1988; Johnson 1992; Payne 1982; Reeves and Clarke 1990; Schauer 1991; Stillings et al. 1987; Varela, Thompson, and Rosch 1991). Examples of propositional statements generated by mainstream OMS referring to organizations are the following: 'If size is large then formalization is high'; 'if technology is routine then complexity is low'; 'if strategy is that of a prospector then centralization is low'; 'if the environment is stable then centralization is high', and so on (see Baligh, Burton, and Obel 1990: 41–4; Glorie, Masuch, and Marx 1990: 87; see also Mintzberg, 1979, 1989; Webster and Starbuck 1988: 128). The preceding conditional statements serve as explanations of certain recurring organizational phenomena and purport to be the basis for formulating rules for guiding managerial action in the future.

Propositional statements are predicated on the assumption that the phenomenon they refer to is patterned, composed of objectively available elements that can be re-presented via an abbreviated formula (Barrow 1991; Cooper 1992; Varela, Thompson, and Rosch 1991). Anything that is assumed to be ordered and non-random is thought to be susceptible to propositional formalization and, thus, to abbreviation or, to use a technical term, to 'algorithmic compressibility' (Barrow 1991: 10–11). For example, the sequence of numbers 1 2 3 1 2 3 1 2 3 1 2 3 can easily be seen to be ordered: there is a pattern in it that allows us to replace the sequence with a rule and, thus, be relieved of the burden of having to carry the whole sequence and list all its contents (Barrow 1995: 46–7). However, in cases where there is no pattern in a sequence to numbers (generated, say, by tossing a coin) there is no abbreviated formula to capture its information content and the whole sequence needs to be listed in full.

Algorithmic compressibility is clearly important in so far as it allows the compression of masses of observational statements into a few clearly stated propositional statements, possessing the same informational content but, more importantly, enabling economy of effort, transferability, and remote control (Cooper 1992; Latour 1986). A revealing defence of the benefits of algorithmic compressibility that come about as a result of the accumulation of scientific knowledge was given, some time ago, by Medawar (cited in Feyerabend 1987: 122, emphasis added):

As science progresses, particular facts are comprehended within, and therefore in a sense annihilated by general statements of steadily increasing explanatory power and compass—whereupon the facts need no longer be known explicitly, i.e. spelled out and kept in mind. *In all sciences we are progressively relieved of the burden of singular instances, the tyranny of the particular.*

Thus, for Medawar, an object of scientific study is, in a very crucial sense, thought to be absorbed ('annihilated') by the discipline that studies it, so that its conceptual re-presentation, derived from a selective attention to certain features deemed crucial by the enquiring discipline, is taken to be more important than the object itself. Any other features of an object of study can, therefore, be disregarded (ibid. 122–3).

As stated earlier, the utility of abbreviated representations stems from their *mobility* (hence their transferability across contexts), their *manipulability*, and from their providing *efficient* ways of achieving results (Cooper 1992; Latour 1986).[2] Consider, for example, what one can do with digital representations of material objects. A two-dimensional square can be represented by four pairs of numbers corresponding to each one of its angles. Having this information on a computer one can play with the digital square: it can be made bigger or smaller by respectively increasing or decreasing its coordinate numbers; or it can be 'moved' around by adding to or subtracting from its coordinate numbers (Wooley 1992: 54). A symbolic world, namely a world consisting of abbreviated representations, is a mobile world (a digitized square can be sent through the network to other computers); it is also a manipulable world (you can experiment with a digitized object and even simulate some of its behaviour); and it is, of course, a world in which you can obtain results more efficiently than by dealing with the objects themselves (a bigger square can be created instantly on the computer without the need physically to design another one).

What is it that makes abbreviated representations mobile and manipulable, and renders their application efficient? A formal representation is independent of the medium in which it is embedded, and, therefore, as Haugeland (1985: 58) remarks, 'essentially the same formal system can be materialized in any number of different media, with no formally significant differences whatsoever'. One may play chess, for example, with chessboard and pawns of all sorts of different materials and sizes without affecting the rules and the syntax of the game. Abbreviated representations are abstract, and are defined exclusively in terms of their syntax (or structure), so that they do not mean anything particular. They are, thus, applicable across a variety of contexts after a particular interpretation (i.e. semantics) has been attached to them in each particular case (Casti 1989: ch. 5). Expert systems are a good example of abbreviated representations whose formal syntax needs to be supplemented with the details of a particular case each time they are used.

In extreme cases once an object of study has been formalized it can be manipulated without its users having to understand what they are doing, thus increasing economy of effort. Reasoning about the object of study can be carried out by purely manipulating symbols, divorced from meaning or interpretative understanding (Casti 1989; Reeves and Clarke 1990). Any time, for example, you use an automatic teller machine you do not need to understand the physics and the engineering principles implicated in its design, as long as you can see the results you expect. Abbreviated representations (and the propositional statements they are associated with) save actors from the burden of interpretative understanding for the sake of efficiently obtaining the desired output.

What must the social world be like for propositional knowledge to be possible? Clearly, it must be, at least to some extent, regularized, patterned, and non-random (Castoriadis 1991) so that it can be described via abbreviated representations in the form of propositional statements. Berger and Luckmann (1966) provided, some time ago, what still remains the best exposition of how the ordered character of reality is socially constructed:

All human activity is subject to habitualization. Any action that is repeated frequently becomes cast into a pattern, which can then be reproduced with an economy of effort and which, *ipso facto*, is apprehended by its performer as that pattern. Habitualization further implies that the action in question may be performed again in the future in the same manner and with the same economical effort. (ibid. 70)

Berger and Luckmann note that habitualization is the precursor to institutionalization. The latter occurs, they argue, 'whenever there is a reciprocal typification of habitualized action by types of actors' (ibid. 72). Notice the link they make between recurring patterns (i.e. habitualization) and quasi-formal cognition (i.e. typification) in the context of institutionalization. Actors attribute motives to each other and, seeing actions recur, they *typify* the motives as recurrent (hence reciprocal typifications). Individuals begin to cease to be—if they ever were—unpredictable, randomly acting atoms, and they gradually develop routines (i.e. roles) for dealing with one another. As Berger and Luckmann put it: 'The institution posits that actions of *type* x will be performed by actors of *type* x' (ibid., emphasis added). The individual and his/her actions are subsumed under broader categories which may formally be related and described.

Institutionalization renders the social world patterned and routinized so that it is possible to 'freeze' patterns and routines, and formally represent them in an abbreviated explanatory-cum-predictive formula (Tsoukas 1992). Or, to put it more generally, the more institutionalized human interaction is, the more likely it is that the patterns and regularities it gives rise to will be describable in an algorithmically compressed formula. For example, Poole and Van de Ven (1989) have highlighted the possibility of explaining the development of innovations in highly institutionalized contexts in terms of relatively deterministic historical-cum-functional models. By contrast, in the absence of highly institutionalized contexts, innovation patterns are better explained, they argue, in terms of emergent processes. In other words, to use the terminology adopted here, algorithmically compressible explanations are less likely to be useful in situations in which there are not well-developed institutional rules for the regulation of social life.

If the above is adopted, it should, I hope, be clear by now that processes of institutionalization imply that actors have delimited modes of interaction and that, therefore, they relate to one another in terms of their roles (see Lee, 1984; Zucker 1977). Roles consist of sets of rules delineating the scope and direction of individual action. This is most clearly manifested in organized contexts, since the latter consist, by design, of sets of processes for reducing equivocality among actors (Weick 1979), thus generating recurring events by means of rules that are usually explicitly defined and their execution monitored. Rules are prescriptive statements mandating or guiding behaviour in a given type of situation (Haugeland 1985; Schauer 1991; Twining and Miers 1991). As Twining and Miers remark, a rule 'prescribes that in circumstances X, behavior of type Y ought, or ought not to be, or may be, indulged in by persons of class Z' (ibid. 131) (see also Argyris and Schon 1974: 6).

Notice the similarities between such a definition of rules and the preceding description of the process of institutionalization by Berger and Luckmann (1966). Rules are necessarily generalizations connecting *types* of behaviour carried out by types of actors to *types* of situations (see Schauer 1991: ch. 2). To assert the existence of a rule is necessarily to generalize, and to institutionalize human interaction implies, of necessity, the existence of rules. As Weber (1948) insightfully remarked, it is the centrality of impersonal rules that marks out formal organization (bureaucracy) from other forms of administration. 'The "objective" discharge of business', observed Weber, 'means a discharge of business according to calculable rules and "without regard for persons"' (Weber 1948: 215). Why are calculable rules so important for bureaucracy? For Weber it is in the very logic of bureaucracy to demand calculability of results. In his words: '(Bureaucracy) develops the more perfectly the more the bureaucracy is "dehumanized", the more completely it succeeds in eliminating from official business love, hatred, and all purely personal, irrational, and emotional elements which escape calculation. This is the specific nature of bureaucracy and it is appraised as its special virtue' (ibid. 216).

The similarities of formal organization to expert systems are evident. Both rely on explicit rules for their functioning, and it is precisely this property of organized contexts that enables some researchers to pursue enthusiastically the formalization of organization theory (Lee 1984; Masuch 1990). However, as we will see below, such formalization is necessarily limited, and in so far as it is considered to be the *raison d'être* of OMS, it is problematic. Organized contexts cannot rely on calculable rules alone. Weber's linear logic, implicit in the preceding extract, can be seen at best as a *ceteris paribus* argument for the development of formal organization. We know enough now about the functioning of formal organizations to be able to question whether they can really function effectively as programmable machines.

Imperfect Rules, Unstable Semantics: The Limits of Propositional Knowledge

It has been argued so far that in organized contexts there is an intrinsic relationship between rules and propositional statements. In fact, as we have seen, they are mirror images of one another. For propositional statements to be possible, rules guiding human action must necessarily be in place. Conversely, the existence of rules can be captured via formal methods of investigation relating factual predicates to consequents. Rules, however, are far from perfect: the links between general categories and the particular instances they seek to relate to is always precarious. In this section it will be explained why this is the case and the implications will be explored.

Particular objects, actions, and events can be subsumed under a number of overlapping categories. A person, for example, can be described using a potentially infinite number of categories (e.g. nationality, race, occupation, state of health, marital status, hobbies, food preferences, and so on—the list is endless), but, in practice, a very limited set will normally do. Category choices are determined not by any of a person's properties—as Schauer (1991: 19) remarks, 'no one of the simultaneously applicable categories of which any particular is a member has a logical priority over another'— but by the discursive context in which a person is described (Watzlawick, Weakland, and Fisch 1974: ch. 8). For example, out of a multiplicity of classificatory candidates, all of which are empirically and logically correct generalizations, we normally choose the category 'patient' to describe someone who enters a hospital for treatment. Within this category even more discriminating choices can be made, depending on the kind of treatment a patient is seeking.

Through generalizing in one direction and, by default, not in another, discursive contexts make organizational action possible (Schauer 1991: ch. 2). Saying, for example, that 'Joanna is a thirty-year-old woman' or that 'Joanna is a teacher' is quite different from saying that 'Joanna is a single mother', because the same Joanna is in the company of different particulars, depending on the category chosen for attention. Thus, in the discursive context of the Child Support Agency (CSA), launched in 1993 by the British government to track down absent fathers who refuse to contribute towards their children's upbringing, women like Joanna are of interest only by virtue of being 'single mothers'. In every other respect these women are bound to be different (each of them is a particular whose properties extend in different directions and can, therefore, be subsumed under different categories) except for the one single category which constitutes the *raison d'être* of the CSA: 'single motherhood'.

By being generalizations, categories are necessarily selective: as selective inclusions they are also selective exclusions; they suppress as much as they reveal (ibid. 21). Furthermore, when categories are joined to make an organizational rule—for example, 'if a single mother is in danger of being harmed by her ex-partner, then the CSA may not force him to pay maintenance to her'—the rule's factual predicate 'consists of a generalization perceived to be causally relevant to some goal sought or evil to be avoided. Prescription of that goal, or proscription of that evil, constitutes the justification which then determines which generalization will constitute the rule's factual predicate' (ibid. 27). Here the evil to be avoided is the ex-partner doing harm to the single mother.

Avoiding this evil is judged to be more important than getting the ex-partner to contribute to the maintenance of his children at all costs.

What is noteworthy about organizational rules is that their consequents ('then the CSA may not force him to pay maintenance to her') are meant to be applied to *future* instances, while their factual predicates ('if a single mother is in danger of being harmed by her ex-partner') are either derived from knowledge of past regularities (which, it is thought, will also obtain in the future), or are based on current assumptions about behaviour in the future.

However, there is an asymmetry between description-cum-explanation and prescription. While propositional knowledge *retro*spectively explains (or at least describes) the functioning of a social system in terms of rules, it cannot *pro*spectively provide actors with the knowledge of how to apply definitively a set of rules in the future, or how to create new rules. This asymmetry can be removed only in closed systems from which internal change and external contingencies have been formally excluded, so that the future is a linear extension of the past.[3] Despite their inbuilt tendencies to closure, however, organizations are inherently open systems in which the above-noted asymmetry can, at best, only temporarily be abolished.

There are two reasons for this. First, there is the inherently unstable semantics of knowledge representation. All formal systems consisting of explicit rules depend for their functioning on the manipulation of representations (i.e. symbols) (see Casti 1989; Haugeland 1985; Lee 1984; Varela Thompson, and Rosch 1991; Winograd and Flores 1987). How do these representations get their meaning? The users of a system interpret the symbols they use in a particular way (that is, the users stabilize the symbols' meaning) so that valid inferences can be drawn. For a formal system to be effective it requires that its representations have stable meanings for as long as is possible. In open systems, however, such stability is always precarious and temporary. New definitions inevitably emerge, eroding the established ones (Tsoukas 1994*b*: 22–7).

For example, in the case of the CSA, a 'single mother applying for maintenance to the CSA' is such a symbol and is incorporated into the agency's knowledge representation. In the CSA's interpretation a single mother is eligible for receiving the full maintenance from the CSA if she discloses the name of her ex-partner and if, in doing so, her safety is not at risk. For its own internal purposes such definition may suffice but in an open social system the stability of the definition is precarious. For some single mothers wishing to receive full maintenance through the CSA, and wishing not to get embroiled in arguments with their ex-partners, or even aiming at obtaining some financial assistance from them which would be less than what their ex-partners would have to pay through the CSA, may collude with their ex-partners in claiming that the latter have been threatening them (see *Independent*, 21 March 1995). So, the initial interpretation of the agency must now be supplemented by another, whereby the genuineness of claims made by single mothers can be verified.

Although the preceding illustration is an example of how definitions can be eroded from 'within', there are also instances whereby definitional control is eroded from 'outside', namely, from competitors or outside stakeholders (see Tsoukas 1994*a*: 8–12; 1994*b*: 22–4). While, for example, initially mobile-tele-communications companies defined the use of mobile phones in terms largely similar to those of fixed-line phones—namely, in terms of transmitting voice messages—technological developments, users' demands, and relentless competition led to seeing mobile phones as electronic personal assistants enabling users to access the Internet, play games, use them as laptops, etc. The question 'What is a mobile phone for?' has had variable answers in a short period of time.

The more general point I am making is that while an organization is compelled to fix the definition of its representations for its own purposes, at a certain point in time, in so far as 'it must interact with the larger social world, it no longer has this definitional control' (Lee 1984: 302). The semantics of knowledge representation in an organized context is intrinsically unstable (although this does not mean permanently unstable) and, therefore, so are the rules underlying its functioning.

Second, several philosophers have pointed out that what ensures that a rule will be followed in the same way repeatedly in the future cannot itself be a rule (Taylor 1993: 57). This is essentially the gist of Wittgenstein's (1958) well-known remark that the application of rules is rooted in customs and public practices, and of Gadamer's claim (1980: 83) that to understand *in concreto* one needs *phronesis* (practical wisdom), since 'the application of rules can never be done by rules'. Anyone, for example, who has attempted to speak a foreign language must have experienced the inadequacy of simply knowing the rules for effectively practising. It is the grounding of language in social practices that makes it necessary for a speaker to learn to discriminate among a large variety of social situations, and this cannot be done effectively except through *participating* in a social practice.

It could be argued, however, that to the extent that contexts, customs, and practices can be studied and classified it is possible to construct increasingly more refined rules. While this has certainly been happening in medicine (see Hunter 1991), in artificial intelligence (Schank and Childers 1984), and in OMS (Masuch 1990), it would be naive to believe that it will eliminate the fundamental imperfection of rules as guides for human action in open social systems (Corbett 1989; Rosenbrock 1988; Schauer 1991). The reason is, as Johannessen (1988) notes (echoing Wittgenstein), as follows:

Since a definition of a rule cannot itself determine how it is to be applied, there is no point in giving a new rule to lay down how the first should be applied. For then the problem will just transfer itself to the new rule, because this also could be interpreted or followed in several different ways. It will continue thus *ad infinitum* if we try to escape this tangle by formulating more and more new rules to determine the use of the first rule. This is a dead end. We must realize that our application of rules cannot itself be determined through a rule. The application must by necessity be ruleless. (ibid. 298–9)

Brown and Duguid (1991), Orr (1990) and Spender (1992) have pointed out the problems associated with the propositional structure of knowledge underlying the application of rules, in their discussion of the role of directive documentation in helping technicians who service broken photocopiers. The machine manuals that are issued to service technicians contain canonical (i.e. rule-full) images of their practice, which are only tenuously related to the non-canonical practices technicians frequently employ to deal with a variety of local problems.[4] This is inescapable: organizations provide the discursive contexts by means of which certain generalizations are preferred, while some others are suppressed (although not negated). For the designers of photocopy manuals a 'broken machine' is of central importance and manuals are about fixing such an abstract entity. Repairing a machine, however, occurs in a social context the details of which cannot be exhaustively known *ex ante* to designers. Furthermore, although certain generalizations are necessarily selected ('If this error code is displayed then check this, or do that') it does not mean that the ones that have been suppressed are irrelevant; indeed, in certain conjunctions of circumstances they may become central (Schauer 1991: 22). The technician, for example, needs not only to fix the machine but to attend simultaneously to several other things (usually of a social nature): he strives not to lose the customer's trust in him, to enquire about the manner in which the customer had been using the machine, to maintain his/her reputation in the community of technicians, and so on (see Brown and Duguid 1991: 43; Orr 1990: 173; see also Vickers, 1983: 42–5). In a particular conjunction of circumstances one or more of those concerns may become particularly salient, although there is no way of telling if or when, or what form such a conjunction may take. Only the technician faced there and then with a concrete concatenation of events can carry out the diagnosis and undertake effective action.

At any point in time, therefore, what is going on in an organized context is not only non-fixed but inherently indeterminate, so that organizational rules (and the underlying propositional knowledge) are bound to be of limited utility. Several processes occur at the same time, and no one can describe them all in advance, since to notice what is going on depends on the (ineluctably partial) perspective of the observer (Hayek 1982: ch. 2; Tsoukas 1994*a*: 16). As MacIntyre has observed, there is no single game that is played, but several, and 'if the game metaphor may be stretched further, the problem about real life is that moving one's knight to QB3 may always be replied to with a lob across the net' (MacIntyre 1985: 98).

Could repair manuals not be made more sophisticated by drawing on past experiences and incorporating increasingly more categories of the social contexts in which broken machines are likely to be found? Should this happen the technicians would surely be offered better-informed, rule-based advice as to how to deal with broken machines. Such advice would certainly be useful but, still, it does not solve the problem. The fact remains that even conditional generalizations are *universal* within their scope of applicability. In Schauer's words: 'Regardless of scope, any rule uses its generalizing factual predicate to make it applicable to *all* of something' (Schauer 1991: 24). To say, for example, 'if in such and such circumstances this error happens, then do that' is to offer advice that is universal within the scope of 'such and such' regardless of how small that scope is.

Managing an organized context by rules alone leads inescapably to paradoxes. The reason is that time is not included in the propositional logic underlying the use of rules. As Bateson (1979: 63) insightfully observed, the 'if, then' of causality contains time, but the 'if then' of propositional statements is timeless (see also Capra 1988: 83). Take, for example, again, the case of the CSA. One of the CSA rules is that if a single mother does not disclose the name of the father to the CSA her benefit will be reduced. What is the justification for this? Obviously, the legitimate need for the CSA to identify irresponsible fathers who have not contributed towards the upbringing of their children and to force them to do so. Putting pressure on the mother (the only person the CSA is likely to have, initially, any contact with) seems a sensible thing to do. But if, for some reason, a mother refuses to tell the CSA the father's name, then her benefit will be reduced. Notice the paradox. On the one hand, here is an agency whose primary goal is to financially support single mothers to be able to bring up their children. On the other hand, if a single mother does not conform to the agency's rules, her maintenance will be reduced. And if the state benefit is reduced, those who will be most likely to suffer will be the children, whose welfare is supposed to be the sole reason for the existence of the CSA. A classic catch-22.

The paradox is created because of a confusion of logical levels induced by timeless propositional logic. One logical level is that of single mothers' real demands; namely, maintenance sufficient for the welfare of their children. A logically higher level is that of single mothers' demands as they are represented by the CSA's rules; namely, state benefits with strings attached. Other things being equal, conflating meeting single mother's demands with 'meeting' their demands as the CSA rules prescribe creates the paradox: if the single mothers' demands are met, then they are not 'met'. If they are 'met', then they are not met! The system oscillates, it cannot get things right.[5]

Organized Contexts as Practices:
The Case for Narrative Knowledge

The impossibility of guiding practical action in organized contexts by rules alone underlines the gnosiological[6] indispensability of examples, anecdotes, and stories (in short: narratives) for stating what rules cannot state. As Wittgenstein famously remarked: 'Not only rules, but also examples are needed for establishing a practice. Our rules leave loopholes open, and *the practice has to speak for itself* (Wittgenstein 1969: 145, emphasis added). We saw earlier why rules leave loopholes open, but in what sense are 'examples' needed for establishing a practice? What does a 'practice' mean, and how can it 'speak for itself'?

In the preceding quotation Wittgenstein uses the word 'example' with a double meaning: I hold someone up as an example, as embodying the standards of excellence I myself aspire to, *and* I use examples, illustrations, and stories to convey to someone else the knowledge that is necessary for engaging in a set of practical activities. In the former sense, I learn a practice through actively participating in it by engaging with and learning from all those who have been there before me. In the latter sense, a community shares a set of narratives through which it articulates its self-understanding, its historically shaped identity, and preserves its collective memory. Thus, a practice speaks for itself *actively* (through its actions); that is, through letting others see what its members are up to. Also, a practice speaks for itself *gnosiologically*; that is, through the narratives articulating the knowledge employed in (the) practice. On this account, therefore, narratives are intimately linked to practices. As will be shown below, organized contexts will not be properly understood unless they are also seen as *practices* (and not merely as institutions).

What are 'practices', and why do we need to distinguish them from 'institutions'? MacIntyre's attempt to sociologically ground his moral philosophy makes use of the concept of 'practice', and in what follows I will draw extensively on his analysis.

By a "practice" I am going to mean any coherent and complex form of socially established cooperative human activity through which goods internal to that form of activity are realized in the course of trying to achieve those standards of excellence which are appropriate to, and partially definitive of, that form of activity, with the result that human powers to achieve excellence, and human conceptions of ends and goods involved are systematically extended. (MacIntyre 1985: 187)

So what might be examples of practices? MacIntyre again: 'Tic-tac-toe is not an example of a practice in this sense, nor is throwing a football with skill; but the game of football is, and so is chess. Bricklaying is not a practice; architecture is. Planting turnips is not a practice; farming is. So are the enquiries of physics, chemistry and biology, and so is the work of the historian, and so are painting and music' (ibid. 187).

There are four crucial features of a practice borne out by MacIntyre's definition. First, a practice is a complex form of social activity that involves the cooperative effort of human beings; it is coherent and, therefore, bound by rules; and it is extended in time. For practices to survive for any length of time they need to be carried out within institutions, for, as we saw earlier, it is the latter that give social life enduring features. Obviously, this is a matter of degree: practices are more or less institutionalized; as, for example, when one is doing solitary research in, say, physics, as opposed to carrying it out within a university laboratory. However, one thing is clear: although practices alone are articulate forms of social action, if they are to be sustained they will inevitably become institutionalized.

Second, every practice establishes a set of what MacIntyre calls 'internal goods'; namely, goods that cannot be achieved in any other way but by *participating* in the practice itself. For example, the particular analytical skills and strategic imagination that are associated with playing chess, the kind of satisfaction derived from caring for patients, or the thrill that comes from exploring new avenues of scientific research cannot be achieved in any other way than by respectively *playing* chess, *nursing* patients, and *researching* in a particular field. Naturally, 'those who lack the relevant experience are incompetent thereby as judges of internal goods' (ibid. 189). By contrast, 'external goods' such as status, money, career, fame, etc., are only contingently attached to a practice and they can, therefore, be achieved in alternative ways without having to participate in a particular practice.

Whereas the achievement of internal goods benefits potentially the whole community who engage in a particular practice (e.g. major conceptual shifts in physics), the achievement of external goods benefits only individuals, and this accounts for the competition that is often associated with acquiring external goods. Practices are intrinsically linked with internal goods, whereas institutions are linked with external goods. The result is conflict: 'the ideals and the creativity of the practices are always vulnerable to the acquisitiveness of the institution' (ibid. 194).

Third, participating in a practice necessarily involves attempting to achieve the standards of excellence operative in the practice at the time. Unless one accepts the standards of the practice into which one has entered, and the inadequacy of one's performance vis-à-vis those standards, one will never learn to excel in that practice.

Fourth, every practice has its own history, which is not only the history of the changes of technical skills relevant to a practice, but also a history of changes of the relevant ends to which the technical skills are put. It is the *historicity* of a practice that impels MacIntyre to argue that 'to enter into a practice is to enter into a relationship not only with its contemporary practitioners, but also with those who have preceded us in the practice, particularly those whose achievements extended the reach of the practice to its present point. It is thus the achievement, and *a fortiori* the authority, of a tradition which I then confront and from which I have to learn' (ibid. 194).

If what has been argued so far is accepted, it follows that organizational rules are intimately connected with the institutional dimension of organized contexts, and are necessarily couched in the language of selective generalizations while, at the same time, remaining inherently open-ended in their future applications. Thus, the task of, say, service technicians is located at the interface between the generic rules mandated by a particular manual *and* the local context of application. It is the ability to mediate between these two levels that marks out an effective technician, and such an ability is largely acquired and enhanced through participating in a practice (i.e. in a community of other technicians) (Brown and Duguid 1991; Orr 1990; Schon 1987: 35–40).

From a gnosiological point of view, what does it mean to participate in a practice? The answer has already been alluded to: it is to share in the narratives a community of practitioners employs. Why is this sharing important, and why sharing in *narratives*? It is because the *history* of the practice into which I have entered and from which I have to learn, if I am to become an effective member of the community of practitioners, is conveyed to me through the *stories* my fellow practitioners tell me. Stories about the good old days, about achievements and failures, about awkward people and memorable episodes; stories about everything that matters to those participating in the practice (Hunter 1991: ch. 4). Narratives, therefore, are context-specific accounts, replete with the actions (or omissions) of concrete individuals, containing events that are temporally arranged and, in an organized context at least, they usually imply suggestions for desirable ways of acting.

Rules cannot have the role that narratives have: rules are impersonal, generic, and atemporal formulae bearing only an apparent relation to what I am exactly experiencing 'on the ground' (Bourdieu 1990: 80–97; Taylor 1993: 56–7). I am an individual with my own aspirations, skills, and vulnerabilities; whatever I am is the result of the particular context-dependent experiences that I have had in the course of my life. As such, I am an inescapably *historical* human being and I have entered into an ineluctably *historical* setting (or context). If I want to find out about why certain patterns of behaviour are dominant in my practice, I have to enquire about the intentions, desires, and goals of the individuals already generating those patterns. But in order to do so, I need to relate those intentions to the settings in which the behaviours occur. Now, to understand the setting(s) of a behaviour I need to find out about its history, for the setting itself consists of individuals and their relationships extended in time (MacIntyre 1985: 204–17). As Mulhall and Swift (1992: 87) have remarked, echoing MacIntyre:

rendering an action intelligible is a matter of grasping it as an episode in the history of the agent's life and of the settings in which it occurs. [...] In other words, narrative history of a certain kind is the basic genre for the characterization of human action. [...] Because action has a basically historical character, our lives are enacted narratives in which we are both characters and authors; a person is a character abstracted from history.

The suggestions for action implied by narratives do not follow the 'if, then' structure of rules.[7] To understand the practical utility of narratives it is helpful to see them as inputs into an individual considered as a black box, the output of which is individual action. Why is the individual thought of as analogous to a black box? In a black box it is not known how inputs are connected to outputs (Beer 1966: 293–8). What is so interesting about a black box? Look at it this way: in a transparent box its internal connections are known, hence its variety (namely, the number of possible states the box can take up) is constrained. Individuals following rules are enjoined to act as if they were transparent boxes: the consequents (i.e. the outputs of action) are linked to the factual predicates (i.e. the inputs) in specific ways—as rules mandate. A particular set of inputs is supposed to lead to an already described set of outputs. No interference from (to quote Weber again) 'love, hatred, and all purely personal, irrational, and emotional elements which escape calculation' is allowed.

The reverse happens with a black box. Because the latter is 'assumed to be able to take on any internal arrangement of input-output connectivity at all' (Beer, 293), a black box can have maximal variety, and thus it is better suited to cope with unforeseen circumstances. Narratives-as-inputs leading to individuals-as-black-boxes can be linked to the specific experiences individuals have already acquired in the course of their lives, in numerous, unforeseeable ways. How is this possible? Three reasons.

First, nobody fully knows what an individual's historical experiences are; or, to put it differently, it cannot be fully known by an observer what an actor's stock of past experiential knowledge consists of (Tsoukas 1994b). Second, no observer can ever possess all the local knowledge each actor *happens* to possess by virtue of his/her particular location in the organization (Hayek 1945, 1982; Tsoukas 1994a). And third, no one is in a position to tell which parts of, and how, an individual's experiential knowledge and local knowledge will be connected with the incoming narratives. Hence, the link between narratives and individual actions is bound to be contingent and, therefore, ambiguous.

From the above it follows that the utility of narratives lies not so much in the particular suggestions for action they may imply as in their mode of use: their contingent connections to individual actions help bridge the gap between generic rules and local circumstances in a flexible and inconclusive manner. Commenting on the extensive narration used by service technicians in their work, Brown and Duguid (1991: 44) aptly remark: 'The stories have a flexible generality that make them both adaptable and particular. They function, rather like the common law, as a usefully underconstrained means to interpret each new situation in the light of accumulated wisdom and constantly changing circumstances'. To the extent that this happens, narratives help provide unexpected clues which may trigger new ways of thinking and thus initiate fresh courses of action (McKelvey and Aldrich 1983; Spender 1992; Weick 1987). Contrary to the linear structure of propositional knowledge, the dynamic structure of narratives is such that it allows events to be flexibly connected along time, social interactions to be preserved, and local contexts to be taken into account. Narratives also have a mnemonic value since they are registered in, and recalled from, human memory more easily than complex sets of propositional statements (Brown and Duguid 1991; Daft and Wiginton 1979: Weick 1987; Weick and Browning 1986).

Narration, therefore, facilitates social interaction, preserves a community's collective memory, and enhances a group's sense of shared identity as participants in a practice (Brown and Duguid 1991; Orr 1990). Starbuck (1985) has given a vivid account of the intimate links between organized-contexts-as-practices and narration. In a research project he investigated how a worker, Charlie Strothman, drafted production schedules, including in particular how he estimated machine run times. No one had taught him an explicit procedure and he could not quite put into words how exactly he was able to estimate run times: 'He had just learned from experience, and he doubted that he always used the same procedure' (ibid. 354). After an in-depth study the researchers concluded that Charlie's complex thought processes could be reduced to a linear equation which produced his speed estimates fairly accurately. Having shown him the linear equation and demonstrated the benefits from using it in his daily work, the researchers expected Charlie to start using it. Alas, this did not happen! 'Six years of habit and the frame of reference that went with it were too strong. The familiar program worked and he trusted it. Who knows what errors lurked in an unfamiliar program?' (ibid. 355). What is more important, however, is the link between narration and organized context *qua* practice that Starbuck alludes to:

[T]he familiar program meshed with other programs used by other people: the whole organization talked and reported data in terms of speeds, not times. [...] *If Charlie were to shift to a time frame of reference, he would isolate himself from other people in his organization, and their talk about speeds would lack meaning for him.* It was no accident that he had earlier told us: "When I first came to work here, I was told what the average speeds were". (ibid., emphasis added)

Starbuck dismisses the possible explanation that Charlie's resistance might stem from apathy, ignorance, or conservatism. Charlie is described as intelligent, extremely cooperative in the research project, having had some engineering training, and being renowned for his willingness to introduce innovations at work. Such apparent resistance cannot be understood unless one sees an organized context as also a communal tradition; that is, as a practice whose main mode of understanding and communication is narration. The particular set of social relationships existing at Charlie's workplace were underwritten by a particular form of organizational knowledge; changing one would inevitably have implications for the other.[8]

An attempt to represent organizational knowledge via an abbreviated propositional formula may be necessary for institutional purposes (e.g. individual or group target setting, efficiency, accountability, etc.), but it highlights the external goods to be achieved in an organized context. A particular abstraction, such as, for example, the productive capacity of individuals (or of *individual* groups, departments, etc.) becomes the prime focus of attention, individual calculation, and potential dispute. The more this happens, the more the institutionalized character of organized contexts is underscored at the expense of their communal dimension and the internal goods the latter is associated with.

An organized context deprived of the experience of a communal form of life manifested in a shared tradition, in stories and memorable episodes, has a truncated collective memory that undermines its ability to cope with novel problems (Weick 1987; see also Engestrom et al. 1990). In so far as organized contexts are inherently open systems, and to the extent that organizational rules are intrinsically open-ended in their application, every problem has some degree of novelty or, as Piaget famously remarked, 'in each act of understanding some degree of invention is involved' (1970: 77). Individuals, therefore, faced with problems will have to transcend their reliance on rules and draw also on narratives shared in their practice if they are to tackle their problems effectively.

Furthermore, Charlie Strothman's resistance to applying the researcher's mathematical formula at work stemmed not only from the important fact that doing so might have distanced him from the community of his fellow-workers, but also from an intuitive appreciation that unless practical knowledge is known tacitly it is ineffectual. Polanyi (1966) and Polanyi and Prosch (1975) cogently argue that all practical knowing is tacit, in the sense that the focal target of our attention (e.g. a pair of stereoscopic pictures) always relies on particulars of which we are only subsidiarily aware (e.g. the individual pictures), and which need to be integrated tacitly by the knower with the focal target. In Polanyi and Prosch's words:

[T]he structure of tacit knowing [. . .] includes a joint pair of constituents. Subsidiaries exist as such by bearing on the focus *to* which we are attending *from* them. In other words, the functional structure of from–to knowing includes jointly a subsidiary 'from' and a focal 'to' (or 'at'). But this pair is not linked together of its own accord. The relation of a subsidiary to a focus is formed by the *act of a person* who integrates one to another. (ibid. 37–8)

Although Polanyi and Prosch's argument refers to the structure of individual knowing, it is also relevant to the structure of collective knowing. As an individual is unable to learn to balance on a bicycle by trying to follow a mathematical formula relating the velocity of the bicycle to its angle of imbalance, so a collectivity of individuals cannot undertake effective action unless its knowledge is known non-explicitly; that is to say, non-propositionally. Narratives provide the subsidiaries which individuals integrate tacitly with the focus of attention.

Thus, what Starbuck's workers practically do with respect to machine run times is based on a host of subsidiaries such as machine speeds and specific features of the production schedule, which they as individuals have tacitly learned to integrate. Collectively, they share a number of stories about machine breakdowns, time miscalculations, successful estimates, etc., which, although they may have little to do directly with the estimates of run time for a particular schedule at a particular point in time, do bear tacitly on it (see also Brown and Duguid 1991). How? Stories make workers (and practitioners in general) aware of the knowledge that has been historically accumulated in a practice, and this subsidiary awareness is merged into the focal awareness of trying to tackle a particular problem. Practitioners watch—namely, they are focally aware of—the effects of their problem solving efforts by keeping subsidiarily aware of the hitherto-known episodes concerning similar problems in the past. Narratively organized experiences (both personal and vicarious ones) provide actors with the subsidiary particulars which bear on the focal activity *to* which actors are attending *from* them (Polanyi and Prosch 1975: 37–8).

Summary and Conclusion

Organizing consists of a set of processes aimed at institutionalizing human interaction and, as such, it is intimately related to quasi-formal cognition. Actors attribute motives to each other and, seeing actions recur, they typify the motives as recurrent. Institutionalized human interaction gives rise to patterns and regularities which are, in principle, amenable to algorithmic compressibility. Knowledge of regularities is cast in a propositional mould so that the right type of action can be initiated in the right type of circumstance. Thus, propositional knowledge is closely linked with the institutional dimension of organizing: organized contexts tend to be, by design, institutionalized systems, replete with regularities which can be represented via propositional knowledge (see Fig. 3.1).

However, knowledge of regularities alone cannot be an effective guide for (prospective) action. The reason is that organized contexts are also open systems in constant flux. Particular organizational practices continue to exist only to the extent that actors' interpretations of them continue to be stable. Also, actors' capacity for learning and self-reflection has the effect that actors have the potential for self-transformation, and thus the social reality they help constitute is also transformable.

The intrinsic openness of organized contexts implies that the future may always be different from the past, and that there is no guarantee that the rules guiding individuals' behaviour now will also be applied in the future as intended. Rules on their own are imperfect coordinating devices: how they will be interpreted and applied in particular situations will always be uncertain. Therefore, rules need to be supplemented by narratives containing the collective memory of a social system and enabling it to cope with novel problems.

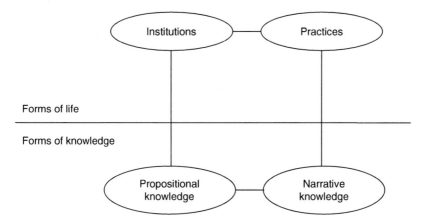

Fig. 3.1: Forms of knowledge and forms of life in organized contexts.

Narrative knowledge is an indispensable input to effective action because organized contexts, in addition to being institutions, are also practices (see Fig. 3.1). As practices, organized contexts are communal traditions having their own standards of excellence as well as their own internal goods which only participants can judge and achieve. To participate in a practice is to share in the narratives that a community of practitioners employs. Narratives are indeed an important category of organizational knowledge and discourse, and are constructed around memorable episodes derived from participating in a practice. Unlike propositional statements, narratives are contingently linked to individual action, thus facilitating individual adaptation to a large number of unforeseeable circumstances. Furthermore, narration facilitates social interaction, preserves a community's collective memory, enhances a group's sense of shared identity as participants in a practice, and serves as a repository of tacit organizational knowledge.

From the above it follows that the knowledge and social domains are inter-dependent: forms of organizational knowledge are rooted in forms of organizational life, and vice versa. In order for actors to be able to realize their plans, their immediate (human and non-human) environment needs to be rendered predictable (i.e. to be institutionalized), and the acquisition (as well as the generation) of propositional knowledge is necessary (as well as feasible). At the same time, however, through participating in a practice, actors need to preserve their free will, their autonomy and creativity, which, valuable though these are in themselves, are also necessary for *en*acting (as opposed to merely *re*acting to) a predictable environment. As MacIntyre has remarked:

It is necessary, if life is to be meaningful, for us to be able to engage in long-term projects, and this requires predictability; it is necessary, if life is to be meaningful, for us to be in possession of ourselves and not merely to be the creations of other people's projects, intentions and desires, and this requires unpredictability. We are thus involved in a world in which we are simultaneously trying to render the rest of society predictable and ourselves unpredictable, to devise generalizations which will capture the behaviour of others and to cast our own behaviour into forms which will elude the generalizations which others frame. (MacIntyre 1985: 104)

Propositional knowledge and narrative knowledge are the two ends of the spectrum of organizational knowledge.[9] In so far as organized contexts are institutions they necessarily generate and use propositional knowledge; to the extent that organized contexts are practices they necessarily generate and draw upon narrative knowledge. Furthermore, other things being equal, the more institutionalized a social system is, the more the propositional type of knowledge will tend to be used in decision-making. Conversely, the more organizational knowledge is understood in terms of propositional knowledge, the more institutionalized a social system will tend to become, and narrative knowledge will tend to be underestimated. In rationalized sociocultural contexts, in which classic scientific argumentation is held to be the paradigm of reliable knowledge, propositional knowledge will tend to dominate over narrative knowledge. In rationalized sociocultural contests organizations have more chance of surviving by adopting a rationalistic discourse manifested in explicit rules. Thus, as well as being gnosiologically indispensable, rules are also politically expedient, for they enhance organizations' chances of survival in rationalized environments. Although exploring the influences that shape the forms of organizational knowledge is important, such exploration is beyond the scope of this chapter.

Notes

1. By 'organizational knowledge' I primarily mean here knowledge used by actors *in* organizations, not knowledge *about* organizations. There is, obviously, a clear relationship between the two. For example, the propositional knowledge used in organizations in the form of rules is certainly related to the formal knowledge about organizational phenomena generated by organizational researchers—the former is supposed to be aided, refined, and, ideally, replaced by the latter. For the sake of conceptual clarity, however, it makes sense to keep these two logical levels of organizational knowledge separate.
2. Transferability is an important property of social-scientific knowledge which was well appreciated by Thompson (1956–7), and was part of his justification for the desirability and possibility of an administrative science. In his words: 'If every administrative action, and every outcome of such action, is entirely unique, then there can be no transferable knowledge or understanding of administration. If, on the other hand, knowledge of at least some aspects of administrative processes is transferable, then those methods which have proved most useful in gaining reliable knowledge in other areas would also seem to be appropriate for adding to our knowledge of administration' (ibid. 103).

Similarly, the efficiency (or economy of effort) that comes with the application of social-scientific knowledge has been praised by Huczynski and Buchanan in their textbook. They write: 'If (for example) we know what motivates you, we then know what buttons to press to make you work harder, we know what levers to pull to make you change your attitudes, we know what rewards and sanctions will get your support for a particular package of changes—so we can influence your behaviour in directions we think desirable' (Huczynski and Buchanan 1991: 54).

3. A social system is intrinsically open in the sense that it is impossible to obtain stable regularities across space and time (see Bhaskar 1979; Saver 1984). Why? Regularities are generated by repeated individual actions (that is, acting similarly in similar circumstances) and are possible only when the following two conditions obtain: first, the mechanisms (that is, individual action) producing regularities must not undergo qualitative change (the intrinsic condition of closure); second, the relationship between mechanisms and the external conditions that matter for their operation must remain constant (the extrinsic condition of closure). To the extent that individuals' meanings and interpretations differ across contexts. and change over time, social systems violate both conditions of closure (Tsoukas 1994*a*: 8–9).

4. It may be noted parenthetically that, although Brown and Duguid, and Orr rightly underline the imperfection of rules in guiding practical action, they do not appreciate the intrinsic relationship between rules and organized contexts. The mismatch between canonical (propositional) knowledge and non-canonical, context-dependent practical action is not so much the result of organizations 'misunderstanding' the work of technicians, as Brown and Duguid (1991: 53) suggest, as an intrinsic property of the generalizations employed in organized contexts.

5. The paradoxes, and the oscillating management of social systems that ensues, have also been explored in the context of the local-government reforms in the UK, focusing in particular on the introduction of league tables (see Tsoukas 1994*a*: 6–8).

6. *Gnosis* is the Greek word for knowledge. 'Gnosiological', therefore, is the adjectival form of 'knowledge'. I use this term here because I want to avoid using the term 'cognitive', which has been related to a particular type of representational thinking in cognitive science (see Stillings et al., 1987) 'Gnosiology' means discourse on knowledge—knowledge in general, not cognition, nor formal knowledge.

7. On the one hand, it could be argued that in so far as knowledge in general implies or suggests propositions for action, all knowledge (including narrative knowledge) is propositional. However, such an assertion would miss the most salient features of propositional knowledge proper—namely, the abbreviated representation of social phenomena via abstract thinking for the purpose of instrumental intervention at a distance (Cooper 1992). Thus, while Spender's 'industry recipes' are sets of knowledge that structure senior managers' ways of looking at particular industries, as well as offering strategists sets of background ideas and elemental judgements concerning their business domains (see Sackmann 1992; Spender 1989: 185–98), the guidance they offer is partial, ambiguous, and inconsistent (Spender 1989: 190). Industry recipes, albeit consisting of actionable knowledge, lack the degree of abstraction, and do not include the systematic covariation of a few salient features of their objects of reference

which are the key characteristic of propositional knowledge as defined above. Later in the chapter it will be argued that individuals applying propositional statements in the form of organizational rules are analogous to 'transparent boxes', while when acting under the influence of narratives they are analogous to 'black boxes'. Both types of knowledge entail or imply action, but in different ways.

On the other hand, it could be argued that all knowledge is narrative in a generic sense—even propositional knowledge is a particular form of narrative. That is true, but the term 'narrative' is used in this chapter in a restricted sense to mean story-like accounts (see Hunter 1991).

8. Of course, it could be that at some point later the same workers might end up using times instead of speeds as the basis for drafting production schedules. However, it would still be the case that for the new metric's daily use to be effective it would have to rely on knowledge cast in a narrative form, albeit one with a different content. New narratives would be expected to be invented, a different set of memorable episodes would become the focus of attention, and the new members would be initiated into the new method of working out machine runs. In short, a more or less different pattern of social interaction would be expected to emerge, and new stories would inevitably be told. But stories there would be!

9. The classification of organizational knowledge suggested here (propositional versus narrative) is not the only one available, although, as I hope has become clear, it is the most suitable for the purpose of showing the links between organized contexts and types of organizational knowledge. Other researchers have suggested different classifications. For example, as is well known, Weber (1947: 184–6) distinguished between 'formal' and 'substantive' rationality, Ryle (1947) between 'knowing that' and 'knowing how', and Habermas between 'strategic' and 'contextual' rationality (see White 1988: 10–21). Similarly, Nonaka (1994), drawing on Polanyi (1966), has made the distinction between 'explicit' and 'tacit' organizational knowledge, which is also one dimension in Spender's (1995) typology of organizational knowledge (the other one being the dimension of the 'individual' versus 'social'). All the above classifications, developed for different purposes, parallel to some extent the distinction between propositional and narrative knowledge used here.

References

Argyris, G., and Schon, D. (1974), *Theory in Practice* (San Francisco, Calif.: Jossey-Bass).

Baligh, H. H., Burton, R. M., and Obel, B. (1990), 'Devising Expert Systems in Organization Theory: The Organizational Consultant', in M. Masuch (ed.) *Organization, Management, and Expert Systems* (Berlin: de Gruyter), 35–57.

Barrow, J. (1991), *Theories of Everything* (London: Vintage).

—— (1995), 'Theories of Everything', in J. Cornwell (ed.), *Nature's Imagination*, (Oxford: Oxford University Press), 45–63.

Bateson, G. (1979), *Mind and Nature* (Toronto: Bantam).

Beer, S. (1966), *Decision and Control* (Chichester: Wiley).

Berger, E., and Luckmann, T. (1966), *The Social Construction of Reality* (London: Penguin).

Bhaskar, R. (1979), *The Possibility of Naturalism* (Brighton: Harvester Wheatsheaf).

Bourdieu, P. (1990), *The Logic of Practice*, trans. R. Nice (Cambridge: Polity).

Brown, J. S., and Duguid, P. (1991), 'Organizational Learning and Communities of Practice: Towards a Unified View of Working, Learning, and Innovation', *Organization Science*, 2: 40–57.

Capra, E. (1988), 'The Pattern which Connects: Gregory Bateson', in E. Capra (ed.) *Uncommon Wisdom* (London: Flamingo), 73–92.

Casti, J. (1989), *Paradigms Lost* (London: Cardinal).

Castoriadis, C. (1991), *Philosophy, Politics, Autonomy*, ed. D. A. Curtis (New York: Oxford University Press).

Cooper, R. (1992), 'Formal Organization as Representation: Remote Control, Displacement and Abbreviation', in M. Reed and M. Hughes (eds.), *Rethinking Organization: New Directions in Organization Theory and Analysis* (London: Sage), 251–72.

Corbett, M. (1989), 'Automate or Innervate? The Role of Knowledge in Advanced Manufacturing Systems', *AI & Society*, 3: 198–208.

Daft, R., and Wiginton, J. (1979), 'Language and Organization', *Academy of Management Review*, 4: 179–91.

Derrida, J. (1976), *Of Grammatology*, trans. G. Spivak (Baltimore, Md.: Johns Hopkins University Press).

Donaldson, L. (1985), *In Defence of Organization Theory* (Cambridge: Cambridge University Press).

Engestrom, Y., Brown, K., Engestrom, R., and Koistinen, K. (1990), 'Organizational Forgetting: an Activity-theoretical Perspective', in D. Middleton and D. Edwards (eds.) *Collective Remembering* (London: Sage), 139–68.

Feyerabend, P. K. (1987), *Farewell to Reason* (London: Verso).

Gadamer, H. G. (1980), 'Practical Philosophy as a Model of the Human Sciences', *Research in Phenomenology*, 9: 74–85.

Glorie, J. C., Masuch, M., and Marx, M. (1990), 'Formalizing Organizational Theory: A Knowledge-based Approach', in M. Masuch (ed.), *Organization, Management, and Expert Systems* (Berlin: de Gruyter), 79–104.

Haugeland, J. (1985), *Artificial Intelligence* (Cambridge, Mass.: MIT Press).

Hayek, E. A. (1945), 'The Use of Knowledge in Society', *American Economic Review* 35: 519–30.

—— (1982), *Law, Legislation and Liberty* (London: Routledge & Kegan Paul).

Huczynski, A., and Buchanan, D. (1991), *Organizational Behaviour* (Hemel Hempstead: Prentice Hall).

Hunter, M. K. (1991), *Doctor's Stories: The Narrative Structure of Medical Knowledge* (Princeton, NJ: Princeton University Press).

Johannessen, K. (1988), 'Rule Following and Tacit Knowledge', *AI & Society*, 2: 287–302.

Johnson, R. (1992), *Human–Computer Interaction* (London: McGraw-Hill).

Latour, B. (1986), 'Visualization and Cognition: Thinking with Eyes and Hands', *Knowledge and Society: Studies in the Sociology of Culture Past and Present*, 6: 1–10.

Lee. R. M. (1984), 'Bureaucracies, Bureaucrats and Information Technology', *European Journal of Operational Research*, 18: 293–303.

Lupton, T. (1983), *Management and the Social Sciences*, 3rd edn. (London: Penguin).

MacIntyre, A. (1985), *After Virtue*, 2nd edn. (London: Duckworth).

Masuch, M. (1990) (ed.), *Organization, Management, and Expert Systems* (Berlin: de Gruyter).

McKelvey, B., and Aldrich, H. (1983), 'Populations, Natural Selection and Applied Organizational Science', *Administrative Science Quarterly*, 28: 101–28.

Mintzberg, H. (1979), *The Structuring of Organizations* (Englewood Cliffs, NJ: Prentice Hall).

—— (1989), *Mintzberg on Management* (New York: Free Press).

Mulhall S., and Swift, A. (1992), *Liberals and Communitarians* (Oxford: Blackwell).

Nonaka, I. (1994), 'A Dynamic Theory of Organizational Knowledge Creation', *Organizational Science*, 5: 14–37.

Orr, J. E. (1990), 'Sharing Knowledge, Celebrating Identity: Community Memory in a Service Culture', in D. Middleton and D. Edwards (eds.) *Collective Remembering* (London: Sage), 168–89.

Payne, R. (1982), 'The Nature of Knowledge and Organizational Psychology', in N. Nicholson and T. Wall (eds.) *Theory and Method in Organizational Psychology* (New York: Academic), 37–67.

Piaget, J. (1970), *Genetic Epistemology* (New York: Norton).

Pinder, C. C., and Bourgeois, W. V. (1982), 'Controlling Tropes in Administrative Science', *Administrative Science Quarterly*, 27: 641–52.

Polanyi, M. (1966), *The Tacit Dimension* (London: Routledge & Kegan Paul).

—— and Prosch, H. (1975), *Meaning*, (Chicago, Ill.: University of Chicago Press).

Poole, M. S., and Van de Ven, A. H. (1989), 'Towards a General Theory of Innovation Processes', in A. Van de Ven, H. L. Angle, and M. S. Poole (eds.) *Research on the Management of Innovation: The Minnesota Studies* (New York: Harper & Row), 637–62.

Pugh, D. S., Mansfield. R., and Warner, M. (1975), *Research in Organizational Behaviour: A British Survey*, (London: Heinemann).

Reeves, S., and Clarke, I. (1990), *Logic for Computer Science* (Wokingham: Addison-Wesley) Robbins, S. (1989), *Organizational Behavior* 4th edn. (Englewood Cliffs, NJ: Prentice Hall). Rosenbrock, H. (1988), 'Engineering as an Art', *AI & Society*, 2: 315–20.

Ryle, G. (1947), *The Concept of Mind* (London: Hutchinson).

Sackmann, S. A. (1992), 'Culture and Subcultures: An Analysis of Organizational Knowledge', *Administrative Science Quarterly*, 37/1: 140–61.

Saver, A. (1984), *Method in Social Science* (London: Hutchinson).

Schank, R., and Childers, P (1984), *The Cognitive Computer* (Reading, Mass.: Addison-Wesley). Schauer, E (1991), *Playing by the Rules* (Oxford: Clarendon).

Schon, D. A. (1983), *The Reflective Practitioner—How Professionals Think in Action* (New York: Basic).

—— (1987), *Educating the Reflective Practitioner* (San Francisco, Calif.: Jossey-Bass).

Simon, H. (1957/76), *Administrative Behavior* 3rd edn. (New York: Free Press).

Spender, J.-C. (1989), *Industry Recipes* (Oxford: Blackwell).

—— (1992), 'Knowledge Management: Putting Your Technology Strategy on Track', in T. Khalil and B. Bayraktar (eds.), *Management of Technology, iii* (Norcross, Ga.: Industrial Engineering and Management Press, Institute of Industrial Engineers), 404–13. (Proceedings of the 3rd International Conference on Management of Technology, 17–21 February, Miami, Florida.)

—— (1995), 'Organizational Knowledge, Collective Practice and Penrose Rents', *International Business Review*, 3: 353–67.

Starbuck, W. H. (1985), 'Acting First and Thinking Later: Theory versus Reality in Strategic Change', in J. M. Pennings et al. (eds.), *Organizational Strategy and Change* (San Francisco, Calif.: Jossey-Bass), 336–72.

Stillings, N., Feinstein, M., Garfield, J., Rissland, E., Rosenbaum, D., Weisler, S., and Baker Ward, L. (1987), *Cognitive Science* (Cambridge, Mass.: MIT Press).

Taylor, C. (1993), 'To Follow a Rule', in C. Calhoun, E. LiPuma, and M. Postone (eds.), *Bourdieu: Critical Perspectives* (Cambridge: Polity), 45–60.

Thompson, J. D. (1956–7), 'On Building an Administrative Science', *Administrative Science Quarterly*, 1/1: 102–11.

Tsoukas, H. (1992), 'Ways of Seeing: Topographic and Network Representations in Organization Theory', *Systems Practice*, 5: 441–56.

—— (1994a), 'Introduction: From Social Engineering to Reflective Action in Organizational Behaviour', in Tsoukas (ed.), *New Thinking in Organizational Behaviour* (Oxford: Butterworth-Heinemann), 1–22.

—— (1994b), 'The Ubiquity of Organizational Diversity: a Social Constructivist Perspective', Warwick Business School Research Paper no. 120.

Twinings, W., and Miers, D. (1991), *How to Do Things with Rules* 3rd edn. (London: Weidenfeld & Nicholson).

Varela, F. J., Thompson, E., and Rosch, E. (1991), *The Embodied Mind* (Cambridge, Mass.: MIT Press).

Vickers, G. (1983), *The Art of Judgment* (London: Harper & Row).

Watzlawick, P., Weakland, J., and Fisch, R. (1974), *Change* (New York: Norton).

Weber, M. (1947), *The Theory of Social and Economic Organization*, trans. A. M. Henderson and T. Parsons (New York: Free Press).

—— (1948), 'From Max Weber: Essays in Sociology', in H. H. Gerth and C. W. Mills (eds.), (London: Routledge).

Webster, J. , and Starbuck, W. (1988), 'Theory Building in Industrial and Organizational Psychology', in C. Cooper and I. Robertson (eds.), *International Review of Industrial and Organizational Psychology* (London: Wiley), 93–138.

Weick, K. E. (1979), *The Social Psychology of Organizing*, 2nd edn. (Reading, Mass.: Addison-Wesley).

—— (1987), 'Organizational Culture as a Source of High Reliability', *California Management Review*, 29: 112–27.

—— and Browning, L. (1986), 'Argument and Narration in Organizational Communication', *Journal of Management*, 12: 243–59.

White, S. (1988), *The Recent Work of Jurgen Habermas* (Cambridge: Cambridge University Press).

Winograd, T. and Flores, F. (1987), *Understanding Computers and Cognition* (Reading, Mass.: Addison-Wesley).

Wittgenstein, L. (1958), *Philosophical Investigations* (Oxford: Blackwell).

—— (1969), *On Certainty* (Oxford: Blackwell).

Wooley B. (1992), *Virtual Worlds* (London: Penguin).

Zucker, L. G. (1977), 'The Role of Institutionalization in Cultural Persistence', *American Sociological Review*, 42: 726–43.

FOUR

The Firm as a Distributed Knowledge System: A Constructionist Approach

Introduction

THERE are two key questions mainstream management researchers have traditionally addressed in their studies of firms' behaviour. First, in what direction should a firm channel its activities? And second, how should a firm be organized? The first is a question of strategy, the second of organization design. What are the typical assumptions behind these questions? What do they take for granted? First, that there is a quasi-optimum in (or at least, a good enough solution to) what a firm should pursue and how it should be organized. And second, that the quasi-optimum can be reached if all the necessary knowledge is possessed by strategists, if a system of preferences is already established, and if the relationship between means and ends is known (Mintzberg 1990: 180–7; Mintzberg, 1994: ch. 5). How could these 'ifs' be turned into certainties? Only if management researchers, through their studies of aggregates of firms, could identify patterns of behaviour which would then codify into 'if, then' propositional (or declarative) statements to be taken as valid under certain specified conditions (Tsoukas 1994a: 4; 1997b). As a result, practitioners would benefit by being able to base their policies on scientific knowledge (Ansoff 1991: 143, 146). Those policies would, ideally, also consist of 'if, then' rules (what Brown and Duguid 1991: 41 call 'canonical practice') which would be drawn upon by organizational members in their daily practices.

The reader may have noticed that the preceding view of what traditional management research has been trying to achieve owes a great deal to Hayek's formulation of what neoclassical economics tried to do (1945, 1982, 1989). For

An earlier version of this chapter was first published in *Strategic Management Journal*, 17 (special winter issue) (1996), 11–25. Reprinted by permission of Wiley, Copyright (1996).

orthodox economists, said Hayek, to construct a rational economic order is synonymous with attempting to find the best way of allocating *given* resources. The economic problem is thus thought to be a mere problem of logic, of economic calculus. Likewise, to view firms as merely allocative devices, as neoclassical economics does, is to treat them as black boxes (Vanberg 1993; Whitley 1987): firm behaviour is identified with the pattern of detectable actions a firm has undertaken in response to environmental stimuli. According to such a view, as Nelson (1991: 64) has noted, 'firms face given and known choice sets [...] and have no difficulty in choosing the action within those sets that is the best for them, given their objectives'. Issues related to how preferences are formed, plans are formulated, and decisions are made, are not normally explored.

It is interesting to note the similarities between a neoclassical view of firms and a behaviourist conception of human agents: just as firms are viewed as black boxes, so too are individuals. Individual behaviour is assumed to be identical with the pattern of detectable body movements in response to environmental stimuli (Harre and Gillett 1994: 2–5). Neoclassical economics and behaviourism make a nice couple: firms as well as individuals are thought to be fixed, bounded, surveyable entities whose behaviour is described by the systematic input–output regularities an observer is able to ascertain.

Hayek convincingly argued that the economic problem of society is not what orthodox economics has taken it to be, for knowledge about resources can never be collected by a single mind (Jacobson 1992). Why? Because

the peculiar character of the problem of a rational economic order is determined precisely by the fact that the knowledge of the circumstances of which we must make use never exists in concentrated or integrated form, but solely as the dispersed bits of incomplete and contradictory knowledge which all the separate individuals possess. (Hayek 1945: 519)

In other words, rational economic calculation does not—it cannot—take into account the factual knowledge of particular circumstances of time and space; such knowledge is essentially dispersed.

Likewise, in order for corporate planners to formulate a strategy they would need, among other things, to be in possession of knowledge which is, to a large extent, fundamentally dispersed (Mintzberg 1990: 186; Tsoukas 1994a: 16). Corporate planners have been historically urged by strategy researchers to cast their strategies in a propositional mould. For example, if environmental turbulence is high, a firm needs to be strategically aggressive (Ansoff 1991: 459); if environmental uncertainty is low, the defender strategy is the best (Miles and Snow 1978), and so on. Propositional knowledge is necessarily concerned with *generalizations*: types of environments are connected to types of strategic behaviour, in types of circumstances (cf. Hayek 1945: 524; Schauer 1991: 18; Tsoukas 1998b; Twining and Miers 1991: 131). However, the circumstances of a particular firm are bound to be, at least to some extent, unique. Furthermore, inside the firm the particular circumstances each individual is faced with are also bound to be, to some extent, unique.

How is a corporate strategist supposed to obtain knowledge of particular circumstances, and use it to formulate a strategy? One answer is that particular circumstances could be taken into account if the conditions under which propositional statements apply were made more and more refined (this is what contingency theorists try to do). This, however, would not solve our problem, since even conditional generalizations are *universal* within their scope of applicability (Schauer 1991: 24; Tsoukas 1998*b*). It turns out, therefore, that the propositional type of knowledge *per se* cannot accommodate knowledge of local conditions of time and space.

If the economic problem of society is not what orthodox economics has taken it to be, then what is it? For Hayek, it is the

problem of how to secure the best use of resources known to any of the members of society, for ends whose relative importance only these individuals know. Or, to put it briefly, *it is a problem of the utilization of knowledge not given to anyone in its totality.*   (Hayek 1945: 520, emphasis added)

Substituting 'the firm' for 'society' in the preceding quotation gives us the organizational problem firms face. Of course, such a formulation would need to take into account the fact that business organizations are deliberately designed systems in a way that societies are not (Bianchi 1994: 233–4; Hayek 1982: 46–52; Vanberg 1993: 189–91). However, there is a similarity between a society and a firm: both face the problem of how to use widely dispersed knowledge and, therefore, how to extend the span of utilization of resources in a way that exceeds the span of control of any one mind. Such a similarity is much stronger today than at the time Hayek was writing (in the 1940s), given the increasing importance of knowledge for the effective functioning of firms in conditions of globalized capitalism (Drucker 1991: ch. 1; Giddens 1991: ch. 1; Reich 1991: chs. 7–10).

The purpose of this chapter is to develop further the insight that firms are distributed knowledge systems. The key question I will address is: In what sense can it be said that organizational knowledge is distributed? To provide an answer I need to enquire into how knowledge in firms is produced, used, and transformed. This, in turn, hinges on exploring the broader issue of how human agents engage in rule-bound practical activities, since, to paraphrase Weick and Roberts (1993: 365), knowledge begins with actions. Hence, I will explore the nature of rules and how agents know how to follow rules, as well as the structure of social practices within which rule-following takes place. My chief claim will be that firms are distributed knowledge systems in a strong sense: they are decentred systems. A firm's knowledge cannot be surveyed as a whole; it is not self-contained; it is inherently indeterminate and continually reconfiguring. As well as drawing on Austrian economics,

I will develop this argument by drawing on insights from interpretative philosophy, Bourdieu's sociology, ethnomethodology, and discursive psychology.

Organizations as Knowledge Systems: A Brief Review

Viewing the firm as a knowledge system focuses our attention not on allegedly given resources that the firm must use but, to use Penrose's language, (1959: 25), on the *services* rendered by a firm's resources. Putting the matter in those terms implies that firms have discretion over how they use their resources and, therefore, over the services derived from them. Such discretion stems from the fact that firms view, and thus utilize, their resources differently, which, in turn, invites us to enquire into the knowledge firms draw upon.

Notice how knowledge is now understood in a much broader sense than the propositional knowledge implied by the traditional perspective: practitioners do not simply use, in an instrumental fashion, already existing (propositional) knowledge; they also draw upon their own factual knowledge, as pointed out by Hayek; and, furthermore, as we will see later, they draw upon collective knowledge (Spender 1996) of which they may not be aware. Finally, practitioners *create* new knowledge, or at least they are capable of doing so (Nonaka and Takeuchi 1995). Thus, not only are resources used differently by firms, but there is no limit to the services rendered by resources, particularly human resources: the more practitioners *invent* new ways of using their resources (themselves included), the more services they can potentially derive (Soros 1987: ch. 1; Tsoukas and Papoulias 1996a: 76).

It is interesting to note how human agents are assumed to behave according to such a view of firms. Individuals are now seen as agents, active co-producers of their surrounding reality. How, therefore, agents construe themselves and their environments becomes the focus of study—hence the emphasis on the interpretation processes through which individuals attach meanings to (and, thus, define and redefine) themselves and their tasks.

The researchers working within a knowledge-based perspective of firms can be grouped, broadly, into two camps: those whose work has been primarily taxonomic in character, and those who have sought to understand the nature of organizational knowledge through making analogies between organizations and human brains on the one hand, and organizations and individual minds on the other. I will briefly discuss each camp below.

The taxonomists seek to classify the different types of organizational knowledge and to draw out each type's implications. Daft and Weick (1984), for example, have suggested a model whereby organizations may be viewed as 'interpretation systems'. The authors' emphasis has been on the distinctive ways in which organizations make sense of the information they deem necessary, and they have suggested the existence of four distinctive interpretation systems. Similarly, Mitroff (1990: 2) has suggested that corporations can be viewed 'as systems for the production and testing of ideas'. Drawing on Churchman's influential work (1971), Mitroff argues that what and how ideas are produced crucially depends on the particular enquiring system that is in place in a corporation. An enquiring system is a social system that is capable of producing knowledge about itself and its environment. Churchman (ibid.) and Mitroff (1990) have distinguished five possible enquiring systems and argued that firms can choose one or more among them.

In his analysis of the information economy Boisot (1998) takes the process of economizing on data processing to be of critical importance. Since data have now become an abundantly available as well as important factor of production, it is crucial that data are processed, otherwise their potential cannot be fruitfully realized. Boisot suggests a framework, called the 'I-Space', in terms of which the economizing and communication of data may be understood. The I-Space consists of three dimensions: codification (the creation of perceptual and conceptual categories that facilitate the classification of phenomena), abstraction (the minimization of the number of categories one needs to drawn upon for a given task), and diffusion (the proportion of a given population of data-processing agents that can be reached with information that is of different degrees of codification and abstraction). The I-Space enables one to explore the information flows in selected populations of agents. Codification and abstraction are mutually reinforcing and, to the extent that this is the case, they facilitate the diffusion of information.

Spender (1995, 1996) has suggested a 'pluralistic epistemology', seeking to capture the different types of knowledge that organizations make use of. For him knowledge can be held by an individual or a collectivity. Also, knowledge can be articulated explicitly or manifested implicitly—that is, it is, respectively, more or less abstracted from practice. Thus, there are four types of organizational knowledge: conscious (explicit knowledge held by the individual); objectified (explicit knowledge held by the organization); automatic (preconscious individual knowledge); and collective (highly context-dependent knowledge manifested in the practice of an organization).

A typology similar, in some respects, to Spender's has been suggested by Nonaka and Takeuchi (1995). Drawing on Polanyi's (1962, 1975) notion of tacit knowledge, their fundamental premiss is that there are two types of organizational knowledge: tacit and explicit (see also Grant 1996; Johnston 1995; Senker 1993). In organizations, they argue, 'knowledge is created and expanded through social interaction between tacit knowledge and explicit knowledge' (Nonaka and Takeuchi 1995: 61). The conversion of tacit to explicit knowledge, and vice versa, gives rise to four modes of knowledge conversion, each one characterized by a particular content. The authors complete their model by suggesting a five-phase process whereby new knowledge is created. The process starts with the sharing of tacit knowledge by a group of individuals; tacit knowledge is subsequently converted into concepts, which then have to be justified in terms of the organization's overarching mission and purpose; a justified concept is then made tangible, usually through the building of an archetype; finally, new knowledge is disseminated to others within the organization.

Although the preceding typologies have undoubtedly advanced our understanding of organizational knowledge by showing its multifaceted nature, they are also marked by certain limitations which stem, primarily, from the 'formistic' type of thinking that is inherent in any typology (Pepper 1942: 141–4; Tsoukas 1994b: 763–4). Typologies are based on the assumption that an observer is able to discern certain systematic similarities and differences (i.e. forms) between the objects of study. That is fine, provided we are also aware of what we lose by doing so: for formistic thinking to be possible, the conceptual categories into which the phenomena are classified must be assumed to be discrete, separate, and stable. The problem is that they hardly ever are (Pepper 1942).

For example, just as, according to Prigogine (1989: 398), 'order and disorder are created simultaneously', so too tacit and explicit knowledge are mutually constituted—they should not be viewed as two separate types of knowledge. Contrary to what Nonaka and Takeuchi argue (1995: 62–3), tacit knowledge can indeed be linguistically expressed *if* we focus our attention on it (Moss 1995:62–3; Polanyi 1975: 39–41). And vice versa: explicit knowledge is always grounded on a tacit component (Polanyi 1975: 41). Tacit knowledge is not explicit knowledge 'internalized', as Nonaka and Takeuchi (1995: 69) claim, nor is it something which a firm may 'lose' during a period of crisis, as Spender (1996: 73) implies. Tacit knowledge is the necessary component of all knowledge; it is not made up of discrete beans which may be ground, lost, or reconstituted. As I will show in the next section, to split tacit from explicit knowledge is to miss the point—the two are inseparably related.

The same applies to Spender's distinction between individual and social knowledge. *Individual* knowledge is possible precisely because of the *social* practices within which individuals engage—the two are mutually defined (Harre and Gillett 1994: 19–21, 99–100; Wetherell and Maybin 1996: 224–6). Indeed, if such a distinction is pushed too far one is tempted to talk, as Spender (1996: 71) does, about 'the privacy of individual thought' versus the 'social' character of publicly available knowledge. The social, however, as I will argue later, following Wittgenstein, is not an aggregation of individual experiences but a set of background distinctions which underlie individual action.

The second group of researchers into organizational knowledge seeks to model organizations on human brains or on individual minds. Those who take the brain as a metaphor for organization tend to highlight the brain's impressively rich connectivity and, by analogy, argue for its heuristic relevance to organizations (Beer 1981; Evers and Lakomski 1991; Garud and

Kotha 1994; Morgan 1986: 77–109; Sanderlands and Stablein 1987). A connectionist imagery has also been invoked by certain psychologists, such as Hutchins (1993: 58), who, through his research on the organization of ship-navigation teams, has shown how the knowledge that is necessary to carry out the navigation task is distributed throughout the team. It is this redundant distribution of knowledge, he argues, that makes a navigation team robust enough to carry out its task even when parts of the team are temporarily inactive.

Taking the individual mind as their metaphor, Weick and Roberts (1993) have developed the notion of collective mind in order to explain the exceptionally high reliability of certain complex organizations. Following Ryle (1949), the mind for the authors is understood to be not a given property but a style of action—a pattern that is manifested in action. Just as the individual mind is 'located' in the specific activities individuals engage in, so the collective mind is manifested in the manner in which individuals *interrelate* their actions. More specifically, drawing on their research on an aircraft carrier, Weick and Roberts argue (1993: 363) that individuals 'construct their actions (contribute) while envisaging a social system of joint actions (represent), and interrelate that constructed action with the system that is envisaged (subordinate)'. Notice that, for the authors, the individual contributions and the collective mind which they enact are mutually constituted: a contribution helps enact the collective mind to the extent to which it is closely (or heedfully) interrelated with the imagined requirements of other contributing individuals in a situation of joint action. This is the main reason why the collective mind is an *emergent joint accomplishment* rather than an already defined representation of any one individual: the collective mind is constituted as individual contributions become more heedfully interrelated in time. Being an emergent phenomenon, the collective mind is known in its entirety to no one, although portions of it are known differentially to all. Hence, as Weick and Roberts (ibid. 365) remark, the collective mind is a distributed system.

The connectionist-cum-distributionist stream of research avoids the dichotomies inherent in the typologies of organizational knowledge. Furthermore, it profitably avoids what Hayek (1982: 14) called 'the synoptic delusion', namely the assumption that knowledge can be surveyed by a single mind, highlighting instead the emergent character of organizational knowledge. However, some onto-epistemological questions are left unexplored: How do individuals construct their actions, and what is individual representation based upon? In other words: How does the distributed character of social systems come about? To explore these questions, one would need to enquire into the nature of practical action, particularly as it occurs in the context of rule-bound social practices. The rest of this chapter will be devoted to exploring those issues from a constructionist sociological perspective.

Knowledge and Action:
Rules, Practices, and Tacit Knowledge

Following Vickers (1983: 42–3), let us imagine a stock controller. What does he do? Clearly, he is formally charged with the task of replenishing supplies of raw materials when their level falls to a certain predetermined point. His job is to adjust the rate of incoming materials by reference to the rate at which they flow outwards. Is that all a stock controller does? Not quite. For Vickers (ibid.) a stock controller's job is more complex than it may seem at first:

He must get good value for his money, yet keep good relations with his suppliers. He must be sensitive to changing nuances in the requirements of the users but only insofar as they can be contained within a practicable buying policy. He must try out new supplies and new suppliers without disturbing uniformity of products and the goodwill of established contacts [...] The buyer [in other words] has to regulate relations not only between flows of material but also between people; nor can the one be reduced to the other.

A stock controller's actions are part of a complex practical activity, which involves the intentional use of both language and tools. Looking at his actions over time we can discern a pattern; there are certain regularities in a stock controller's behaviour, which indicate that he follows certain rules in carrying out his job. But these rules (whatever they may be) do not just give shape to his actions; they function as normative constraints; that is, as criteria by which his behaviour may be guided and assessed. How does the stock controller know how to follow those rules? He knows because he has been trained to follow them: he has acquired certain skills which enable him to engage in the normatively bound activity that his job entails.

To put it more generally, a stock controller, a production scheduler (Starbuck, 1985), a photocopier-repair technician (Orr 1990), a blacksmith (Harper 1987; Keller and Keller 1993), a forest ranger (Pea 1993), a ship navigator (Hutchins 1993), or a physician (Engestrom 1993) each engages in a particular *discursive practice*. As Harre and Gillet (1994: 28–9) note, 'a discursive practice is the use of a sign system, for which there are norms of right and wrong use, and the signs concern or are directed at various things'. Why call a practice discursive? Because a practice is what it is by virtue of the background distinctions that are embodied in it (Taylor 1985: 34: Tsoukas and Papoulias 1996b: 855); the meaning of those distinctions is established through their use in discourse (Harre and Gillett 1994: 26). For example, even apparently trivial dialogues such as: '*Chairman*: Do you have the minutes? *Secretary*: Yes, here they are. I think 2.4.3 is what you will need' (Scollon and Scollon 1995: 20) are based on a set of distinctions with reference to what is taken to constitute proper behaviour. For the dialogue to be meaningful to the participants and intelligible to outsiders, one needs to know the meaning of certain utterances as they tend to be used in a particular discourse over time.

In what sense does a stock controller *know* how to follow rules? One way of answering this question is to suppose that somewhere in his mind there is a premiss that tells him how to do certain things. Or, to put it more philosophically, the human agent may be seen as 'primarily a subject of representations: representations about the world outside and depictions of ends desired or feared' (Taylor 1993: 49). According to this view, understanding resides in the head; the agent is the locus of representations. Indeed, the cognitivist approach has been largely based on such an assumption (cf. Harre and Gillet 1994: 13–16; Taylor 1993: 46).

However, if a thought resides somewhere in the head telling the agent how to follow a rule, how is it possible that a particular rule, no matter how well illustrated its use may have been, may always be misunderstood in its application? For example, I ask a friend to follow the rule '+ 2', as in the series: 0, 2, 4, 6, 8, 10, etc. My friend may continue the series until he/she reaches 1000, and then write: 1004, 1008, 1012. If I say that what he/she is doing is wrong, he/she might respond by saying that his/her understanding of the rule was: 'Add 2 up to 1000, 4 up to 2000, 6 up to 3000, and so on' (Stueber 1994: 1516; Taylor 1993: 46; Winch 1958: 29–30; Wittgenstein 1958, para. 185).

One way of answering the preceding question is to say that another rule is necessary to determine how the first one is to be applied. This is not a satisfactory solution, however, because it leads to infinite regress. Another way out of this tangle would be to say that a rule follower would need to be shown in advance all the possible misinterpretations of a rule. This, however, is again problematic for it would require that we have 'an infinite number of thoughts in our heads to follow even the simplest instructions' (Taylor 1993: 46). Clearly, this is impossible. The only sensible solution we are left with is to accept that the 'application of rules cannot be done by rules' (Gadamer 1980: 83). This is what Garfinkel (1984) wanted to underscore with his 'et cetera principle': no set of rules can ever be self-contained, complete. Thus, we are led to the conclusion that every act of human understanding is essentially based on an unarticulated background of what is taken for granted (Taylor 1993: 47). It is when we lack a common background that misunderstandings arise, in which case we are forced to articulate the background, and explain it to ourselves and to others (Winograd and Flores 1987: 36–7).

If this conclusion is accepted, it means that the common-sense view (or 'representational' or 'intellectualist' or 'rationalist' view, as it is variously called by philosophers) that we understand the world 'out there' by forming representations of it 'inside' our minds which we subsequently process is seriously deficient (Rorty 1991). It does not mean, of course, that we never form representations of the world, but that such representations are 'islands in the sea of our unformulated practical grasp on the world' (Taylor 1993: 50). According to this view the human agent's understanding resides, first and foremost, in the practices in which he/she participates. The locus of the agent's knowing how to follow a rule is not in his/her head but in practice, that is to say, his/her understanding is implicit in the activity in which he/she engages.

A quartermaster, for example, does not need to form explicit representations of his sensing instruments. His ability to act comes from his familiarity with *navigating* a ship, not from his representation of the navigation instruments in his mind (Hutchins 1993). The world for him is, to use Heidegger's expression, (1962) 'ready-to-hand', and it is so through the social activity in which the practitioner engages. The social activity (e.g. navigating, hammering, teaching, nursing, stock controlling), not the cognizing subject, is the ultimate foundation of intelligibility (Winograd and Flores 1987: 33).

How exactly is the unarticulated background related to human understanding? Polanyi (1962, 1975) provides an interesting answer. When I am aware of something, he argues, I know it focally, as a whole. But I know it by integrating certain particulars, which are known by me subsidiarily. I integrate the particulars tacitly. Tacit knowing has a from–to structure: the particulars bear on the focus *to* which I attend *from* them. Thus, tacit knowing requires three elements: subsidiary particulars, a focal target, and a person who links the two. When, for example, I probe with my stick into a cavity, I 'attend subsidiarily to the feeling of holding the probe in the hand, while the focus of [my] attention is fixed on the far end of the probe' (Polanyi 1975: 36). For my attention to focus on something (on anything), the subsidiaries must remain 'essentially unspecifiable' (ibid. 39): the moment I look at them I cease to see their meaning.

To sum up, three themes have emerged in the discussion thus far. First, all articulated knowledge is based on an unarticulated background, a set of subsidiary particulars which are tacitly integrated by individuals. Those particulars reside in the social practices—our forms of life—in which we happen to participate. Before we are cognizing subjects we are *Daseins* (beings-in-the-world). An utterance is possible only by the speaker's dwelling in a tacitly accepted background.

Second, a practitioner's ability to follow rules is grounded on an unarticulated background. Hence, the rules an *observer* is able to postulate in a practice (rules-as-represented) are different from the rules actually operating in the activities of the *agents* (rules-as-guides-in-practice).

And third, the unarticulated background in which we dwell is known by us through our having been *socialized* into it by others. The background understanding that socialization imparts to us is not only cognitive but also embodied (Taylor 1993:50); we acquire particular skills through training our bodies to relate in certain ways to the world (Polanyi 1975: 31). Through our socialization into a practice we internalize a set of background distinctions which are constitutive of the practice. By dwelling in a set of distinctions 'we are dwelling in our own memory and indirectly in the numberless experiences through which we learnt the language in the first place' (Moss 1995: 3). Hence, the process of learning is constitutive of what is learnt (Williams 1994: 200).

The Structure of Social Practices: Positions, Dispositions, and Interactive Situations

We have explained so far what it means to know a rule in the context of practical action, but where do those rules come from? Moreover, if rules do make social life patterned, where does novelty come from? These questions are particularly important for organizations, since in them one finds both order and disorder, stability and change (Cooper 1986; Stacey 1996). In this section these questions will be answered and, by doing so, the distributed character of organizational knowledge will be shown.

Attempting to synthesize the work of Parsons, Bourdieu, and of several ethnomethodologists, Mouzelis (1995: ch. 6) has suggested that social practices be viewed as consisting of three dimensions. First, the social position or *role dimension*; namely, the normative expectations that are associated with the carrying out of a particular role. Thus, in the case of the stock controller this would involve the normative expectations held of him by his superiors, his peers, and his associates in other firms. To find out about those normative expectations one would need to enquire into how the stock controller has been socialized into his particular role by formal and informal means.

Second, the *dispositional dimension*; namely, the system of mental patterns of perception, appreciation, and action which has been acquired by an individual via past socializations and is brought to bear on a particular situation of action. This is Bourdieu's notion of *habitus*. More specifically, 'the *habitus*', says Bourdieu (1990: 54):

is a product of history, produces individual and collective practices—more history—in accordance with the schemes generated by history. It ensures the active presence of past experiences, which, deposited in each organism in the form of schemes of perception, thought and action, tend to guarantee the 'correctness' of practices and their constancy over time, more reliably than all formal rules and explicit norms.

For Bourdieu it is the 'active presence of the whole past'; that which gives social practices both a continuity and 'a relative autonomy with respect to external determinations of the immediate present' (ibid. 56).

In other words, history leaves its marks on how actors see the world; every time we act we do so by means of the habits of thinking we have acquired through our past socializations. At any point in time our habits of thinking have been historically formed through our participation in historically constituted practices. Thus, to understand why our stock controller behaves the way he does we need also to enquire into his *habitus*: the past socializations to which he was subjected in the context of his involvement in several social practices (e.g. education, family, religion, etc.).

Finally, the *interactive-situational dimension*; namely, the specific context of a social activity within which normative expectations and the *habitus* are activated. This dimension is similar to Goffman's 'interaction order' (1983) and, according to Mouzelis (1995: 104), it is what gives social interaction its open-ended character. Thus, to complete our enquiry into why the stock controller behaves the way he does we would also need to investigate the dynamic unfolding of his concrete interactions with others, within a particular socio-temporal context.

Stepping back to view the stock controller's behaviour as a whole, no doubt we will notice that it is patterned—certain actions tend to be repeated. In the course of his role-related socialization as well as through his past socializations (i.e. his *habitus*) he has developed certain ways of thinking which are activated every time he acts. From this we might be tempted to formulate the rules underlying the stock controller's actions and argue that the rules-as-represented completely describe his practice. But this would be a mistake for, as argued in the previous section, the rules-as-represented are always formulated from the point of view of the observer. There is an important asymmetry between the rules-as-represented and the rules-as-guides-in-practice (Boden 1994: 42; Bourdieu 1990: 39; Taylor 1993: 55–7), which can be put in terms of the law of requisite variety (Ashby 1956: 206–13): a practice is always richer than any formal representation of it. The time-related aspects of a stock controller's practice as well as the rich variety of his experiences cannot appear in a formal account, just as the experience of driving through a place cannot be captured by a map (Taylor 1993: 56–7; Tsoukas 1998*b*).

It is the richness of experiences associated with any particular role that Vickers (1983) highlights with his example of the stock controller. For an observer, the latter regulates the flow of incoming and outgoing materials, and certain rules can be inferred from studying his behaviour. However, at the same time there are other things that the stock controller does, or might want to do, which cannot be formally represented by rules. His concern is also with maintaining a web of human relationships which, strictly speaking, is not part of the job *per se*, but without it he would be unable to do his job properly.

If at this point the reader feels somewhat uneasy, this is because there is something elusive about social practices, no matter how replete with regularities they may be: at any point in time one cannot offer a comprehensive description of a social practice, since to do so presupposes first that one is able to foresee all future events that may occur in a practice, and second that one possesses an unambiguous language which can faithfully reflect what is going on. Neither of these presuppositions applies. As Popper insightfully pointed out, (1988: 12–16, 24), in order to be able to predict an event one would have to state with sufficient accuracy what kind of data one would need for such a prediction task, which is impossible to do. (That is why lotteries are unpredictable games!) (See also Penrose 1994: 22–3). In other words, our problem is not only that we do not know enough but, more fundamentally, that we do not know what we need to know. This kind of 'radical uncertainty' (Piore 1995: 120), or second-order ignorance, adds additional force to Hayek's insight that in a social system knowledge is essentially dispersed. It is dispersed not only in the sense that knowledge is not, and cannot be, concentrated in a single mind but also that no single mind can specify in advance what kind of practical knowledge is going to be *relevant*, when and where.

Moreover, a social practice has no essence, or intrinsic nature, which can be faithfully captured by language (Rorty 1991: 100). What at any point in time a social practice is, depends on how human agents interpret it to be (Morgan 1986; Rorty 1991; Soros 1987; Tsoukas and Papoulias 1996a). As noted in the previous section, language is constitutive of reality—there is no privileged position from which reality might objectively be viewed. As marriage counsellors know all too well, different interpretations constitute different realities (Shotter 1993; Watzlawick et al., 1974). Thus, at any point in time what is going on in a social system is not only not fixed but is inherently indeterminate. Several transactions take place at once, and no one is in a position to fully describe them in advance. To recall MacIntyre's apt remark (1985: 98), there is no single game that is played but several, and 'if the game metaphor may be stretched further, the problem about real life is that moving one's knight to QB3 may always be replied to with a lob across the net'.

The indeterminacy of social practices has been richly illustrated by Orr (1990) in his ethnographic study of photocopier-repair technicians. In their work technicians need to make use of the explicit rules (i.e. rules-as-represented) provided to them by their repair manuals. The activity of repairing photocopiers, however, occurs in a social context the details of which cannot be fully described *ex ante*. In attempting to repair the machine, the technician needs to attend simultaneously not only to the strictly technical aspects of the machine but also to the social context within which it functions. He needs to enquire about how the customer has been using the machine. He must also perform a delicate balancing act in striving to gain and maintain the customer's trust in him and, at the same time, to maintain his reputation in the community of technicians (see Brown and Duguid 1991: 43; Orr 1990: 173; Vickers 1983: 42–5). In a particular interactive situation one or more of those concerns may become salient, although there is no way of telling in advance if, when, and what will exactly happen (Tsoukas 1998b).

Given that positions and dispositions entail, each in their own way, certain types of quasi-automatic behaviour on the part of actors (Mouzelis 1995: 112), how are we to account for the diversity of actors' behaviour? For example, why do all photocopier-repair technicians not act either in the same manner or totally differently when they try to repair a broken machine? Clearly, they do not behave randomly or erratically, but neither do they behave uniformly; there is both consistency and diversity across the technicians' patterns of behaviour (Orr 1990). Why is this the case?

The answer lies in the effort agents make to manage the unavoidable tensions between social positions (roles), dispositions, and interactive situations (Mouzelis, 1995: 105). Through the explicit rules associated with a particular role as well as through training and informal socialization a firm attempts to define the normative expectations of the technicians' role—thus, in effect, trying to homogenize their behaviour. But normative expectations are extremely unlikely to be identical to an individual's *habitus*.

The set of dispositions of each individual technician (i.e. his *habitus*) is the result of past socializations, reflecting the diverse social contexts each technician has gone through in the course of his life. The history of each technician will, no doubt, have left its mark on how he tends to think and behave. It is the persistence of this historically formed habit of thinking and acting that Bourdieu points out, when he underlines its 'relative autonomy with respect to external determinations of the immediate present' (Bourdieu 1990: 56).

Normative expectations and dispositions are activated within particular interactive situations, and how such activation occurs is always a *local* matter. Human agency is '*always* and *at every moment* confronted with specific conditions and choices. Those conditions are not [...] simply historically given, but are instead made relevant (or irrelevant) as a local matter' (Boden 1994: 13; emphasis in the original). Boden draws our attention here to a valuable ethnomethodological insight: human agents *select out* on the one hand what they understand to be the *relevant* aspects of both their role-related normative expectations and their sets of dispositions, and on the other those *relevant* aspects of the local conditions within which their actions take place, and they try to fit the two together.

Thus, social structure, understood as a set of normative expectations and dispositions, is neither ignored nor seen as exogenous to action (Giddens 1984). On the contrary, as Boden (1994:5) elegantly observes, 'the tiniest local moment of human intercourse contains *within* and *through* it the essence of society, and vice versa' (emphasis in the original; see also Wetherell and Maybin 1996: 245). But how social structure is instantiated is always a local matter: '*how*, *where*, with *whom*, and even *why* particular aspects of social structure, biographical elements or historical conditions are made relevant in concrete situations is a matter of members' methods' (Boden 1994: 46, 215; emphasis in the original). Although she does not say so, what Boden alludes to is the distributed character of organizational knowledge: agents possess local knowledge which cannot be surveyed as a whole and, furthermore, part of their knowledge originates from outside the organization.

But how concrete are 'concrete situations'? How particular are 'particular circumstances'? How relevant are 'the relevant aspects of local conditions'? The answer is: infinitely concrete; infinitely particular; infinitely relevant. As pointed out earlier, a social practice is inherently indeterminate. One can indefinitely go on and on redescribing it (Rorty 1991: 100–3); it all depends on how many and how good are the viewing positions one takes. The reason, however, why we are not paralysed by a potentially infinite number of redescriptions is that they are brought to an end by the *institutional* context within which they are enunciated (Schauer 1991: 18–22).

For example, a photocopier may be described in all sorts of ways, but only a few descriptions are selected out by the engineers of a photocopier company for the purpose of issuing a repair manual. The purpose of the task at hand, and the institutional context within which it occurs, impose limits on how a photocopier may be described. The fact, however, that only a few descriptions are selected does not mean that there are not others (Tsoukas 1998*b*). Indeed, in certain conjunctions of circumstances other descriptions may become central (e.g. I use the machine not only to make 'official' copies but also to make copies for my friends; the machine is not just a machine but also an object over which I, its official user, have control, while others have not; etc.). The point to note here is that no one can know in advance what are going to be the relevant descriptions of a machine within a particular context. The diagnosis and, therefore, the action a technician will undertake are irredeemably local.

An Illustration: 'Industry Recipes'

A rich description of what Taylor (1993: 57) aptly calls 'the "phronetic gap" between the formula and its enactment' has been offered by Spender (1989) in his study of several British firms in three industries. Firms in a particular industry, Spender argues, draw upon an 'industry recipe'; namely, a shared pattern of managerial judgements concerning issues of product, technology, marketing, personnel, etc. An industry recipe is closely tied to the field of experience in which it is generated and enables managers to make sense of their particular environment. A recipe emerges as 'an *unintended consequence* of managers' need to communicate, because of their uncertainties, by word and example within the industry' (ibid. 188; emphasis added).

An industry recipe is essentially a discourse, developed over time within a particular industry context. To use a term mentioned earlier, a recipe consists of a set of background distinctions tied to a particular field of experience. The distinctions pertain to a number of issues which managers in a firm must grasp if they are to 'get things under control' (ibid. 181). For example, Spender (ibid. 191–2) points out the different ways in which firms in different industries segment their markets, or, to put it differently, the market-related distinctions which are drawn in particular industries. Thus, in the dairy industry the market is segmented into territories; in the fork-lift-rental industry the market is segmented by the variety of user needs. Likewise, in every industry there are different distinctions made between different kinds of employees firms must employ. For example, the dairy industry distinguishes between the transients and long-servers; the foundry industry between skilled and semi-skilled moulders.

Through a process of socialization, managers internalize industry-specific distinctions. Managers are introduced into a universe of meanings which is not related to their firm-specific roles as such, but pertains to the broader industrial field within which their roles are carried out. To paraphrase Wetherell and Maybin (1996: 228), internalizing industry-specific distinctions is not 'a matter of learning definitions in dictionaries, or knowledge which might be gained from [...] books. [Recipes] are always embedded in conversations and social interactions'. The recipe is learned within the context of discursive practices. It forms the unarticulated background which underlies managers' representations of their firms; it is the ' "tacit knowledge" that enables managers to construct some order in a hostile environment' (Whitley 1987: 134). Or, to use Bourdieu's language, the recipe is part of each manager's *habitus*; that is, it is part of the set of dispositions which a manager has historically acquired, ensuring 'the active presence of past experiences' (Bourdieu 1990: 54).

An industry recipe offers managers not only a vocabulary but also a grammar. Says Spender (1989: 194): 'The essence of the recipe is more in the way its elements come together and synthesize into a coherent rationality than in the particular elements themselves'. But such a rationality offers 'mere guidance' (ibid. 192); it is 'open and somewhat ambiguous' (ibid. 194). A firm's circumstances are bound to be different and 'may prevent it acting in the way the recipe implies' (ibid. 192). As a result of the *particular* conditions within which a firm operates (remember that particularity and relevance are in the eye of the beholder), its managers will inevitably have to improvise (Weick 1993)—they will have to close Taylor's 'phronetic gap' (1993: 57). How managers understand a recipe is always influenced by 'immediate circumstances and local agendas' (Boden 1994: 18). As Spender (1989: 192) notes, 'the strategist is forced to make a *personal judgment* about the *relevance* of the recipe to his firm's situation' (emphasis added). It is this tension between the industry-specific *habitus* and the *local* conditions within which it is instantiated that explains why a firm's strategy is neither a replication of an idealized industry recipe nor an *ex nihilo* construction.

It needs to be said that a manager's *habitus* includes more than the distinctions involved in an industry recipe: it also includes the dispositions that stem from past socializations he/she has been through in his/her life. Spender's study was not designed to go into biographical details of the managers involved. Nor did it aim to address the tension between the normative expectations of specific managerial roles and managers' historically acquired dispositions. But, if what has been said so far is accepted, one can see how such additional evidence might fit in.

For example, the by now legendary manner in which the 'Post-it' notepads were developed by 3M (see *Financial Times*, 30 May 1994) is a good illustration of how the innovative capacity of a firm depends on its members' efforts to alleviate tensions between positions, dispositions, and interactive situations (for similar examples see Mintzberg and Waters 1982, 1985). Thus, to understand Arthur Fry's key contribution to the development of Post-it notepads one needs to know about his 3M formal position as a chemist, and the normative expectations associated with such a role (among those expectations was 3M's well-known policy of encouraging innovation through 'bootlegging'). One also needs to know about Fry's religious disposition (part of his historically formed *habitus*). Normative expectations and dispositions were activated within the local context of a church in Minnesota. Fry used to sing in a church choir and realized how convenient it would be if he had a sticky, yet easily removable, note to mark the pages in his books of religious hymns. The invention of the Post-it note pads can be conceptualized as the outcome of what Schutz (1964) called the 'congruency of relevances' (cf. Boden 1994: 192)—an outcome that is inherently contingent and locally produced.

Conclusions

My claims in this chapter have been as follows. First, the resources a firm uses are neither given, nor discovered, but created (Bianchi 1995; Buchanan and Vanberg 1991; Joas 1993). It is not so much the resources *per se* that are important to a firm as the services rendered by those resources (Penrose 1959). The services depend on how resources are viewed, which is a function of the knowledge applied to them. The carriers of organizational knowledge are a firm's routines (Nelson and Winter 1982) and members. Hence, a firm can be seen as a knowledge system (Grant 1996).

Second, the organizational problem firms face is the utilization of knowledge which is not, and cannot be, known in its totality by a single mind (cf. Hayek 1945, 1982, 1989; Tsoukas 1994*a*).

Third, the firm is a distributed knowledge system. A firm's knowledge is distributed not only in a computational sense (Hutchins 1993; Kiountouzis and Papatheodorou 1990), or in Hayek's sense (1945: 521) that the factual knowledge of the particular circumstances of time and place cannot be surveyed as a whole. More radically, a firm's knowledge is distributed in the sense that it is inherently indeterminate: nobody knows in advance what that knowledge is or need be. Firms are faced with *radical uncertainty*: they do not, they cannot, know what they need to know. Viewed this way, firms are not only distributed, but decentred systems—they lack the cognitive equivalent of a 'control room' (Stacey 1995, 1996).

Fourth, a firm's knowledge is distributed in an additional sense; namely, that it is partly derived from the broader industrial and societal context within which a firm is embedded (Granovetter 1992; Spender 1989; Whitley 1996). Furthermore, a firm's knowledge is continually (re)constituted through the activities undertaken within it. The latter's knowledge is not, and cannot be, self-contained. The reason is as follows. Social practices within a firm consist of three dimensions: role-related normative expectations, dispositions, and interactive situations. A firm has (greater or lesser) control over normative expectations, whereby the behaviour of its members is to be made consistent across contexts. However, a firm has no control over its members' dispositions, which are derived from their past socializations in contexts outside the firm. Finally, the normative expectations and dispositions of the members of a firm are instantiated within particular interactive situations, whose features cannot be fully known by anyone *ex ante*, but are actively shaped by practitioners as they confront local circumstances. Thus, a firm's knowledge is *emergent* (Weick and Roberts 1993): it is not possessed by a single agent; it partly originates 'outside' the firm; and it is never complete at any point.

Fifth, normative expectations, dispositions, and interactive situations are inevitably in tension. There are always gaps between these three dimensions (Boden 1994: 18); between 'canonical practice' and 'noncanonical practice' (Brown and Duguid 1991); between 'universalistic' and 'particularistic' practices (Heimer 1992: 146–54); between 'formal' and 'substantive rationality' (Weber 1964); between 'ideal' and 'practical action' (Boden 1994); between 'rules-as-represented' and 'rules-as-guides-in-practice' (Taylor 1993); between 'the model of reality' and 'the reality of the model' (Bourdieu 1990: 39). Those phronetic gaps are closed only through practitioners exercising their judgement: they select out what they take to be the relevant features of each one of the three dimensions making up social practices, and attempt to fit them together.

From the preceding analysis it follows that how normative expectations, dispositions, and interactive situations are matched is always a contingent, emergent, indeterminate event. From a research point of view, what needs to be explained is not so much 'why firms differ' (Nelson 1991) (they inevitably do), as what are the processes that make them similar—how the infinitude of particularities is tamed, how tensions are managed, and gaps are filled; how, in short, in a distributed knowledge system coherent action emerges over time (Araujo and Easton 1996).

Finally, as to its management implications, viewing the firm as a distributed knowledge system helps us refine our view of what organizations are and, consequently, of what management is about. Organizations are seen as being in constant flux, out of which the potential for the emergence of novel practices is never exhausted—human action is inherently creative. Organizational members do follow rules, but how they do so is an inescapably contingent-cum-local matter. In organizations, both rule-bound action and novelty are present, as are continuity and change, regularity and creativity. Management, therefore, can be seen as an open-ended process of coordinating purposeful individuals, whose actions stem from applying their partly unique interpretations to the local circumstances confronting them. Those actions give rise to often unintended and ambiguous circumstances, the meaning of which is open to further interpretations and further actions, and so on. Given the distributed character of organizational knowledge, the key to achieving coordinated action does not so much depend on those 'higher up' collecting more and more knowledge, as on those 'lower down' finding more and more ways of getting connected and interrelating the knowledge each one has. A necessary condition for this to happen is to appreciate the character of a firm as a discursive practice: a form of life, a community, in which individuals come to share an unarticulated background of common understandings. Sustaining a discursive practice is just as important as finding ways of integrating distributed knowledge.

References

Ansoff, I. H. (1991), 'Critique of Henry Mintzberg's "The Design School: Reconsidering the Basic Premises of Strategic Management"', *Strategic Management Journal*, 12(6): 449–61.

Araujo, L., and Easton, G. (1996), 'Strategy: Where is the pattern?', *Organization*, 3: 361–83.

Ashby, R. (1956), *An Introduction to Cybernetics* (London: Chapman & Hall).

Beer, S. (1981), *Brain of the Firm* (Chichester: Wiley).

Bianchi, M. (1994), 'Hayek's Spontaneous Order: The "Correct" Versus the "Corrigible" Society', in J. Birner and R. van Zijp (eds.), *Hayek, Co-ordination and Evolution* (London: Routledge), 232–51.

—— (1995), 'Markets and Firms: Transactions Costs versus Strategic Innovation', *Journal of Economic Behavior and Organization*, 28: 183–202.

Boden, D. (1994), *The Business of Talk* (Cambridge: Polity).

Boisot, M. H. (1998), *Knowledge Assets* (Oxford: Oxford University Press).

Bourdieu, P. (1990), *The Logic of Practice* (Cambridge: Polity).

Brown, J. S., and Duguid, P. (1991), 'Organizational Learning and Communities of Practice: Toward a Unified View of Working, Learning, and Innovation', *Organization Science*, 2: 40–57.

Buchanan, J., and Vanberg, V. (1991), 'The Market as a Creative Process', *Economics and Philosophy*, 7: 167–86.

Churchman, C. W. (1971), *The Design of Inquiring Systems* (New York: Basic).

Cooper, R. (1986), 'Organization/Disorganization', *Social Science Information*, 25: 299–335.

Daft, R., and Weick, K. (1984), 'Toward a Model of Organizations as Interpretation Systems', *Academy of Management Review*, 9: 284–95.

Drucker, P. (1991), *Post-capitalist Society* (Oxford: Butterworth/Heinemann).

Engestrom, Y. (1993), 'Developmental Studies of Work as a Testbench of Activity Theory: The Case of Primary Care Medical Practice', in S. Chaiklin and J. Lave (eds.), *Understanding Practice* (Cambridge: Cambridge University Press), 64–103.

Evers, C., and Lakomski, G. (1991), *Knowing Educational Administration* (Amsterdam: Elsevier Science).

Gadamer, H.-G. (1980), 'Practical Philosophy as a Model for the Human Sciences', *Research in Phenomenology*, 9: 74–85.

Garfinkel, H. (1984), *Studies in Ethnomethodology* (Cambridge: Polity).

Garud, R., and Kotha, S. (1994), 'Using the Brain as a Metaphor to Model Flexible Production Systems', *Academy of Management Review*, 19: 671–98.

Giddens, A. (1984), *The Constitution of Society* (Cambridge: Polity).

—— (1991), *Modernity and Self-Identity* (Cambridge: Polity).

Goffman, E. (1983), 'The Interaction Order', *American Sociological Review*, 48: 1–17.

Granovetter, M. (1992), 'Problems of Explanation in Economic Sociology', in N. Nohria and R. G. Eccles (eds.), *Networks and Organizations* (Boston, Mass.: Harvard Business School Press), 25–56.

Grant, R. M. (1996), 'Prospering in Dynamically-Competitive Environments: Organizational Capability as Knowledge Integration', *Organization Science*, 7: 375–87.

Harper, D. (1987), *Working Knowledge* (Berkeley, Calif.: University of California Press).

Harré, R., and Gillett, G. (1994), *The Discursive Mind* (Thousand Oaks, Calif.: Sage).

Hayek, F. A. (1945), 'The Use of Knowledge in Society', *American Economic Review*, 35: 519–30.

—— (1982), *Law, Legislation and Liberty*, (London: Routledge & Kegan Paul).

—— (1989), 'The Pretense of Knowledge', *American Economic Review*, 79: 3–7.

Heidegger, M. (1962), *Being and Time* (New York: Harper & Row).

Heimer, C. A. (1992), 'Doing Your Job and Helping Your Friends: Universalistic Norms about Obligations to Particular Others in Networks', in N. Nohria and R. G. Eccles (eds.), *Networks and Organizations* (Boston, Mass.: Harvard Business School Press) 143–64.

Hutchins, E. (1993), 'Learning to Navigate', in S. Chaiklin and J. Lave (eds.), *Understanding Practice* (Cambridge: Cambridge University Press), 35–63.

Jacobson, R. (1992), 'The "Austrian" School of Strategy', *Academy of Management Review*, 17: 782–807.

Joas, H. (1993), 'Conclusion: The Creativity of Action and the Intersubjectivity of Reason: Mead's Pragmatism and Social Theory', in Joas, *Pragmatism and Social Theory* (Chicago, Ill.: University of Chicago Press) 238–61.

Johnston, R. B. (1995), 'Making Manufacturing Practices Tacit: A Case Study of Computer-aided Production Management and Lean Production', *Journal of the Operational Research Society*, 46: 1174–83.

Keller, C., and Keller, J. (1993), 'Thinking and Acting with Iron', in S. Chaiklin and J. Lave (eds.), *Understanding Practice* (Cambridge: Cambridge University Press) 125–43.

Kiountouzis, E., and Papatheodorou, C. (1990), 'Distributed Artificial Intelligence and Soft Systems: A Comparison', *Journal of the Operational Research Society*, 41: 441–6.

MacIntyre, A. (1985), *After Virtue*, 2nd edn.) (London: Duckworth).

Miles, R. E., and Snow, C. S. (1978), *Organizational Strategy, Structure, and Process* (New York: McGraw-Hill).

Mintzberg, H. (1990), 'The Design School: Reconsidering the Basic Premises of Strategic Management', *Strategic Management Journal*, 11(3): 171–95.

—— (1994), *The Rise and Fall of Strategic Planning* (Hemel Hempstead: Prentice Hall).

—— and Waters, J. (1982), 'Tracking Strategy in an Entrepreneurial Firm', *Academy of Management Journal*, 25: 465–99.

Mintzberg, H. (1985), 'Of Strategies, Deliberate and Emergent', *Strategic Management Journal*, 6(3): 257–72.

Mitroff, I. (1990), 'The Idea of the Corporation as an Idea System: Commerce in the Systems Age', *Technological Forecasting and Social Change*, 38: 1–14.

Morgan, G. (1986), *Images of Organization* (London: Sage).

Moss, E. (1995), *The Grammar of Consciousness* (Houndmills: St Martin's).

Mouzelis, N. (1995), *Sociological Theory: What Went Wrong?* (London: Routledge).

Nelson, R. (1991), 'Why Do Firms Differ, and How Does It Matter?', *Strategic Management Journal* (special winter issue): 12: 61–74.

—— and Winter, S. (1982), *An Evolutionary Theory of Economic Change* (Cambridge, Mass.: Harvard University Press).

Nonaka, I., and Takeuchi, H. (1995), *The Knowledge-creating Company.* (New York: Oxford University Press).

Orr, J. E. (1990), 'Sharing Knowledge, Celebrating Identity: Community Memory in a Service Culture', in D. Middleton and D. Edwards (eds.), *Collective Remembering* (London: Sage), 168–89.

Pea, R. (1993), 'Practices of Distributed Intelligence and Designs for Education', in G. Salomon (ed.), *Distributed Cognitions* (Cambridge: Cambridge University Press), 47–87.

Penrose, E. (1959), *The Theory of the Growth of the Firm* (New York: Wiley).

Penrose, R. (1994), *Shadows of the Mind* (Oxford: Oxford University Press).

Pepper, S. (1942), *World Hypotheses* (Berkeley, Calif.: University of California Press).

Piore, M. J. (1995), *Beyond Individualism* (Boston, Mass.: Harvard University Press).

Polanyi, M. (1962), *Personal Knowledge* (Chicago, Ill.: University of Chicago Press).

—— (1975), 'Personal Knowledge', in M. Polanyi and H. Prosch (eds.), *Meaning* (Chicago, Ill.: University of Chicago Press), 22–45.

Popper, K. (1988), *The Open Universe* (London: Hutchinson).

Prigogine, I. (1989), 'The Philosophy of Instability', *Futures*, 21: 396–400.

Reich, R. B. (1991), *The Work of Nations* (London: Simon & Schuster).

Rorty, R. (1991), *Objectivity, Relativism, and Truth* (Cambridge: Cambridge University Press).

Ryle, G. (1949), *The Concept of Mind* (Chicago, Ill.: University of Chicago Press).

Sanderlands, L. E., and Stablein, R. E. (1987), 'The Concept of Organization Mind', in S. Bacharach and N. DiTomaso (eds.), *Research in the Sociology of Organizations*, v. (Greenwich, Conn.: JAI), 135–61.

Schauer, F. (1991), *Playing by the Rules* (Oxford: Clarendon).

Schutz, A. (1964), *Collected Papers, i* (The Hague: Martinus Nijhoff).

Scollon, R., and Scollon, S. (1995), *Intercultural Communication* (Oxford: Blackwell).

Senker, J. (1993), 'The Contribution of Tacit Knowledge to Innovation', *AI & Society*, 7: 208–24.

Shotter, J. (1993), *Conversational Realities* (London: Sage).

Soros, G. (1987), *The Alchemy of Finance*, 2nd ed. (New York: Wiley).

Spender, J.-C. (1989), *Industry Recipes* (Oxford: Blackwell).

—— (1995), 'Organizations are Activity Systems, Not Merely Systems of Thought', in P. Shrivastava and C. Stubbart, *Advances in Strategic Management*, il (Greenwich, Conn.: JAI), 153–74.

—— (1996), 'Organizational Knowledge, Learning and Memory: Three Concepts in Search of a Theory', *Journal of Organizational Change Management*, 9: 63–78.

Stacey, R. (1995), 'The Science of Complexity: An Alternative Perspective for Strategic Change Processes', *Strategic Management Journal*, 16(6): 477–95.

—— (1996), *Complexity and Creativity in Organizations* (San Francisco, Calif.: Berrett-Koehler).

Starbuck, W. H. (1985), 'Acting First and Thinking Later: Theory versus Reality in Strategic Change', in J. M. Pennings et al. (eds.), *Organizational Strategy and Change* (San Francisco, Calif.: Jossey-Bass), 336–72.

Stueber, K. (1994), 'Practice, Indeterminacy and Private Language: Wittgenstein's Dissolution of Scepticism', *Philosophical Investigations*, 17: 14–36.

Taylor, C. (1985), *Philosophy and the Human Sciences*, ii. (Cambridge: Cambridge University Press).

—— (1993), 'To Follow a Rule . . .', in C. Calhoun, E. LiPuma and M. Postone (eds.), *Bourdieu: Critical Perspectives* (Cambridge: Polity), 45–59.

Tsoukas, H. (1994a), 'Introduction: From Social Engineering to Reflective Action in Organizational Behavior', in H. Tsoukas (ed.), *New Thinking in Organizational Behavior.* (Oxford: Butterworth/Heinemann), 1–22.

—— (1994b), 'Refining Common Sense: Types of Knowledge in Management Studies', *Journal of Management Studies*, 31: 761–80.

—— (1998a), 'The Word and the World: A Critique of Representationalism in Management Research', *International Journal of Public Administration*, 21: 781–817.

—— (1998b), 'Forms of Knowledge and Forms of Life in Organized Contexts', in R. Chia (ed.), *In the Realm of Organization* (London: Routledge), 43–66.

—— and Papoulias, D. B. (1996a), 'Creativity in OR/MS: From Technique to Epistemology', *Interfaces*, 26: 73–9.

—— (1996b), 'Understanding Social Reforms: A Conceptual Analysis', *Journal of the Operational Research Society*, 47: 853–63.

Twining, W., and Miers, D. (1991), *How to Do Things with Rules*, 3rd edn. (London: Weidenfeld & Nicolson).

Vanberg, V. (1993), 'Rational Choice, Rule-following and Institutions: An Evolutionary Perspective', in U. Maki, B. Gustafsson, and C. Knudsen (eds.), *Rationality, Institutions and Economic Methodology* (London: Routledge), 171–200.

Vickers, G. (1983), *The Art of Judgement* (London: Harper & Row).

Watzlawick, P., Weakland, J. and Fisch, R. (1974), *Change* (New York: Norton).

Weber, M. (1964), *The Theory of Social and Economic Organization* (New York: Free Press).

Weick, K. (1993), 'Organization Design as Improvisation', in G. P. Huber and W. H. Glick (eds.), *Organization Change and Redesign* (New York: Oxford University Press), 346–79.

—— and Roberts, K. (1993), 'Collective Mind in Organizations: Heedful Interrelating on Flight Decks', *Administrative Science Quarterly*, 38: 357–381.

Wetherell, M., and Maybin, J. (1996), 'The Distributed Self: A Social Constructionist Perspective', in R. Stevens (ed.), *Understanding the Self* (London: Sage), 219–79.

Whitley, R. (1987), 'Taking Firms Seriously as Economic Actors: Towards a Sociology of Firm Behaviour', *Organization Studies*, 8: 125–47.

—— (1996), 'The Social Construction of Economic Actors: Institutions and Types of Firm in Europe and Other Market Economies', in R. Whitley and P. H. Kristensen (eds.), *The Changing European Firm* (London: Routledge), 39–66.

Williams, M. (1994), 'The Significance of Learning in Wittgenstein's Later Philosophy', *Canadian Journal of Philosophy*, 24: 173–204.

Winch, P. (1958), *The Idea of Social Science and its Relation to Philosophy* (London: Routledge & Kegan Paul).

Winograd, T., and Flores, F. (1987), *Understanding Computers and Cognition* (Reading, Mass.: Addison-Wesley).

Wittgenstein, L. (1958), *Philosophical Investigations* (Oxford: Blackwell).

FIVE

What is Organizational Knowledge?

Haridimos Tsoukas and Efi Vladimirou

Introduction

THE aim of this chapter is to explore the links between individual knowledge, organizational knowledge, and human action undertaken in organized contexts. Those links have remained relatively unexplored in the relevant
literature, a large part of which, captive within a narrowly Cartesian understanding of knowledge and cognition, has tended to privilege 'pure' knowledge and thinking at the expense of outlining the forms of social life which
sustain particular types of knowledge (Tsoukas 1996, 1997, 1998; Varela,
Thompson, and Rosch 1991; Winogrand and Flores 1987).

Moreover, although most people intuitively identify knowledge with *individual* knowledge, it is not quite evident how knowledge becomes an individual possession and how it is related to individual action, nor is it clear in what
sense knowledge merits the adjective *organizational*. Despite the insights
gained through the research of leading experts on organizational knowledge,
there are still crucial questions unresolved. For example, Nonaka and Takeuchi
(1995: 58–9) argue that:

Information is a flow of messages, while knowledge is created by that very flow of
information, anchored in the beliefs and commitment of its holder. This understanding emphasizes that *knowledge is essentially related to human action.* (emphasis
in the original)

Other researchers have similarly stressed the close connection between knowledge and action: whatever knowledge is, it is thought to make a difference to

An earlier version of this chapter was first published in the *Journal of Management Studies*,
38(7) (2001), 973–93. Reprinted by permission of Blackwell, Copyright (2001).

We would like to thank Jacky Swan and two anonymous *JMS* reviewers for their
valuable comments on that version.

individuals' actions (Choo 1998; Davenport and Prusak 1998; Leonard and Sensiper 1998; Suchman 1987; Wigg 1997). However, while this is a useful insight, it is not clear *how* knowledge is connected to action, nor, more fundamentally, what knowledge is. True, knowledge makes a difference, but how? How is knowledge brought to bear on what an individual does? What are the prerequisites for using knowledge effectively in action?

Davenport and Prusak (1998: 5) have provided the following definition of knowledge:

Knowledge is a flux mix of framed experiences, values, contextual information, and expert insight that provides a framework for evaluating and incorporating new experiences and information. It originates and is applied in the minds of knowers. In organizations, it often becomes embedded not only in documents or repositories but also in organizational routines, processes, practices, and norms.

While this definition correctly highlights the dynamic character of knowledge (i.e. knowledge is both an *outcome*—'a framework'—and a *process* for 'incorporating new experiences and information'), it is not clear in what sense knowledge is different from information, nor how it is possible for values and contextual information to originate and apply in the minds of individuals alone. Moreover, Davenport and Prusak pack into knowledge too many things, such as 'values', 'experiences', and 'contexts', without specifying their relationships, thus risking making 'knowledge' an all-encompassing, and, therefore, little-revealing, concept. Also, while it is acknowledged that knowledge becomes embedded in organizations, it is not mentioned in what form, nor how individuals draw on it.

For some researchers and practitioners (see Gates 1999; Lehner 1990; Terrett 1998), organizational knowledge tends to be viewed as synonymous with information, especially digital information, in which case the interesting issue is thought to be how knowledge-as-information is best stored, retrieved, transmitted, and shared (cf. Brown and Duguid 2000; Hendriks and Vriens 1999). In contrast, for some researchers, such as Kay (1993), organizational knowledge becomes the essence of the firm. For example, as Kay (ibid. 73) remarks, '[organizational knowledge] is distinctive to the firm, is more than the sum of the expertise of those who work in the firm, and is not available to other firms'. Here knowledge is thought to be profoundly collective, above and beyond discrete pieces of information individuals may possess; it is a pattern formed within and drawn upon by a firm, over time. While few would take issue with this definition, it does not quite reveal what are the characteristic features of organizational knowledge, and does not even hint at the relationship between individual and organizational knowledge.

From the above admittedly cursory review, it follows that it is still not clear what knowledge is, nor what makes it organizational. Realizing that knowledge is indeed a tricky concept, some researchers have gone as far as to suggest (mostly in the context of academic conferences) that, perhaps, we do not need more formal definitions of knowledge, since they very probably end up complicating things further. We do not agree with this view. Our understanding of organizational knowledge (or any other topic of interest) will not advance if we resign ourselves to merely recycling commonsensical notions of knowledge, for if we were to do so we would risk being prisoners of our own unchallenged assumptions, incapable of advancing our learning. On the contrary, what we need is ever more sophisticated theoretical explorations of our topic of interest, aiming at gaining a deeper insight into it. Those who think such an attempt is futile need to ponder the great extent to which Polanyi's notion of 'personal knowledge' has advanced our understanding of what knowledge is about and, accordingly, how impoverished our understanding would have been without that notion. If theoretical confusion is in evidence, the answer cannot be 'drop theory', but 'develop more and better theory'.

In this chapter we will argue that our difficulties in getting to grips with organizational knowledge stem from a double failure: to understand the generation and utilization of knowledge we need a theory of knowledge, *and* to understand *organizational* knowledge we need a theory of organization. Moreover, it needs to be pointed out that, although no self-respecting researchers have so far failed to acknowledge their debt to Polanyi for the distinction he drew between tacit and explicit knowledge, Polanyi's work, for the most part, has not been really engaged with. If it had been, it would have been noticed that, since all knowledge has its tacit presuppositions, tacit knowledge is not something that can be converted into explicit knowledge, as Nonaka and Takeuchi (1995) have claimed (cf. Cook and Brown 1999; Tsoukas 1996). Moreover, and perhaps more crucially, it would have been acknowledged that Polanyi (1962), more than anything else, insisted on the *personal* character of knowledge—hence the title of his magnum opus, *Personal Knowledge*. In his own words: '*All* knowing is personal knowing—participation through indwelling' (Polanyi 1975: 44, emphasis in the original).

In this chapter we will take on board Polanyi's profound insight concerning the personal character of knowledge and fuse it with Wittgenstein's claim that all knowledge is, in a fundamental way, collective, in order to show on the one hand how individuals appropriate knowledge and expand their knowledge repertoires, and, on the other hand how knowledge, in organized contexts, becomes organizational, and with what implications for its management. We will ground our theoretical claims on a case study undertaken at a call centre at Panafon (now Vodafone), the leading mobile-telecommunications company in Greece.

The structure of the chapter is as follows. In the next section we describe what personal knowledge is and develop further the notion of organizational knowledge. In a nutshell, our claim is that knowledge is the individual capability to draw distinctions, within a domain of action, based on an appreciation of context or theory, or both. Similarly, organizational knowledge is the capability members of an organization have developed to draw distinctions in the process of carrying out their work, in particular concrete contexts, by enacting sets of generalizations whose application depends on historically evolved collective understandings. Following our theoretical exploration of organizational knowledge, we report the findings of a case study carried out at a call centre in Panafon, in Greece. In line with our argument that all organizations can be seen as collections of knowledge assets (cf. Wenger 1998: 46), we investigate how call operators at a call centre—a unit which, conventionally, would not be called knowledge-intensive—answer customer calls by drawing on and modifying organizational knowledge to suit their particular circumstances. Finally, we explore the implications of our argument by focusing on the links between knowledge and action on the one hand, and the management of organizational knowledge on the other.

On Personal and Organizational Knowledge

The distinction between data, information, and knowledge has often been made in the literature (Boisot 1995; Choo 1998; Davenport and Prusak 1998; Nonaka and Takeuchi 1995). What differentiates knowledge from information, it has been argued, is that knowledge presupposes values and beliefs, and is closely connected with action. Similarly, Bell (1999; lxi–lxiv) has provided a neat definition of these terms, which is particularly useful for our purpose here. For Bell *data* is an ordered sequence of given items or events (e.g. the name index of a book). *Information* is a context-based arrangement of items whereby relations between them are shown (e.g. the subject index of a book). And *knowledge* is the judgement of the significance of events and items which comes from a particular context and/or theory (e.g. the construction of a thematic index by a reader of a book).

What underlies Bell's definition of knowledge is his view that data, information, and knowledge are three concepts that can be arranged on a single continuum, depending on the extent to which they reflect human involvement with, and processing of, the reality at hand. For example, the name index of a book is merely data, since it involves minimal effort on the part of an individual to make such an index—the names are there, it is just a matter of arranging them alphabetically. The subject index of a book, however, requires more processing on the part of the individual, since it depends on his/her judgement to construct the appropriate headings for such an index. Finally, when a reader relates the content of a book to his/her own interests, he/she may construct his/her own analytical index—in other words, the reader in this case has a far greater degree of involvement and exercises far greater judgement in organizing the material at hand. Put simply, data require minimal human judgement, knowledge maximum judgement. Knowledge is the capacity to exercise judgement on the part of an individual, which is either based on an appreciation of context or is derived from theory, or both (ibid. 1999: lxiv).

Drawing on Dewey's conception of aesthetic experience (1934), Bell (1999: lxiv) goes on to argue that 'judgement arises from the self-conscious use of the prefix *re*: the desire to *re*-order, to *re*-arrange, to *re*-design what one knows and thus create new angles of vision or new knowledge for scientific or aesthetic purposes'. The self-conscious desire to rearrange what one knows implies that the individual wishes to see things differently, to disclose aspects of a phenomenon that were hitherto invisible, or simply to see more clearly than before. But this is not all: the individual will rearrange his/her knowledge while being located somewhere—a certain standpoint or tradition. Thus, the capacity to exercise judgement involves two things. First, the ability of an individual to draw distinctions (Reyes and Zarama 1998; Vickers 1983) and second, the location of an individual within a collectively generated and sustained domain of action—a 'form of life' (Wittgenstein 1958), a 'practice' (MacIntyre 1985), a 'horizon of meaning' (Gadamer 1989), or a 'consensual domain' (Maturana and Varela 1988)—in which particular criteria of evaluation hold.

Why does the capacity to exercise judgement imply the capability of drawing distinctions? Because when we draw a distinction we split the world into 'this' and 'that', we bring into consciousness the constituent parts of the phenomenon we are interested in (Dewey 1934: 310). Through language we name, and constantly bring forth and ascribe significance to, certain aspects of the world (including, of course, our own behaviour) (Schutz 1970; Taylor 1985; Winograd and Flores 1987). When our language is crude and unsophisticated, so are our distinctions and the consequent judgements. The more refined our language, the finer our distinctions. Our attempt to understand and act on reality is simultaneously enabled and limited by the cultural tools we employ—with language being one of the most important (Vygotsky 1978; 23–30; Wertsch 1998; 40). Just as someone with a rudimentary knowledge of English cannot easily differentiate between different English accents (that is, he/she cannot draw fine distinctions related to accent), so a person untrained in a particular activity has only a rule-based, undifferentiated outline of it in mind, rather than a set of refined distinctions (Dreyfus and Dreyfus 1986). Polanyi (1962; 101) has perceptively captured this point in the following illustration:

Think of a medical student attending a course in the X-ray diagnosis of pulmonary diseases. He watches in a darkened room shadowy traces on a fluorescent screen placed against a patient's chest, and hears the radiologist commenting to his assistants, in technical language, on the significant features of these shadows. At first the student is completely puzzled. For he can see in the X-ray picture of a chest only the shadows of the heart and the ribs, with a few spidery blotches between them. The experts seem to be romancing about figments of their imagination; he can see nothing that they are talking about. Then as he goes on listening for a few weeks, looking carefully at ever new pictures of different cases, a tentative understanding will dawn on him; he will gradually forget about the ribs and begin to see the lungs. And eventually, if he perseveres intelligently, a rich panorama of significant details will be revealed to him: of physiological variations and pathological changes, of scars, of chronic infections and signs of acute disease. He has entered a new world. He still sees only a fraction of what the experts can see, but the pictures are definitely making sense now and so do most of the comments made on them.

The medical student refines his/her ability to read an X-ray picture through his/her bodily exposure to the relevant material (what Lakoff (1987: 297) calls 'the basic-level interactions with the environment') *and* the specialized language he/she is taught to apply to that material (Schon 1983). How does this happen? Having a body, the medical student is capable of obtaining preconceptual experience; namely, experience that is tied to gestalt perception, mental imagery, and motor movement (Lakoff 1987: 267–8, 302–3). At the same time, being a language user, the medical student operates in the cognitive domain; namely, a domain within which he/she recursively interacts with his/her own descriptions (i.e. thoughts). What initially appears only as a shadow of the heart and the ribs (i.e. a description) is further processed, through language and with the help of an instructor or with peers, until a much more refined picture emerges. As Mercer (1995: 13) remarks, 'practical, hands-on activity can gain new depths of meaning if it is *talked about*' (emphasis added). Relating his/her existing knowledge to the X-ray picture and talking about it with his/her instructor, the medical student is forced to revise and refine his/her understanding about the matter at hand (Hunter 1991). In Foerster's second-order-cybernetics language (1984: 48), cognitive processes are never-ending processes of computation. Cognition consists in computing descriptions of descriptions; that is, in recursively operating on—modifying, transforming—representations. In doing so, cognizing subjects rearrange and reorder what they know, thus creating new distinctions and, therefore, new knowledge (Bell 1999: lxiv; Dewey 1934).

Individuals draw distinctions within a collective domain of action; that is, within a language-mediated domain of sustained interactions. For the medical student to be able to discern the medically significant pattern of an X-ray picture, he/she necessarily draws on medical knowledge; that is, on a collectively produced and sustained body of knowledge (Hunter 1991). Likewise, for an individual copier technician to be able to diagnose a faulty photocopier he needs to draw on a specific body of expertise, which is produced and sustained by the company making photocopiers and by the community of technicians as a whole (Orr 1996; cf. Wenger 1998). Why is this so? The reason is that the key categories implicated in human action, for example 'physiological variation', 'pathological change' (Polanyi 1962: 101), 'faulty photocopier' (Orr 1996), or 'clunky flute' (Cook and Brown 1999: 396; Cook and Yanow 1996), derive their meanings from the way they have been used within particular forms of life (the medical community, or the community of photocopier technicians, or the community of flute makers). One learns how to recognize a pathology on the lungs or a 'clunky flute' only because one has been taught to use the category 'pathological lung' or 'clunky flute' within a domain of action (Toulmin 1999).

In other words, knowing how to act within a domain of action is learning to make competent use of the categories and the distinctions constituting that domain (Wenger 1998). As Spender (1989) has shown, upon entering a particular industry, managers learn a particular 'industry recipe'; that is, a set of distinctions tied to a particular field of experience. The distinctions pertain to a number of issues ranging from how markets are segmented to the kind of employees suited to an industry or to the technology used. To put it broadly, to engage in collective work is to engage in a discursive practice; that is, in the normative use of a sign system which is directed at influencing aspects of the world and whose key categories and distinctions are defined through their use in discourse (Harre and Gillet 1994; 28–9; Taylor 1993; Tsoukas 1996, 1998).

On the basis of the preceding analysis, the definition of knowledge mentioned earlier may be reformulated as follows: Knowledge is the individual ability to draw distinctions within a collective domain of action, based on an appreciation of context or theory, or both. Notice that such a definition of knowledge preserves a significant role for human agency, since individuals are seen as being inherently capable of making (and refining) distinctions, while also taking into account collective understandings and standards of appropriateness, on which individuals necessarily draw in the process of making distinctions, in their work.

The individual capacity to exercise judgement is based on an appreciation of *context* in the ethnomethodological sense that a social being is (or, to be more precise, becomes) knowledgeable in accomplishing routine and taken-for-granted tasks within particular contexts (e.g. taking measurements, driving, holding a conversation, filling in a medical-insurance form, etc.), as a result of having been through processes of socialization (Berger and Luckmann 1966; Garfinkel 1984; Schutz 1970). We do not need a Ph.D. in linguistics to carry out a conversation, nor do we need specialized training in economics or agricultural science to buy cheese at the grocer's. We know how to deal with the practical things in life because we have picked up through interaction (with the world and with others) what is expected of us, or what works (Heritage 1984; Wenger 1998). 'We bring to situations of interaction', notes McCarthy (1994: 65), a 'tacit awareness of the normative expectations relevant to them and an intuitive appreciation of the consequences that might follow from breaking them'.

The individual capacity to exercise judgement is based on an appreciation of *theory* in the epistemic sense that, as Bell (1999: lxiii) has noted, 'theory allows one to take a finding and generalize from any one context to another context. From verified theory—Newton's laws of motion—we can accept the finding in a new context as knowledge'. Choosing a theory and applying it in a new context involves judgement, and the capacity to make such judgements is knowledge. The notion of 'theory' here is a broad one to include any framework, set of generalizing principles, or abstract instructions. Just as a judge brings a set of legal principles to bear on a particular situation, so a copier technician draws upon, among other things, a set of abstract instructions in order to repair a faulty photocopier. Whatever abstract principle enables an individual to generalize across contexts counts as theory and forms an additional basis for exercising judgement.

If the above is accepted then it becomes possible for us to see the sense in which knowledge becomes organizational. In a weak sense, knowledge is organizational simply by its being generated, developed, and transmitted by individuals within organizations. That is obvious but unrevealing. In a strong sense, however, knowledge becomes organizational when, as well as drawing distinctions in the course of their work by taking into account the contextuality of their actions, *individuals draw and act upon a corpus of generalizations in the form of generic rules, produced by the organization.*

Why is this the case? A distinguishing feature of organization is the generation of recurring behaviours by means of institutionalized roles that are explicitly defined. For an activity to be said to be organized implies that *types* of behaviour in *types* of situations are connected to *types* of actors (Berger and Luckmann 1966: 22; Scott 1995). An organized activity provides actors with a given set of cognitive categories and a typology of action options (Scott 1995; Weick 1979). Such a typology consists of rules of action—typified responses to typified expectations (Berger and Luckmann 1966: 70–3). Rules are prescriptive statements guiding behaviour in organizations, and take the form of propositional statements; namely, 'If X, then Y, in circumstances Z'. As Twining and Miers (1991: 131) remark, 'a rule prescribes that in circumstances X, behavior of type Y ought, or ought not to be, or may be indulged in by persons of class Z'.

On this view, therefore, organizing implies *generalizing*: the subsumption of heterogeneous particulars under generic categories. In that sense, formal organization necessarily involves abstraction. Since in an organization the behaviour of its members is formally guided by a set of propositional statements, it follows that an organization may be seen as a *theory*—a particular set of concepts (or cognitive categories) and the propositions expressing the relationship between concepts. Organization-as-theory enables organizational members to generalize across contexts. For example, the operators of the call centre we researched had been instructed to issue standardized responses to standardized queries: If this type of problem appears, then this type of solution is appropriate. From a strictly organizational point of view, the contextual specificity surrounding every particular call (a specificity that callers tend to expand upon in their calls) is removed through the application of generic organizational rules.

Rules, however, exist for the sake of achieving specific goals. The generaliza-tions selected and enforced are selected from among numerous other possibil-ities. To have as a rule, for example, that 'no caller should wait for more than one minute before his/her call is answered' is not self-evident. It has been selected by the company, in order to increase its customer responsiveness, hoping that, ultimately, it will contribute to attracting more customers, thus leading to a higher market share, and so on. In other words, a rule's factual predicate ('If X...') is a generalization selected because it is thought to be causally relevant to a *justification*—some goal to be achieved or some evil to be avoided (Schauer 1991: 27). A justification (or, to be more precise, a set of logically ordered justifications) determines which generalization will consti-tute a rule's factual predicate. This is an important point, for it highlights the fact that rules exist for the sake of some higher-order goals.

Moreover, rules do not apply themselves; members of a community of practice, situated in specific contexts, apply them (Gadamer 1980; Tsoukas 1996; Wittgenstein 1958). Members of a community must share an interpret-ation as to what a rule means before they apply it. As Barnes (1995: 202) remarks, 'nothing in the rule itself fixes its application in a given case, [...] there is no 'fact of the matter' concerning the proper application of a rule, [...] what a rule is actually taken to imply is a matter to be decided, when it is decided, by contingent social processes'. Since rules codify particular previous examples, an individual following a rule needs to learn to act in proper analogy with those examples. To follow a rule is, therefore, to extend an analogy. Barnes (ibid. 55) has put it so felicitously that we cannot resist the temptation to quote him in full:

To understand rule-following or norm-guided behavior in this way immediately highlights the normally open-ended character of norms, the fact that they cannot themselves fix and determine what actions are in true conformity with them, that there is no logical compulsion to follow them in a particular way. Every instance of a norm may be analogous to every other, but analogy is not identity: analogy exists between things that are similar yet different. And this means that, although it is always possible to assimilate the next instance to a norm by analogy with existing examples of the norm, it is equally always possible to resist such assimilation, to hold the analogy insufficiently strong, to stress the differences between the in-stance and existing examples. If norms apply by analogy then it is up to *us* to decide where they apply, where the analogy is sufficiently strong and where not.

Notice that, on this essentially Wittgensteinian view, the proper application of a rule is not an individual accomplishment but is fundamentally predicated on collectively shared meanings. If formal organization is seen as a set of propos-itional statements, then those statements must be put into action by organ-izational members, who 'must be constituted as a *collective* able to sustain a shared sense of what rules imply and hence an agreement in their practice when they follow rules' (ibid. 204, emphasis added). The justification (pur-pose) underlying a rule needs to be elaborated upon and its meaning agreed by the organizational collective. Organizational tasks are thus accomplished by individuals being able to secure a shared sense of what rules mean (or by agreeing upon, reinforcing, and sustaining a set of justifications) in the course of their work. This suggests an organization as a densely connected network of communication through which shared understandings are achieved.

A collectivist understanding of organizational knowledge has been evident in Penrose's work on the theory of the firm (1959). The key to understanding firms' growth, wrote Penrose, is to focus not on the given resources a firm possesses but on the *services* rendered by those resources. This means that, according to Penrose, firms have discretion over how they use their resources and, therefore, over the services derived from them. Such discretion stems from the fact that firms view, and thus utilize, their resources differently. On this view, organizational knowledge is the set of collective understandings embedded in a firm, which enable it to put its resources to particular uses. Penrose's view of organizational knowledge identifies the latter with cultural or collective knowledge (cf. Blackler 1995; Collins 1990)—*it is a distinctive way of thinking and acting in the world.*

There is an interesting parallel between the preceding Wittgensteinian view of rule-following and Polanyi's conception of personal knowledge. Both philosophers showed that even the most abstract formalisms we use ultimately depend, for their effective deployment, on social definitions. Abstract systems cannot be self-sustained; they are necessarily grounded on collective definitions; hence, they depend on human judgement (Toulmin 1999). Polanyi extended this argument further. For him, human judgement is manifested not only at the level of collective significations that happen to have evolved historically; it is equally manifested at the individual level. All knowledge is personal knowledge.

Seeking to highlight the nature of science as a skilful practice, Polanyi has described, time and again, the exact sciences as 'a set of formulae which have a bearing on experience' (e.g., Polanyi 1962; 49). It is precisely the establishment of this 'bearing on experience' that renders all scientific knowing, ultimately, *personal* knowing. In so far as even the most abstract mathematical formalisms need to be empirically checked—that is, predictions to be made, measurements to be taken, and predictions to be compared with measurements—there are bound to be discrepancies between theory and observations, no matter how minor, which will need to be assessed by personal judgement on the part of the scientist (Polanyi 1975; 30). In his various illustrations, from map-reading, through piano playing and bicycle riding, to scientific work, Polanyi consistently pointed out that all abstract systems, from the shortest set of instructions right down to the most abstract and comprehensive set of formalisms, ultimately encounter experience—the real world, with all its messiness, imperfection, and complexity—and that encounter is inevitably mediated through human judgement. In Polanyi's words (ibid. 31):

even the most exact sciences must therefore rely on our personal confidence that we possess some degree of personal skill and personal judgement for establishing a valid correspondence with—or a real deviation from—the facts of experience.

Acknowledging that all knowledge contains a personal element or, to put it differently, '[recognizing] personal participation as the universal principle of knowing' (Polanyi 1975; 44) implies that knowing always is, to a greater or lesser extent, a skilful accomplishment, an art.

What is the structure of such a skill? What does it consist of? Whether we refer to everyday or expert knowledge or, to use Bell's terminology, to knowledge based on an appreciation of context or theory, the structure of knowing-as-a-skill is identical. In order to know something, the individual acts to integrate a set of particulars of which he/she is subsidiarily aware. To make sense of our experience we necessarily rely on some parts of it subsidiarily in order to attend to our main objective focally. We comprehend something as a whole (focally) by tacitly integrating certain particulars, which are known by the actor subsidiarily. Knowing has a *from–to* structure: the particulars bear on the focus *to* which I attend *from* them. Subsidiary awareness and focal awareness are mutually exclusive. Action is confused if the individual shifts his/her focal attention to the particulars of which he/she had been previously aware in a subsidiary manner.

Thus, knowing consists of three elements: subsidiary particulars, a focal target, and, crucially, a person who links the two. Polanyi's classic example (ibid. 36) is the blind man probing a cavity with his stick. The focus of his attention is at the far end of the stick, while he attends subsidiarily to the feeling of holding the stick in his hand. The difference between a seeing man blindfolded and a blind man is that for the former probing feels like a series of jerks in his palm, whereas for the latter probing indicates the presence of certain obstacles of a specific hardness and shape. In the first case the stick has not yet been assimilated (and as a result it receives focal awareness), while in the latter case the stick is being subsidiarily noticed and, as a result, it is used as a tool to a certain end.

On Polanyi's view practical knowledge has two features. First, it is inevitably and irreducibly *personal*, since it involves personal participation in its generation. In his words, 'the relation of a subsidiary to a focus is formed by the *act of a person* who integrates one to another' (ibid. 38). And second, for knowledge to be effectively applied it needs to be *instrumentalized*—to be used as a tool. On this point Polanyi was very clear, echoing the Heideggerian line of thinking (Winograd and Flores 1987). 'Hammers and probes', he wrote, 'can be replaced by intellectual tools' (Polanyi 1962: 59). As we learn to use a tool, any tool, we gradually become unaware of how we use it to achieve results. Polanyi called this 'indwelling'—dwelling in the tool, making it feel as if it is an extension of our own body (ibid. 1975). We make sense of experience by assimilating the tool through which we make sense. The lapse into unawareness of the manner in which we use a tool is accompanied by an expansion of awareness of the experiences at hand, on the operational plane. We refine our ability to get things done by dwelling in the tools (both physical and intellectual) through which we get things done. The increasing instrumentalization of certain actions in the service of some purpose (or what we earlier called 'justification') enables the individual to expand his/her awareness of the situation he/she encounters and thus to refine his/her skills (Dreyfus and Dreyfus 1986). The ongoing process of transforming experience into subsidiary awareness, or, in Polanyi's (1962; 64) words, 'the pouring of ourselves into the subsidiary awareness of particulars', allows one to reach ever higher levels of skilful achievement (e.g. the improvement of the medical student's ability to read the X-ray picture).

To sum up, knowledge is the individual capability to draw distinctions, within a domain of action, based on an appreciation of context or theory, or both. Organizations are three things at once: concrete settings within which individual action takes place; sets of abstract rules in the form of propositional statements; and historical communities. Organizational knowledge is the capability members of an organization have developed to *draw distinctions* in the process of carrying out their work, in particular *concrete contexts*, by enacting sets of generalizations (*propositional statements*) whose application depends on historically evolved *collective understandings* and experiences. The more propositional statements and collective understandings become instrumentalized (in Polanyi's sense of the term), and the more new experiences are reflectively processed (both individually and collectively) and then gradually driven into subsidiary awareness, the more organizational members dwell in all of them, and the more able they become to concentrate on new experiences, on the operational plane.

Having developed the notion of organizational knowledge and shown its links with personal knowledge and human action, we will proceed below empirically to investigate these claims through a case study.

Organizational Knowledge in Action: A Case Study

Research Setting

A case study on organizational knowledge was undertaken at the customer-care department at Panafon, Greece's leading mobile-phone operator. The company was formed in 1992; at the time of writing (in 2001) it employed 900 people and was controlled by the UK-based Vodafone group. (Now it has been completely absorbed by Vodafone and adopted its name.) With more than two million subscribers in 2001, Panafon holds a 38 per cent share of the mobile-phone market in Greece, one of the fastest growing markets in Europe (*Financial Times*, 28 December 2000). The company is listed on the Athens stock exchange and provides a wide range of standard and enhanced GSM services as well as services such as voicemail, short-message services, personal numbering and data, fax transmission services, and internet-related services (Panafon 1998).

The quality of customer care is, along with price, network coverage, and range of services, a determining factor for customers in choosing to subscribe to one of the three providers of mobile telecommunications services in Greece. Considering the great importance of customer care for Panafon's ability to maintain and attract customers, the empirical part of this study focuses on organizational knowledge within the customer-care department (CCD), although the latter is not what might be called a knowledge-intensive department. This however, is immaterial for us, since, as was, we hope, made clear in the preceding section, knowledge is de facto implicated in all types of organizational work (Wenger 1998). Indeed, one of our claims in the preceding section was that human action in organizations (all kinds of organizations) *necessarily* draws on organizational knowledge; namely, on sets of generalizations underlain by collective understandings, activated in particular contexts. Of course, this is not to deny that there are, indeed, important differences between organizational forms concerning the dominant types of knowledge to be found in each one of them (Lam 2000). But such differences are not analytically relevant in the context of the present argument, just as differences between societies are not analytically relevant in the context of an enquiry that sets out to investigate the structuring and enactment of social relations (Garfinkel 1984).

The customer-care department (CCD) has been in operation since the start of Panafon's commercial operation, and it was the first customer-care centre in Greece to operate twenty-four hours a day. At the time of writing (2001) the CCD has a total of 250 employees and consists of four call centres. The volume of calls to the CCD has increased significantly in recent years, due to both the growth in the customer base and new services introductions. Currently the department receives an average of 60,000 calls a day, although volumes fluctuate by month of the year, day of the week, time of day, and maturity of service. Operators, working in eight-hour shifts, are responsible for answering calls about specific Panafon services according to their experience of, and training in, such services.

The aim of the CCD is to provide information support to Panafon subscribers, including directory enquiries, connection through directory assistance, secretarial messaging services, general information on the company's services (e.g. tariffs, network coverage), voicemail enquiries, as well as general information and assistance, including information about mobile phones, to both contract and pre-paid customers. Customer care is provided by customer-care operators (hereafter referred to as operators), all of whom have been formally trained in Panafon's products and services and in the techniques of providing customer support. In addition, operators have received on-the-job training before taking on their duties.

Data Collection and Analysis

Data collection was conducted in two phases. In Phase 1, we participated in a two-day induction programme designed for new employees. Our aim was to familiarize ourselves with the company, and get an overall picture of its operation, products and services, departments, etc. In Phase 2 data about the CCD were collected using unstructured and semi-structured interviewing and document review. In addition, Phase 2 involved extensive on-the-job observation, and review of relevant work-related material.

Observation took the form of sitting with operators when they were on and off the phones as well as attending their coffee breaks, and taking notes on their work practices. Operators were encouraged to give explanations about what they were doing, and these descriptions were supplemented with questions probing particular issues, especially for explanations and clarifications both of the use of the available technology and work manuals, and of operators' initiatives and tacit understandings in dealing with customer calls. Materials reviewed included the work manuals provided by Panafon to employees and operators' personal notes. Detailed interviews in Phase 2 were taken from three CCD operators, the fault coordinator, the shift supervisor, and the supervisor of one of the four call centres, as well as three employees at engineering and one at operations and Support departments, who liaise with customer care. Qualitative techniques were used to analyse the data collected, in line with the recommendations of Miles and Huberman (1984).

Knowledge Practices within
Panafon's Customer Care Department

To answer most customer queries operators draw upon electronically provided and printed information. Concerning electronically provided information, operators use computerized databases containing pertinent information for each of the services provided by the CCD. For example, for general enquiries concerning contract customers the computerized database contains, among other things, information about which services the customer has subscribed to and who is his/her service provider. This information enables operators to help customers identify whether, for example, a customer has indeed subscribed to a particular service the customer has enquired about (e.g. whether the customer has subscribed to voicemail). The system can also help operators to activate the connection of pre-paid customers or even to activate call recognition for these customers if they wish.

The system is also used for directory enquiries. Every day operators are required to check their computer screens for new information that may have become available (concerning, for example, network-coverage problems, tariff changes, etc.), which operators need to know about in order to answer customer queries accurately and efficiently. As for the printed material operators draw upon, it consists of company manuals containing information about a range of issues, such as details about all services provided by Panafon, countries in which roaming may be activated, information on different types of mobile phones, etc.

Drawing on both printed and electronically available information, operators are, in principle, in a position to handle customer queries. As an experienced operator put it:

Answers to 95% of the questions we are asked exist somewhere in the computer system, or in the manuals, or somewhere. Most likely the subscriber will be given the information he wants. The only question is how fast this will be done.

Indeed, the question of speed is an important indicator of high-quality service since if a particular customer is served quickly he/she will very probably be a satisfied customer. Prompted to explain what she meant by 'somewhere', the above-mentioned operator went on to exalt the significance of 'work experience' in that it provides operators with a repository of instances upon which they may regularly draw in their work.

Viewed this way, the information systems used by the operators include not only the organizationally-provided technical means for accessing relevant information, but also the informal memory system (both individual and collective) which has gradually been built up over time, consisting of the individual stocks of experience held by each operator, and by the stories shared in their community. As the operators often pointed out in their interviews with us, accessing that informal collective stock of knowledge is a valuable source of information for them. This is quite important because it highlights the significance of the web of social relations at work, since it is within those relations that such informal knowledge is preserved and drawn upon (Davenport and Prusak 1998).

Indeed, all the operators interviewed stressed how important it is for them to be able to draw upon each other's accumulated experience and knowledge at work. We noticed that operators, while carrying out their tasks, often consulted one another about matters unknown to them. Communication about work-related issues also occurs during their breaks. It is noteworthy that such communication occurs naturally; it is part of the informal storytelling that goes on among operators. Narrating work-related episodes to one another about, for example, awkward customers and uncommon questions tackled creates an environment in which the ties of community are reinforced, collective memory is enriched, and individual knowledge is enhanced. Researchers such as Brown and Duguid (1991), Orr (1996), Weick, (1995), and

Wenger (1998) have also mentioned the strong links between community ties, individual learning, and storytelling.

Providing customer support is not as easy a job as it might first appear. Operators must be able continuously to provide efficient, courteous, and helpful customer-support services to subscribers—at least that is the official company policy. Moreover, customers are not always 'sophisticated' mobile-phone users, which often makes communication between operators and customers difficult: customers do not always express themselves in a clear and articulate manner, and sometimes they are not even sure what exactly they want. For example, we noticed that when asking for information several customers tended to provide plenty of contextual details while describing their query. Often such contextual information was, strictly speaking, redundant and actually tended to blur, to some extent, the point of their query.

Customer queries, thus, contain some ambiguity. Such ambiguity requires that operators be adept in helping customers articulate their problems, probe them further in order to get customers to clarify what they want, and locate the appropriate information that will answer customers' queries. As well as doing all this, operators must be courteous towards customers and efficient in carrying out their tasks. Given that, as stated earlier, information about customers' calls normally exists 'somewhere' in the call centre, the primary task for the operator is to dispel the ambiguity surrounding customer calls and understand what the problem really is, and how, consequently, it ought to be solved. Even seemingly simple problems require diagnostic skills on the part of operators.

For example, a particular customer complained that he did not have the identification call service, whereby a caller's phone number appears on the receiver's mobile-phone display, although he had paid for it. This could have been a technical problem (i.e. something wrong with his mobile phone), it could have been an error on the part of the company in having failed to activate that service, or it could have been because certain callers do not wish their phone numbers to appear on other people's mobile-phone displays. An inexperienced operator would probably have investigated all these possibilities in turn. An experienced operator, however, would know that the first two possibilities are not very common and would, therefore, focus on the third. Indeed, through appropriate questioning, the particular operator observed first asked the customer about the extent to which the problem appeared, and when told that it tended to occur only in relation to one particular caller was immediately able to reach the conclusion that the caller, in all probability, did not wish for his/her number to be identified. The operator's ability to see through a customer's query, that is to make ever finer distinctions, is an important skill, which is developed and constantly refined on the job.

Through experience and their participation in a 'community of practice' (Brown and Duguid 1991; Wenger 1998), operators develop a set of diagnostic skills which, over time, become instrumentalized; that is to say, tacit. This enables them to think quickly 'on their feet' and serve customers speedily. Over time operators learn to dwell in these skills, feel them as extensions of their own body, and, thus, gradually become subsidiarily aware of them, which enables operators to focus on the task at hand.

For example, for operators to become effective in their job they need to develop sophisticated perceptual skills in the context of mediated interaction (Thompson 1995). Hearing only a voice deprives an operator of the multiple clues associated with face-to-face communication. The message a customer conveys to the operator is communicated not only through words but also through the tone of voice and other associated verbal clues. An operator realizes that he/she is dealing with an unhappy customer, a confused customer, or a puzzled customer not only by what they say to her but also by *how* they say it. High-quality service means that the operator has instrumentalized his/her ability to discern such nuances in customer behaviour (i.e. to draw fine distinctions) and act accordingly.

An operator's perceptual skills, therefore, in understanding what is going on at the other end of the line are very important. It may be perhaps interesting to note that operators had refined their perceptual skills to the extent that they could tell straight away whether the caller at the other end was an electrical-appliances retailer acting on behalf of a customer or whether it was the customer himself/herself. Recognizing nuances in callers' voices and acting accordingly (for example, to pacify an angry customer, to reassure a panic-stricken customer, or to instruct an utterly ignorant customer) was an important part of an effective operator's skill.

The tacitness of operators' knowledge was manifested when they were asked to describe how and why they tackled a particular problem in a particular way. Faced with such questions, operators were at a loss for words: 'You feel it', 'You know it', 'I just knew it', were some of the most often repeated expressions they used (cf. Cook and Yanow 1996). Such knowledge was difficult to verbalize, let alone codify. Although operators did make use of the information systems provided by the company, they did so in a manner whose distinguishing features were, on the one hand, the exercise of operators' judgement in diagnosing problems, while, on the other hand, the way in which operators' judgement was exercised had been crucially shaped by the overall company culture. Given that the latter placed heavy emphasis on high-quality service, which was constantly reinforced through corporate announcements, induction programmes, training, and performance-appraisal systems, the operators had internalized a set of values which helped them orient their actions accordingly.

Operators were drawing on a plethora of data and information (in Bell's sense of these terms) provided to them by the company in electronic and printed forms. Such data consisted of discrete items (e.g. addresses and phone numbers), while information consisted of generic propositional statements in the form of 'If this problem appears, then look at this or that' (Devlin 1999). What was interesting to notice was the transformation of such information to knowledge by the operators themselves. To enact abstract 'if, then' statements, operators had to take into account the particular context of their conversation with a caller and quickly make a judgement as to what was required. To do so, the operators did not simply (and mindlessly) put the organizational rules into action, but they adapted those rules to the circumstances at hand.

As argued earlier, the encounter of a formalism with experience necessitates the exercise of human judgement, out of which new experience emerges, which is drawn upon on subsequent occasions. If Polanyi's claim that all knowledge is personal knowledge is accepted, it follows that, at least as far as organizational knowledge is concerned, there always is an improvisational element in putting knowledge into action. Indeed, this is the sense in which Bell differentiates knowledge from information: the former involves an active rearrangement of the latter; it 'involves judgements, and judgements are derived from the knowledge of the "that it is so", or from a theory of the subject' (Bell 1999: lxiv).

For example, through her experience, one operator knew that a particular type of mobile phone presented certain problems. The same operator also came to know that the set of instructions to customers to activate another type of card-based mobile phone were perceived as somewhat confusing by a number of customers. Having such knowledge, and faced with a particular problem, an operator might first ask what type of mobile phone a particular customer had been using and, depending on his/her answer, the operator would then proceed accordingly. Notice that such knowledge was not to be found in the official information system: it rather developed as a result of operators repeatedly facing (and learning from) particular types of problems to which they developed (i.e. for which they improvised) particular solutions.

As Orlikowski (1996) has persuasively shown, operators improvise in order to meet the demands of their tasks more effectively. Several operators observed were constructing their own personal information systems, which contained photocopies of the relevant corporate manuals plus personal notes. The latter consisted of notes they had taken during their training and notes they had scribbled in response to customer queries they had faced in the past, without, at the time, being able to locate the requisite information through the use of the formal information system. This is an important point that has not been given adequate coverage in the literature on knowledge management, although the phenomenon of 'improvisation' *per se* has received attention (Orlikowski 1996; Weick 1998): alongside formal organizational knowledge there exists informal knowledge that is generated in action. This type of knowledge (what Collins (1990) calls 'heuristic knowledge') is gained only through the improvisation employees undertake while carrying out their tasks. Heuristic knowledge resides both in individuals' minds and in stories shared in communities of practice. Such knowledge may be formally captured and, through its casting into propositional statements, may be turned into organizational knowledge. While this is feasible and desirable, the case still remains that, at any point in time, abstract generalizations are in themselves incomplete to capture the totality of organizational knowledge. In action an improvisational element always follows it as a shadow follows an object.

Discussion and Implications

From the preceding analysis it follows that what makes knowledge distinctly organizational is its codification in the form of propositional statements underlain by a set of collective understandings. Given that individuals put organizational knowledge into action by acting inescapably within particular contexts, there is always, however, room for individual judgement and for the emergence of novelty. It is the open-endedness of the world that gives rise to new experience and learning, and gives knowledge its not-as-yet-formed character. As Gadamer (1989: 38) has perceptively noted, at issue is more than the correct application of general principles. Our knowledge of the latter is 'always supplemented by the individual case, even productively determined by it'. What Gadamer points out is that 'application is neither a subsequent nor merely an occasional part of the phenomenon of understanding, but codetermines it as a whole from the beginning' (ibid. 324). In other words, individuals are not given generalizations which must be first understood before afterwards being applied. Rather, individuals understand generalizations only *through* connecting the latter to particular circumstances facing them; they comprehend the general by relating it to the particular they are confronted with. In so far as this process takes place, every act of interpretation is necessarily creative and, in that sense, heuristic knowledge is not accidental but a necessary outcome of the interpretative act.

A condition for organizational members to undertake action is to be placed within a conceptual matrix woven by the organization. Such a conceptual matrix contains generic categories (e.g. 'service quality', 'happy customer', 'efficient service') and their interrelations (e.g. 'high-quality service makes customers happy'). By categorizing and naming the situation at hand, organizational members begin to search for appropriate responses. Commenting on Joas's *The Creativity of Action* (1996), McGowan (1998: 294) aptly remarks: 'My judgement takes the raw data and raw feels of the present and names them. I decide to take this action because I deem this situation to be of this kind. The novelty of situations, the newness of the present, is tempered by this judgement'. Of course, my judgement may be wrong. After all, it is only a guide to action, a tentative hypothesis, which may prove erroneous. The expected results may not occur; I need to reflect on this fact and revise my judgement. In other words, categorization and abstraction are conditions of possibility for human action (Lakoff 1987). But categories qua categories may fail to match the particularities of the situation at hand. However, the abstract indeterminacy of categories is not a problem in practice, for it is situationally dealt with by the practical reasoning of competent language users. What gives organizational knowledge its dynamism is the dialectic between the general and the particular. Without the general no action is possible. And without the particular no action can be effective (McCarthy 1994: 68).

If all organizational work necessarily involves drawing on knowledge, then the management of organizational knowledge must be an age-old managerial activity. In one sense this is as true as the realization that marketing has been around since the dawn of the market economy. But in another sense this is not quite the case, if by management we mean the distinctly modern activity of authoritative coordination of socio-technical processes. For organizational knowledge to be managed, an unreflective practice needs to be turned into a reflective practice, or, to put it differently, practical mastery needs to be supplemented by a quasi-theoretical understanding of what individuals are doing when they exercise that mastery.

An unreflective practice involves us acting, doing things, effortlessly observing the rules of our practice, but finding it difficult to state what they are. In that sense we are all *un*reflective practitioners: in so far as we carry out the tasks involved in our practice, we do so having instrumentalized, appropriated, the tools (i.e. abstract rules and collective understandings) through which we get things done. As Strawson (1992: 5) elegantly notes:

When the first Spanish or, strictly, Castilian grammar was presented to Queen Isabella of Castile, her response was to ask what use it was ... [Her response was quite understandable since] the grammar was in a sense of no use at all to fluent speakers of Castilian. In a sense they knew it already. They spoke grammatically correct Castilian because grammatically correct Castilian simply *was* what they spoke. The grammar did not set the standards of correctness for the sentences they spoke; on the contrary, it was the sentences they spoke that set the standard of correctness for the grammar. However, though in a sense they knew the grammar of their language, there was another sense in which they did not know it.

What was that? If Queen Isabella had been asked to judge whether a particular sequence of Castilian words was grammatically correct, she would have had to state the rules of the language in terms of which she would need to make her judgement. The speaking of Castilian sentences by the Queen and her subjects showed that they, indeed, observed such rules, but they could not easily state what they were, unless there was a grammar available.

The point of this example is that we may have (unreflectively) mastered a practice, but this is not enough. If we need efficiently to teach new members to be effective members of the practice, or if we need to reflect on ways of improving our practice, or if we want to rid ourselves of likely confusions, we need to elucidate our practice by articulating its rules and principles. Knowledge management then is primarily the dynamic process of turning an unreflective practice into a reflective one by elucidating the rules guiding the activities of the practice, by helping give a particular shape to collective understandings, and by facilitating the emergence of heuristic knowledge.

Without any doubt the management of organizational knowledge today certainly implies the ever more sophisticated development of electronic corporate-information systems, which enable a firm to abstract its activities and codify them in the form of generic rules (Gates 1999). In this way, a firm provides its members with the requisite propositional statements for acting efficiently and consistently. Ideally, on this view, an organizational member should have all the information that he/she needs instantly. To a considerable extent that was the case in the call centre under study, although the relative simplicity of operators' tasks (in technical terms) does not make it seem a very impressive achievement.

However, the above is only one aspect of organizational-knowledge management. Another less appreciated aspect, one that has, we hope, been made more evident in this chapter, is the significance of heuristic knowledge developed by employees while doing their jobs. This type of knowledge cannot be 'managed' in the way formally available information can, because it crucially depends on employees' experiences and perceptual skills, their social relations, and their motivation. Managing this aspect of organizational knowledge means that a company must strive to sustain a spirit of community at work, to encourage employees to improvise and undertake initiatives of their own, as well as actively maintain a sense of corporate mission. To put it differently, and somewhat paradoxically, the management of the heuristic aspect of organizational knowledge implies more the sensitive management of social relations and less the management of corporate digital information (Tsoukas 1998). In addition, the effective management of organizational knowledge requires that the relationship between propositional and heuristic knowledge be a two-way street: while propositional knowledge is fed into organizational members and is instrumentalized through application (thus becoming tacit), heuristic knowledge needs to be formalized (to the extent that this is possible) and made organizationally available. Managing organizational knowledge does not narrowly imply efficiently managing hard bits of information but, more subtly, sustaining and strengthening social practices (Kreiner 1999). In knowledge management, digitalization cannot be a substitute for socialization.

References

Barnes, B. (1995), *The Elements of Social Theory* (London: UCL Press).

Bell, D. (1999), 'The Axial Age of Technology Foreword: 1999', in D. Bell, *The Coming of the Post-Industrial Society*, special anniversary edn. (New York: Basic), pp. ix–lxxxv.

Berger, P., and Luckmann, T. (1966), *The Social Construction of Reality* (London: Penguin).

Blackler, F., (1995), 'Knowledge, Knowledge Work and Organizations: An Overview and Interpretation', *Organization Studies*, 16(6): 1021–1046.

Boisot, M. H. (1995), *Information Space: A Framework for Learning in Organizations, Institutions and Culture* (London: Routledge).

Brown, J. S., and Duguid, P. (1991), 'Organizational Learning and Communities-of-Practice: Toward a Unified View of Working, Learning and Innovation', *Organization Science*, 2(1): 40–57.

—— (2000), *The Social Life of Information* (Boston, Mass.: Harvard Business School Press).

Choo, C. W. (1998), *The Knowing Organization: How Organizations Use Information to Construct Meaning, Create Knowledge, and Make Decisions* (New York: Oxford University Press).

Collins, M. H. (1990), *Artificial Experts: Social Knowledge and Intelligent Machines* (Cambridge, Mass.: MIT Press).

Cook, S. D., and Brown, J. S. (1999), 'Bridging Epistemologies: The Generative Dance between Organizational Knowledge and Organizational Knowing', *Organization Science*, 10: 381–400.

Cook, S. D., and Yanow, D. (1996), 'Culture and Organizational Learning', in M. D. Cohen and L. S. Sproull (eds.), *Organizational Learning* (Thousand Oaks, Calif.: Sage), 430–59.

Davenport, T. H., and Prusak, L. (1998), *Working Knowledge* (Cambridge, Mass.: Harvard University Press).

Devlin, K. (1999), *Infosense: Turning Information into Knowledge* (New York: Freeman).

Dewey, J. (1934), *Art as Experience* (New York: Perigee).

Dreyfus, H. L., and Dreyfus, S. E. (1986), *Mind over Machine* (New York: Free Press).

Foerster, H. von (1984), 'On Constructing a Reality', in P. Watzlawick (ed.), *The Invented Reality* (New York: Norton), 41–61.

Gadamer, H.-G. (1980), 'Practical Philosophy as a Model of the Human Sciences', *Research in Phenomenology*, 9: 74–85.

—— (1989), *Truth and Method*, 2nd edn. (London: Sheed & Ward).

Garfinkel, H. (1984), *Studies in Ethnomethodology* (Cambridge: Polity).

Gates, B. (1999), *Business @ the Speed of Thought* (London: Penguin).

Harre, R. and Gillett, G. (1994), *The Discursive Mind* (Thousand Oaks, Calif.: Sage).

Hendriks, P. H. J., and Vriens, D. J. (1999), 'Knowledge-based Systems and Knowledge Management: Friends or Foes?', *Information and Management*, 35: 113–25.

Heritage, J. (1984), *Garfinkel and Ethnomethodology* (Cambridge: Polity).

Hunter, K. M. (1991), *Doctors' Stories: The Narrative Structure of Medical Knowledge* (Princeton, NJ: Princeton University Press).

Joas, H. (1996), *The Creativity of Action* (Cambridge: Polity).

Kay, J. (1993), *Foundations of Corporate Success* (New York: Oxford University Press).

Kreiner, K. (1999), 'Knowledge and Mind', *Advances in Management Cognition and Organizational Information Processing*, 6: 1–29.

Lakoff, G. (1987), *Women, Fire, and Dangerous Things* (Chicago, Ill.: University of Chicago Press).

Lam, A. (2000), 'Tacit Knowledge, Organizational Learning and Societal Institutions: An Integrated Framework', *Organization Studies*, 21(3): 487–514.

Lehner, F. (1990), 'Expert Systems for Organizational and Managerial Tasks', *Information and Management*, 23(1): 31–41.

Leonard, D., and Sensiper, S. (1998), 'The Role of Tacit Knowledge in Group Innovation', *California Management Review*, 40(3): 112–32.

McCarthy, T. (1994), 'Philosophy and Critical Theory', in D. C. Hoy, and T. McCarthy, *Critical Theory* (Oxford: Blackwell) 5–100.

McGowan, J. (1998), 'Toward a Pragmatist Theory of Action', *Sociological Theory*, 16: 292–7.

MacIntyre, A. (1985), *After Virtue*, 2nd edn. (London: Duckworth).

Maturana, H., and Varela, F. (1988), *The Tree of Knowledge* (Boston, Mass.: New Science).

Mercer, N. (1995), *The Guided Construction of Knowledge* (Clevedon: Multilingual Matters).

Miles, M. B., and Huberman, A. M. (1984), *Qualitative Data Analysis: A Sourcebook of New Methods*, (Newbury Park, Calif.: Sage).

Nonaka, I., and Takeuchi, H. (1995), *The Knowledge-Creating Company: How Japanese Companies Create the Dynamics of Innovation* (New York: Oxford University Press).

Orlikowski, W. J. (1996), 'Improvising Organizational Transformation Over Time: A Situated Change Perspective', *Information Systems Research*, 7(1): 63–92.

Orr, J. E. (1996), *Talking about Machines* (Ithaca, NY: ILR/Cornell University Press).

Panafon, November 1998, initial public offering.

Penrose, E. (1959), *The Theory of the Growth of the Firm* (New York: Wiley).

Polanyi, M. (1962), *Personal Knowledge* (Chicago, Ill.: University of Chicago Press).

—— (1975), 'Personal Knowledge', in M. Polanyi and H. Prosch, *Meaning* (Chicago, Ill.: University of Chicago Press), 22–45.

Reyes, A., and Zarama, R. (1998), 'The Process of Embodying Distinctions—A Reconstruction of the Process of Learning', *Cybernetics and Human Knowing*, 5: 19–33.

Schauer, F. (1991), *Playing by the Rules* (Oxford: Clarendon).

Schon, D. (1983), *The Reflective Practitioner* (New York: Basic).

Schutz, A. (1970), *On Phenomenology and Social Relations*, ed. H. R. Wagner (Chicago, Ill.: University of Chicago Press).

Scott, W. R. (1995), *Institutions and Organizations* (Thousand Oaks, Calif.: Sage).

Spender, J.-C. (1989), *Industry Recipes* (Oxford: Blackwell).

Strawson, P. F. (1992), *Analysis and Metaphysics* (Oxford: Oxford University Press).

Suchman, L. A. (1987), *Plans and Situated Actions: The Problems of Human–Machine Communication* (Cambridge: Cambridge University Press).

Taylor, C. (1993), 'To Follow a Rule ...', in C. Calhoun, E. LiPuma and M. Postone (eds.), *Bourdieu: Critical Perspectives* (Cambridge: Polity), 45–59.

—— (1985), *Philosophy and the Human Sciences*, ii. (Cambridge: Cambridge University Press).

Terrett, A. (1998), 'Knowledge Management and the Law Firm', *Journal of Knowledge Management*, 2(1): 67–76.

Thompson, J. B. (1995), *The Media and Modernity* (Cambridge: Polity).

Toulmin, S. (1999), 'Knowledge as Shared Procedures', in Y. Engestrom, R. Miettinen and R-L. Punamaki (eds.), *Perspectives on Activity Theory* (Cambridge: Cambridge University Press), 53–64.

Tsoukas, H. (1996), 'The Firm as a Distributed Knowledge System: A Constructionist Approach', *Strategic Management Journal*, 17 (special winter issue): 11–25.

Tsoukas, H.(1997), 'The Tyranny of Light: The Temptations and the Paradoxes of the Information Society', *Futures*, 29(9): 827–44.

—— (1998), 'Forms of Knowledge and Forms of Life in Organized Contexts', in R. C. H. Chia, *In the Realm of Organization* (London: Routledge), 43–66.

Twining, W., and Miers, D. (1991), *How to Do Things with Rules*, 3rd edn. (London: Weidenfeld and Nicolson).

Varela, F. J., Thompson, E., and Rosch, E. (1991), *The Embodied Mind* (Cambridge, Mass.: MIT Press).

Vickers, G. (1983), *The Art of Judgement* (London: Harper & Row).

Vygotsky, L. S. (1978), *Mind in Society* (Cambridge, Mass.: Harvard University Press).

Weick, K. E. (1979), *The Social Psychology of Organizing*, 2nd edn. (Reading, Mass.: Addison-Wesley).

—— (1995), *Sensemaking in Organizations* (Thousand Oaks, Calif.: Sage).

—— (1998), 'Improvisation as a Mindset of Organizational Analysis', *Organization Science*, 9(5): 543–55.

Wenger, E. (1998), *Communities of Practice* (Cambridge: Cambridge University Press).

Wertsch, J. V. (1998), *Mind as Action* (New York: Oxford University Press).

Wigg, K. M. (1997), 'Integrating Intellectual Capital and Knowledge Management', *Long Range Planning*, 30(3): 399–405.

Winograd, T., and Flores, F. (1987), *Understanding Computers and Cognition* (Reading, Mass.: Addison-Wesley).

Wittgenstein, L. (1958), *Philosophical Investigations* (Oxford: Blackwell).

SIX

Do We Really Understand Tacit Knowledge?

Nisi credideritis, non intelligitis (Unless ye believe, ye shall not understand)

> (St Augustine, cited in Polanyi 1962: 266)

Something that we know when no one asks us, but no longer know when we are supposed to give an account of it, is something that we need to *remind* ourselves of

> (Ludwig Wittgenstein 1958: no. 89, emphasis in the original)

The act of knowing includes an appraisal; and this personal coefficient, which shapes all factual knowledge, bridges in doing so the disjunction between subjectivity and objectivity

> (Michael Polanyi 1962: 17)

I⊤ is often argued that knowledge is fundamental to the functioning of late modern economies (Drucker 1993; Stehr 1994; Thurow 2000). 'Well, what's new here?', a sceptic might ask. 'Knowledge has always been implicated in the process of economic development, since anything we do, how we transform resources into products and services, crucially depends on the knowledge we have at our disposal for effecting such a transformation. An ancient artisan, a medieval craftsman and his apprentices, and a modern manufacturing system all make use of knowledge: certain skills, techniques, and procedures are employed for getting things done'.

What is distinctly new, if anything, in the contemporary so-called 'knowledge economy'? Daniel Bell answered this question more than thirty years ago: theoretical (or codified) knowledge has acquired a central place in late modern societies, in a way that was not the case before. Says Bell:

An earlier version of this chapter was first published in M. Easterby-Smith and M. Lyles (eds.), *The Blackwell Handbook of Organizational Learning and Knowledge Management* (Oxford: Blackwell, 2003), 410–27. Reprinted by permission of Blackwell, Copyright (2003).

Knowledge has of course been necessary in the functioning of any society. What is distinctive about the post-industrial society is the change in the character of knowledge itself. What has become decisive for the organization of decisions and the direction of change is the centrality of *theoretical knowledge*—the primacy of theory over empiricism and the codification of knowledge into abstract systems of symbols that, as in any axiomatic system, can be used to illustrate many different and varied areas of experience. (1992: 20, emphasis in the original)

Indeed, it is hard today to think of an industry that does not make systematic use of 'theoretical knowledge'. Products increasingly incorporate more and more specialized knowledge, supplied by R&D departments, universities, and consulting firms; and production processes are also increasingly based on systematic research that aims to optimize their functioning (Drucker 1993; Mansell and When 1998; Stehr 1994).

Taking a historical perspective on the development of modern market economies, as Bell does, one can clearly see the change in the character of knowledge over time. To simplify, modernity has come to mistrust intuition, preferring explicitly articulated assertions; it is uncomfortable with ad hoc practices, opting for systematic procedures; it substitutes detached objectivity for personal commitment (MacIntyre 1985; Toulmin 1990, 2001). Yet if one takes a closer look at how theoretical (or codified) knowledge is actually *used* in practice, one will see the extent to which theoretical knowledge itself, far from being as objective, self-sustaining, and explicit as it is often taken to be, is actually grounded on personal judgements and tacit commitments. Even the most theoretical form of knowledge, such as pure mathematics, cannot be a completely formalized system, since it is based for its application and development on the *skills* of mathematicians and how such skills are used in practice. To put it differently, codified knowledge necessarily contains a 'personal coefficient' (Polanyi 1962: 17). Knowledge-based economies may indeed be making great use of codified forms of knowledge, but that kind of knowledge is inescapably used in a *non-codifiable* and *non-theoretical* manner.

The significance of 'tacit knowledge' for the functioning of organizations has not escaped the attention of management theorists. Ever since Nonaka and Takeuchi (1995) published their influential *The Knowledge-Creating Company*, it has been nearly impossible to find a publication on organizational knowledge and knowledge management that does not make a reference to or use the term 'tacit knowledge'. And quite rightly so: as common experience can verify, the knowledge people use in organizations is so practical and deeply familiar to them that when people are asked to describe how they do what they do they often find it hard to express it in words (Ambrosini and Bowman 2001; Cook and Yanow 1996: 442; Eraut 2000; Harper 1987; Nonaka and Takeuchi 1995; Tsoukas and Vladimirou 2001). Naturally, several questions arise: What is it about organizational knowledge that makes it so hard to describe? What is the significance of the tacit dimension of organizational knowledge? What are the implications of tacit knowledge for the learning and exercise of skills? If skilled knowing is largely tacit, how is it possible to improve it?

The purpose of this chapter is to explore the preceding questions. My argument will be that popular as the term 'tacit knowledge' may have become in management studies, it has, on the whole, been misunderstood. By and large, tacit knowledge has been conceived in opposition to explicit knowledge, whereas it is simply its other side. As a result of such a misunderstanding, the nature of organizational knowledge and its relation to individual skills and social contexts has been inadequately understood. In this chapter I will first explore the nature of tacit knowledge by drawing primarily on Polanyi (the inventor of the term), an author who is frequently referred to but little understood. Then I will explore how Polanyi's understanding of tacit knowledge has been interpreted by Nonaka and Takeuchi, the two authors who, more than anyone else, have helped popularize the concept of 'tacit knowledge' in management studies and whose interpretation has been adopted by several management authors (see e.g. Ambrosini and Bowman 2001; Baumard 1999; Boisot 1995; Davenport and Prusak 1998; Devlin 1999; Dixon 2000; Krogh et al. 2000; Leonard and Sensiper 1998; Spender 1996; for exceptions see Brown and Duguid 2000; Cook and Brown 1999: 385, 394–5; Kreiner 1999; Tsoukas 1996: 14; 1997: 830–1; Wenger 1998: 67). Finally, I will end this chapter by fleshing out the implications of tacit knowledge, properly understood, for an epistemology of organizational practice.

A Primer in Polanyi

One of the most distinguishing features of Polanyi's work is his insistence on overcoming well-established dichotomies, such as theoretical versus practical knowledge, sciences versus humanities, or, to put it differently, his determination to show the common structure underlying all kinds of knowledge. Polanyi, a chemist turned philosopher, was categorical that all knowing involves *skilful action*, and that the knower necessarily participates in all acts of understanding. For him the idea that there is such a thing as 'objective' knowledge, self-contained, detached, and independent of human action, was wrong and pernicious. '*All* knowing', he insists, 'is personal knowing—participation through indwelling' (Polanyi and Prosch 1975: 44, emphasis in the original).

Take, for example, the use of geographical maps. A map is a representation of a particular territory. As an explicit representation of something else, a map is, in logical terms, not different from a theoretical system, or a system of rules: they all aim at enabling purposeful human action, that is, respectively, to get from A to B, to predict, and to guide behaviour. We may be very familiar with a map *per se* but to *use* it we need to be able to relate it to the world outside the map. More specifically, to use a map we need to be able to do three things. First, we must identify our current position on the map ('You are here'). Second, we must find our itinerary on the map ('We want to go to the National Museum, which is there'). And third, to actually get to our destination, we must identify the itinerary by various landmarks in the landscape around us ('You go past the train station and then turn left'). In other words, a map, no matter how elaborate it is, cannot read itself; it requires the judgement of a skilled reader who will relate the map to the world by both cognitive and sensual means (Polanyi 1962: 18–20; Polanyi and Prosch, 1975: 30).

The same personal judgement is involved whenever abstract representations encounter the world of experience. We are inclined to think, for example, that Newton's laws can predict the position of a planet circling the sun at some future point in time, provided its current position is known. Yet this is not quite the case: Newton's laws can never do that, only *we* can. The difference is crucial. The numbers entering the relevant formulae, from which we compute the future position of a planet, are readings on our instruments—they are not given, but need to be worked out. Similarly, we check the veracity of our predictions by comparing the results of our computations with the readings of the instruments—the predicted computations will rarely coincide with the readings observed and the significance of such a discrepancy needs to be worked out (Polanyi 1962: 19; Polanyi and Prosch 1975: 30). Notice that, as in the case of map reading, the formulae of celestial mechanics cannot apply themselves; the personal judgement of a human agent is necessarily involved in applying abstract representations to the world.

The general point to be derived from the above examples is this: in so far as a formal representation has a bearing on experience, that is to the extent to which a representation encounters the world, personal judgement is called upon to make an assessment of the inescapable gap between the representation and the world encountered. Given that the map is a representation of the territory, I need to be able to match my location in the territory with its representation on the map, if I am to be successful in reaching my destination. Personal judgement cannot be prescribed by rules but relies essentially on the use of our senses (Polanyi 1962: 19; 1966: 20; Polanyi and Prosch 1975: 30). To the extent that this happens, the exercise of personal judgement is a skilful performance, involving both the mind and the body.

The crucial role of the body in the act of knowing has been persistently underscored by Polanyi (cf. Gill 2000: 44–50). As said earlier, the cognitive tools we use do not apply themselves; we apply them and, thus, we need to assess the extent to which our tools match aspects of the world. In so far as our contact with the world necessarily involves our somatic equipment—'the trained delicacy of eye, ear, and touch' (Polanyi and Prosch 1975: 31)—we are engaged in the art of establishing a correspondence between the explicit formulations of our formal representations (be they maps, scientific laws, or organizational rules) and the actual experience of our senses. As Polanyi (1969:

147) remarks, 'the way the body participates in the act of perception can be generalized further to include the bodily roots of all knowledge and thought. [...] Parts of our body serve as tools for observing objects outside and for manipulating them'.

If we accept that there is indeed a 'personal coefficient' (Polanyi 1962: 17) in all acts of knowing, which is manifested in a skilful performance carried out by the knower, what is the structure of such a skill? What is it that enables a map reader to make a competent use of the map to find his/her way around, a scientist to use the formulae of celestial mechanics to predict the next eclipse of the moon, and a physician to read an X-ray picture of a chest? For Polanyi the starting point towards answering this question is to acknowledge that 'the aim of a skilful performance is achieved by the observance of a set of rules which are not known as such to the person following them' (Polanyi 1962: 49). A cyclist, for example, does not normally know the rule that keeps his/her balance, nor does a swimmer know what keeps him/her afloat. Interestingly, such ignorance is hardly detrimental to their effective carrying out of their respective tasks.

The cyclist keeps himself/herself in balance by tilting through a series of curvatures. One can formulate the rule explaining why he/she does not fall off the bicycle—'for a given angle of unbalance the curvature of each tilt is inversely proportional to the square of the speed at which the cyclist is proceeding' (Polanyi 1962: 50)—but such a rule would hardly be helpful to the cyclist. Why? Partly because, as we will see below, no rule is helpful in guiding action unless it is assimilated and lapses into unconsciousness. And partly because there is a host of other particular elements to be taken into account, which are not included in this rule and, crucially, are not known by the cyclist. Skills retain an element of opacity and unspecificity; they cannot be fully accounted for in terms of their particulars, since their practitioners do not ordinarily know what those particulars are; even when they do know them, as, for example, in the case of topographic anatomy, they do not know how to integrate them (ibid. 88–90). It is one thing to learn a list of bones, arteries, nerves, and viscera, and quite another to know how precisely they are intertwined inside the body (ibid. 89).

How then do individuals know how to exercise their skills? In a sense they don't. 'A mental effort', says Polanyi (ibid. 62), 'has a heuristic effect: it tends to incorporate any available elements of the situation which are helpful for its purpose'. Any particular elements of the situation which may help the purpose of a mental effort are selected in so far as they contribute to the performance at hand, without the performer knowing them as they would appear in themselves. The particulars are subsidiarily known in so far as they contribute to the action performed. As Polanyi (ibid. 62) remarks,

this is the usual process of unconscious trial and error by which *we feel our way* to success and may continue to improve on our success without specifiably knowing how we do it—for we never meet the causes of our success as identifiable things which can be described in terms of classes of which such things are members. This is how you invent a method of swimming without knowing that it consists in regulating your breath in a particular manner, or discover the principle of cycling without realizing that it consists in the adjustment of your momentary direction and velocity, so as to counteract continuously your momentary accidental unbalance. (emphasis in the original)

There are two different kinds of awareness in exercising a skill. When I use a hammer to drive in a nail (one of Polanyi's favourite examples—(see ibid. 55); Polanyi and Prosch 1975: 33), I am aware of both the nail and the hammer, but in a different way. I watch the effects of my strokes on the nail, and try to hit it as effectively as I can. Driving the nail down is the main object of my attention and I am focally aware of it. At the same time, I am also aware of the feelings in my palm of holding the hammer. But such awareness is subsidiary: the feelings of holding the hammer in my palm are not an object of my attention but an instrument of it. I watch hitting the nail by being aware of them. As Polanyi and Prosch (ibid. 33) remark: 'I know the feelings in the palm of my hand *by relying on them for attending to the hammer hitting the nail*. I may say that I have a *subsidiary* awareness of the feelings in my hand which is merged into my *focal awareness* of my driving the nail' (emphasis in the original).

If the above is accepted, it means that we can be aware of certain things in a way that is quite different from focusing our attention on them. I have a subsidiary awareness of my holding the hammer in the act of focusing on hitting the nail. In being subsidiarily aware of holding a hammer I see it as having a meaning that is wiped out if I focus my attention on how I hold the hammer. Subsidiary awareness and focal awareness are mutually exclusive (Polanyi 1962:56). If we switch our focal attention to particulars of which we had only subsidiary awareness before, their meaning is lost and the corresponding action becomes clumsy. If a pianist shifts her attention from the piece she is playing to how she moves her fingers; if a speaker focuses his attention on the grammar he is using instead of the act of speaking; or if a carpenter shifts his/her attention from hitting the nail to holding the hammer, they will all be confused. We must rely (to be precise, we must learn to rely) subsidiarily on particulars to attend to something else, hence our knowledge of them remains *tacit* (Polanyi 1966: 10; Winograd and Flores 1987: 32). In the context of carrying out a specific task, we come to know a set of particulars without being able to identify them. In Polanyi's (1966: 4) memorable phrase, 'we can know more than we can tell'.

From the above it follows that tacit knowledge forms a triangle, at the three corners of which are the *subsidiary particulars*, the *focal target*, and the *knower* who links the two (see Fig. 6.1). It should be clear from the above that the linking of the particulars to the focal target does not happen automatically but is a result of the *act* of the knower. It is in this sense that Polanyi talks about all knowledge being *personal* and all knowing being *action*. No knowledge is

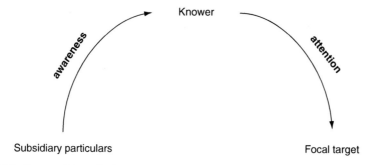

Fig. 6.1: Personal knowledge

possible without the integration of the subsidiaries to the focal target by a person. However, unlike explicit inference, such integration is essentially tacit and irreversible. Its tacitness was discussed earlier; its irreversible character can be seen if juxtaposed to explicit (deductive) inference, whereby one can unproblematically traverse between the premises and the conclusions. Such traversing is not possible with tacit integration: once you have learned to play the piano you cannot go back to being ignorant of how to do it. While you can certainly focus your attention on how you move your fingers, thus making your performance clumsy to the point of paralysing it, you can always recover your ability by casting your mind forward to the music itself. With explicit inference no such break-up and recovery are possible (Polanyi and Prosch 1975: 39–42). When, for example, you examine a legal syllogism or a mathematical proof you proceed in an orderly way from the premises, in a sequence of logical steps, to the conclusions. You lose nothing and you recover nothing—there is complete reversibility. You can go back to check the veracity of each constituent statement separately and how it logically links with its adjacent statements. Such reversibility is not, however, possible with tacit integration. Shifting attention to subsidiary particulars entails the loss of the skilful engagement with the activity at hand. By focusing on a subsidiary constituent of skilful action one changes the character of the activity one is involved in. There is no reversibility in this instance.

The structure of tacit knowing has three aspects: the functional, the phenomenal, and the semantic. The functional aspect consists in the *from–to* relation of particulars (or subsidiaries) to the focal target. Tacit knowing is a from–to knowing: we know the particulars by relying on our awareness of them for attending to something else. Human awareness has a 'vectorial' character (Polanyi 1969: 182): it moves from subsidiary particulars to the focal target (cf. Gill 2000: 38–9). Or, to repeat the words of Polanyi and Prosch (1975: 37–8): 'Subsidiaries exist as such by bearing on the focus *to* which we are attending *from* them' (emphasis in the original). The phenomenal aspect involves the transformation of subsidiary experience into a new sensory experience. The latter appears through—it is created out of—the tacit integration of subsidiary sense perceptions. Finally, the semantic aspect is the meaning of subsidiaries, which is the focal target on which they bear.

Dimension	
Functional	From–to knowing: we know the particulars by relying on our awareness of them for attending to something else
Phenomenal	The transformation of subsidiary experience into a new sensory experience
Semantic	The meaning of subsidiaries (i.e. the focal target on which they bear)

The above aspects of tacit knowing will become clearer with an example. Imagine a dentist exploring a tooth cavity with a probe. His/her exploration is a from–to knowing (the functional aspect): she relies subsidiarily on her feeling of holding the probe in order to attend focally to the tip of the probe exploring the cavity. In doing so the sensation of the probe pressing on her fingers is lost and, instead, she feels the point of the probe as it touches the cavity. This is the phenomenal aspect whereby a new coherent sensory quality appears (i.e. her sense of the cavity) from the initial sense perceptions (i.e. the impact of the probe on the fingers). Finally, the probing has a semantic aspect: the dentist gets information by using the probe. That information is the meaning of her tactile experiences with the probe. As Polanyi (1966: 13) argues, the dentist becomes aware of the feelings in her hand in terms of their meaning located at the tip of the probe, to which she is attending.

We engage in tacit knowing in virtually anything we do: we are normally unaware of the movement of our eye muscles when we observe, of the rules of language when we speak, of our bodily functions as we move around. Indeed, to a large extent, our daily life consists of a huge number of small details of which we tend to be focally unaware. When, however, we engage in more complex tasks, requiring even a modicum of specialized knowledge, then we face the challenge of how to assimilate the new knowledge—to interiorize it, dwell in it—in order to get things done efficiently and effectively. Polanyi gives the example of a medical student attending a course in X-ray diagnosis of pulmonary diseases, which was discussed in the previous chapter. The student is initially puzzled: 'he can see in the X-ray picture of a chest only the shadows of the heart and the ribs, with a few spidery blotches between them. The experts seem to be romancing about figments of their imagination; he can see nothing that they are talking about' (Polanyi 1962: 101).

At the early stage of his training the student has not assimilated the relevant knowledge; unlike the dentist with the probe, he cannot yet use it as a tool to carry out a diagnosis. The student, at this stage, is at a remove from the diagnostic task as such: he cannot think about it directly; he rather needs to think about the relevant radiological knowledge first. If he perseveres with his training, however, 'he will gradually forget about the ribs and begin to see the lungs. And eventually, if he perseveres intelligently, a rich panorama of significant details will be revealed to him: of physiological variations and pathological changes, of scars, of chronic infections and signs of acute disease. He has entered a new world' (ibid. 101).

We see here an excellent illustration of the structure of tacit knowledge. The student has now interiorized the new radiological knowledge; the latter has become tacit knowledge, of which he is subsidiarily aware while attending to the X-ray itself. Radiological knowledge exists now not as something unfamiliar which needs to be learned and assimilated before a diagnosis can take place, but as a set of particulars—subsidiaries—which exist as such by bearing on the X-ray (the focus) *to* which the student is attending *from* them. In so far as this happens, a phenomenal transformation has taken place: the heart, the ribs, and the spidery blotches gradually disappear and, instead, a new sensory experience appears—the X-ray is no longer a collection of fragmented radiological images of bodily organs, but a representation of a chest full of meaningful connections. Thus, as well as having functional and phenomenal aspects, tacit knowledge has a semantic aspect: the X-ray conveys information to an appropriately skilled observer. The meaning of the radiological knowledge, subsidiarily known and drawn upon by the student, is the diagnostic information he receives from the X-ray: it tells him what it is that he is observing by using that knowledge.

It should be clear from the above that for Polanyi, from a gnosiological point of view, there is no difference whatsoever between tangible things like probes, sticks, or hammers on the one hand, and intangible constructions such as radiological, linguistic, or cultural knowledge on the other—they are all *tools* enabling a skilled user to get things done. To use a tool properly we need to assimilate it and dwell in it. In Polanyi's words (1969: 148), 'we may say that when we learn to use language, or a probe, or a tool, and thus make ourselves aware of these things as we are our body, we *interiorize* these things and *make ourselves dwell in them*' (emphasis in the original). The notion of *indwelling* is crucial for Polanyi and turns up several times in his writings. It is only when we dwell in the tools we use, make them extensions of our own body, that we amplify the powers of our body and shift outwards the points at which we make contact with the world outside (Polanyi 1962: 59; 1969: 148; Polanyi and Prosch 1975: 37). Otherwise our use of tools will be clumsy and will get in the way of getting things done.

For a tool to be unproblematically used it must not be the object of our focal awareness; it rather needs to become an instrument through which we act—of which we are subsidiarily aware—not an object of attention. To dwell in a tool implies that one *uncritically* accepts it, is unconsciously committed to it. Such uncritical commitment is a necessary pre-supposition for using the tool effectively and, as such, cannot be asserted. Presuppositions cannot be asserted, says Polanyi (1962: 60), 'for assertion[s] can be made only *within* a framework with which we have identified ourselves for the time being; as they are themselves our ultimate framework, they are essentially inarticulable' (emphasis in the original).

The interiorization of a tool—its instrumentalization in the service of a purpose—is beneficial to its user, for it enables him/her to acquire new experiences and carry out more competently the task at hand (Dreyfus and Dreyfus 2000). Compare, for example, one who is learning to drive a car to one who is an accomplished driver. The former may have learned how to change gear and to use the break and the accelerator, but cannot, yet, integrate those individual skills—he has not constructed a coherent perception of driving, the phenomenal transformation has not taken place yet. At the early stage the driver is conscious of what he needs to do and feels the impact of the pedals on his foot and the gear stick on his palm; he has not learned unconsciously to correlate the performance of the car with the specific bodily actions he undertakes as a driver. The experienced driver, by contrast, is unconscious of the actions by which she drives—car instruments are tools whose use she has mastered, that is interiorized, and she is therefore able to use them for the purpose of driving. By becoming unconscious of certain actions, the experienced driver expands the domain of experiences she can concentrate on as a driver (i.e. principally road conditions and other drivers' behaviour).

The more general point to be derived from the preceding examples is formulated by Polanyi (1962: 61) as follows: 'we may say [...] that by the effort by which I concentrate on my chosen plane of operation I succeed in absorbing all the elements of the situation of which I might otherwise be aware in themselves, so that I become aware of them now in terms of the operational results achieved through their use'. This is important because we get things done, we achieve competence, by becoming unaware of how we do so. Of course, one can take an interest in, and learn a great deal about, the gearbox and the acceleration mechanism but, to be able to drive, such knowledge needs to lapse into unconsciousness. 'This lapse into unconsciousness', remarks Polanyi (ibid. 62), 'is accompanied by a newly acquired consciousness of the experiences in question, on the operational plane. It is misleading, therefore, to describe this as the mere result of repetition; it is a structural change achieved by a repeated mental effort aiming at the instrumentalization of certain things and actions in the service of some purpose'.

Notice that, for Polanyi, the shrinking of consciousness of certain things is, in the context of action, necessarily connected with the expansion of consciousness of other things. Particulars such as 'changing gear' and 'pressing the accelerator' are subsidiarily known, as the driver concentrates on the act of driving. Knowing something, then, is always a contextual issue and fundamentally connected to action (the 'operational plane'). My knowledge of gears is in the context of driving, and it is only in such a context that I am subsidiarily aware of that knowledge. If, however, I were a car mechanic, gears would constitute my focus of attention, rather than being an assimilated particular. Knowledge has, therefore, a *recursive* form: given a certain context, we 'black-box'—assimilate, interiorize, instrumentalize—certain things in order to concentrate—focus—on others. In another context, and at another level of analysis (cf. Bateson 1979: 43), we can open up some of the previously blackboxed issues and focus our attention on them. In theory this is an endless process, although in practice there are institutional and practical limits to it. In this way we can, to some extent, 'vertically integrate' our knowledge, although, as said earlier, what pieces of knowledge we *use* depends, at any point in time, on context. If the driver happens to be a car mechanic as well as an engineer he/she will have acquired three different bodies of knowledge, each having a different degree of abstraction, which, taken together, give his/her knowledge depth and make him/her a sophisticated driver (cf. Harper 1987: 33). How, however, he/she draws on each one of them—that is, what is focally and what is subsidiarily known—depends on the context in use. Moreover, each one of these bodies of knowledge stands on its own, and cannot be reduced to any of the others. The practical knowledge I have of my car as a driver cannot be replaced by the theoretical knowledge of an engineer; the practical knowledge I have of my own body cannot be replaced by the theoretical knowledge of a physician (cf. Polanyi 1966: 20). In the social world, specialist, abstract, theoretical knowledge is necessarily refracted through the 'life-world'—the taken-for-granted assumptions by means of which human beings organize their experience, knowledge, and transactions with the world (cf. Bruner 1990: 35).

The Appropriation of 'Tacit Knowledge' in Management Studies: The Great Misunderstanding

As mentioned in the introductory section to this chapter, 'tacit knowledge' has become very popular in management studies since the mid 1990s, to a large extent because of the publication of Nonaka and Takeuchi's influential *The Knowledge-Creating Company* (1995). The cornerstone of Nonaka and Takeuchi's theory of organizational knowledge is the notion of 'knowledge conversion'—how tacit knowledge is 'converted' to explicit knowledge, and vice versa. As the authors argue, 'our dynamic model of knowledge creation is anchored to a critical assumption that human knowledge is created and expanded through social interaction between tacit knowledge and explicit knowledge. We shall call this interaction "knowledge conversion"' (ibid. 61).

Nonaka and Takeuchi distinguish four modes of knowledge conversion: from tacit knowledge to tacit knowledge (socialization); from tacit knowledge to explicit knowledge (externalization); from explicit knowledge to explicit knowledge (combination); and from explicit knowledge to tacit knowledge (internalization). Tacit knowledge is converted to tacit knowledge through observation, imitation, and practice, in those cases where an apprentice learns from a master. Tacit knowledge is converted to explicit knowledge when it is articulated and it takes the form of concepts, models, hypotheses, metaphors, and analogies. Explicit knowledge is converted to explicit knowledge when different bodies of explicit knowledge are combined. And explicit knowledge is converted to tacit knowledge when it is first verbalized and then absorbed, internalized by the individuals involved.

The organizational knowledge-creation process proceeds in cycles (in a spiral-like fashion), with each cycle consisting of five phases: the sharing of tacit knowledge among the members of a team; the creation of concepts whereby a team articulates its commonly shared mental model; the justification of concepts in terms of the overall organizational purposes and objectives; the building of an archetype which is a tangible manifestation of the justified concept; and the 'cross-levelling' of knowledge, whereby a new cycle of knowledge creation may be created elsewhere in (or even outside) the organization.

To illustrate their theory Nonaka and Takeuchi describe the product-development process of Matsushita's Home Bakery, the first fully automated bread-making machine for home use, which was introduced on to the Japanese market in 1987. There were three cycles in the relevant knowledge-creation process, each cycle being initiated to either remove the weaknesses of the previous one or improve upon its outcome. The first cycle ended with the assemblage of a prototype which, however, was not up to the design team's standards regarding the quality of bread it produced. This triggered the second cycle, which started when Ikuko Tanaka, a software developer, took an apprenticeship with a master baker at the Osaka International Hotel. Her purpose was to learn how to knead bread dough properly in order later to 'convert' this know-how into particular design features of the bread-making machine under development. Following this, the third cycle came into operation, in which the commercialization team, consisting of people drawn from the manufacturing and marketing sections, further improved the prototype that came out of the second cycle, and made it a commercially viable product.

To obtain a better insight into what Nonaka and Takeuchi mean by 'tacit knowledge' and how it is related to 'explicit knowledge', it is worth zooming in on their description of the second cycle of the knowledge-creation process, since this is the cycle most relevant to the acquisition and 'conversion' of tacit knowledge. In the section below I quote in full the authors' description of this cycle (references and figures have been omitted) (ibid. 103–6).

A Case Study: The Second Cycle of the Home Bakery Spiral

The second cycle began with a software developer, Ikuko Tanaka, sharing the tacit knowledge of a master baker in order to learn his kneading skill. A master baker learns the art of kneading, a critical step in bread making, following years of experience. However, such expertise is difficult to articulate in words. To capture this tacit knowledge, which usually takes a lot of imitation and practice to master, Tanaka proposed a creative solution. Why not train with the head baker at Osaka International Hotel, which had a reputation for making the best bread in Osaka, to study the kneading techniques? Tanaka learned her kneading skills through observation, imitation, and practice. She recalled:

At first, everything was a surprise. After repeated failures, I began to ask where the master and I differed. I don't think one can understand or learn this skill without actually doing it. His bread and mine [came out] quite different even though we used the same materials. I asked why our products were so different and tried to reflect the difference in our skill of kneading.

Even at this stage, neither the head baker nor Tanaka was able to articulate knowledge in any systematic fashion. Because their tacit knowledge never became explicit, others within Matsushita were left puzzled. Consequently, engineers were also brought to the hotel and allowed to knead and bake bread to improve their understanding of the process. Sano, the division chief, noted, "If the craftsmen cannot explain their skills, then the engineers should become craftsmen."

Not being an engineer, Tanaka could not devise mechanical specifications. However, she was able to transfer her knowledge to the engineers by using the phrase "twisting stretch" to provide a rough image of kneading, and by suggesting the strength and speed of the propeller to be used in kneading. She would simply say, "Make the propeller move stronger", or "Move it faster". Then the engineers would adjust the machine specifications. Such a trial-and-error process continued for several months.

Her request for a "twisting stretch" movement was interpreted by the engineers and resulted in the addition inside the case of special ribs that held back the dough when the propeller turned so that the dough could be stretched. After a year of trial and error and working closely with other engineers, the team came up with product specifications that successfully reproduced the head baker's stretching technique and the quality of bread Tanaka had learned to make at the hotel. The team then materialized this concept, putting it together into a manual, and embodied it in the product. [. . .]

In the second cycle, the team had to resolve the problem of getting the machine to knead dough correctly. To solve the kneading problem, Ikuko Tanaka apprenticed herself with the head baker of the Osaka International Hotel. There she learned the skill through *socialization*, observing and imitating the head baker, rather than through reading memos or manuals. She then translated the kneading skill into explicit knowledge. The knowledge was *externalized* by *creating the concept of "twisting stretch"*. In addition, she *externalized* this knowledge by expressing the movements required for the kneading propeller, using phrases like "more slowly" or "more strongly". For those who had never touched dough before, understanding the kneading skill was so difficult that engineers had to *share experiences* by spending hours at the baker to experience the touch of the dough. Tacit knowledge was *externalized* by lining special ribs inside the dough case. *Combination* took place when the "twisting stretch" concept and the technological knowledge of the engineers came together to produce a prototype of Home Bakery. Once the prototype was *justified* against the concept of "Rich," the development moved into the third cycle. (ibid., emphasis in the original.)

How Should We Understand Tacit Knowledge?

The preceding account of tacit knowledge has very little in common with that of Polanyi. Nonaka and Takeuchi assume that tacit knowledge is knowledge-not-yet-articulated: a set of rules incorporated in the activity an actor is involved in, which it is a matter of time for him/her to first learn and then formulate. The authors seem to think that what Tanaka learned through her apprenticeship with the master baker can be ultimately crystallized in a set of propositional 'if, then' statements (Tsoukas 1998: 44–8), or what Oakeshott (1991: 12–15) called 'technical knowledge' and Ryle (1963: 28–32) 'knowing that'. In that sense, the tacit knowledge involved in kneading that Tanaka picked up through her apprenticeship—in Oakeshott's terms, (1991: 12–15), the 'practical knowledge' of kneading, and in Ryle's terms (1963: 28–32), 'knowing how' to knead—the sort of knowledge that exists only *in use* and cannot be formulated in rules, is equivalent to the set of statements that articulate it, namely to technical knowledge.

Tacit knowledge is thought to have the structure of a syllogism, and as such can be reversed and, therefore, even mechanized (cf. Polanyi and Prosch 1975: 40). What Tanaka was missing, the authors imply, were the premises of the syllogism, which she acquired through her sustained apprenticeship. Once they had been learned, it was a matter of time before she could put them together and arrive at the conclusion that 'twisting stretch' and 'the [right] movements required for the kneading propeller' (Nonaka and Takeuchi 1995: 103–6) were what was required for designing the right bread-making machine.

However, although Nonaka and Takeuchi rightly acknowledge that Tanaka's apprenticeship was necessary because 'the art of kneading' (ibid. 103) could not be imparted in any other way (e.g. 'through reading memos and manuals', ibid. 105), they view her apprenticeship as merely an alternative mechanism for transferring knowledge. In terms of content, knowledge acquired through apprenticeship is not thought to be qualitatively different from knowledge acquired through reading manuals, since in both cases the content of knowledge can be articulated and formulated in rules—only the manner of its appropriation differs. The mechanism of knowledge acquisition may be different, but the result is the same.

The 'conduit metaphor of communication' (Lakoff 1995: 116; Reddy 1979; Tsoukas 1997) that underlies Nonaka and Takeuchi's perspective—the view of ideas as objects which can be extracted from people and transmitted to others through a conduit—reduces practical knowledge to technical knowledge (cf. Costelloe 1998: 325–6). However, while clearly Tanaka learned a technique during her apprenticeship, she acquired much more than technical knowledge, without even realizing it: she learned to make bread in a way which could not be formulated in propositions but only manifested in her work. To treat practical (or tacit) knowledge as having a precisely definable content, which is initially located in the head of the practitioner and then 'translated' (Nonaka and Takeuchi 1995: 105) into explicit knowledge, is to reduce what is known to what is articulable, thus impoverishing the notion of practical knowledge. As Oakeshott (1991: 15) remarks,

a pianist acquires artistry as well as technique, a chess-player style and insight into the game as well as a knowledge of the moves, and a scientist acquires (among other things) the sort of judgement which tells him when his technique is leading him astray and the connoisseurship which enables him to distinguish the profitable from the unprofitable directions to explore.

As should be clear from the preceding section, by viewing all knowing as essentially 'personal knowing' (Polanyi 1962: 49) Polanyi highlights the skilled performance that all acts of knowing require: the actor does not know all the rules he/she follows in the activity he/she is involved in. Like Oakeshott (1991), Polanyi (1962: 50) notes that 'rules of art can be useful, but they do not determine the practice of an art; they are maxims, which can serve as a guide to an art only if they can be integrated into the practical knowledge of the art. They cannot replace that knowledge'. It is precisely because what needs to be known cannot be specified in detail that the relevant knowledge must be passed from master to apprentice.

To learn by example [says Polanyi] is to submit to authority. You follow your master because you trust his manner of doing things even when you cannot analyse and account in detail for its effectiveness. By watching the master and emulating his efforts in the presence of his example, the apprentice unconsciously picks up the rules of the art, including those which are not explicitly known to the master himself. These hidden rules can be assimilated only by a person who surrenders himself to that extent uncritically to the imitation of another. (1962: 53)

Like Polanyi's medical student discussed earlier, Tanaka was initially puzzled by what the master baker was doing—'At first, everything was a surprise' (Nonaka and Takeuchi 1995: 104), as she put it. Her 'repeated failures' (ibid.) were not from lack of knowledge as such, but from not yet having interiorized—dwellt in—the relevant knowledge. When, through practice, she began to assimilate the knowledge involved in kneading bread—that is, when she became subsidiarily aware of how she was kneading—she could, subsequently, turn her focal awareness to the task at hand: *kneading* bread, as opposed to imitating the master. Knowledge now became a tool to be tacitly known and uncritically used in the service of an objective. 'Kneading bread' ceased to be an object of focal awareness and became an instrument for actually kneading bread—a subsidiarily known tool for getting things done (Winograd and Flores 1987: 27–37). For Tanaka to 'convert' her kneading skill into explicit knowledge, she would need to focus her attention on her subsidiary knowledge, thereby becoming focally aware of it. In that event, however, she would no longer be engaged in the same activity, namely bread kneading, but in the activity of thinking about bread-kneading, which is a different matter. The particulars of her skill are 'logically unspecifiable' (Polanyi 1962: 56), in the sense that their specification would logically contradict and practically paralyse what is implied in the carrying out of the performance at hand.

Of course, one might acknowledge this and still insist, along with Ambrosini and Bowman (2001) and Eraut (2000), that Tanaka could, *ex post facto*, reflect on her kneading skill, in the context of discussing bread-kneading with her colleagues—the engineers—and articulate it as explicit knowledge. But this would be an erroneous claim to make, for in such an event she would no longer be describing her kneading skill *in toto* but only its technical part: that which it is possible to articulate in rules, principles, maxims—in short, in propositions. What she has to say about the 'ineffable' (Polanyi 1962: 87–95) part of her skill, that which is tacitly known, she has 'said' already in the bread she kneads and cannot put into words (cf. Janik 1992: 37; Oakeshott 1991: 14). As Polanyi so perceptively argued, you cannot view subsidiary particulars as they allegedly are in themselves for they always exist in conjunction with the focus to which you attend from them, and that makes them unspecifiable. In his words:

Subsidiary or instrumental knowledge, as I have defined it, is not known in itself but is known in terms of something focally known, to the quality of which it contributes; and to this extent it is unspecifiable. Analysis may bring subsidiary knowledge into focus and formulate it as a maxim or as a feature in a physiognomy, but such specification is in general not exhaustive. Although the expert diagnostician, taxonomist and cotton-classer can indicate their clues and formulate their maxims, they know many more things than they can tell, knowing them only in practice, as instrumental particulars, and not explicitly, as objects. The knowledge of such particulars is therefore ineffable, and the pondering of a judgement in terms of such particulars is an ineffable process of thought. (Polanyi 1962: 88)

If the above is accepted, it follows that Tanaka neither 'transferred' her tacit knowledge to the engineers nor did she 'convert' her kneading skill into explicit knowledge, as Nonaka and Takeuchi (1995: 104, 105) suggest. She could do neither of these things, simply because, following Polanyi's and Oakeshott's definitions of tacit and practical knowledge respectively, skilful knowing contains an ineffable element; it is based on an act of personal insight that is essentially inarticulable.

How are we then to interpret Tanaka's concept of 'twisting stretch', which turned out to be so useful for the making of Matsushita's bread-making machine? Or, to put it more generally, does the ineffability of skilful knowing imply that we can never talk about a practical activity at all; that the skills involved in, say, carpentry, teaching, ship navigation, or scientific activity will ultimately be mystical experiences outside the realm of reasoned discussion?

Not at all. What we do when we reflect on the practical activities we engage in is to re-punctuate the distinctions underlying those activities, to draw the attention of those involved to certain hitherto unnoticed aspects of those activities—to see connections among items previously thought unconnected (cf. Weick 1995: 87, 126). Through instructive forms of talk (e.g. 'Look at this', 'Have you thought about this in that way?', 'Try this', 'Imagine this', 'Compare this to that') practitioners are moved to *re*-view the situation they are in, to relate to their circumstances in a different way. From a Wittgensteinian perspective, Shotter and Katz (1996: 230) summarize succinctly this process as follows:

> to gain an explicit understanding of our everyday, practical activities, we can make use of the very same methods we used in gaining that practical kind of understanding in the first place—that is, we can use the self-same methods for drawing *our* attention to how people draw each other's attention to things, as they themselves (we all?) in fact use!

Notice what Shotter and Katz are saying: we learn to engage in practical activities through our participation in social practices, under the guidance of people who are more experienced than us (MacIntyre 1985: 181–203; Taylor, 1993); people who, by drawing our attention to certain things, make us 'see connections' (Wittgenstein 1958: no. 122; see also Shotter 2005), pretty much as the master baker was drawing Tanaka'a attention to certain aspects of bread-kneading. Through her subsequent conversations with the engineers Tanaka was able to form an explicit understanding of the activity she was involved in, by having her attention drawn to how the master baker was drawing her attention to kneading—hence the concept of 'twisting stretch'. It is in this sense that Wittgenstein talks of language as issuing 're-minders' of things we *already* know: 'Something that we know when no one asks us, but no longer know when we are supposed to give an account of it, is something that we need to *remind* ourselves of' (ibid. no. 89; emphasis in the original).

In her apprenticeship Tanaka came eventually to practise 'twisting stretch', but she did not know it. She needed to be 'reminded' of it. When we recursively punctuate our understanding, we see new connections and '[give] prominence to distinctions which our ordinary forms of language easily make us overlook' (ibid. no. 132). Through the instructive (or directive) use of language we are led to notice certain aspects of our circumstances that, because of their simplicity and familiarity, remain hidden ('one is unable to notice something—because it is always before one's eyes'; (ibid. no. 129). This is, then, the sense in which although skilful knowing is ultimately ineffable it nonetheless can be talked about: through reminding ourselves of it we notice certain important features which had hitherto escaped our attention and can now be seen in a new context. Consequently, we are led to relate to our circumstances in new ways and thus see new ways forward.

Conclusions

Tacit knowledge has been misunderstood in management studies—or so I have argued in this chapter. While Nonaka and Takeuchi were possibly the first to see the importance of tacit knowledge in organizations and systematically explore it, their interpretation of tacit knowledge as knowledge-not-yet-articulated—namely, knowledge awaiting its 'translation' or 'conversion' into explicit knowledge—an interpretation that has been widely adopted in management studies, is erroneous: it ignores the essential ineffability of tacit knowledge, thus reducing it to what can be articulated. Tacit and explicit knowledge are not two ends of a continuum but two sides of the same coin: even the most explicit kind of knowledge is underlain by tacit knowledge. Tacit knowledge consists of a set of particulars of which we are subsidiarily aware as we focus on something else. Tacit knowing is vectorial: we know the particulars by relying on our awareness of them for attending to something else. Since subsidiaries exist as such by bearing on the focus *to* which we are attending *from* them, they cannot be separated from the focus and examined independently; for if this is done, their meaning will be lost. While we can certainly focus on particulars, we cannot do so in the context of action in which we are subsidiarily aware of them. Moreover, by focusing on particulars after a particular action has been performed, we are *not* focusing on them as they bear on the original focus of action, for their meaning is necessarily derived from their connection to that focus. When we focus on particulars we do so in a new context of action which itself is underlain by a new set of subsidiary particulars. Thus, the idea that somehow one can focus on a set of particulars and convert them into explicit knowledge is unsustainable.

The ineffability of tacit knowledge does not mean that we cannot discuss the skilled performances in which we are involved. We can—indeed, should— discuss them, provided we stop insisting on 'converting' tacit knowledge and, instead, start recursively drawing our attention to how we draw each other's attention to things. Instructive forms of talk help us reorientate ourselves to how we relate to others and the world around us, thus enabling us to talk and act differently. We can command a clearer view of our tasks at hand if we 're-mind' ourselves of how we do things, so that distinctions which we had previously not noticed, and features which had previously escaped our attention, may be brought forward. Contrary to what Ambrosini and Bowman (2001) suggest, we need not so much to operationalize tacit knowledge (as explained earlier, we could not do this, even if we wanted) as to find new ways of talking, fresh forms of interacting, and novel ways of distinguishing and connecting. Tacit knowledge cannot be 'captured', 'translated', or 'converted', but only displayed—manifested—in what we do. New knowledge comes about not when the tacit becomes explicit, but when our skilled performance—our praxis—is punctuated in new ways through social interaction (Tsoukas 2001).

References

Ambrosini, V., and Bowman, C. (2001), 'Tacit Knowledge: Some Suggestions for Operationalization', *Journal of Management Studies*, 38: 811–29.
Banmard, P. (1999), *Tacit Knowledge in Organizations*, trans. S. Wanchope (London: Sage).
Bateson, G. (1979), *Mind and Nature: A Necessary Unity* (Toronto: Bantam).
Bell, D. (1999), 'The Axial Age of Technology Foreword: 1999, in D. Bell, *The Coming of the Post-Industrial Society*, special anniversary edn. (New York: Basic), pp. ix–lxxxv.
Boisot, M. H. (1995), *Information Space: A Framework for Learning in Organizations, Institutions and Culture* (London: Routledge).
Brown, J. S., and Duguid, P. (2000), *The Social Life of Information* (Boston, Mass.: Harvard Business School Press).
Bruner, J. (1990), *Acts of Meaning* (Cambridge: Harvard University Press).
Cook, S. D. N., and Brown, J. S. (1999), 'Bridging Epistemologies: The Generative Dance between Organizational Knowledge and Organizational Knowing', *Organization Science*, 10: 381–400.
Cook, S. D. N., and Yanow, D. (1996), 'Culture and organizational learning', in M. D. Cohen and L. S. Sproull (eds.), *Organizational Learning* (Thousand Oaks, Calif.: Sage), 430–59.
Costelloe, T. (1998), 'Oakeshott, Wittgenstein, and the Practice of Social Science', *Journal for the Theory of Social Behaviour*, 28: 323–47.
Davenport, T. H., and Prusak, L. (1998), *Working Knowledge* (Cambridge, Mass.: Harvard University Press).
Devlin, K. (1999), *Infosense* (New York: Freeman).
Dixon, N. M. (2000), *Common Knowledge* (Boston, Mass.: Harvard Business School Press).
Dreyfus, L. H., and Dreyfus, S. E. (2000), *Mind Over Machine* (New York: Free Press).
Drucker, P. (1993), *Post-Capitalist Society* (Oxford: Butterworth/Heinemann).
Eraut, M. (2000), 'Non-formal Learning and Tacit Knowledge in Professional Work', *British Journal of Educational Psychology*, 70: 113–36.
Gill, J. H. (2000), *The Tacit Mode* (Albany, NY: State University of New York Press).
Harper, D. (1987), *Working Knowledge* (Berkeley, Calif.: University of California Press).
Janik, A. (1992), 'Why is Wittgenstein Important?', in B. Goranzon and M. Florin (eds.), *Skill and Education* (London: Springer-Verlag), 33–40.
Kreiner, K. (1999), 'Knowledge and mind', *Advances in Management Cognition and Organizational Information Processing*, 6: 1–29.
Krogh, G. von, Ichijo, K., and Nonaka, I. (2000), *Enabling Knowledge Creation* (New York: Oxford University Press).

Lakoff, G. (1995) (interviewed by I. A. Boal), 'Body, Brain, and Communication', in J. Brook and I. A. Boal (eds.), *Resisting the Virtual Life* (San Francisco, Calif.: City Lights), 115–29.

Leonard, D., and Sensiper, S. (1998), 'The Role of Tacit Knowledge in Group Innovation', *California Management Review*, 40(3): 112–32.

MacIntyre, A. (1985), *After Virtue*, 2nd edn. (London: Duckworth).

Mansell, R., and When, U. (1998), *Knowledge Societies* (New York: Oxford University Press).

Nonaka, I., and Takeuchi, H. (1995), *The Knowledge-creating Company* (New York: Oxford University Press).

Oakeshott, M. (1991), *Rationalism in Politics and Other Essays*, new and expanded edn. (Indianapolis, Ind.: Liberty).

Our Competitve Future: Building the Knowledge Driven Economy (1998), Paper presented to Parliament by the Secretary of State for Trade and Industry (London: Stationery Office).

Polanyi, M. (1962), *Personal Knowledge* (Chicago, Ill.: University of Chicago Press).

—— (1966), *The Tacit Dimension* (London: Routledge & Kegan Paul).

—— (1969), *Knowing and Being*, ed. M. Grene (Chicago, Ill.: University of Chicago Press).

—— and Prosch, H. (1975), *Meaning*, (Chicago, Ill.: University Of Chicago Press).

Reddy, M. J. (1979), 'The Conduit Metaphor—A Case of Frame Conflict in our Language about Language', in A. Ortony (ed.), *Metaphor and Thought* (Cambridge: Cambridge University Press), 284–324.

Ryle, G. (1963), *The Concept of Mind*, (London: Penguin).

Shotter, J. (forthcoming) 'Inside the Moment of Managing': Wittgenstein and the Everyday Dynamics of our Expressive-Responsive Activities', *Organization Studies*.

—— and Katz, A. M. (1996), 'Articulating a Practice from Within the Practice Itself: Establishing Formative Dialogues by the Use of a 'Social Poetics', *Concepts and Transformation*, 1: 213–37.

Spender, J.-C. (1996), Making Knowledge the Basis of a Dynamic Theory of the Firm', *Strategic Management Journal*, 17 (special winter issue): 45–62.

Stehr, N. (1994), *Knowledge Societies* (London: Sage).

Taylor, C. (1993), 'To Follow a Rule . . .', in C. Calhoun, E. LiPuma, and M. Postone (eds.), *Bourdieu: Critical Perspectives* (Cambridge: Polity), 45–59.

Thurow, L. (2000), *Creating Wealth* (London: Nicholas Brealey).

—— (1990), *Cosmopolis* (Chicago, Ill.: University of Chicago Press).

Toulmin, S. (2001), *Return to Reason* (Cambridge, Mass.: Harvard University Press).

Tsoukas, H. (1996), 'The Firm as a Distributed Knowledge System: A Constructionist Approach', *Strategic Management Journal*, 17 (special winter issue): 11–25.

—— (1997), 'The Tyranny of Light: The Temptations and the Paradoxes of the Information Society', *Futures*, 29: 827–43.

—— (1998), 'Forms of Knowledge and Forms of Life in Organized Contexts', in R. C. H. Chia, *In the Realm of Organization* (London: Routledge), 43–66.

—— (2001), 'Where Does New Organizational Knowledge Come From?', keynote address at the international conference 'Managing Knowledge: Conversations and Critiques', Leicester University, 10–11 April 2001.

—— and Vladimirou, E. (forthcoming), 'What Is Organizational Knowledge?', *Journal of Management Studies*.

Weick, K. (1995), *Sensemaking in Organizations* (Thousand Oaks, Calif.: Sage).

Wenger, E. (1998), *Communities of Practice* (Cambridge: Cambridge University Press).

Winograd, T., and Flores, F. (1987), *Understanding Computers and Cognition*, (Reading, Mass.: Addison-Wesley).

Wittgenstein, L. (1958), *Philosophical Investigations* (Oxford: Blackwell).

World Development Report 1998/9, World Bank (1998), *Knowledge for Development* (Oxford: Oxford University Press).

II

ORGANIZATION AS *CHAOSMOS*: COPING WITH ORGANIZATIONAL COMPLEXITY

SEVEN

Understanding Social Reforms: A Conceptual Analysis

Haridimos Tsoukas and Demetrios B. Papoulias

Introduction

I N an article on the role of operational research/management science (OR/ MS) in the management of social reforms Papoulias and Tsoukas (1994) argued that the more important social reforms are, the more conflict-ridden and complex they will tend to be and, as a result, the more difficult it will be for them to be subjected to systematic analysis (i.e. analysis based on models and techniques from OR/MS). 'Having such a nature', the authors concluded, 'the success of important social reforms seems to hinge more on the articulation of a coherent social philosophy along with the existence of political and symbol-management skills on the part of policy makers than on merely systematic analysis' (Papoulias and Tsoukas 1994: 985).

In this chapter it is our aim to expand on this claim and examine why and how a coherent socio-economic philosophy (or discourse) plays such a significant role in the management of social reforms. Our goal is set within the broader context of rethinking the texture of policy-making in the light of recent developments in systems theory, philosophy, and organization theory. Our focus is primarily conceptual: we both provide an explanation of the difficulties often encountered in pushing through social reforms and offer some generic suggestions as to how such difficulties might be overcome. What is beyond the scope of the present chapter, however, is the also

This chapter was first published in the *Journal of the Operational Research Society*, 47 (1996), 853–63. It was awarded the Operational Research Society President's Medal for Best Paper in 1996. Reprinted by permission of Palgrave Macmillan, Copyright (1996). The authors would like to thank the two anonymous referees of the *JORS* for their very useful comments and suggestions on that version.

important issue of the technologies of social reforms (that is, techniques for managing effectively social reforms), which is primarily an empirical issue and needs to be discussed separately.

The chapter is structured as follows. First, we examine Vickers's seminal contribution to policy-making, focusing in particular on his concept of 'appreciative systems', which serves as the cornerstone for much of our subsequent analysis. Next, it is shown that appreciative systems are grounded on social practices which are self-referential in nature and, thus, resistant to reform. It is argued that the role of reformist policy makers should be seen as consisting of two elements: first, inventing and supplying the social practices under reform with new appreciative systems; and second, regularly providing social practices with information about both their own functioning and the functioning of other, similar practices. To such information the systems under reform are encouraged to respond by, potentially, *re*-forming themselves. Finally, we illustrate these claims with examples from the UK and America.

'Appreciative Systems' and Policy Making

According to Vickers (1983), the business of government is 'the regulation of institutions'. The latter need to be regulated in order to function according to commonly agreed purposes and values, rather than according to the inherent logic of the situation concerned. There is no doubt, for example, that, left alone, traffic volume or the provision of health services eventually regulates itself, but in ways which not only may be deemed unacceptable by a particular social unit (be it a group, a community, or a society), but also may not have been discussed and agreed upon by those concerned. Institutional regulation therefore presupposes a set of human values which it seeks to enact (Adams and Catron 1994; Checkland 1994; Forester 1994).

For Vickers (1983), the regulation of institutions consists in maintaining relationships in time. Traffic regulation, for example, aims at maintaining an acceptable relation between road capacity and traffic volume. Vickers chose to define institutional regulation in terms of *relationships* rather than, more conventionally, in terms of goals, for he wanted to emphasize, among other things, the dynamic nature of institutions (and, of course, of institutional regulation). The dynamic nature of institutions stems primarily from two sources.

First, it stems from the time-dependent and open-ended character of institutions. As a result of the very institutional regulation itself (exercised over time), and of the often unpredictable and contingency-dependent texture of social life, new problems appear to which an institution must constantly respond—the regulation of traffic, the handling of crime, and the provision of health services are good examples of this.

Second, it stems from changes in the social values underlying institutional regulation. Such value changes result in the need for the resetting of standards (or governing norms) according to which institutions are regulated. After the Second World War, for example, the free, universal provision of health services was the number-one priority for those who designed the NHS in Britain. Today, however, although such a value has not changed, it is supplemented with (or, some might even say, overshadowed by) other values concerning costs and efficiency. Similar value changes can be seen in the reorganization of the welfare state in several western economies in the last fifteen years (Osborne and Gaebler 1992).

According to Vickers, institutional regulation consists of two elements. The *policy-making* element, which seeks to set (or, more often, to reset) the governing norms underlying institutional functioning, so that the latter corresponds to human wishes; and the *executive* element, which aims at maintaining the functioning of an institution within the limits set by the governing norms. At the risk of oversimplification, it can be said that policy-making is the primarily conceptual element, and policy execution is the primarily technical element. Whereas for the manager of executive problems the latter are usually presented in a more or less well-defined form, for the policy maker problems are far from given but, on the contrary, must be first defined—indeed, problem definition is his/her most significant task (Vickers 1983).

Policy-making and execution, being two phases in the regulative cycle, call for two different types of judgement. In the former case we have what Vickers (ibid.) called *appreciative judgement*, and in the latter case *instrumental judgement*. Appreciative judgements involve making *reality* judgements, namely judgements of fact about the state of the system, and *value* judgements, namely judgements about the significance of those facts. As Vickers observed: 'the relation between judgements of fact and value is close and mutual; for facts are relevant only in relation to some judgement of value and judgements of value are operative only in relation to some configuration of fact' (ibid. 40). Reality and value judgements make up what Vickers called an 'appreciative system' (Adams and Catron 1994; Checkland 1994; Checkland and Scholes 1990). Instrumental judgements concern particular ways of doing things and suggesting possible modes of action.

For Vickers, the main feature of institutional regulation is the 'endless dialogue between appreciative and instrumental judgement, in which appreciative judgement always has the last word, testing the solutions offered to it against judgements of fact or of value and rejecting them until an acceptable one is found' (Vickers 1983: 47; see also Schon 1983, 1987). It is worth noting that Vickers's definition of policy-making can be interpreted as having been made from the standpoint of the individual policy maker; he attempted 'to set out what mental processes the individual must engage in when he embarks on an act of policy-making and has to take a decision of policy' (Johnson, 1994: 31). Indeed, in the extract quoted above it is implied that the 'endless dialogue' takes place in the individual mind, and in his several illustrations of policy-making Vickers explicitly dealt with the latter from the point of view of the policy makers involved (see e.g. Vickers 1983: 42–8).

In what follows we build on Vickers's arguments concerning policy-making by developing further his concept of an appreciative system (i.e. the set of reality and value judgements made in a particular situation). Through the latter Vickers introduced the important idea that the problems policy makers manage are always problems for *someone*; that is, perceived problems. On this view, therefore, policy makers are active shapers of problem situations—problems have no values and speak no language; only humans do (Tsoukas 1998; Tsoukas and Papoulias 1996). In other words, instead of focusing on 'the demands of the object' (as traditional OR/MS, organization theory, and the decision sciences have done), Vickers, as well as Checkland (1981) and Churchman (1971), sensitized us to the need to pay attention to 'the demands of the purpose which a particular inquiry is supposed to serve' (Rorty 1991: 110).

We extend this line of reasoning by focusing more closely on appreciative systems, why they emerge, and how they may be changed. We do so by drawing selectively on certain strands of interpretative philosophy, and on relatively recent developments in systems theory and organization theory. We argue that appreciative systems are socially established ways of perceiving and acting, grounded on social practices, and embodying particular self-understandings which are normally resistant to change. While Vickers in his pioneering analyses underscored the *subjective* nature of appreciative systems, thus paying attention to the role of individual creativity and experimentation and to the concomitant changeability of appreciative systems (Flood and Jackson 1991), we highlight here a less discussed feature of appreciative systems; namely, their *self-referential* nature and their resultant resistance to change. In line with such an analysis, we conclude that the role of policy makers is not only that of understanding the appreciative settings of their fellows (as Vickers argued), but also that of redefining and helping to establish new self-understandings through conceptual innovation and the management of information. These arguments are illustrated with examples from UK and US public life.

The Self-Referentiality of Social Practices and the Possibility of Reform

Vickers persistently argued that in social life findings of fact are essentially judgements, for their identification depends on the appreciative system of the enquirer (Churchman, 1971; Flood and Jackson, 1991; Morgan, 1986). In his own words: 'there is no more basic reality than the appreciative settings of our fellows—except for ourselves, our own' (Vickers 1983: 71). Furthermore, although social systems are causally efficacious—that is, they trigger individual action—it is also the case that social systems are constituted by certain self-understandings (i.e. appreciative settings) expressed as sets of language-based background distinctions shared by individuals. In other words, social phenomena are language-dependent (Berger 1963; Berger and Luckmann 1966; Taylor 1985). As Taylor (ibid. 34) remarks, 'the language is constitutive of the reality, is essential to its being the kind of reality it is'. To the extent, therefore, that social theories (or cognitive categories, frameworks, and models) modify the background distinctions that are constitutive of those self-understandings that make up particular social systems, they change the systems themselves (see Fig. 7.1).

In other words, there is an *internal* relationship between policy makers' cognitive categories and the social practices they attempt to influence. The models through which policy makers view the world are not mere mirrors in which the world is passively reflected, but, in an important sense, policy makers' models also help *constitute* the world they subsequently experience (Beer 1973; Giddens 1976; Schon 1983; Taylor 1985; Tsoukas 1998a; Watzlawick 1984). This is illustrated below with an example (Tsoukas, 1998a).

Until 1987 the US government barred car makers from pursuing joint R&D projects, on the assumption that if they were allowed to collaborate they

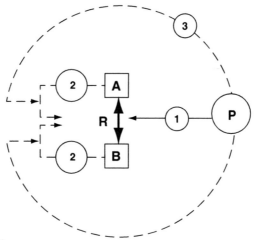

Key :
A, B : individuals
R   : the relationship between A and B
P   : policy maker
(1)   : P intervenes into R
(2)   : A's and B's self-understandings
(3)   : P's understanding of A's and B's self-understandings

Fig. 7.1: Social phenomena are language-dependent.
Source: Adapted from Ritsert (1978)

would delay the introduction of new technologies. The notion of a purely competitive market in which firms only compete against each other but never collaborate (because if they did they would probably spoil the purity of the market) has long been a distinguishing feature of American capitalism (Reich 1991). Largely under the influence of competition from Japan and of Japanese industrial practices, such an assumption has subsequently been relaxed. In the late 1980s, and increasingly more in the 1990s, R&D collaboration was no longer anathema, while antitrust legislation was also softened (see *The Economist*, 13 June 1992, 89–90).

Thus, a social practice, such as the way business organizations in the same industry relate to one another, is what it is by virtue of the key self-understandings embodied in the practice. Such self-understandings are not reflections of the world as it is (relationships between firms are neither competitive nor collaborative by nature) but intersubjective meanings 'which are constitutive of the social matrix in which individuals find themselves and act' (Taylor 1985: 36). When policy makers' self-understandings change (as happened in the case of the American government) so do the constitutive features of social practices. If this is accepted, it follows that the identity of social systems derives, at least in part, from cognitive schemata and meaning categories which have developed in particular contexts over time.

If a social system is constituted by a set of self-understandings, where do those self-understandings come from? What are they based upon? Or, to use Vickers's language, if the existence of an appreciative system implies, at least to some extent, 'shared experiences, a common language and purposes that are also shared or compatible with each other' (Johnson 1994: 31), what must the social form that sustains such a collective consciousness be? In his influential *After Virtue* (1985) MacIntyre explored, among other things, the forms of social life which sustain different forms of morality. His concept of a 'practice', which is also discussed in Chapter Three, is quite useful to our attempt to provide answers to the questions raised above.

By a 'practice' I am going to mean [says MacIntyre] any coherent and complex form of socially established cooperative human activity through which goods internal to that form of activity are realized in the course of trying to achieve those standards of excellence which are appropriate to, and partially definitive of, that form of activity, with the result that human powers to achieve excellence, and human conceptions of the ends and goods involved, are systematically *extended*. (ibid. 187)

What might examples of 'practices' so defined be? MacIntyre again:

Tic-tac-toe is not an example of a practice in this sense, nor is throwing a football with skill; but the game of football is, and so is chess. Bricklaying is not a practice; architecture is. Planting turnips is not a practice; farming is. So are the enquiries of physics, chemistry and biology, and so is the work of the historian, and so are painting and music (ibid.)

There are several constitutive features of a practice inherent in MacIntyre's definition but for our purposes here, two are particularly relevant (for a more analytical commentary see Tsoukas 1998*b*). First, a practice is a complex form of social activity that involves the cooperative effort of human beings; it is coherent and, therefore, bound by rules; and it is extended in time. Second, every practice establishes a set of what MacIntyre calls 'internal goods', meaning those goods that cannot be specified, recognized, and achieved in any other way than by *participating* in a particular practice (e.g. *playing* chess, *nursing* patients, *doing* scientific research, etc.). 'Those who lack the relevant experience are incompetent thereby as judges of internal goods' (MacIntyre 1985: 189). By contrast, 'external goods' such as status, money, fame, etc. are only contingently attached to practices and they can, therefore, be achieved by alternative means without having to participate in a particular practice.

Notice that, in MacIntyre's definition, a practice derives its key features—its identity—from 'within': it constitutes a self-referential system. How? A practice's 'internal goods', namely those values and cognitive categories that make it *this* distinctive practice and not that, are rooted in the particular experiences actors derive from participating in the practice. To the extent that this is the case, the particular cognitive categories that have developed in the history of a practice condition the manner in which its members interact with the outside world. This is the point at which MacIntyre's work comes very close to the claims of constructivist epistemologists such as Glaserfeld (1984) and Foerster (1984), systems theorists such as Maturana and Varela (1980), organization theorists such as Morgan (1986), and sociologists such as Luhmann (1990).

All the above-mentioned scholars converge on the view that social systems do not interact with an objectively given environment, but rather with whatever they *perceive* their environment to be (Bateson 1979; Weick 1979). Accordingly, a social system is not determined by its environment, although it may be triggered by it; a social system's response is rather dependent on its particular structure. As Mingers (1995: 30) remarks, 'the actual changes that the system undergoes depend on the structure itself at a particular instant'. Through their appreciative systems (or, to use MacIntyre's term, through their 'internal goods') social systems assign patterns of variation and significance to their 'environment', and it is with those self-created patterns that they interact. Or to borrow Morgan's (1986: 238) formulation, a system 'creates images of reality as expressions or descriptions of its own organization and interacts with these images, modifying them in the light of actual experience'. In other words, rather than the knowledge of a system passively reflecting what stands outside it, it emerges as the product of a system's activity within its environment. As Piaget (quoted in Glaserfeld 1984: 24, 32) so aptly observed, 'intelligence organizes the world by organizing itself'.

Focusing on living systems, Maturana (1980) has argued that they are self-producing; that is, organized in such a way that they preserve their organization when faced with perturbations. As Mingers (1995: 33) has noted, 'the product of their organization is that very organization itself'. How do systems do this? Morgan has summarized Maturana and Varela's arguments, and extended them to social systems, as follows:

They do so by engaging in circular patterns of interaction whereby change in one element of the system is coupled with changes elsewhere, setting up continuous patterns of interaction that are always self-referential. They are self-referential because a system cannot enter into interactions that are not specified in the pattern of relations that define its organization. Thus a system's interaction with its 'environment' is really a reflection and part of its own organization. It interacts with its environment in a way that facilitates its own self-production, and in this sense we can see that its environment is really part of itself. (Morgan 1986: 236)

Social systems, therefore, interact with their environments in terms of how they are internally organized. They have historically developed their own cognitive categories, values, and appreciative settings—in short: their own organization—and it is in terms of that organization that systems interact with their environments. Put simply, a system's organization determines what it will perceive, and vice versa; namely, a system perceives those things that will enable it to maintain its organization (i.e. its identity). This means that social systems, as self-referential entities, find it difficult to change—they tend to dampen perturbations in order to preserve their organization (Goldstein 1988; Morgan 1986). System-wide change *may* occur if a social system regularly receives information from its environment, and/or generates information about its own functioning (Goldstein 1988; Hirschhorn and Gilmore 1980).

Why does information have such a reorganizing potential? The reason is to be found in the very nature of information. As Bateson (1979) has so perceptively noted, information is a difference that makes a difference. If a system regularly receives information about other systems and/or generates information about its own functioning, it creates a set of differences; namely, differences between its knowledge of itself and its knowledge of other systems, and differences between what the system-in-focus knows about itself at a particular point in time and what it knows at another point in time. These differences have the potential to help the system reorganize itself. In other words, a system regularly supplied with information, provided the information is spread throughout it, is forced to take that information into account, reflect on it, and somehow respond to it, thus creating the conditions for the system's potential transformation.

Why might such a transformation come about? Foerster (1984) and Maturana (1980) have argued that in a self-referential system novelty may occur from a process of recursive application of descriptions (or, in Bateson's terms, of 'information'; in Vicker's terms, of 'appreciative judgements'). Says Maturana:

Through language we interact in a domain of *descriptions* within which we necessarily remain even when we make assertions about the universe or about our knowledge of it. This domain is both bounded and infinite; bounded because everything we say is a *description*, and infinite because every *description* constitutes in us the basis for *new orienting interactions*, and hence for *new descriptions*. [...] The *new* then is a necessary result of the historical organization of the observer that makes of every attained state the starting point for the specification of the next one, which thus cannot be a strict repetition of any previous state; creativity is the cultural expression of this unavoidable feature. (1980: 50, 51, emphasis in the original)

What Maturana, in effect, is saying is this. We humans operate in the cognitive domain; that is, a domain within which we interact with our own descriptions (i.e. thoughts) as if they were independent entities (Popper 1979). Such interaction gives rise to further descriptions with which we subsequently interact in an endlessly recursive manner (for Maturana this is possible because of the nature of our nervous system, but this need not concern us here). Notice the cycle: at each stage a set of descriptions provides the basis for interactions, and interactions give further rise to new descriptions, leading to new inter-actions, and so on. In other words, novelty comes about as a result of the intrinsically human capability of being reflexive: of reflecting on one's behav-iour in a recursive manner. Potentially endless reflexivity creates the condi-tions for potentially endless novelty (Berger 1963; Castoriadis 1991; Giddens 1991; Soros 1987; Tsoukas and Papoulias 1996).

Reforming Social Practices: Three Illustrations

(1) The internal relationship between actors' cognitive categories (or apprecia-tive systems) and social practices is richly demonstrated in Osborne and Gaebler's 1992 account of administrative reforms in the USA, in the 1980s. Describing the socio-economic background against which those grass-roots reforms took place, Osborne and Gaebler remark as follows:

Washington remained mired in an ideological stalemate between one party still wedded to the laissez-faire paradigm, but visionary state and local leaders gradually begun to adjust, developing new practices and new vocabularies. Suddenly the field of government was brimming with new catch phrases: 'public–private partner-ships', 'alternative service delivery', 'contracting out', 'empowerment', 'Total Qual-ity Management', 'participatory management', 'privatization', 'load shedding'. (ibid. 323–4, emphasis added)

This is not simply an exercise in 'new speak', although there are cases in management and policy-making when it is no more than that. Throughout their book Osborne and Gaebler show how new practices and new ways of thinking are mutually constituted in a recursive manner. Provided new defin-itions of reality start gaining ground and persuading actors, new ways of *doing* things (i.e. new interactions) emerge. And vice versa: provided new ways of doing things start taking place, new *definitions* of reality (i.e. new descriptions) emerge. For example, the unprecedented financial hardship that American local governments found themselves in, in the early 1980s, impelled them to do something. The initiative *some* of them *happened* to take (for example, the market-oriented educational reforms initially undertaken by local leaders in Minnesota—see Osborne and Gaebler 1992: 325), and the practices thus adopted, gave rise to a new set of self-understandings, which gradually gained ascendancy, were further refined in the process, and helped spread the new practices further.

(2) Similarly, reflecting on the radical reforms introduced by Conservative governments in the UK after 1979, focusing in particular on how a not-so-Thatcherite institution such as the Open University had changed, Hall observed:

One of the key lessons I learned from Thatcherism was that first of all you struggle about conduct, and hearts and minds follow later. I learned that through the institution in which I work, the Open University. It is filled with good social democrats. Everybody there believes in the redistribution of educational opportunities and seeks to remedy the exclusiveness of British education. And yet, in the past ten years, these good social-democratic souls, without changing for a minute what is in their hearts and minds, have learned to speak a brand of metallic new entrepreneurialism, a new managerialism of a horrendously closed nature. They believe what they always believed, but *what they do*, how they write their mission statements, how they do appraisal forms, *how they talk* about students, how they calculate the cost—that's what they are really interested in now. The result is that the institution has been transformed. (1993: 15, emphasis added)

Although in the preceding extract Hall is, as one might expect, hostile to Thatcherism, and irrespective of what one makes of it, his description of social reforms has a generic application. It shows that, from a policy-making point of view, appreciating the language-dependent (and, thus, malleable) character of social reality is very significant in reforming it. A new way of thinking about a social practice leads to a new way of talking about it and then to a new way of acting towards (in) it. Social practices do not have an intrinsic nature but rather a texture consisting of a set of self-understandings expressed in language. When the language underlying the functioning of a practice changes, so do the self-understandings expressed in it—hence, the purpose and the functioning of the practice change too. Hall's reflections on the changes that tork place in the Open University is a useful reminder of the intimate relationship between language and social practices. It brings out the importance of the political discourse of those initiating the changes (in this case the British government), for it is the coherence, plausibility, and legitimacy of such a discourse that grant it its ideological (and therefore political) hegemony (Rosenhead 1992) and provide it with the momentum that enables its supporters to displace (or at least significantly influence) the already existing self-understandings embodied in a social practice.

(3) As mentioned above, social reformers usually encounter resistance to their attempts to reform social systems, mainly because of the latter's self-referential nature. Consider, for example, the debate in the UK in the 1990s concerning important changes in police organization. Both Sir Patrick Sheehy's committee's recommendations on police pay and conditions in 1993, and a Home Office review of police tasks in 1994 converged in their business-oriented conclusions. Urged by the rise in crime rates in the previous twenty years, the falling clear-up rate, and the soaring cost of policing, the philosophy of the proposed reforms was to pattern the police on the model of business firms: a reduced starting salary for policemen, payment by results, dismissal of those deemed inadequate, living off non-essential tasks to other agencies, charities, and private firms, etc. No doubt, at the heart of the reforms is the often implicit question: What is the role of the Police in our society?

The Conservative government's view, consistent with its wider neo-liberal agenda, was that the police needed to concentrate their efforts on fighting crime alone, and to do so as efficiently as possible—hence the need for some of the principles underlying the organization and behaviour of business firms to be adopted by the police. The latter's view, however, is different. 'Rather than narrowly focusing on crime', the police seemed to argue, 'our task is, more broadly, to soothe conflict and solve local problems in communities—at least that is what the public expects of us'. In an informative article in *The Economist* this was put as follows:

Citizens ask for directions, or request that drunks be moved on. Officers are called out to prevent suicides, to direct traffic and to soothe disputes among neighbours or families. 'We can't avoid responding to whatever it is that concerns people', says Sir John Smith, deputy head of London's police. [. . .] The police argue that many apparently marginal duties are essential to the fight against crime. For instance, when officers deal with lost property or teach road-safety to children, they are building contacts among the communities they have to work with. The police say that locals are more likely to volunteer information on crimes to a trusted and familiar bobby than to an unknown officer who deals solely with catching crooks. Research shows that the police solve crimes far more often by using tip-offs from the public than through their own detective work (*The Economist*, 6 August 1994, 35)

The Government might acknowledge all this but, furthermore, insist on asking: 'Yes, but is it efficient? Are there not other, more efficient, ways for officers to glean information? Might it be preferable to use paid informants (as the Audit Commission suggested) instead of relying on casual witnesses? Would not the police become more effective in boosting clear-up rates if they shifted resources to computerizing the analysis of crime patterns, and to sharpening their forensic and detective skills?' Now, to do all these things, the government might argue, resources must be found, and to save money the police must consider withdrawing from some of the many community commitments they have traditionally undertaken (see *The Economist*, 6 August

1994; 15 October 1994). Moreover, linking policemen's pay to results will help make policemen more effective and accountable.

About such a policy, however, the police are deeply sceptical, even cynical: 'How many arrests must I make', asks a police sergeant, 'to pay the mortgage? How many to meet the car repayments? How do you measure the comfort given by a young community constable to an old lady living alone in a village?' *(Sunday Times,* 25 July 1993).

We can properly understand comments such as these if we view police work as a social practice (as defined earlier). What we have here is a set of 'internal goods', or an 'appreciative system', developed over time, whose main features are those normally associated with professional work. The police appear to be saying to the government: 'We know what policing is, you don't. Furthermore, you misunderstand the nature of policing. It is extremely important for effective policing, for example, to win the trust of local communities. What you propose is going to hinder us in achieving this. You just cannot run police stations like business units. Our work is different'. Being members of a self-referential practice, the police have developed their own cognitive categories, professional values, norms, and interests—that is, their distinctive appreciative system—which accounts for the practice's reactions to the proposed reforms. These reforms are viewed in terms of the perceptions generated by the appreciative system of this particular practice. Hence their members' hostile reaction to the 'outrageous' idea that business practices may serve as a model.

In this case, policy-making can be conceptualized as providing the practice-in-focus with an alternative set of self-understandings. Thus, to the question 'What is the role of the Police?' the Conservative British Government, in line with its broader neo-liberal socio-economic philosophy, gave an answer which was at variance with the traditional professional work ethic espoused by the police. 'The role of the police', the government appeared to be saying, 'is to fight crime as efficiently and effectively as possible. To do this, we believe that it would be useful for the police to borrow some well-tested ideas and practices from the business world that are known to work'. Notice that such a view of policing-as-a-practice is unlikely to be generated from within the practice itself. The latter's self-referential nature ensures that its historically developed identity is maintained and, therefore, that any proposed reform will be viewed from the appreciative system underlying that identity. It takes an outsider, one with legitimate authority and a radical agenda, to shake up the system and introduce an alternative set of self-understandings with regard to what policing is about.

The role of policy makers extends further to regularly supplying the system under reform with information about both other systems and its own functioning. Thus, in the UK there has been a wealth of crime data as well as data pertaining to the effectiveness of the police in handling crime which, in the form of publications by Home Office committees or Royal Commissions, or, more recently, in the form of league tables and press reports, are used by the government to perturb the system and force it to respond. It is interesting, for example, that published regional clear-up rates compel those police constables underperforming to provide explanations for their performance (see *Financial Times*, 12 April 1995). Similarly, published league tables of hospitals, local authorities, schools, or universities provide the systems concerned with comparative information, and force them to take corrective action, for, in a competitive environment, no one enjoys bad publicity (see *Financial Times*, 21 November 1994). Management by embarrassment seems to be a particularly powerful tool in forcing social systems to ask certain questions about themselves and, in so doing, to contemplate modes of self-reform.

It appears, therefore, that when reformist policy makers (a) have a particular agenda to implement, supported by a popularly backed socio-economic philosophy, and (b) supply the system under reform with information about its functioning and about other systems, they create the necessary conditions for pushing through their reforms with success. They do so by establishing a discourse in terms of which debate is structured, the key categories of which those resisting the reforms are forced to employ. It is interesting, for example, that even those who actively sought to resist the sweeping Conservative reforms in the UK in the 1980s found it very difficult to avoid using the government's language—something that may help explain, at least to some extent, the remarkable success the Conservative government had in pushing through most of these reforms. As the police sergeant who quoted earlier remarked: 'I don't doubt that we should be making ourselves more efficient and more cost-conscious. [...] But [...]' (*Sunday Times*, 25 July 1993). Notice that her particular objection is not of great importance; what matters is that she (and many others like her) talks (and therefore *thinks)* now in a manner that is consistent with the philosophy of the very reforms she is otherwise prepared to resist. To paraphrase Hall's earlier statement, she may continue believing in the traditional police values, but how she now *talks* and how she now *works* have changed remarkably. And this is what matters from the policy makers' point of view.

Summary and Conclusions

It is widely accepted that pushing through important social reforms is not an easy job (Rosenhead 1989, 1992; Vickers 1983, 1984). We have attempted here to explain why this is the case by re-examining and further developing Vickers's concept of appreciative systems. An appreciative system consists of a set of reality and value judgements that underlie individuals' perceptions of a situation. We have argued that appreciative systems are not just properties of individuals, merely different ways of looking at things chosen at will. More than that, appreciative systems are socially established ways of perceiving, consisting of a set of cognitive categories, values, and interests, which are grounded in social practices. The latter are constituted by certain historically developed self-understandings and internal goods which are expressed as sets of background distinctions shared by individuals.

A key feature of social practices is their self-referential character. Members of social practices interact not with an objectively given environment but rather with *perceptions* of the 'environment'. Those perceptions are derived from the way a practice is organized; namely, from the set of cognitive categories, values, and interests by which it is historically constituted. In other words, the manner in which the members of a social practice relate to their environment is conditioned by their historically developed appreciative system. They act the way they do because they think the way they do; and they think the way they do because they act the way they do—that is why we describe them as self-referential, and as being concerned with maintaining their identity.

How then may this cycle be broken so that practices may be re-formed? There are two ways, both necessary. First, by recognizing the language-dependent character of social practices one is able to appreciate their malleability. Policy makers' models of social practices are internally related to social practices (see Fig. 7.1). This is the most important reason why it is necessary for policy makers to have developed a coherent, plausible, and legitimate discourse: it provides them with the new distinctions, definitions, and self-understandings which may constitute the new appreciative system of the practice under reform. In other words, if policy makers want to change the particular way a certain practice functions, they need to win the contest of ideas, the battle for language. They need to envisage an alternative mode of institutional functioning, and this can be done only if they can articulate an alternative mission and establish an alternative discourse in terms of which reforms may be contemplated. Ideological hegemony, far from being pernicious, as Rosenhead (1992) seems to imply, is a necessary prerequisite for challenging the status quo.

Second, the normal identity-preserving functioning of a social system may be counteracted if the latter regularly receives information about other systems and/or about its own functioning. In such a case information has potentially reorganizing effects, for, in principle, it enables a system to reflect on it and thus come up with new descriptions of itself, leading to potentially novel patterns of action. Institutional reflexivity is likely to stir things up and *may* lead to self-reform or at least it can aid policy-makers' efforts to establish a new appreciative system.

If the claims put forward in this chapter are accepted, it follows that the management of change in social practices is as much a conceptual as a technical matter. Reforming self-referential systems hinges crucially on policy makers' ability to articulate a vision, define institutional reality afresh, and manage information creatively. We are aware that the picture we have painted here is very broad. Its details will need to be worked out through empirical research, for it is only then that we will learn more about the intricacies of social reforms and acquire a concrete understanding of the process, the dynamics, and the techniques used and the role of contingencies, all of which are crucial in determining the effectiveness of social-reform projects.

References

Adams, G. B., and Catron, B. (1994), 'Communitarianism, Vickers and Revisioning American Public Administration', *American Behavioral Scientist*, 38: 44–63.

Bateson, G. (1979), *Mind and Nature* (Toronto: Bantam).

Beer, S. (1973), 'The Surrogate World We Manage', *Behavioral Science*, 18: 198–209.

Berger, P. (1963), *Invitation to Sociology*. (London: Penguin).

—— and Luckmann, T. (1966), *The Social Construction of Reality* (London: Penguin).

Castoriadis, C. (1991), *Philosophy, Politics, Autonomy*, trans. and ed. D. A. Curtis (New York: Oxford University Press).

Checkland, P. (1981), *Systems Thinking, Systems Practice*, (Chichester: Wiley).

—— (1994), 'Systems Theory and Management Thinking', *American Behavioral Scientist*, 38: 75–91.

—— and Scholes, J., (1990), *Soft Systems Methodology in Action* (Chichester: Wiley).

Churchman, C. W. (1971), *The Design of Inquiring Systems* (New York: Basic).

Flood, R. L., and Jackson, M. C. (1991), *Creative Problem Solving* (Chichester: Wiley).

Foerster, H. von (1984), 'On Constructing a Reality', in P. Watzlawick (ed.), *The Invented Reality* (New York: Norton), 41–61.

Forester, J. (1994), 'Judgment and the Cultivation of Appreciation in Policy-making', *American Behavioral Scientist*, 38: 64–74.

Giddens, A. (1976), *New Rules of Sociological Method* (London: Hutchinson).

—— (1991), *Modernity and Self-Identity* (Cambridge: Polity).

Glaserfeld, E. von (1984), 'An Introduction to Radical Constructivism', in P. Watzlawick (ed.), *The Invented Reality* (New York: Norton, 17–40).

Goldstein, J. (1988); 'A Far-from-Equilibrium Systems Approach to Resistance to Change', *Organizational Dynamics*, 17: 16–26.

Hall, S. (1993), 'Thatcherism Today', *New Statesman and Society*, 26 November 1993, 14–16.

Hirschhorn, L., and Gilmore, T. (1980), 'The Application of Family Therapy Concepts to Influencing Organizational Behavior', *Administrative Science Quarterly*, 15: 18–37.

Johnson, N. (1994), 'Institutions and Human Relations: A Search for Stability in a Changing World', *American Behavioral Scientist*, 38: 26–43.

Luhmann, N. (1990), *Essays in Self-Reference*. (New York: Columbia University Press).

Macintyre, A. (1985), *After Virtue*, 2nd edn. (London: Duckworth).

Maturana, H. (1980), 'Biology of Cognition', in H. Maturana and F. Varela, *Autopoiesis and Cognition* (Dordrecht: Reidel), 5–62.

—— and Varela, F. (1980), *Autopoiesis and Cognition*. (Dordrecht: Reidel).

Mingers, J. (1995), *Self-Producing Systems*. (New York: Plenum).

Morgan, G. (1986), *Images of Organization* (Beverly Hills, Calif.: Sage).

Osborne, D., and Gaebler, T., (1992), *Reinventing Government*, (Reading, Mass.: Addison-Wesley).

Papoulias, D. B., and Tsoukas, H. (1994), 'Managing Reforms on a Large Scale: What Role for OR/MS?', *Journal of the Operational Research Society*, 45: 977–86.

Popper, K. (1979), *Objective Knowledge* (Oxford: Clarendon).

Reich, R. B. (1991), *The Work of Nations* (London: Simon & Schuster).

Ritsert, J. (1978) (ed.), *Arbeitsgruppe Soziologie: Denkweissen und Grundbegriffe der Soziologie: Eine Einführung* (Frankfurt: Campus Verlag).

Rorty, R. (1991), *Objectivity, Relativism and Truth*, (Cambridge: Cambridge University Press).

Rosenhead, J. (1989), *Rational Analysis for a Problematic World*. (Chichester: Wiley).

—— (1992), 'Into the Swamp: The Analysis of Social Issues', *Journal of the Operational Research Society*, 43: 293–305.

Schon, D. (1983), *The Reflective Practitioner* (Aldershot: Avebury).

—— (1987), *Educating the Reflective Practitioner* (San Francisco, Calif.: Jossey-Bass).

Soros, G. (1987), *The Alchemy of Finance* (New York: Wiley).

Taylor, C. (1985), *Philosophy and the Human Sciences: Philosophical Papers*, ii, (Cambridge: Cambridge University Press).

—— (1998a), 'The Word and the World: A Critique of Representationalism in Management Research', *International Journal of Public Administration*, 21: 781–817.

Tsoukas, H., and Papoulias, D. B., (1996), 'Creativity in OR/MS: From Technique to Epistemology', *Interfaces*, 26(2): 73–9.

—— (1998b), 'Forms of Knowledge and Forms of Life in Organized Contexts', in R. C. H. Chia (ed.), *In the Realm of Organization* (London: Routledge), 43–66.

Vickers, G. (1983), *The Art of Judgement* (London: Harper & Row).

—— (1984), *The Vickers Papers*, (London: Harper & Row).

Watzlawick, P. (1984) (ed.), *The Invented Reality* (New York: Norton).

Weick, K. (1979), *The Social Psychology of Organizing*, 2nd edn. (New York: McGraw-Hill).

EIGHT

On Organizational Becoming: Rethinking Organizational Change

Haridimos Tsoukas and Robert Chia

The point is that usually we look at change but we do not see it. We speak of change, but we do not think about it. We say that change exists, that everything changes, that change is the very law of things: yes, we say it and we repeat it; but those are only words, and we reason and philosophize as though change did not exist. In order to think change and see it, there is a whole veil of prejudices to brush aside, some of them artificial, created by philosophical speculation, the others natural to common sense.

(Henri Bergson 1946: 131)

What really *exists* is not things made but things in the making. Once made, they are dead, and an infinite number of alternative conceptual decompositions can be used in defining them. But put yourself *in the making* by a stroke of intuitive sympathy with the thing and, the whole range of possible decompositions coming into your possession, you are no longer troubled with the question which of them is the more absolutely true. Reality *falls* in passing into conceptual analysis; it *mounts* in living its own undivided life—it buds and bourgeons, changes and creates (emphasis in the original).

(William James 1909/96: 263–4)

The future is not given. Especially in this time of globalization and the network revolution, behavior at the individual level will be

This chapter was first published in *Organization Science*, 13(5) (2002), 567–82. Reprinted by permission of the Institute for Operations Research and the Management Sciences, 901 Elkridge Landing Road, Suite 400, Linthicum, MD 21090 USA, Copyright (2002).

The authors would like to thank Marshall Scott Poole, Senior Editor of *Organization Science*, three anonymous *OS* reviewers, and Royston Greenwood for their very helpful comments on earlier drafts.

the key factor in shaping the evolution of the entire human species. Just as one particle can alter macroscopic organization in nature, so the role of individuals is more important now than ever in society

(Ilya Prigogine 2000: 36–7)

S EVERAL calls have recently been made to reorient both organization science and management practice to embrace change more openly and consistently (Eccles, Nohria, and Berkley 1992; Ford and Ford 1995; Orlikowski 1996; Pettigrew 1992; Van de Ven and Poole 1995; Weick 1993, 1998; Weick and Quinn 1999). This is easier said than done. As Orlikowski (1996: 63) admits, 'for decades, questions of transformation remained largely backstage as organizational thinking and practice engaged in a discourse dominated by questions of stability'. Similarly, Weick (1998) has pointed out the difficulties one has in understanding the proper nature of concepts such as 'improvisation' and the subtle changes in the texture of organizing, unless one sees change in its own terms, rather than as a special case of 'stability' and 'routine'. 'When theorists graft mechanisms for improvisation onto concepts that basically are built to explain order', notes Weick (1998: 551), the result is 'a caricature of improvisation that ignores nuances'.

What would be the benefits if 'organizational change', both as an object of study and as a management preoccupation, were to be approached from the perspective of ongoing change rather than stability? Why would such a reversal of ontological priorities be helpful? It would be helpful for three reasons.

First, it would enable researchers to obtain a more complete understanding of the micro-processes of change at work. In their avowedly macro, neo-institutionalist approach to organizational change Greenwood and Hinings (1996: 1044) have argued that future research ought to address the question of how 'precipitating' and 'enabling' dynamics interact in response to pressures for change. What makes organizations actually move from and change the 'archetype' (template for organizing)? How are new archetypes uncovered and legitimated? By whom, using what means? To explore such micro-questions is of considerable importance in understanding the dynamics of change and will 'permit the careful assessment of non-linear processes' (ibid. 1045). Although the authors do not expand on those 'non-linear processes', they do imply that to properly understand organizational change we must allow for emergence and surprise, meaning that we must take into account the possibility of organizational change having ramifications and implications beyond those initially imagined or planned.

Second, as well as not knowing a lot about the micro-processes of change, we do not know enough about how change is actually *accomplished*. Even if we can explain, *ex post facto*, how and why organization A moved from archetype X to archetype Y, or from position A to position B (which is the hitherto dominant approach—more about this later), our explanation would look like a 'post-mortem dissection' (James 1909/96: 262); it would not be fine-grained enough to show how change was actually accomplished on the ground—how plans were translated into action and, in so being, how they were modified, adapted, changed. If organizational change is viewed as a *fait accompli*, its dynamic, unfolding, emergent qualities (in short: its potential) are devalued, even lost from view. If change is viewed in juxtaposition to stability, we tend to lose sight of the subtle micro-changes that sustain and, at the same time, potentially corrode stability. If change is viewed as the exception, the occasional episode in organizational life, we underestimate how pervasive change already is. Feldman (2000), for example, has empirically shown how organizational routines, far from being the repeated stable patterns of behaviour that do not change very much from one iteration to another, are actually 'emergent accomplishments'; they are 'flows of connected ideas, actions, and outcomes' (ibid. 613) that perpetually interact and change in action. In so far as routines are *performed* by human agents, they contain the seeds of change. In other words, even the most allegedly stable parts of organizations, such as routines, are potentially unstable—change is always potentially there if we only care to look for it.

Third, a major cause of dissatisfaction with the traditional approach to change—the approach that gives priority to stability and treats change as an epiphenomenon—is pragmatic: change programmes that are informed by that view often do not produce change (Beer and Nohria 2000; Taylor, 1993). Taylor (ibid.), for example, has described how an office computerization programme sponsored by the Canadian government in the 1980s failed to achieve its goals (i.e. to lead to major productivity improvements). The explanation Taylor advances is that the project was motivated by a 'particulate vision of reality' (ibid. 185); namely, by the atomistic ontological assumption that organizations are collections of individual 'pieces' (human and non-human) rather than situation-specific webs of social relations which technology enters and modifies and by which, in turn, it is modified. As Taylor (ibid. 241) remarks, the approach to change that was taken by the technologists 'assumed that information is particulate, that decisions are taken from the top, and that interpersonal dynamics can be safely disregarded. It conceptualized the organization as constructed from the outside, by a managerial corps, much in the way a computer program is written by a computer programmer, rather than an entity that builds itself up from the inside'. Interestingly, the one exception in the office-automation project was a government agency whose members took the initiative to improvise and adapt the project to their own local context, and made the effort to integrate the technology into their patterns of work (ibid. 242).

To put it more generally, as ethnographic research has shown, change programmes, like organizational routines, need to be *made* to work on any given occasion, they do not work themselves out (Barley 1990; Boden 1994; Orlikowski 1996). Change programmes 'work' in so far as they are fine-tuned and adjusted by actors in particular contexts—that is, in so far as they are further changed on an ongoing basis (Orlikowski 1996). Unless we have an image of change as an ongoing process, a stream of interactions, and a flow of situated initiatives, as opposed to a set of episodic events, it will be difficult to overcome the implementation problems of change programmes reported in the literature.

From the above it follows that, prima facie at least, it will be helpful to move beyond the assumptions of stability that have underlain for so long our understanding of organizational change, and attempt to think of the latter on its own terms. While there has been no paucity of explanations as to how assumptions of stability have historically dominated organization science and other fields alike (see Shenhav 1995; Toulmin 1990: ch.3), it is less clear how a reconceptualization of change might occur. How could change be thought of in its own terms? What might the Heraclitean dictum that 'everything changes and nothing abides' mean in the context of organizations?

Weick (1998) has observed that the main barriers to rethinking change are the ontological and epistemological commitments that have underpinned research into the subject. He is not the first to point in that direction. Nearly ninety years ago William James expressed his dissatisfaction with 'the ruling tradition in philosophy' for its adherence to 'the Platonic and Aristotelian belief that fixity is a nobler and worthier thing than change' (James 1909/ 96: 237). It is now realized, across scientific fields, that we lack the vocabulary to talk meaningfully about change as if change mattered—that is, not to treat change as an epiphenomenon, as a mere curiosity or exception, but to acknowledge its centrality in the constitution of socio-economic life (North 1996; Prigogine 1989; Stacey 1996; Sztompka 1993).

Nonetheless, there are already interesting developments in progress, especially in organization science. Dissatisfied with traditional approaches to organizational change, Orlikowski (1996) has conceptualized the latter as ongoing improvisation. Rather than seeing organizational change as orchestrated from the top, Orlikowski (ibid. 65) sees it as 'grounded in the ongoing practices of organizational actors, and [emerging] out of their (tacit and not so tacit) accommodations to and experiments with the everyday contingencies, breakdowns, exceptions, opportunities, and unintended consequences that they encounter'. Similarly, Weick and Quinn (1999: 382) have concluded that a shift in vocabulary from 'change' to 'changing' will make theorists and practitioners more attentive to the dynamic, change-full character of organizational life. Feldman, in her 'performative model of organizational routines' (2000: 611), has described how a routine changes as participants respond to outcomes of previous iterations of it. She notes that we get a richer picture of routines when we do not separate them from the people applying them. So long as human actors *perform* the routines, there is an intrinsic potential for ongoing organizational change. Echoing similar calls by Barley (1986, 1990) and Pentland and Rueter (1994), Feldman (2000: 626) has argued for a focus 'on the role of agency in the way structures are transformed and modified through processes of everyday organizational life'.

Our purpose in this chapter is to build on and extend Orlikowski's, Weick's, and Feldman's intriguing arguments (as well as on those of others who share similar concerns—see Barley 1986, 1990; Brown and Eisenhardt 1997; Choi 1995; Ford and Ford 1994, 1995; March 1981; Marshak 1993; Van de Ven and Poole 1995). We start from the assumption that to properly understand *organizational change* (in the sense argued by Orlikowski, Weick, and Feldman) we need to stop giving ontological priority to organization, thereby making change an exceptional effect produced only under specific circumstances by certain people (change agents). We should rather start from the premiss that change is pervasive and indivisible; that, to borrow James's apt phrase (1909/96: 253) 'the essence of life is its continuously changing character', and *then* see what this premiss entails for our understanding of organizations.

Much as we have been inspired by the work of writers such as Orlikowski, Weick, and Feldman, we wish to argue here for an even more radically process-oriented approach to organizational change. These writers have contributed enormously to sensitizing organizational theorists to the significance of seeing change as an ongoing process, but they do not go far enough, or at least not as far as their own approach would allow them to go.

For example, traces of the traditional way of thinking about change are not absent from Weick's thinking (see Weick and Quinn 1999). Weick and Quinn (ibid. 370, 377), for instance, are ambivalent about the ontological status of continuous change: while arguing for an appreciation of continuous change, they also think that the latter ceases to take place in certain types of organizations, such as machine bureaucracies (ibid. 381). Similarly, Orlikowski makes her improvisational model of organizational change conditional on the kind of technology introduced: groupware technologies allow individuals to adapt and customize them—hence the need for ongoing change—whereas traditional technologies do not (Orlikowski and Hofman 1997: 18). As we will show later, and as Trist et al.'s classic study of work organization in UK coal mines (1963) has shown, this is not the case. Change is far more pervasive than Orlikowski allows. Moreover, her conception of change as being 'situated and endemic to the practice of organizing' (Orlikowski 1996: 91), helpful and refreshing as it undoubtedly is, does not go far enough in theoretically explicating the driving forces of 'improvisation'. Finally, Feldman (2000) has perceptively argued that the key to understanding change as an ongoing process is to pay attention to the transformational character of ordinary human action, but she has not elaborated on what it is about human action that contributes to such ongoing change, other than pointing at the continuous feedback of outcomes to plans.

In this chapter we aim to show that the implications that follow from Weick's, Feldman's, and Orlikowski's insights (and those of other process-oriented organizational writers mentioned above) will be drawn out only if their calls for a greater attention to process lead to a consistent reversal of the ontological priority accorded to organization and change. Change must not be thought of as a property of organization. Rather, organization must be understood as an emergent property of change. Change is ontologically prior to organization—it is the condition of possibility for organization. With this ontological reversal in mind, the central question we address in this chapter is as follows: What must organization(s) be like if change is constitutive of reality? Wishing to highlight the pervasiveness of change in organizations, we talk about *organizational becoming*. Drawing on process-oriented philosophers and ethnomethodologists we argue that change is the re-weaving of actors' webs of beliefs and habits of action as a result of new experiences obtained through interactions. In so far as this is an ongoing process, that is to the extent that actors try to make sense of, and act coherently in, the world, change is inherent in human action. Organization is an attempt to order the intrinsic flux of human action, to channel it towards certain ends, to give it a particular shape, through generalizing and institutionalizing particular meanings and rules. At the same time, organization is a pattern that is constituted, shaped, *emerging* from change. Viewed this way, organization is a secondary accomplishment, in a double sense: first, it is a socially defined set of rules aiming at stabilizing an ever mutating reality, by making human behaviour more predictable. Second, organization is an outcome, a pattern, emerging from the reflective application of the very same rules in local contexts, over time. While organization aims at stemming change, it is also the outcome of change. We will illustrate this claim by drawing on relevant parts of the organizational literature.

The chapter is organized as follows. First, we describe an approach for making sense of change by drawing on, primarily, the writings of Bergson and James. Next, we discuss the notion of organizational becoming and explain the sense in which change in organizations is pervasive as well as how organization emerges from change. Finally, we outline the implications of our view of organizational becoming for theory and practice.

Understanding Change

As several reviews of the literature on organizational change have shown (Porras and Silvers 1991; Van de Ven and Poole 1995; Weick and Quinn 1999), the bulk of research has been oriented towards providing *synoptic* accounts of organizational change. Synoptic accounts view change as an accomplished event, whose key features and variations, and causal antecedents and consequences, need to be explored and described. Such knowledge is generated by approaching 'change' from the outside and, typically, it takes the form of a stage model in which the entity that undergoes change is shown to have distinct *states* at different points in time. Synoptic accounts have been useful in so far as they have provided us with snapshots of key dimensions of organizations at different points in time, along with explanations for the trajectories organizations followed (Donaldson 1999; Greenwood and Hinings 1996; Miller 1982; Tushman and Romanelli 1985). That knowledge, however, indispensable as it is, has certain limitations: given its synoptic nature, it does not do justice to the open-ended micro-processes that underlie the trajectories described; it does not quite capture the distinguishing features of change—its fluidity, pervasiveness, open-endedness, and indivisibility.

Why is this? Why cannot stage models of change, such as, for example, Lewin's classic 'unfreezing-moving-refreezing' model (1951), incorporate the distinguishing features of change? To begin to address this question we must appreciate that change is an age-old philosophical puzzle. Zeno's famous paradox illustrates the source of this puzzle (see James 1909/96: 228–32; Sainsbury 1988: ch. 1). The fast runner Achilles can never overtake the slow-moving tortoise, for by the time Achilles reaches the tortoise's starting point the tortoise has already moved ahead of that starting point, and by the time Achilles reaches the tortoise's new position the tortoise will have moved on, and so on *ad infinitum*. Zeno's paradox is created by the assumption that space and time are infinitely divisible. According to James (1909/96: 216–19), the basis for the assumption that space and time are infinitely divisible is our 'intellectualist' impulse: our readiness to transform the perceptual order (what our senses can apprehend) into a conceptual order (making sense of our experience through concepts). The trouble with concepts, James (ibid. 253) remarks, is that they are discontinuous and fixed, and, as such, unable to capture the continuously mutating character of life. The only way to make concepts coincide with life is to arbitrarily suppose 'positions of arrest therein' (ibid.). Thus, on intellectualist premises, we try to understand change by transforming it into a succession of positions. This tendency is best illustrated in the case of motion.

Motion is normally defined as 'the occupancy of serially successive points of space at serially successive instants of time' (ibid. 234). Notice how such a definition fails to capture what is distinctive of motion—*getting* from A to B. Oddly, on this definition motion is made up of immobilities: an object occupies this position now, that position later, and so on indefinitely (Bergson 1946: 145). It could be argued that the more 'positions' we identify in an object's movement, the better we describe its motion. But no matter how many such positions are created to represent the trajectory of an object, the fact remains that they contain no element of movement (James 1909/96: 234). As James (ibid. 236) aptly remarks, 'the stages into which you analyze a change are *states*, the change itself goes on between them. It lies along their intervals, inhabits what your definition fails to gather up, and thus eludes conceptual explanation altogether' (emphasis in the original).

The critique of the intellectualist approach to change by 'process philo-sophers' (Rescher 1996) such as James and Bergson helps us see the difficulties we face when we try to understand change by breaking it down into stages: by doing so, change is reduced to a series of static positions—its distinguishing features are lost from view. Change *per se* remains elusive and unaccounted for—strangely, it is whatever goes on *between* the positions representing change (James 1909/96: 236). Notice the paradox: a conceptual framework for making sense of change (namely, the stage model of change) cannot deal with change *per se*, except by conceiving of it as a series of immobilities; it makes sense of change by denying change!

If an intellectualist understanding of change leads to paradoxes and, ultim-ately, denies the very nature of change, what is the alternative? How can change be made sense of in a way that will acknowledge its distinguishing features? Bergson's advice (1946) is useful at this point: dive back into the flux itself, he says; turn your face toward sensation; bring yourself in touch with reality through *intuition*; get to know it from *within* or, to use Wittgenstein's famous aphorism, (1958, para. 66), 'don't think, but look'. Only a direct perception of reality will enable one to get a glimpse of its most salient characteristics—its constantly changing texture; its indivisible continuity; the conflux of the same with the different over time.

How does one get to know the continuously shifting flux of reality from within? For Bergson and James this is achieved when we experience reality directly, or when we sympathetically divine someone else's inner life. Only by placing ourselves at the centre of an unfolding phenomenon can we hope to know it from within. Take the example of the character Tom Sawyer, whose adventures are the subject of Mark Twain's eponymous novel. Mark Twain vividly paints Tom's personality in different circumstances, ranging from the funny to the horrifying, and we get to know him and life in the American south quite well. However, this is still knowledge from the outside. We would get knowledge from the inside through intuitively sympathizing with Tom Sawyer; that is, if we were to draw on our experiences and identify with the character himself. Then we would experience a feeling that we truly know the character, in all his complexity, in the same way that we know a city through walking its streets rather than via photographs of it (Bergson 1946: 160; James 1909/96: 262–3). To change metaphor, knowing from within is like mindfully listening to a melody: when we do so we have a perception of movement, of flow, of indivisible continuity (Bergson 1946: 145).

Intuition, knowledge from within, and direct acquaintance make up Berg-son's and James's method for apprehending the flux of reality. Perceiving for them is more important than conceiving. The former is more likely than the latter to be attentive to qualitative differences, to appreciate particular experi-ences, and to acknowledge the ever mutating character of life, where partial decay and partial growth, continuity and difference all coexist. But how does perception do this?

Whereas concepts help us name and package experience and, thus, obliterate differences (James, 1909/96: 217, 250–60; Wittgenstein 1967, para. 568), in perception, on the contrary, we are responsive to *difference*, to change (Bateson 1979: 102). I can feel the bump in the road because of the difference between the level of the road and the level of the top of the bump. I can see that morale in the department has dropped because of the difference between how people feel now and the time when the department was full of life. The undifferentiated is imperceptible.

According to Bateson (ibid.), our sensory system is activated by difference. The more sensitive one is to differences, ever more subtle, the more perceptive one will be. Artists do this all the time. A good painter, notes Bergson (1946: 135–6), brings to our attention something we had seen but not noticed. Art (and, incidentally, philosophy for Bergson and James) extends our faculty of perceiving by focusing our attention on hitherto unnoticed aspects of our lives. But how does art achieve this? Interestingly, it achieves it by taking a distance from reality. Our attachment to everyday reality, that is our concern with living and acting, necessarily narrows our vision; it obliges us to 'look straight ahead in the direction we have to go' (ibid. 137), at the expense of peripheral vision. This happens because in action we are less interested in the things themselves than in the use we can make of them. We normally look at the categories things belong to, rather than things *per se*. Artists, however, do exactly the opposite. By detaching their faculty of perceiving from their faculty of acting, 'when they look at a thing they see it for itself, and not for themselves. [. . .] It is because the artist is less intent on utilizing his perception that he perceives a greater number of things' (ibid. 138). The general point here is that we obtain a much more direct vision of reality, and thus begin to really appreciate its dynamic complexity, by occasionally turning our attention away from practical matters towards reflection.

Perception, however, has its limits. There are differences so small we cannot detect them; or we may have become accustomed to the new state of affairs before our senses could tell us that it is new. As Bateson (1979: 105) notes, 'there is necessarily a threshold of gradient below which gradient cannot be perceived'. Moreover, what we directly experience or concretely engage with is very limited in duration. The weather is changing from hour to hour and from day to day, but is it changing from year to year? How many of us have detected the decrease of birds in our gardens? We know how downsizing in the 1980s affected our company, but do we know how the entire American corporate landscape changed in the same period? Our perceptual knowledge is ill suited to answer such questions—we need conceptual knowledge instead. Bergson and James were well aware of this. 'If what we care most about', observes James (1909/96: 251), 'be the synoptic treatment of phenomena, the vision of the far and the gathering of the scattered alike, we must follow the conceptual

method'. Direct knowledge (intuition) and conceptual knowledge are complementary to each other. One provides what the other cannot.

Looked at synoptically, reality appears more stable than it actually is, something already noted by Weick and Quinn (1999: 362) and Feldman (2000: 622).
The acrobat on the high wire maintains his/her stability, we say. But he/she
does so by continuously correcting his/her imbalances (Bateson 1979: 65).
From this, a more general principle may be inferred: 'when we use *stability* in
talking about living things or self-corrective circuits, we should *follow the
example of the entities about which we are talking*' (ibid., emphasis in the original). What does this mean in practice? It means that statements
about stability and change should be labelled by reference to some descriptive
proposition, so that the logical type to which 'what changes' and 'what
stays stable' belong should be clear (Keeney 1983: 29–31; Roach and Bednar
1997).

For example, at a certain level of analysis (or logical type)—that of the
body—the statement 'the acrobat maintains his/her balance' is true, as is
also the statement 'the acrobat constantly adjusts his/her posture', but at
another level of analysis, that of the *parts* of the body, the apparent stability
of the acrobat does not preclude change; on the contrary, it presupposes it.
Similarly, in the case of organizational routines, at a certain level of analysis—
that of the routine itself—a synoptic account highlights the routine's self-
contained, thing-like, and stable character. However, at another level of analysis—that of individual action and interaction through which routines are
implemented—a process-oriented, or 'performative' (Feldman 2000: 622), account, which takes human agency seriously, would show that routines are
situated 'ongoing accomplishments' (ibid. 613) and, as such, they keep changing, depending on the dynamic between ideals, action, and outcomes.

From the above it follows that both 'synoptic' and 'performative' accounts
of organizational change are necessary—they serve different needs. Synoptic
accounts enable us to attain, in James's memorable phrase (1909/96: 251),
'vision of the far and the scattered alike', and make us notice patterns at
different points in time that normally escape our perceptions (Boulding
1987); performative accounts, on the other hand, through their focus on
situated human agency unfolding in time, offer us insights into the actual
emergence and accomplishment of change—they are accounts of change par
excellence. Given that (as mentioned at the beginning of this section) the
relevant literature has been dominated by synoptic accounts, it is important
that sophisticated performative accounts of change redress the balance. This is
especially so since performative accounts are more directly connected to
practitioners' lived experiences and actions. Indeed, the 'change' that is synoptically explained *ex post facto* is *experienced* by practitioners as an unfolding
process, a flow of possibilities, a conjunction of events and open-ended interactions occurring in time. If we are to understand how change is actually
accomplished (Eccles, Nohria, and Berkley 1992), change must be approached

from within—not as an 'abstract concept' (James 1909/96: 235) but as a performance enacted in time. In the following section we will put forward a performative model of organizational change.

Organizational Becoming

One of Weick's landmark contributions to organization science has been his shift in attention from organizations to organizing, and the conception of the latter as a set of processes for reducing equivocality amongst actors (Weick 1979). In Weick's view, organizing consists of *reducing differences* among actors; it is the process of generating *recurring* behaviours through institutionalized cognitive representations. For an activity to be said to be organized, it implies that *types* of behaviour in *types* of situations are systematically connected to *types* of actors (Berger and Luckmann 1966: 72; Tsoukas 1998). An organized activity provides actors with a given set of cognitive categories and a typology of actions (Weick 1979).

Thus, organizing implies generalizing; it is the process of subsuming particulars under generic categories. However, although the generic categories and the purposes for which they may be used are, at any moment, given to organizational members, they are nonetheless socially defined. Moreover, those categories are subject to potential change: the stability of their meanings is precariously maintained. The organization is both a given structure (i.e. a set of established generic cognitive categories) *and* an emerging pattern (i.e. the constant adaptation of those categories to local circumstances). Institutionalized cognitive categories are drawn upon by individuals-in-action but, in the process, established generalizations may be supplemented, eroded, modified, or, at any rate, interpreted in oftentimes unpredictable ways.

Why does this happen? Because although an organization fixes the definition of its representations (generic cognitive categories) for certain purposes, it does not have total definitional control over them (Lee 1984: 302). The semantics of knowledge representation in an organization is intrinsically unstable. To put it differently, for organizational action to be possible—that is, for recurrent behaviours to take place in accordance with established purposes—closure of meaning must be effected (Beer 1981: 58): cognitive categories must be stable enough in order to be consistently and effectively deployed. However, such closure, while it certainly occurs, is potentially temporary. This is so for two reasons.

First, definitional control is compromised because of organizational interactions with the outside world. For example, Orr's ethnographic study of photocopier-repair technicians (1996) has shown the amount of improvisation involved in their work, which stems from the open-endedness of the social contexts within which photocopiers break down (for similar findings see also Brown and Duguid 1991: 43; Orlikowski 1996; Orr 1990: 173; Vickers 1983: 42–5). The repair manuals issued to technicians typically contain definitions of what a broken machine is and how it may be repaired. Such definitions, however, though undoubtedly helpful, are of limited use: machines break down in particular contexts, and as a result of the particular uses they are put to. The possible contexts, and the kinds of machine use, are, potentially, so diverse that they cannot be fully anticipated (Tsoukas 1996: 19). Having to interact with the outside world, a technician is forced to adapt his/her knowledge to local contexts—to undertake situated action which compels him/her to partially revise his/her plans and the rules he/she is working with. To put it more generally, the carrying out of an organizational activity involves simultaneously the existence of certain generic rules containing a canonical image of the activity to be carried out (i.e. 'If X happens, do Y, in circumstances Z') *and* the non-canonical, particularistic practices of the actors involved in it, which are consequences of the inherent open-endedness of the context within which organizational action takes place.

Interaction with the outside world is conducive to altering established organizational meanings because of the 'prototype' (or 'radial)' structure of categories organizational members work with (Johnson 1993; Lakoff 1987; Lakoff and Johnson 1999). The classical theory of category structure postulates that categories (or concepts) are exhaustively defined by a list of features, which all members of a category must possess. According to this view, categories have no internal structure: 'since every member must possess all of the features on the list that define the category, there is nothing in the structure of the category that could differentiate one member from another. They are all equally in the category' (Johnson 1993: 78). However, as Rosch's pioneering research has shown, there is a great deal of structure to a category (Rosch and Lloyd 1978). Some members are more centrally placed in—are more representative of—a category than others. For example, robins are more central to our understanding of the category 'bird' than ostriches are. A woman who gave birth to a child, nurtured him/her, supplied half the genes to him/her, is married to the child's father, and is a generation older than the child is more representative of the category 'mother' than a stepmother or a surrogate mother (Lakoff 1987: 83). Categories, in other words, are radially structured: there is a stable core in a category, consisting of prototypical members, which accounts for the stability with which the category is often applied. However, there is also an unstable part, consisting of non-prototypical members, which accounts for the potential change in a category, which its situated application may bring about (more about this later).

What explains the stable core that exists in most categories, and what do we do with the non-prototypical cases that are not part of the stable core? According to Lakoff (1987) and Johnson (1993), categories cannot be understood in themselves—they have no essence. Rather, they derive their meaning from the broader web of background assumptions, experiences, and understandings shared in a culture. As Johnson (ibid. 90) remarks, 'the fact that there is a core to [a] concept is not typically a result of properties alleged to be inherent in the concept, but, instead, it is a result of continuity within the social background of a culture's shared experience by virtue of which the concept can mean what it does'. In other words, concept stability is conditional upon the stability of the cognitive models shared within a culture. We agree, for example, on what constitutes 'lying' in so far as we share the same background understandings and are thus able to easily and non-controversially recognize 'lies'. Alongside such prototypical cases, however, there are non-prototypical ones (e.g. white lies, social lies, official lies, oversimplifications, jokes, mistakes) where we are not sure, in varying degrees, as to whether they are 'lies' and how to assess them (ibid. 91–8).

Non-prototypical members of a category are variants of the stable core; they are 'imaginative extensions' (ibid. 100) that are not generated from the stable core by general rules but instead are generated 'by convention and must be learned one by one' (Lakoff 1987: 91). The indeterminacy of extension does not indicate arbitrariness. We are still able to make intelligent judgements about problematic cases, because we can understand in what ways they diverge from the conditions of prototypicality. Making such judgements involves an imaginative projection of a category beyond prototypical cases to marginal ones. Indeed, applications of a particular concept in non-prototypical cases have the potential for extending the radius of application of the concept, thus transforming it.

Take, for example, the case of a statute banning the use of wheeled vehicles in parks. While we all certainly know the cases to which this statute non-controversially applies (i.e. prototypical cases), there is 'a penumbra of debatable cases in which words are neither obviously applicable nor obviously ruled out' (Hart 1958: 593). For instance, would roller skates be included in the ban? What about toy cars? Applying the statute in such non-prototypical cases, a judge is not simply unpacking the category of 'wheeled vehicles', sorting out cases to fixed categories; rather he/she partially determines the law by putting forward an evaluation (Hart 1958; Johnson 1993).

More generally, the application of a concept is always a *normative* act in so far as it presupposes background knowledge, which is inherently value-laden (Taylor 1985). For example, in the case of the ban on wheeled vehicles in the park, there is a host of background assumptions concerning the purposes parks serve for us, what are the standards of proper behaviour in parks, etc. Similarly, as Tsoukas and Vladimirou (2001) found in their case study of call centre operators working in the customer-services department of a mobile-telecommunications company, in deciding the length to which operators should go to answer customers' enquiries was not a matter of mere 'application' of given company rules and guidelines but of active determination of those rules *in practice*—an imaginative extension of company rules in marginal cases. Additional acts of 'normation or evaluation' (Hare, cited in Johnson 1993: 89) are required to decide what counts as 'good customer service' on certain occasions. Such acts further transform the existing company rules and guidelines.

To summarize, most categories (or concepts) are *radially* structured. They have a stable part made up of prototypical (central) members and an unstable part made up of non-prototypical (peripheral, marginal) members radiating out at various conceptual distances from the central members. Conceptual stability comes from the prototype structure of categories *and* the stability of the background assumptions and understandings that define a communal practice. All this makes it possible for us to talk about clear and unproblematic cases in which we know what to do. Patterns of action stemming from acting on central cases tend to be stable. But the stability of action is precarious. The world also throws at us peripheral cases in which we are, in varying degrees, puzzled as to what to do and how to respond. Organizational ethnographers have shown that such cases are far from rare—in fact, even routine actions are quite likely to have an element of indeterminacy; hence their susceptibility to change (Feldman 2000; Orr 1996). As a result of the radial (or prototype) structure of categories, there is an intrinsic indeterminacy when organizational members interact with the world—hence the potential for change. Responding to non-prototypical (peripheral) cases requires imaginative extension beyond central cases to peripheral ones (Johnson 1993; Lakoff 1987).

But there is a second reason why definitional control of organizational representations is limited. As well as interacting with the outside world, humans have the intrinsic ability to interact with their own thoughts and, therefore, to draw new distinctions, imagine new things, and employ metaphor, metonymy, and mental imagery (Lakoff 1987; Rorty 1989, 1991). Maturana (1980) and Foerster (1984) have argued that the new comes about as a result of a process of recursive application of descriptions. In Maturana's and Foerster's view (1980: 50–1; 1984: 46–9), we humans operate in the cognitive domain; that is, a domain within which we interact with our own descriptions (e.g. thoughts) as if they were independent entities (see Popper 1986: 180–93 for a similar argument). Such interactions give rise to further descriptions with which we subsequently interact in an endlessly recursive manner. (For Maturana and Foerster this is possible because of the nature of the human nervous system, but this need not concern us here.) New descriptions (i.e. new understandings) are the result of the intrinsically human ability to be reflexive—to reflect on one's behaviour, as an observer.

Of course, both at the individual and collective levels of analysis, whether such ability will be exercised is a contingent matter. For example, for some social theorists what differentiates modernity from previous epochs is its pervasive reflexivity—'the susceptibility of most respects of social activity, and material relations with nature, to chronic revision in the light of new information or knowledge' (Giddens 1991: 20; see also Beck, Giddens, and Lash 1994). In other words, in modern societies it is more likely than in other kinds of societies for people to exercise their inherent capacity for reflexive thinking and, thus, to change their behaviours. Likewise, in some organizations reflexivity is more encouraged and, therefore, more likely to be encountered than in others (Argyris 1992). In other words, reflexivity requires certain conditions for it to flourish, although detailing those conditions would be beyond the scope of this chapter.

From the preceding analysis it follows that organizational closure is only temporarily established, because of the inevitability of *human interactions*—interactions with oneself and interactions with others (both individuals and objects). Although treated here as analytically distinct, in real life both kinds of interactions tend to be interwoven. Individuals often interact with others and with themselves at the same time: they undertake action while being mindful of earlier patterns of actions. In this view, actors are conceived as webs of beliefs and habits of action that keep re-weaving (and thus altering) as they try coherently to accommodate new experiences, which come from new interactions over time (Rorty 1991: 93–110). The human ability for re-flexivity and reinterpretation, and the radial structure of categories render an actor's web of beliefs continually reconfigurable. Even if, *in extremis*, new experiences are not obtained, actors can always reflect on their old stock of experiences and rearrange them, thus generating new patterns of meaning. As Berger (1963: 70) noted some time ago, 'memory itself is a reiterated act of interpretation. As we remember the past, we reconstruct it in accordance with our present ideas of what is important and what is not'. Actors' re-weaving may be minimal, such as, for example, in instances of single-loop learning or Weick's 'embellishments' (1998). Alternatively, it may be maximal, such as when entirely new ways of doing things emerge, through metaphorical re-description (Lakoff 1987; Rorty 1989: 3–22). In either case, change there is , the web is reconfigured and change is brought about.

Illustrations

Feldman (2000) provides an illustration of how interactions potentially alter established categories in her study of organizational routines in a student-housing department of a large US state university. One of her vignettes is that of the damage-assessment routine, itself part of the broader routine of closing the halls of residence at the end of the academic year. In carrying out the damage-assessment routine, building directors became increasingly uncomfortable because 'the routine simply placed them in the role of simply procuring funds and did not allow them to act as educators with respect to this one aspect of the job' (ibid. 620). Falling short of the building directors' ideals of primarily being educators and secondarily collectors of repair bills (borne out of frustration with having to interact with students' parents and their parents' secretaries in order to collect repair bills, thus allowing students to 'get off lightly' without taking personal responsibility for damage they had done to their rooms), building directors gradually changed the routine to reflect their new self-understanding. This is clearly a case in which performing the routine, namely having to interact with others in the context of carrying out the routine, and reflecting on the purpose the routine has been serving generate new experiences which actors need to accommodate, thereby re-forming, modifying, transforming the routine.

Feldman's second vignette—the moving-in routine—is even more revealing, because it shows how interactions within an increasingly wider context may generate non-prototypical cases, which are dealt with by extending the categories applied to prototypical cases. The moving-in routine consisted of a set of guidelines to staff and students concerning students' move into the halls of residence at the beginning of the academic year. Initially, the housing department announced the three moving-in days to students, leaving it to each hall of residence to handle the move-in in its own way. However, long queues, traffic jams, and angry students and parents caused the housing department to change the routine. Now a central administrator would coordinate with the city police department to change traffic flows, and a set of rules was announced concerning the logistics of the move-in (e.g. cars were given thirty minutes to unload in front of a hall of residence, parking arrangements were made, etc). Once these changes were in place, housing staff turned their attention to further refinements. Vendors selling carpets and other things to students, who had traditionally sold their wares in the lobbies and just outside halls of residence, were given a special small area. Furthermore, when, unexpectedly, one year, the sports department scheduled the first home fixture on the first day of the move-in, the routine was in trouble. An accommodation had to be reached and the routine had to change so that, from now on, it would include coordination with the sports department.

Notice the pattern. Rather than having the move-in routine algorithmically applied year after year in a stable and unchanging manner, it kept being refined and modified in practice on an ongoing basis in order to handle new problems, offer a better service, take advantage of new opportunities—in short, to accommodate new experiences. As Feldman (ibid. 618) remarks: 'Clearly Housing had extended its outreach schema. The first outreach was to the city officials and had resulted in closed streets. [The] new outreach was to the athletic department, and we can assume involved increased communication with the athletic department about such things as football schedules'. The move-in routine was initially about students simply moving into their halls of residence within a certain period. That was a prototypical case—clear enough in its application. When problems with traffic jams and long queues cropped up, were they the housing department's problems too? Should housing have tried to accommodate the vendors, and when the sports department made a decision that threatened to subvert the rationale of the move-in process, should the housing department have been concerned about it as well? Notice what we are getting at: accommodating the vendors, handling traffic jams, and fitting a football game into the move-in process are non-prototypical cases calling for an imaginative extension of current policies designed to handle the prototypical case of simply letting students into the halls. Confronted with experience, in an open-ended world, the routine gradually changed, extended its reach, and provided opportunities for further changes. With every change the notion of what was possible expanded and new levels of expectations were established (ibid. 621).

The benefit of the preceding analysis is that it enables us to see through the façade of organizational stability to the underlying reality of ongoing change. Organizations are in a state of perpetual becoming, since situated action in them is inherently creative (Tenkasi and Boland 1993): established categories and practices are potentially on the verge of turning into something different to enable new experiences to be accommodated. For some scholars, such an image of pervasive change is an inherent characteristic of social and economic change at large (North 1996; Sztompka 1993). As economic historian North (ibid. 346) remarks: 'economic change is a ubiquitous, ongoing, incremental process that is a consequence of the choices individual actors and entrepreneurs of organizations make every day'. What is interesting to note in North's statement is his view of the very *ordinariness* of economic change. There is no object as such which undergoes change; there are, instead, choices, actions, decisions, and people ordinarily going about their businesses (March 1981). Change is all there is. As Bergson would have put it, the indivisible continuity of change is what constitutes economic reality.

The argument for organizational becoming finds strong support in the recent work of several organizational ethnographers. Orr's insightful study (1996) was mentioned earlier. Orlikowski's (1996) studies are another excellent case. In her study of the customer-support department (CSD) of a software company Orlikowski has shown how the introduction of an information system for tracking customer calls (the incident-tracking support system) provided the stimulus for the emergence of a stream of events and actions, several of which were unanticipated, over time. This happened as specialists and managers attempted to cope with the everyday contingencies, breakdowns, opportunities, and unanticipated outcomes in the use of the ITSS, and improvised techniques and norms for its effective incorporation into their working practices. Orlikowski documents in detail the appropriation of the ITSS by CSD members, as well as the adaptations and adjustments they enacted over time as they tried to incorporate the ITSS into their working practices. Orlikowski shows organizational change to be 'an ongoing improvisation enacted by organizational actors trying to make sense of and act coherently in the world' (ibid. 65).

Finally, it is worth noting that the view of change suggested here helps us understand better the process of jazz improvisation discussed by Barrett (1998), Hatch (1999), and Weick (1998), without, at the same time, reifying it. In the case of jazz, improvisation is the process of a jazz musician adjusting his/her music in response to his/her own earlier music and/or to the music played by others. It is the effort to accommodate new experiences which is the key to improvisation, rather than the conscious effort to be creative. In that sense, improvisation (hence, change) is just as much an inherent feature of the activity of a photocopier-repair technician (Orr 1996), or a ship navigator (Hutchins 1993), as it is of a jazz musician (Barrett 1998; Hatch 1999; Weick 1998). The degree to which improvisation is empirically manifested is a function of the degree to which organizational members are involved in *inter-actions*—interactions with themselves and with others (individuals and objects).

Conclusions and Implications

As should be clear by now, the argument advanced in this chapter owes a lot to the insights of process philosophers and ethnomethodologists. The latter in particular have long emphasized the local (or situated) character of human agency and the importance of social interaction as a primary locus of social order (Boden 1994: 35, 36; Wenger 1998). As Boden (1994: 1) remarks, 'organizations are taken to be locally organized and interactionally achieved contexts of decision-making and of enduring institutional momentum'. Human agency, that is the actions and inactions of social actors, is '*always* and at *every moment* confronted with specific conditions and choices' (ibid. 13, emphasis in the original). Those conditions are not just given but are locally made relevant (or irrelevant) by actors. Organizational categories and rules are constantly adjusted, modified, or even ignored in the carrying out of actual organizational tasks. What is so distinctive about the ethnomethodological approach to organizations, which makes it particularly well suited to the argument advanced in this chapter, is its insistence on capturing the dynamism and ever mutating character of organizational life. Organizational phenomena are not treated as entities, as accomplished events, but as enactments—unfolding processes involving actors making choices interactively, in inescapably local conditions, by drawing on broader rules and resources. In Boden's words (ibid. 42): 'What looks—from outside—like behavior controlled by rules and norms is actually a delicate and dynamic series of interactionally located adjustments to a continual unfolding and working out of "just what" is going on and being made to go on, which is to say, the organizing of action'. To put it briefly, organizations do not simply work; they are *made* to work.

With these ethnomethodological insights in mind, we have argued here that organizations are sites within which human action takes place. Drawing on institutionalized categories, which (as discussed earlier) are radially structured, organizational members make their behaviours more predictable. However, in so far as organizational members try reflectively to adapt those radially structured categories to local conditions, they cannot help but modify them, minimally or maximally. Minimal modification occurs when action involves dealing with more-or-less prototypical cases, whereas maximal modification occurs when action involves dealing with non-prototypical ones. When actors respond to non-prototypical cases (as, for example, Feldman's housing staff did) that are encountered in an open-ended world, they imaginatively extend the radius of application of an organizational category, thus changing it. In that sense, change is immanent *in* organizations: in carrying out their tasks, actors are compelled to interact with the outside world and, thus, to accommodate new experiences; and actors, having the inherent ability to be reflexive, are prone to drawing new distinctions and making fresh metaphorical connections. Action in an open-ended world is potentially creative, in so far as individuals need to improvise (i.e. to re-weave their webs of beliefs and their habits of action) to act coherently.

From a practical point of view, however, as James (1909/96: 247) acknowledged, 'sensible reality is too concrete to be entirely manageable'; we need to abstract it, to harness its fluidity and concreteness to our conceptual systems in order to act systematically on it. It is, therefore, not only the case that change is immanent in organizations but also the case that change is channelled, guided, led—in short, is *organizational* change. Notice the double meaning of 'organization(s)' here: *organizations* are sites of continuously changing human action; and *organization* is the making of form, the patterned unfolding of human action. Organization in the form of institutionalized categories is an input into human action, while in the form of emerging pattern it is an outcome of it; organization aims at stemming change, but in the process of doing so it is generated by it.

Orlikowski's, Orr's, and Weick's work (1996; 1996; 1998) enables us empirically to appreciate both the ongoing character of *change in organizations* and the emergence of *organization*. Orr's repair technicians improvise as they go about their work. Orlikowski's specialists enact ongoing situated accommodations, adaptations, and alterations in response to previous variations, while anticipating future ones. Jazz musicians constantly improvise as they listen to themselves and to each other. Change, in other words, is not an exceptional or special activity individuals undertake, as one might be tempted to think from the perspective of stability. On the contrary, as March (1981: 564) has so aptly remarked, 'change takes place because most of the time most people in an organization do about what they are supposed to do; that is they are intelligently attentive to their environments and jobs'. At the same time, all this flow of tinkering, experimenting, and adapting is not incoherent. On the contrary, it is patterned as a result of individuals closely *interrelating* their actions with those of others (Weick and Roberts 1993). The organization (i.e. a pattern) emerges as situated accommodations become heedfully interrelated in time.

The above does not at all imply that all organizational change is endogenously generated. To be precise, if the main thrust of our argument is accepted, the very distinction between endogenously and exogenously generated change collapses (cf. Barrett et al., 1995: 367). Of course, organizations routinely respond to external influences (hence they have to change), be they competitive pressures, takeovers and mergers, government regulations, technological changes, personnel turnover, members' personal trajectories. However, *how* organizations respond is endogenously conditioned, and it cannot be fully anticipated. There is a world out there which causes the organization to respond, but the pattern of response depends on an organization's self-understanding—the historically created assumptions and interpretations of itself and its environment (Barrett et al. 1995; Granovetter 1992: 49–50; Morgan 1997: 253–61; Tsoukas and Papoulias 1996: 857). Moreover, an organization's response to an exogenously generated pressure over time is complex, multi-layered and evolving, rather than simple, fixed, and episodic. What our approach highlights is the ethnomethodological insight that 'social order is organized *from within*' (Boden 1994: 46; emphasis in the original), and that what is interesting to explore is what, how, where, with whom, and why particular aspects of an organization's self-understanding are *made relevant* in concrete situations, over time.

For example, to return to an illustration discussed earlier, Orlikowski and Hofman (1997) have described the case of the customer-services department (CSD) at Zeta, one of the top fifty software companies in the world, which introduced a new incident-tracking supprt system (ITSS), based on the Lotus Notes groupware technology, to help it improve the way it tracked and generally handled customers' problems. Such a technological change was deemed necessary because of the antiquated nature of the existing tracking system, advances in groupware technology, and management's desire to offer a better customer service. Notice how change here is both exogenously *and* endogenously generated. Changes in the environment put pressure on management to improve the customer service, but it was also management's receptivity to, and appreciation of, those changes that ultimately determined the precise organizational response. As Orlikowski and Hofman (ibid. 19) perceptively point out, this cannot always be assumed. Management may rationalize problems, defer decisions, or simply pay lip service to change (Argyris 1990, 1992; Johnson and Scholes 1997: 75–6).

However, this is not the end of the story. After the groupware technology was introduced and people began to *experience* it, they also started appreciating its capabilities and imagining new possibilities for it. What from the outside could be seen as a mere episode of technical change, whereby one tracking system replaces another, became, from the perspective of ongoing change, an increasing momentum, a flow of opportunity-driven choices, and unanticipated changes. For example, to leverage the ITSS's capabilities managers introduced a change in the structure of the department; now having a much better idea of how CSD specialists went about their work, managers expanded the evaluation criteria to include work-in-progress documentation; further changes were introduced in the CSD when specialists began to realize that they could use the information generated by ITSS to train newcomers (Orlikowski and Hofman 1997).

However, this series of ongoing changes, several of which were emergent and opportunity-based as the system was put into action, does not occur only when 'the technology being implemented is new, [...] open-ended and customizable', as Orlikowski and Hofman (ibid. 18) argue, although clearly such technologies invite further modifications, customization, and local adaptation. Ongoing change and improvisation is a fundamental feature of all change programmes. Barrett et al. (1995), for example, described the introduction of total quality (TQ) in the computer and telecommunication command of the US Navy in the early 1990s. Their analysis shows how even in a machine bureaucracy, such as the Navy, a change programme acquires its own momentum and is continually modified and adapted by those involved in it. Rather than a change programme such as the introduction of TQ changing something specific in an anticipated way, it actually opens up possibilities for ongoing changes, some anticipated and some not. Notice how Barrett et al. (ibid. 367) describe the unfolding of changes made possible by the TQ programme:

When an enlisted person at the telecommunications command hears that he or she is encouraged to offer suggestions for process improvements, he or she may interpret this as an opportunity to make suggestions about the work schedule and ask that the organization consider a flex time program. (Or it might trigger nothing at all.) As others discuss or ignore the suggestion as useful or irrelevant, members begin to extend various versions of process improvement: Perhaps it is now legitimate to suggest changes in task design without fear of jumping the chain of command.

There is a common thread in both preceding illustrations: change programmes trigger ongoing change; they provide the discursive resources for making certain things possible, although what exactly will happen remains uncertain when a change programme is initiated—it must first be experienced before the possibilities it opens up are appreciated and taken up (if they are taken up). Change programmes are *made* to work and, in so far as this happens, they are locally adapted, improvised, and elaborated by human agents; institutionalized categories are imaginatively extended when put into action.

If this is accepted, what is, then, the meaning of 'planned change'? For several theorists focusing on change at the level of the organization (as opposed to populations of organizations or organizational fields) change has been taken to mean that which occurs as a consequence of deliberate managerial action. In the argument put forward here, such a view is limited (cf. Orlikowski and Hofman 1997). Although managers certainly aim at changing established ways of thinking and acting through implementing particular plans, nonetheless change in organizations occurs without necessarily intentional managerial action, as a result of individuals trying to accommodate new experiences and realize new possibilities. On the view suggested here, an excessive preoccupation with planned change risks failing to recognize the *always already changing* texture of organizations.

What is, then, the role of managerial intentionality? To paraphrase Wittgenstein (1958), managers need to clear their vision in order to *see* what is going on and, at the same time, help fashion a coherent and desirable *pattern* out of what is going on. As Burgelman (1983, 1988), Frohman (1997) and Kanter (1983), among others, have shown, change in organizations often occurs locally when certain individuals reflect on their circumstances and experiences, and decide to intervene in order to change organizational policies and systems. Whether local changes are amplified and become institutionalized depends on the 'structural context', created to a large extent, as Burgelman (1983) has convincingly demonstrated, by senior managers. Looking at change from within, managers need to be attentive to the historically shaped interpretative codes (i.e. the discursive template) underlying organizational practices, and how such codes and the associated practices mutate over time as a result of individuals' attempting to cope with new experiences. In short, managers need to refine their sensitivity in order to be able to *perceive* subtle differences.

From this view, deliberate intervention acquires a new meaning. It is not so much focusing on the realization of a particular change plan as intended, as seeing the change plan as a new discursive template—a set of new interpretative codes—which enables a novel way of talking and acting. A new discursive template such as, for example, the introduction of TQ in the US Navy works *recursively*: it allows some of the *already ongoing changes* to be amplified, thus reinforcing the new set of interpretative codes, which, in turn, are likely to further facilitate novel practices (Barrett et al. 1995; Keeney, 1983). Whereas within the old discursive template junior officers' ideas and suggestions were bureaucratically handled (e.g. they would be channelled in a very time-consuming and frustrating manner through the chain of command), after the launch of TQ it was discursively possible for junior officers to attach different attributions to talk about their suggestions (Barrett et al. 1995:363). Whereas before unsolicited suggestions tended to be viewed as nuisance and a bypassing of the chain of command, now they have gained legitimacy as a part of 'participation' and 'continuous improvement'—two key values (interpretative codes) in the new TQ discourse. At the very minimum such practices cannot be frowned upon as easily as before.

Moreover, for the first time it became possible for junior officers to discuss the manner in which 'upper management looks at ideas' (ibid.). That was not possible before, because 'looking at ideas' was not part of the discursive template in the Navy and, therefore, was not thought to be part of upper management's job. Through upholding the values of 'empowerment', 'participation', and 'continuous improvement', the new discursive template of TQ provided certain junior officers with the resources to reinterpret their experiences, and furnished a common language to enable individuals heedfully to interrelate their actions. Junior officers in the Navy always put forward suggestions, always adapted orders received to their local circumstances, but it was only after the introduction of TQ and its associated new discourse that such subtle changes were brought into focus, were amplified, and earned legitimacy.

According to the approach adopted here, managerial interventions are not external to the organization, but are another locally realized act expressed in language. A manager is as much an agent of change as everybody else is, the only important difference being that a manager is endowed with 'declarative powers' (Taylor and Van Every 2000: 143). The power to 'declare' is to be institutionally empowered to bring about 'a change in the world by representing it as having been changed' (Searle 1998: 150). In other words, a new state of affairs is created by the successful carrying out of a declarative statement (e.g., 'You are fired', 'You do this', 'We will buy this system', 'We will adopt this reward system') (Searle 1995: 34). Being endowed with declarative powers, managers are ex officio in a privileged position to introduce a new discursive template that will make it possible for organizational members to notice new things, make fresh distinctions, see new connections, and have novel experiences, which they will seek to accommodate by re-weaving their webs of beliefs and desires (Morgan 1997: 263–70; Weick and Quinn 1999: 380). However, seen from the perspective of ongoing change, the introduction of a new discursive template is only the beginning of the journey of change or, to be more precise, it is a punctuation of the flow of organizational life. As the illustrations of Zeta and the Navy show, managerial intentions are best understood as an author's text, which is interpreted and further reinterpreted by those it addresses, depending on the interpretative codes and the local circumstances of its addressees.

If the argument advanced in this chapter is accepted, namely if change is indeed an ongoing process in organizations, how can it be squared with what is known about organizational inertia and resistance to change? As has been well documented by relevant research, organizational routines, systems, and strategies tend to persist, even when there is strong evidence that they should change (Argyris 1990, 1992; Cyert and March 1963; Hannan and Freeman 1984; Levitt and March 1988; Miller 1982, 1993). Our argument in this chapter has been that there are ongoing processes of change *in* organizations. That, however, should not be taken to mean that *organizations* constantly change. The local initiatives, improvisations, and modifications individuals engage in may go unrecognized; opportunities may not be officially taken up, imaginative extensions may not break through existing organizational culture—in short, local adaptations may never become institutionalized (Goodman and Dean 1982). If we focus our attention only on what becomes institutionalized, an approach largely assumed by synoptic accounts of organizational change, we risk missing all the subterranean, microscopic changes that always go on in the depths of organizations, changes which may never acquire the status of formal organizational systems and routines, but are no less important.

As Wittgenstein might have argued, the source of the confusion that 'change in organizations' may be taken necessarily to mean 'organizational change' is language—the expression 'organizational change' is used to refer to both phenomena. Organizations are both sites of continuously changing human action (hence our argument that to the extent that individuals try to accommodate new experiences change occurs constantly in organizations) *and* sets of institutionalized categories (hence the organizational inertia and resistance to change several researchers have documented). The statement 'organizations tend to resist change' is a shorthand expression for saying that change initiatives, either locally or centrally undertaken, remain 'improvisations' or plans, without becoming institutionalized. If, however, we were to take an ethnographic look at what is really going on *in* organizations, as Barley (1986), Boden (1994), Feldman (2000), and Orlikowski (1996) have done, we would most probably see some sort of Brownian motion taking place, with actors constantly re-weaving their webs of beliefs and actions in order to accommodate new experiences. It is because the human mind is not like a computer that human *experiences* are cognitively significant, and the accommodation of new experiences is a practically important task (Reed 1996; Tenkasi and Boland 1993; Varela, Thompson, and Rosch 1991). Whether the re-weaving of individual webs of beliefs and habits of action leads to microscopic changes becoming *organizational* is a different issue. It may or may not happen, or, to be more precise, the extent to which it happens is an interesting topic for empirical research and further theoretical development.

In the view proposed here, organization scientists need to give theoretical priority to *microscopic* change. As, we hope, has been shown in this chapter, such change occurs naturally, incrementally, and inexorably through 'creep', 'slippage', and 'drift', as well as natural 'spread'. It is subtle, agglomerative, often subterranean, heterogeneous, and often surprising. It spreads like a patch of oil. Microscopic change takes place by adaptation, variations, restless expansion, and opportunistic conquests. Microscopic change reflects the actual becoming of things (Chia 1999). Looking at change in organizations from within, that is noticing how organizational members re-weave their webs of beliefs and habits of action in response to local circumstances and new experiences, and how managers influence and intervene in the stream of organizational actions, is a perspective organizational scientists must take if they are determined to convey a sense of the organizational flow. Needless to say, capturing and making sense of the cognitive, political, and cultural dynamics of such a process of organizational becoming is extremely important (Pettigrew 1992). For this to happen we need to see organizations both as quasi-stable structures (i.e. sets of institutionalized categories) *and* as sites of human action in which, through the ongoing agency of organizational members, organization emerges.

References

Argyris, C. (1990), *Overcoming Organizational Defenses* (Boston: Allyn and Bacon).

—— (1992), *On Organizational Learning* (Oxford: Blackwell).

Barley, S. (1986), 'Technology as an Occasion for Structuring: Evidence from Observations of CT Scanners and the Social Order of Radiology Departments', *Administrative Science Quarterly*, 31: 78–108.

—— (1990), 'The Alignment of Technology and Structure Through Roles and Networks', *Administrative Science Quarterly*, 35: 61–103.

Barrett, F. J. (1998), 'Creativity and Improvisation in Jazz and Organizations: Implications for Organizational Learning', *Organization Science*, 9: 605–22.

—— Thomas, G. F., and Hocevar, S. P. (1995), The Central Role of Discourse in Large-scale Change: A Social Construction Perspective', *Journal of Applied Behavioral Science*, 31: 352–72.

Bateson, G. (1979), *Mind and Nature* (Toronto: Bantam).

Beck, U., Giddens, A., and Lash, S. (1994), *Reflexive modernization* (Cambridge: Polity).

Beer, M., and Nohria, N. (2000), 'Cracking the Code of Change', *Harvard Business Review*, 78 (May–June), 133–41.

Beer, S. (1981), *Brain of the firm* (Chichester: Wiley).

Berger, P. (1963), *Invitation to Sociology* (London: Penguin).

—— and Luckmann, T. (1966), *The Social Construction of Reality* (London: Penguin).

Bergson, H. (1946), *The Creative Mind* (New York: Carol).

Boden, D. (1994), *The Business of Talk* (Cambridge: Polity).

Boulding, K. (1987), 'The Epistemology of Complex Systems', *European Journal of Operational Research*, 30: 110–16.

Brown, J. S., and Duguid, P. (1991), 'Organizational Learning and Communities of Practice: Towards a Unified View of Working, Learning, and Innovation', *Organization Science*, 2: 40–57.

Brown, S. L., and Eisenhardt, K. M. (1997), 'The Art of Continuous Change: Linking Complexity Theory and Time-paced Evolution in Relentlessly Shifting Organizations', *Administrative Science Quarterly*, 42: 1–34.

Burgelman, R. A. (1983), 'A Process Model of Internal Corporate Venturing in the Diversified Major Firm', *Administrative Science Quarterly*, 28: 223–44.

—— (1988), 'Strategy Making as a Social Learning Process: The Case of Internal Corporate Venturing', *Interfaces*, 18: 74–85.

Chia, R. (1999), 'A "Rhizomic" Model of Organizational Change and Transformation: Perspective From a Metaphysics of Change', *British Journal of Management*, 10: 209–27.

Choi, T. Y. (1995), 'Conceptualizing Continuous Improvement: Implications for Organizational Change', *Omega*, 23: 607–24.

Cyert, R. M., and March, J. G. (1963), *A Behavioral Theory of the Firm* (Englewood Cliffs, NJ: Prentice Hall).

Donaldson, L. (1999), *Performance-driven Organizational Change* (Thousand Oaks, Calif.: Sage).

Eccles, R. G., Nohria, N., and Berkley, J. D. (1992), *Beyond the Hype* (Boston, Mass.: Harvard Business School Press).

Feldman, M. (2000), 'Organizational Routines as a Source of Continuous Change', *Organization Science*, 11(6): 611–29.

Foerster, H. (1984), 'On Constructing a Reality', in P. Watzlawick (ed.), *The Invented Reality* (New York: Norton), 41–61.

Ford, J. D. and Ford, L. W. (1994), 'Logics of Identity, Contradiction, and Attraction in Change', *Academy of Management Review*, 19: 756–85.

—— (1995), 'The Roles of Conversations in Producing Intentional Change in Organizations', *Academy of Management Review*, 20: 541–70.

Frohman, A. L. (1997), 'Igniting Organizational Change from Below: The Power of Personal Initiative', *Organizational Dynamics*, 25: 39–53.

Giddens, A. (1991), *Modernity and Self-identity* (Cambridge: Polity).

Goodman, P. S., and Dean, J. W. (1982), 'Creating Long-term Organizational Change', in P. S. Goodman (ed.), *Change in Organizations* (San Francisco, Calif.: Jossey-Bass), 226–79.

Granovetter, M. (1992), 'Problems of Explanation in Economic Sociology', in N. Nohria and R. G. Eccles (eds.), *Networks and organizations*, (Boston Mass.: Harvard Business School Press), 25–56.

Greenwood, R., and Hinings, C. R. (1996), 'Understanding Radical Organizational Change: Bringing Together the Old and New Institutionalism', *Academy of Management Review*, 21(4): 1022–54.

Hannan, M. T., and Freeman, J. (1984), 'Structural Inertia and Organizational Change', *American Sociological Review*, 49: 149–64.

Hart, H. L. A. (1958), 'Positivism and the Separation of Law and Morals', *Harvard Law Review*, 71: 593–629.

Hatch, M. J. (1999), 'Exploring the Empty Spaces of Organizing: How Improvisational Jazz Helps Redescribe Organizational Structure', *Organization Studies*, 20: 75–100.

Hutchins, E. (1993), 'Learning to Navigate', in S. Chaiklin and J. Lave (eds.), *Understanding practice* (Cambridge: Cambridge University Press), 35–63.

James, W. (1909/96), *A Pluralistic Universe*, (Lincoln, Nebr.: University of Nebraska Press).

Johnson, G., and Scholes, K. (1997), *Exploring Corporate Strategy*, 4th edn. (London: Prentice Hall).

Johnson, M. (1993), *Moral Imagination* (Chicago, Ill.: University of Chicago Press).

Kanter, R. M. (1983), *The Change Masters* (New York: Touchstone).

Keeney, B. P. (1983), *Aesthetics of Change* (New York: Guilford).

Lakoff, G. (1987), *Women, Fire, and Dangerous Things* (Chicago, Ill.: University of Chicago Press).

—— and Johnson, M. (1999), *Philosophy in the Flesh*, (New York: Basic).

Lee, R. M. (1984), Bureaucracies, Bureaucrats, and Information Technology, *European Journal of Operational Research*, 18: 293–303.

Levitt, B. and March, J. G. (1988), 'Organizational Learning', *Annual Review of Sociology*, 14: 319–40.

Lewin, K. (1951), *Field Theory in Social Science*, (New York: Harper & Row).

March, J. (1981), 'Footnotes to Organizational Change', *Administrative Science Quarterly*, 26: 563–77.

Marshak, R. J. (1993), 'Lewin Meets Confucius: A Review of the OD Model of Change', *Journal of Applied Behavioral Science*, 29: 393–415.

Maturana, H. (1980), 'Biology of Cognition', in H. Maturana and F. Varela, *Autopoiesis and Cognition* (Dordrecht: Reidel), 5–62.

Miller, D. (1982), 'Evolution and Revolution: A Quantum View of Structural Change in Organizations', *Journal of Management Studies*, 19: 131–51.

—— (1993), 'The Architecture of Simplicity', *Academy of Management Review*, 18: 116–38.

Morgan, G. (1997), *Images of Organization* (Thousand Oaks, Calif.: Sage).

North, D. (1996), 'Epilogue: Economic Performance Through Time', in L. J. Alston, T. Eggertsson, and D. North (eds.), *Empirical Studies in Institutional Change* (Cambridge: Cambridge University Press), 342–55.

Orlikowski, W. J. (1996), 'Improvising Organizational Transformation Over Time: A Situated change Perspective', *Information Systems Research*, 7: 63–92.

—— and Hofman, D. J. (1997), 'An Improvisational Model for Change Management: The Case of Groupware Technologies', *Sloan Management Review*, 38: 11–21.

Orr, J. (1990), 'Sharing Knowledge, Celebrating Identity: Community Memory in a Serving Culture', in D. Middleton and D. Edwards (eds.), *Collective Remembering* (London: Sage), 168–89.

—— (1996), *Talking About Machines* (Ithaca, NY: ILR).

Pentland, B. T., and Rueter, H. H. (1994), 'Organizational Routines as Grammars of Action', *Administrative Science Quarterly*, 39; 484–510.

Pettigrew, A. (1992), 'The character and Significance of Strategy Process Research', *Strategic Management Journal*, 13: 5–16.

Popper, K. (1986), *Unended quest.* (London: Flamingo).

Porras, J. I., and Silvers, R. C. (1991), 'Organization Development and Transformation', *Annual Review of Psychology*, 42: 51–78.

Prigogine, I. (1989), 'The Philosophy of Instability', *Futures*, 21: 396–400.

—— I (2000), 'The Future is Not Given, in Society or Nature', *New Perspectives Quarterly*, 17(2): 35–7.

Reed, E. S. (1996), *The Necessity of Experience* (New Haven, Conn.: Yale University Press).

Rescher, N. (1996), *Process Metaphysics* (New York: State University of New York Press).

Roach, D. W. and Bednar, D. A. (1997), 'The Theory of Logical Types: A Tool for Understanding Levels and Types of Change in Organizations', *Human Relations*, 50: 671–99.

Rorty, R. (1989), *Contingency, irony and solidarity* (Cambridge: Cambridge University Press).

—— (1991), *Objectivity, relativism, and truth* (Cambridge: Cambridge University Press).

Rosch, E., and Lloyd, B. B. (1978) (eds.), *Cognition and Categorization* (Hillsdale, NJ: Lawrence Erlbaum).

Sainsbury, R. M. (1988), *Paradoxes* (Cambridge: Cambridge University Press).

Searle, J. R. (1995), *The Construction of Social Reality* (London: Penguin).

—— (1998), *Mind, Language and Society* (New York: Basic).

Shenhav, Y. (1995), 'From Chaos to Systems: The Engineering Foundations of Organization Theory, 1879–1932', *Administrative Science Quarterly*, 40: 557–85.

Shotter, J. (1993), *Conversational Realities* (London: Sage).

Stacey, R. (1996), *Complexity and Creativity in Organizations* (San Francisco, Calif.: Berrett-Koehler).

Sztompka, P. (1993), *The Sociology of Social Change* (Oxford: Blackwell).

Taylor, C. (1985), *Human Agency and Language* (Cambridge: Cambridge University Press).

Taylor, J. R. (1993), *Rethinking the Theory of Organizational Communication* (Norwood, NJ: Ablex).

—— and Van Every, E. J. (2000), *The Emergent Organization* (Mahwah, NJ: Lawrence Erlbaum).

Tenkasi, R. V. and Boland, R. J. (1993), 'Locating Meaning Making in Organizational Learning: The Narrative Basis of Cognition', *Research in Organizational Change and Development*, 7: 77–103.

Toulmin, S. (1990), *Cosmopolis* (Chicago, Ill: University of Chicago Press).

Trist, E. L., Higgin, G. W., Murray, H., and Pollock, A. B. (1963), *Organizational Choice* (London: Tavistock).

Tsoukas, H. (1996), 'The Firm as a Distributed Knowledge System: A Constructionist Approach', *Strategic Management Journal*, 17(special winter issue): 11–25.

—— (1998), 'Forms of Knowledge and Forms of Life in Organized Contexts', in R. Chia (ed.), *In the Realm of Organization* (London: Routledge), 43–66.

—— and Papoulias, D. (1996), 'Understanding Social Reforms: A Conceptual Analysis', *Journal of the Operational Research Society*, 47: 853–63.

—— and Vladimirou, E. (2001), 'What is Organizational Knowledge?', *Journal of Management Studies*, 38: 973–93.

Tushman, M., and Romanelli, E. (1985), 'Organizational Evolution: A Metamorphosis Model of Convergence and Reorientation', in L. L. Cummings and B. M. Staw (eds.), *Research in Organizational Behavior*, (Greenwich, Conn.: JAI), 355–89.

Van de Ven, A., and Poole, M. S. (1995), 'Explaining Development and Change in Organizations', *Academy of Management Review*, 20: 510–40.

Varela, F. J., Thompson, E., and Rosch, E. (1991), *The Embodied Mind* (Cambridge, Mass.: MIT Press).

Vickers, G. (1983), *The Art of Judgement* (London: Harper & Row).

Watzlawick, P., Weakland, J., and Fisch, R. (1974), *Change* (New York: Norton).

Weick, K. (1979), *The Social Psychology of Organizing* 2nd edn. (Reading, Mass.: Addison-Wesley).

—— (1993), 'Organization Design as Improvisation', in G. P. Huber and W. H. Glick (eds.), *Organization Change and Redesign* (New York: Oxford University Press), 346–79.

—— (1998), 'Improvisation as a Mindset for Organizational Analysis', *Organization Science*, 9: 543–55.

—— and Roberts, K. (1993), 'Collective Mind in Organizations: Heedful Interrelating on Flight Decks', *Administrative Science Quarterly*, 38: 357–81.

—— and Quinn, R. E. (1999), 'Organizational Change and Development', *Annual Review of Psychology*, 50: 361–86.

Wenger, E. (1998), *Communities of practice* (Cambridge: Cambridge University Press).

Wittgenstein, L. (1958), *Philosophical investigations*, trans. G. E. M. Anscombe (Oxford: Blackwell).

—— (1967), *Zettel*. trans. G. E. M. Anscombe. ed. G. E. M. Anscombe and G. H. von Wright, (Oxford: Blackwell).

NINE

Chaos, Complexity, and Organization Theory

The New Cosmopolis?

A t first glance it might seem odd that organization theory should concern itself with chaos. Since the study of organizational phenomena is its *raison d'être*, it could plausibly be argued that organization theory has very little (if anything) to do with the study of the absence of organization; that is, with the study of disorganization or chaos. Such an argument, however, would not be convincing. Moreover, not only can organization and disorganization not be separated (one presupposes the other—see Cooper 1986); the very concept of disorganization, upon closer inspection, does not make much sense.

If the traffic in London were left to itself, there would be little doubt that it would eventually become a self-regulating system (just as in Cairo and, sometimes, in Athens or Lisbon). The problem in such a case would not be so much disorganization as *undesirable* organization: the traffic patterns which would eventually emerge perhaps would not satisfy most people's criteria of efficiency and fairness, but patterns—organization of some sort—there would be (Vickers 1983: 28–9). Similarly, crime-infested areas in Los Angeles are no more disorderly than Wall Street is: there is only a different kind of order—set up, organized and reproduced by the underworld, which, simply because it is 'under', is no less a 'world'—an organized socio-technical ensemble with its own rules of order. For most people, however, that kind of world is organized to serve the wrong purposes, making use of unacceptable means; it is the wrong kind of order. In other words, as ethnomethodologists keep reminding us (Boden 1994; Garfinkel 1984), social life is de facto organized: we, as sentient beings, have no choice but to organize our world and our actions in it. The interesting questions are how we do it; what we do it for.

An earlier version of this chapter was first published in *Organization*, 5(3) (1998), 291–313. Reprinted by permission of Sage, Copyright (1998).

The reason why the distinctions 'organization versus chaos', 'order versus disorder' have been so firmly entrenched in both lay and social-scientific discourses is that organization and order have been historically identified with classification, generalizability, and predictability. Notice that all of these terms presuppose a subject: someone who classifies, generalizes, predicts. In formal organizations that subject is normally the managerial elite; looking across societies, it has been the hitherto dominant western values through which non-western practices have been described and judged (Bauman 1992: 76–90). In his novel *A Passage to India* Forster (1952) describes, among other things, how 'chaotic' India looked to colonial British administrators, in contrast with how natural (i.e. 'orderly') local customs and practices appeared to the indigenous people. The culturally alien appears, at first sight, incomprehensible and, thus, 'disorganized', 'chaotic' (Said 1995).

The significance of the relatively recent fascination with 'chaos' lies in the growing recognition that organization coexists with surprise; that unpredictability does not imply the absence of order; that recurrence does not exclude novelty. Of course, the fact that these pairs are not mutually exclusive but, quite the contrary, mutually implied, has not escaped the attention of those philosophers and social scientists who are not positivists (Bateson, 1979; Castoriadis 1987, 1991, 1997; Cooper 1986). In organization theory, more specifically, the preceding conceptual oppositions were seriously challenged by Weick's ground-breaking *The Social Psychology of Organizing* (1979) and March and Olsen's insightful *Ambiguity and Choice in Organizations*, (1976), although it is fair to say that mainstream organization theory, at least the kind taught in most organizational behaviour (OB) and organizational theory (OT) textbooks, has been extremely slow in incorporating this new thinking.

What, however, is particularly interesting today is that, thanks to advances in mathematics and the sciences, what was hitherto regarded as marginal in the social sciences now has the chance to move closer to the mainstream. As is so often the case with conceptual and social change, legitimacy is the key that helps explain such a development. To understand why even popular management books nowadays are filled with (mostly simplistic) references to 'chaos', one needs to understand that ever since 'chaos', somewhat unusually, entered the vocabulary of the sciences it is no longer considered eccentric to make systematic use of related concepts in the social sciences. If mathematicians are discovering, as Lorenz did back in 1963, that merely rounding off a set of numbers and feeding them back to very simple equations suffices to generate unpredictability about the outcome, how much stronger is the case for unpredictability in the social realm? If nature turns out to be much less deterministic than we hitherto thought; if equilibrium is far from being the norm in nature; and if new patterns emerge from the iterative interactions of a number of agents on a computer, then perhaps our hitherto mechanistic approach to understanding the messiness we normally associate with the social world may need revising.

Why should advances in the sciences lend credibility to similar advances in the social sciences? There are two reasons. First, for historical reasons. Just as the 'Newtonian style' (Cohen 1994) historically found a large number of imitators in economics and the social sciences, so does the approach of new physics today. The sciences have historically set the tone in intellectual enquiry (Murphy 1995: 157). Second, and perhaps more importantly, there seems to be a fundamental human urge, evidence for which can be traced as far back as the Stoics and beyond, to want to understand both the *cosmos* (nature) and the *polis* (society) as a unified whole—as a *cosmopolis* (Toulmin 1990). The order of nature and the order of society are expressions of a deeper unity of the world (Bateson 1979). Since the seventeenth century such an urge has been expressed in a predominantly Newtonian vocabulary (Shapin 1996): the social order reflects the order of nature which, in turn, reflects the will of God. Social order is stable, predictable, with individuals containing fixed (i.e. 'natural') positions in it. That such an imagery has often been used to legitimate inequality and domination is beyond doubt (Bauman 1992; Toulmin 1990: 194). Such a realization, however, should not lead one to jump to the conclusion that the very ideal of cosmopolis needs to be abandoned—only its Newtonian version.

True, as a political tool, the regulative ideal of cosmopolis—the reflection of Newtonian order in society—has had authoritarian implications, but a different imagery of nature might enter into a feedback loop with a different understanding of society. Indeed, as Toulmin (1990: 175–209) observes, this is what is largely happening today: the softening of conceptions of nature is linked with the softening of conceptions of society. A humanized modernity— an 'ecological cosmopolis', in Toulmin's (ibid. 195) terms—has come to understand itself not so much by looking into the Newtonian mirror, but by seeing itself as part of the broader cosmic pattern. Diversity, change, and adaptability are much more valued today than hierarchy, rigidity, standardization, and uniformity—all of which have been associated with the Newtonian view. In these post-Newtonian times, developments across diverse sites in culture lead one to conclude that intellectual enquiry is driven by the desire to achieve an alternative unified understanding of nature and society ('a new synthesis of mind and matter', as Capra (1996) has subtitled one of his books). Such an understanding tends to be expressed today not in the language of classical physics but in a largely ecosystemic vocabulary (Toulmin 1990: 180–4). Chaos theory should be seen as part of such an emerging new vocabulary (Capra 1996; Cilliers 1998; Prigogine 1997).

From the above it should not be assumed that chaos theory alone has brought about changes in the cultural milieu within which we think today. The picture is more complex. A number of developments after World War II has led to a general awareness of feedback loops, interconnectivity, and non-linear processes (Hayles 1991: 7). The growing importance of information, the spectacular expansion of information and communication technologies, and the rapidly increasing economic and political interdependence in the world have shaped new attitudes, fostered a new language, and, more generally, formed the cultural milieu within which chaos theory has grown. In turn, chaos theory has reinforced that new language and helped shape a certain attitude towards non-linearity, disorder, and noise. At the same time, changes in other sites within western culture have followed a similar path. Post-structuralism, for example, with its emphasis on fragmentation, unpredictability, and the marginal, has also grown out of, and, in turn, reinforced, this general awareness of chaotic processes (Cilliers 1998; Hayles 1990, 1991).

Such an awareness is the reason why it is perhaps better to talk about *chaotics* rather than chaos, since chaotics 'signifies certain attitudes towards chaos that are manifest at diverse sites within the culture, among them poststructuralism and chaos' (Hayles 1991: 7). How such parallel developments and mutual influences have emerged would be an interesting question for sociologists of science to explore. What is important for us, however, is to note that chaotics fosters a new awareness of dynamic processes; it encourages a positive attitude towards unpredictability and novelty; it reconciles order and disorder; and it invites us to rethink the character of human intervention in the social and natural world. Naive rationalism is out; reflexive reason is in.

The Newtonian Style

So far several references have been made to both the Newtonian style and chaotics, but in a general sense; it is time now to define these terms more precisely. What is the Newtonian style? What does it consist of? What has its influence been in the social sciences and in organization theory in particular? While all these questions cannot be answered in detail here, a few important points can be made.

The defining feature of the Newtonian style of thinking is the pursuit of what Toulmin calls the 'decontextualized ideal': the search for the universal, the general, and the timeless (Toulmin 1990: 30–6). Ontologically, a phenomenon is supposed to consist of discrete, objective elements, whose law-like associations the analyst will identify through the construction of an abstract model, for the purpose of predicting and, if possible, controlling the phenomenon at hand. The Newtonian view assumes an objectivist ontology, works with a mechanistic epistemology, and enacts an instrumental praxeology (Tsoukas and Cummings 1997: 656).

The Newtonian style of thinking operates by constructing an idealized world in the form of an abstract model, in order to approximate the complex behaviour of real objects. For example, Newton's laws of motions describe the behaviour of bodies in a frictionless vacuum—a mathematically handy approximation, good enough for several real-life occasions. Moreover, the core of the Newtonian style consists of two assumptions (Murphy 1995: 160). First, the extremal principle; namely, that the objects of study behave in such a way as to optimize the values of certain variables. And, second, prediction is possible by abstracting causal relations from the path-dependence of history. As Mirowski (1984, 1989) has brilliantly shown, neoclassical economics developed by adopting the paradigm of mid-nineteenth-century energy physics.

The Newtonian style of thinking has dominated the development of organization theory. By way of illustration, consider the following two examples. Mintzberg (1979) starts his influential book *The Structuring of Organizations* with a chapter on 'The Essence of structure'. What is the essence of structure? His answer: division of labour and coordination. '*Every organized human activity*', says Mintzberg (ibid. 2), 'gives rise to two fundamental and opposing requirements: the division of labour into various tasks to be performed and the coordination of these tasks to accomplish the activity' (emphasis in the original). Notice the sweeping generalization: 'every organized activity'. That there have been other societies, at other times, for which division of labour and coordination were not focal issues (at least not in the sense they are pressing issues for us moderns today) is never mentioned.

The a-contextual and ahistorical perspective Mintzberg holds on organizations is manifested in his (fictional?) illustration of how Ms Raku, an independent pot maker, gradually builds her business and, as a result, the organization of her firm grows and passes from a simple structure, through a machine bureaucracy, to a divisionalized form. The reader is led to think that it is the endogenous growth of the organization in response to growing market demand that accounts for these organizational forms and the associated coordination mechanisms. The organization responds optimally to the demands placed on it by its economic environment.

Notice the abstraction: nothing is mentioned about Ms Raku's background (an ethnic entrepreneur perhaps, as her surname suggests?); nor is her business situated within a broader societal context—it is as if Ms Raku's firm exists in a social vacuum; nor is the particular path the firm has taken within a particular social, economic, and political milieu ever charted. The divisionalized form succeeds the machine bureaucracy which, in turn, succeeds the simple structure as the optimally adaptive structural forms to suit the firm at its different stages of growth. It is the immanent, atemporal, history-independent logic of organization that accounts for the developmental trajectory of Ms Raku's organization.

However, it is doubtful whether a structural form that seems optimally adaptive is better explained by its current utility rather than by historical processes which pre-adapted it to its current function (Murphy 1995: 168). As Granovetter (1992: 49–50) observes:

Institutions do not typically arise in any simple way as solutions to problems presented in the environment. Rather, ways of doing things begin for reasons that relate to the various purposes of the actors involved and to the structures of relations they are embedded in. Further, economic institutions may seem well matched to their economic environment precisely because they have modified that environment to make it more suitable. Static analysis could not reveal such a process, but would instead see only the good match and jump to the functionalist conclusion that the institution was created by the environmental characteristics.

Mintzberg's account of the development of Ms Raku's firm fails to address questions such as: What are the institutional demands made of the organization? What is the mode of financing its growth, and why? How is its trade union organized (if there is one) and what is its influence? How is the firm's work organization related to the broader issues of, say, trust and authority structures developed in the particular societal context within which Ms Raku's firm is embedded? An analysis motivated by the decontextualized ideal would find it very difficult to give convincing answers to questions such as the above.

Of course, it could be plausibly objected that some simplification is inevitable and that for the purpose of illustrating the importance of division of labour and coordination Mintzberg's example is highly effective, which it is. Such an objection would be valid in terms of its own presuppositions, except that it is those presuppositions that are the problem. If one is in search of timeless and generic mechanisms to explain specific real-life phenomena, one is forced to drop from one's narrative a host of important features (abstracting them as mere 'details') which make organizations the complex, ambiguous, and culturally specific entities that our common experience tells us they are. A-contextual, ahistorical, optimality-searching thinking gets in the way of complex understanding. Mintzberg's rhetoric, the way his narrative is developed and presented, is, as any narrative, not merely ornamental: it is a mode of thought which invites the reader to think in a particular manner; the narrative connects events in a specific way (here in an a-contextual and ahistorical way) and leads the reader to form certain expectations (here universalistic expectations) about what needs to be done (Bruner 1996: 98). The crucial questions are: What is thought of as important for an organization theorist? What should his/her narrative include and what should it leave out? How should the story of organizational growth be told? In this example Mintzberg tells his story in Newtonian style—privileging the timeless, the general, and the adaptively optimal at the expense of the timely, the contextual, and the historical.

Much mainstream organization theory not only assumes that organizations operate in a societal vacuum, it also takes them to function in a frictionless manner. Decision-making is a good case in point. Decision-making has traditionally been seen as a rational exercise involving the translation of management talk into decisions and then into action (cf. Brunsson 1989; Langley et al. 1995). It has rarely been acknowledged that the capacity of economic agents for decision-making is a limited and, thus, costly resource which, if not taken into account, leads to a self-reference problem. As Knudsen (1993: 161) puts it:

to make a decision is cost consuming, therefore it must be decided whether it is worth making a decision. But to make a decision implies costs; therefore we must decide, whether it is worth making a decision on whether it is worth making a decision, etc. Since this infinite regress can only be stopped at an arbitrary point, it will be impossible to find an optimal solution to this decision.

Thus, echoing Hayek (1967), Knudsen concludes that firms must ground their decisions on a historically developed body of collective knowledge, a way of doing things, which is not—it cannot be—fully articulated (see also Knudsen 1995). As Wittgenstein (1958) observed, our ways of thinking are rooted in our forms of life, and treating the former in purely cognitive terms leads to undecidability and infinite regress.

What is Chaos?

The world envisioned by chaos theory differs significantly from the Newtonian view. Before explaining in what way it differs, it is important to emphasize that chaos theory is a branch of what is technically known as 'dynamical systems theory' (Kellert 1993: ch. 1). The latter is not a theory of physical phenomena but a mathematical theory which is applied to a variety of different phenomena (Capra 1996: 112).

Chaos theory, according to Kellert (1993: 2), is *'the qualitative study of unstable aperiodic behavior in deterministic nonlinear dynamical system'* (emphasis in the original). This is a densely phrased definition, so let me unpack it. A system is dynamic when its state—how the system is, that is what the numerical values of the variables describing the system are, at a point in time—changes with time. The rules specifying how the system changes (what are called 'evolution' or 'structural' equations) are normally written in the form of differential equations which represent the rate of change of its variables. Differential equations allow one to calculate the state of the system at other times, given its state at one specific point in time. The rate of change of each variable is expressed in either linear or non-linear terms. Linearity means that a unit change in variable X will always cause a specific change in variable Y. By contrast, non-linearity means that the change in variable y brought about by a unit change in variable X will depend on the magnitude of variable X (Contractor 1994: 49–50). More simply, non-linearity means that a small change in a system variable can have a disproportionate effect on another variable.

Linear equations can easily be solved, in the sense that they can be collapsed into a general formula from which a future state is calculated, if only the initial condition and the time period under consideration are provided (Johnson and

Burton 1994: 321). Non-linear equations are much more difficult to deal with: there is no general formula for obtaining solutions for successive points in time. This is the reason why a qualitative account of the behaviour of a non-linear dynamical system is sought. Instead of finding a formula which will yield the prediction of a future state from a present one, mathematical techniques can be used to enquire about the general pattern of the long-term behaviour of a system.

Chaos theorists are interested in system behaviour which is unstable and aperiodic. *Unstable behaviour* means, as Kellert (1993: 4) observes, 'that the system never settles into a form of behavior that resists small disturbances'. *Aperiodic behaviour* means that the variables describing the state of a system do not undergo a repetition of values—the system does not repeat itself. 'Unstable aperiodic behavior is highly complex', notes Kellert (ibid.): 'it never repeats and it continues to manifest the effects of any small perturbation. Such behavior makes exact predictions impossible and produces a series of measurements that appear random' (ibid.). In other words, how unstable systems evolve depends on small disturbances—the famous 'butterfly effect'. As Lorenz (1963) found with his deterministic model of the earth's atmosphere, an infinitesimal change in the values of the three variables depicting the initial state of the atmosphere generated, in a short period of time, markedly different results. This *sensitive dependence on initial conditions* is a distinguishing feature of chaotic systems.

If the variables of a chaotic system are pictured in Cartesian coordinate space (what is technically known as 'phase space'), with a single point describing the entire system, then as the system changes the point traces out a trajectory. The state towards which a system tends—the set of points in phase space 'attracting' the trajectories—is called an *attractor*. The attractor of a chaotic system has an irregular shape (that is why it is called a 'strange attractor'), so that two very close points on the attractor will, after a while, diverge exponentially, while remaining within the confined area of the attractor. As Kellert (1993: 14–15) remarks, the strange attractor has two features: 'nearby points evolve to opposite sides of the attractor, yet the trajectories are confined to a region of phase space with a particular shape'. The existence of strange attractors shows that chaotic systems combine pattern with unpredictability, determinism with chaos, order with disorder. Indeed, it is *orderly disorder* that is so typical of chaotic systems. In that sense, chaos theory has made it possible, as well as legitimate, to overcome hitherto accepted conceptual dichotomies.

The pattern of a strange attractor is produced by the systematic operation of *feedback*—the dependence of a future state of a system upon an earlier state or, more technically, the iterative operation of a function upon itself. In non-linear systems small changes are amplified through self-reinforcing feedback, giving rise to instabilities and the emergence of new patterns of order. This is important, for it shows that 'often the total system resulting from the operation of simple equations with feedback terms included begins to manifest *emergent properties* that could never have been predicted ahead of time by looking only at the original very simple rules for interaction among concepts' (Eve et al. 1997: xxx). In other words, the amazing thing is that very simple rules of interaction, involving self-reinforcing feedback, may give rise to highly complex structures that no one thought of before.

To sum up, chaos theory shows mathematically that with simple non-linear deterministic equations (deterministic in the sense that given the initial conditions a unique solution may be derived from an equation) small changes in initial conditions can generate unpredictable outcomes. New patterns may emerge from very simple rules of non-linear feedback. The implications of chaos theory for organization theory are explored in the next section.

The Chaotic Style

The basic elements of chaos theory presented in the preceding section were described less for their specific content (admittedly simplified here) but more for the particular style of thinking they encourage. Chaos theory highlights the *impossibility* of long-term prediction for non-linear systems, since the task of prediction would require knowledge of initial conditions of impossibly high accuracy (see also Popper 1988: ch. 1). Such a limitation stems from our inherent finitude as human beings.

To appreciate the significance of this realization one needs only to be reminded of the Laplacian view of the human intellect, a view that has underlain the development of both the natural and the social sciences over the last three centuries. For Laplace, if an intellect was 'vast enough' to know 'all the forces that animate nature and the mutual positions of the beings that comprise it', then 'for such an intellect nothing could be uncertain, and the future just like the past would be present before its eyes' (Laplace, quoted in Stewart 1993: 25–6). Chaos theory, on the contrary, underscores the fact that our intelligence is inherently limited, and this has real consequences for scientific enquiry (Kellert 1993: 41–2; Turner 1997: xiv).

Human finitude means that social actors do not possess the infinite (or even bounded) optimizing capacity that mainstream organization theory has often thought them to have. The organizational capability for rational decision-making is grounded on the *arational* body of collective knowledge that a socially embedded organization has historically developed.

The finitude and historicity of human beings have been a central concern of Gadamer's philosophical hermeneutics. For him, finitude and historicity are not contingent but ontological features of human beings. We view the world from the hermeneutic horizon of the tradition in which we happen to have been embedded. 'The historicity of our existence', notes Gadamer (1976: 9), 'entails that prejudices, in the literal sense of the word, constitute the initial directedness of our whole ability to experience. Prejudices are biases of our openness to the world. They are simply conditions whereby we experience something—whereby what we encounter says something to us.' In other words, a collective actor's stock of knowledge always develops from a set of initial conditions which, arbitrary though they are, nonetheless form the ground, and are the necessary preconditions, for all understanding. Echoing Heidegger (1962), Gadamer privileges the particular ground, the concrete tradition, as a *conditio sine qua non* for human understanding and action, rather than the abstract, situationless, transhistorical *cogito* of Cartesian and Kantian philosophy (Gadamer 1989: 265–84).

Moreover, the fact that actors are possessed by history (rather than the other way round);[2] that they lack comprehensive knowledge of their own initial conditions;[3] and, thus, that they cannot base their knowledge and action on transhistorical epistemic foundations makes organizations (and social systems in general) inherently *political* entities. Politics is possible only to the extent that the human world is not fully ordered and our knowledge of it is never complete. 'If a full and certain knowledge (episteme) of the human domain were possible', observes Castoriadis (1991: 104), 'politics would immediately come to an end'. It is because we do not—we cannot—obtain an Archimedean point from which to view the world and our position in it that we need collectively to deliberate and, thus, to engage in political activity in order to settle our differences and decide on the course of action to be taken. The human domain is fundamentally the domain of *doxa* (opinion), not of *episteme* (science).

It is worth noticing how the impossibility of prediction invites us to reconsider the concept of *freedom*, which has long been ignored in a mechanistically oriented social science. In a deterministic world, a world of known causes leading to predictable effects, freedom makes no sense. A mechanistic social science modelled on Newtonian physics does not need freedom, in the same way that Laplace did not need God in his equations. Yet, paradoxically, it is in terms of purposes, free will, and moral accountability that we still make sense of our humanity—and rightly so. Our modern predicament has been that 'our success in understanding nature has generated deep problems for understanding our place in it and, indeed, for understanding *human nature*' (Shapin 1996: 163).

To continue making sense of what it is that makes us truly human, we cannot dispense with the concept of freedom. Freedom does not imply disorder or randomness. It rather implies 'discoverable meaning in an act—indeed, it distinguishes an act from an event' (Turner 1997: xiv). A free act may be unpredictable but not unintelligible: after it has occurred, it can be made sense of—it is retrodictable. Given that organization theory (and management studies in general) is a practically oriented discipline, it is necessary to make a central concern of the field the human capacity for making things happen as well as making sense of acts after they have happened, rather than emphasize the need for predictability. As Aristotle very well knew, in *prakta* (practical matters) judgement, imagination, ability to understand, and *phronesis* (practical wisdom) are more important qualities than the ability to predict (Berlin 1996).

Free will has always been an embarrassment to organization theory. Even those arguing for strategic choice, while rightly emphasizing the role of managerial discretion in the selection of organization structures, have been unable to provide an alternative explanatory form (a form other than the contingency approach). As soon as 'managerial choice' becomes the focus of attention, contingency-approach explanations of the 'If X, then Y, in circumstances Z' type are utilized. When organization theorists attempt to explain organizational phenomena, they tend to transform them into objects to be dissected in a mechanistic way.

The reason for such an approach is not difficult to identify. In a mechanistic epistemology, phenomena are regarded as objects which must be taken apart, abstracted, and packaged into propositional statements (Ackoff 1981: 6–12; Gharajedaghi and Ackoff 1984), so that practitioners can be instructed to apply those statements in an instrumental manner (Thompson 1956-7). Freedom is epistemologically redundant—it appears only as instrumental application. But this is not really freedom, since, from a contingency point of view, practitioners must apply the formulae organization theorists prescribe if their organizations are to be optimally adaptive (Donaldson 1996; Masuch 1990).

Even researchers prepared to lend a sympathetic ear to postmodern voices are trapped in the contingency style of thinking and the associated mechanistic approach. Clegg (1990), for example, seeks to explain the emergence of what he describes as 'postmodern organizations' by matching them to a 'postmodern' context. In this manner, he leaves decision-makers very little choice, since the choice of an organizational form is dictated by the demands of its context (postmodern or not doesn't matter). As said earlier, within such a mode of thinking, choice, creative action, and free will cannot be accommodated—they are dispensable. Mechanistic explanations perpetuate the divide between the world as experienced by actors vis-à-vis the world as functionally explained by an outside, allegedly objective, observer.

In classical physics, time is either ignored or thought to be an illusion. In the deterministic Newtonian world past and future play the same role—their only difference is that the future is depicted as $+t$, the past as $-t$ (Prigogine 1997: 18). Prediction is symmetrical with explanation. Popper (1988: 5) likened the role of time in a world deterministically conceived to a motion-picture film: 'In the film, the future co-exists with the past; and the future is fixed, in exactly the same sense as the past' (ibid.). However, the time-symmetric view of classical physics conflicts with our experience of time. In the world as experienced there is *change*: organisms grow and decay, people change their minds, hardly anything stays the same.

The emergence of complexity arising from non-linear feedback relation-ships, underlined by chaos and complexity theory, makes it now possible to appreciate the role of time and to reconcile our intuitive understanding of time with that of the sciences. Moreover, the arrow of time need not be associated with disorder: in fact, as is shown in non-equilibrium physics, time-irreversible processes are a source of order (Prigogine 1997: 26).

An appreciation of the role of time in the production of complexity brings with it the appreciation of *history* which, as earlier argued, has been a source of problems for Newtonian thinking. Just as a psychotherapist cannot hope to understand a particular quarrel between a couple unless he/she sees the inter-actively produced pattern of quarrels, part of which is the latest episode (Watzlawick et al. 1974), so it is important for an organization theorist to appreciate the historically developed pattern of interactions between actors that forms the background to the phenomena he/she wants to understand. As Senge (1990: 13) succinctly put it, 'our actions create the problems we experience', and what he means, of course, is that our previous inter-actions have brought about what we currently experience (see also Weick 1979: 65–80). Similarly, the notion is now gaining acceptance that the emer-gence of particular technological and economic changes is path-dependent: the form and direction they take depend on the particular sequence of events that precedes them (Arthur 1994, 1996; Garud and Karnoe 2001; Granovetter 1992; Rosenberg 1994; Turner 1997).

Acknowledging the role of history leads, in turn, to an appreciation of the *circularity* of organizational (and more generally social) phenomena (Tsoukas 1998). As March (1988) and Starbuck (1985) have shown, in organizations it is not only problems that are looking for solutions but also solutions that are looking for problems. Cooper (1992) has demonstrated how key features of the organizational environment are reproduced inside organiza-tions and vice versa (see also Granovetter 1992). Institutional theorists have convincingly argued that the way we organize our lives, far from being guided by ahistorical ironclad laws, reflects dominant societal, historically formed self-understandings (Dobbin 1995). Organizations reproduce the beliefs and institutional practices of the society in which they are embedded, and in so doing they help perpetuate them (Powell and DiMaggio 1991; Scott and Chris-tensen 1995; Whitley, 1992). Circularity, produced in systems replete with feedback loops unfolding in time, is the norm in organizations. As Eve et al. (1997: xxix) have observed, 'there are very few problems in the social sciences where the value of one or more of the so-called explanatory variables has not been influenced at some point in time by that which we wish to explain'.

As noted earlier, the mathematics of chaos privileges a *qualitative* approach to the understanding of chaotic systems by seeking to provide an analysis of the general pattern of a system's behaviour rather than the precise values of its variables at a certain point in time (see also Hayek 1989). In chaos theory such a qualitative approach takes the form of topological analysis (i.e. the study of patterns and relationships in the transformation of geometric figures). In organization theory the limited success of variance models of explanation (Webster and Starbuck 1988) has led researchers to seek *process* explanations (Pettigrew 1985), and even to calls for the narrative understanding of organizational phenomena (Czarniawska 1997; Hatch and Tsoukas 1997; Weick 1990).

Indeed, qualitative descriptions seem to be best suited for capturing the circular texture of organizational phenomena. How else could one hope to do justice to the historicity of the phenomena to be explained, if not by narrating how the actions of interacting agents and the occurrence of chance events, unfolding in time, have been intertwined to generate the phenomena at hand? Using the stock-market crash of 19 October 1987 as an example, Reisch (1991) has shown how a covering-law explanation for this event would be impossible. Instead, he argues, the events linked with the stock-market crash could be convincingly connected in a narrative explanation: 'a scene by scene description of the particular causal paths by which events are realized as consequences of certain causes and conditions occurring in the past' (ibid. 17). A qualitative approach does not reduce the phenomena at hand to their constituent parts, searching for the law-like rules governing them, but seeks to understand social phenomena in terms of patterns of interactions and feedback loops developed in time (Weick 1979). Mintzberg's qualitative research in strategy (1989) and Pettigrew's research on organizational change (1985) are, to some extent, illustrations of such an approach.

Chaosmos

Are organizations, and social systems in general, chaotic? This type of question has often been raised in organization theory. Several research programmes have sought to add to our understanding of organizational behaviour by drawing on analogies between, for example, organizations and organisms (Miller, 1978; Baum and Singh 1994; Beer 1981). Usually, those advocating analogically developed knowledge tend to answer the question in the affirmative (Gregersen and Sailer 1993; Holland 1995; Stacey 1995; Thietart and Forgues 1995).

In contrast, other researchers have had strong doubts about the applicability of concepts from chaos and complexity theory to the study of organizations, and other social-science fields in general. The reason? Johnson and Burton (1994: 328) are very clear: 'Human systems are not like other systems in the physical world, and researchers should not expect to model them in precisely the same way' (see also Gould 1987). Others underscore the different meanings certain key terms such as iteration, initial conditions, bifurcation, etc. have in chaos theory compared to the meanings they have acquired in fields as different as Foucauldian social theory (Price 1997), and deconstructionist analyses in literary theory (Matheson and Kirchhoff 1997). Since the discourses as well as the disciplinary requirements in each of these fields are different, so are the key concepts employed and the overall tenor of intellectual enquiry pursued. Ergo, transferring knowledge from chaos theory to organization theory is unilluminating.

Neither the defenders nor the opponents of the use of chaos and complexity metaphors in organization theory, and the rest of the social sciences, get it right. They are answering a misconceived question, thus missing the point about what analogies are for. To say that organizations *are* (or they *are not*) chaotic systems implies that one can elevate oneself to an extralinguistic terrain from which one can settle the matter. Such an Olympian high ground, however, does not exist (Rorty 1989: 3–22). We can never escape the maze of language. Our statements about the world are formulated in the language of a particular community of speakers and, as such, they do not represent the world; they only describe it in a particular way. As Rorty (ibid. 6) notes, 'the world does not speak. Only we do. The world can, once we have programmed ourselves with a language, cause us to hold beliefs. But it cannot propose a language for us to speak. Only other human beings can do that.' One cannot, therefore, be certain whether one has captured the 'nature' of an object of study; we cannot be sure whether our particular language cuts reality at the joins.

What then, are, metaphors and analogies for? See first what they are not for: they do not reveal aspects of a language-independent reality, since for such a task we would need to have direct access to reality (which we, being historically situated, 'self-interpreting animals' (Taylor 1985: 3–4), do not) in order to decide the degree of match between a certain metaphor and the reality it refers to. Metaphors and analogies, like the rest of language, are *tools*, enabling their users to do certain things in the world by drawing people's attention to what is thought to be important or relevant (Rorty 1989: 93–110).

Analogies are not discovered; they are constructed. To say that 'organizations are chaotic systems' is not to make a factual statement about organizations but rather to say to others: 'Try to imagine organizations as if they were chaotic systems and see what might be the consequences of this' (Rorty 1991: 78–92, 162–72; Stern 1995; Tavor Bennet 1997). A metaphor, therefore, does not disclose an antecedently existing meaning but causes us to shift attention to hitherto unsuspected, or only peripherally relevant, features of an object of study. A metaphor acquires meaning if and when it begins to resonate with other people's experiences (Rorty 1991).

Whether or not the metaphors of chaos and complexity theory are widely adopted will depend on a host of factors: their analytical capacity to allow us comprehensively to redescribe organizations and society at large; their acceptance by other fields; their match with the rest of culture[4]—and, of course, on social contingencies, which cannot be foreseen.[5]

One thing, however, is certain. Chaos and complexity metaphors draw our attention to certain features of organizations about which organization theorists have been, on the whole, only subliminally aware. Notions like 'non-linearity', 'sensitivity to initial conditions', 'iteration', 'feedback loops', 'novelty', 'unpredictability', 'process', and 'emergence' make up a new vocabulary in terms of which we may attempt to redescribe organizations (Poley 1997; Tsoukas 1994). True, these concepts may have acquired somewhat different meanings in the social sciences compared to the meanings they have in the disciplines in which they were first developed. But there is nothing sacrosanct about meaning anyway: concepts from different sites in the culture are in feedback loops with each other. Their meanings are inevitably modified when they cross to discourses different from the ones in which they originated. In today's late-modern context, chaos and complexity concepts have been transformed into *chaotics*—a new generalized imagery in terms of which the world may be redescribed. Chaotics arises out of, and contributes to, a Zeitgeist that makes certain questions interesting to pursue and renders others uninteresting or irrelevant (Hayles 1984: 22).

Of course, there are very good reasons to believe that it is highly unlikely that we will ever come up with the 'evolution equations' for an organization or a society. Even if we could find such equations, the human capacity for learning and radical self-creation would render them obsolete and redundant. Gould (1987: 220) is right: the human world cannot be mathematized because 'it is a world *defined* by beings with the capacity to reflect upon, and so contradict, any mathematical description made of them' (see also Castoriadis 1993: 98–9). Chaos and complexity theory, however, provides us with an alternative imagery, different from that of classical mechanics. Such an imagery helps us recover the classical Greek insight of chaos as the gaping void, the abyss, the *apeiron*, from which cosmos—form—arises. As Castoriadis (1987, 1991, 1997) is never tired of reminding us, being is not a system but a radical imaginary: the creation of new forms from chaos.

The social world is, to use Morin's apt term, *chaosmos* (see Kofman 1996: ch. 5): it has the features of a *cosmos*, without which human thinking would be impossible; and also, at its roots, is *chaos*, without which socio-historic creation would be unachievable (Castoriadis 1987: 340–4; 1991: 81–123). It is the interdependence of chaos and cosmos, so well understood by Presocratic Greek philosophy, that makes social life patterned yet indeterminate, and enables the human mind to account for it, though in an irremediably incomplete way.

Our attempts to theorize about the social world understood as *chaosmos* need to reflect such an awareness. We badly need complex theories which will take into account context, time, history, process, meaning, politics, emergence, contingency, feedback, novelty, change (Emirbayer 1997). Chaos and complexity theory will be most profitably used in the social sciences if it is seen not so much as a set of mathematical formalisms, but as an alternative imagery, a source of inspiration: a repository of insights which will, one hopes, be so stimulating as to impel us to complexify our theories. It is with such an understanding of chaos and complexity, I suggest, that we should use these concepts in organization theory. We should pay attention to chaos theorists not so much for what they say as for what they point at.

Notes

1. Disorganization is a concept which, strictly speaking, makes no sense. Says Castoriadis (1987: 341): 'What is, is not and cannot be, absolutely disordered chaos—a term to which, moreover, no signification can be assigned: a random ensemble still represents as random a formidable organization, the description of which fills the volumes expounding the theory of probabilities. If this were the case, it could not lend itself to any organization or it would lend itself to all; in both cases, all coherent discourse and all action would be impossible.'
2. Says Gadamer (1989: 276–7): 'In fact history does not belong to us; we belong to it. Long before we understand ourselves through the process of self-examination, we understand ourselves in a self-evident way in the family, society, and state in which we live. The focus of subjectivity is a distorting mirror. The self-awareness of the individual is only a flickering in the closed circuits of historical life. That is why the prejudices of the individual, far more than his judgements, constitute the historical reality of his being'. In other words, the human capacity to reason is rooted in circumstances which the subject has not, and could not have, rationally chosen.
3. In Gadamer's words: 'to be historical means that one is not absorbed into self-knowledge' (quoted in Linge 1976: xv). The subject, in other words, being historically situated, cannot have complete knowledge of itself—its initial conditions will always be beyond its cognitive mastery.
4. By comparison, think how the clock metaphor of classical physics enabled early moderns to make comprehensive sense of both the world and human behaviour (see Shapin 1996; Smith 1997).
5. Drawing on relevant historical material, Toulmin (1990) has shown how the devastation caused by the religious wars in seventeenth-century Europe made the Cartesian quest for 'pure reason' highly desirable and believable—contingency shaped, at least to some extent, intellectual developments.

References

Ackoff, R. (1981), *Creating the Corporate Future* (New York: Wiley).
Arthur, W. B. (1994), *Increasing Returns and Path Dependence in the Economy* (Ann Arbor, Mich.: University of Michigan Press).
—— (1996), 'Increasing Returns and the New World of Business', *Harvard Business Review*, 74: 100–9.

Bateson, G. (1979), *Mind and Nature* (Toronto: Bantam).

Baum, J. A. C., and Singh, J. V. (1994), *Evolutionary Dynamics of Organizations* (New York: Oxford University Press).

Bauman, Z. (1992), *Intimations of Postmodernity* (London: Routledge).

Beer, S. (1981), *Brain of the Firm* (Chichester: Wiley).

Berlin, I. (1996), *The Sense of Reality*, ed. H. Hardy (London: Chatto & Windus).

Boden, D. (1994), *The Business of Talk* (Cambridge: Polity).

Bruner, J. (1996), 'Frames for Thinking: Ways of Making Meaning', in D. R. Olson and N. Torrance (eds.), *Modes of Thought: Explorations in Culture and Cognition* (Cambridge: Cambridge University Press), 93–105.

Brunsson, N. (1989), *The Organization of Hypocrisy* (Chichester: Wiley)

Capra, F. (1996), *The Web of Life* (London: HarperCollins).

—— (1999), *The Web of Life* (London: HarperCollins).

Castoriadis, C. (1987), *The Imaginary Institution of Society* (Cambridge: Polity).

—— (1991), *Philosophy, Politics, Autonomy*, trans. and ed. D. A. Curtis (New York: Oxford University Press).

—— (1993), 'Pseudo-chaos, Chaos and Cosmos', in C. Castoriadis, *Anthropology, Politics, Philosophy* (in Greek) (Athens: Ypsilon), 91–116.

—— (1997), *World in Fragments*, trans. and ed. D. A. Curtis (Stanford, Calif.: Stanford University Press).

Cilliers, P. (1998), *Complexity and Postmodernism* (London: Routledge).

Clegg, S. (1990), *Modern Organizations* (London: Sage).

Cohen, B. (1994), 'Newton and the Social Sciences, with Special Reference to Economics, or, the Case of the Missing Paradigm', in P. Mirowski (ed.), *Natural Images in Economic Thought* (Cambridge: Cambridge University Press), 55–90.

Contractor, N. (1994), 'Self-organizing Systems Perspective in the Study of Organizational Communication', in B. Kovacic (ed.), *New Approaches to Organizational Communication* (New York: State University of New York Press), 39–66.

Cooper, R. (1986), 'Organization/Disorganization', *Social Science Information*, 25: 299–335.

—— (1992), 'Formal Organization as Representation: Remote Control, Displacement and Abbreviation', in M. Reed and M. Hughes (eds.), *Rethinking Organization* (London: Sage), 254–72.

Czarniawska, B. (1997), *Narrating the Organization* (Chicago, IU.: University of Chicago Press).

Dobbin, F. (1995), 'The Origins of Economic Principles: Railway Entrepreneurs and Public Policy in Nineteenth-century America', in W. R. Scott and S. Christensen (eds.), *The Institutional Construction of Organizations* (Thousand Oaks, Calif.: Sage), 277–301.

Donaldson, L. (1996), *For Positivist Organization Theory* (London: Sage).

Emirbayer, M. (1997), 'Manifesto for a Relational Sociology', *American Journal of Sociology*, 103: 281–317.

Eve, R., Horsfall, S., and Lee, M. (1997), Preface to R. Eve, S. Horsfall, and M. Lee (eds.), *Chaos, Complexity, and Sociology* (New York: Sage), pp. xxviii–xxxii.

Forster, E. M. (1952), *A Passage to India* (New York: Harcourt, Brace).

Gadamer, H.-G. (1976), *Philosophical Hermeneutics*, trans. and ed. D. E. Linge (Berkeley, Calif.: University of California Press).

—— (1989), *Truth and Method*, (2nd rev. edn., translation revised by J. Weinsheimer and D. G. Marshall) (London: Sheed & Ward).

Garfinkel, H. (1984), *Studies in Ethnomethodology* (Cambridge: Polity). Gharajeda-ghi, J. and Ackoff, R. (1984), 'Mechanisms, Organisms, and Social Systems', *Strategic Management Journal*, 5: 289–300.

Garud, R., and Karnoe, P. (2001), *Path Dependence and Creation* (Mahawa, NJ: Lawrence Erlbaum).

Gould, P. (1987), 'A Critique of Dissipative Structures in the Human Realm', *European Journal of Operational Research*, 30: 211–21.

Granovetter, M. (1992), 'Problems of Explanation in Economic Sociology', in N. Nohria and R. G. Eccles (eds.), *Networks and Organizations* (Boston: Harvard Business School Press), 25–56.

Gregersen, H., and Sailer, L. (1993), 'Chaos Theory and its Implications for Social Science Research', *Human Relations*, 46: 777–802.

Hatch, M. J., and Tsoukas, H. (1997), 'Complex Thinking about Organizational Complexity: The Appeal of a Narrative Approach to Complexity Theory', paper presented to the American Academy of Management, Boston, August 1997.

Hayek, F. A. (1967), *Studies in Philosophy, Politics and Economics* (London: Routledge & Kegan Paul).

—— (1989), 'The Pretence of Knowledge', *American Economic Review* 79: 3–7.

Hayles, N. K. (1984), *The Cosmic Web* (Ithaca: Cornell University Press).

—— (1990), *Chaos Bound* (Ithaca: Cornell University Press).

—— (1991), 'Introduction: Complex Dynamics in Literature and Science', in Hayles (ed.), *Chaos and Order*, (Chicago, Ill.: University of Chicago Press), 1–33.

Heidegger, M. (1962), *Being and Time* (New York: Harper & Row).

Holland, J. (1995), *Hidden Order: How Adaptation Builds Complexity* (Reading, Mass.: Addison-Wesley).

Johnson, J., and Burton, B. (1994), 'Chaos and Complexity Theory for Management', *Journal of Management Inquiry*, 3: 320–8.

Kellert, S. (1993), *In the Wake of Chaos* (Chicago, IU: University of Chicago Press).

Knudsen, C. (1993), 'Equilibrium, Perfect Rationality and the Problem of Self-reference in Economics', in U. Maki, B. Gustafsson, and C. Knudsen (eds.) *Rationality, Institutions, and Economic Methodology* (London: Routledge), 133–70.

—— (1995), 'The Competence View of the Firm: What Can Modern Economists Learn from Philip Selznick's Sociological Theory of Leadership?', in W. R. Scott and S. Christensen (eds.), *The Institutional Construction of Organizations* (Thousand Oaks, Calif.: Sage), 135–63.

Kofman, M. (1996), *Edgar Morin* (London: Pluto).

Langley, A., Mintzberg, H., Pitcher, P., Posada, E., and Saint-Macary, J. (1995), 'Opening up Decision Making: The View from the Back Stool', *Organization Science*, 6: 260–79.

Linge, D. E. (1976), editor's introduction to H.-G. Gadamer, *Philosophical Hermeneutics*, trans. and ed. D. E. Linge (Berkeley, Calif.: University of California Press), pp. xi–lviii.

Lorenz, E. (1963), 'Deterministic Nonperiodic Flows', *Journal of the Atmospheric Sciences*, 20: 130–41.

March, J. (1988), *Decisions and Organizations* (Oxford: Blackwell).

—— and Olsen, J. P. (1976), *Ambiguity and Choice in Organizations* (Bergen: Universitetsforlaget).

Masuch, M. (1990) (ed.), *Organization, Management, and Expert Systems* (Berlin: de Gruyter).

Matheson, C., and Kirchhoff, E. (1997), 'Chaos and Literature', *Philosophy and Literature*, 21: 28–45.

Miller, J. G. (1978), *Living Systems* (New York: McGraw-Hill).

Mintzberg, H. (1979), *The Structuring of Organizations* (Englewood Cliffs, NJ: Prentice Hall).

—— (1989), *Mintzberg on Management* (New York: Free Press).

Mirowski, P. (1984), 'Physics and the "Marginalist Revolution" ', *Cambridge Journal of Economics*, 8: 361–79.

—— (1989), *More Heat than Light: Economics as Social Physics, Physics as Nature's Economics* (Cambridge: Cambridge University Press).

Murphy, J. B. (1995), 'Rational Choice Theory as Social Physics', *Critical Review*, 9: 155–74.

Pettigrew, A. (1985), *The Awakening Giant* (Oxford: Blackwell).

Poley, D. (1997), 'Turbulence in Organizations: New Metaphors for Organizational Research', *Organization Science*, 8: 445–57.

Popper, K. (1988), *The Open Universe* (London: Hutchinson).

Powell, W., and DiMaggio, P. (1991), *The New Institutionalism in Organizational Analysis* (Chicago, Ill.: The University of Chicago Press).

Price, B. (1997), 'The Myth of Postmodern Science', in R. Eve, S. Horsfall, and M. Lee (eds.), *Chaos, Complexity, and Sociology* (New York: Sage), 3–14.

Prigogine, I. (1997), *The End of Certainty* (New York: Free Press).

Reisch, G. (1991), 'Chaos, History, and Narrative', *History and Theory*, 30: 1–20.

Rorty, R. (1989), *Contingency, Irony, and Solidarity* (Cambridge: Cambridge University Press).

—— (1991), *Objectivity, Relativism, and Truth* (Cambridge: Cambridge University Press).

Rosenberg, N. (1994), *Exploring the Black Box* (Cambridge: Cambridge University Press).

Said, E. (1995), *Orientalism* (London: Penguin).

Scott, V. R., and Christensen, S. (1995) (eds.), *The Institutional Construction of Organizations* (Thousand Oaks, Calif.: Sage).

Senge, P. (1990), *The Fifth Discipline* (New York: Doubleday).

Shapin. S. (1996), *The Scientific Revolution* (Chicago, Ill.: University of Chicago Press).

Smith, R. (1997), *The Fontana History of the Human Sciences* (London: Fontana).

Stacey, R. (1995), 'The Science of Complexity: An Alternative Perspective for Strategic Change Processes', *Strategic Management Journal*, 16: 477–95.

Starbuck, W. H. (1985), 'Acting First and Thinking Later: Theory versus Reality in Strategic Change', in J. M. Pennings et al. (eds.), *Organizational Strategy and Change* (San Francisco, Calif.: Jossey-Bass), 336–72.

Stern, D. G. (1995), *Wittgenstein on Mind and Language* (Oxford: Oxford University Press).

Stewart, I. (1993), 'Chaos', in L. Howe and A. Wain (eds.), *Predicting the Future* (Cambridge: Cambridge University Press), 24–51.

Tavor Bennet, E. (1997), 'Analogy as Translation: Wittgenstein, Derrida, and the Law of Language', *New Literary History*, 28: 655–72.

Taylor, C. (1985), *Philosophy and the Human Sciences, ii* (Cambridge: Cambridge University Press).

Thietart, R. A. and Forgues, B. (1995), 'Chaos Theory and Organization', *Organization Science*, 6: 19–31.

Thompson, J. D. (1956–7), 'On Building an Administrative Science', *Administrative Science Quarterly*, 1: 102–11.

Toulmin, S. (1990), *Cosmopolis: The Hidden Agenda of Modernity* (Chicago, Ill.: University of Chicago Press).

Tsoukas, H. (1994), 'Introduction: From Social Engineering to Reflective Action in Organizational Behaviour', in H. Tsoukas (ed.), *New Thinking in Organizational Behaviour* (Oxford: Butterworth/Heinemann), 1–22.

—— (1998), 'The Word and the World: A Critique of Representationalism in Management Research', *International Journal of Public Administration*, 5: 781–817.

—— and Cummings, S. (1997), 'Marginalization and Recovery: The Emergence of Aristotelian Themes in Organization Studies', *Organization Studies*, 18: 655–83.

Turner, F. (1997), 'Foreword: Chaos and Social Science', in R. Eve, S. Horsfall, and M. Lee (eds.), *Chaos, Complexity and Sociology* (Thousand Oaks, Calif.: Sage), pp. xi–xxvii.

Vickers, G. (1983), *The Art of Judgement* (London: Harper & Row).

Watzlawick, P., Weakland, J. and Fisch, R. (1974), *Change* (New York: Norton).

Webster, J. , and Starbuck, W. (1988), 'Theory Building in Industrial and Organizational Psychology', in C. Cooper and I. Robertson (eds.), *International Review of Industrial and Organizational Psychology* (Chichester: Wiley), 93–138.

Weick, K. (1979), *The Social Psychology of Organizing*, 2nd edn. (New York: McGraw-Hill).

—— (1990), 'Introduction: Cartographic Myths in Organizations', in A. S. Huff (ed.), *Mapping Strategic Thought* (Chichester: Wiley), 1–10.

Whitley, R. (1992), *Business Systems in East Asia* (London: Sage).

Wittgenstein, L. (1958), *Philosophical Investigations* (Oxford: Blackwell).

TEN

Complex Thinking, Complex Practice: The Case for a Narrative Approach to Organizational Complexity

Haridimos Tsoukas and Mary Jo Hatch

Introduction

A central assumption in organization science has been that organization is an intrinsic feature of the social world. Social systems in general, and business organizations in particular, are thought to be organized in one way or another, and it is the task of organization scientists to find out how and why. To this end two schools of thought can be broadly distinguished. One is sociological-historical-anthropological in orientation; it seeks to produce accounts explaining the specific features of organization(s), either by employing what Mohr (1982) called the 'variance model' of explanation, or through tracing back the lineage of organizational features to historical-cum-institutional or cultural factors (e.g. Geertz 1973; Granovetter 1992). There is a great deal of methodological and theoretical diversity within this school, but there is also a common theme: the *social* sciences can offer an account of *social* organization.

The second school is the cybernetic-systemic one. Here organization is much more broadly conceived: it is thought to be a feature of the cosmos at large, not just of social collectivities (Capra 1996). Both living forms and non-living matter are taken as being organized, and the suggestion is that there is a great deal to be learned about social organization by looking at the organization of the non-social world. Indeed, organizational cybernetics and systems

This chapter was first published in *Human Relations*, 54(8) (2001), 979–1013. Reprinted by permission of Sage, Copyright (2001).

theory have been built upon this premises (Beer 1981; Miller 1978). The recent surge of interest in exploring social organization(s) through the science of complexity falls firmly within this category. Proponents of this school argue that we can enhance our understanding of social organization(s), in particular of business organizations operating within a market economy, through modelling them on, that is by finding analogies with, natural and biological systems (Holland 1995; Stacey 1996).

Both schools of thought have been heuristically useful; they have helped generate a great deal of research and have significantly advanced our understanding of organization(s). However, less often has the question been asked whether organization might be not only a feature of the world (social and/or natural) but also of our thinking *about* the world. In other words, in order for cognitive beings to be able to act effectively in the world we must organize our thinking. As Piaget so aptly remarked, 'intelligence organizes the world by organizing itself' (quoted in Glaserfeld 1984: 24). Following this reasoning, one way of viewing organizations as complex systems is to explore complex ways of thinking about organizations-as-complex-systems; in this chapter we explicate this view, which we will call second-order complexity. We further note that entering the domain of second-order complexity—the domain of the thinker thinking about complexity—raises issues of interpretation (and, we argue, narration) that have heretofore been ignored by complexity theorists.

In shifting the focus from first- to second-order complexity we expose epistemological and methodological issues that have important implications for how we position ourselves and our approach to organizational complexity. Put most simply, is it better to explore complex thought processes (second-order complexity) in relation to an assumed objective world (first-order complexity), in which case the variance model-based methods of natural science appear to be indicated? Or should we, instead, explore along the lines of sociological-historical-anthropological approaches that employ interpretative methods and are more likely to view the objectivity of the world as a social construction? Although few within the cybernetic school may have considered the second option, our thesis is that not only does interpretative research within the social-science school suggest the value of doing so, but also the developing logic of complexity theory itself is entirely compatible with an interpretative, and in our case a narrative, approach.

Indeed, similarities between complexity theory and literary studies have been explored by a number of authors (Argyros 1992; Dyke 1990; Hayles 1990, 1991; Reisch 1991; Stonum 1989), although these have tended to focus on post-structural analysis rather than the narrative aspects of second-order complexity, which is our focus here. Although there are important connections between post-structuralism and the narrative approaches we will explore, our ambition is not to compare traditions or analyse developments within literary theory, but rather to suggest ways to apply narrative literary theory to the study of organizational complexity. There is, however, one sense in which our approach to complexity is similar to that of post-structural literary theorists who have addressed this topic. Like them, we take the view that the key concepts of complexity science constitute not so much a theory with predictive validity as a guide for interpretation (Hayles 1990: 36).

From the interpretative perspective, chaos and complexity are metaphors that posit new connections, draw our attention to new phenomena, and help us see what we could not see before (Rorty 1989: ch.1). This is the contribution they make to our understanding of organizational complexity. Such a perspective departs radically from the established orthodoxy, which is mainly derived from the Santa Fe Institute (Waldrop 1992). Whereas most Santa Fe scientists tend to conceive of complexity in the classic reductionist manner of searching for the common principles underlying a variety of utterly different systems (see e.g. Holland 1995: 36), the perspective adopted here seeks to generate new insights, and thus contribute to expanding the possibilities for thought and action, through the use of the narrative perspective and of the metaphor of complexity (Morgan 1997: chs. 1, 12; Rorty 1989: ch.1).

To frame our thesis we employ a distinction between logico-scientific and narrative modes of thought developed by Bruner (1986, 1996). We use this framework to make a comparison of cybernetic and interpretative social-science approaches and use this comparison to suggest the value of developing a narrative approach to complexity theory. We then explicate and critique the logico-scientific mode of thinking within the context of complexity theory itself and point out the multiple ways in which the narrative mode compensates for the inherent limitations of logico-scientific thinking. We conclude with a peek at what we believe developing a narrative approach to understanding organizational complexity would offer.

Complexity and its Interpreters: Logico-Scientific and Narrative Modes of Thought

In *Actual Minds, Possible Worlds*, Bruner (1986: 11) claimed that:

There are two modes of cognitive functioning, two modes of thought, each providing distinctive ways of ordering experience, of constructing reality. The two (though complementary) are irreducible to one another. Efforts to reduce one mode to the other or to ignore one at the expense of the other inevitably fail to capture the rich diversity of thought.

Bruner called the two modes of thought 'logico-scientific' (or paradigmatic) and 'narrative', arguing that:

the types of causality implied in the two modes are palpably different. The term *then* functions differently in the logical proposition 'if X, then Y' and in the narrative *récit* 'The king died, and then the queen died.' One leads to a search for universal truth conditions, the other for likely particular connections between two events—mortal grief, suicide, foul play. (ibid.)

To compare the two modes, Bruner claimed, is to understand the difference between a sound argument and a good story. He contrasts the logico-scientific and narrative modes in a variety of dimensions, which we have summarized in Table 10.1 and will expand upon in later sections of this chapter.

Viewed from a higher logical level, it could be said that the logico-scientific mode itself constitutes a particular type of narrative—and, indeed, a narrative it is. However, following Bruner, it is analytically useful to keep the two modes distinct, since they are characterized by a different logical organization and, as shown later, are connected to different types of action. Moreover, the usefulness of this distinction for the study of second-order complexity comes in recognizing that the two modes capture much of the difference between the understanding we glean from variance models and from interpretative accounts in the fields of organization science mentioned above. Of course, when social organization is described using such different modes of thought,

Table 10.1: Comparison of Bruner's two modes of thought

	Logico-scientific mode	**Narrative mode**
Objective	Truth	Verisimilitude
Central problem	To know truth	To endow experience with meaning
Strategy	Empirical discovery guided by reasoned hypothesis	Universal understanding grounded in personal experience
Method	Sound argument	Good story
	Tight analysis	Inspiring account
	Reason	Association
	Aristotelian logic	Aesthetics
	Proof	Intuition
Key characteristics	Top-down	Bottom-up
	Theory-driven	Meaning-centred
	Categorical	Experiential
	General	Particular
	Abstract	Concrete
	Decontextualized	Context-sensitive
	Ahistorical	Historical
	Non-contradictory	Contradictory
	Consistent	Paradoxical, ironic

Source: Bruner (1986: 11–43)

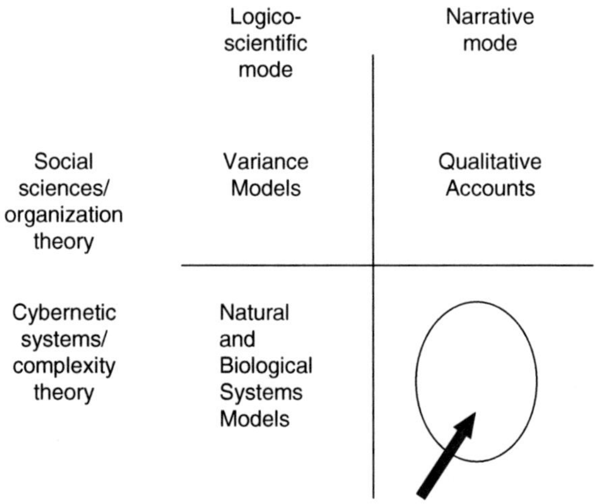

	Logico- scientific mode	Narrative mode
Social sciences/ organization theory	Variance Models	Qualitative Accounts
Cybernetic systems/ complexity theory	Natural and Biological Systems Models	

Fig. 10.1: Framing the interpretative approach to complexity theory.

it is not surprising that different views should emerge. What is intriguing about structuring the comparison between social-science and cybernetic approaches in this way is that it points to the absence of the narrative mode within complexity theory (see Fig. 10.1). If Bruner is correct in arguing that narrative-mode thinking is important, then this absence in the discussion of complexity deserves discussion. It is this absence that we intend to address in this chapter. In the sections that follow we will briefly review narrative approaches within interpretative organization studies, then make the case for considering complexity to be a matter for interpretative study, consider the limitations of the logico-scientific mode of thinking, and finally specify what we mean by a narrative approach to complexity.

Narrative Approaches to
Interpretative Organization Studies

One of the foremost proponents of narrative in the study of organizations, Czarniawska (1997*a*, 1997*b*, 1998), defines three narrative approaches offered to organization studies thus far: narrating organizations, collecting stories, and organizing as narration. Narrating organizations consists of telling about organizations using a narrative structure (e.g. a sequence of events or plot, in literary terminology). This approach most often produces case studies, though Czarniawska also includes in this category fictional stories and novels relating organizational life (e.g. Joseph Heller's *Something Happened*). Czarniawska says that the second category, collecting stories, initially focused on documenting cultural artefacts (e.g. Martin 1982; Martin et al. 1983; Smircich and Morgan 1982; Wilkins 1983) but has recently turned to storytelling within organizations as an approach to capturing the narrative mode of meaning construction (e.g. Boje 1991; Boyce 1995; Gabriel 1995; Shaw, Brown, and Bromiley 1998).

Czarniawska's final category of organizing as narration is where she places interpretative organizational research, to which she sees her work as contributing (Czarniawska 1997a, 1997b, 1998). This grouping applies the interpretative devices of literary theory to the narratively structured data of interpretative research (e.g. Barry 1997; Corvellec 1997; O'Connor 1995). However, because not all interpretative organizational research derives from literary theory (e.g. much was developed on the basis of anthropological or sociological traditions), we feel that, to a large extent, the narrative approach falls within interpretative studies rather than the other way around. In any case, we are in full agreement with Czarniawska (1997a: 29) when she claims that the interpretive approach 'further[s] our understanding of the complex and unpredictable—the major concern and interest of current organization studies'.

Why Complexity is a Matter of Interpretation

What is complexity? It is our contention that the puzzle of defining the complexity of a system leads directly to concern with description and interpretation and therefore to the issue of second-order complexity. There is apparently no consensus about when a system should be regarded as complex. As Waddington (1977: 30) remarks: 'no one has yet succeeded in giving a definition of "complexity" which is meaningful enough to enable one to measure exactly how complex a system is'. Casti (1994: 10) concurs and admits that 'the line of demarcation between the simple and the complicated is a fuzzy one'. Waddington notes that complexity has something to do with the number of components of a system as well as with the number of ways in which they can be related. But is it indisputably clear what the components of a system are or how they are related?

Echoing mathematical information theory (Hayles 1990; Shannon and Weaver 1949), Casti (1994: 9) defines complexity as being 'directly proportional to the length of the shortest possible description of [a system]' (see also Gell-Mann 1994: 30–41). If, for example, in a series of numbers there is a clear pattern, whereas in another series the numbers are randomly placed, the latter is more complex than the former, because no shorter description of it can be given other than repeating the series itself (Barrow 1995: 10–11). However, the length of a description cannot be determined objectively: it depends on the chosen language of description, as well as on the two parts of the communication process. A stone, says Casti (1994: 276), is a very simple object to most of us (that is, according to a common-sense description of it), but to a geologist it is rather more complicated. The conclusion Casti draws from this is that complexity is, in effect, in the eye of the beholder: 'system complexity is a contingent property arising out of the interaction *I* between a system *S* and an observer/decision-maker *O*' (Casti 1986: 149). To put it more formally, the complexity of a system, as seen by an observer, is directly proportional to the number of inequivalent descriptions of the system that the observer can generate (Casti 1986: 157; 1994: 276). The more inequivalent descriptions an observer can produce, the more complex the system will be taken to be.

Casti's definition of complexity is an interesting one, for it admits that the complexity of a system is not an intrinsic property of that system; it is observer-dependent; that is, it depends upon how the system is described and interpreted. Consequently, if an observer's language is complex enough that is, contains enough inequivalent descriptions), the system at hand will be described in a complex way and thus will be interpreted as a complex system. What complexity science has done is to draw our attention to certain features of systems' behaviours which were hitherto unremarked, such as non-linearity, scale-dependence, recursiveness, sensitivity to initial conditions, emergence. It is not that those features could not have been described before, but that they have now been brought into focus and given meaning (Hayles 1991: 5; Prigogine 1989: 396; Shackley, Wynne, and Waterton 1996: 202).

To put it another way, physics has discovered complexity by complicating its own language of description. We argue that a similar refocusing occurred in organization science when interpretative approaches were developed drawing attention to issues such as reflexivity (e.g. Chia 1996; Cooper and Burrell 1988; Giddens 1991; Woolgar 1988), narrativity (e.g. Czarniawska 1997*b*; Czarniawska-Joerges 1994; Hatch 1996; Van Maanen 1988; Weick and Browning 1986), and paradox, ambiguity, and contradiction (e.g. Feldman 1991; Filby and Willmott 1988; Hatch and Ehrlich 1993; March and Olsen 1976; Meyerson 1991; Poole and Van de Ven 1989; Putnam 1985; Quinn and Cammeron 1988; Weick 1979; Westenholz 1993).

Weick (1979) was one of the first to argue for an observer-dependent definition of organization. His notion of organizing made us realize that what we experience as organization is the outcome of an interactive sense-making process. Moreover, a constant theme of Weick's thought, like Bateson's, has been an appreciation of the paradoxical nature of organizational behaviour (see also Brunsson 1989: 194–205; Hatch 1997; Pascale 1990: 110–11; Perrow 1977; Price Waterhouse Change Integration Team 1996; Quinn and Cameron 1988). For instance, Weick (1979: 222) gives the example of a bank whose very functioning is inherently paradoxical. A bank's motto is: 'To make money you have to lend it rather than store it.' But the bank acts as if this statement is both true and false. Says Weick:

[The bank] acts as if the statement is true by continuing to select from enacted inputs those occasions where there is an opportunity to lend money at a profit. It acts as if this statement is false by urging customers to be thrifty and use the bank as a repository for the results of that thrift. It is good to save and bad to borrow, it's good to borrow and bad to save. That complicated definition is something a bank must manage as a routine matter. (ibid.)

Notice how appreciating the paradox of the bank demands appreciation of second-order complexity (i.e. statements describing a bank's behaviour). The bank is pursuing two contradictory policies simultaneously. Since more than one (in this case, two) inequivalent descriptions of the bank's behaviour can be generated, it is seen as being more complex than it would otherwise be.

How could one practitioner-cum-observer hope to make sense of such behaviour? What might be an appropriate mode of thought able to accommodate contradictions? If practitioners are to increase their effectiveness in managing paradoxical social systems, they should, as Weick (ibid. 261) recommends, 'complicate' themselves (see also Bateson 1979: 77–82; Beer 1973: 204–5; Weick 1995). But complicate themselves in what way? By generating and accommodating multiple inequivalent descriptions, practitioners will increase the complexity of their understanding and, therefore, will be more likely, in logico-scientific terms, to match the complexity of the situation they attempt to manage (Bartunek et al. 1983; Bolman and Deal 1991; Bruner 1996: 147; Morgan 1997), or, in narrative terms, to enact it (Weick 1979).

Hatch and Ehrlich (1993) provide an example of managers complicating themselves via narrative activities. In their study of the sense of humour of a management team these researchers found that managing security issues (i.e. finding effective means of securing the assets of the corporation against pilfering and theft) placed managers in the role of guarding their own employees. However, the guard role contradicted their attempts to encourage trust and teamwork in their unit, another important item on the corporate agenda. Reflection on their status as guards in a system demanding a collaborative form of organization was a recurrent theme in their joke-making. As Koestler (1964) has shown, humour is built upon 'bisociation'—the ability mentally and emotionally to traverse both paths of a bifurcating line of thought, the recognition of which provokes laughter (see also Mulkay 1988). Thus, any potential choice point can become a point of bisociation by shifting from one level of complexity (serious, rational, linear) to another (humorous, playful, paradoxical). Bisociation through humour permitted the managers in Hatch and Ehrlich's study a more complex view of their organization, complex in the sense that it offered a both/and rather than an either/or orientation to the contradictions of managing and organizing. What is more, in taking the form of a joke the bisociation becomes linked to narrative, because joking is one way for managers to narrate their experiences (and their organizations).

We argue that the features of complex systems described by complexity theory (non-linearity, scale-dependence, recursiveness, sensitivity to initial conditions, and emergence) can only be appreciated and acted upon from the position of second-order complexity. This claim is based on our assumption that the features of complexity are descriptions and interpretations assigned by complex observers to systems whose existence itself is a matter of definitional agreement. Expanding the focus from the system itself (first-order complexity) to also include those who describe the system as complex (second-order complexity) exposes the interpretative-cum-narrative dimensions of complexity.

The Interpretative Dimensions of Complexity

Complexity science highlights at least five properties that are proposed to be held in common by natural, biological, and social systems (see Casti 1994; Crutchfield et al. 1986; Davis 1990; Hayles 1989, 1990, 1991; Kamminga 1990; Kellert 1993; Stewart 1993):

1. Complex systems are non-linear: there is no proportionality between causes and effects. Small causes may give rise to large effects. Non-linearity is the rule, linearity is the exception.
2. Complex systems are fractal: irregular forms are scale-dependent. There is no single measurement that will give a true answer; it depends on the measuring device. For example, to the question 'How long is the coastline of Britain?' there is no single answer, for it hinges on the scale chosen to measure it. The smaller the scale, the larger the measurement obtained.
3. Complex systems exhibit recursive symmetries between scale levels: they tend to repeat a basic structure at several levels. For example, turbulent flow can be modelled as small swirls nested within swirls nested, in turn, within yet larger swirls.
4. Complex systems are sensitive to initial conditions; even infinitesimal perturbations can send a system off in a wildly different direction. Given that initial conditions cannot be adequately specified with infinite accuracy, complex systems have the tendency to become unpredictable.
5. Complex systems are replete with feedback loops. Systemic behaviour is the emergent outcome of multiple chains of interaction. As the level of organization increases, complex systems have the tendency to shift to a new mode of behaviour, the description of which is not reducible to the previous description of the system's behaviour. These emergent novelties represent points of bifurcation.

Positioning the narrator as the interpreter of these five properties moves us from the logico-scientific to the narrative mode and presents complexity as a second-order phenomenon. To see this, imagine yourself in the position of the person describing a system in the terms listed above. Though you may call non-linearity, scale dependence, recursiveness, sensitivity to initial conditions, and emergence properties of the system, they are actually your descriptive terms—they are part of a vocabulary, a way of talking about a system. Why use such a vocabulary? Is it because it corresponds to how the system really is? Not quite. Since the system cannot speak for itself, you do not know what the system really is (Rorty 1989: 6). Rather, you use such a vocabulary because of its suspected utility—it may enable you to *do* certain things with it. A new vocabulary, notes Rorty (ibid. 13), 'is a tool for doing something which could not have been envisaged prior to the development of a particular set of descriptions, those which it itself helps to provide'. Our language cannot be separated from our goals and beliefs (Taylor 1985: 23). Switching to the narrative mode of thinking makes this obvious because in narrative mode the researcher making claims about systems is in full view—his/her goals and desires are reflected in his/her language. It is thus that second-order complexity is engaged—the complexity (subjectivity) of the researcher (i.e. narrator) attempting to understand complexity is revealed and made available for analysis.

To see the transformation of properties into descriptors by means of bringing the researcher–narrator into our frame of reference, take the case of non-linearity. The lack of proportionality between causes and effects captures our attention precisely because we expect linearity. We interpret the non-linearity of complex systems as counter-intuitive or surprising, but the surprise rests on our perspective and in our violated expectations, not in the system we describe in this way. Similarly, scale-dependence is not a property of systems, but of our interpretation of them; it is our concepts that are indeterminate, not the system we describe using these concepts. From a position of second-order complexity, recursiveness, sensitivity to initial conditions, and emergence are likewise revealed as interpretations. To shift perspective from one level to another, to define where an event begins and ends, and even to consider some congregation of occurrences to be a system, are all interpretative moves, not properties of systems (Checkland 1981). In other words, the complexity we discover when we apply the methods of complexity science is a function of the second-order complexity we introduce by our involvement.

We claim that the narrative approach gives us access to second-order complexity, which we will demonstrate below by taking a narrative approach to recursiveness. However, this is not the only case we can make for the narrative approach to organizational complexity; a strong case can be made from within complexity science itself. To develop this case we will critique the logico-scientific mode of thinking and examine its limitations, for it is in relation to the limits of logico-scientific thought that the contribution of the narrative approach is perhaps most easily understood by those who have never before considered taking a narrative approach.

The Logico-scientific Mode of Thinking and its Limitations

As historians of science and philosophers have shown, the rise of scientific rationalism in post-seventeenth-century Europe involved a radical shift in how humans thought about the world (see Feyerabend 1987; Foucault 1966; MacIntyre 1985; Shapin 1996; Toulmin 1990). Toulmin (1990: 200) sums up the shift as a search for a 'rational method' motivated by a 'decontextualized ideal'—the ideal of universal, general, and timeless knowledge (ibid. 30–6). Nowhere have the principles of the 'rational method' been manifested more clearly than in Newton's work, whose influence on the social and economic sciences has been profound (Cohen 1994; Mirowski 1989; Smith 1997).

The 'Newtonian style' (Cohen 1994: 77), or what other researchers call the 'Galilean style' (Varela, Thompson, and Rosch 1991: 17), involves a particular approach towards the world, the main features of which are as follows. First, the scientific method deals with the 'primary qualities' (Goodwin 1994: 184; Pepper 1942: 192) of the phenomena under investigation (e.g. mass, velocity, position, etc.), which can be quantified and measured. Second, science constructs *idealized* models of the phenomena it studies, either with the help of mathematics or through the creation of controlled conditions in a laboratory, or both (Latour 1987). A consequence of the Newtonian style is that it is both *a-contextual* and *ahistorical*. It is a-contextual in so far as it involves 'switching off' all contextual influences upon the phenomenon under study so that its intrinsic properties may be revealed to the scientist (Ackoff 1981: 11; Kallinikos 1996: ch. 1). It is ahistorical because it is marked by *synchrony* (Kellert 1993:93): the state of a system is thought to be known solely in terms of the way the system is at a particular moment. As Kellert (ibid.) remarks: 'Physics considers that we know everything relevant about a system if we know everything about it at one point in time'.

There are several examples of the Newtonian style of thinking in the social sciences. Cohen (1994: 76–9) relevantly discussed the case of Malthus' theory of population, and Mirowski (1984, 1989) showed that neoclassical price theory was developed in the late nineteenth century as an imitation of energy physics. In psychology the study of cognition has long been conducted in the laboratory (Lave 1988; Salomon 1993: xii; Varela et al. 1991). For example, commenting on memory research, Banaji and Crowder (1989: 1192) are only slightly able to conceal their distaste for complexity. 'The more complex a phenomenon', they note, 'the greater the need to study it under controlled conditions, and the less it ought to be studied in its natural complexity'. Finally, in organization science, Barnard (1976: xlvi) remarked that 'abstract principles of structure may be discerned in organizations of great variety, and that ultimately it may be possible to state principles of general organization'. Notice how easily Barnard moves from talking about organizations to talking about organization. Behind the awesome variety of organizations there is an underlying set of universal principles of organization. How does one discover those principles? Through the study of aggregates of the phenomenon at hand under statistically controlled conditions (Ansoff 1991: 459). In other words, as soon as one dispenses with the contingent, as well as deceptive, experience of diversity, one comes upon a small set of generally applicable principles. Experiential contingency gives way to theoretically contrived necessity (Reed 1996).

From the above it follows that social scientists should search for regularities obtained under well-specified conditions, establish their validity, and, ideally, codify them in the form of rules to be followed by practitioners (Tsoukas 1994: 4; 1998). Notice how well scientific rationalism fits within Bruner's logico-scientific mode of thought (Table 10.11, p. 233), and how equally well Bruner's narrative mode represents the other against which logico-scientific thinkers have defined themselves.

What form does logico-scientific knowledge take? How is it organized? Ideally, it consists of propositional statements: 'if, then' statements relating a set of empirical conditions, called the *factual predicate* ('If X ...'), to the *consequent*; that is, to a set of consequences that follow when the conditions specified in the factual predicate obtain ('... then Y') (see Holland 1995: 6–10 and ch. 2; Johnson 1992: ch. 4; Schauer 1991: 23). As Bruner (1986: 12–13) notes, propositional knowledge:

employs categorization or conceptualization and the operations by which categories are established, instantiated, idealized, and related one to the other to form a system. [...] It deals in general causes, and in their establishment, and makes use of procedures to assure verifiable reference and to test for empirical truth. Its language is regulated by requirements of consistency and non contradiction.

What might be examples of propositional knowledge in organization studies? There are plenty: 'if size is large, then formalization is high'; 'if technological complexity is high (or low), then work is non-routine'; 'if the organization uses a prospector strategy, then centralization is low'; 'If environmental uncertainty is low, then centralization is high'; and so on (see Baligh, Burton, and Obel 1990: 41–4; Glorie, Masuch, and Marx 1990: 87; see also Mintzberg 1979, 1989; Webster and Starbuck 1988: 128). These conditional statements serve as explanations of certain recurring organizational phenomena *and* purport to be the basis for formulating rules for guiding human action in the future.

Propositional knowledge is recursively employed: organizational scientists explain and predict organizational phenomena by means of propositional

Table **10.2**: The limits to logico-scientific thinking, and some narrative 'Correctives'

Logico-scientific limits	Narrative 'Correctives'
Imperfect generalizations	Contextuality and reflexivity
Tacit justification	Expression of purposes and motives
Requires consistency and non-contradiction	Temporal sensitivity

statements like those mentioned above; *and* practitioners are guided in their work by *rules*, namely by statements prescribing that 'In circumstances X, behavior of type Y ought, or ought not to be, or may be, indulged in by persons of class Z' (Twinning and Miers 1991: 131). The factual predicate of rules is derived from events that occurred in the past and is meant to guide action in the future. Thus, any novel situation is described by breaking it down into familiar parts, the behaviour of which can be described by tested rules (Holland 1995: 51). In that sense, the future is understandable in (i.e. reducible to) the terms of the past; time does not really matter since the new is comprehensible in terms of the old.

Thinking propositionally and managing by rules has certain advantages which mainly stem from the fact that propositional statements are abstract and defined exclusively in terms of their syntax. Thus, they are applicable across a variety of contexts after a particular interpretation (i.e. semantics) has been attached to them in each particular case (Casti 1989: ch. 5; Kallinikos 1996: 42–6; Tsoukas 1998). However, an excessive reliance on the propositional mode of thinking has certain limitations. What are they? First, propositional statements are generalizations which, by themselves, cannot deal with particular circumstances or singular experiences. Second, propositional statements incorporate purposes and motives that cannot be formulated propositionally. And third, propositional statements do not include time, thus leading to paradoxes. It is each of these limitations of propositional knowledge to which the narrative mode of thinking offers a complementary strength (see Table 10.2). Below we will expand on each of the limitations and point out how a narrative approach offers an important 'corrective' to knowledge about organizational complexity. Each 'corrective' will be developed more fully in the following section, where we will suggest how a narrative approach to complexity might look.

Imperfect Generalizations

Rules are generalizations connecting types of behaviour by types of actors to types of situations. To assert the existence of a rule is necessarily to generalize (and categorize, label), just as to institutionalize human interaction is, of necessity, to imply the existence of rules (Berger and Luckmann 1967:

70–96). Rules, however, are implemented *locally*, that is, within contexts in which idiosyncratic configurations of events may occur in a manner that has not been specified by a rule's factual predicate (Shackley et al. 1996: 206; Tsoukas 1996: 19–20). The circumstances confronting a practitioner always have an element of uniqueness that is not, and cannot be, specified by a rule. In other words, the indeterminacy of local implementation cannot be eliminated (Brown and Duguid 1991; Orr 1990). In common-sense terms; what can go wrong, will go wrong. Only the practitioner possessing 'the knowledge of the particular circumstances of time and place' (Hayek 1945: 521) can undertake effective action in the moment. The 'tyranny' of the local, the particular, and the timely cannot be escaped in the context of *practical* reasoning (MacIntyre 1985; Taylor 1993).

Notice that the rules the practitioner applies are derived from what is known about previous failures or successes; thus, the practitioner comes already equipped with historical understanding of sorts. But this aggregate, codified, past-derived knowledge is not very useful when it comes to examining a *particular* problem (Orr 1996). To comprehend a particular problem, the practitioner needs to follow a bifurcation path (Kellert 1993: 95). As Prigogine (1980: 106) observes with reference to natural systems, 'interpretation of state C implies a knowledge of the history of the system, which has to go through bifurcation points A and B'. Put very simply, one cannot understand why a system is at point C without understanding *how* it came to be there. That historical 'know-how', cannot be provided by propositionally organized renderings of human experience in organizational settings; instead it requires a contextually sensitive narrative understanding—in short, it needs a story with a plot (see Bruner 1996; Dyke 1990; MacIntyre 1985: 206–18; Reisch 1991). The question is: What mode of thinking might take the features of practical reasoning and historically based know-how into account? As shown below, narratively organized knowledge provides such a mode.

Tacit Justification

Underlying the implementation of rules is the achievement of a certain goal or the fulfilment of what Schauer (1991: 26) calls 'justification'. For example, the manual issued by a photocopier company to service technicians includes rules such as: 'If this error code is displayed then check this or do that.' The justification for this rule is obviously the company's desire to satisfy the customer in the most efficient manner. A rule's factual predicate ('If this error occurs') is *causally* related to the rule's justification—the satisfaction of the customer will be brought about by following the rule.

Why does one need justifications? 'Justifications exist', says Schauer (ibid. 53), 'because normative generalizations are ordinarily instrumental and not ultimate, and justifications are what they are instrumental to'. A justification lies behind the rule, it is the reason for having a rule. As such, justifications are *implied*; they are not explicitly contained in the rule. This is important, for in order to fulfil the justification one may occasionally need to break the rules (e.g. when the machine displays a misleading error code). However, within a purely propositional framework of knowledge such a paradoxical requirement cannot be accommodated. As Bruner (1986: 13) noted, the 'requirements of consistency and noncontradiction' are *constitutive* of this mode of thinking. The conclusion should deductively flow from the premises (Hayek 1982: 10).

Moreover, given that a justification is implicit, it cannot be conveyed to practitioners in a propositional form. Just like Polanyi's (1975: 39) tacit knowledge, a justification is 'essentially unspecifiable': the moment one focuses on it, one ceases to see its meaning. If a justification were to be propositionally articulated it would inevitably be based upon a further implicit justification, and this implicit–explicit polarity would be reproduced ad infinitum. Justification is to a rule what a shadow is to an object. It follows, therefore, that, in the propositional mode of thinking, *why* practitioners should follow a particular rule cannot be conveyed; what a rule is *for* cannot be stated. A rule provides the method but not the purpose. As we show below, the exploration of purposes (and motives) is in the domain of narrative mode thinking.

Consistency and Non-contradiction

In an organized context, managing by rules alone leads inescapably to paradoxes that cannot be accommodated by logico-scientific thinking. The reason is that time is not included in the logic of propositional statements. As Bateson (1979: 63) insightfully noted, 'the *if ... then* of causality contains time, but the *if ... then* of logic is timeless'. For example, the 'if ... then' in 'If the temperature falls below 0 °C, then the water begins to freeze' is different from the 'if ... then' in 'If Euclid's axioms are accepted, then the sum of all angles in a triangle is 180 degrees'. The first statement makes reference to causes and effects, whereas the second is part of a syllogism; the first includes time, the second is timeless (Prigogine 1992: 23–5). When causal sequences become circular (von Foerster 1981: 103), their description in terms of logic becomes self-contradictory—it generates paradoxes (Bateson 1979: 61; Beer 1973: 199; Capra 1988: 83; Clemson 1984: 109). However, as we show below, narrative, because of its sensitivity to the temporal dimension of experience, is well suited to avoid (or reveal) such conflations of logic and causality.

To sum up, the key features of the propositional mode of thinking are as follows: it deals in generalizations, its justification of rules is tacit, it is regulated by the requirements of consistency and non-contradiction, and it ignores time. If, as argued above, second-order complexity is seen as a property of the interaction between an observer O and a system S, and considering that a propositionally thinking observer is led to neglect the particular, the local, and the timely, all of which are important features of the life world (the world as experienced) (Varela et al. 1991: ch. 2), it follows that the quality of interaction between *O* and *S* for such an observer will tend to be poor. This is because an observer guided by propositional thinking alone will be unable to handle paradoxical requirements or contradictions like those illustrated previously with examples from Weick (1979) and Hatch and Ehrlich (1993). Such paradoxes and contradictions, by definition, cannot be handled by propositional logic, according to which one should aim for consistency and non-contradiction in (as well as between) one's thinking and one's acting.

Finally, it is interesting to note that while propositional thinking requires that paradoxes be formally avoided, action that is exclusively guided by propositional thinking tends to generate paradoxes. Ironically, what is avoided in logic turns up in practice! Thus, a propositionally thinking observer will find it difficult to manage a system that is characterized by non linearity, feedback loops, and sensitivity to initial conditions—the very features used to define a system as complex. It is precisely these features, however, that favour the narrative mode and argue for the narrative approach, to which we will now turn.

The Narrative Approach

More important than the novelty of its knowledge claims in mathematics and physics, the wider appeal of complexity science stems from its contribution to the emergence of a new imagery in terms of which the world may be understood (Prigogine 1997). Such an imagery, as has already been mentioned, fosters an awareness of dynamic processes, unpredictability, novelty, and emergence, leading to what Kellert (1993: 114) calls 'dynamic understanding'. The main features of dynamic understanding in the sciences are that it 'is holistic, historical, and qualitative, eschewing deductive systems and causal mechanisms and laws' (ibid.).

It is interesting to see that notions like 'holistic', 'historical', and 'qualitative', which have traditionally been the trademark of interpretative social science, are now appearing in the language of physicists. As several researchers have noted (see Capra 1996; Goodwin 1994; Hayles 1990, 1991; Prigogine 1997; Shotter 1993: ch. 10; Toulmin 1990: ch. 5), the appeal of such a vocabulary in scientific discourse signifies the disenchantment with the Newtonian ideal, and the attempt to pursue, instead, more meaningful, open-ended, and systemic modes of enquiry. It is precisely the sense of dynamic understanding, as we argued earlier, that the narrative mode of thinking conveys, and in the remainder of this chapter we intend to explore what this approach might contribute.

In this part of the chapter we will illustrate the narrative approach and second-order complexity via an exploration of the ways in which narrative corrections to logico-scientific thinking produce new insights into complexity issues. However, to adequately illustrate the potential contribution of the narrative approach we feel that we must narrow our ambition to considering but one of the features of complex systems articulated by complexity scientists. Therefore, we will concentrate our focus on recursiveness. We do this in order to develop the narrative approach to complexity in a way that reveals its own (i.e. second-order) complexity, as well as illuminating the holistic, historical, and qualitative features of the dynamic understanding in which it deals.

Contextuality and Reflexivity

Genette (1980) argues that narrative can refer to three separate things: the written or spoken narrative statement; the events and their relationships that are the subject of the narrative (he calls this the story); or the act of narrating. When the narrative statement and the story are considered together, the issues of interpretation and context become pronounced. This is because the difference between what is told about and what is told gives rise to questions about the meaning of a narrative and the context in which it is interpreted. (The act of narrating and the act of listening are both considered to be interpretative acts taking place in specific contexts which inspire and support the development of particular meanings.) When the narrative statement and the act of narrating are considered together, the position of the narrator (along with the motives of the narrator, discussed later) becomes an issue for reflection. That is, the difference between the statement and the act of making it causes the narrator to come into view.

Ricoeur (1984) claimed, building on Aristotle's notion of *muthos* ('emplotment'), that narrative thinking produces plots. According to Aristotle's *Poetics*, narrative is plot-driven. Events, mental states, happenings—in short, the constituents of a narrative (Burke 1945 described these dramatistically as act, agent, agency, scene, and purpose)—are sequentially placed within the overall configuration that is the plot. To make sense of the particular constituents of a narrative, one needs to grasp its plot. And vice versa: in order for one to understand a plot one needs to grasp the sequence of events that relate its constituent elements (Taylor 1985: 18). Thus, the parts and the whole are mutually defined and defining, or, in the terms offered by complexity theory, they are recursively ordered. However, the narrative perspective allows us to carry the insight of recursivity further than simply suggesting we look for structural similarity between narratives and plots or between plots and their constitutive elements. Second-order thinking about complexity focuses our attention on how, in making plots, we construct and use narrative thinking. This is what Ricouer addresses with the concept of emplotment and Bruner with the concept of narrative mode.

Emplotment raises several important issues, the most obvious of which is sequencing. According to Ricoeur (1984: 38) emplotment organizes the continuous flux of experience into describable sequences with beginnings, middles, and ends. We will return to the issue of sequencing below in our discussion of temporality. Two others, to be addressed here, concern context and reflexivity.

Context. As Polkinghorne (1988: 36) explained: 'The narrative scheme serves as a lens through which the apparently independent and disconnected elements of existence are seen as related parts of a whole'. Thus, plots give meaning and connection that would otherwise be absent. The connection that plots give is, in part at least, the context provided by the sequence of events and the relationships between them that are highlighted by the sequencing. What happens in a narrative happens situationally (or situatedly). Providing or invoking a context for meaning-making is thus an important part of narrating.

Whereas in logico-scientific thinking, propositions or rules connect categories of behaviour to categories of actors and situations, narrative thinking places these elements in a sequenced, contextualized statement with a plot. But once the plot has been constructed the elements are explicit, local, tangible instances engaged in events with consequences. The narrative mode of thinking enlivens and energizes the emploted characters and events. In narrating, a narrator communicates and captures nuances of event, relationship, and purpose that are dropped in the abstraction process that permits categorization and correlation in the logico-scientific mode. In narrative we have a more concrete rendering of causality. It is historical and specific, not general and contingent (see Table 10.1, p. 233). 'This did happen in this way', versus 'This should happen if the following conditions hold'. In terms of addressing organizational complexity, this concreteness is a contribution that narrative approaches make to understanding in that it supplies the specific context within which events have occurred. Whereas within logico-scientific thinking context becomes contingency, in narrative mode context is situation and circumstance. Thus, narrative thinking gives us access to and appreciation of context that logico-scientific thinking cannot provide.

Boje (1991) argued that context is essential for interpreting narratives that occur in organizational settings. He claimed that without participating in the organization that contextualizes a narrative its meaning will be difficult, if not impossible, to grasp. O'Connor shows how context can be revealed using narrative analysis. Hers is a view informed by literary theory in which contextualism refers to the self-containment of a work of literature (i.e. the view that literary works have no reference to things beyond themselves). The literary view supports text analysis (which O'Connor 1995 illustrates) as a means to reveal the context and embedded assumptions of narrative processes. Boje's work, in contrast, positions the narratives he examines within a broader framework. This broader framework is the organization that provides context for the narrative act (i.e. the telling and interpreting of stories), which is what he means by his phrase 'the storytelling organization'. Thus, Boje places narratives within a context of both narrating and organizing, whereas

O'Connor looks to texts produced by organizational members for insights into the assumptions, motives, and orientations that frame their narrative statements. In either approach narrative thinking provides sensitivity to the situational particularity missing from the propositional statements favoured by the logico-scientific mode of thinking. As can be seen, the narrative mode, in contrast, both demands and engages contextualized understanding, and this contextualized understanding contributes to second-order complexity.

Each interpretation invokes a new context producing recursive symmetry of a narrative sort. If complexity is a matter of interpretation, as we have argued, then each 'reading' will produce another layer of context. Thus, taken together, O'Connor and Boje illustrate the connection between complexity theory and narrative. O'Connor's work addresses the fact that narrative statements contain references to the context of the events they tell about, while Boje points out that narrative acts also have a context—the context of the teller and their telling which helps to interpret the narrative act. But interpreting the narrative act produces further contextualizing *ad infinitum* (von Foerster 1984: 45–9)—a narrative form of recursive symmetry involving sensitivity to the context of interpretation and the paradox of inescapability from context no matter how many interpretive moves we make. Acknowledgement of this paradox brings narrative consciousness of our embeddedness; which brings us to reflexivity.

Reflexivity. The narrative mode of thinking reminds one that behind every narrative there is a narrator. A story told presupposes a storyteller; it is not an outcome of logical necessity but a product of contingent human construction. As White (1987: 178) argues, echoing Ricoeur, 'narrative discourse does not simply reflect or passively register a world already made; it works up the material in perception and reflection, fashions it, and creates something new, in precisely the same way that human agents by their actions fashion distinctive forms of historical life out of the world they inherit as their past'. In other words, the domain of narrative discourse has verisimilitude. The closest we can come to explaining verisimilitude in logico-scientific terms is to say that narrative discourse is isomorphic with the domain of action: humans reproduce as narrators what they do as agents, and vice versa (MacIntyre 1985: 204–25; White 1987: 173–81). However, in narrative terms verisimilitude means more than this: it is the subjective resonance that occurs between the listener's/reader's experience of the world and the narrator's rendition of it. It imparts credibility to the narrative, the narrator, and the narrative act (Fisher 1987), but also provides experience with authenticity (ibid.).

As we have already argued at some length above, appreciating complexity requires a second order of thinking about complexity. That is, not only must we engage with the system under study, we must also confront our own complexity. In narrative terms, complexity theorists are part of the stories they tell about complex systems—they are narrators of complexity (in both senses of that ambiguous phrase: they narrate about complexity and they are complex narrators). Once inside the frame of the story, complexity-theorists-as-narrators are subject to narrative analysis which can be conducted in a variety of ways. One of these ways is suggested by narratology.

Inspired by Genette (1980; 1982; 1988; 1992; see also Hatch 1996 for an application of narratology to organization theory), narratology concerns the positioning of the narrator in relation to the story told and the narrative act. Genette offered two analytical dimensions to the study of narrative position: narrative perspective (Who sees?) and narrative voice (Who says?). Genette explained narrative perspective in terms of the relationship between the narrator and the story told, which he claimed defines whether the story is seen from an internal or an external point of view. Building on Genette, Hatch (1996: 361) claimed that narrative perspective parallels social scientists' concerns with epistemology (i.e. subjectivism versus objectivism). Genette explained narrative voice in terms of the relationship between the narrator and the narrative act, which he claimed is captured by whether or not the narrator includes him- or herself as a character in the story told. Hatch compared this dimension with social scientists' concerns with reflexivity (e.g. Giddens 1984, 1991; Woolgar 1988) and pointed out that the question for social scientists is one of deciding whether or not the researcher will be represented in the research story told, which is our interest here.

A step toward appreciating and understanding second-order complexity would be achieved by analysing the positioning of narrators in writing on complexity theory. We are inclined to argue that narrative positions that are reflexive are more complex than those occupied by the non-reflexive narrators who dominate contemporary social-science writing, particularly writing about complexity theory. Because a reflexive narrator does not balk at entering the domain of explicating and commenting upon meaning and interpretation, such narrative positioning should help complexity researchers to reflect critically on the features they attribute to systems (i.e. non-linear, scale-dependent, recursive, sensitive to initial conditions, and emergent) and expose the purposes and motivations that link them to the systems they seek to address (e.g. the desire for predictability).

Reflexivity is related to contextuality in the sense that inclusion of the narrator in the narrative involves another layer of context. Narrative thinking reveals a story told by a narrator, occupying a particular position, interpreted by listeners, engaged together in a narrative act. Stories are contextualized by narrators whose positions give context via insight operating inside the context of narrative acts, etc. The recursiveness of context extends to the recursiveness of narrative thinking, so that thinker and thought become so intertwined as to render the possibility of disentanglement unimaginable, and ourselves more complex.

A deep understanding of second-order complexity has been shown by certain reflexive practitioners who have been aware of their own complexity (subjectivity). For example, the late Sir Geoffrey Vickers (1983), a senior British civil servant, manifested such an awareness in his writings on policy-making through his concept of 'appreciative systems'— the value judgements underlying executive decision-making. More recently, the financier George Soros (1994) made 'reflexivity' a central concept of his theory of the operation of financial markets. To the extent that the actor's thinking is part of the situation to which it relates, notes Soros, there is no reality independent of human perceptions. Since an actor's understanding of a situation influences the situation, such an understanding is always imperfect. Being aware of such imperfection (what Soros calls 'participant's bias') makes an actor see social processes as open-ended and brings into focus his/her own role in shaping them.

In other words, for Soros a reflexive actor—an actor aware of the interplay between his/her thinking and acting—is a more complex actor than a non-reflexive one, since more inequivalent descriptions of a situation can be generated. While for a non-reflexive actor reality has certain definite features which can be captured by a limited number of descriptions, for a reflexive actor reality is, partly at least, dependent for its description on an observer's vocabulary. In defining a situation, being aware of the role of your own as well as of others' vocabularies enables you to generate more descriptions of it (Tsoukas and Papoulias 1996: 75).

Purposes and Motives

Narrative organization is causal: in narrative accounts it is not only sequence that is important but, crucially, consequence (Randall 1995: 121). Indeed, causality is what distinguishes a plot from a mere story. As Forster famously remarked, ' "The king died and then the queen died" is a story'. ' "The king died and then the queen died of grief" is a plot' (Forster quoted ibid.). In the first instance (in a story) we ask: 'And then?', while in the second instance (in a plot) we ask: 'Why?' Whereas in the logico-scientific mode of thinking an event is explained by showing that it is an instance of a general law, in the narrative mode of thinking an event is explained by relating it to human purpose. Narrative preserves both time (to which we return later) and human agency.

Narrative is infused with motive. Burke (1945, 1954) claims that motive is a linguistic product because motives are interpretations of our own and others' reasons for acting. As such, they are framed by the discourses in which they and we operate and are couched in terms provided by that discourse. Thus, when we narrate, we give evidence of our motives in a way that is largely (though not completely) absent from our logico-scientific mode of speaking and writing. As a matter of interpretation, motives are presented throughout narratives and may be imputed by the narrators themselves, and/or by their listeners/readers. As interpretations, motives are not fixed entities, they are open to multiple readings framed by the contexts and orientations of the readers caught up in the narrative act (which may include the narrator him- or herself).

As a discourse, organization provides the terms in which motives are spoken of. That is, when organizational members are asked to justify their actions, they do so in the terms provided by the organizational discourses in which they participate. For example, downsizing is justified by the necessity of economic circumstance; acquisition in terms of opportunities for revenue creation or profit-taking. As discourses change, so justifications change. In the knowledge age, downsizing becomes a matter of reducing redundancies in competence; acquisitions are performed to take advantage of another company's database or to acquire its knowledge resources. As language shifts, so do the terms in which we speak about our motives.

In Part I entitled of *Permanence and Change*, 'On Interpretation', Burke (1954) presented his thesis on motives as interpretations and as linguistic products (see also Taylor 1985: 23–8). Burke positioned his arguments in contrast to the enterprise of reductionist natural science, claiming that what this orientation excludes from view is 'social motives as such' (Burke 1954: li). In relating motives to interpretations and positioning both against rationalizing science, Burke (ibid. 62) pointed out that:

Those who look upon science as the final culmination of man's rationalizing enterprise may be neglecting an important aspect of human response. Even a completely stable condition does not have the same meaning after it has continued for some time as it had when first inaugurated.

In positioning his argument thus, we find Burke's thesis entirely compatible with Bruner's distinction between logico-scientific and narrative modes of thinking. Thus, when Burke discusses motives as absent from rationalizing science but present in ordinary language, we cannot help equating his position with what Bruner called the narrative mode. Moreover, Burke also positions language, and thus the motives that he claimed are constituted by language, within the confines of a particular context, or 'orientation', to use his term. A motive, according to Burke (ibid. 25) is 'a term of interpretation, and being such it will naturally take its place within the framework of our *Weltanschauung* as a whole'. Motives as interpretations are 'centered in the entire context of judgments as to what people ought to do, how they [prove] themselves worthy, on what grounds they [can] expect good treatment, what good treatment [is], etc.' That is another way of saying that motives, as interpretations, require cultural context to recover or create their meaning. Thus, Burke (ibid.) concluded, attributions of motive by which people explain their conduct are 'but a fragmentary part of [their] larger orientation', and 'a terminology of motives [...] is moulded to fit our general orientation as to purposes, instrumentalities, the "good life," etc.'

Burke permits a clear view of what we have called second-order complexity. In describing motivation as a linguistic product situated in a dominant discourse, he suggests a more complicated understanding of motives, an understanding once removed from the psychological level and placed instead at the organizational level where the discourse itself, which defines the terms in which motivation can be spoken of, is located (Harre and Gillett 1994: 97–111). By seeing motives in relation to discourse, Burke complicates our understanding and offers a narratological viewpoint. We say this because to speak about second-order complexity, or the discourse of motives, is to express what is meant by the narrative mode of thinking. That is, the narrative mode, because it instantiates the discourse as well as the story told within it, matches the requirements of addressing second-order complexity.

Organizational complexity, in our view, is well-served by a narrative approach precisely because of its relationship to motives. Both being 'linguistic products' in Burke's terms, they have an affinity that we might profit from recognizing. To give just one example, in considering the five features of complex systems presented earlier, acknowledgement of the narrator describing systems in these terms makes us aware of the discourse (i.e. the discourse of complexity theory) that the narrator invokes, and of the positioning of the narrator within that discourse, which gives us our appreciation of his or her motives; in other words, a way to frame the narrator that produces a motivation-rich sense of understanding. Weick, of course, would call this sense-making. But either way, having a device for framing motives leads us to a narrative approach to complexity, and narrative in turn provides a more complex orientation (i.e. both first- and second-order appreciations are accommodated) to the study of organizing. Once again, we engage (enact, employ) recursiveness when we switch to the narrative mode of thinking.

Temporality

Narrative is factually indifferent but temporally sensitive: its power as a story is determined by the sequence of its constituents, rather than the truth or falsity of any of them (Bruner 1990: 44; Czarniawska 1998: 5). Temporality, therefore, is a key feature of narrative organization, helping also to preserve particularity. As Hunter (1991:46) notes with respect to medical narratives: 'By means of the temporal organization of detail, governed by the "plots" of disease, physicians are able to negotiate between theory and practice, sustaining medicine as an inter-level activity that must account for both scientific principle and the specificity of the human beings who are their patients.'

Ricoeur's (1984) treatise on *Time and Narrative* supports the claim that a narrative approach to complexity theory uniquely emphasizes the temporal dimension of experience and simultaneously explores the issues of consciousness that are raised by the juxtaposition of narrative and time. As Ricoeur (ibid.) argued, one cannot engage in narrative as either a narrator or reader/ listener without the experience of time. In his study Ricoeur (ibid.: 20) demonstrated this with a passage from Augustine's *Confessions*:

Suppose that I am going to recite a psalm that I know. Before I begin my faculty of expectation is engaged by the whole of it. But once I have begun, as much of the psalm as I have removed from the province of expectation and relegated to the past now engages my memory, and the scope of the action which I am performing is divided between the two faculties of memory and expectation, the one looking back to the part which I have already recited, the other looking forward to the part which I have still to recite. But my faculty of attention is present all the while, and through it passes what was the future in the process of becoming the past. As the process continues, the province of memory is extended in proportion as that of expectation is reduced, until the whole of my expectation is absorbed. This happens when I have finished my recitation and it has all passed into the province of memory.

According to Ricoeur, this passage illustrates how memory (past) and expectation (future) interact to influence attention and thereby produce the three-fold present of our experience (the present of the past, the present of the present, and the present of the future). Although this example may seem trivial, Augustine went further, generalizing his point to other levels of experience (ibid. 22, from Augustine's *Confessions*):

What is true of the whole psalm is also true of all its parts and each syllable. It is true of any longer action in which I may be engaged and of which the recitation of the psalm may only be a small part. It is true of a man's whole life, of which all his action are parts. It is true of the whole history of mankind, of which each man's life is a part.

These last statements evoke images of fractals and recursive symmetries, but portray them along their temporal rather than their spatial axes. We believe that increasing sensitivity to the ways in which memory and expectation contribute to complexity is a valuable contribution narrative approaches can make to the study of complexity (in this instance with respect to recursiveness) and organizations.

To carry on a little further exploring what this contribution might look like, we consider another Augustinian idea promoted by Ricoeur—*distensio*. Following Augustine, Ricoeur suggested that, when engaged, memory and expectation extend us across time, allowing us to bridge past and future in the present moment. Things in memory and in imagination are potentially present and *distensio* occurs when we stretch our consciousness across past, present, and future. Furthermore, Ricoeur argued, it is the relationship between expectation, memory, and attention forged by *distensio* that gives us the experience of time.

Could it be that through distended experience we construct and make use of the temporal dimension, as Ricoeur suggested? If so, it could likewise be that narrative is part of our distensive capability, both in the sense of invoking memory and expectation, and, as Augustine also showed, via engagement in the process of relegating the future to the past on a moment-by-moment basis. Only that to which we attend can make the journey from expectation to memory, and in this regard narrative may be an important attention-giving device. If this is the case, then narrative helps us experience time by offering a means of passing expectation into memory. Furthermore, memory and expectation, once engaged, enlarge our consciousness in (and of) the present. Such enlargement increases our complexity.

Ricouer's *distensio* and the way it contributes towards the compexification of the subject can be illustrated nicely by drawing on Weick and Roberts' study (1993) of high-reliability organizations. Weick and Roberts developed the notion of 'collective mind', which they take to be not a given property of a collectivity but the pattern whereby individuals heedfully interrelate their actions. The more heedfully individuals interrelate their actions, the more likely it is that unexpected events will be handled adequately. The significance of this cannot be overestimated because in high-reliability organizations it is extremely important that interactions between small, unexpected events do not escalate to yield catastrophes.

How might heedful interrelating be increased? Weick and Roberts (ibid. 366) suggest three ways, the first of which is directly relevant to our discussion of *distensio*: by making connections across time, activities, and experience. Weick and Roberts (ibid.) explain: '[By connecting longer stretches of time] more know-how is brought forward from the past and is elaborated into new contributions and representations that extrapolate farther into the future'. By making connections between the past, the present, and the future, collective mind becomes more complex and, thus, is strengthened, since 'the scope of heedful action reaches more places' (ibid.). In this regard, Weick and Roberts (ibid. 368) extol the significance of organizational members developing their 'narrative skills', because it is through them that collective mind becomes richer and more complex. 'Stories', argue the authors, 'organize know-how, tacit knowledge, nuance, sequence, multiple causation, means–ends relations, and consequences into a memorable plot' (ibid.).

In their study of the use of history by decision-makers, Neustadt and May (1986: ch. 14) have similarly extolled the virtues of what they call 'thinking in time-streams'—looking at an issue in the present with a sense of the past and an awareness of the future (see also Schon 1983). Citing examples of several influential US policy makers, the authors make it clear how the interlacing of past, present, and future complexifies policy makers' thinking, making them potentially more effective. Commenting on General George Marshall in particular, Neustadt and May note Marshall's acute sense of history which, while informing his decisions at a point in time, made Marshall focus his eyes 'not only to the coming year but well beyond. [...] By looking back, Marshall looked ahead, identifying what was worthwile to preserve from the past and carry into the future' (Neustadt and May 1986: 248). Policy makers' skills in making such connections across time are necessarily of a narrative kind.

As argued earlier, narrative plots can be far more intricate than logico-scientific causal models can, because narrative connections can also be forged through associations that are not causal in the logico-scientific sense. In narrative, for example, things can be connected by co-occurrence, spatial proximity, formal similarity, or metaphor, all types of association that logico-scientific modes of thinking try to eliminate as distractions from the discovery of scientific generalizations. Nevertheless, these connections may well help us understand, in addition to recursiveness (explored above), the non-linearity, indeterminacy, unpredictability, and emergence of complex systems. We leave these explorations for future development of the narrative approach.

Narratives not only allow for multiple connections among events across time, they also preserve multiple temporalities. As well as being linked to clock time, narrative time is primarily humanly relevant time (Ricouer 1984): its significance is not derived from the clock or the calendar, but from the meanings assigned to events by actors (Bruner 1996: 133). In this sense narrative time is not symmetrical. Returning to Forster's and Bruner's example quoted earlier, the moment after the King's death is for the Queen qualitatively different from the moment before his death. Burke (1954: 62) similarly noted that: 'Even a completely stable condition does not have the same meaning after it has continued for some time as it had when first inaugurated.' It is this asymmetry of time (so elegantly argued for in the sciences by Prigogine—see Prigogine 1992, 1997; Prigogine and Stengers 1984) that gives narrative its dynamic texture. For some researchers narrative time is like a turbulent current 'characterized by an overall vector, the plot, itself composed of areas of local turbulence, eddies where time is reversed, rapids where it speeds ahead, and pools where it effectively stops' (Argyros 1992: 669). By accommodating multiple temporalities, narratives are far more complex than propositional statements, in which, as we saw earlier, time is absent.

Conclusions

To summarize; a narrative approach to complexity theory suggests that our understandings of complex systems and their properties will always be grounded in the narratives we construct about them. When we characterize initial conditions as perturbations of a system, we construct the beginning of a plot (the system is a character or protagonist and the perturbation is a situation or antagonist) that may conclude with the system moving off in a direction that is surprising. As with unpredictable characters in other stories or in life, the complex system is interpreted as volatile or capricious. When the multiple interactions of systemic behaviour in complex systems produce emergent (new) modes of behaviour, in narrative terms the plot thickens, the characters develop. To put this more reflexively, when we theorize about complexity, we narrate. Being conscious of our narrativity develops the second order of complexity upon which we earlier claimed complexity itself rests. This chapter has been about developing second-order complexity alongside our appreciation of organizational complexity via a narrative approach.

In presenting arguments in favour of taking a narrative approach to complexity theory, we analysed the primary mode of thinking typical of complexity theorists and suggested a role that the narrative mode of thinking could play in compensating for the limitations of complexity theory's well-practised logico-scientific mode of thought. Interpretative organization theory was used to show how the narrative mode complements and extends the findings of complexity theory and complexifies our thinking about organizational complexity. A few ideas from narrative theory were presented to give a sense of the contribution that further development of narrative approaches to understanding complexity theory might offer to organization theory. A critique of the logico-scientific mode of thinking indicated absences in complexity theory that narrative theory might fill, and these possibilities were explored in relation to contextuality, reflexivity, purposes/motives, and temporal sensitivity, all of which were related to recursiveness in order to demonstrate how the narrative approach contributes to understanding organizational complexity.

References

Ackoff, R. (1981), *Creating the Corporate Future* (New York: Wiley).

Ansoff, I. H. (1991), 'Critique of Henry Mintzberg's "The Design School: Reconsidering the Basic Premises of Strategic Management"', *Strategic Management Journal*, 12: 136–48.

Argyros, A. (1992), 'Narrative and Chaos', *New Literary History*, 23: 659–73.

Baligh, H. H., Burton, R. M., and Obel, B. (1990), 'Devising Expert Systems in Organization Theory: The Organizational Consultant', in M. Masuch (ed.), *Organization, Management, and Expert Systems* (Berlin: de Gruyter), 35–57.

Banaji, M., and Crowder, R. (1989), 'The Bankruptcy of Everyday Memory', *American Psychologist*, 44: 1185–93.

Barnard, C. (1976), 'Foreword' to H. Simon, *Administrative Behavior*, (New York: Free Press), pp. xlvii–xlvi.

Barrow, J. (1995), 'Theories of Everything', in J. Cornwell (ed.), *Nature's Imagination* (Oxford: Oxford University Press), 45–63.

Barry, D. (1997), 'Strategy Retold: Toward a Narrative View of Strategic Discourse', *Academy of Management Review*, 22: 429–52.

Bartunek, J., Gordon, J., and Weathersby, R. (1983), 'Developing "Complicated" Understanding in Administrators', *Academy of Management Review*, 8: 273–84.

Bateson, G. (1979), *Mind and Nature* (Toronto: Bantam).

Beer, S. (1973), 'The Surrogate World We Manage', *Behavioral Science*, 18: 198–209.

—— (1981), *Brain of the Firm* (Chichester: Wiley).

Berger, P., and Luckmann, T. (1967), *The Social Construction of Reality* (London: Penguin).

Boje, D. (1991), 'The Storytelling Organization: A Study of Story Performance in an Office-supply firm', *Administrative Science Quarterly*, 36: 106–26.

Bolman, L., and Deal, T. (1991), *Reframing Organizations* (San Francisco, Calif.: Jossey-Bass).

Boyce, M. (1995), 'Collective Centring and Collective Sense-making in the Stories and Storytelling of One Organization', *Organization Studies*, 16: 107–37.

Brown, J. S., and Duguid, P. (1991), 'Organizational Learning and Communities of Practice', *Organization Science*, 2: 40–57.

Bruner, J. (1986), *Actual Minds, Possible Worlds* (Cambridge, Mass.: Harvard University Press).

—— (1990), *Acts of Meaning* (Cambridge, Mass.: Harvard University Press).

—— (1996), 'The Narrative Construal of Reality', in J. Bruner, *The Culture of Education* (Cambridge, Mass.: Harvard University Press), 130–49.

Brunsson, N. (1989), *The Organization of Hypocrisy* (Chichester: Cambridge, Mass.: Wiley).

Burke, K. (1945), *A Grammar of Motives* (Berkeley, Calif.: University of California Press).

—— (1954), *Permanence and Change: An Anatomy of Purpose*, 3rd edn. (Berkeley, Calif.: University of California Press).

Capra, F. (1988), *Uncommon Wisdom*, (London: Fontana).

—— (1996), *The Web of Life* (New York: Anchor).

Casti, J. (1986), 'On System Complexity: Identification, Measurement, and Management', in J. Casti and A. Karlqvist (eds.), *Complexity, Language, and Life: Mathematical Approaches* (Berlin: Springer-Verlag), 146–73.

—— (1989), *Paradigms Lost* (London: Cardinal).

—— (1994), *Explaining a Paradoxical World Through the Science of Surprise* (London: Abacus).

Checkland, P. (1981), *Systems Thinking, Systems Practice* (Chichester: Wiley).

Chia, R. (1996), 'The Problem of Reflexivity in Organizational Research: Towards a Postmodern Science of Organization', *Organization*, 3: 31–59.

Clemson, B. (1984), *Cybernetics* (Cambridge, Mass.: Abacus).

Cohen, B. (1994), 'Newton and the Social Sciences, with Special Reference to Economics, or, the Case of the Missing Paradigm', in P. Mirowski (ed.), *Natural Images in Economic Thought* (Cambridge: Cambridge University Press), 55–90.

Cooper, R. and Burrell, G. (1988), 'Modernism, Postmodernism and Organisational Analysis: An Introduction, *Organization Studies*, 9: 91–112.

Corvellec, H. (1997), *Stories of Achievements: Narrative Features of Organizational Performance*, (New Brunswick, NJ: Transaction).

Crutchfield, J., Farmer, D., Packard, N., and Shaw, R. (1986), 'Chaos', *Scientific American*, 255: 46–57.

Czarniawska-Joerges, B. (1994), 'Narratives of Individual and Organizational Identities', in S. A. Deetz (ed.), *Communication Yearbook*, xvii (Thousand Oaks, Calif.: Sage), 193–221.

—— (1997a), *Narrating the Organization: Dramas of Institutional Identity* (Iowa, Ia.: University of Iowa Press).

Czarniawska-Joerges, B. (1997*b*), 'A Four Times Told Tale: Combining Narrative and Scientific Knowledge in Organization Studies', *Organization*, 4: 7–30.

—— (1998), *A Narrative Approach to Organization Studies* (Thousand Oaks, Calif.: Sage).

Davis, P. (1990), 'Chaos Frees the Universe', *New Scientist*, 1737: 48–51.

Dyke, C. (1990), 'Strange Attraction, Curious Liaison: Clio Meets Chaos', *Philosophical Forum*, 21: 369–92.

Feldman, Martha (1991), 'The Meanings of Ambiguity: Learning from Stories and Metaphors', in P. Frost, L. Moore, M. Reis Louis, C. Lundberg, and J. Martin (eds.) *Reframing Organizational Culture*, (Newbury Park, Calif.: Sage), 145–56.

Feyerabend, P. (1987), *Farewell to Reason* (London: Verso).

Filby, I., and Willmott, H. (1988), 'Ideologies and Contradictions in a Public Relations Department: The Seduction and Impotence of Living Myth', *Organization Studies*, 9: 335–49.

Fisher, W. R. (1987), *Human Communication as Narration: Toward a Philosophy of Reason, Value and Action* (Columbia, SC: University of South Carolina Press).

—— (1981), 'On Cybernetics of Cybernetics and Social Theory', in G. Roth and H. Schwegler (eds.), *Self-Organizing Systems* (Frankfurt: Campus Verlag), 102–5.

Foucault, M. (1966), *The Order of Things* (London: Tavistock/Routledge).

Gabriel, Y. (1995), 'The Unmanaged Organization: Stories, Fantasies and Subjectivity', *Organization Studies*, 16: 477–501.

Geertz, C. (1973), *The Interpretation of Cultures*, (New York: Basic).

Gell-Mann, M. (1994), *The Quark and the Jaguar* (London: Little, Brown).

Genette, Gerard (1980), *Narrative Discourse: An Essay in Method*, trans Jane E. Lewin (Ithaca, Cornell University Press).

—— (1982), *Figures of Literary Discourse*, trans. Alan Sheridan (New York: Columbia University Press).

—— (1988), *Narrative Discourse Revisited* trans. Jane E. Lewin (Ithaca, NY: Cornell University Press).

—— (1992), *The Architext*, trans Jane E. Lewin (Berkeley, Calif.: University of California Press).

Giddens, A. (1984), *The Constitution of Society: Outline of the Theory of Structuration* (Berkeley, Calif.: University of California Press).

—— (1991), *Modernity and Self-identity: Self and Society in the Late Modern Age* (Stanford, Calif.: Stanford University Press).

Glaserfeld, E. (1984), 'An Introduction to Radical Constructivism', in P. Watzlawick (ed.) *The Invented Reality* (New York: Norton) 17–40.

Glorie, J. C., Masuch, M., and Marx, M. (1990), 'Formalizing Organizational Theory: A Knowledge-based Approach', in M. Masuch (ed.), *Organization, Management, and Expert Systems* (Berlin: de Gruyter), 79–104.

Goodwin, B. (1994), *How the Leopard Changed its Spots* (London: Phoenix).

Granovetter, M. (1992), 'Problems of Explanation in Economic Sociology', in N. Nohria and R. G. Eccles (eds.), *Networks and Organizations* (Boston, Mass.: Harvard Business School Press).

Harre, R., and Gillett, G. (1994), *The Discursive Mind* (Thousand Oaks, Calif.: Sage).

Hatch, M. J. (1996), 'The Role of the Researcher: An Analysis of Narrative Position in Organization Theory', *Journal of Management Inquiry*, 5(4):359–74.

—— (1997), 'Irony and the Social Construction of Contradiction in the Humor of a Management Team', *Organization Science*, 8: 275–88.

—— and Ehrlich, S. B. (1993), 'Spontaneous Humor as an Indicator of Paradox and Ambiguity in Organizations', *Organization Studies*, 14(4): 505–26.

Hayek, F. A. (1945), 'The Use of Knowledge in Society', *American Economic Review*, 35: 519–30

—— (1982), *Law, Legislation and Liberty* (London: Routledge & Kegan Paul).

Hayles, N. K. (1989), 'Chaos as Orderly Disorder: Shifting Ground in Contemporary Literature and Science, *New Literary History*, 20: 305–22

—— (1990), *Chaos Bound: Orderly Disorder in Contemporary Literature and Science* (Ithaca, NY: Cornell University Press).

—— (1991), (ed.), *Chaos and Order: Complex Dynamics in Literature and Science* (Chicago, Ill.: University of Chicago Press).

Holland, J. (1995), *Hidden Order: How Adaptation Builds Complexity* (Reading, Mass.: Addison-Wesley).

Hunter, K. M. (1991), *Doctors' Stories: The Narrative Structure of Medical Knowledge* (Princeton, NJ: Princeton University Press).

Johnson, P. (1992), *Human-Computer Interaction* (London: McGraw-Hill).

Kallinikos, J. (1996), *Technology and Society* (Munich: Accedo).

Kamminga, H. (1990), 'What is This Thing Called Chaos?', *New Left Review* 181: 49–59.

Kellert, S. (1993), *In the Wake of Chaos* (Chicago, Ill.: University of Chicago Press).

Koestler, A. (1964), *The Act of Creation* (New York: Macmillan).

Latour, B. (1987), *Science in Action* (Milton Keynes: Open University Press).

Lave, J. (1988), *Cognition in Practice* (Cambridge: Cambridge University Press).

MacIntyre, A. (1985), *After Virtue*, 2nd edn. (London: Duckworth).

March, J. G., and Olsen, J. P. (1976), *Ambiguity and Choice in Organizations* (Bergen: Universitetsforlaget).

Martin, J. (1982), 'Stories and Scripts in Organizational Settings', in A. H. Hastorf and A. M. Isen (eds.) *Cognitive Social Psychology* (New York: Elsevier), 255–305.

—— Feldman, M., Hatch, M. J., and Sitkin, S. (1983), 'The Uniqueness Paradox in Organizational Stories', *Administrative Science Quarterly*, 28: 438–53.

Meyerson, D. (1991), ' "Normal" Ambiguity?', in P. Frost, L. Moore, M. Reis Louis, C. Lundberg, and J. Martin (eds.) *Reframing Organizational Culture* (Newbury Park, Calif.: Sage), 131–44.

Miller, J. G. (1978), *Living Systems* (New York: McGraw-Hill).

Mintzberg, H. (1979), *The Structuring of Organizations* (Englewood Cliffs, NJ: Prentice-Hall).

—— (1989), *Mintzberg on Management* (New York: Free Press).

Mirowski, P. (1984), 'Physics and the "marginalist revolution" '. *Cambridge Journal of Economics* 8: 361–79.

—— (1989), *More Heat than Light: Economics as Social Physics, Physics as Nature's Economics* (Cambridge: Cambridge University Press).

Mohr, L. (1982), *Explaining Organizational Behavior* (San Francisco, Calif.: Jossey-Bass).

Morgan, G. (1997), *Images of Organization*, 2nd edn. (Thousand Oaks, Calif.: Sage).

Mulkay, M. (1988), *On Humour* (Oxford: Blackwell).

Neustadt, R. E., and May, E. R. (1986), *Thinking in Time* (New York: Free Press).

O'Connor, E. S. (1995), 'Paradoxes of Participation: Textual Analysis and Organizational Change', *Organization Studies*, 16(5): 769–803.

Orr, J. E. (1990), 'Sharing Knowledge, Celebrating Identity: Community Memory in a Service Culture', in D. Middleton and D. Edwards (eds.), *Collective Remembering* (London: Sage), 168–89.

—— (1996), *Talking About Machines* (Ithaca, NY: ILR/Cornell University Press).

Pascale, R. (1990), *Managing on the Edge* (London: Viking).

Pepper, S. (1942), *World Hypotheses* (Berkeley, Calif.: University of California Press).

Perrow, C., (1977), 'The Bureaucratic Paradox: The Efficient Organization Centralizes in Order to Decentralize', *Organizational Dynamics*, 5: 3–14.

Polanyi, M. (1975), 'Personal Knowledge', in M. Polanyi and H. Prosch, *Meaning* (Chicago, Ill.: University of Chicago Press), 22–45.

Polkinghorne, D. (1988), *Narrative Knowing and the Human Sciences* (Albany, NY: State University of New York Press).

Poole, S. and Van de Ven, A. (1989), 'Using Paradox to Build Management and Organization Theories', *Academy of Management Review*, 14: 562–78.

Price Waterhouse Change Integration Team (1996), *The Paradox Principles: How High-Performance Companies Manage Chaos, Complexity, and Contradiction to Achieve Superior Results*, (Chicago, Ill.: Irwin).

Prigogine, I. (1980), *From Being to Becoming* (San Francisco, Calif.: Freeman).

—— (1989), 'The Philosophy of Instability', *Futures*, 21: 396–400.

—— (1992), 'Beyond Being and Becoming', *New Perspectives Quarterly*, 9: 22–8.

—— (1997), *The End of Certainty* (New York: Free Press).

—— and Stengers, I. (1984), *Order Out of Chaos* (London: Fontana).

Putnam, Linda (1985), 'Contradictions and Paradoxes in Organizations', in L. Thayer (ed.), *Organization—Communication: Emerging Perspectives* (Norwood, NJ: Ablex), 151–67.

Quinn, R., and Cameron, K. (1988), *Paradox and Transformation* (Cambridge, Mass.: Ballinger).

Randall, W. L. (1995), *The Stories We Are* (Toronto: University of Toronto Press).

Reed, E. S. (1996), *The Necessity of Experience* (New Haven, Conn.: Yale University Press).

Reisch, G. (1991), 'Chaos, History, and Narrative', *History and Theory*, 30: 1–20.

Ricoeur, P. (1984), *Time and Narrative*, i. (Chicago, Ill: University of Chicago Press).

Rorty, R. (1989), *Contingency, Irony, and Solidarity* (Cambridge: Cambridge University Press).

Salomon, G. (1993), editor's introduction to G. Salomon (ed.), *Distributed Cognitions* (Cambridge: Cambridge University Press), pp.xi–xxi.

Schauer, F. (1991), *Playing by the Rules* (Oxford: Clarendon Press).

Schon, D. (1983), *The Reflective Practitioner* (Aldershot: Avebury).

Shackley, S., Wynne, B., and Waterton, C. (1996), 'Imagine Complexity: The Past, Present and Future Potential of Complex Thinking', *Futures*, 28: 201–25.

Shannon, C., and Weaver, W. (1949), *The Mathematical Theory of Communication* (Urbana, Ill.: University of Illinois Press).

Shapin, S. (1996), *The Scientific Revolution* (Chicago, Ill.: University of Chicago Press).

Shaw, G., Brown, R., and Bromiley, P. G. (1998), 'Strategic Stories: How 3M is Rewriting Business Planning', *Harvard Business Review*, 50(3): 41–50.

Shotter, J. (1993), *Conversational Realities* (London: Sage).

Smircich, L., and Morgan, G. (1982), 'Leadership: The Management of Meaning', *Journal of Applied Behavioral Science*, 18: 257–73.

Smith, R. (1997), *The Fontana History of the Human Sciences* (London: Fontana).

Soros, G. (1994), *The Alchemy of Finance* (New York: Wiley).

Stacey, R. (1996), *Complexity and Creativity in Organizations* (San Francisco, Calif.: Barrett-Koehler).

Stewart, I. (1993), 'Chaos', in L. Howe and A. Wain (eds.) *Predicting the Future* (Cambridge: Cambridge University Press), 24–51.

Stonum, G. L. (1989), 'Cybernetic Explanation as a Theory of Reading', *New Literary History*, 20: 397–410.

Taylor, C. (1985), *Philosophy and the Human Sciences*, ii, (Cambridge: Cambridge University Press).

—— (1993), 'To Follow a Rule . . .', in C. Calhoun, E. Lipuma, and M. Postone (eds.), *Bourdieu: Critical Perspectives* (Cambridge: Polity), 45–59.

Toulmin, S. (1990), *Cosmopolis: The Hidden Agenda of Modernity* (Chicago, Ill.: University of Chicago Press).

Tsoukas, H. (1994), 'Introduction: From Social Engineering to Reflective Action in Organizational Behavior', in H. Tsoukas (ed.), *New Thinking in Organizational Behavior* (Oxford: Butterworth/Heinemann), 1–22.

—— (1996), 'The Firm as a Distributed Knowledge System: A Constructionist Approach', *Strategic Management Journal*, 17, special winter issue: 11–25.

—— (1998), 'Forms of Knowledge and Forms of Life in Organized Contexts', in R. Chia (ed.), *In the Realm of Organization* (London: Routledge) 43–66.

—— and Papoulias, D. (1996), 'Creativity in OR/MS: From Technique to Epistemology', *Interfaces*, 26: 73–9.

Twining, W., and Miers, D. (1991), *How To Do Things With Rules*, 3rd edn. (London: Weidenfeld and Nicolson).

Van Maanen, John (1988), *Tales of the Field: On writing Ethnography* (Chicago, Ill.: University of Chicago Press).

Von Foerster, H. (1984), 'On Constructing a Reality', in P. Watzlawick (ed.), *The Invented Reality* (New York: Norton), 41–61.

Varela, F., Thompson, E., and Rosch, E. (1991), *The Embodied Mind: Cognitive Science and Human Experience* (Cambridge, Mass.: MIT Press).

Vickers, G. (1983), *The Art of Judgement* (London: Harper & Row).

Waddington, C. (1977), *Tools for Thought* (Frogmore: Paladin).

Waldrop, M. M. (1992), *Complexity* (London: Penguin).

Webster, J., and Starbuck, W. (1988), 'Theory Building in Industrial and Organizational Psychology', in C. Cooper and I. Robertson (eds.), *International Review of Industrial and Organizational Psychology* (Chichester: Wiley), 93–138.

Weick, K. E. (1979), *The Social Psychology of Organizing* (Reading, Mass: Addison-Wesley).

—— (1995), *Sensemaking in Organizations* (Thousand Oaks, Calif.: Sage).

—— and Browning, L. (1986), 'Argument and Narration in Organizational Communication', *Journal of Management* 12: 243–59.

—— and Roberts (1993), 'Collective Mind in Organizations: Heedful Interrelating on Flight Decks', *Administrative Science Quarterly*, 38: 357–81.

Westenholtz, A. (1993), 'Paradoxical Thinking and Change in the Frames of Reference', *Organization Studies*, 14(1): 37–58.

White, H. (1987), *The Content of the Form*, (Baltimore, Mass.: Johns Hopkins University Press).

Wilkins, A. (1983), 'Organizational Stories as Symbols which Control the Organization', in P. J. Frost, L. F. Moore, M. R. Louis, C. C. Lundberg, and J. Martin (eds.), *Reframing Organizational Culture*, (Beverly Hills, Calif.: Sage), 81–91.

Woolgar, Steve (1988), 'Reflexivity is the Ethnographer of the Text', in S. Woolgar (ed.) *Knowledge and Reflexivity: New Frontiers in the Sociology of Knowledge*: (London: Sage), 14–34.

ELEVEN

What is Organizational Foresight and How can it be Developed?

Deliberation is irrational in the degree in which an end is so fixed, a
passion or interest so absorbing, that the foresight of consequences is
warped to include only what furthers execution of its predetermined
bias. Deliberation is rational in the degree in which forethought flexibly remakes old aims and habits, institutes perception and love of new
ends and acts

(John Dewey 1988: 138)

The dominance of retrospect in sensemaking is a major reason why
students of sensemaking find forecasting, contingency planning, strategic planning, and other magical probes into the future wasteful and
misleading if they are decoupled from reflective action and history

(Karl E. Weick 1995: 30)

M ANAGEMENT is historically taken to be about effecting and managing
closure: buffering the organization so that uncertainty is minimized,
external dependencies are reduced, and, thus, closure is achieved (Thompson
1967). Such a view, a thoroughly modern one, assumes time to be symmetrical
(or reversible) and, therefore, inconsequential—the future is, more or less, the
past played forward. A closed system is one in which time reversibility has been
established; such a system maximizes efficiency, perhaps, but is short on novelty. In a closed system planning is possible, since external sources of uncertainty have been minimized. Interestingly, a view of time as reversible goes hand
in hand with a view of time as controllable. For planning to be possible, time
must be seen as merely metric, not productive of novelty (Prigogine 1997).

This chapter draws heavily on H. Tsoukas and J. Shepherd, 'Introduction: Organizations
and the Future: From Forecasting to Foresight', in H. Tsoukas and J. Shepherd (eds.),
Managing the Future (Oxford: Blackwell, 2004), 1–17. Parts are reprinted by permission of
Blackwell, Copyright (2004)

The obsession with planning has been a hallmark of modernity. As several leading social theorists have pointed out, one of the most significant features of modern individuals is their attitude to time in general and the future in particular. Giddens (1990, 1991), for example, has repeatedly argued that, whereas for pre-modern societies the future is something that just happens, with individuals exercising only a limited influence over it, for modern societies the future is something to be carefully thought about, influenced, and, ideally, planned. Nowhere is this modern tendency better manifested than in the field of strategy. Companies are advised to plan ahead meticulously, and several techniques have been on offer to that effect.

However, research has shown the limits of the planning-cum-design approach to strategy (Mintzberg 1994; Mintzberg, Ahlstrand, and Lampel 1998), as well as the inherent limits to the ability of organizations to forecast, especially discontinuities and radically new developments (Hogarth and Makridakis 1981; Makridakis 1990; Makridakis and Hibon 1979). Popper (1988) famously remarked that for radically new innovation to occur at all, the future must be *unknowable*, since otherwise innovation would, in principle, be already known and would occur in the present and not in the future. As MacIntyre (1985: 93) has observed, commenting approvingly on Popper's claim, 'any invention, any discovery, which consists essentially in the elaboration of a radically new concept cannot be predicted, for a necessary part of the prediction is the present elaboration of the very concept whose discovery or invention was to take place only in the future. The notion of the prediction of radical conceptual innovation is itself conceptually incoherent'. If we are to take the idea of the future seriously, we must accept that the future is inherently open-ended—it will always surprise us (Rorty 1989).

While such an agnostic attitude towards the future points out the limits of a purely cognitive attitude to it—that is, it highlights the limits of trying to forecast and plan for what lies ahead—it makes it possible, at the same time, to emphasize an *active* attitude to the future: although the latter may not be known *ex ante*, it is however *created* by human beings. Therefore, the question of foresightful action—action that aims at influencing and shaping what will be—becomes relevant and important to investigate. In an organizational context at least, the main questions to explore include: What does an active stance to the future imply for organizations? What is organizational foresight and how can it be developed?

Organizations and the Future

In a celebrated lecture given at the Harvard Business School in 1931 Alfred North Whitehead (1967) posed similar questions. The distinguished philosopher identified *foresight* as the crucial feature of the competent business mind.

Anticipating contemporary notions of 'sense-making', 'double-loop learning', and 'scenario planning', Whitehead perspicuously saw that business organizations need to cultivate foresight in order to cope with the relentless change that modernity generates. Foresight is rooted in deep understanding, he remarked. It marks the ability to see through the apparent confusion, to spot developments before they become trends, to see patterns before they fully emerge, and to grasp the relevant features of social currents that are likely to shape the direction of future events. While Whitehead (and other philosophers, such as Dewey and Popper, who also addressed the question of foresight) had individual actors (entrepreneurs) in mind, his remarks can be extended to organizations as well. However, to appreciate what foresight may mean in an organizational context, we need to revisit some key properties of organizations.

It has been suggested that organizing is about reducing equivocality between actors and generating recurrent patterns of behaviour over time (Weick 1979). Another way of putting this is to point out that organizing is a process for institutionalizing cognitive representations, routines, and sequences of predictable behaviour. Moreover, strictly speaking, when a social system is organized it creates the conditions for a standardization of time, whereby events and processes are placed in a patterned chronological order. Take, for example, the case of a university. Classes are scheduled, meetings are planned, office hours are announced, events are put on the calendar—university life has its own patterned rhythms. Chronological time is superimposed over the subjective time of individuals so that the synchronized carrying out of organizational tasks is possible (Hassard 2002; see Das in that volume). Or, to use Giddens's language (1991), experienced (subjective) time is 'disembedded'—it is lifted out of its subjective individual context and placed in an abstract (organizational) context (Tsoukas 2001). In so far as this happens, an organized social system creates quasi-predictability: its internal life is structured along standardized routines sequenced over time.

That predictability, however, is never complete. Partly this is because of the, ultimately, non-programmable human nature: the 'disruptive' student, the 'awkward' academic, the 'indifferent' administrator, all conspire to make university life more interesting than it would otherwise have been. Predictability, moreover, is mainly limited by changes in the external environment. Although this is more difficult to see in a regulated academic environment, it is clearly visible in the case of business organizations operating in the market place. Changes in competition, legislation, customer tastes, and technology are some of the most important changes that make a market-based business environment truly unpredictable in the long term. And if those researchers who have studied 'high-velocity' environments (Brown and Eisenhardt 1998; Ilinitch, Lewin, and D'Aveni 1998) are to be believed, such changes are faster and more frequent than ever in the history of capitalism.

The environment is thus a source of uncertainty for business organizations, much more so than human behaviour within organizations is. The reason for this is not difficult to see. Human behaviour in organizations is regularized and normalized to some extent (but never completely) through the authority relationship. The latter standardizes expectations, homogenizes to some degree individual cognitive maps and, through management control systems, elicits certain intended behaviours. The environment, however, is, to a large degree, beyond an organization's control; hence, it is not clear how it will change over time. Think of how disruptive technologies have reshaped the semiconductor and the watch industries (Glasmeier 1997; Tushman, Anderson, and O'Reilly 1997), or how legislation has influenced the activities of accounting firms, in the aftermath of corporate scandals in the USA in 2002. Precisely because of the uncertainty of the environment—the uncertainty generated by the interactions of all those factors that make up the business environment over time—strategy-making is important: it represents senior managers' intention to steer a distinctive and coherent course of organizational action over time (Mintzberg 1994: 239). But how do organizations do that? How do they deal with the uncertainty of the future?

How organizations deal with the future depends on how they answer the following two questions. First, to what extent is there a knowledge base on the basis of which important events may be anticipated? And second, to what extent is there a stock of knowledge on which to draw for undertaking action? Or, to put it differently, to what degree do we know what will happen? To what extent do we know how to deal with it? Depending on how these two questions are answered, we obtain four different ways in which organizations attempt to deal with the future (see Fig. 11.1).

When important events are anticipated (that is, when we have knowledge of forthcoming events) and there is a stock of knowledge as to how to deal with them, organizations use forecasting methods. Seasonal demand, for example, is such an event that may be anticipated, which a, say, beverages company knows how to deal with. Such events are typically extrapolations from the past, and a relevant knowledge base has been developed over time. The future in this case is not qualitatively different from the past; it rather is a pattern that is being repeated over time (Makridakis 1990).

When, however, certain events may be anticipated but a stock of knowledge as to how to deal with them does not yet exist, forecasting is of limited utility. In such cases *analogies* are the most often used method for drawing conclusions. In politics, nation-building is a good example. Overthrowing a government and disrupting the political and institutional status quo in a country leads, typically, to a power vacuum, lawlessness, and a breakdown of institutions (at least initially). Such events may be anticipated, but how to deal with them—how, in other words, to create new institutions, which will command the loyalty of the local people—is far from clear. Iraq is a good case in point. Building institutions (especially democratic ones that will reflect the values

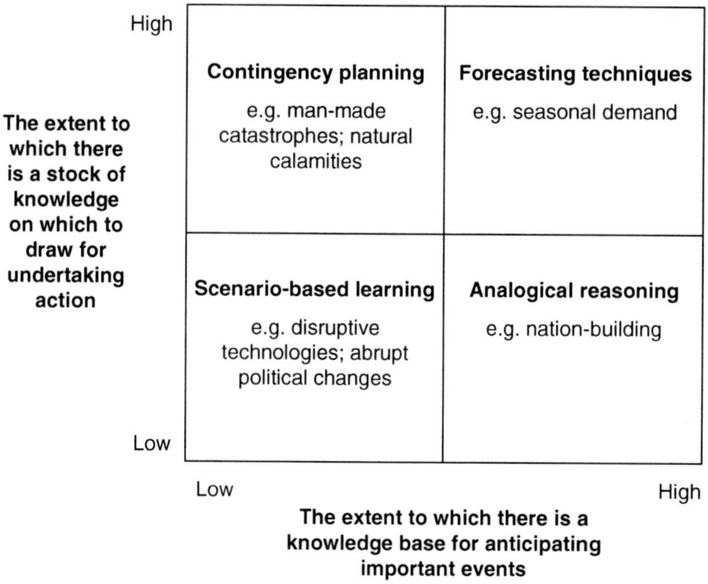

Fig. 11.1: Organizations and the future: a typology

and culture of the indigenous population) for post-Saddam Iraq is fraught with huge difficulties and uncertainty. As is seen in the debate about the future of Iraq, drawing analogies with similar situations concerning nation-building in post-war Japan and Germany, as well as more contemporary ones in Bosnia, Kosovo, and Afghanistan, is the best policy makers can do in order to figure out what to do. The same applies to policy-making at large. How to create a functioning market economy and a liberal democracy in former communist countries is far from clear (Elster, Offe, and Preuss 1998). Analogies with the development of capitalism in other parts of the world help to derive lessons for what to do.

In cases where knowledge about the extent to which certain events may be anticipated is low but there is a stock of knowledge of how to deal with them, this leads typically to the use of 'what-if' contingency planning and scenarios. Forecasting in this case is inadequate, since forecasting relies heavily on the established patterns of past behaviours and/or a good understanding of cause–effect relationships in order to predict what may happen in the future. Some events, however, may be novel or rare, about which there is very little prior knowledge, hence they cannot be predicted. There are, however, certain events which, although uncommon, nonetheless should they occur there is a stock of knowledge in how to deal with them. For example, a biological terrorist attack on the London underground is an event concerning which no policy maker knows whether it will happen, but, if it does, hospitals need to be ready to treat the patients in certain ways. The same applies to some environmental catastrophes. There is now a certain know-how concerning, for example, the treatment of oil leaks in the sea or earthquakes. Policy makers know, broadly, how to respond to such events, although they do not know if and when they will happen.

It is far more difficult for managers and policy makers to respond to events concerning which (a) they know very little about the probability of their happening, or even cannot imagine what form they will take (think, for example, of the terrorist attack on the Twin Towers—who would have imagined it?), and (b) they have very little knowledge about how to deal with them. Such events represent *discontinuities*—they are rare events that happen on an ad hoc basis (Mintzberg 1994: 228). Rapid price increases, draconian legislation, dramatic political changes, disruptive technologies, and abrupt shifts in consumer attitudes are discontinuities whose occurrence and/or timing are difficult to predict and for which there is no developed knowledge base as to how to deal with them.

Scenario-based organizational learning (SBOL) is currently the most widely used method to deal with such discontinuities. Notice that the use of scenarios is not an attempt to attach probabilities to a set of events, but a *process* to prepare the organization to see such discontinuities 'soon enough [. . .] and to do so earlier or at least better than anyone else' (ibid. 233; see also Van der Heijden et al., 2002: 176). SBOL does not attempt to eliminate uncertainty; it rather recognizes its irreducible character and, consequently, the fundamentally unpredictable changes in the environment (Van der Heijden 1996: 103). Uncertainty now is not so much a threat to be eliminated as an opportunity to be taken up and given form (Tsoukas 1999). The burden is on the organization: how clearly and quickly it can see developments in its environment, how sensitive it is to environmental changes, how quickly it can spot differences both within and outside the organization.

SBOL is not so much about the future *per se* as about sharpening the organizational ability of *perceiving* the present. As Van der Heijden (1996: 118) remarks,

The language of scenarios is about the future, but they should make a difference in what is happening now. If it is successful in embedding different models of the business environment in the consciousness of the organisation, it will make the organisation more aware of environmental change. Through early conceptualisation and effective internal communication scenario planning can make the organisation a more skilful observer of its business environment. By seeing change earlier the organisation has the potential to become more responsive.

In this view, a foresightful organization is an organization that has sharpened its ability to see, to observe, to perceive what is going on both externally and internally, and to respond accordingly (Chia 2004). Organizational awareness is enhanced by the extent to which members of an organization collectively become skilful perceivers of the business environment (Schwandt and Gorman 2004). The ability to perceive is sharpened through increasing the individual and organizational capacity to see *differences*. This is easier in the case of individuals, such as, for example, the retailer Sam Steinberg, who was the first to launch his business into shopping centres, in the early 1950s, in Canada (Mintzberg and Waters 1982). As Mintzberg (1994: 232) points out, incipient discontinuities in the business environment tend to be spotted by individuals who have a deep understanding of an industry and its context (see Fuller, Argyle and Morgan, 2004).

However, as some artifical-intelligence researchers have shown, such a sophisticated form of pattern recognition for discontinuities cannot be formalized and, in so far as this is the case, it cannot be turned into formal organizational systems and routines (Dreyfus and Dreyfus 1986, 1997; Penrose 1994; Searle 1997). Ansoff's 'weak signals' (1984)—the signals that give an organization a clue for discontinuities to come—are potentially infinite. Which ones will turn out to be critical cannot be formally articulated but only informally intuited (Mintzberg 1994: 233; Seidl 2004), which is why foresight tends to be an important feature of successful entrepreneurs who do not have to articulate and justify their choices and actions to outside audiences.

For an organization to sharpen its collective capacity to perceive is more difficult than in the case of individuals. The reason is that, as argued at the beginning of this chapter, organizing is the process of generating recurrent behaviours; that is, a process for reducing differences among individuals through institutionalized cognitive representations (Tsoukas and Chia 2002: 571). This is what gives organized systems predictability and efficiency; but this is also what gives them rigidity and crudeness. Organizing induces abstraction and generalization in social activities for coordinated purposeful action to become possible. Thus, in strictly organizational terms, a 'broken photocopier' is an abstract entity, as malfunctioning as any other, and this is what enables a photocopier company to issue repair manuals to its service technicians (Orr 1996). Organizations, however, are far more than abstract systems: they are *activity* systems (Blackler 1995; Spender 1996). A particular broken photocopier is not an abstract entity that simply features in repair manuals, but a material machine that is used in specific contexts by specific individuals, which will be repaired by specific technicians.

An organization develops its ability to see differences to the extent to which its members do not merely draw on institutionalized cognitive representations and routines ('a broken machine', 'If this happens, then do that') but *improvise* and adapt them to local contexts, and undertake situated action that compels organizational members to partially revise the cognitive representations they draw upon (Cunha 2004). The more sensitive organizational members are to differences between institutionalized representations and routines on the one hand and the local contexts of action on the other, the more perceptive they will be. Just as a good painter brings to our attention something we had seen but not noticed (Bergson 1946), so an organization becomes perceptive by sharpening its members' attention through helping them spot differences between how things canonically and routinely should be, on the one hand, and how they actually are and/or might be, on the other. Notice that what is important here is not forecasting what exactly 'might be' but using plausible versions of the latter in order to juxtapose them with current representations, routines, and assumptions, and draw out the implications. Maintaining the difference—the tension—between 'what should be' and 'what is', as well as between 'what is' and 'what might be' activates the organizational sensory system, just as the human sensory system is activated by difference (Bateson 1979).

It is in that sense that SBOL creates 'memories of the future' (Ingvar 1985). Through preparing scenarios about different futures an organization can get to see plausible changes in the environment and how they will probably impact on the organization. Although none of those scenarios may come true, the jolt that is delivered to the organization through them is often strong enough to make the organization challenge its business-as-usual assumptions, its current cognitive models and routines (Van der Heijden et al., 2002: 176; Wright and Goodwin 1999).

Van der Heijden et al. (ibid. 177) describe how a scenario project in an Asian multinational corporation made the company perceive more clearly the changes in its environment and their implications for the organization, as follows:

The 'jolt' in this case was that on considering the scenarios, there was a realization within the senior management team that their success formula—which had served them well for 20 years—was unlikely to generate the same success in the future. It did not matter much which scenario one looked at; there were a number of changes in the contextual environment which they had not previously heeded, and which made it unlikely that the organization could continue to succeed in the future without fundamental rethinking taking place in the organization.

In other words, the scenario project refocused senior managers' attention and made them notice changes which they had probably seen but not noticed—the price of being both an organization in general (reducing differences) and a successful organization in particular (complacency) (Miller, 1990). The process of constructing and reflecting on a scenario set enabled senior managers to 'visit' the future ahead of time, thereby creating 'memories of the future', and juxtapose those 'memories' with current practices. It is the difference between 'how things may turn out to be' and 'how they currently are' that spurred managers into action. The organization could not now go on as before pretending it did not know: things would have to change.

Notice that, seen this way, foresightful action—action in conditions of limited knowledge concerning both the extent to which future events may be anticipated and how to deal with them—is possible through greater *self-knowledge*. Knowledge about the future and how to handle it may be difficult to obtain, but it is within our power to enhance what we know about ourselves. This should not be confused with the case of self-prediction—self-knowledge is valuable not because it leads to self-prediction but because it sharpens one's ability to perceive and, thus, enhances one's capacity for action.

As MacIntyre (1985: 95–6) persuasively argued, self-prediction is impossible because an actor's future actions cannot be predicted by him/her since they depend on the outcomes of decisions as yet unmade by him/her. Self-knowledge is clarity about one's behavioural tendencies. In organizations, it is particularly strengthened when senior managers envisage different ways in which the future may turn out and how the organization would accordingly respond. That kind of knowledge makes the organization more aware of its potentiality and, to the extent that this happens, it contributes to organizational self-knowledge.

This is in line with Dewey's understanding of 'potentiality'. For him potentiality is not teleologically defined—that is, defined as the unfolding of an inner essence in the pursuit of a fixed end—but interactively produced (Dewey 1998: 223). Potentialities are known after interactions have occurred. There are, at a given time, unactualized potentialities in an organization in so far as there are in existence other things with which it has not as yet interacted. Scenarios of the future are such things with which an organization is asked to simulate 'interacting', and by doing so it obtains a clearer picture of its potentiality.

Dewey (ibid. 143) has observed that 'the object of foresight of consequences is not to predict the future. It is to ascertain the meaning of present activities and to secure, so far as possible, a present activity with a unified meaning'. And, later on, he continues:

Hence the problem of deliberation is not to calculate future happenings but to appraise present proposed actions. We judge present desires and habits by their tendency to produce certain consequences. [...] Deliberation is not calculation of indeterminate future results. The present, not the future is ours. No shrewdness, no store of information will make it ours. But by constant watchfulness concerning the tendency of acts, by noting disparities between former judgements and actual outcomes, and tracing that part of the disparity that was due to deficiency and excess in disposition, we come to know the meaning of present acts, and to guide them in the light of that meaning. (ibid. 143–4)

Dewey's argument can be seen as a wonderful advocacy of organizational learning. While he points out the futility of trying to forecast the future, he is sensitive enough to realize that an intelligent (or, in his terms, 'deliberative') action is one that (a) springs from knowledge of past experience that reveals current tendencies, and (b) is quick enough to link outcomes to expectations in a continuous manner (Lipshitz, Ron, and Popper 2004). Dewey seems to have in mind here both retro-knowledge and how important it is in helping actors understand current tendencies, *and* fore-knowledge and how significant it is in inducing reconsideration of old aims and habits in the light of expected outcomes. Like the executives of the Asian multinational mentioned above, organizations need to keep ascertaining the meaning of their current activities—their active tendencies—since by doing so they keep their activities alive, stop them from becoming routine habits. The meaning of current activities is ascertained by juxtaposing them with activities in the past and, more importantly, with likely activities in the future.

While organizational learning partly relies on retrospective sense-making, whereby we obtain a clearer picture of our actions through making sense of them *ex post facto* (Weick 1995), it also partly relies on prospective sense-making, whereby an organization ascertains its tendency to yield certain results through comparing its current modus operandi with the anticipated challenges of the future. In other words, in Dewey's terms, an organization is likely to act foresightfully when it obtains the necessary self-knowledge regarding its current tendencies. This happens when it systematically links both expectations to outcomes and current practices to anticipated futures. Foresightful action is thus inextricably linked to learning and sense-making. Dealing effectively with the future is not so much about getting it right *ex ante* as about preparing for it. Whereas forecasting focuses on outcomes, organizational learning (especially scenario-based and analogical organizational learning) focuses on *process*—preparing the organization to spot differences soon enough and act before or more effectively than others.

Foresightfulness as Coping

From the above it follows that an actor is foresightful when it has the propensity to act in a manner that coherently connects past, present, and future (Tsoukas and Hatch 2001; Weick and Roberts 1993). At an elementary level, this happens when an organization forecasts, for example, demand for next year and adjusts its policies accordingly (e.g. production capability, prices, marketing campaign) in anticipation of the new demand. Forecasting techniques tackle this sort of problem rather well. For this simple form of foresightfulness to be effective, organizations need to have a memory in which past incidents are recorded, and to have deciphered certain relations between the items stored in memory, which enable the organization to anticipate future incidents.

A second, more complex way of relating past, present, and future is for an organization to hypothesize that certain events will take place in the future and work backwards to the present state to decide what it would need to do should these prognostications come true. This, as argued above, can take the form of contingency planning or scenario planning.

Third, an organization fully develops the pervasive *skill* of foresightfulness when its members systematically treat time as a stream; that is, when they forge a coherent relationship between past, present and future or, respectively, between memory, attention, and expectation (ibid.). Through the use of stories, scenario-based organizational learning provides practitioners with flexible means to connect data dispersed in time. Plausible futures need to be narratively connected to current tendencies and past experiences.

The pitfall for organizations here is threefold. Too heavy an influence by the *past* results in incapacity to see what has changed in the present and what is the likely shape of things to come. This is a problem inherent in formal organization. The latter tends to perceive the world predominantly in terms of its own cognitive categories, which are necessarily derived from past experiences. The world may be changing but the cognitive system underlying formal organization, a system that reflects and is based on past experiences, changes slowly (Blackman and Henderson 2004).

Too much concentration on the *present* task makes the organization unappreciative of all the small changes that are taking place in the wider environment. Van der Heijden (1996: 115–16) mentions a major company in the mainframe computer industry in the 1980s that found it nearly impossible to notice the huge changes that were taking place in its industry. They were very capable of forecasting demand for computing power (tellingly, expressed in 'millions of instructions per second'—a key term in the mainframe business) but unable to work out the *form* the market was slowly taking before their own eyes (i.e. the emergence of distributed computing).

Finally, too tight a focus on the *future per se* risks making the organization a victim of fashions. As Mintzberg (1994) has pointed out, moving in and out of diverse markets, following the fashion of the day, without properly considering the organizational capabilities a firm has historically developed, may lead a company to reckless decisions. Diversifying into new businesses should not be a mere exercise in linguistic redescription ('reinvent your business') but a balanced consideration of a firm's capabilities. 'Knowing thyself' is as important as 'daring to be different'.

Foresightfulness becomes an *organizational skill* when future-oriented thinking ceases to be a specialized activity undertaken by experts and/or senior managers, in which they engage from time to time, in order to deal with something called 'the future', and acquires the status of expertise that is widely distributed throughout the organization and is spontaneously put into action. Forecasting techniques, simulation methods, even scenario planning, all are designed to be used or engaged in by experts, or senior managers, who focus explicitly on the future and treat it as if it were a separate entity. While this is important, for all the reasons mentioned above, it is even more important that foresightfulness becomes an embedded organizational capability, a set of actions which do not spring so much from explicit reasoning about 'the future' as from an 'immediate coping' (Varela 1999: 5) with what is confronting the organization. Just as 'a wise (or virtuous) person is one who knows what is good and spontaneously does it' (ibid.), so a foresightful organization is one whose members spontaneously forge connections between past, present, and future. In other words, organizational foresightfulness is fully developed when it becomes an institutionalized capacity for unobtrusively responding to an organization's circumstances so that the organization may get along in the world.

The notion of *coping*, drawn from Heideggerian philosophy (see Dreyfus 1991; Wrathall and Malpas 2000), implies that dealing with the future is a pervasive, *background* organizational skill, not a focal act. In executing its primary task—be it treating patients, serving customers, teaching students, or whatever—an organization acts necessarily in the present. The future is not some entity to engage with in the same way that, for example, a bank engages with a customer. A bank sells its services in the present and organizes itself to be able to carry out this task in the future as effectively as it can. To be able, however, to *continue* selling services to customers, it needs to be concerned not just with the present but with the future as well. A foresightful bank is *subsidiarily* aware of the past and the future while focally engaging in the present (Tsoukas 2003)—it is aware of the fact that it ought to be able to continue to be attractive to customers in the future, while serving them in the present, on the basis of abilities it has acquired in the past. While engaging in its primary task it is unobtrusively adjusting its service to carry on drawing in customers in the future (McSweeney 2000).

An organization develops its subsidiary awareness of the future by developing its *distensive* capability—the ability narratively to link past, present, and future. As we saw in Chapter 10, *distentio* is an Augustinian idea offered by Ricouer (1984) to describe the stretching of consciousness through simultaneous attention to memory and expectation. When memory and expectation are engaged, they enlarge the consciousness of the present—know-how is brought forward from the past and extrapolations to the future are made. Narratives are a means of letting us experience time by bringing memory and expectation to bear on the present. Narratives enable us to appreciate the temporal dimension of human experience and think in 'time-streams' (Neustadt and May 1986).

An excellent example of such a highly developed 'distentive' capability—the ability to be subsidiarily aware of the past and the future—was shown by George Marshall, the Chief of Staff of the US Army during the Second World War. In the spring of 1943, in the midst of the war, Marshall called John Hilldring to his office to discuss how Hilldring, a two-star general, should go about organizing military governments for countries that had been liberated or conquered by the Allies. Hilldring reported what Marshall said to him as follows (cited ibid. 247–8):

I'm turning over to you a sacred trust and I want you to bear that in mind every day and every hour you preside over this military government and civil affairs venture. Our people sometimes say that soldiers are stupid. I must admit at times we are. Sometimes our people think we are extravagant with the public money, that we squander it, spend it recklessly. I don't agree that we do. We are in a business where it's difficult always to administer your affairs as a businessman can administer his affairs in a company, and good judgement sometimes requires us to build a tank that turns out not to be what we want, and we scrap that and build another one ... But even though people say we are extravagant, that in itself isn't too disastrous ...

But we have a great asset and that is that our people, our countrymen, do not distrust us and do not fear us. Our countrymen, our fellow citizens, are not afraid of us. They don't harbor any ideas that we intend to alter the government of the country or the nature of this government in any way. This is a sacred trust that I turn over to you today ... I don't want you to do anything, and I don't want to permit the enormous corps of military governors that you are in the process of training and that you're going to dispatch all over the world, to damage this high regard in which the professional soldiers in the Army are held by our people, and it could happen, it could happen, Hilldring, if you don't understand what you are about.

This is a remarkable piece of talk, for it skilfully weaves together past, present, and future, and shows how a policy maker may indeed be foresightful. Marshall, remember, was busy fighting a terrible war, and yet he was capable of seeing far ahead to ponder the post-war situation. He looked ahead with a clear awareness of the past. He showed a deep understanding of US military–civilian relations (the criticism of, but also the crucial trust in, its armed forces by the US people) and, implicitly, of how the same relations had had a different history in other countries. He urged Hilldring to make day-to-day decisions while thinking of their long-term consequences. Marshall coped with the future spontaneously: the situation (advising a subordinate) brought forth the action; the future did not become a separate object of analysis but was spontaneously brought to the present and was coherently linked to the past. Foresightfulness is shown here to be not a specialized activity, to be occasionally engaged in, but a pervasive mode of being. As Neustadt and May (ibid. 248) aptly remark: 'By looking back, Marshall looked ahead, identifying what was worthwhile to preserve from the past and carry into the future. By looking around, at the present, he identified what could stand in the way, what had potential to cause undesired changes of direction. Seeing something he had power to reduce, if not remove, he tried to do so'.

Conclusions

Traditionally, strategic planning and forecasting have been the main methods by which organizations have attempted to deal with the future (Das 2004; Narayanan and Fahey 2004). Such an approach was predicated on a closed-world ontology: the assumption that the future will be, more or less, an extension of the past, or at least predictable. However, the occurrence of radically new innovation shows the inadequacy of such an assumption. The future is open-ended and, in principle, unknowable. An open-world ontology is required to deal with a future full of possibilities. Consequently, organizations should move from a narrow preoccupation with forecasting to cultivating the capability of foresight. Forecasting is needed when future events can be anticipated and the organization knows how to deal with them. However, in situations in which this is not possible (that is to say, most of the time) organizations need to develop a different set of skills: to think analogically, to engage in 'what-if' contingency planning, and practice scenario-based organizational learning (SBOL). Moving from forecasting to SBOL implies moving from a focus on probable outcomes to a focus on organizational processes or, to put it differently, shifting from prediction to perception. A foresightful organization is one that has sharpened its ability to perceive—to see differences between how things may turn out to be and how they currently are. The ability to perceive is enhanced if the meaning of current activities is ascertained by juxtaposing them with activities in the past and likely activities in the future. Ultimately, foresightfulness becomes a generic organizational capability when it is not so much an explicit activity practiced by specialists, but becomes a background skill practiced spontaneously by as great a number of organizational members as possible. This happens when individuals in an organization engage in the present by being subsidiarily aware of the past and the future. In other words, seen as an organizational capability, foresightfulness is the institutionalized ability to cope unobtrusively with the world, whereby connections between the past, the present, and the future are forged.

References

Ansoff, H. I. (1984), *Implanting Strategic Management* (Englewood Cliffs, NJ: Prentice Hall).
Bateson, G. (1979), *Mind and Nature* (Toronto: Bantam).
Bergson, H. (1946), *The Creative Mind* (New York: Carol).
Blackler, F. (1995), 'Knowledge, knowledge Work and Organizations: An Overview and Interpretation, *Organization Studies*, 16: 1021–46.
Blackman, D., and Henderson, S. (2004), 'Autopoietic Limitations of Probing the Future', in H. Tsoukas and J. Shepherd (eds.), *Managing the Future* (Oxford: Blackwell), 189–205.
Brown, S. L., and Eisenhardt, K. M. (1998), *Competing on the Edge* (Boston: Harvard Business School Press).
Chia, R. (2004), 'Re-educating Attention: What is Foresight and How is it Cultivated?', in H. Tsoukas and J. Shepherd (eds.), *Managing the Future* (Oxford: Blackwell), 20–37.

Cunha, M. P. E. (2004), Time Traveling: Organizational Foresight as Temporal Reflexivity, in H. Tsoukas and J. Shepherd (eds.), *Managing the Future* (Oxford: Blackwell), 135–52.

Das, T. K. (2004), 'Strategy and Time: Really Recognizing the Future', in H. Tsoukas and J. Shepherd (eds.), *Managing the Future* (Oxford: Blackwell), 58–74.

Dewey, J. (1988), *Human Nature and Conduct* (Carbondale, Ill: Southern Illinois University Press).

—— (1998), 'Time and Individuality', in L. A. Hickman and T. M. Alexander (eds.), *The Essential Dewey, i,* (Bloomington, Ind.: Indiana University Press), 217–26.

Dreyfus, H. L. (1991), *Being-in-the-World: A Commentary on Heidegger's Being and Time, Division I* (Cambridge, Mass.: MIT Press).

—— (1997), 'From Micro-worlds to Knowledge Representation: AI at an Impasse', in J. Haugeland (ed.), *Mind Design, ii* (Cambridge, Mass: MIT Press), 143–82.

—— and Dreyfus, S. E. (1986), *Mind over Machine* (New York: Free Press).

Elster, J., Offe, C., and Preuss, U. K. (1998), *Institutional Design in Post-communist Societies* (Cambridge: Cambridge University Press).

Fuller, T., Argyle, P., and Morgan, P. (2004), 'Meta-rules for Entrepreneurial Foresight'. in H. Tsoukas and J. Shepherd (eds.), *Managing the Future* (Oxford: Blackwell), 171–88.

Giddens, A. (1990), *The Consequences of Modernity* (Cambridge: Polity).

—— (1991), *Modernity and Self-identity* (Cambridge: Polity).

Glasmeier, A. (1997), 'Technological Discontinuities and Flexible Production Networks: The Case of Switzerland and the World Watch Industry', in M. L. Tushman and P. Anderson (eds.), *Managing Strategic Innovation and Change* (New York: Oxford University Press), 23–42.

Hassard, J. (2002), 'Organizational Time: Modern, Symbolic and Postmodern Reflections', *Organization Studies*, 23: 885–92.

Hogarth, R. M., and Makridakis, S. (1981), 'Forecasting and Planning: An Evaluation', *Management Science*, 27: 115–38.

Ilinitch, A. Y., Lewin, A. Y., and D'Aveni, R. (1998), *Managing in Times of Disorder*, (Thousand Oaks, Calif.: Sage).

Ingvar, D. (1985), 'Memories of the Future: An Essay on the Temporal Organization of Conscious Awareness', *Human Neurobiology*, 4: 127–36.

Lipshitz, R., Ron, N., and Popper, M. (2004), 'Retrospective Sensemaking and Foresight: Studying the Past to Prepare for the Future', in H. Tsoukas and J. Shepherd (eds.), *Managing the Future* (Oxford: Blackwell), 98–108.

MacIntyre, A. (1985), *After Virtue*, 2nd edn. (London: Duckworth).

McSweeney, B. (2000), 'Looking Forward to the Past', *Accounting, Organizations and Society*, 25: 767–86.

Makridakis, S. (1990), *Forecasting, Planning, and Strategy for the Twenty-first Century* (New York: Free Press).

—— and Hibon, M. (1979), 'Accuracy of Forecasting: An Empirical Investigation', *Journal of the Royal Statistical Society*, 142: 97–145.

Miller, D. (1990), *The Icarus Paradox* (New York: Harper).

Mintzberg, H. (1994), *The Rise and Fall of Strategic Planning* (New York: Prentice Hall).

—— and Waters, J. A. (1982), 'Tracking Strategy in an Entrepreneurial Firm', *Academy of Management Journal*, 25: 465–99.

—— Ahlstrand, B., and Lampel, J. (1998), *Strategy Safari* (London: Prentice Hall).

Narayanan, V. K., and Fahey, L. (2004), 'Invention and Navigation as Contrasting Metaphors of the Pathways to the Future', in H. Tsoukas and J. Shepherd (eds.), *Managing the Future* (Oxford: Blackwell), 38–57.

Neustadt, R. E., and May, E. R. (1986), *Thinking in Time: The Uses of History for Decision Makers* (New York: Free Press).

Orr, J. (1996), *Talking About Machines* (Ithaca, NY: ILR).

Penrose, R. (1994), *Shadows of the Mind* (Oxford: Oxford University Press).

Popper, K. (1988), *The Open Universe* (London: Hutchinson).

Prigogine, I. (1997), *The End of Certainty* (New York: Free Press).

Ricoeur, P. (1984), *Time and Narrative, i* (Chicago, Ill.: University of Chicago Press).

Rorty, R. (1989), *Contingency, Irony and Solidarity* (Cambridge: Cambridge University Press).

Schwandt, D., and Gorman, M. (2004), 'Foresight or Foreseeing? A Social Action Explanation of Complex Collective Knowing', in H. Tsoukas and J. Shepherd (eds.), *Managing the Future* (Oxford: Blackwell), 77–97.

Searle, J. (1997), 'Minds, Brains and Programs', in J. Haugeland (ed.), *Mind Design, ii* (Cambridge, Mass: MIT Press), 183–204.

Seidl, D. (2004), 'The Concept of "Weak Signals" Revisited: A Re-description from a Constructivist Perspective', in H. Tsoukas and J. Shepherd (eds.), *Managing the Future* (Oxford: Blackwell), 153–70.

Spender, J.-C. (1996), 'Making Knowledge the Basis of a Dynamic Theory of the Firm', *Strategic Management Journal*, 17, (special winter issue): 45–62.

Thompson, J. D. (1967), *Organizations in Action* (New York: McGraw-Hill).

Tsoukas, H. (1999), 'Reading Organizations: Uncertainty, Complexity, Narrativity', University of Essex, Department of Accounting, Finance and Management, working paper series no. 16.

—— (2001), 'Re-viewing Organization', *Human Relations*, 54: 7–12.

—— (2003), 'Do We Really Understand Tacit Knowledge?', in M. Easterby-Smith and M. A. Lyles (eds.), *Handbook of Organizational Learning and Knowledge* (Oxford: Blackwell).

—— and Chia, R. (2002), 'On Organizational Becoming: Rethinking Organizational Change', *Organization Science*, 13: 567–82.

—— and Hatch, M. J. (2001), 'Complex Thinking, Complex Practice: A Narrative Approach to Organizational Complexity', *Human Relations*, 54: 979–1013.

Tushman, M. L., Anderson, P. C., and O'Reilly, C. (1997), 'Technology Cycles, Innovation Streams, and Ambidextrous Organizations: Organizational Renewal through Innovation Streams and Strategic Change', in M. L. Tushman and P. Anderson (eds.), *Managing Strategic Innovation and Change* (New York: Oxford University Press), 3–23.

Van der Heijden, K. (1996), *Scenarios: The Art of Strategic Conversation* (Chichester: Wiley).

—— Bradfield, R., Burt, G., Cairns, G., and Wright, G. (2002), *The Sixth Sense*, (Chichester: Wiley).

Varela, F. J. (1999), *Ethical Know-How* (Stanford, Calif.: Stanford University Press).

Weick, K. E. (1979), *The Social Psychology of Organizing*, 2nd edn. (Reading, Mass.: Addison-Wesley).

—— (1995), *Sensemaking in Organizations* (Thousand Oaks: Calif.: Sage).

—— and Roberts, K. H. (1993), 'Collective Mind in Organizations: Heedful Inter-relating on Flight decks, *Administrative Science Quarterly*, 38: 357–81.

Whitehead, A. N. (1967), *Adventures of Ideas* (New York: Free Press).

Wrathall, M., and Malpas, J. (2000), *Heidegger, Coping, and Cognitive Science, ii,* (Cambridge, Mass.: MIT Press).

Wright, G., and Goodwin, P. (1999), Future-focussed Thinking: Combining Scenario Planning with Decision Analysis, *Journal of Multi-criteria Decision Analysis,* 8: 311–21.

TWELVE

Noisy Organizations: Uncertainty, Complexity, Narrativity

Noise destroys and horrifies. But order and flat repetition are in the vicinity of death. Noise nourishes a new order. Organization, life and intelligent thought live between order and noise, between disorder and perfect harmony. If there were only order, if we only heard perfect harmonies, our stupidity would soon fall down towards a dreamless sleep; if we were always surrounded by the shivaree, we would lose our breath and our consistency, we would spread out among all the dancing atoms of the universe. We are; we live; we think on the fringe, in the probable fed by the unexpected, in the legal nourished with information

(Michel Serres 1982*a*: 127)

I F every discipline needs to have a demon, a never-disappearing intruder threatening the orderly system of thought that scientific activity seeks to create, a demon which must be constantly fought otherwise systematic knowledge becomes impossible (ibid.), it is probably fair to say that in organization theory (OT) *uncertainty* qualifies for such a disruptive role. Concluding his influential *Organizations in Action*, Thompson (1967: 159) put it with enviable clarity: 'Uncertainty appears as the fundamental problem for complex organizations, and coping with uncertainty, as the essence of the administrative process'. Similarly, for Galbraith (1977) an information-processing view of organization design aims primarily at enabling organizations to manage uncertainty. 'Uncertainty', remarks Galbraith (ibid. 36), 'is the core concept upon which the organization design frameworks are based'. Since uncertainty in-

Previously unpublished. An earlier version of this paper was presented as a keynote address at the conference on 'Uncertainty, Knowledge and Skill', Limburg University, Belgium, 6–8 November 1997.

creases the amount of information that must be processed during task execution, organizational forms vary depending on the extent to which organizations are capable of processing information about events that could be
anticipated in advance.

What is uncertainty and where does it comes from? Uncertainty, remarks
Galbraith (ibid. 36–7), is the difference between the amount of information
required and the amount of information possessed by the organization.
According to Thompson (1967: 159–61), there are three sources of organizational uncertainty. The first, and most important, source is the lack of causal
knowledge—being unable to identify relations between causes and effects
(generalized uncertainty). The second source is contingencies—organizational
dependence on an environment that may not be cooperative. And the third
source is internal interdependence—the way internal components of an organization depend on one another. The worst kind of uncertainty is the first,
followed by the other two in descending order.

Fighting uncertainty seems sensible if organizations are understood as well-
bounded entities that aim at maximizing the effectiveness of their actions;
how else could an organization decide what needs to be done and, at the same
time, be sure that it made the right decisions? As Thompson (ibid. 160)
eloquently put it: 'Purpose without cause/effect understanding provides no
basis for recognizing alternatives, no grounds for claiming credit for success or
escaping blame for failure, no pattern of self-control'.

The more, therefore, one knows about what causes what, the more rational
action one is likely to undertake. Just as you cannot optimize the allocation of
a given set of resources unless you have all the relevant information in your
hands, so you cannot optimally make a host of business decisions, ranging
from strategy through operations management and maintenance policy, to
organizational and behavioural issues, unless you possess all the requisite
information. Decision-making involves information processing: to make decisions rationally you need information—Thompson's 'causal knowledge'—
which, alas, you may not possess. Hence, you need to minimize the ensuing
uncertainty by collecting, codifying, and processing more and more information about relevant issues. In short: maximum information implies minimum
uncertainty, and vice versa.

This is, broadly, how OT has tended to approach the matter (Crozier 1964;
Cyert and March 1963; Galbraith 1977; Mintzberg 1979), and this is the
message most organizational behaviour/theory/design textbooks seek to pass
on to students. Notice that in this mode of reasoning uncertainty is thought to
be the *absence of (relevant) information*. Such an assumption raises certain
questions: 'Relevant' to whom? Information about what? And, of course,
what is 'information' anyway? The answers that have typically been given
in the OT literature presuppose a homogeneous organization populated by
self-similar agents, having nearly identical information needs, which can be
well described in advance. For example, according to this view, the same

information about the pattern of, say, machine breakdowns is thought to be equally relevant to maintenance workers and engineers. Moreover, versions of formally articulated and codified information are normally accepted as being organizationally relevant. Information is commonsensically thought to be a specific, expected message, pretty much like the instructions given at an airport's information desk: 'What is the cheapest way of getting to the city?'; 'Buy a bus ticket from the desk opposite and wait over there for the green bus to arrive.'

Such a view of uncertainty (what I call here a defensive view) is beset with problems. Ethnographic studies show that the information organizational members need differs according to the demands of the *task* at hand and the *institutional* context in which information is used. Take, for example, Orr's aforementioned fascinating study of photocopier-repair technicians (1996), a study whose insights will often be drawn upon in this chapter. A photocopier may be described in all sorts of ways but, typically, only a particular set of descriptions is selected out by the engineers of a photocopier company, for the purpose of issuing a repair manual. For the engineers, a photocopier is an *abstract* machine, a primarily technical object, whose reliable operation can be statistically described. The engineer's role is to investigate patterns of machine breakdowns, codify them, relate types of breakdowns to types of repair action that need to be undertaken (in the form of 'if, then' rules), and incorporate this information into the repair manual. It isn't that a photocopier cannot be described in any other way; but it is the role of an engineer to think and act in this particular way, in order for a repair manual to be produced. Both institutional context and the task at hand set limits on how a photocopier may be formally described.

Consider now how a repair technician typically approaches a photocopier. Called on to repair a *particular* machine, the technician wants to know not only the generic technical aspects of the machine's operation (which are described, in an abstract fashion, in the repair manual), but also the particular *social setting* within which the machine functions. He needs to know, for example, how the customer has been using the machine. Moreover, in doing his job the technician must perform a delicate balancing act: on the one hand he needs to gain and maintain the customer's trust in him; on the other hand, he is concerned with maintaining his reputation in the community of technicians of which he is a member. In other words, in the case of a repair technician, both the task and the institutional context are different from those of the engineer. The information needed is, therefore, different in its content as well as in its degree of codifiability; what constitutes information is understood differently (ibid.).

According to the defensive view of uncertainty, from an organizational point of view repair technicians will maximize their effectiveness the more information they possess in advance; that is to say, the more sophisticated the repair manual becomes. If past experiences, both successful and unsuccessful, can be codified and find their way into the manual, and if this entire exercise occurs in an ongoing process, organizational intelligence will be enhanced, since more and more information will become available. The problem with this view, however, is that it sets an impossible task: one cannot know in advance, with sufficient detail, what is going to be the *relevant* information about a broken machine. This is because one cannot foresee all the contexts in which a machine may break down. Although, technically speaking, the operation of a machine may be statistically described in a context-independent manner (the machine qua machine is a relatively predictable object), the breakdown of a particular machine is an inescapably context-dependent phenomenon, whose particular configuration evades prediction in the strict sense of the word. As Popper (1988: 12–16, 24) pointed out, in order to be able to predict an event one would have to state with sufficient accuracy what kind of data one would need for such a prediction task, which is not possible to do. In other words, prediction requires closure (that is what laboratories are for—see Bhaskar 1978), which is impossible to achieve in social systems. Thus, the strategy of collecting, codifying, and disseminating more and more information, useful as it certainly is, cannot solve the more fundamental problem of 'radical uncertainty' (Piore 1995: 120): one cannot specify in advance, with sufficient detail, what kind of practical information is going to be relevant, when, and where.

An alternative way of thinking about uncertainty, what I call here a *receptive view of uncertainty*, is to see the latter not just as the absence of relevant—that is, expected—information but, more subtly, as the *presence of unexpected information*. Suppose, for example, that you switch on the radio and hear that the Cabinet met yesterday to finalize the government's policy on next year's budget. This is not big news: that's what a Cabinet normally does; that's what one would expect a government to do. But suppose that instead of the Cabinet meeting you hear that three of the Cabinet's most senior ministers resigned. Now, that's unusual; most people will be taken by surprise; the media will thrive on it. This piece of news is more informative than the first simply because it is more unexpected, more improbable. To put it more generally, the more meaningful a message is, the more probable and predictable it is. And vice versa: a message is more informative, the more improbable it is, in the context of a certain system or certain rules (Eco 1989: 54; Hayles 1990).

Associating information with originality, novelty, and improbability poses certain communication problems. The larger the amount of information, the more difficult its communication; the clearer the message, the smaller the amount of information it conveys (Eco 1989: 55). For example, the series 1, 3, 5, 7, 9 ... is a very clear message; in fact, so clear that if I start this series you can easily continue it. There is a pattern in this message which allows it to be algorithmically compressed and, therefore, easily communicated (Hayles 1990: 6). If, however, I were to write the series produced by a random-number generator and ask you to continue with it, you couldn't. The message is too unpredictable, and in order for it to be communicated to someone it is necessary that it be reproduced in its entirety.

Thus, from a communication point of view, there is a balance to be struck. For a message to be simultaneously informative and communicable, it should be improbable but not too improbable; it should also contain elements which may be regarded as probable or redundant. The correlation between information and probability makes sense from an engineering point of view, if one thinks that the most probable elements need the shortest code in which to be transcribed for transmission, whereas the most improbable elements need longer codes (ibid. 52).

Think, for example, about the repair manual mentioned earlier. Knowing which types of machine breakdown occur most often is communicatively useful, since they can be efficiently codified and, for a channel of given capacity such as a repair manual, more information on probable breakdowns will be transmitted to the technician. If, however, the technician knows as a matter of routine what the message in the manual will most likely be, the message, easy though it is to communicate, conveys very little information. Conversely, a surprising message—a message whose probability of occurrence is low—is more informative.

To see more clearly how, from the point of view of communication, information is a function of both redundancy and surprise, consider the following example discussed by Hayles (ibid. 52–3):

Suppose that I ask you to guess the missing letter in 'ax-'. It is of course e, the most probable letter in an English text. Because it is so common, e can often be omitted and the word will still be intelligible. In 'axe', the letter e carries so little information that 'ax' is an alternate spelling. Suppose, by contrast, that I ask you to guess the word 'a-e'. You might make several guesses without hitting the choice I had in mind—'ace,' 'ale,' 'ape,' 'are,' 'ate.' When you find out that the expected letter is x [*NB* one of the most improbable letters in an English text], you will gain more information than you did when you learned that the final letter was e. Shannon's equation recognizes this correspondence by having the information content of a message increase as elements become more improbable.

Thus, a message which is highly expected (such as the series of odd numbers mentioned above) is not particularly informative. At the other extreme, a message which is so overwhelmingly surprising that there aren't any discernible patterns in it (such as the output of a random-number generator) is not informative either. For maximum information we need a mixture of redundancy and surprise; the message must be partly anticipated and partly surprising (Hayles 1990; Paulson 1988, 1991; Shannon and Weaver 1949). Eco (1989: 58) has succinctly summarized what information is, from a communication perspective, as follows: 'I have information when (1) I have been able to establish an order (that is, a code) as a system of probability within an original disorder; and when (2) within this new system I introduce—through the elaboration of a message that violates the rules of the code—elements of disorder in dialectical tension with the order that supports them (the message challenges the code)'. Information, in short, is the interplay of probability with improbability, code with noise, system with chance.

Self-organization from Noise

> We are building a kind of unified cultural identity at the end of the 20th century. We can move beyond the classical conflict between being and becoming. Being is no longer the primordial element, just as becoming is no longer an illusion, the product of ignorance. Today, we see that becoming, which is the expression of instability in the universe, is the primordial element. Yet, in order to express this, we also need elements that are permanent. We cannot have becoming without being, just as we cannot have light without darkness or music without silence.
>
> (Ilya Prigogine 1992: 26)

From the preceding discussion it follows that, according to the defensive view of uncertainty, the latter is equivalent to information which one knows one needs but does not have. (Remember Galbraith's (1977: 36–7) definition: uncertainty is information you need but do not currently have.) By contrast, according to the receptive view of uncertainty, the latter is equivalent to (partly) unexpected information—that is, information which is partly surprising, noisy, random, and, as a result, one does not know what to do with it. Notice the difference: in the first view uncertainty is not knowing enough about something given; in the second view uncertainty is not knowing what to do with something which is puzzling.

A system characterized by a high degree of information is complex, since the shortest possible description of it involves repeating the (partially unexpected) information itself—the latter is not algorithmically compressible (Barrow 1995: 10–11; Casti 1994: 9; Hatch and Tsoukas 1997). A complex system, puzzling as it is, may appear difficult to make sense of, since it cannot be compressed to something simpler, but it can be made meaningful if placed in an appropriate context. What appears as noisy (or random) at one level may be entirely meaningful at another (Popper 1987; Tsoukas 1993). While for the experienced reader of poetry, for example, a poem may be full of evocative analogies, for the novice it may appear as an incomprehensible set of lines. As Atlan remarks (quoted in Paulson 1988: 73), 'randomness is a kind of order, if it can be made meaningful; the task of making meaning out of randomness is what self-organization is all about' (see also Atlan 1974).

The creation of meaning out of what is noisy depends crucially upon the observer: on his/her willingness and ability to invent new codes in terms of which, what appears as noisy may be accounted for; what seems initially to be interference may seen as part of a new signifying structure and, therefore, be integrated into a new level of understanding.

Nowhere is this process of self-organization from noise more clearly manifested than in artistic communication. Whereas in scientific communication language is used as a mere instrument for the efficient communication of ideas about an extra-textual world, in artistic communication language is simultaneously the medium and the message (Barthes 1986). In science noise must be reduced to the minimum and transparency must be enhanced to the maximum, so that the truth-conditions of theories can be tested. But in literature, especially poetry, noise is deliberately sought, since the self-referential world of literature grows opportunistically by attempts to go beyond established literary conventions, rather than because it does not agree with the 'facts' (Paulson 1988). It isn't that literary works have nothing to do with the 'real' world but, as Bruner (1986: 24) aptly remarks, their purpose is to 'render that world newly strange, rescue it from obviousness', to make it noisy, more complicated. The ambiguity of a poetic text, a result of the rhetorical use of language which makes words depart from linguistic norms (de Man 1982; Paulson 1988: 66), is a constant challenge to the reader to invent new signifying codes in terms of which the poem may be interpreted. Paulson (1991: 43–4) has brilliantly described this process, and it is worth quoting him here in full:

The artistic text begins as an attempt to go beyond the usual system of language—in which the word is a conventional sign—to a specifically artistic system such as that of poetry, in which sounds, rhythms, positional relations between elements will signify in new ways. The poetic text, in other words, demands of its reader that she create new codes, that she semanticize elements normally unsemanticized. [...] Whereas in nonartistic communication there can be *extrasystemic* facts, which are simply ignored or discarded because they are not dealt with by the codes being used to interpret the message, in an artistic text there are only *polysystemic* facts, since whatever is extrasystemic at a given level, and thus destructive of regularity or predictability on that level, must be taken as a possible index of another level, another textual system with a new kind of coding. The multiplication of codes, or rather the creation of new and specific codes within a given genre and a given text, is the essence of artistic communication and the emergence of meaning in artistic texts. (emphasis in the original; references omitted)

Notice that in artistic communication the reader is not simply a recipient of information or a mere decoder of messages, but an *actor*, a constructor of meaning. As Iser (quoted in Bruner 1986: 25) remarks, 'literary texts initiate "performances" of meaning rather than actually formulating meaning themselves'. In constructing meaning, the reader attempts to integrate 'elements that ordinary codes of reading do not account for' (Paulson 1988: 90), and, in this sense, he/she is forced to *complexify* herself. The reader is made up of the reader-as-receiver-of-a-message plus his/her own understanding of it, which is different from the understanding of the author-sender. What at the level where transmission takes place may be seen as a loss in information (what the reader receives is not what the writer sends, hence the message is noisy), at the higher level, where the writer and the reader are seen as a *system*, there is gain in information: the quantity of information emitted by the system (writer → reader) includes the information received by the reader plus the ambiguity (the reader's interpretation of the message received). Since the poetic message is modified (interpreted), the information the reader now has is not identical to that of the writer; thus the system (writer → reader) contains more information (that is, it is more complex) than if each one of them had the same information (ibid. 74).

A reader brings to a poem his/her linguistic skills plus whatever experience he/she has in reading poetry. The fact that he/she shares with the author the same natural language makes him/her, in principle, competent in gaining access to the poem's meaning. In this sense a poem is not an entirely unique entity—there is sufficient redundancy in the system (author → reader) without which the poem would be inaccessible. At the same time, although the reader shares with the author a common linguistic structure, the textual effect of the poem remains unknown; a reader's logical and grammatical skills do not suffice to determine its meaning *ex ante* (de Man 1982).

To some extent the poem is meant to be noisy; it purposefully contains variety (noise) which our current interpretative codes are too limited to make sense of. This is so not because of our own inadequacy but because of the nature of literature. 'Under an aesthetic of formal innovation and uniqueness', observes Paulson (1991: 48), 'the specific relations between elements of a text are to some degree unique to that text and so cannot have been learnt anywhere else'. The poem is partly redundant, thus enabling our access to it, and partly unique, thus forcing us to invent new codes in terms of which we can derive meaning from it. It is this deliberately produced strangeness of the literary text that 'solicits our entry into a learning process, [inciting] us to learn to become its reader' (Paulson 1988: 99). By doing so we are led to 'modify ourselves, to shift position, to change and adapt our ways of mind a little so that [the text] can become a part of them' (ibid.).

Uncertainty, Complexity, Narrativity

Narrative doesn't represent an object, idea, signified, bit of information, or cognitive structure; on the contrary, narrative is self-similar to the dynamics of nature—the cruelty and beauty of the deep, dialectical, interpenetration between conservation and creation

(Alex Argyros 1992: 673)

The preceding analysis has, I hope, shown how meaning may come out of noise, order out of disorder, sense out of nonsense (Serres 1982*a*, 1982*b*; White 1991). Noise, disorder, nonsense may have destructive effects but, approached from another angle, they may also lead to novelty and a more complex order. By relentlessly waging war on uncertainty, early organization theorists privileged the organizational need for 'self-control' (Thompson 1967: 160, 161). The most significant task for organizations was thought to be the creation of stable conditions within which organizational action could predictably unfold as designed. Generalized uncertainty was seen as the arch-enemy, since it threatened predictability.

In order to receive and process as much information about the environment as possible, organizations need, on this view, to possess in advance all the necessary codes. Translated into organizational action, such a strategy entails careful boundary management (ibid.; Lawrence and Lorsch 1967)—coping with uncertainty by creating certain parts specifically to deal with it (Thompson 1967: 13). Uncertainty, in other words, was seen as something undesirable but unavoidable: 'Let someone deal with it so that the rest of us can get on with our work' was the suggested solution.

The defensive view of uncertainty sets uncertainty against certainty and conceives of the two in zero-sum terms. If what has been said in the previous section is accepted, it follows that uncertainty is as valuable as certainty; it is not the intrusive stranger to be expelled, but the unfamiliar other whose behaviour needs to be understood. It is, in short, the necessary condition for order to emerge, the source of all novelty and renewal. As will be seen below, a receptive view of uncertainty strengthens the organizational ability to cope with the unknown and the unforeseen, by seeking not so much to predict as to act and transform.

Consider again the work of photocopier-repair technicians. A faulty photocopier is like the word 'a-e' mentioned earlier. Something has gone wrong, the message is noisy, and it is the task of the repair technician to find out what is the matter. The information he gets from the machine is partly redundant and partly surprising. It is partly redundant in so far as he has repaired machines before, and by drawing on the repair manual he shares a common language with the machine, so to speak (to be precise, with its designer). If the machine failure is of a type that happens often and is, therefore, anticipated and documented by the manual designers, the manual conveys little information and tends, indeed, to be ignored by the technician (Orr, 1996: 109, 112). The technician will most probably repair the machine efficiently, but the system (designer → technician) will be poor in information since, on this occasion, the technician possesses nearly identical information with the designer.

If, however, the failure is rather rare and unusual, the information the technician gets from the machine is partly surprising. He needs to develop as comprehensive an understanding of the machine as possible, and for this task he needs to understand both what the documentation is testing *and* the social setting in which the machine has been used. Most probably, the technician will engage in a process of trial and error or, more appropriately, in a process of *bricolage*: 'the reflective manipulation of a set of resources accumulated through experience' (ibid. 122).

The technician will seek to create an account of the situation by synthesizing clues gleaned from the machine, its setting, and the customer. Deciphering the causes will not normally be easy and to do so the technician will most probably need to go beyond what is in the manual. Indeed, as Orr (ibid. 110) observes, 'the technicians' talk about using the service documentation is full of cautions about the perils of following the diagnostic procedures'. The technician must develop new codes to make sense of the problem at hand; relying on what he already knows is not enough.

Like the reading process described earlier, the diagnostic process is a complex system in action (Hayles, 1991: 20). When the technician first reads the situation, the latter contains a lot of noise—there are several puzzling things he cannot understand. As a result of the first reading, his cognitive process is becoming slightly more complex (he now knows more than before). When he reads the situation again, also trying new checks out, more noise is processed as information because he now reads at a higher level of complexity. As Hayles (ibid.) remarks, 'the reading process instantiates the symbiotic relationship between complexity and noise, for it is the presence of noise that forces the system to reorganize itself at a higher level of complexity'. And as Orr (1996: 124) confirms, 'in most of the hard diagnoses I observed, solution was discovered through *reinterpretation* of known facts and following the new interpretation with new investigations' (emphasis added).

An outcome of the diagnostic process is the complexification of the system (designer → technician), since what the technician now knows is different from what the manual indicates. How might the organization take advantage of this more complex order? By tapping into the technicians' experience and codifying it, on an ongoing basis, the organization will be able to design more sophisticated documentation to be used by technicians in the future. In other words, the organization can act as a broker of knowledge that is widely distributed among its various parts (Tsoukas 1996).

That is certainly useful and desirable, provided the organization realizes the limits of such an attempt. No matter how sophisticated the repair manual may be, at the end of the day it is always the technician who will carry out a particular diagnosis, and this implies that he will have to rely on his initiative and judgement. As Gadamer (1989: 334) notes,

The criterion of understanding is clearly not in the order's actual words, nor in the mind of the person giving the order, but solely in the understanding of the situation and in the responsible behavior of the person who obeys. [...] Thus there is no doubt that the recipient of an order must perform a definite creative act in understanding its meaning'. (see also Garfinkel 1984: ch.1; Orr 1996:110; Suchman 1987: 61)

In other words, the knowledge that is relevant to a technician's diagnosis cannot be determined *ex ante, in abstracto*; it rather is an unavoidably local matter, to be decided by the technician engaged in situated action (Brown and Duguid 1991; Hutchins 1993; Lave and Wenger 1991; Orr 1996: 107; Schon 1987: 35–40; Tsoukas 1996: 20; 1998).

From the above it follows that, partly at least, the complexity of the organization stems from the uncodified (informal) knowledge its members have. This should be obvious by now since, on the one hand, complexity was earlier defined as the length of the shortest possible description of a system and, on the other hand, uncodified knowledge is, by definition, something which cannot be algorithmically compressed. When uncodified knowledge is converted to 'if, then' instructions, the system it refers to loses some of its 'requisite variety' (Ashby, 1956: 206–13). To maintain complexity, the system needs to preserve uncodifiability. In that sense, contrary to the common belief often attributed to senior managers, namely 'I wish we knew what we know', it is preferable that the organization does not formally know what it knows, since such formal organizational knowledge would inevitably lead to some sort of codification strategy and would, thus, reduce complexity. After all, only variety can absorb variety (Beer 1985: 26).

Where does lay, uncodified knowledge reside? What form does it take? Orr makes it abundantly clear, throughout his book, that the primary element in the technician's work is *narrative*—both the accounts individual technicians need to create in order to make sense of broken machines *and* the stories technicians tell one another. '[D]iagnosis happens through a narrative process', notes Orr (1996: 2). 'A coherent diagnostic narrative constitutes a technician's mastery of the problematic situation. Narrative preserves such diagnoses as they are told to colleagues; the accounts constructed in diagnosis become the basis for technicians' discourse about their experience and thereby the means for the social distribution of experiential knowledge through community interaction' (ibid.).

Narrative is the currency of the life-world, of practice. Stories are widely circulated in a practice and, as a result, they contribute to the cognitive as well as the social development of a community of practitioners (Brown and Duguid 1991; Tsoukas 1998). The cognitive value of narratives stems from the fact that they are a type of discourse which, by its very nature, helps 'recruit whatever is most appropriate and emotionally lively in the [reader hearer's] repertoire' (Bruner 1986: 35). This happens mainly because, to use Bruner's term (ibid. 26), narratives help to 'subjunctivize reality': they 'keep meaning open, "performable" by the reader' (ibid.). As in poetic reading, reality is not seen as a *fait*

accompli but as possibility; meaning is not something already existing in the reality-as-text but something *emerging* from the reality-as-text.

How does the subjunctivization of reality take place? Bruner suggests three ways. First is the triggering of *presupposition*: 'the creation of implicit rather than explicit meanings' (ibid. 25). Poetry is the case par excellence. Consider the first part of Seferis's poem 'Argonauts' (1986:4)

> And if the soul
> is to know itself
> it must look
> into a soul:
> the stranger and enemy, we've seen him in the mirror

What does Seferis mean here? What does the 'mirror' stand for? Could he be talking about the process of self-knowledge; namely, that we get to know ourselves through direct contact with others? And why does he talk about the 'soul' and not the 'person'? Is it important? Could the 'mirror' be a metaphor for the modern forms of surveillance (CCTVs), which turn others into 'strangers' or 'enemies'? Could the mirror symbolize narcissism? You see, I hope, what I am getting at: implicit language mobilizes and enlists the reader into making sense of it; it 'forces "meaning performance" upon the reader' (Bruner, 1986: 27).

Second is *subjectification*: 'the depiction of reality not through an omniscient eye that views a timeless reality, but through the filter of the consciousness of protagonists in the story' (Bruner 1986: 25). The stories technicians tell fit exactly this definition. They are stories about the good old days, about achievements and failures, about awkward customers and stubborn machines. Stories are about real people and refer to concrete situations; they tell of particular departures from the expected, the canonical, and they are narrated by someone (Bruner 1990: 49).

Third is *multiple perspective*: 'beholding the world not univocally but simultaneously through a set of prisms each of which catches some part of it' (Bruner 1986: 26). Again, narratives are unique for this. As stories are passed around a community of practitioners, different perspectives are circulated, several voices are heard, a multiplicity of subjectivities is brought forward.

The overall cognitive effect of narratives, as Orr (1996: 2) perceptively notes, is that their 'circulation among the community of practitioners is the principal means by which the technicians stay informed of the developing subtleties of machine behavior in the field'. But there is more to narratives than being cognitively useful. Storytelling facilitates social interaction, preserves a community's collective memory, and enhances a group's sense of shared identity as members of a practice (Weick 1987, 1990). As ethnographers illustrate (Burawoy 1979; Collinson 1992; Kunda 1992; Orr 1996), when practitioners get together it is stories they typically exchange, and in doing so they reaffirm their membership of a particular community.

Conclusions

> For Hesiod, in the beginning there is chaos. In the proper, initial sense
> 'chaos' in Greek means void, nothingness. It is out of the total void
> that the world emerges. But already in Hesiod, the world is also chaos
> in the sense that there is no complete order in it, that it is not subject to
> meaningful laws. First there is total disorder, and then order, cosmos, is
> created. But at the 'roots' of the world, beyond the familiar landscape,
> chaos always reigns supreme. The order of the world has no 'meaning'
> for man: it posits the blind necessity of genesis and birth, on the one
> hand, of corruption and catastrophe—death of the forms—on the
> other.
>
> (Cornelius Castoriadis 1997: 273)

As some philosophers have argued, the fear of uncertainty has been a
central feature of modern thinking, right from the time of the Enlightenment
to the present day (MacIntyre 1985; Reed 1996; Toulmin 1990). Descartes
was notoriously suspicious of sensory experience, for he thought it was inherently unreliable. As he put it, reality was a malicious demon 'deliberately
trying to deceive me in any way he can' (Descartes quoted in Reed 1996: 53).
Pure thought, finding its ideal expression in mathematics, was elevated to
the status of the most reliable knowledge, since it deals in ideas 'clear and
distinct'.

Such a view of uncertainty has historically pervaded the social sciences
(Bauman 1992: ch. 3), and OT in particular. Organization was conceived as
the very antithesis to uncertainty. True, the latter was acknowledged to be a
feature of the world, but a feature which organized activity needed to fight
against (cf. Chia 1996; Cooper 1986; Stacey 1996). Such an attitude was
probably understandable given that the concern of early organization theorists was to outline the conditions in which organizations could attain high
levels of performance. For this to happen organizations need to have increasingly more sophisticated causal knowledge both about themselves and their
environment, so that they can rationally decide what courses of action to
embark upon. Uncertainty, thus, was seen as the absence of knowledge,
which is known to be needed but, unfortunately, is not at hand.

Such an argument is based on the assumption that, since organizations are
systems for the recurrent production of events and processes, one should know
what knowledge one needs, not only now, but, also, in the future. Such an
assumption is, however, unsustainable: to predict what knowledge I am going
to need tomorrow implies that I can specify *now* the sort of information I
would need for such a prediction task, which is impossible. The future is
radically open-ended and, as such, it may surprise us.

The key word here is 'surprise'. To acknowledge and accept the open-endedness of the world means that we must find a symbiotic relationship with uncertainty. I suggested above that uncertainty should not be seen as the absence, but as the presence, of information—the presence of (some) surprise. Notice that surprise does not necessarily imply incomprehensibility; it rather denotes a departure from the canonical, which our present interpretative codes cannot make sense of. Surprise is a call to action; a challenge to invent new codes in order to understand what previously was only marginally understood. Moreover, if complexity is defined as being proportional to the length of the shortest possible description of a system, it follows that a system rich in information—rich, in other words, in surprise—is a more complex system than one containing self-identical pieces of information.

Realizing how uncertainty leads to higher complexity is one thing, knowing what to do with it is another. Whereas the defensive view of uncertainty leads us to seek more information (to be precise, expected items of information) in order to cope with uncertainty, the receptive view outlined here seeks to embrace uncertainty (unexpected information) and integrate it within a new context; it views uncertainty as the occasion—the trigger—for creating a pattern out of what disrupts patterns. Just as in reading a poem the reader must *create* new codes in order to make sense of it, so does a practitioner confronting a particular situation. Both a literary work and a situation calling for action have elements which are unique to each of them. In the case of literary work, uniqueness stems from the rhetorical use of language, which is inherent in literature. In the case of a situation calling for action, uniqueness comes from the particular configuration of events that, at a particular point in time, happened to form a distinctive pattern. In both cases, however, informational variety (uniqueness) is tempered by redundancy: as language speakers we know enough about the language a poem is written in; as skilful participants in society, we know enough about the grammar of social action to be able to extract, in principle, meaning from individual cases. But in both cases meaning needs to be 'performed'—to be created out of what is available.

The knowledge practitioners derive from reading a situation as if it were a text is partly uncodified and had better stay that way, for it enriches the corpus of organizational knowledge. Uncodified knowledge exists in a narrative form and is both an input into, and an outcome of, practitioners' work. It is an input in so far as practitioners, in order to make sense of problematic situations, need to create coherent accounts of them. For this purpose practitioners partly rely on what stories have been passed to them by their colleagues, stories which may convey valuable information regarding the particular problems they face. Stories are also an output of practitioners' work, since stories are circulated in the community of practitioners, thus enhancing its collective memory and strengthening human interaction. Their very uncodifiability makes stories ideal for subjunctivizing reality—making it appear as a continuing process, full of possibilities, rather than a *fait accompli*.

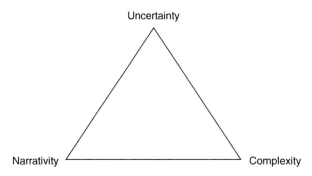

Fig. 12.1:   Reading organizations: uncertainty, complexity, narrativity.

To sum up, I have argued in this chapter that uncertainty, complexity, and narrativity form a triangle (see Fig. 12.1). An open (uncertain) world is a complex world, forcing us to keep reinventing (thus complexifying) ourselves in order to deal with it. New knowledge, preserved in a narrative form, contributes to organizational complexification, for the narrative discourse is a reminder that what we see is not all there is. Rather than uncertainty being the enemy, uncertainty is a challenging other: it renews the conversation and keeps us from entropic decay. By seeing complexity coming out of surprise, and meaning arising from noise, we are recovering the classical Greek insight that cosmos emerges from chaos, and to see the two as being mutually exclusive is to miss the dialectic of creation.

References

Argyros, A. (1992), 'Narrative and chaos', *New Literary History*, 23: 659–73.

Ashby, R. (1956), *An Introduction to Cybernetics* (London: Chapman & Hall).

Atlan, H. (1974), 'On a Formal Definition of Organization', *Journal of Theoretical Biology*, 45: 295–304.

Barrow, J. (1995), 'Theories of everything', in J. Cornwell (ed.), *Nature's Imagination* (Oxford: Oxford University Press), 45–63.

Barthes, R. (1986), *The Rustle of Language*, trans. (New York: R. Howard Hill & Wang).

Bauman, Z. (1992), *Intimations of Postmodernity* (London: Routledge).

Beer, S. (1985), *Diagnosing the System* (Chichester: Wiley).

Bhaskar, R. (1978), *A Realist Theory of Science* (Hassocks: Harvester).

Brown, J. S., and Duguid, P. (1991), 'Organizational Learning and Communities of Practice: Toward a Unified View of Working, Learning, and Innovation', *Organization Science*, 2: 40–57.

Bruner, J. (1986), *Actual Minds, Possible Worlds* (Cambridge, Mass.: Harvard University Press).

—— (1990), *Acts of Meaning* (Cambridge, Mass.: Harvard University Press).

Burawoy, M. (1979), *Manufacturing Consent* (Chicago, IU.: University of Chicago Press).

Casti, J. (1994), *Complexification* (London: Abacus).

Castoriadis, C. (1997), 'The Greek *polis* and the Creation of Democracy', in D. A. Curtis (ed.), *The Castoriadis Reader* (Oxford: Blackwell), 267–89.

Cavafy, C. P. (1984), *Collected Poems*, trans. E. Keeley and P. Sherrard, ed. G. Savidis (London: Hogarth Press).

Chia, R. (1996), 'The Problem of Reflexivity in Organizational Research: Towards a Postmodern Science of Organization', *Organization*, 3: 31–60.

Collinson, D. (1992), *Managing the Shopfloor* (Berlin: de Gruyter).

Cooper, R. (1986), 'Organization/Disorganization', *Social Science Information*, 25: 299–335.

Crozier, M. (1964), *The Bureaucratic Phenomenon* (London: Tavistock).

Cyert, R. M., and March, J. G. (1963), *A Behavioral Theory of the Firm*, Englewood Cliff, NJ: Prentice Hall).

De Man, P. (1982), 'The Resistance to Theory', *Yale French Studies*, 63: 3–20.

Eco, U. (1989), *The Open Work*, trans. A. Cancogni (Cambridge, Mass.: Harvard University Press).

Gadamer, H.-G. (1989), *Truth and Method*, second, revised, edn. trans. and rev. J. Weinsheimer and D. G. Marshall (London: Sheed & Ward).

Galbraith, J. R. (1977), *Organization Design* (Reading, Mass.: Addison-Wesley).

Garfinkel, H. (1984), *Studies in Ethnomethodology* (Cambridge: Polity).

Hatch, M. J., and Tsoukas, H. (1997), 'Complex Thinking about Organizational Complexity: The Appeal of a Narrative Approach to Complexity Theory', paper presented at the American Academy of Management, Boston, August 1997.

Hayles, N. K. (1990), *Chaos Bound* (Ithaca, NY: Cornell University Press).

—— (1991), 'Introduction: Complex Dynamics in Literature and Science', in N. K. Hayles (ed.), *Chaos and Order* (Chicago, Ill.: University of Chicago Press) 1–33.

Hutchins, E. (1993), 'Learning to Navigate', in S. Chaiklin and J. Lave (eds.) *Understanding Practice* (Cambridge: Cambridge University Press), 35–63.

Kunda, G. (1992), *Engineering Culture* (Philadelphia, Pa.: Temple University Press).

Lave, J., and Wenger, E. (1991), *Situated Learning* (Cambridge: Cambridge University Press).

Lawrence, P. R., and Lorsch, J. W. (1967), *Organization and Environment* (Cambridge, Mass.: Harvard Graduate School of Business Administration).

MacIntyre, A. (1985), *After Virtue*, second edn. (London: Duckworth).

Mintzberg, H. (1979), *The Structuring of Organizations* (Englewood Cliffs, NJ: Prentice Hall).

Orr, J. (1996), *Talking About Machines* (Ithaca, NY: ILR/Cornell University Press).

Paulson, W. (1988), *The Noise of Culture* (Ithaca, NY: Cornell University Press).

—— (1991), 'Literature, Complexity, Interdisciplinarity', in N. K. Hayles (ed.), *Chaos and Order* (Chicago, Ill.: University of Chicago Press). 37–53.

Piore, M. J. (1995), *Beyond Individualism* (Boston, Mass.: Harvard University Press).

Popper, K. (1987), 'Natural Selection and the Emergence of Mind', in G. Radnitzky and W. W. Barley III (eds.), *Evolutionary Epistemology* (LaSalle, Ill.: Open Court), 139–55.

—— (1988), *The Open Universe* (London: Hutchinson).

Prigogine, I. (1992), 'Beyond Being and Becoming', *New Perspectives Quarterly*, 9: 22–8.

Reed, E. S. (1996), *The Necessity of Experience* (New Haven, Conn.: Yale University Press).

Schon, D. (1987), *Educating the Reflective Practitioner* Aldershot: Avebury.

Seferis, G. (1986), *Collected Poems*, trans. ed., and introd. E. Keeley and P. Sherrard (London: Anvil).

Serres, M. (1982a), *The Parasite*, trans., with notes L. R. Schehr (Baltimore, Md.: Johns Hopkins University Press).

—— (1982b), *Hermes: Literature, Science, Philosophy*, ed. J. V. Harari and D. F. Bell (Baltimore, Md.: Johns Hopkins University Press).

Shannon, C. E., and Weaver, W. (1949), *The Mathematical Theory of Communication* (Urbana, iii.: University of Illinois Press).

Stacey, R. (1996), *Complexity and Creativity in Organizations* (San Francisco, Calif.: Berrett-Koehler).

Suchman, L. (1987), *Plans and Situated Actions* (Cambridge: Cambridge University Press).

Thompson, J. D. (1967), *Organizations in Action* (New York: McGraw-Hill).

Toulmin, S. (1990), *Cosmopolis* (Chicago, iii.: University of Chicago Press).

Tsoukas, H. (1993), 'Organizations as Soap Bubbles: An Evolutionary Perspective on Organization Design', *Systems Practice*, 6: 501–15.

—— (1996), 'The Firm as a Distributed Knowledge System: A Constructionist Approach', *Strategic Management Journal*, 17 (special winter issue): 11–25.

—— (1998), 'Forms of Knowledge and Forms of Life in Organized Contexts', in R. Chia (ed.), *In the Realm of Organization* (London: Routledge), 43–66.

Weick, K. (1987), 'Organizational Culture as a Source of High Reliability', *California Management Review*, 29: 112–27.

—— (1990), 'Introduction: Cartographic Myths in Organizations', in A. S. Huff (ed.), *Mapping Strategic Thought* (Chichester: Wiley), 1–10.

White, E. C. (1991), 'Negentropy, Noise, and Emancipatory Thought', in N. K. Hayles (ed.), *Chaos and Order* (Chicago, iii.: University of Chicago Press) 263–77.

III

META-KNOWLEDGE: TOWARDS A COMPLEX EPISTEMOLOGY OF MANAGEMENT RESEARCH

THIRTEEN

Refining Common Sense: Types of Knowledge in Management Studies

Introduction

M ANAGEMENT studies has historically been a very diverse field. Its diversity has been manifested not only through the many different (often disconnected) problems management scholars choose to study, or through the multiple and shifting membership of the management-studies community, which includes academics, consultants, and occasionally practitioners, but also through the conceptual fragmentation of the field (Whitley 1984*b*). It appears to be no accident that some of the most influential books in management studies (such as (e.g.) Mintzberg 1979; Morgan 1986) owe their success, partly at least, to suggesting a conceptual reorganization (i.e. a novel categorization) of the plethora of theories and models one encounters in the field. Such classifications organize their extremely diverse material, and help the reader to make some sense of it.

The chief problem, however, of such conceptual categorizations is that their heuristic power is not as great as it could be. In Burrell and Morgan's typology (1979: 22–35), for example, one can ignore, without much loss, the 'regulation versus radical change' dimension, which appears to be more a property of social theories and less an ontological assumption about features of the social world. As Donaldson (1985: 27–34, 40–6) has pointed out, there is no reason why 'functionalism', for example, should be concerned exclusively with stability-cum-regulation as Burrell and Morgan suggest, rather than with radical change as well. Burrell and Morgan's typology is ultimately reducible to the ontological 'subjective versus objective' dimension concerning the

An earlier version of this chapter was first published in the *Journal of Management Studies*, 31(6) (1994), 761–80. Reprinted by permission of Blackwell, Copyright (1994).

I would like to thank Alan B. Thomas, Richard Whitley, and the two anonymous *JMS* reviewers for their very helpful comments and suggestions to improve earlier drafts.

assumptions social theories make about the nature of the social world (see Evered and Louis 1981; Morgan and Smirich 1980). Such a set of assumptions, however, useful as it certainly is, is not sufficient for spelling out the logical organization that social theories attribute to the social world. Slicing the cake in the way Burrell and Morgan propose does not, for example, bring out sufficiently the differences between researchers as diverse as, say, Ansoff (1991), Donaldson (1985), Hersey (1984), Miller and Friesen (1980), Mintzberg (1990), and Pettigrew (1990).

It is the purpose of this chapter to suggest a framework that will be rich enough for understanding the different types of knowledge produced in management studies. I will borrow such a framework from Pepper (1942), and will illustrate it with examples from management studies, particularly from organizational behaviour (OB) and strategic management (SM). I will focus later on the debate between Mintzberg and Ansoff in order to investigate in more detail the different assumptions, methodologies, and knowledge claims each one of these scholars makes, which, as will be suggested later, stem from their subscribing to very different types of knowledge. It is the claim of this chapter that Pepper's framework enables us to appreciate the nature of competing knowledge claims made by management scholars as well as understand the subtleties of their disagreements. Throughout the chapter, by the term 'types of knowledge' I mean types of *formal* knowledge; that is, knowledge that is generated by social scientists through the systematic study of the social world (Whitley 1993).

Pepper's *World Hypotheses*

In his *World Hypotheses* (1942) Pepper argued that human knowledge is an endless process of cognitive refinement: the criticism and improvement of common-sense claims (cf. Payne 1975/6, 1982). Cognitive refinement occurs in two ways. First, by a process of what Pepper called 'multiplicative corroboration'; that is, a process of merely obtaining intersubjective confirmation of certain phenomena. And second, by 'structural corroboration'; that, is by constructing theories or hypotheses about the world and comparing them with empirical data. For Pepper, structural hypotheses do not merely produce predictions whose validity is decided on comparison with real data; structural hypotheses also organize the evidence they encounter and try to accommodate it even when anomalous. In other words, structural hypotheses are enquiry systems for obtaining knowledge (Churchman 1971), and as such they do not merely reflect aspects of social reality but also impose a cognitive organization on it (Burrell and Morgan 1979).

Pepper distinguishes four 'world hypotheses', which he considers to be the most adequate ways of refining common sense. He also argues that world hypotheses are epistemologically incommensurate—one cannot reject one

Table 13.1. World hypotheses

	Analytic theories	**Synthetic theories**Synthetic theories
Dispersive theories	Formism (root metaphor: similarity)	Contextualism (root metaphor: the historic event)
Integrative theories	Mechanism (root metaphor: the machine)	Organicism (root metaphor: the integrated whole)

Source: Pepper (1942)

on the basis of another and, thus, they cannot be synthesized into an over-arching world hypothesis. These four world hypotheses are the following: formism, mechanism, contextualism, and organicism. Each one is associated with a different 'root metaphor' (Pepper 1942) and characterized by a different set of assumptions concerning the logical structure of the social world (see Table 13.1). Below, each type of knowledge is described and illus-trated with relevant examples from management studies, particularly from OB and SM.

Formism

Formism is based on, and profits from, the human capacity to identify simi-larities and differences—in short, to categorize (cf. Mitroff and Mason 1982). Its root metaphor is similarity. Objects, events, processes—all sorts of phenom-ena—are construed as discrete facts that can be classified in several ways. Formism is characterized by two main features. First, it is an *analytic* theory: complexes or contexts are derivative, not an essential part of categorization. And second, it is a *dispersive* theory: '[F]acts are taken one by one from what-ever source they come and are interpreted as they come and so are left. The universe has for these theories the general effect of multitudes of facts rather loosely scattered about and not necessarily determining one another to any considerable degree' (Pepper 1942; 142–3). In other words, those advancing formistic knowledge claims seek to capture similarities and differences be-tween discrete objects of study without being necessarily concerned to offer an account of the underlying mechanisms that are responsible for any simi-larities and differences identified.

In so far as human thinking inevitably involves making conceptual distinc-tions, and highlighting selectively only certain aspects of phenomena, it may be argued that all human knowledge is inescapably formistic to some extent. Indeed, Pepper's attempt (and, equally, for that matter, my aim here) to delineate four distinctive types of knowledge and describe them in terms of two dimensions (see Table 13.1, above) is a typically formistic way of making sense of an object of study. Similarly, Burrell and Morgan's classification of theories and paradigms in organizational analysis, (1979), as well as Morgan's presentation of the organizational literature in terms of eight 'images of organization' (1986) are both illustrations of formistic thinking.

The preceding examples, however, are examples of a 'soft' (or 'weak') version of formistic thinking. The principle purpose of such authors (with Morgan being a notably good example) is discursive, communicative, and interpretative. Usually, no assumption is made that those conceptual distinctions that researchers favour reflect the 'true' state of things; more modestly, it is assumed that analytical categories are a researcher's invention to enable him/her to talk intelligibly and coherently about an object of study (see also Rorty 1991). Like Wittgenstein's ladder, such concepts, categories, and distinctions may be thrown away after one has used them to climb a wall. As will be seen later, such a 'soft' version of formism is close to a contextualist approach to knowledge, since they both share an anti-realist stance: our knowledge is conceived of more as a social construction and less as a supposedly true reflection of an independent reality.

By contrast, a 'hard' version of formism tends to attribute conceptual categories not merely to an author's ingenuity and to a community's acceptance of them, but to the real world itself. Objects of study are thought to exhibit certain systematic, observer-independent similarities and differences, and the task of the social scientist is to find out what they are. Zoology, botany, and chemistry are the paradigmatic sciences for those subscribing to such an approach to socialscientific knowledge; the ultimate taxonomy is the Holy Grail they are after.

In management studies, in particular, more often than not the construction of typologies has been underpinned by the logic of 'hard' formism. Environments, structures, technologies, control systems, leadership styles, organizational cultures, or whatever else happens to be of interest to academics or practitioners, have been predominantly understood through relentless categorization (see Daft 1989; Robbins 1990). Samples of 'excellent' or 'awful' organizations, for example, have been dissected for similarities which, once revealed, are assumed (but only assumed, not demonstrated) to be the causes of organizational excellence or failure respectively (see Peters and Waterman 1982).

As we will see later, in our discussion of Ansoff's claims, 'hard' formists assume that their typologies reflect the world as it is, and that the relationship between actors and the phenomena they seek to influence is predominantly instrumental. For Ansoff (1991), for example, 'environmental turbulence' is not merely a concept invented by researchers seeking to understand a particular class of phenomena; rather, it is an objective property of all business environments, which researchers ought to capture with their research instruments as finely as possible. Having done so, that is having represented business environments by a set of logically connected categories, practitioners can then begin to think how to influence business environments at will.

It is when formists attempt to use knowledge instrumentally that they usually take one further step and become mechanists. For simply to identify the similarities and differences between objects of study is not enough to influence social reality; one needs also to know how similarities and differences have come about, what are the mechanisms responsible for their appearance. To do so, 'hard' formists need to transcend the merely taxonomic character of their enquiry, and search explicitly for causes. Hence, they usually turn to mechanism.

Mechanism

The root metaphor of mechanism is the machine. Like formism, mechanism is an *analytical* world theory: discrete elements or factors, not complexes or contexts, are what mechanistic thinking is interested in. Unlike formism, however, mechanism is *integrative*: the world appears well ordered, it somehow hangs together, and 'facts occur in a determinate order and where, if enough were known, they could be predicted, or at least described, as being necessarily just what they are to the minutest detail' (Pepper 1942: 142). There are six features that are immanent in the mechanistic type of knowledge, and they are described below.

First, the object of study is regarded as ontologically given, fully describable, and algorithmically compressible. It is assumed to consist of discrete parts whose *locations* can be specified. In the case of a social object of study this means that its parts, as well as the relationships among them, can be represented in an abbreviated form (Cooper 1992; Tsoukas 1993a). Leavitt's representation (1965) of an organization as consisting of tasks, a structure, people, and technology is a good example of such thinking. Obviously, the parts of an object of study determine its functioning, and the more refined representations of them we can make, the better our understanding of the functioning of the entire object (cf. Mitroff and Mason 1982).

Second, the parts of an object of study are redescribed in some quantitative form that is different from our common-sense perception of them. Organizational structure, for example, may be reduced to three dimensions: formalization, centralization, and complexity (Daft 1989; Mintzberg 1979; Robbins 1990). In OB, in particular, there has not always been agreement about the operationalization of key constructs (cf. Mohr 1982), but the conviction is that operationalization is not only possible but indispensable. Pepper calls such measures *primary qualities*.

Third, there is an effective relationship (ideally a *lawful* one) between the parts making up a study object. In the natural sciences such laws are represented in the form of function equations. In OB and SM, more modestly, statistical correlations are the closest we can get to describing empirical regularities between parts.

Fourth, although parts are quantitatively redescribed, there are always some *secondary qualities* which are temporarily relegated to the status of background characteristics. At any point in time such qualities may not be directly relevant to a particular investigation, but they are not forgotten since they are related to the study object. Organizational culture, for example, was such a secondary quality in the Aston studies (see Donaldson 1985).

Fifth, secondary qualities are somehow connected with the study object by some *principle* and, as Pepper (1942: 193) remarked, making an analogy with a machine, 'if we were to make a complete description of the machine we should want to find out and describe just what the principle was which kept certain secondary qualities attached to certain parts of the machine'. Notice the insatiable appetite of mechanistic thinking for ever more complete descriptions and finer representations, so that an abbreviated representation of the logic by which the parts of a study object hang together may ultimately be achieved (Barrow 1991). The point being made here is not that such an abbreviation may or may not be achieved at any point in time, but that such an abbreviation is *achievable*. In OB, for example, the increasing attention paid to organizational culture and cognitive processes in organizations (cf. Kilmann et al. 1985; Sims et al. 1986), and the desire to find out if and how they are related systematically to other organizational characteristics exemplify this feature of mechanistic thinking.

Sixth, just as there are stable relationships between the primary qualities, it is possible that secondary qualities may exhibit stable relationships among themselves (ideally expressed by *secondary* laws).

The reader may have already recognized the sort of thinking we have described above: the contingency approach by another name. Indeed, as Payne (1975/6, 1982) has remarked, mechanistic thinking has long dominated OB. For example, the larger the size of an organization, the higher the degree of formalization, the larger the number of hierarchical levels, the higher the degree of centralization, and so on (see Donaldson 1985: 161).

In spite of its widespread use, however, it is doubtful whether mechanistic thinking has been really successful in OB. In a survey of organizational psychology Payne (1975/6) noticed the little variance that mechanistic models have been able to account for; the unsatisfactory level of correlation coefficients reported by several studies; the poor control of alternative propositions; and the fundamental difficulties in obtaining representative samples (for similar remarks see also Mohr 1982). Similarly, Webster and Starbuck (1988) have made comparable claims about industrial and organizational psychology. Having analysed data on effect sizes for the five most common variables organizational psychologists have studied (i.e. job satisfaction, absenteeism, turnover, job performance, and leadership) between 1944 and 1983, Webster and Starbuck concluded that theories in organizational psychology have failed to explain increasingly higher percentages of variance over time—the largest of the correlations reported is only 0.22.

Like formism, mechanism views the relationship between actors and phenomena in instrumental terms. It thus underplays actors' reflexivity and their potential for transforming the very reality a mechanistic theory seeks to explain and predict. As Payne (1975/6) argued, even if the predictive power of mechanistic types of knowledge were adequate, the amount of data one would need in order to make use of them would be inordinately high. Fiedler's (1967) contingency model of leadership, for example, requires organizations regularly to assess leaders' LPC scores, measures of the group atmosphere, task structure, and the leader's position of power in the organization. Such a regular exercise would turn organizational members into form fillers. What, however, is even more important is that actors' reflexivity vitiates attempts to represent reality as it supposedly is: the very fact of such a leadership-assessment exercise taking place at all is likely to influence actors' assessment of the situation and thus modify their responses to the relevant questions. It is precisely actors' reflexivity that makes Payne (ibid. 209) sceptical about Fiedler's model, and about the utility of this type of knowledge more generally: 'Would the model hold up if these measures were regularly taken in the organization and people knew they were being related to the assessment of the leader's performance? [...] Research results of this kind do not transfer easily to the actual world' (see also Tsoukas 1994).

Contextualism

Unlike formism and mechanism, contextualism is *synthetic:* it takes a pattern, a gestalt, as the object of study, rather than a set of discrete facts. Like formism, contextualism is *dispersive:* the multitudes of facts it seeks to register are assumed to be loosely structured, not systematically connected by virtue of a lawful relationship. There is no search for underlying structures, and the distinction between appearances and an underlying reality is not accepted. Its root metaphor is the historic event, continuously changing over time. A historic event is assumed to lie at the intersection of several trajectories whose origins and destinations are unknown to an enquirer (Barrett and Srivastava 1991).

Change and *novelty* are two fundamental features of contexualism. Change is regarded as endemic in social systems: taking their cue from Heraclitus, contextualists believe that one cannot step into the same river twice. Every event reconfigures an already established pattern, thus altering its character. Every moment is qualitatively different and should be treated as such. Every event, specified at a particular point in time, can be apprehended in terms of two additional features: *quality* and *texture.* Quality is the intuited wholeness of an event; texture is the details and relations making up the quality. We understand events by grasping intuitively the whole pattern (a face, a mood, a song, a painting, etc.), and when we wonder why we are so sure of our intuitions we start analysing their texture.

Historic events always have a certain quality and texture which continuously mutate into something novel over time. Notice that quality and texture are like two sides of the same coin: when we intuit the whole we suppress its details (i.e. its texture), and when we analyse a pattern we tend to underplay its wholeness (i.e. its quality). As Pepper (1942: 239) put it, 'qualities are most commonly in the focus of our attention but never (except for philosophic or aesthetic purposes) in the focus of analysis'.

The quality of an event has a *spread*, an interpenetration of past and future. An event is never what is immediately available, but also includes its contiguous past and present. This very paragraph I am writing draws on the preceding text, and although I haven't finished writing it you may have already realized what I am getting at. To a mechanist, of course, such a statement sounds unnecessarily vague. The only notion of time mechanists accept is that of schematic (chronological) time: the temporal ordering of distinct events (e.g. 'the' is the first word in this sentence, 'only' is the second word, and so on). While contextualists do not deny the usefulness of schematic time, they also insist on the notion of qualitative time. In Pepper's words (ibid. 242): 'In an actual event the present is the whole texture which directly contributes to the quality of the event. The present therefore spreads over the whole texture of the quality, and for any given event, can only be determined by intuiting the quality of the event.'

It has, I hope, become clear that contextualists categorically accept *change* as an inherent feature of the world, and seek to accommodate the ontological claim that the social world is incessantly on the move (Cooper and Fox 1990). It is also clear that contextualists work from the present event outward. They can make some definite claims about the present event but they are less confident of making claims about underlying mechanisms that may have caused the present event. This is indeed both the strength and the weakness of contextualism. By privileging the historic event, contextualists are able to highlight its uniqueness and aid our understanding of it, but are unable to offer (and are uninterested in offering) generalized statements about empirical regularities underpinned by more fundamental structures. For contextualists the world is not algorithmically compressible, hence there is no systematic way of investigating it—only loose, temporary, and ever revisable frameworks that guide human understanding.

Thus, contextualists always face a dilemma: either they can confine their analyses only to facts of direct verification, with the result being that their frameworks will be lacking in scope; or they may increase the scope of their claims by conceding the validity of indirect verification, in which case they would have to admit that the world has a determinate structure, thus falling back on one of the other world hypotheses. To such a dilemma, however, contextualists might playfully reply, 'How can you be so sure that nature is not intrinsically changing and full of novelties?' (Pepper 1942: 279). How, indeed?

The links between interpretivism and contextualism are obvious; the very language of contextualists often draws on literary metaphors. Contextualists' emphasis on the construction of narratives and stories for the interpretation of unique episodes makes them the prime exponents of 'narrative rationality' (Hunter 1991: ch. 2; Weick 1987: Weick and Browning 1986). In management studies, qualitative research has usually been based on contextualist premisses (Morgan and Smircich 1980). Pettigrew's investigation of organizational change (1987, 1990), for example, is an attempt to generate relevant knowledge within an avowedly contextualist framework. His account of change eschews invoking deeper structures, it avoids recording regularities, and is not concerned with outlining forms of organizational change congruent with situational characteristics. Instead, loose frameworks are offered which purport to help practitioners with organizing their material so that rich portraits of change episodes may be painted.

An additional stream of publications written within a loose contextualist framework are those offering advice to managers from the vantage point of either personal or documented experience (Blanchard and Johnson 1983; Harvey-Jones 1988; Iacocca 1985; Kanter 1983). Using lay language, such books are directly accessible to practitioners and inform them about 'how others do it' as well as advising about 'what works, and what doesn't' (cf. Thomas 1989; Whitley 1988, 1989). The fact that such collections of stories have proved so popular highlights the limits of the types of knowledge produced by formism and mechanism: it is almost impossible to establish closed systems in the social world in order to obtain stable forms and regularities (Tsoukas 1992, 1993a). Narratives, being loose, flexible frameworks, are close to the activities of practitioners, are richer in content, and have a higher mnemonic value (Daft and Wiginton 1979; Weick 1987). The practitioner is invited to connect them flexibly to his/her personal experience and interpret them liberally, something which he/she is not encouraged to do with formistic and mechanistic knowledge.

Organicism

The root metaphor of organicism is the integrated whole. Although its name is loaded with biological connotations, this need not be the case. Organicism deals with historic processes which are regarded as essentially organic processes: the unfolding of a logic that is immanent in the object of study. Through a sequence of specified steps, an organic process eventually culminates in a *telos*—that is, an ultimate, most inclusive structure. The process unfolds in the direction of greater inclusiveness, determinateness, and organicity—organic processes are progressive. The Hegelian and Marxian views of the 'laws of history' are some of the best examples of organicist thinking on a grand scale.

Organicism does not leave much to chance. The world may not appear to be, but it really is coherent and well integrated—so the argument goes. The world is a cosmos, and we can identify the manner in which it hangs together. Organicism is characterized by seven features, which Pepper (1942: 283) describes as follows:

(1) Fragments of experience which appear with (2) *nexuses* or connections or implications, which spontaneously lead as a result of the aggravation of (3) *contradictions*, gaps, opposition, or counteractions to resolution in (4) an *organic whole*, which is found to have been (5) *implicit* in the fragments, and to (6) *transcend* the previous contradictions by means of a coherent totality, which (7) *economizes*, saves, preserves all the original fragments of experience without any loss.

Organicism sees fragments of events connected in meaningful, though often incomplete or contradictory, ways. The conflicts in a nexus of events are resolved via a higher synthesis, which, while recognizing the particularity of fragments, transcends them and harmonizes them in a more complete *holon*. Notice that for organicists fragments of experience do not matter as such, since it is their ultimate explanation in terms of underlying structures that is epistemically important. Thus, organicism is more prone than other world hypotheses to explaining away empirical anomalies or dismissing as unimportant 'secondary qualities'. In so far as the integrated whole is of such ontological significance, organicism strives for comprehensiveness and underlying structures, but it leaves little room for autonomous human action (Castoriadis 1987: Pt. 1).

In management studies there have been increasingly influential streams of research dealing with evolutionary processes, configurations of organizational and environmental characteristics, and modelling organizations on biological organisms, all of which are broadly within the organicist type of knowledge (cf. Gersick 1991). The contrast between Pettigrew's, Mangham's, and Johnson's contextual approaches to organizational change on the one hand (1987, 1990; 1988; 1987), and Miller and Friesen's and Tushman and Romanelli's quantum models of change on the other (1980; 1985) is a vivid example of the widely different thinking styles between contextualism and organicism (see also Poole and Van de Ven 1989).

Another example of organicist thinking is Mintzberg's set of organizational configurations (1979, 1989), arranged along time in evolutionary terms. Organizational features and behaviour, for Mintzberg, are explained in terms of a set of five underlying components which are put together in five characteristic ways. Thus, the behaviour of ideal-type configurations provides the conceptual template for the explanation and prediction of actual organizational behaviour. As organizations grow, there are conflicts among the various structural components they are made of, which are resolved by the organization jumping on to a new arrangement of these components (i.e. a new configuration).

Similarly, models of organization that have developed via analogical reasoning (Tsoukas 1991, 1993*b*) exhibit several traits of organicist thinking. Beer's viable-system model (VSM) (1981) is a good case in point, although it lacks an evolutionary dimension. The VSM is a model that has been developed by modelling organizations on the human nervous system. The five subsystems and their relationships that make up the nervous system are the source models for similar organizational systems. The integrated wholeness that characterizes the nervous system is transferred into the domain of organizations. Thus, organizational problems are diagnosed in terms of dysfunctions between parts of the whole system, and the aim is to redesign it in order to eliminate such dysfunctions.

A Case Study: The Mintzberg–Ansoff Debate on the Nature of Strategic Management

For Pepper, the types of knowledge outlined above are incommensurate and resist synthesis. Not infrequently their exponents have found it difficult to communicate with one another despite working in the same disciplinary field. However, this should not come as a surprise. Fundamental assumptions about the organization and functioning of the social world do not stand outside it, but are crucially involved in its constitution (Rosenberg 1988: ch. 2; Sayer 1984; Winch 1958: ch. 4). Furthermore, the kinds of research questions asked, the objects selected for study, and the criteria for evaluating knowledge claims are all intimately connected with the underlying assumptions of what is valid knowledge and how it may be obtained (see Burrell and Morgan 1979; Morgan 1980, 1986; Pinder and Bourgeois 1982).

Pepper's four world hypotheses provide a framework for appreciating the different types of knowledge generated in management studies and, as I will show below, they help us to understand better the arguments involved when researchers who have different conceptions of knowledge engage in a debate. I will illustrate these points below by focusing on the relatively recent exchange between Mintzberg and Ansoff (see Ansoff 1991; Mintzberg 1990, 1991), which provides an excellent example of the different types of knowledge these scholars espouse, and the nature of disagreements that ensue.

Echoing themes of his earlier work on strategy, Mintzberg (1990) sought in the early 1990s to describe and critique the main tenets of what he calls 'the design school of strategic management'. The latter, according to Mintzberg, has historically been the most influential school of thought in SM; it proposes a model of strategy that views it as a conscious process of design to achieve a fit between a firm's external threats and opportunities on the one hand and its internal strengths on the other. Such a view of strategy is predicated on three premises, he argues. First, the formulation of strategy precedes clearly its implementation. Second, the process of strategy formulation is one of consciously controlled thought, involving senior managers and, more specifically (and crucially), the CEO. And third, such a process is explicit, and the strategy produced should also be explicit, simple, and unique. In short, from an onto-epistemological point of view, the most fundamental assumption of the design school is that of the split between thinking and acting, and the consequent identification of thinking with strategy formulation and of acting with strategy implementation.

For Mintzberg strategies are formulated in the manner prescribed by the 'design school' only in a minority of cases, in which information is simple, so that it can be comprehended by a single brain (or a few brains), and the environment is stable, so that the strategy can be implemented as intended. More often than not these conditions do not obtain, and, therefore, strategies are never as deliberate as the design school assumes (or requires) them to be; they, inescapably, have elements of emergence. More realistically, strategies can form as well as be formulated. Thinking and acting are intertwined, and truly creative strategies are more probably the result of experiential trial and error than of detached analytical thinking (see also Mintzberg 1978, 1987, 1989).

Ansoff (1991), as one familiar with his work might expect, will have none of this. In his reply to Mintzberg he criticizes him for lack of coherence in his argument, for deriving prescriptive from merely descriptive statements, and, on the whole, for exaggerating his claims about emergent strategies, which for Ansoff, in an inversion of Mintzberg's argument, are encountered only in a minority of contexts. Ansoff's critique reveals a mechanistic-cum-formistic conception of knowledge, which is in sharp contrast to Mintzberg's avowedly contextualist thinking with regard to strategy. Ansoff's critique consists essentially of two parts. The first part replies to Mintzberg's criticisms (a) that the design school has denied itself the chance to adapt, and (b) that other prescriptive schools of thought in SM have also remained frozen in time. However, these claims attributed to Mintzberg are only contingently linked to the main core of Mintzberg's argument against the design school. One could even agree with Ansoff's reply on these points and still adhere to Mintzberg's core argument. For this reason, therefore, I will not examine the first part of Ansoff's reply more closely.

The second part, attempting to rebut Mintzberg's core assertions, reveals Ansoff's mechanistic-cum-formistic epistemology for SM. Ansoff charges Mintzberg with lack of precision and vagueness when referring to the environment of firms. Says Ansoff (ibid. 455):

One learns that managers:

cannot be sure of the future. Sometimes organizations need to function during periods of unpredictability. Sometimes organizations come out of a period of changing circumstances into a period of operating stability. (Mintzberg, 1990: 184)

Nothing is said about how often is 'sometimes', what is meant by 'unpredictability', by 'changing circumstances', or how long and how prevalent are the 'periods of operating stability'. The only complete sentence devoted to the environment does not help very much:

... environment is not some kind of pear to be plucked from the tree of external appraisal, but a major and sometimes unpredictable force .... (Mintzberg 1990: 185)

This cryptic statement begs all kinds of questions: whose environment is being discussed; what kind of influence does the force exert on organizations; under what circumstances is it exerted; what impact does it have on strategic behavior, etc.

Ansoff's discourse exhibits all the main characteristics of mechanistic thinking. His remarks are primarily concerned with questions of representation and frequency. The business environment is construed as a potentially fully describable entity which can be adequately represented via a set of dimensions, categories, or variables, expressed, ideally, in quantitative terms. Such measures, called by Pepper 'primary qualities', should be investigated statistically so that certain regularities, obtaining under certain empirically verifiable conditions, may be ascertained. Indeed, the bulk of Ansoff's criticism precisely consists of a torrent of references to empirical studies aiming to demonstrate the validity of his contingency model of strategy.

Ansoff does not seem to be beset by philosophical doubts about the nature of reality that his model of strategy seeks to reflect. For a descriptive statement to be valid, he remarks, 'it must be an accurate observation of reality' (Ansoff 1991: 455–6). Empirical research, according to Ansoff, seeks to describe the regularities the world consists of, and then, on the basis of these empirically established regularities, to recommend prescriptions to decision makers for future action. Prescriptions for strategic action in the future become possible if the conditions that make such action possible are similar enough to the conditions that have been empirically established in the past, so that action in the future can follow the patterns of action in the past.

A mechanistic view of strategy differs radically from that based on contextualist premises. For contextualists, strategy making is 'a creative process (of synthesis) for which there are no formal techniques (analysis)' (Mintzberg 1991: 465), nor can it be objectively operationalized by a researcher, because it then loses its context-derived distinctiveness. Strategy-making stems from a deep direct knowledge of local contexts and from the intimate understanding that is generated by actors engaged with the world in trial and error (Mintzberg 1987, 1989). To attempt to detach strategy-making from its intrinsic embedment in local contexts for the purpose of aggregating empirical findings and compressing them in a quasi-algorithmic formula, is to destroy the very features of strategy-making that make it a uniquely creative process, inextricably bound up with personal, especially tacit, knowledge (Polanyi and Prosch 1975: ch. 2).

Such personal knowledge is possessed and utilized only by those who are intimately involved with the details of a business, and should a researcher want to objectify such knowledge for the purpose of a mechanistic investigation he/she would destroy it. Instead, a qualitative approach, employing narratives as the main medium of exposition, is better suited to capture the many context-dependent nuances, details, and flexible temporal connections that characterize strategy making (see Brown and Duguid 1991; Hunter 1991; Morgan and Smircich 1980; Susman and Evered 1978; Tsoukas 1993*a*; Weick 1987; Weick and Browning 1986).

Thus, for contextualists like Mintzberg the concept of strategy does not indicate a centrally formulated plan for a substantial commitment of resources to particular products and processes over fairly long periods of time (as it does for Ansoff 1965, 1984, and the design school more generally), but simply patterns in a stream of decisions that have not necessarily been made at the centre (see Mintzberg 1979, 1987, 1989). Such a view of strategy allows for patterns not to be viewed as fixed but as inherently changeable and reconfigurable, depending on the observer ('Patterns, like beauty, are in the mind of the beholder, of course', writes Mintzberg (1987: 67)). It also offers the investigator the possibility of looking for connections over a wider span of real time (what Pepper in his discussion of contextualism calls 'spread') and over a broader spectrum of concrete events than would be allowed by the linear structure and the abstract form of statements produced by mechanistic-cum-formistic thinking.

By contrast, mechanists privilege the researcher's 'scientific method', which is modelled on the method of the natural sciences (Rosenberg 1988: 19). Ansoff's reply is indeed permeated by the tone of the serious-looking scholar reprimanding an amateur social scientist for not using properly or adequately the canons of 'scientific method', identifying abstract facts which stand for objective properties of the object of study, and then connecting those facts statistically to identify lawful regularities. Of course, what Ansoff does not appreciate, and Mintzberg (1991) in his rejoinder is curiously reticent to point out, is that his precepts lack the universality he assumes they have; the epistemological categories as well as the evaluation criteria he employs are formulated only within a certain template of formal knowledge (that of mechanism-cum-formism) which, although historically dominant in the social-scientific discourse, is only one type of knowledge among others.

Discussion

As we have already seen, mechanists eschew studying uniqueness and singularity, preferring instead the investigation of abstract properties, which are assumed to be generic and lawfully connected. Attempting to distinguish an abstract property of all business environments, Ansoff (1991: 459) singles out the concept of 'environmental turbulence'. In contrast, faithful to his mistrust of objective variables, Mintzberg (1991: 464) remains sceptical: 'What in the world does "turbulence" mean anyway? And who has ever made a serious claim of measuring it?' Adhering to mechanistic thinking, Ansoff presupposes that an independent mind can measure an objective feature of the environment (in this case, turbulence) which may then be correlated with the appropriate strategic behaviour:

[A]n organization will optimize its success when the aggressiveness of its strategic behavior in the environment and its openness to the external environment are both aligned with the turbulence level of the organization's external environment[...] The levels of success in organizations which are aligned with the environment were substantially higher than in organizations which were out of alignment. (Ansoff 1991: 459)

The identification of past empirical regularities enables Ansoff to put forward prescriptions for future action. But on what grounds are such prescriptions valid? A prescription is valid, writes Ansoff (ibid. 456), only when it can 'offer evidence that use of the prescription will enable an organization to meet the objective by which it judges its success'. The implied symmetry between explanations of past regularities and predictions of (or recommendations for) future action is a characteristic feature of mechanistic thinking, although Ansoff implies that it is (or ought to be) a feature of all knowledge.

It is the assumption that regularities in the past can be extrapolated into the future that lends mechanistic thinking its 'scientific' authority and its consequent capacity to authorize (in both senses of the word) courses of action (MacIntyre 1985: 104). Indeed, as MacIntyre (ibid. 107) aptly observed, should this assumption be undermined, the very basis of authoritative managerial action would become questionable. Yet in so far as human praxis is under-determined by the past (conditioned to be sure, but not completely), the nature of organizational action is necessarily open-ended (open yes, but not infinitely open), potentially creative (creative certainly, but not a *de novo* construction), and, thus, able to break away from past regularities (Briskman 1980; Tsoukas 1992, 1993*a*).

The capability of social theories to predict (and therefore prescribe) a future course of action is not as strong as mechanists seem to think it is (although this is not to suggest that it is entirely absent). There are two reasons for this. First, in so far as current practices partly depend on current systems of knowledge, predictions about the likely results of future practices depend on predictions of the growth of knowledge. However, as Popper (1982: 62) has remarked, 'we cannot predict, scientifically, results which we shall obtain in the course of the growth of our knowledge'. As noted above, the logical contradictions besetting self-prediction are well known: if we were to know today what theories we will know tomorrow then these theories would occur to us today and not tomorrow (MacIntyre 1985; ch. 8; Popper 1982: 60–5). If the opposite were true, radical innovation would be impossible (Whitley 1989). Thus, if conventional western notions of organization and criteria of commercial success had been in some sense fixed and absolute, the rise of, say, Japan as an economic superpower in the 1980s would not have occurred. For radical innovation to be possible, the future ought to remain not only unknown but *unknowable* (Tsoukas 1992).

The point about the potentially creative nature of human praxis is also brought out by Mintzberg in his discussion of Honda's strategy that captured two-thirds of the American motorcycle market. Says Mintzberg (1991: 464):

> Honda's success, if we are to believe those who did it and not those who figured it, was built precisely on what they initially believed to be one of Igor's 'probable non-starters'—namely the small motorcycle. Their own priors were that a market without small motorcycles would not buy small motorcycles. Had they a proper planning process in place, as Igor describes it in these pages, this non-starter would have been eliminated at the outset—plan 'rationally' and be done with it.

Mintzberg underscores here the experimental character of successful strategies as well as the vicious self-fulfilling prophesies in which one is embroiled as soon as one takes knowledge of past regularities as an absolute guide for future action. By contrast, as we saw, Ansoff privileges the certainty that such knowledge provides to practitioners.

While contextualist thinking construes prospective action as potentially novel and open-ended, mechanistic thinking conceives of it as being, essentially, a modified extension of the past. To the extent that social life is institutionalized and follows certain patterns and routines, the mechanistic assumption is not mistaken: prospective action does not always break away from the patterns of the past (Berger and Luckmann 1966: 65–84; Tsoukas 1993*a*). Similarly, to the extent that social life historically often evolves in ways that no one can really predict or anticipate, the contextualist assumption is not incorrect either. The problem, of course, is to know the scope of each 'extent' respectively. Knowing the area of their applicability, however, is beyond the scope of all four types of knowledge discussed here. This is because for a type of knowledge to be aware of its own limits, there should be a meta-perspective from which to view itself and the other types of knowledge. But, as Pepper and others have argued, such a meta-perspective does not exist (Who could tell us where it is? Who could tell us what 'strategy' *really* is?), and that is why Pepper's world hypotheses are more than mirrors reflecting aspects of the social world; they are competing discourses that view (and shape) the social world in terms of their own categories (see also Foucault 1971).

Ansoff's defence of the design school is as good an illustration as any of the taken-for-granted nature of the basic categories and premises of a particular type of knowledge. Revealingly, Ansoff not only defends his perspective as one would expect, but he also attempts to *reconstruct* Mintzberg's perspective in terms of the categories of mechanistic-cum-formistic thinking. Positioning the epistemic rival is as important as defending one's own position. Says Ansoff (1991: 459):

Thus empirical research described above shows that Mintzberg's Prescriptive Model is a valid prescription for organizations which seek to optimize their performance in environments in which strategic changes are incremental and the speed of the changes is slower than the speed of the organizational response.

Similarly, while Ansoff cites a wealth of quantitative empirical studies to support his claims, Mintzberg resorts to 'the sample of one'—singular cases such as his favourite examples of Honda, or Sam Steinberg's retailing business, which best exemplify what he thinks are the key features of strategy-making.

Conclusions

I have described in this chapter four different approaches to obtaining formal knowledge in management studies, drawing on Pepper's *World Hypotheses*. Those subscribing to these four approaches vary widely in terms of the research questions they pose, the research methodologies they utilize, and the evaluation criteria they adopt. Epistemological differences can indeed be so great that, as the exchange between Mintzberg and Ansoff indicates, even foundational concepts (such as, for example, that of 'strategy') are conceptualized and researched in radically different ways. Mintzberg and Ansoff, subscribing to incommensurate types of knowledge, clearly cannot agree on what strategy is.

From a contextualist point of view, strategy-making is rooted in local contexts so that, stripped of its contextuality, it is no longer strategy-making proper. By way of analogy, as Winch (1958: 107) aptly observed, both the Aristotelian and Galilean systems of mechanics use the notion of 'force', but its meaning within each system is substantially different: 'the relation between idea and context is an *internal* one. The idea gets its sense from the role it plays in the system' (ibid.). For Mintzberg strategy-making is an inherently *creative* process which can neither be formalized nor abstracted out of its context. All academic research can do is to offer an account of the local context-in-time, as well as give voice to the intimate experience actors have developed over time. The richness of strategy-making, therefore, can be brought out only through the narrative mode of exposition. Thus, in contextualist epistemology, actors are given their voice in the researcher's narrative; they speak in their own words, and the researcher is the 'interpreter' (Bauman 1987: 4–6) between the community he/she describes and the audience to which he/she reports his/her findings.

Contrast this picture of strategy-making with that drawn by mechanists. For Ansoff, strategy-making is an objective process and it is the task of the researcher to describe and explain it. Strategy, therefore, is construed as having certain generic properties that can be abstracted out of their local contexts and correlated with other generic organizational properties under certain specified conditions. Once such correlations have been established ('at 0.05 or better confidence level', as Ansoff is at pains to point out (1991: 459)), they can serve as the basis for recommending prospective action. Researchers, therefore, are seen as 'legislators' (Bauman 1987: 4–6) whose authority to prescribe solutions is based on the allegedly superior knowledge that is generated by the application of the scientific method to management problems.

In a practically oriented field such as management studies (Whitley 1984*a*) prescriptions to guide practitioners have historically been extremely important. For Ansoff (and for mechanists in general) practical action in the future ought to be guided (determined?) by practitioners' knowledge of past regularities. What this view assumes is that the future action of an individual firm can be guided reliably by the past actions of a large number of firms that have been aggregated (and thus their context-dependent features have been abstracted) for certain research purposes. Uniqueness and singularity are not particularly valued by mechanists, and this shows in their research designs and the questions they investigate. Thompson (1956–7: 103), for example, expressed his disdain for 'the tyranny of the particular' (Medawar cited in Feyerabend 1987: 122) as follows:

If every administrative action, and every outcome of such action, is entirely unique, then there can be no transferable knowledge or understanding of administration. If, on the other hand, knowledge of at least some aspects of administrative processes is transferable, then those methods which have proved most useful in gaining reliable knowledge in other areas would also seem to be appropriate for adding to our knowledge of administration.

For contextualists, by contrast, such a view of management studies and of practical reason is unacceptable. As Susman and Evered (1978: 590) have put it:

Appropriate action is based not on knowledge of the replications of previously observed relationships between actions and outcomes. It is based on knowing how particular actors define their present situations or on achieving consensus on defining situations so that planned actions will produce their intended consequences.

Mintzberg's research on strategy-making has echoed similar concerns. He has consistently emphasized the importance of experience and non-programmable personal knowledge as the most essential prerequisites for strategy-making. What Mintzberg sees as the most salient feature of strategy-making is *creative action*: the inherent potential of human praxis for novelty. Judgement, personal knowledge, and experimental action are his mottos; by contrast, for Ansoff, effective managerial action is informed by formally generated knowledge of past regularities.

Well, 'Who is right?' would be a tempting question to ask. Tempting though it may be, it would also be the wrong question to try to answer. As Pepper emphasized, there is no independent ground, no Archimedean point, from which one may pass a judgement. World hypotheses are epistemologically incommensurate. They all capture aspects of reality and in doing so they legitimate themselves for making more universal knowledge claims. Epistemological incommensurability, however, need not be translated into sociological incommensurability. In so far as types of knowledge are not disembodied epistemic artefacts but *social constructions* which fight for acceptance within particular institutional settings, there are social rules that help arbitrate between them. It would be interesting to investigate how, in management studies, incommensurate types of knowledge are legitimated in particular socio-temporal junctures and gain institutional ascendancy. Expanding on such a project, however, would be beyond the scope of this chapter.

References

Ansoff, I. (1965), *Corporate Strategy* (New York: McGraw-Hill).
—— (1984), *Implanting Strategic Management* (Englewood Cliffs, NJ.: Prentice Hall).
—— (1991), 'Critique of Henry Mintzberg's "The Design School: Reconsidering the Basic Premises of Strategic Management"', *Strategic Management Journal*, 12: 449–61.
Barrett, F., and Srivastava, S. (1991), 'History as a Mode of Inquiry in Organizational Life: A Role for Human Cosmogony', *Human Relations*, 44, 231–54.
Barrow, J. (1991), *Theories of Everything* (London: Vintage).
Bauman, S. (1987), *Legislators and Interpreters* (Cambridge: Polity).
Beer, S. (1981), *Brain of the Firm* (Chichester: Wiley).
Berger, P., and Luckmann, T. (1966), *The Social Construction of Reality* (London: Penguin).
Blanchard, K., and Johnson, S. (1983), *The One Minute Manager* (Glasgow: Collins/Fontana).
Bolman, L., and Deal, T. (1991), *Reframing Organizations* (San Francisco Calif.: Jossey-Bass).
Briskman, L. (1980), 'Creative Product and Creative Process in Science and Art', *Inquiry*, 23: 83–106.
Brown, J. S., and Duguid, P. (1991), 'Organizational Learning and Communities of Practice: Toward a Unified View of Working, Learning, and Innovation', *Organization Science*, 2: 40–57.
Burrell, G., and Morgan, G. (1979), *Sociological Paradigms and Organisational Analysis* (Aldershot: Gower).
Castoriadis, C. (1987), *The Imaginary Institution of Society*, trans. K. Blarney, (Cambridge: Polity).
Churchman, C. W. (1971), *The Design of Inquiring Systems* (New York: Basic).
Cooper, R. (1992), 'Formal Organization as Representation: Remote Control, Displacement and Abbreviation', in M. Reed and M. Hughes (eds.), *Rethinking Organization* (London: Sage), 254–72.
—— and Fox, S. (1990), 'The "Texture" of Organizing', *Journal of Management Studies*, 27: 575–82.

Daft, R. L. (1989), *Organization Theory and Design*, 3rd edn., (St Paul, Minn: West).

—— and Wiginton, J. (1979), 'Language and Organization', *Academy of Management Review*, 4: 179–91.

Donaldson, L. (1985), *In Defence of Organization Theory* (Cambridge: Cambridge University Press).

Evered, R., and Louis, M. R. (1981), 'Alternative Perspectives in the Organizational Sciences: "Inquiry from the Inside" and "Inquiry from the Outside"', *Academy of Management Review*, 6: 385–95.

Feyerabend, P. (1987), *Farewell to Reason* (London: Verso).

Fiedler, F. E. (1967), *A Theory of Leadership Effectiveness* (New York: McGraw-Hill).

Foucault, M. (1971), 'Orders of Discourse', *Social Science Information*, 10: 7–30.

Gersick, C. (1991), 'Revolutionary Change Theories: A Multi-level Exploration of the Punctuated Equilibrium Paradigm', *Academy of Management Review*, 16: 10–36.

Harvey-Jones, J. (1988), *Making It Happen* (London: Fontana).

Hersey, P. (1984), *The Situational Leader* (New York: Warner).

Hunter, M. K. (1991), *Doctors' Stories: The Narrative Structure of Medical Knowledge* (Princeton, NJ: Princeton University Press).

Iacocca, L., with Novak, W. (1985), *Iacocca: An Autobiography* (London: Sidgwick and Jackson).

Johnson, G. (1987), *Strategic Change and the Management Process* (Oxford: Blackwell).

Kanter, R. M. (1983), *The Change Masters* (London: Allen & Unwin).

Kilmann, R., Saxton, M., Serpa, R., et al. (1985), *Gaining Control of the Corporate Culture* (San Francisco, Calif.: Jossey-Bass).

Leavit, H. J. (1965), 'Applied Organizational Change in Industry: Structural, Technological and Humanistic Approaches', in J. March (ed.), *Handbook of Organizations* (Chicago, Ill: Rand-McNally), 1144–70.

Macintyre, A. (1985), *After Virtue*, 2nd edn. (London: Duckworth).

Mangham, I. (1988), *Effecting Organizational Change* (Oxford: Blackwell).

Miller, D., and Friesen, P. (1980), 'Momentum and Revolution in Organizational Adaptation', *Academy of Management Journal*, 23: 591–614.

Mintzberg, H. (1978), 'Patterns in Strategy Formation', *Management Science*, 24: 934–48.

—— (1979), *The Structuring of Organizations* (Englewood Cliffs, NJ: Prentice Hall).

—— (1987), 'Crafting Strategy', *Harvard Business Review*, 65: 66–75.

—— (1989), *Mintzberg on Management* (New York: Free Press).

—— (1990), 'The Design School: Reconsidering the Basic Premises of Strategic Management', *Strategic Management Journal*, 11: 171–95.

—— (1991), 'Learning 1, Planning 0: Reply to Igor Ansoff', *Strategic Management Journal*, 12: 463–6.

Mitroff, I., and Mason, R. (1982), 'Business Policy and Metaphysics: Some Philosophical Considerations', *Academy of Management Review*, 7: 361–71.

Mohr, L. (1982), *Explaining Organizational Behavior* (San Francisco, Calif.: Jossey-Bass).

Morgan, G. (1980), 'Paradigms, Metaphors and Puzzle-solving in Organization Theory', *Administrative Science Quarterly*, 25: 605–22.

—— (1986), *Images of Organization* (London: Sage).

—— and Smircich, L. (1980), 'The Case for Qualitative Research', *Academy of Management Review*, 5: 491–500.

Payne, R. (1975/6), 'Truisms in Organizational Behaviour', *Interpersonal Development*, 6: 203–20.

—— (1982), 'The Nature of Knowledge and Organizational Psychology', in N. Nicholson, and T. Wall, (eds.), *Theory and Method in Organizational Psychology* (New York: Academic), 37–67.

Pepper, S. (1942), *World Hypotheses* (Berkeley, Calif.: University of California Press).

Peters, T., and Waterman, R. (1982), *In Search of Excellence* (London: Harper & Row).

Pettigrew, A. (1987), 'Context and Action in the Transformation of the Firm', *Journal of Management Studies*, 24: 650–70.

—— (1990), 'Longitudinal Field Research on Change: Theory and Practice', *Organization Science*, 1: 267–92.

Pinder, C. C., and Bourgeois, W. V. (1982), 'Controlling Tropes in Administrative Science', *Administrative Science Quarterly*, 27: 641–52.

Polanyi, M., and Prosch, H. (1975), *Meaning* (Chicago, Ill.: University of Chicago Press).

Poole, M. S., and Van De Ven, A. H. (1989), 'Toward a general theory of innovation processes', in A. Van de Ven, H. L. Angle, and M. S. Poole (eds.), *Research on the Management of Innovation* (Minnesota studies) (New York: Harper & Row), 637–62.

Popper, K. (1982), *The Open Universe* (London: Hutchinson).

Robbins, S. P. (1990), *Organization Theory: Structure, Design, and Applications*, 3rd edn. (Englewood Cliffs, NJ: Prentice Hall).

Rorty, R. (1991), *Objectivism, Relativism, and Truth* (Cambridge: Cambridge University Press).

Rosenberg, A. (1988), *Philosophy of Social Science* (Oxford: Clarendon).

Sayer, A. (1984), *Method in Social Science* (London: Hutchinson).

Sims, H. P., Giola, D. A., et al. (1986), *The Thinking Organization* (San Francisco, Calif.: Jossey-Bass).

Susman, G., and Evered, R. (1978), 'An Assessment of the Scientific Merits of Action Research', *Administrative Science Quarterly*, 23: 582–603.

Thomas, A. B. (1989), 'One-Minute Management Education: A Sign of the Times?', *Management Education and Development*, 20: 23–38.

Thompson, J. D. (1956–7), 'On Building an Administrative Science', *Administrative Science Quarterly*, 1: 102–11.

Tsoukas, H. (1991), 'The Missing Link: A Transformational View of Metaphors in Organizational science', *Academy of Management Review*, 16: 566–85.

—— (1992), 'The Relativity of Organizing: Its Knowledge Presuppositions and its Pedagogical Implications for Comparative Management', *Journal of Management Education*, 16, special issue, S147–S162.

—— (1993a), 'Beyond Social Engineering and Contextualism: The Narrative Structure of Organisational Knowledge', Warwick Business School research paper no. 69, Warwick University.

—— (1993b), 'Analogical Reasoning and Knowledge Generation in Organization Theory', *Organization Studies*, 14: 323–46.

—— (1994), 'Introduction: from Social Engineering to Reflective Action in Organizational Behaviour', in H. Tsoukas (ed.), *New Thinking in Organizational Behaviour* (Oxford: Butterworth/Heinemann), 1–21.

Tushman, M., and Romanelli, E. (1985), 'Organizational evolution: A Metamorphosis Model of Convergence and Reorientation', in L. L. Cummings, and

B. M. Staw (eds.), *Research in Organizational Behavior*, 7 (Greenwich, Conn.: JAI), 171–222.

Webster, J. , and Starbuck, W. (1988), 'Theory Building in Industrial and Organizational Psychology', in C. Cooper, and I. Robertson (eds.), *International Review of Industrial and Organizational Psychology*, Chichester: Wiley, 93–138.

Weick, K. (1979), *The Social Psychology of Organizing*, 2nd edn. (Reading, Mass.: Addison–Wesley).

—— (1987), 'Organizational Culture as a Source of High Reliability', *California Management Review*, 29: 112–27.

—— and Browning, L. (1986), 'Argument and Narration in Organizational Communication', *Journal of Management*, 12: 243–59.

Whitley, R. (1984a), 'The Status of Management Research as a Practically Oriented Social Science', *Journal of Management Studies*, 21: 369–90.

—— (1984b), 'The Fragmented State of Management Studies: Reasons and Consequences', *Journal of Management Studies*, 21: 331–48.

—— (1988), 'The Management Sciences and Managerial Skills', *Organization Studies*, 9, 47–68.

—— (1989), 'Knowledge and Practice in the Management and Policy Sciences', working paper no. 174, Manchester Business School.

—— (1993), 'Formal Knowledge and Management Education', in L. Engwall, and E. Gunnarsson, (eds.), *Management Studies in an Academic Context* (Uppsala: Series Acta Universitatis, Upsaliensis Studia Oeconomica Negotiorum).

Winch, P. (1958), *The Idea of a Social Science and its Relation to Philosophy* (London: Routledge & Kegan Paul).

FOURTEEN

The Practice of Theory: A Knowledge-based View of Theory Development in Organization Studies

THE prevailing view of theory development in organization studies (OS) has, for quite some time, been that theory development takes place within incommensurate paradigms. This claim is typically made by theorists of an anti-positivist or 'critical' epistemological bent. Another widespread view has been that if the knowledge produced in OS is to be instrumentally used by practitioners, such knowledge needs necessarily to be tested for its generality and scope of application. This claim is put forward by, typically, positivist and some action-oriented researchers. While both meta-theoretical views have elements of truth, they conceal more than they reveal. What they have in common is a mentalistic understanding of research, whereby the latter is predominantly seen as a series of competing abstract knowledge claims. In this chapter I challenge this mentalisitc understanding by conceiving of organizational research as knowledge-based work, and explore the implications for paradigm incommensurability, theory development, and theory use.

From Theory to Meta-theory: The Paradox of Reflexivity

The number-one problem in OS has been suggested to be the fragmentation of the field into so many, often unconnected, perspectives and paradigms. This is

This chapter draws heavily on H. Tsoukas and C. Knudsen, 'Introduction: The Need for Meta-theoretical Reflection in Organization Theory', in H. Tsoukas and C. Knudsen (eds.), *The Oxford Handbook of Organization Theory: Meta-theoretical Perspectives* (Oxford: Oxford University Press, 2003), 1–36. Parts are reprinted by permission of Oxford University Press, Copyright (2003).

a problem, it has been alleged, for it makes the field less influential among policy makers; less capable of obtaining resources; it obstructs communication within the field; and, ultimately, it makes scientific progress difficult, if not impossible (Miner 1984; Pfeffer 1993; Webster and Starbuck 1988; Zammuto and Connolly 1984). It has been alleged that OS appears to be close to becoming a Tower of Babel (Burrell 1996: 644; Kaghan and Philips 1998), and this cannot be good to anyone. Add to this concern the perennial anxiety regarding the extent to which a policy science such as OS is indeed relevant to practitioners (Abrahamson and Eisenman 2001; Lawler et al., 1999; Mowday 1997; Pettigrew 2001; Starkey and Madan 2001; Tranfield and Starkey 1998), and you have the makings of a crisis of self-confidence: How good are we as a field to develop valid knowledge which is of relevance to practitioners?

The moment such questions are raised, meta-theoretical reflection—reflexivity—begins. What is valid knowledge and how is it to be generated? To whom exactly should it be made relevant? For what purpose? What does 'relevant' mean anyway, and how is 'relevant' knowledge best produced? How should competing knowledge claims be evaluated? Raising such questions implies taking a step back from ordinary theoretical activity to reflect on what the latter should be aiming at and how it ought to be conducted—it is for this reason that such reflection is called '*meta*-theoretical'. By raising those 'meta' questions the purpose is not to generate theory about particular organizational topics but to make the generation of theory itself an object of analysis (see Fig. 14.1).

Notice, however, the paradox here, a paradox intrinsic to all acts of reflexivity. Ordinarily we go about doing our theoretical work (i.e. trying to make sense of a particular organizational phenomenon) without too much concern for what theory is and how it is best generated—as *practitioners* engaged in the generation of theoretical knowledge, we normally take such things for granted. The moment, however, we step back to enquire about theory— the moment, that is, we stop being practitioners and become, instead, *observers* of our theoretical practice (our research)—we are faced with questions which cannot be conclusively answered. Meta-theoretical questions have an air of undecidability about them, and this explains the inconclusive arguments concerning paradigm incommensurability among organizational theorists.

The reason for this inconclusiveness—the reason, in other words, for not being able to arrive at a rational consensus concerning the validity claims of knowledge produced within different paradigms—is not only the intrinsically high degree of difficulty in answering such questions anyway, stemming in large measure from the ambiguity of, and the controversy surrounding, key concepts, but, principally, the abstract and decontextualized manner in which such questions are raised. If, for example, we ask *in abstracto*, 'Is organizational structure best explained by contingency or political models?' (see respectively

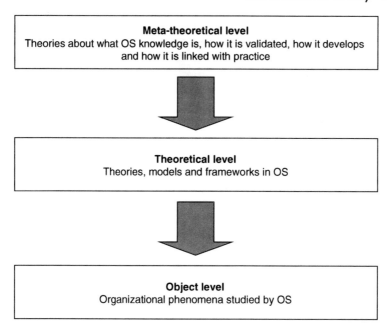

Fig. 14.1: What meta-theoretical reflection is about.

Donaldson 1996; Pfeffer 1981), we will find it very difficult to demonstrate the superiority of one or the other position (McKinley et al., 1999) (which is not to deny that some arguments in defence of one or the other position may be more *persuasive* than others). The reason is that putting the question in purely abstract terms assumes that all we need to do is to engage in a process of abstract reasoning in which we, as observers, scrutinize and compare different paradigmatic assumptions. When such assumptions widely differ, as they normally do, how are we to choose? We would need to step back and seek another set of paradigmatically neutral meta-assumptions that would enable us to adjudicate between the rival sets of assumptions we began with. But this would involve us in infinite regress: since no such set of meta-assumptions exists, we would need to step back further, and so on. This process of abstract reasoning is inconclusive, since there is no ultimate conceptual common ground upon which we may stand to make paradigmatic comparisons (MacIntyre, 1985: ch.2)—hence incommensurability (Burrell 1996; Burrell and Morgan 1979; Jackson and Carter 1991; Scherer and Steinmann 1999: 525; Tsoukas 1994).

As researchers we are both participants in the field *and* observers of our actions. Echoing Kierkegaard, Weick (2002) remarks that the way we live when we are engaged in our research practice is different from the way we live when we subsequently reflect on it. Acting in the world is necessarily somewhat opaque; we increase our awareness of what our acting has involved when we reflect *ex post facto* on the way we habitually act. Reflexivity enables us to detect the biases that creep into our research—biases that constitute likely threats to the validity of our knowledge claims—and, one hopes, try to overcome them next time we engage in research. As Weick (ibid: 895) remarks, 'We are reminded in no uncertain terms of the ways in which our culture, ideology, race, gender, class, language, advocacy, and assumed basis of authority limit, if not destroy, any claim our work has to validity in some interpretive community. These threats to validity are treated as objects that can be labeled, separated, differentiated, and treated as decisive flaws'.

It is the participant–observer duality that creates the paradox mentioned earlier: to carry out our theoretical work effectively we cannot afford to wonder too much about its key categories; but to improve it, to increase the validity of our knowledge claims, we need to reflect on what we do and how we do it. But the more we do so, the more we risk engaging in inconclusive meta-theoretical quandaries—we may end up infinitely regressing in search of some Archimedean original point. Reflexivity can easily turn into self-obsession and narcissism (ibid: 894). Indeed, a sceptic might argue that most of the debate on incommensurability in OT could be seen in that light—an excessive preoccupation with our own practice rather than with the practice of those we study. It is perhaps for this reason that Weick makes a plea for 'disciplined reflexivity' (Weick 1999). Polanyi would certainly agree. 'Unbridled speculation' for him is detrimental to the effective carrying out of science (Polanyi 1962). But how should we view our work in OS so that we do justice to both its tacit component (the taken-for-granted assumptions which our research practice necessarily incorporates) *and* the possibility of meaningfully elucidating our research practice in order to reduce the likely threats to the validity of knowledge claims we make? This question is explored next.

Organization Studies as a Practical Social Activity

Saying that the production of academic knowledge is a social activity is perhaps stating the obvious. The generation of knowledge involves both work and communicative interaction (Habermas 1972; Sayer 1992). By 'work' I mean the transformation of matter and/or symbols for human purposes. For an object of study to reveal itself to the researcher, it needs to be probed, and such probing takes the form of several kinds of interventions (i.e. work), such as experiments, surveys, and/or fieldwork. By 'communicative interaction' I mean the sharing of meaning in a community of enquirers, typically through learning a particular scientific language and a set of procedures for thinking and arguing about the object of study (Sayer 1992: 17–22). Both work and communicative interaction are necessary, and one cannot be reduced to the other, although in real life they are closely interwoven. Researchers act on their object of study by following a set of communication protocols, which they learn as members of a particular academic community.

The production of academic knowledge is a collective effort, embedded in historical time: to carry out his/her enquiry, a researcher draws on the conceptual resources and modes of thinking and arguing of a historically developed language community. Given that in OS the object of study is a *social object*, the relationship between the researcher and his/her object is also a social one (Weber 1993: 63). We do not stand in a social relationship to a tree or a planet, but we do vis-à-vis an organization. The latter is a concept-dependent object; what it is depends on the particular self-interpretations and sets of meanings it incorporates. Unlike non-social objects, which are impervious to the meanings enquirers attach to them, social objects are socially defined—they are constituted by certain distinctions of worth marked in a conceptual space (Taylor 1985*a*, 1985*b*). Since organizations are social objects of study, they constitute language communities. There is a conceptual symmetry between a research community and a social object of study (see Fig. 14.2), in so far as they are both constituted by language (Giddens 1993). As shown in Figure 14.2, developing new knowledge is a *practical* activity in which a researcher, drawing on the conceptual, symbolic, and material resources of his/her

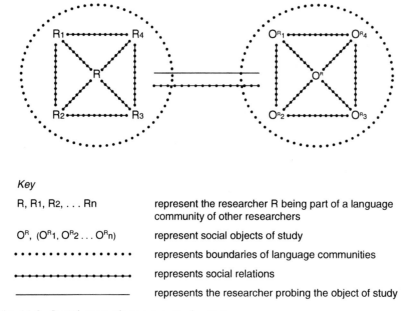

Key

R, R1, R2, . . . Rn	represent the researcher R being part of a language community of other researchers
O^R, (O^R1, O^R2 . . . O^Rn)	represent social objects of study
• • • • • • • • • • • • • • •	represents boundaries of language communities
•—•—•—•—•—•—•—	represents social relations
—————————	represents the researcher probing the object of study

Fig. 14.2: Social research as a practical activity.
Source: Adapted from Sayer (1992: 27)

language community, attempts to account for what is going on in another language community by probing it in particular ways.

Accepting that knowledge production is a practical social activity puts it on the same level with any other practical social activity: for work to be carried out effectively, a set of procedures, principles, and assumptions need to be internalized and unreflectively practised—they need, in other words, to enter the pre-theoretical praxis, the life-world, of a community (Polanyi 1962; Scherer and Steinmann 1999: 527; Tsoukas and Vladimirou 2001; Winogrand and Flores 1987). Since research is a form of work, its practitioners have internalized a host of particulars (assumptions), of which they normally are not aware, while at work. Only when researchers reflexively raise the question of any likely threats to the validity of their knowledge claims will they become aware of, and start scrutinizing, their assumptions, thus engaging in meta-theoretical reflection.

Adopting a Heideggerian perspective for social-scientific enquiry, Weick (2003) has argued that there is always something tacit, opaque, and indeterminate in human action. Actors become aware of the assumptions, the presuppositions, and the point of their actions only *after* they have obtained some distance from their actions, by looking back at them. Greater awareness comes about when we reflect on the way we reflect. This is as true of those we observe (organizational members) as it is of ourselves, the observers (researchers). As professional enquirers, enquiry is our form of action, our *praxis*. When we change level of analysis and detach ourselves from the situation that was the focal object of our enquiry, in order to study the tacit assumptions that informed our enquiry, we normally become aware of our probable biases and of the contingency of our descriptions.

The point here is that over time OS practitioners will improve the validity of their knowledge claims by systematically thinking about the way they habitually think about their objects of study (Antonacopoulou and Tsoukas 2002). What sort of unreflective biases (what phenomenologists and interpretative philosophers call 'prejudgements'; see Gadamer 1989), such as, for example, those concerning 'gender', 'race', and 'class', has OS research manifested over time? What are the historically contingent institutional arrangements and dominant societal and metaphysical understandings that have influenced research in a particular direction? What forms of explanation have dominated the field, and why? How have human agency and social structure—two age-old issues in social theory—been treated in OS? What modes of arguing and what rhetorical forms have been considered appropriate? What notions of 'practicality' and 'usefulness' have been put forward or implied in OS? How have normative principles of ethics been considered in relation to the descriptive-explanatory knowledge produced in OS? And so on.

How Should We Make Sense of the Development of Organization Studies?

Notice that while it is important that the preceding questions are articulated and discussed, since by doing so we become more aware of the taken-for-granted assumptions we have unreflectively followed, the conceptual dilemmas they engender cannot be settled *in abstracto*. To the extent, however, that we have become convinced of the importance of certain issues, hitherto underestimated—for example, of the boundedness of rationality; the conflict-ridden nature of organizations; the cultural context of organizing, etc.—we cannot go on as if we did not know all this. Over time our new awareness enters our pre-theoretical (tacit) stock of knowledge—it joins the internalized assumptions we take for granted. Put in those terms, it is possible to picture OS as a field which has been becoming ever more complex in its assumptions and investigations over time. As March and Olsen (1986: 28) have remarked with reference to organizational decision-making, 'theories of limited rationality relaxed the assumptions about cognitive capacities and knowledge. Theories of conflict relaxed the assumptions about the unity of objectives. Theories of ambiguity and temporal order relaxed the assumptions about the clarity of objectives and causality, as well as the centrality of decisions to the process of decision making'.

The movement from initially rigid and limited assumptions to ever more realistic and complex assumptions has been one of the most encouraging features of the field. While initially organizations were viewed as rationally designed systems, it is now accepted that organizations are historically constituted social collectivities, embedded in their environments (Scott 1987). From this realization, now more or less taken for granted, stem most new investigations, such as those exploring the social embeddedness of organizations (Granovetter 1992; Granovetter and Swedberg 1992; Scott and Christensen 1995; Scott et al., 1994; Whitley 1992); the profoundly cultural aspects of organizations (Frost et al., 1991; Kunda 1992); the social construction of organizational identity (Brown 1997; Whetten and Godfrey 1998); the irreducibly emergent texture of organizing (Stacey et al., 2000; Taylor and Van Every 2000; Weick and Roberts 1993); the importance of history in accounting for aspects of organizations (Dobbin 1995; Kieser 1998; Roe 1994; Zald 1996); the processes through which sense-making in organizations takes place (Weick 2001); the centrality of learning and knowledge to organizational functioning (Cohen and Sproull 1996; Grant 1996; Spender 1996; Tsoukas 1996); the importance of power and the significance of gender in organizational life (Calas and Smircich 1996; Gherardi 1995; Martin 1990); and the influence of unconscious processes and psychic needs on organizational functioning (Gabriel 1999).

What all these admittedly diverse perspectives have in common is the assumption about the profoundly social, historically shaped, and context-cum-time-dependent nature of organizing, which they approach from different angles, focusing on different levels of analysis. In other words, in the early steps of the field, individuals and organizational environments were 'given' to organizations, with the latter being seen, in quasi-algorithmic terms, as 'abstract systems' (Barnard 1968: 74) geared towards the optimization of certain key variables (typically the maximization of performance, the minimization of uncertainty or transaction costs) (Donaldson 2001; Thompson 1967; Williamson 1998). Following the 'Newtonian style' of analysis (Cohen 1994: 76; Toulmin 1990), organization theorists were supposed to uncover the calculus of organization. As Barnard (1976: xlvi) revealingly put it, 'abstract principles of structure may be discerned in organizations of great variety, and ... ultimately it may be possible to state principles of general organization' (see also Thompson 1956/7). In other words, if the contingent, historical, time-dependent, contextual influences on organizations were somehow to be discarded, the essence of organizations, their invariant properties across space and time, would be revealed.

Over time, however, the limits of such an analysis became apparent. If nothing else, the Newtonian style of enquiry hardly illuminated what common experience told practitioners was important: organizations vary widely across time and space; history matters; extra-organizational institutions matter too; gender, race, and ethnicity are hot issues at the workplace; there are multiple rationalities in an organization; sense-making is an important part of action; decision-making and strategy-making do not quite happen as formal theories prescribe. It is precisely the divergence between OS knowledge produced by following the Newtonian style and the common experience of practitioners that accounts, to a large extent, for the perception some practitioners have that OS is 'irrelevant' to their practice (Argyris 1980; Lawler et al., 1999; Mowday 1997; cf. Nowotny et al., 2001; Pfeffer 1993; Weber and Starbuck 1988). Indeed, one of the challenges for OS is to find ways in which practitioners' lived experiences may be incorporated (rather than ignored as 'unscientific') into OS accounts. This is where the 'ecological' style of analysis (to use Toulmin's apt term (1990: 193–4)) comes in.

Gradually individuals and environments have been 'brought into' organizational analysis, and a whole new set of questions has opened up: How do individuals make sense of their tasks, with what consequences? What exactly do people do when they work in organizations? What makes a group of people working together an organization? How do organizational members sustain a sense of community? How do gender and ethnicity influence organizational politics? How are organizational objectives and policies set, by whom, with what consequences? How does the environment, as it changes over time, influence what is going on in organizations? What is the impact of history on key organizational features? Such questions purport to explain organizations in a *substantive* way by embracing the complexity of the issues involved, rather than abstracting them away for the sake of analytical rigour.

Viewing research as a practical social activity makes us see more clearly than before that researchers rarely are idealistic paradigm warriors but, more realistically, while they certainly do have certain paradigmatic predilections, they remain open to borrowing from other paradigms and perspectives as they see fit, and are subjected to normative institutional criteria regarding the evaluation of their work. In other words, in order to get their work done, researchers are, to some extent, *bricoleurs* (Brown and Duguid 1991): they purposefully work with whatever conceptual resources are available. Their work is shaped by their own paradigmatic preferences, the prevailing Zeitgeist, and the institutional frameworks and norms within which their work takes place. In so far as we *work* with others within certain institutional and cultural contexts, our work rarely adheres to idealized paradigms.

Sometimes paradigms are erroneously given an anthropomorphic status, which obscures the obvious fact that it is not paradigms that do the research, but researchers. It is not paradigms that 'cannot speak unto each other', for example, as Burrell (1996: 648) asserts, for paradigms have no voice. It is researchers engaged in practical work, interacting with other researchers, who influence and are influenced by others in what they do, and, to the extent that this happens, there is a certain inevitable osmosis between paradigms. Child, for example, one of the most important contributors to the contingency theory of organizational structure, has revised his views to formulate a strategic-choice perspective, which gives a far more prominent role to managers as agents exercising choice within certain contexts than contingency theory would allow for (Child 1997). Similarly, in his four desiderata for a 'dynamic theory of strategy', Porter (1991) has shown an appreciation for the limits of an industrial-economics approach to the firm, arguing for the need for theories of strategic management to take into account, among other things, endogenous change, creative action, and historical accident and chance. Finally, responding to the ascendancy of interpretative OS in the 1970s and 1980s, in which meaning and human agency are strongly highlighted, positivist accounts have expanded their scope to include aspects of agency and meaning, such as cognition and culture, in their agenda (Tenbrunsel et al., 1996).

This should not be surprising. In so far as interaction and dialogue go on among researchers, new syntheses are likely to come up. We learn more about new research agendas and cross-paradigmatic exchange by looking at what OS practitioners *do*, rather than by hypostasizing paradigms and then getting ourselves caught in conceptual traps regarding paradigmatic 'incommensurability'. Paradigms appear incommensurable only to an observer who, seeking *in abstracto* a neutral set of 'translation rules', cannot find any and proclaims that, well, there aren't any (Burrell 1996: 650). Instead, paradigms do provide challenges for thinking and learning to anyone engaged in research *in concreto*.

For example, reflecting on his own work, Deetz (1996: 200) remarks as follows:

I often draw on conceptions from critical and dialogic writings. For me, critical theory conceptions of ideology and distorted communication provide useful *sensitizing* concepts and an analytic framework for looking for micro-practices of control, discursive closure, conflict suppression, and skewed representation in organizational sites. But rarely are these conceptions closely tied to the full critical theory agenda. They require considerable *reworking* in specific sites, and the results of my studies aim more at finding and giving suppressed positions a means of expression than realizing an ideal speech situation or reaching a purer consensus. What is important is not whether I am a late-modern critical theorist or a dialogic post-modernist, but rather the meaning and implications of concepts that I draw from these two competitive orientations. My degree of consistency is of less interest than how I handle the tension and whether the two conceptual resources provide an interesting analysis or intervention. (references omitted; emphasis added)

In this passage Deetz draws attention to the fact that a researcher may have multiple paradigmatic sympathies, and, at any rate, subscribing to a paradigm means that one is more likely to be inspired and sensitized by it than to be buying wholesale into it. It is surprising how often it is forgotten that paradigms are our own constructions—artefacts we have invented *ex post facto* to make sense of competing sets of assumptions social scientists habitually make—and, as such, they are somewhat idealized descriptions. When we engage in research we do not necessarily buy into an entire paradigm; more realistically, we are oriented by it to explore particular kinds of questions. Moreover, the effective carrying out of research into particular topics of interest entails the 'reworking' of key paradigmatic assumptions *in concreto* ('in specific sites') and this reworking may well bring about new concepts and syntheses (Moldoveanu and Baum 2002).

Like any other kind of work, empirical research is not a matter of mere 'application' of a given set of paradigmatic assumptions, but of active determination of those assumptions *in practice* (cf. Boden 1994: 19). Researchers do not so much 'apply' or 'follow' paradigms in their work as they explore particular topics, in particular sites, and, having to cope coherently with all the puzzles and tensions stemming from the complexity of the phenomena they investigate, they extend, synthesize, and/or invent concepts (cf. Rorty 1991: 93–110). Paradigmatic exchange occurs before our nose but we do not recognize it as such until well *after* such exchange has led to new concepts and conceptual syntheses. Certain insights from Silverman's interpretative critique of positivist OS (1971) and Weick's phenomenological model of organizing (1979) have been 'translated' into other research traditions and have led to interesting developments in, for example, the institutional school of OS and the cognitive perspective on organizations. Conceptual translation 'on the ground' inevitably takes place, all the time, and this is what makes intellectual developments so potentially interesting.

What is OS Knowledge For?

Figure 14.2 (p. 325) shows the double relationship that exists between a researcher and an object of study. The researcher probes the object (the solid line in Fig. 14.2) and, at the same time, he/she is involved in a social relationship with it (the dotted-cum-solid line). What Figure 14.2 does not show is that these two relationships occur in *time*. Probing an object of study means using systems of representation, such as vocabularies and conceptual frameworks, and certain research techniques and modes of thinking, such as ideal-type models, *ceteris paribus* clauses, surveys, experiments, and fieldwork, whereby the salient features of an object of study may be revealed and explained (Searle 1995: 151).

Acts of probing are acts of construction: they *bring forth* aspects of the object under investigation. There are several vocabularies, conceptual frameworks, and modes of thinking to be used, and which ones are chosen is bound, to some extent, to depend on contingent institutional arrangements, the material and symbolic resources available, and the historical and cultural context. While an object of study is often independent of the researcher and his/her vocabulary, the moment it is framed in a particular language it acquires a *contingent* existence—systems of representation contain particular distinctions of worth enacted in specific spatio-temporal junctures, and approach the study object from only certain angles. In that sense, theories in OT, and in the social sciences in general, are *generative* of meaning (Gergen 1994: ch.3): they provide practitioners with certain symbolic resources for making sense of their objects of study.

Moreover, systems of representation incorporate certain assumptions concerning how they are related to their objects and to the users of the knowledge produced, and locate their object within a wider social and political vision (Heilbroner and Milberg 1995). For example, a positivist epistemology assumes that the language of the researcher represents, more clearly than lay language, what is really going on in an object of study (cf. Deetz 1996: 196; McKelvey 1997). Moreover, the knowledge produced by a positivist epistemology is thought to be external to its users, by whom it is used instrumentally in order to optimize a particular performance variable, and is devoid of any intrinsic ethical commitments (cf. Tsoukas and Cummings 1997). To be precise, ethics enters the scene in the way knowledge is *used* rather than in the manner and the form it is produced. A positivist epistemology aims at enhancing the effectiveness of formal organizations in the context of a rationalized society (Burrell 1996; Marsden and Townley 1996; Reed 1996). It is that distinctly modern socio-political vision that animates positivist work in OS. Moreover, each paradigm in OS has its own particular assumptions about these matters.

The social relationship between the OS research community and its object of study implies that knowledge produced is fed back to its users, altering their beliefs and understandings. This is very important for two reasons. First, because it shows that practitioners may change their behaviour in a non-instrumental manner: simply by changing the vocabulary in terms of which they think of themselves and of what they do, they may alter their practice. Think, for example, how the notions of 'total quality management', 'Business-process re-engineering', 'organizational competences', 'strategic learning', and 'chaos', as well as the rhetoric of 'business excellence' have influenced how practitioners view organizations and their role in them (Abrahamson and Fairchild 1999). In this sense academic knowledge is profoundly political and rhetorical (Astley 1985; Astley and Zammuto 1992; Czarniawska 1999). As Van Maanen (1995: 135) remarks, 'the discourse we produce as organization theory has an action component which seeks to induce belief among our readers. Our writing is then something of a performance with a persuasive aim. In this sense, when our theories are well received they do practical work. Rather than mirror reality, our theories help generate reality for readers'.

Second, the intrinsic relationship between theory and action implies that any regularities organization theorists uncover are bound to be perishable, since as soon as they are announced to practitioners the latter will probably modify their beliefs and expectations, thus altering those very regularities (Bhaskar 1978; Tsoukas 1992). As Numagami (1998: 10) has shown in his game-theoretical models of OS knowledge dissemination, provided we accept that practitioners are reflective agents, the search for invariant laws in OS is futile in most cases. (The only exception is when a game with a dominant strategy can be established.) This is far from denying the presence of observable regularities, but merely to point out that such regularities do not rest upon invariant social laws, but upon the stability of the beliefs and expectations of the actors involved.

Numagami (ibid.) has put it convincingly as follows:

What we must not forget, however, is that stable macro patterns in social phenomena are stable not because they are supported by inhuman forces, but because they are reproduced by human conduct. Most observable stability and universality are not generated by invariant and universal laws, but are supported by the stability of knowledge and beliefs shared steadily and universally [...] If practitioners and researchers are able to predict the future course of events, it may not be because they know any invariant laws but because they have a good understanding of what the agents involved would expect in a specific situation and excellent skills in synthesizing the actions, and/or because they are powerful enough to redefine the original situation into a game structure that has a dominant equilibrium. That is, for a person to predict the future course of events, he or she should at least have either knowledge or power.

If the search for invariant laws in OS is futile, what should OS be aiming at? It should be aiming at generating 'reflective dialogue', says Numagami (ibid. 11–12) (see also Flyvbjerg 2001; Gergen and Thatchenkery 1998; Tsoukas and Knudsen 2002). Espousing a hermeneutical model of knowledge, Numagami points out that OS knowledge should aim at producing explanations (redescriptions) of organizational phenomena, which must include references to actors' meanings and conceptual schemata, because it is only then that we as researchers understand what generates the regularities we have noticed. Moreover, such explanations will be, in principle, useful to practitioners, since they invite them to engage in 'sympathetic emulation' Numagami (1998: 11) of the situation described in the explanandum, thus stimulating their thinking. In other words, a hermeneutical model of knowledge does not pretend to be able to offer practitioners universal generalizations and invariant laws, since such knowledge is logically impossible to attain. It does, however, empower practitioners by enabling them to make links with, and reflect on, others' experiences (i.e. the explananda organizational theorists redescribe), thus leading practitioners to undertake potentially novel forms of action. By re-entering the world of practitioners hermeneutically, OS knowledge can connect with practitioners' concrete experiences, thus inviting them to reflect on their circumstances in novel ways (Tsoukas and Knudsen 2002: 432). Hermeneutically conceived, OS knowledge does not tell practitioners how things universally are, but how they locally become.

Conclusions

I have argued here that a knowledge-based view of OS (and of social science in general) dissolves some of the meta-theoretical difficulties encountered in the field, since it makes us see that we are not merely observers and debaters of the theories we produce but practitioners as well. As practitioners our main task is to produce theory, and in order to do so we must necessarily internalize certain assumptions that we take for granted in our intellectual work. In other words, qua practitioners, we must unreflectively practice our research skills. As observers of our work, however, we want to improve our work, to teach it to new members of our practice, and remove likely threats to the validity of our knowledge claims. We become *reflective practitioners* when we both unreflectively carry out our research tasks to generate new knowledge about organizational phenomena of interest *and* engage in discussions about the validity of our knowledge claims.

Seeing this way, namely seeing organizational research as knowledge-based work, throws new light on paradigm incommensurability. Paradigms are our own convenient idealizations and should be seen as such. It is researchers who explore relevant phenomena of interest and, in so far as they put their paradigmatic assumptions to work, they extend, synthesize, or invent concepts as they try to cope coherently with the tensions arising from intellectual work. Researchers do not do anything qualitatively different from what all other practitioners do: they try to cope with the practical demands of their tasks and, in doing so, they necessarily innovate—they extend, synthesize, modify, and/ or recontextualize ideas—although they come to frame their innovations subsequently. Looking at the development of OS this way one is struck by the osmosis between ideas stemming from different research traditions and the gradual complexification of the field over time.

Moreover, it is not only organizational researchers who are embedded in the life-world of their practice; so are those practitioners whose actions and choices researchers study. The two life-worlds interact. Practitioners draw on the conceptual-cum-symbolic resources provided by researchers to carry out their work, and researchers include in their redescriptions of organizational phenomena practitioners' beliefs and desires. Such a symbolic exchange sustains novelty for both sides. Practitioners may undertake novel forms of action by changing their beliefs and desires through the influence of knowledge generated by organizational researchers, and the latter may innovate intellectually by probing, in multiple ways, into the practices and meaning systems underlying the work of practitioners.

References

Abrahamson, E., and Eisenman, M. (2001), 'Why Management Scholars Must Intervene Strategically in the Management Knowledge Market', *Human Relations*, 54: 67–75.

Abrahamson, E., and Fairchild, G. (1999), 'Management Fashion: Life Cycle, Triggers and Collective Learning Processes', *Administrative Science Quarterly*, 44: 708–40.

Alvesson, M., and Deetz, S. (1996), 'Critical Theory and Postmodern Approaches to Organization Studies', in S. R. Clegg, C. Hardy, and W. R. Nord (eds.), *Handbook of Organization Studies* (London: Sage), 191–217.

Alvesson, M., and Willmott, H. (1992) (eds.), *Critical Management Studies* (London: Sage).

Antonacopoulou, E., and Tsoukas, H. (2002), 'Time and Reflexivity in Organization Studies: An Introduction', *Organization Studies*, 23/6: 857–62.

Argyris, C. (1980), *Inner Contradictions of Rigorous Research* (San Diego, Calif.: Academic).

Astley, W. G. (1985), 'Administrative Science as Socially Constructed Truth', *Administrative Science Quarterly*, 30: 497–513.

—— and Van de Ven, A. H. (1983), 'Central Perspectives and Debates in Organization Theory', *Administrative Science Quarterly*, 28: 245–73.

—— and Zammuto, R. F. (1992), 'Organization Science, Managers, and Language Games', *Organization Science* 3: 443–60.

Barnard, C. (1968), *The Functions of the Executive* (Cambridge, Mass.: Harvard University Press).

—— (1976), Foreword to H. Simon, *Administrative Behavior* (New York: Free Press), pp. xlvii–xlvi.

Bhaskar, R. (1978), *A Realist Theory of Science* (Herts.: Harvester Wheatsheaf).

Boden. D. (1994), *The Business of Talk* (Cambridge: Polity).

Brown, A. (1997), 'Narcissism, Identity and Legitimacy', *Academy of Management Review*, 22: 643–86.

Brown, J. S., and Duguid, P. (1991), 'Organizational Learning and Communities of Practice: Toward a Unifying View of Working, Learning and Innovation', *Organization Science*, 2: 40–57.

Burrell, G. (1996), 'Normal Science, Paradigms, Metaphors, Discourse and Genealogies of Analysis', in S. R. Clegg, C. Hardy, and W. R. Nord (eds.), *Handbook of Organization Studies* (London: Sage), 642–58.

—— (1997), *Pandemonium* (London: Sage).

—— and Morgan, G. (1979), *Sociological Paradigms and Organizational Analysis* (London: Heinemann).

Calas, M., and Smircich, L. (1996), 'From "the Woman's" Point of View: Feminist Approaches to Organization Studies', in S. R. Clegg, C. Hardy, and W. R. Nord (eds.), *Handbook of Organization Studies* (London: Sage), 218–57.

Child, J. (1997), 'From the Aston Programme to Strategic Choice: A Journey from Concepts To theory', in T. Clark (ed.), *Advancement in Organizational Behaviour* (Aldershot: Ashgate).

Cohen, I. B. (1994), 'Newton and the Social Sciences, with Special Reference to Economics, or the Case of the Missing Paradigm', in P. Mirowski (ed.), *Natural Images in Economic Thought* (Cambridge: Cambridge University Press), 55–90.

Cohen, M. D., and Sproull, L. S. (1996) (eds.), *Organizational Learning* (Thousand Oaks, Calif.: Sage).

Czarniawska, B. (1998), 'Who is Afraid of Incommensurability?', *Organization*, 5: 273–5.

—— (1999), *Writing Management* (Oxford: Oxford University Press).

Deetz, S. (1996), 'Describing Differences in Approaches to Organization Science: Rethinking Burrell and Morgan and their Legacy', *Organization Science*, 7: 190–207.

Dobbin, F. (1995), 'The Origins of Economic Principles: Railway Entrepreneurs and Public Policy in Nineteenth-century America', in W. R. Scott, and S. Christensen (1995) (eds.), *The Institutional Construction of Organizations* (Thousand Oaks, Calif.: Sage), 277–301.

Donaldson, L. (1996), *For Positivist Organization Theory* (London: Sage).

—— (1998), 'The Myth of Paradigm Incommensurability in Management Studies: Comments by an Integrationist', *Organization*, 5: 267–72.

—— (2001), *The Contingency Theory of Organizations* (Thousand Oaks, Calif.: Sage).

Flyvbjerg, B. (2001), *Making Social Science Matter* (Cambridge: Cambridge University Press).

Frost, P. J., Moore, L. F., Louis, M. R., Lundberg, C. C., and Martin, J. (1991), *Reframing Organizational Culture* (Newbury Park, Calif.: Sage).

Gabriel, Y. (1999), *Organizations in Depth* (London: Sage).

Gadamer, H. G. (1989), *Truth and Method*, 2nd edn. (London: Sheed & Ward).

Gergen, K. (1994), *Toward Transformation in Social Knowledge*, 2nd edn. (London: Sage).

—— and Thatchenkery, T. J. (1998), 'Organizational Science in a Postmodern Context', in R. Chia (ed.), *In the Realm of Organization* (London: Routledge), 15–42.

Gherardi, S. (1995), *Gender, Symbolism and Organizational Culture* (London: Sage).

Giddens, A. (1993), *New Rules of Sociological Method*, 2nd edn. (Oxford: Polity).

Granovetter, M. (1992), 'Problems of Explanation in Economic Sociology', in N. Nohria and R. G. Eccles (eds.), *Networks and Organizations* (Boston, Mass.: Harvard Business School Press), 25–56.

—— and Swedberg, R. (1992), *The Sociology of Economic Life* (Boulder, Colo.: Westview).

Grant, R. M. (1996), 'Toward a Knowledge-based Theory of the Firm', *Strategic Management Journal*, 17 (special winter issue): 109–22.

Guillen, M. F. (1994), *Models of Management* (Chicago, Ill.: University of Chicago Press).

Habermas, J. (1972), *Knowledge and Human Interests* (London: Heinemann).

Heilbroner, R., and Milberg, W. (1995), *The Crisis of Vision in Modern Economic Thought* (Cambridge: Cambridge University Press).

Jackson, N., and Carter, P. (1991), 'In Defense of Paradigm Incommensurability', *Organization Studies*, 12: 109–27.

Kaghan, W., and Philips, N. (1998), 'Building the Tower of Babel: Communities of Practice and Paradigmatic Pluralism in Organization Studies', *Organization*, 5: 191–215.

Kieser, A. (1998), 'From Freemasons to Industrious Patriots: Organizing and Disciplining in Eighteenth-century Germany', *Organization Studies*, 19: 47–71.

Knorr, K. (1981), *The Manufacture of Knowledge* (Oxford: Pergamon).

Kuhn, T. (1962), *The Structure of Scientific Revolutions* (Chicago, Ill.: University of Chicago Press).

Kunda, G. (1992), *Engineering Culture* (Philadelphia, Pa.: Temple University Press).

Latour, B., and Woolgar, S. (1986), *Laboratory Life* (Princeton, NJ: Princeton University Press).

Lawler, E. E., Mohrman, A. M., Mohrman, S. A., Ledford, G. E., Cummings, T. G., et al. (1999), *Doing Research that is Useful for Theory and Practice*, 2nd edn. (Lanham, Md.: Lexington).

McCloskey, D. N. (1985), *The Rhetoric of Economics* (Madison, Wisc.: University of Wisconsin Press).

MacIntyre, A. (1985), *After Virtue*, 2nd edn. (London: Duckworth).

McKelvey, B. (1997), 'Quasi-natural Organizational Science', *Organization Science*, 8: 352–80.

McKinley, W., and Mone, M. A. (1998), 'The Re-construction of Organization Studies: Wrestling with Incommensurability', *Organization*, 5: 169–89.

—— and Moon, G. (1999), 'Determinants and Development of Schools in Organization Theory', *Academy of Management Review*, 24: 634–48.

March, J. G. (1988), *Decisions and Organizations* (Oxford: Blackwell).

—— and Olsen, J. (1986), 'Garbage Can Models of Decision Making in Organizations', in J. March and R. Weissinger-Baylon (eds.), *Ambiguity and Command* (Marshfield, Mass.: Pitman).

Marsden, R., and Townley, B. (1996), 'The Owl of Minerva: Reflections on Theory in Practice', in S. R. Clegg, C. Hardy, and W. R. Nord (eds.), *Handbook of Organization Studies* (London: Sage), 659–75.

Martin, J. (1990), 'Deconstructing Organizational Taboos: The Suppression of Gender Conflict in Organizations', *Organization Science*, 1: 339–59.

Miner, J. B. (1984), 'The Validity and Usefulness of Theories in an Emerging Organizational Science', *Academy of Management Review*, 9: 296–306.

Mintzberg, H. (1979), 'An Emerging Strategy of "Direct" Research', *Administrative Science Quarterly*, 24: 582–89.

Mirowski, P. (1989), *More Heat Than Light* (Cambridge: Cambridge University Press).

Moldoveanu, M. C., and Baum, J. A. C. (2002), 'Contemporary Debates in Organizational Epistemology', in J. A. C. Baum (ed.), *The Blackwell Companion to Organizations* (Oxford: Blackwell).

Morgan, G. (1983) (ed.), *Beyond Method* (Beverly Hills, Calif.: Sage).

—— and Smircich, L. (1980), 'The Case for Qualitative Research', *Academy of Management Review*, 5: 491–500.

Mowday, R. T. (1997), 'Presidential Address: Reaffirming our Scholarly Values', *Academy of Management Review*, 22: 335–45.

Nkomo, S. (1992), 'The Emperor Has No Clothes: Rewriting "Race in Organizations" ', *Academy of Management Review*, 17: 487–513.

Nowotny, H., Scott, P., and Gibbons, M. (2001), *Re-Thinking Science* (Cambridge: Polity).

Numagami, T. (1998), 'The Infeasibility of Invariant Laws in Management Studies: A Reflective Dialogue in Defense of Case Studies', *Organization Science*, 9: 1–15.

Pettigrew, A. (2001), 'Management Research After Modernism', *British Journal of Management*, 12(special issue): S61–S70.

Pfeffer, J. (1981), *Power in Organizations* (Marshfield, Mass.: Pitman).

—— (1982), *Organizations and Organization Theory* (Boston, Mass.: Pitman).

—— (1993), 'Barriers to the Advance of Organizational Science: Paradigm Development as a Dependent Variable', *Academy of Management Review*, 18: 599–620.

Pickering, A. (1992), *Science as Practice and Culture* (Chicago, Ill.: University of Chicago Press).

Polanyi, M. (1962), *Personal Knowledge* (Chicago, Ill.: University of Chicago Press).

Porter, M. (1991), 'Towards a Dynamic Theory of Strategy', *Strategic Management Journal*, 12: 95–117.

Reed, M. (1996), 'Organizational Theorizing: A Historically Contested Terrain', in S. R. Clegg, C. Hardy, and W. R. Nord (eds.), *Handbook of Organization Studies* (London: Sage), 31–56.

Roe, M. J. (1994), *Strong Managers, Weak Owners* (Princeton, NJ: Princeton University Press).

Rorty, R. (1989), *Contingency, Irony, and Solidarity* (Cambridge: Cambridge University Press).

—— (1991), *Objectivity, Relativism, and Truth* (Cambridge: Cambridge University Press).

Sayer, A. (1992), *Method in Social Science*, 2nd edn. (London: Routledge).

Scherer, A. G. (1998), 'Pluralism and Incommensurability in Strategic Management and Organization Theory: A Problem in Search of a Solution', *Organization*, 5: 147–68.

Scherer, A. G. and Steinmann, H. (1999), 'Some Remarks on the Problem of Incommensurability in Organization Studies', *Organization Studies*, 20: 519–44.

Scott, W. R. (1987), *Organizations: Rational, Natural, and Open Systems* (Englewood Cliffs, NJ: Prentice Hall).

—— and Christensen, S. (1995) (eds.), *The Institutional Construction of Organizations* (Thousand Oaks, Calif.: Sage).

—— Meyer, J. W. et al. (1994), *Institutional Environments and Organizations* (Thousand Oaks, Calif.: Sage).

Searle, J. R. (1995), *The Construction of Social Reality* (London: Allen Lane).

Sennett, R. (1998), *The Corrosion of Character* (New York: Norton).

Shenhav, Y. (1999), *Manufacturing Rationality* (Oxford: Oxford University Press).

Silverman, D. (1971), *The Theory of Organizations* (London: Heinemann).

Spender, J.-C. (1996), 'Making Knowledge the Basis for a Dynamic Theory of the Firm', *Strategic Management Journal*, 17 (special winter issue): 45–62.

Stacey, R. D., Griffin, D., and Shaw, P. (2000), *Complexity and Management* (London: Routledge).

Starkey, K., and Madan, P. (2001), 'Bridging the Relevance Gap: Aligning Stakeholders in the Future of Management Research', *British Journal of Management*, 12 (special issue): S3–S26.

Taylor, C. (1985*a*), *Human Agency and Language: Philosophical Papers, i* (Cambridge: Cambridge University Press).

—— (1985*b*), *Philosophy and the Human Sciences: Philosophical Papers, ii* (Cambridge: Cambridge University Press).

Taylor, J. R. and Van Every, E. J. (2000), *The Emergent Organization* (Mahwah, NJ: Lawrence Erlbaum).

Tenbrunsel, A. E., Galvin, T., Neale, M. A., and Bazerman, M. (1996), 'Cognition in Organizations', in S. R. Clegg, C. Hardy, and W. R. Nord (eds.), *Handbook of Organization Studies* (London: Sage), 313–37.

Thompson, J. D. (1956–7), 'On Building an Administrative Science', *Administrative Science Quarterly*, 1: 102–11.

—— (1967), *Organizations in Action* (New York: McGraw-Hill).

Toulmin, S. (1990), *Cosmopolis* (Chicago, Ill.: University of Chicago Press).

Tranfield, D., and Starkey, K. (1998), 'The Nature, Social Organization and Promotion of Management Research: Towards Policy', *British Journal of Management*, 9: 341–53.

Tsoukas, H. (1992), 'The Relativity of Organizing: Its Knowledge Presuppositions and its Pedagogical Implications for Comparative Management', *Journal of Management Education*, 16 (special issue): S147–S162.

—— (1994), 'Refining Common Sense: Types of Knowledge in Management Studies', *Journal of Management Studies*, 31: 761–80.

—— (1996), 'The Firm as a Distributed Knowledge System: A Constructionist Approach', *Strategic Management Journal*, 17 (special winter issue): 11–26.

—— (1998), 'The World and the Word: A critique of Representationalism in Management Research', *International Journal of Public Administration*, 21: 781–817.

—— and Cummings, S. (1997), 'Marginalization and Recovery: The Emergence of Aristotelian Themes in Organization Studies', *Organization Studies*, 18: 655–83.

—— and Knudsen, C. (2002), 'The Conduct of Strategy Research', in A. Pettigrew, H. Thomas, and R. Whittington (eds.), *Handbook of Strategy and Management* (London: Sage), 411–35.

—— and Vladimirou, E. (2001), 'What Is Organizational Knowledge?', *Journal of Management Studies*, 38: 973–94.

Van Maanen, J. (1988), *Tales of the Field* (Chicago, Ill.: University of Chicago Press).

—— (1995), 'Style as Theory', *Organization Science*, 6: 133–43.

Weber, M. (1993), *Basic Concepts in Sociology* (New York: Citadel).

Webster, J., and Starbuck, W. H. (1988), 'Theory Building in Industrial and Organizational Psychology, in C. L. Cooper and I. Robertson (eds.), *International Review of Industrial and Organizational Psychology 1988* (London: Wiley), 93–138.

Weick, K. (1979), *The Social Psychology of Organizing*, 2nd edn. (New York: McGraw-Hill).

—— (1999), 'Theory Construction as Disciplined Reflexivity: Tradeoffs in the 1990s', *Academy of Management Review*, 24: 797–806.

—— (2001), *Making Sense of the Organization* (Oxford: Blackwell).

—— (2002), '*Essai* Real-Time Reflexivity: Prods to Reflection', *Organization Studies*, 23: 893–8.

—— (2003), 'Theory and Practice in the Real World', in H. Tsoukas and C. Kundsen (eds.), *The Oxford Handbook of Organization Theory: Metatheoretical Perspectives* (Oxford: Oxford University Press), 453–75.

—— and Roberts, K. (1993), 'Collective Mind in Organizations: Heedful Interrelating on Flight Decks', *Administrative Science Quarterly*, 38: 357–81.

Whetten, D., and Godfrey, P. (1998) (eds.), *Identity in Organizations* (Thousand Oaks, Calif.: Sage).

Whitley, R. (1984), 'The Scientific Status of Management Research as a Practically Oriented Social Science', *Journal of Management Studies*, 21: 369–90.

—— (1992), *Business Systems in East Asia* (London: Sage).

—— (2000), *The Intellectual and Social Organization of the Sciences*, 2nd edn. (Oxford: Oxford University Press).

Wicks, A. C., and Freeman, R. E. (1998), 'Organization Studies and the New Pragmatism: Positivism, Anti-positivism, and the Search for Ethics', *Organization Science*, 9: 123–40.

Williamson, O. (1998), 'Transaction Cost Economics and Organization Theory', in G. Dossi, D. J. Teece, and J. Chytry (eds.), *Technology, Organization, and Competitiveness* (Oxford: Oxford University Press), 17–66.

Willmott, H. (1993), 'Breaking the Paradigm Mentality', *Organization Studies*, 14: 681–719.

Winograd, T., and Flores, F. (1987), *Understanding Computers and Cognition* (Reading, Mass.: Addison-Wesley).

Zald, M. N. (1996), 'More Fragmentation? Unfinished Business in Linking the Social Sciences and the Humanities', *Administrative Science Quarterly*, 41: 251–61.

Zammuto, R. F., and Connolly, T. (1984), 'Coping with Disciplinary Fragmentation', *Organizational Behavior Teaching Review*, 9: 30–7.

FIFTEEN

The Conduct of Strategy Research: Meta-theoretical Issues

Haridimos Tsoukas and Christian Knudsen

Parameter: [...] The question is, what is management science? Most of it these days sells itself as corporate strategy. I'm not well up on this, but it seems to be mostly platitudes. Invest in R&D, but not too much. Be ruthlessly efficient, but be nice to your workers. Manage decisively, but empower your subordinates. Be big but not too big. On the other hand, don't be too small. Listen to your customers. Concentrate on quality. Concentrate on value for money. On market share. On shareholder value.

Platitudes plus lists [...] Let's not forget the highest form of this literature of lists and platitudes—lists of platitudes. The Four Principles, the Seven Dilemmas, the 102 Dalmatians. What was it in your last one, the Nine Fallacies? That plus a snappy title and you're in for the money

> (Howard Parameter, Lucky Goldstar Fellow in Economics,
> in conversation with Susan Emolument, formerly Professor of
> Corporate Taxonomy, currently a business consultant,
> (*The Economist*, 21 December 1991, 107–9))

Introduction

MORE than in any other field in management studies, the study of corporate strategy is the study of reason in action. What course of action a firm

An earlier version of this chapter was first published in A. Pettigrew, H. Thomas and R. Whittington (eds), *Handbook of Strategy and Management* (London: Sage, 2002), 411–35. Reprinted by permission of Sage, Copyright (2002).

chooses to follow over time, with what effects; how such choices are made and put into action; and how continuity and novelty are interwoven in corporate behaviour are some of the most important questions studied in strategic management (SM). As Mintzberg et al. (1998: 299) have aptly remarked, what distinguishes SM from other fields in management is 'its very focus on *strategic choice*: how to find it and where to find it, or else how to create it when it can't be found, and then how to exploit it' (emphasis added).

Focusing on strategic choice raises all sorts of interesting questions: What is choice and how is it best explained? To what extent can it be said that human choices are an expression of free will rather than a deterministic reflection of circumstances? How is thinking related to action? How are choices made at one point in time related to choices made at earlier points in time, and to what extent do they foreclose choices to be made at later points in time? Are there certain strategic choices that are systematically connected to creating competitive advantage? Do such choices already exist waiting to be discovered, or are they uniquely created? How are both corporate coherence and corporate renewal achieved over time?

Grappling with these questions, SM has been predominantly preoccupied with studying choice in different types of situations and finding optimal solutions that may be prescribed for these situations. In fact, much of the literature in SM that has its origin in economics (such as the 'positioning school' and 'modern game theory') starts from such a clear rational-choice foundation. However, much of this literature seems to be limited to decision-making situations that are relatively stable and repetitive, involving no surprises and few uncertainties (no changes). The development of the rational-choice approach in economics has shown that there are strict limitations as to how complex a problem may be if it is to have an optimal solution (March 1994; Simon 1983).

More recently, several SM scholars have been arguing for a better theoretical understanding of the change processes that are fundamentally transforming firms and industries in the contemporary global economy. However, attempting to conceptualize change processes, some researchers have tended to build models that reduce the element of human agency to a minimum, relying on selection forces rather than on human intentionality to design viable organizations and strategies. Within this stream of research, the process rather than the content of strategy is emphasized, and 'emergent' rather than 'planned' strategies are highlighted (Nelson and Winter 1982).

The field of SM seems to be confronted with a dilemma: strategy thinkers have either drawn on theories that account for strategic choices but no changes, or they have drawn on theories that account for changes but no strategic choices. However, the crucial question is: How can strategy thinkers model change processes involving genuine uncertainties and non-repetitive situations *and*, at the same time, model individuals and organizations as being able to make strategic choices? As in other fields, the existence of such a dilemma may motivate a thorough investigation of the philosophical foundations of SM. It is often by making more explicit the ontological, epistemological, and praxeological presuppositions of existing perspectives that we identify the reasons for the existence of a dilemma. Identifying the limiting constraints and presuppositions may also give us some idea of how to build a framework that would allow us simultaneously to model 'strategic choices' and 'change processes'; that is, a theory of how individuals and/or organizations make 'strategic choices' by gradually building their 'opportunity sets' in fast-changing and partly unpredictable 'environments'.

Motivated by presumably similar concerns, Porter (1991) argued that SM has been in need of a 'dynamic theory of strategy'. Coming from an orthodox industrial-economics perspective that has traditionally put its emphasis almost exclusively on 'choice' rather than 'change', Porter interestingly formulated the following four desiderata which a 'dynamic theory of strategy' would need to fulfil. First, such a theory should simultaneously deal with the firm and its environment. Second, it should allow for endogenous change. Third, it should make room for creative action. And fourth, such a theory should acknowledge the roles of historical accident and chance.

Porter's first desideratum refers to the tendency in strategy research to focus exclusively either on the *firm* (as in the resource-based approach) or on its *environment* (as in the positioning approach). Porter's first contribution to strategy (1980) took its point of departure from the structure-conduct-performance (SCP) paradigm, with its black-box view of the firm. As a consequence, his theory presupposes that competitive advantages may be explained by the firm's ability to exploit the opportunities and threats in its industry, rather than by the building of its strengths and the minimization of its weaknesses (as in the resource-based view). One suggestion for overcoming the one-sidedness of each theory would be to synthesize the positioning school and the resource-based school. However, such a solution neglects the that fact one theory takes a rather static and short-term view of industries while the other assumes a much more long-term and dynamic view.

Porter's second desideratum is that a 'dynamic theory of strategy' should allow for *endogenous change*. Most economic approaches to SM build on the neoclassical paradigm that assumes that preferences and technology are exogenous variables. In this paradigm, changes would be explained by assuming certain shifts in these exogenous variables. However, since the process of obtaining competitive advantage has often been associated with processes of endogenous changes in the technology and knowledge structure of the firm, relying only on exogenous changes would be highly unsatisfactory from the point of view of a dynamic theory of strategy.

The third desideratum is that a dynamic theory of strategy should make room for *creative action*. This desideratum derives from the fact that several of the major approaches to SM have viewed human behaviour and strategies as 'situationally determined' or 'externally enforced', rather than intentionally chosen or constructed. As we will argue later in this article, desiderata (2) and (3) are interrelated. If the 'strategizing subject' is viewed as an evolving and creative actor that co-constructs, through a historical process, his or her own 'set of opportunities', we have not only fulfilled the third but also the second desideratum (by having modelled an endogenous process of an expanding set of opportunities). Desiderata (2) and (3) imply, therefore, a view of the 'strategizing subject' as an evolving historical entity.

Finally, according to Porter's fourth desideratum, a 'dynamic theory of strategy' must acknowledge the *historicity* of strategy development. An important implication of this desideratum is that strategy researchers should abandon the classic view of scientific method and explanation founded on the covering law (or deductive-nomological) model. As will be argued later in this chapter, a 'dynamic theory of strategy' is unlikely to be developed if SM researchers persist in merely recording 'social regularities' or discovering allegedly 'invariant laws' by which firms' strategic behaviour may be explained and predicted. Rather, a dynamic theory of strategy should aim to outline the processes or generative mechanisms that produce specific empirical events (Hedstrom and Swedberg 1998). A 'process approach' should replace the standard 'variance approach' (Mohr 1982: ch. 2).

Despite the enormous significance of the preceding issues for SM, one is surprised by the paucity of systematic reflection on them. True, there have been notable attempts to explicate some of the philosophical issues involved (see Calori 1998; Scherer and Dowling 1995; Singer 1994), and focusing especially on questions of epistemology and theory development (Camerer 1985; Mahoney 1993; Schendel and Hofer 1979; Spender 1993; Thomas and Pruett 1993). However, the bulk of research has been in the tradition of 'normal science' (Kuhn 1970): the meaning of key notions such as 'choice' and 'rational action' has been taken as given (that is to say, unproblematically borrowed from positivist approaches to the social sciences and neoclassical economics) with the view of generating knowledge of relevant empirical regularities (Ansoff 1987, 1991). As sociologists of science would probably tell us, this may have been a necessary feature of the process of maturation of a relatively young field (as SM undoubtedly is—see Rumelt et al., 1994), whereby the meaning of fundamental concepts is established, albeit provisionally, to enable the accumulation of empirical findings. It was to be expected that a field anxious to legitimate itself would most probably adopt the language and method of 'science' (as SM did) rather than let itself be permeated by a speculative, self-questioning spirit (Cohen 1994; Mirowski 1989; Toulmin 1990). As we will see later, and as some SM researchers have already pointed out (Mintzberg et al., 1998: 37–8), the type of knowledge claims made in SM is crucially shaped by the audiences they are addressed to. If to be seen as relevant and useful meant that one needed to be 'scientific', it was to be expected that the knowledge produced would exhibit certain analogous features. Nothing surprising, at least to those remotely familiar with the history and the sociology of sciences.

Be that as it may, it will be enlightening to critically examine the key assumptions that have characterized the conduct of research in SM. Such meta-theoretical reflection will elucidate the manner in which certain key notions have been used in SM and will contribute to outlining alternative sets of assumptions that may guide research in the future. Our goal is to enable researchers to see more clearly what is implicitly involved in adopting particular theoretical perspectives and, by so doing, to better appreciate what is at stake when different conceptualizations of strategy are suggested (Tsoukas 1994).

This chapter is in two (long) parts. In the first part we undertake an epistemological exploration of the theoretical foundations of strategy research, which mostly lie in economic models. The purpose of that part is to assess the different modes of explanation that have been adopted in strategy research and tease out their implications. This analysis is followed, in the second part, by an outline of a meta-theoretical framework that enables us to see where different perspectives in SM stand with regard to the following two questions: How is thinking related to action? Who sets strategy? Our thesis will be that SM has been dominated by one particular mode of explanation (the covering-law model) and one particular view of how thinking is related to action (representationalism), both of which have their problems. We argue that strategy research will become more relevant, encompassing, and subtle if it moves closer towards a process-oriented view of the firm and opens itself up to a constructivist view of strategy-making.

Economic Models and Strategy Research: Two Conceptions of Explanation

The core argument of this and the following sections is that there seem to be at least two very different sets of ideas concerning what a good explanation is and, therefore, how to build theories within the field of SM. By identifying these differences we think that it is also possible to identify at least two sets of very different ontological and epistemological presuppositions that separate two major research streams in SM.

The dominant tradition in SM argues that the goal of strategic management is to find statistical associations between important variables in order to identify regularities, causal statements, and even laws in firms' behaviour. This tradition builds on what some organization researchers have called the 'variance approach' (Mohr 1982) and philosophers of science refer to as the 'deductive-nomological model' or the 'covering-law model' of explanation (Bohman 1991; Camerer 1985; Rosenberg 1988). According to this model, a social regularity or law takes the form 'If conditions C1, C2, C3 ... Cn then always E'. The conditions used to explain are called the explanans and the phenomenon E to be explained is called the 'explanandum'. A covering-law explanation consists in explaining an instance of E by demonstrating the presence of C1, C2, C3, ... Cn. Furthermore, the covering-law model postulates that explanations have the same logical structure as predictions (the *symmetry thesis*). If we are able to predict an empirical phenomenon, we have simultaneously explained it, and vice versa. And if we are able to identify a regularity, we may make use of it to control or intervene in the social world.

It is this view of what constitutes an explanation or a 'good theory' that researchers subscribing to a 'process approach' (Mohr 1982; Pettigrew 1990, 1992, 1997) or a 'mechanism approach' (Elster 1983; Hedstrom and Swedberg 1998) criticize. Let's assume now that some strategy researchers have observed a systematic relationship between two variables; for instance, between market share and profitability. Such a correlation does not constitute an explanation, because it could be a 'spurious relationship', should it be caused by a third variable. From the perspective of the process/mechanism approach we have not established a social regularity, say between I and O, before a mechanism/ process M describing how O is produced by I has been specified. Giving an explanation is therefore closely associated with the possibility of showing *how* I and O are linked to each other; that is, how the cause I produces the effect O through a mechanism M. By specifying a mechanism and thereby providing the details of a causal story we will reduce the risk of spurious explanations. The problem with the covering-law model is, according to Elster (1983), that it is too coarse-grained. It allows too wide a gap between causes and effects. Such a gap may exist if there is too long a time lag between the cause and the effect, or if we provide a too aggregated description by using a macro-variable instead of a micro-variable. For the process researcher the goal is to close such gaps and to 'open up the black box and show the nuts and bolts, the cogs and wheels of the internal machinery' (ibid. 24–5). While the covering-law approach is very outcome-oriented, the process/mechanism approach focuses on the process that produces an outcome.

Equilibrium Models as 'Outcome' Explanations

Having formulated the main difference between the covering-law model and the process/mechanism approach, we will try now to show how these two basic approaches to explanation pervade the different research traditions within the field of SM.

Historically, the covering-law model has been by far the most influential in SM, since both equilibrium models (used by industrial economics, including the SCP paradigm, the positioning school, and part of modern game theory) and structural-functionalist models (early business-policy models, contingency theory, transaction-cost economics, nexus-of-contract theory) build on it.

Let us start by studying the structure of equilibrium models and the closely related comparative-static method in economics. Drawing on Machlup (1955) we can show how the covering-law model lies at the very foundation of equilibrium models and the comparative-static type of analysis that is so common in economics. For Machlup (ibid.) an economic theory may be viewed as a 'machine' that consists of fixed and variable parts (see right side of Fig. 15.1). Let us take the case of the neoclassical theory of the firm. The fixed part of the theory is the 'assumed type of action' or the profit-maximizing hypothesis. The variable part consists of assumptions about which type of situation a firm is confronted with (type of economy, type of market structure, etc.) and what information the firm has access to when taking decisions.

It is from such a machine model of fixed and variable assumptions that we may derive comparative static theorems that tell us what happens when an exogenous variable is changed; that is, when we have a 'disequilibrium variation'. Assuming that the system studied is a stable equilibrium system, we will then be able to get an 'equilibrium variation' that tells us what happens to an endogenous variable. The predictions/explanations of the 'machine' consist of conditional statements of the type: 'If the exogenous variable Y is increased under the conditions X1, X2, X3 ... Xn, then the endogenous variable Z will decrease.'

This description of the comparative static method can tell us something about what equilibrium theorists presuppose about the reality or the empirical systems they study. By looking more closely at these models we can reveal what ontological assumptions they make about reality. To make these assumptions more explicit, we can ask the following question: Why have economists (and especially equilibrium theorists) not been interested in studying social systems without equilibria, systems with several equilibria, and systems with unstable equilibria?

An answer to this question was given by Samuelson (1947: 5) in his famous book *The Foundation of Economic Analysis*: 'Positions of unstable equilibrium, even if they exist are transient, non persistent states, and hence on the crudest probability calculation would be observed less frequently than stable states. How many times has the reader seen an egg standing upon its ends?' A necessary condition for obtaining empirical knowledge (i.e. identifying empirical regularities) about a social system is that the system demonstrates a relatively high degree of stability or it is relatively invariant. According to Samuelson's *correspondence principle*, a necessary condition for deducing what he somewhat misleadingly calls 'operationally meaningful' (i.e. falsifiable) comparative static theorems about a system is that the system has a stable equilibrium. It is only within such a stable system that a change in an exogenous variable, by introducing a disequilibrium variation, will lead to a new equilibrium position (or an equilibrium variation) which may be compared to the original equilibrium position. The main argument is therefore that it

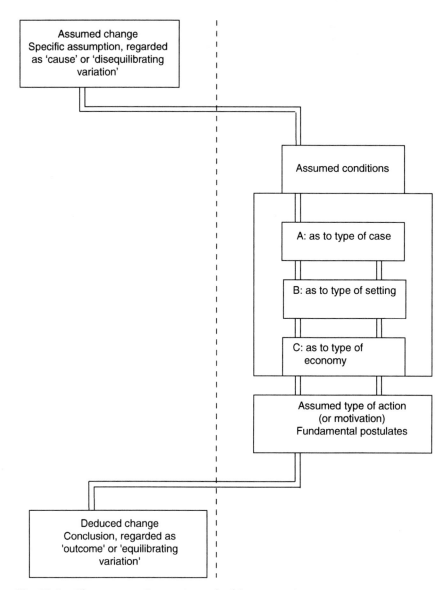

Fig. 15.1: The comparative-static method in economics.
Source: F. Machlup (1955: 13).

will be impossible to obtain any knowledge (i.e. comparative static theorems) about systems that are not stable, i.e. systems that after a disequilibrium variation do not return to a new equilibrium position. As a consequence, economists have restricted themselves to the study of systems with stable equilibria and reproductive processes, thereby avoiding the study of irreversible and cumulative change processes (cf. Boudon 1981).

The underlying world-view that economists have taken as an exemplar for setting up equilibrium models is Newtonian mechanics (cf. Mirowski 1989). If we want to obtain knowledge (empirical regularities or causal statements) about a mechanical system, it needs to fulfil, according to Bhaskar (1978), two criteria of closure. First, it should be possible to isolate the system from its environment so that it is not influenced by external variables. This is the criterion of *external closure* (or *isolationism*) (cf. Lawson 1997). However, even if we are able to isolate the system from external influences, we may still not be able to derive social regularities or laws from it. The reason for this is that most systems have a specific internal structure or complexity, which implies that a system will not necessarily behave in the same way when exposed to the same external conditions. Complete closure of a system will therefore imply, according to Bhaskar (1978) and Lawson (1997), that the system must also meet the criterion of *internal closure* or (*atomism*). According to this criterion, not only the environment but also the internal structure of a system must remain constant over time, in order for us to be able to derive laws or regularities describing a system's behaviour. The condition of internal closure implies a preference for a purely atomistic type of analysis, as well as for a unit of analysis that is not allowed to change endogenously but responds identically to identical environmental changes (Gharajedaghi and Ackoff 1984).

In the standard microeconomic paradigm, we find the criterion of internal closure expressed in the methodological rule of 'de gustibus non est disputandum' (cf. Stigler and Becker 1977). This rule prescribes that the behaviour of consumers and firms should be explained by considering their preferences and production functions as constant, and that changes in behaviour have to be explained by changes in their situational constraints. This rule implies that consumers and firms are viewed as the 'atoms' or the basic units of analysis, whose behavioural dispositions are invariant over time, since the possibility of behavioural changes as a result of endogenous changes in preferences and production functions has been ruled out by definition. For instance, had we assumed that 'learning-by-doing', 'learning-by-using', or other endogenous changes in knowledge had been taking place inside the firm, then the criterion of internal closure would not have been fulfilled and we would have been unable to discover social regularities.

It was exactly this feature of the standard microeconomic theory of the firm that caused Latsis (1976) to describe it as a research programme. In his words: 'Viewing economic actions as highly constrained reactions has provided a research program for the neoclassical theory of the behaviour of the firm. That is, the approach to the explanation of the decisions and actions of sellers in all the diversity of market structures is handled in a unified way, in accordance with certain principles and certain problem solving rules' (ibid. 17). The most important of these rules is, according to Latsis (ibid.), that the behaviour of the firm should be seen as determined by its external situational constraints. As a consequence, Latsis (1972) uses the term *situational determinism* to describe this programme. He argues that the goal of this programme is to reduce the number of alternatives by putting more and more external constraints on the firm, until a 'single-exit' solution emerges as the maximizing outcome.

The fulfilment of the criteria of 'external' and 'internal closure' has several implications for how the firm has been conceptualized within the standard microeconomic research programme, as well as for how this programme has been used within SM. First, since the primary intellectual task of the microeconomic research programme has been to explain the formation of prices within different market structures or industries rather than to account for the behaviour of the single firm, they have used a 'black-box' or at least a 'grey-box' view of the firm. And precisely because microeconomists, including many modern game theorists, see the industry as their primary level of analysis, all explanatory factors are located in the environment of the firm rather than inside the firm and its organization. Strategy theorists who build on this tradition (such as Porter 1980) retain a similar 'black-box' view and identify strategy with the positioning of the firm in an industry. Strategy is therefore mainly concerned with the opportunities and threats of the market, rather than related to the internal strengths and weaknesses of the firm.

Second, in accordance with the criterion of internal closure, the firm is viewed as an unchanging atom that displays identical behaviour in identical situations. In accordance with the research programme of situational determinism, the firm is viewed as an entity that has no history and can only change behaviour through changes in exogenous situational variables, rather than through endogenous change processes. This may be substantiated by looking at how orthodox microeconomists have conceptualized changes in knowledge over time as related to production possibilities. In accordance with the 'production-function' view, firms are conceptualized as having access to a set of different production techniques that can be matched with different relative factor prices in order to produce a certain product in the most efficient way. All these production techniques are assumed to be common knowledge among the firms in an industry; that is, all firms are assumed to have access to exactly the same 'cookbook' of production techniques (cf. Nelson 1991). According to the criterion of internal closure of the model, only exogenous changes in the knowledge of the firm are allowed. In the world of standard microeconomic theory, firms cannot be seen as building competitive advantages through firm-specific knowledge-accumulation processes, since firms are analysed from a cross-sectional rather than a longitudinal perspective.

Third, the criterion of internal closure in microeconomic models does not only imply that firms in an industry are viewed as entities without a history. Firms in the same industry are also viewed as identical, in the sense that they are assumed to face the same demand curve and to have identical cost curves. Often industries are studied from the point of view of a 'representative firm', or firms have been assumed to be homogeneous within an industry. This has been very unfortunate for the field of SM, since it made it impossible for the microeconomic paradigm to answer the fundamental question: Why do firms differ?

Structural Functionalist Models as 'Outcome' Explanations

The structural-functionalist (SF) model that has dominated both organizational sociology and organizational economics has both similarities and differences with the standard-equilibrium SE model. Like equilibrium models, SF models are based on the covering-law model of explanation. Both types of models study social phenomena from an 'outcome' rather than a 'process' perspective. However, SF models differ from SE models by studying a much wider variety of systems. Structural functionalists argue that more enduring social structures, such as institutions, organizational structures, norms, social conventions, etc., are solutions to repeated problems of social interaction (cf. Ullmann-Margalit 1977). In order to understand the specific functions that an institution, organizational structure, norm, or convention may have, we need to reconstruct the social problem of interaction that it solves.

For instance, we explain the right-hand rule in traffic as an efficient solution to an underlying coordination game with at least two players that have two strategies: right-hand driving (R) and left-hand driving (L), and the four outcomes: (R, L) (R, R), (L, R) and (L,L). In this case, structural functionalists start by studying a system with two Nash equilibrium solutions—(R, R) and (L, L)—and analyse the institution as the selection of, or convergence towards, one of these two equivalent Nash equilibria. The underlying assumption in the SF explanations is that the most 'efficient' institution will emerge as the solution to the repeated problem of social interaction, either through a reinforcing learning process or through a selection process.

In SF models the existence of a firm and the structure of its organization are the main phenomena to account for (its explanandum). In transaction-cost economics the existence of the firm has been explained as an institutional solution to a market-failure problem that economizes on transaction costs. In the nexus-of-contracts theory the capitalist firm has been assumed to emerge as a solution to a team-production problem that helps to solve a metering problem. In the case of agency theory, the firm has been assumed to emerge as a solution to the separation between ownership and control by minimizing agency costs. And finally, in the case of contingency theory, a firm's organizational structure has been considered as being adaptive to its environment to make it as efficient as possible. Compared to orthodox equilibrium theorists, structural functionalists take their point of departure in systems without any equilibria, systems with several equilibria, as well as systems with different types of coordination failures, such as market failures, organization failures, etc. The goal of the analysis has been to account for the institutional framework that emerges as a solution to this problem, arguing that it is the most efficient solution by either minimizing or at least economizing on some type of costs (agency costs, transaction costs, adaptation costs, metering costs, etc.).

While equilibrium models have had their foundation in Newtonian mechanics, SF models have taken their point of departure from the Darwinian theory of natural selection. Organizations and firms are studied as if they were organisms in need of fitness for their environment. In fact, many of the early contributions in SM (at that time called business policy) build on an SF model. Among the most important works are Ansoff's *Corporate Strategy* (1965), Chandler's *Strategy and Structure* (1990), and Learned et al.'s *Business Policy* (1965).

While an orthodox equilibrium model tries to explain and predict what happens within a stable system by comparing two states of equilibrium before and after a change in exogenous variables, an SF model tries to explain the existence of the different institutional structures that are taken as given in the orthodox equilibrium model. The comparative static type of analysis that is used in an orthodox equilibrium model to explain *empirical events* within an existing institutional structure is replaced, in the SF model, with a comparative institutional model used for explaining the existence of different *structural arrangements* as a response to different situational circumstances (cf. Simon 1978).

Process Explanations in Strategy Research

Although equlibrium theorists and SF theorists have different explananda, they are both using the covering-law model of explanation. Both camps share the common feature of studying social phenomena from an 'outcome' rather than a 'process' perspective. This implies that social systems are studied when they are in a stationary state and when there is no further tendency for changes in terms of new learning or new knowledge. The regularities studied within such systems are of a 'synchronous' rather than of a 'diachronous' nature. Though most 'outcome'-oriented models only study the end state of social processes, they often have an ad hoc story of how the 'outcome' may have been produced tacked on to a more formal model. In most equilibrium models a so-called 'adjustment' story is tacked on to the formal equilibrium analysis in order to legitimate why it is relevant to study a specific equilibrium outcome and how the equilibrium came about. In a similar way, many structural functionalists try to legitimate the study of an efficient institutional arrangement by arguing that it has been produced by a 'natural-selection' process or through a reinforcement learning process.

However, as Hayek (1948) stated some time ago, most equilibrium models do not provide us with an explanation as to *how* the equilibrium state has been produced in the first place:

The statement that, if people know everything, they are in equilibrium is true simply because that is how we define equilibrium. The assumption of a perfect market in that sense is just another way of saying that equilibrium exists, but does not get us any nearer an explanation of when and how such a state will come about. It is clear that if we want to make the assertion that under certain conditions people will approach the state *we must explain by what process they will acquire the necessary knowledge.* (ibid. 46, emphasis added)

In a similar fashion, SF researchers have studied the efficient outcomes of social processes without demonstrating what process or mechanism may in fact have produced such a state. In most cases structural functionalists just assume that an adjustment process has been operative without demonstrating that empirically.

The choice between an 'outcome perspective' and a 'process perspective' is a choice between two very different ontologies: a closed-world ontology and an open-world ontology. Following the outcome perspective, one sees the world as closed (i.e. as having a finite set of states), which implies that economic agents can never be surprised. Following the process perspective one views the world as open-ended, allowing fundamentally new and unexpected events to happen (cf. Popper 1988; Rorty 1991: 93–7). But what implications do these two different onto-epistemological views have with regard to the way we model firms and, consequently, to the way we understand the concept of strategy? We may address this question by first finding out in what ways the process approach diverges from the outcome approach as exemplified by the standard microeconomic theory or the research programme of situational determinism.

As argued, earlier, it was according to the outcome approach it is possible to obtain knowledge (i.e social regularities) about a social system only if it fulfils the criterion of internal closure. This criterion implies that firms should be conceptualized as entities without a history, identically responding to identical situations. It was in opposition to the criterion of internal closure that the behavioural theory of the firm emerged. According to Simon, both the internal structure of the firm and its historical evolution were important factors in understanding its behaviour:

Responses to environmental events [notes Simon], can no longer be predicted simply by analyzing the 'requirements of the situation', but depend on the specific decision processes that the firm employs [. . .] If in the face of identical environmental conditions, different decision mechanisms can produce different firm behaviors, this sensitivity of outcomes to processes can have important consequences for analysis at the level of the markets and the economy. (1979: 509)

According to this 'multiple-exit' heuristic of the behavioural research programme, one should never assume that goals, technology, and preferences are exogenous, but they must instead be accounted for within an endogenous-process perspective (cf. Latsis 1976).

The most important implication of abandoning the criterion of internal closure is that it enables us to model organizations as *historical* entities. In the behavioural theory of Cyert and March (1963), the firm is characterized as an adaptive institution whose short-term behaviour is determined by its 'standard operating procedures'. The latter are viewed as the memory of the organization, since they contain solutions to standard problems the firm has confronted in the past. The firm's knowledge of how to solve repeated problems is embodied in its behavioural rules. The key for understanding the short-term behaviour of a firm consists in the analysis of its procedural rules. The conception of strategy following from the behavioural theory of Cyert and March (ibid.) has been described as 'logical incrementalism' (Quinn 1980). In the behavioural theory the firm is often viewed as a 'political coalition' between different interest groups that the strategist must constantly try to build a truce between (Lindblom 1968). However, from a classical-strategy perspective, logical incrementalism is thought to lead to a 'purposeless' or even an 'anti-strategic' view of the firm (Andrews 1980).

It was Nelson and Winter's *An Evolutionary Theory of Economic Change* (1982) that extended Cyert and March's short-term behavioural analysis of the firm into a long-term analysis of how firms within an industry adapt to new environments through a process of search for new and more profitable routines. In the evolutionary theory of Nelson and Winter the firm has been conceptualized as a historical entity more consistently than in the short-term analysis of Cyert and March (1963). By viewing the firm as a bundle of routines in which knowledge is stored, the productive knowledge of the firm is seen to be the result of an endogenous and historical learning process. In opposition to the criterion of internal closure in orthodox equilibrium and SF models, evolutionary economists find it necessary to uncover the cumulative process leading to the firm's current ways of doing things.

By viewing the firm as a historical entity that has emerged through a cumulative causal process, the evolutionary theory not only clashes with orthodox equilibrium theories but also with SF models, such as Williamson's transaction-cost economics. As Winter argues:

In the evolutionary view—perhaps in contrast to the transaction cost view—the size of a large firm at a particular time is not to be understood as the solution to some organizational problems. General Motors' [. . .] position at the top [of the Fortune 500] reflects [alternatively] the cumulative effect of a long string of happenings stretching back into the past [. . .] A position atop the league standing is not a great play. It does not exclude the possibility that there were several not-so-great plays. (1988: 178)

Indirectly this is a critique of the assumption of internal closure and of the ahistoric view of the firm adopted by SF models. Transaction-cost theory breaks the firm down into a series of interdependent transactions, arguing that the firm organizes transactions in a way that economizes on transaction costs. Since the firm consists of complex networks of interdependent transactions, it is the totality of the transactions, and not the individual transaction, that is subject to the 'market test' of efficiency. In such a bundle of transactions it is very likely that some will be inefficient. From the perspective of the evolutionary theory of Nelson and Winter, a firm should rather be viewed from a *holistic* perspective, since it is assumed to emerge from a cumulative causal process. According to the 'process approach' favoured by Winter, the selection mechanism will always have to mould already existing structures rather than create them *de novo*. Therefore, changes will consist of incremental adaptations to a complex and interdependent system and the selection mechanism will, according to Winter, 'produce progress, but [...] not [...] an "answer" to any well-specified question or list of questions about how activities should be organized', as in SF models of Williamson's transaction-cost economics (ibid. 177).

The process approach questions the rather simplistic view of causality that is often assumed by the outcome approach. Well-known examples that are relevant to SM can be found both within equilibrium models and within SF models. The best-known example within equilibrium models is the structure-conduct-performance (SCP) paradigm that assumes a one-way causal relationship from the market structure to the performance variable. According to the so-called market-concentration doctrine in the SCP paradigm, the higher the concentration of an industry, the higher the profitability in that industry. However, as argued by Demsetz (1973), the causal relationship between concentration and profitability may be a spurious relationship, since the causal relationship may just as well go the other way; that is, from profitability to market structure. According to Demsetz, it is even more likely that a higher concentration is caused by the fact that more efficient/profitable firms outcompete less efficient/profitable firms, thereby increasing the concentration of the industry.

Similarly, a simplistic view of causality can be seen in the SF model of the strategy-structure-performance (SSP) paradigm. It was Chandler's *Strategy and Structure* (1990) that first established this paradigm. According to contingency theorists such as Donaldson (1995: ch. 2), Chandler's major thesis was that the introduction of the M-form in four major American corporations was the result of a prior diversification strategy and could be reconstructed as 'structure follows strategy'. Corporations such as General Motors, Sears, Dupont, etc. had all introduced the M-form, the argument goes, in order to solve 'control loss' and other 'inefficiency' problems that had been caused by an earlier diversification strategy. Later empirical studies within the SSP paradigm viewed 'strategy' as the independent variable and 'structure' as the dependent variable. However, such an interpretation may be too simplistic.

From a process perspective, the simple one-way causal relationship assumed in the SSP paradigm needs to be replaced with a more complex cumulative causal model that, over time, allows causality to go both ways. Though the emergence of the M-form may be explained by a strategy of diversification, an explanation of the persistence and later diffusion of the M-form may be built on the opposite causal relationship. When first introduced, the main advantage of the M-form over the U-form was the superior ability of the M-form to 'digest' acquisitions. In the M-form, an acquired firm only needs to be assigned the status of profit centre to become part of the new firm. In the U-form the integration of a new firm is much more difficult, since all the new assets need to be integrated with the old assets. However, after the introduction of the M-form, the diversification strategy may be reinforced by the M-form structure. In this case, 'strategy follows structure' rather than the reverse. As Chandler himself remarks in a new introduction to his *Strategy and Structure*:

structure had as much impact on strategy as strategy had on structure. But because the changes in strategy came chronologically before those of structure, and perhaps also because an editor at The MIT Press talked me into changing the title from *Structure and Strategy* to *Strategy and Structure*, the book appears to concentrate on how strategy defines structure rather than on how structure affects strategy. My goal from the start was to study the complex interconnections in a modern industrial enterprise between structure and strategy, and an ever changing external environment. (1990, unpaginated)

In fact, Chandler (1992) has recently opposed the atomistic and ahistorical perspective of firms that characterizes SF models, in favour of a more holistic and historical perspective that is characteristic of process models.

A process approach has been claimed to be at the core of game-theoretical approaches to strategy and it is worth considering here the modelling of strategic rational agents in modern game theory. The shift from the SCP paradigm (Scherer 1970) to game theory (Tirole 1988) has been described as a shift from 'old' industrial organization to 'new' industrial organization (cf. Ghemawat 1997). Compared with the SCP paradigm, the introduction of game theory presents several advantages. First, while the SCP paradigm took the industry structure as an independent and given variable, industry structure has been endogenized in much of modern game theory. Second, compared with the rather static framework of the SCP paradigm, the introduction of extensive games has given game theorists a language for modelling intertemporal or dynamic competitive interactions. Third, compared with the SCP paradigm, game theory has been able not only to accommodate situations with imperfect information but also to handle the much more difficult situations with asymmetric information.

However, like much of the SCP paradigm, game theory has mostly been applied to the study of competitive interactions at the industry level and has, therefore, to a large degree, adopted the black-box view of the firm from orthodox microeconomics and the SCP paradigm (Saloner 1991). This seems to stem more from tradition than from methodological limitations of game theory itself. With the diffusion of extensive games, an increasing number of game theorists have abandoned the view of the firm as an *ahistoric* entity and have either modelled the firm as an entity that builds its reputation over time (cf. Kreps 1990) or as an entity that makes different types of pre-commitments in order to constrain its future behaviour (cf. Besanko et al. 1996: ch. 9; G. Ghemawat 1997; P. Ghemawat 1991). However, it seems to us that even if game theory has made major progress in terms of modelling strategic rational agents in an inter-temporal perspective, there are still some deep-seated methodological and ontological problems to be solved in this research programme.

The solution to intertemporal games is found through *backward induction* (Selten 1975). This method advises us to unravel the game backwards by solving the very last subgame first. After we have solved the last sub-game, we may then move on to the next-to-last sub-game. Since we know the outcome of the last sub-game, it will then be possible to determine what is a rational choice in this sub-game. Continuing in this way we will be able to unravel the whole game, finding a rational strategy for the whole game.

Besides being haunted by a number of logical paradoxes (cf. Bicchieri 1993; Binmore 1990; Knudsen 1993), the backward-induction method in extensive games raises some important ontological questions. By using this method, game theorists seem to have broken down an inter-temporal game in which time plays an important role into a set of separate static games in which time (and therefore process) is no longer an essential variable. Indeed, it seems to be a general principle not only in game theory but more generally within economics, that what constitutes a rational choice is never allowed to depend on what happened earlier. In economics, the status quo has no special advantage over its alternatives. In defining rational behaviour, only future states matter. This implies that we overlook, by definition, the path-dependency of our decisions, since each new decision is assumed to be taken *de novo*. All decisions are therefore fully reversible and there are no historical constraints. McClelland (1993) argues that strategic players in extensive games make use of what he calls a *principle of separability*, which is the foundation of Selten's sub-game perfect equilibrium (1975):

It is separability that drives the form that backward reasoning, or 'folding backward,' takes in the analysis of sequential choice games. Separability implies that in evaluating any coordination plan, what that plan calls upon a given agent to choose, at any given point, must be consistent with what that agent would choose, were she to make a *de novo* choice at that point. This is what licenses proceeding from the evaluation of the last segment of that plan, *taken in isolation from the rest of the plan*, successively backward, to the evaluation of the whole plan. (McClelland 1993: 192–3)

It is by using the principle of separability as a foundation for defining rational behaviour in extensive games that it becomes impossible to model the decision maker as being able to coordinate his/her decisions over time and, therefore, as an adequate behavioural foundation for a truly process approach.

Moreover, game theory treats all firms (players) in an industry as fundamentally uniform. For example, when defining what constitutes rational behaviour, the principle of symmetry is assumed to hold, implying that a player has to ascribe the same form of rationality to his opponent that he/she applies to himself/herself (i.e. maximizing expected utility). However, by applying the principle of symmetry, game theorists ignore information about the *identity* of opponents that real-world actors will typically use to make 'rational' decisions. As Schelling (1960) remarks: 'If a man knocks at the door and says that he will stab himself on the porch unless given 10 dollars, he is more likely to get the 10 dollars if his eyes are bloodshot'. To signal what type of an agent one is (i.e. one's identity) is therefore of great importance to the outcome of the social processes studied by game theorists. This implies that the conception of the firm as an invariant entity in game theory needs to be replaced by a conception of the firm in which firm-specific *history* is important for understanding differences in firms' behaviour within the same industry.

It is this emphasis on the historicity of the firm that has been the hallmark of Penrose's work (1959). While Nelson and Winter (1982) have primarily been interested in developing an evolutionary theory of industries and firms, Penrose (1959) was more focused on building a theory of the individual firm and its growth process. She based her theory on what she described as an 'unfolding perspective' (Penrose 1955), and used the gradual unfolding of an organism as an analogy for studying the growth of the firm. Penrose's focus was especially directed towards understanding how resources, capabilities, and knowledge are gradually created through an irreversible and cumulative causal process. New knowledge is gradually built into the formal and informal structure of the organization, thereby becoming a significant factor for the direction of future knowledge accumulation, where more complex knowledge structures are created on the basis of already existing structures. As opposed to both the research programme of situational determinism (orthodox microeconomics) and Porter's strategy framework, Penrose emphasized the internal over the external limits to growth (cf. Knudsen 1996).

Theories of Action in Strategy Research: A Meta-theoretical Framework

Most researchers agree that the chief purpose of corporate strategy is the creation of sustainable competitive advantage. They also seem to agree that such an advantage is created through a continuous effort on the part of managers to align their organization's strengths with the opportunities and limitations present in their environment. There is near unanimity that whatever else strategy may be thought to be, it certainly is *consistent corporate action over time*. Strategic behaviour, in other words, is a systematic attempt to shape the future in a coherent way (Araujo and Easton 1996).

There are two crucial issues in seeking to understand strategic behaviour. First, how does organizational consistency develop? To a large extent (although not exclusively) this is a question concerning the role of human intentionality in setting up patterns of corporate actions. Put differently, how is thinking related to acting? Second, who is responsible for the development of strategy? Who sets it? As soon as these questions are raised, differences between the several perspectives in SM start to crop up. For example, there are those who believe that, more than anything else, strategy is systematic thinking by a single person (or, at most, a few individuals), using relevant concepts and analytical techniques in order to decide on an appropriate course of action, which will be implemented in the future. At the other end, there are those for whom strategy-making is primarily a social process of continuous experimentation, the outcome of which is the formation of a distinct (as well as unique) pattern of action over time. What is worth noting is that behind a seemingly common understanding of strategy as corporate consistency over time, there are significant differences over the way thought is related to action, generating contrasting interpretations of strategy (Tsoukas 1994). Ultimately, as we hope to show in this chapter, these differences are the result of competing theories of action implicit in the different perspectives.

Strategic management is a very diverse field. It is commonly acknowledged that the diversity of SM is, by and large, the result of, on the one hand, the different disciplines which take corporate strategy as their object of study, ranging from economics to sociology and psychology, and, on the other hand, the multiple audiences addressed by strategy researchers (Gopinath and Hoffman 1995; Shrivastava 1987). To cope with an ever increasing theoretical pluralism, there have been several attempts to bring some taxonomic order to the field by grouping research findings into distinct schools of thought (Bowman 1995; Gilbert et al., 1988; Mintzberg 1990a; Mintzberg et al., 1998; Scherer and Dowling, 1995; Zan, 1990). Such an attempt is inherently fraught with conceptual difficulties, given the contrasting disciplinary allegiances of competing perspectives. However, after nearly forty years of research in SM, we have seen enough to be able to make meaningful comparisons.

The ten schools of thought identified by Mintzberg (Mintzberg, 1990a; Mintzberg et al., 1998) serve as a useful guide to an already large SM literature. Mintzberg's scheme is comprehensive enough to cover most developments in the field, and will be used throughout this chapter as a point of reference. The ten schools of thought are the following: (1) the design school (strategy formation as a process of conception); (2) the planning school (strategy formation as a formal process of analysis); (3) the positioning school (strategy formation as an analytical process of positioning the firm in its industry); (4) the entrepreneurial school (strategy formation as a process of envisioning new possibilities and taking advantage of opportunities); (5) the cognitive school (strategy formation as a mental process); (6) the learning school (strategy formation as a social learning process); (7) the power school (strategy formation as a process of negotiation); (8) the cultural school (strategy formation as a process for building collective uniqueness); (9) the environmental school (strategy formation as a reactive process); and (10) the configuration school (strategy formation as a process of quantum-like transformation) (Mintzberg et al., 1998: 5–6).

There are several ways that these perspectives may be classified. For example, Mintzberg et al. (ibid.) group them in two categories. The first three schools are avowedly *prescriptive*: their proponents do not attempt to describe or explain how strategies form, but rather they seek to prescribe how strategies should be formulated. The reverse is the case with all the other perspectives. Another way of grouping them would be to distinguish between those schools concerned with the *content* of strategy (the positioning school) vis-à-vis those concerned with either prescribing the *process* of strategy formulation (the design school, the planning school, and the entrepreneurial school), or *explaining the process of strategy formation* (the learning school, the power school, and the cultural school).

Despite what the authors of several leading textbooks in SM have argued (Johnson and Scholes 1997; Mintzberg et al., 1998), the environmental and the configuration schools are not really concerned with describing, explaining, or prescribing *strategy*—at least, not if we take human agency to be a necessary feature of strategy—and, therefore, we will not include them in our discussion in the rest of this chapter. There are good reasons for this. To the extent that strategy involves making choices, it cannot be said that the environmental school is in any way concerned with strategy since, on the environmental view, corporate actors do not choose but they are chosen (selected by the environment). One may certainly discern, *ex post facto*, failed strategies or strategies selected by the environment, but this hardly constitutes an argument concerning corporate strategy *per se*. As said earlier, strategy implies coherent action over time, and any theoretical framework which does not engage with (or assume) it cannot properly be said to be about strategy *per se*; it may well be about the evolution of corporate behaviour, but, in order to qualify as an account of strategy, it needs to make provisions for human agency unfolding in time.

Similarly, the configuration school seeks to explain organizational change, drawing on the model of paradigmatic change. Within such a model, particular types of strategy are shown to match particular types of structure and particular types of context. However, how strategies form or should form are not issues with which the configuration school is preoccupied. A particular strategy is simply seen to occupy a place within a particular configuration. Why this should be the case and how it came to be the case are not dealt with. In fact, when it comes to the nitty-gritty of strategy, the proponents of the configuration school offer extremely general advice to practitioners (of the type 'everything matters' (see Mintzberg et al.), 1998: 305–6) to the point where such advice, because it leaves almost nothing out, risks being vacuous. This is not to belittle the contribution of the configuration school, only to point out that it is not a theory of strategy but a theory of corporate change.

Representationalism versus Enactivism in Strategy Research

As mentioned earlier, there are two key questions the answers to which will help us distinguish the different theories of action underlying perspectives on strategy. First, how is thinking related to action? By and large, there have been two answers to this question. First, thinking is a basically representational activity, according to which the mind represents the world 'outside' as well as depicts ends desired 'within' the individual (Rorty 1980, 1991; Taylor 1993). Action is following the rules dictated by such representations. In its strong version, which is the one most often found in SM, the representationalist approach consists, more precisely, of the following principles: (a) The world has certain pre-given features; (b) there is a cognitive system which represents those features; and (c) the cognitive system acts on the basis of those representations (Varela et al., 1991: 135). It is assumed that, ontologically, the world is pre-given and that, epistemologically, its features can be specified prior to any cognitive activity. Moreover, as Varela et al. (ibid. 147) remark, a representationalist approach tacitly assumes that 'the world can be divided into regions of discrete elements and tasks. Cognition consists in problem solving, which must, if it is to be successful, respect the elements, properties, and relations within these pregiven regions'.

According to this view, largely Cartesian in origin, human experience is made up of atoms of subjective sensation. Knowledge of the world is built by assembling those atomic sensations to make up a picture of the world (Reed 1996: 24; Rorty 1991). Cognition consists of two stages: first the gathering of sensations, and then the drawing of inferences (i.e. thinking) on the basis of those sensations. In other words: first we experience, then we think. However, according to Descartes (1968), the two steps are not equally trustworthy. Sensory experience, gathered through the bodily mechanisms, is not dependable. Our senses may deceive us: we may mistake (as we often do) one thing for another, and, therefore, we cannot possibly base our judgements on such shaky foundations. In Descartes's graphic language (ibid. 103), 'there is some deceiver both very powerful and very cunning, who constantly uses all his wiles to deceive me'. For true knowledge of the world to be obtained, sensory experience needs to be purified through the rigorous scrutiny of Reason. Hence, for Descartes, only pure thought can ever be completely reliable. The second step in the process of cognition (that of inference) is more trustworthy than the first (that of sensory experience). The evil demon lurking to deceive the individual can eventually be defeated. 'Let him deceive me as much as he likes', says Descartes (ibid.), 'he can never cause me to be nothing, so long as I think I am something.' In other words, I may mistake that robot for a person, my rival's silence for cowardice, my competitor's new product for a short-lived project, but I cannot deceive myself that I am thinking—hence *cogito, ergo sum* (I think, therefore I am).

Because thinking is more reliable than sensing, we should base our actions on a set of distinct and clear ideas, which we know to be true and, therefore, we trust. This has been the mainstream theory of knowledge in the twentieth century: 'knowledge involves taking one's subjective states and trying to test whether they fit current or upcoming realities' (Reed 1996: 58; see also MacIntyre 1985; Rorty 1991; Taylor 1985). For example, a firm wants to enter a new market. What, on this view, should it do? For a start, it should identify what are the formally known (that is, scientifically validated) ways of entering new markets and establishing competitive advantage, and then connect this generic knowledge with the knowledge of the particular market the firm is interested in (see Ansoff 1991). Actors, on this view, are deductive reasoners: from an abstract set of generically valid premises and from a particular set of current observations, they deduce conclusions which they proceed to implement (Devlin 1997). Another way of putting it is to say that actors are propositional thinkers: they follow explicit rules of the type 'If X, then Y, in conditions Z' (Tsoukas 1998a).

Thus, to sum up, the representational approach is characterized by the following principles. Ontologically, it assumes a pre-given world. Epistemologically, it is based on the belief that only pure thinking can yield reliable knowledge, by allowing a deductive approach. And praxeologically, it adheres to instrumental action: actors follow explicit rules or apply explicit precepts, in order to achieve their goals. Action is driven by reliable prior knowledge.

The second answer to the question of how thinking is related to action, is the *enactive* approach. According to this, knowing is action. In Varela et al.'s words (1991: 149): 'knowledge is the result of an ongoing interpretation that emerges from our capacities of understanding. These capacities are rooted in the structures of our biological embodiment but are lived and experienced within a domain of consensual action and cultural history. They enable us to make sense of our world'. On this view, rather than the mind passively reflecting a pre-given world, the mind actively engages with the world and, by so doing, it helps shape the world. Meaning is enacted (constructed)—it is brought forward from a taken-for-granted background of understanding (Winograd and Flores 1987: 36–7; Taylor 1993: 47; Varela et al., 1991: 49). It is when we lack a common background that misunderstandings arise, in which case we are forced to articulate the background, and explain it to ourselves and to others (Winograd and Flores 1987: 36–7).

The world causes us to form beliefs but does not dictate the content of our beliefs (Rorty 1991). Objects 'out there' are the loci of causal powers providing the stimuli for manifold uses of language. But the moment we ask for *facts* about an object we are asking how it should be described in a particular language, and that language is not—it cannot be—neutral: its vocabulary is necessarily loaded with meaning. Notions, for example, such as 'trust', 'work', or 'authority' do not mirror an independent reality, but are inextricably bound up with having certain *experiences* (concerning trust, work, authority, etc.), which involves seeing that certain *descriptions* apply. Particular languages mark particular qualitative distinctions concerning what *are* trust, work, authority, etc., and how actors ought to respond to them. Therefore the language actors use to describe their goals, beliefs, and desires also defines the meaning these terms have for them (Taylor 1985: 71; Tsoukas 1998*b*).

Moreover, as well as goals, beliefs, and desires being language-dependent, so are social practices and institutions: they incorporate particular background distinctions (distinctions of worth). Without such distinctions a particular practice would not be what it is. What, for example, a firm is (its particular competencies, the way it combines resources) incorporates a particular self-understanding as to what matters and what does not. Knowledge, therefore, is action in the sense that when statements about the world are made, these are not merely denotative but connotative: utterances do not merely describe the world but, by interpreting it, they help create it (Austin 1962; Moch and Huff 1983; Tsoukas 1998*b*; Winograd and Flores 1987). Seeing a particular market as saturated, a competitor as threatening, or a product as fulfilling a particular need, a firm is helping to create those objects and properties it describes by undertaking appropriate action (Soros 1987). Thinking *is* doing.

If social institutions and practices are what they are by virtue of the particular sets of background distinctions they incorporate, from where do those distinctions derive their meaning? As Wittgenstein (1958) insightfully observed, the meaning of our signs and symbols comes from the use we put them to. Social practices and meanings are mutually constituted. Without a particular practice, a set of meanings would be unintelligible. And without a set of meanings, a practice could not exist. Actors learn to follow certain rules by being socialized into the meanings constituting a particular practice. An actor's understanding, therefore, does not reside in his/her head but in the *practices* in which he/she participates. In other words, understanding is implicit in the social activity in which the individual participates.

This Heideggerian and Wittgensteinian insight is perhaps the single most important difference between representationalism and enactivism: the social activity, rather than the cognizing subject, is the ultimate foundation of intelligibility (Heidegger 1962; Wittgenstein 1958). For example, a quarter-master does not need to form explicit representations of his sensing instruments. His ability to act comes from his familiarity with *navigating* a ship, not from his representation of the navigation instruments in his mind (Hutchins 1993). The world for him is, to use Heidegger's expression (1962), 'ready-to-hand'. Activity is much more fundamental than representational knowledge. Doing comes before thinking.

Knowing may be understood as action in an additional sense. As Polanyi (1975) observed, in order to make sense of our experience we necessarily rely on some parts of it subsidiarily in order to attend to our main objective focally. We comprehend something as a whole (focally) by tacitly integrating certain particulars, which are known by the actor subsidiarily. As noted above, Polanyi's classic example (ibid: 36) is the man probing a cavity with his stick. The focus of his attention is at the far end of the stick while attending subsidiarily to the feeling of holding the stick in his hand. This is an important point, for it underscores the personal-cum-constructed character of knowledge—something which Polanyi (1962) was so keen to point out. All knowledge, for Polanyi, involves personal participation (action): the individual *acts* to integrate the particulars of which he/she is subsidiarily aware in order to *know* something focally. Knowing is action.

To sum up thus far, the enactive approach consists of the following three principles. Ontologically, it assumes that actors are beings-in-the-world and, thus, takes social activity as the fundamental building-block of the social world. Epistemologically, it highlights the personal-cum-constructed character of human knowledge. And praxeologically, it conceives of action as experimentation, or, to put it differently, thinking and acting are seen as being perpetually engaged in a dialogue (Schon 1983).

The second question is about who sets strategy. This is an important question since, in focusing our attention on who is involved in the formation of strategy, it enables us to see how different perspectives in SM have conceptualized organizational agency. Three answers can be found in the literature. First, the strategy is set by the strategist(s) who, typically, is the CEO or, at any rate, a few designated individuals in the organization. The important thing to note is that the formation of strategy is a largely *individual* responsibility. Second, the strategy is set by the planning system. By this is meant an administrative system of data collection and analysis which, on a routine basis, is charged with formulating the strategy of the organization. Like an expert system, a planning system is supposed to tap into formal knowledge concerning the organization and its environment in a systematic manner, in order to suggest particular courses of action. It is a machine-like version of human cognition: the planning system stands to the strategist as artificial intelligence stands to natural intelligence (Devlin 1997; Haugeland 1985). It is recognized that the formulation of strategy is a complex task involving

Table 15.1. Theories of action in strategy research: a meta-theoretical framework

		How is thinking related to action?	
		Representationalism	Enactivism
Who	Individual	Design school	Entrepreneurial school
		Game-theoretical approaches	Constructionist approach
Sets		Cognitive school	
	Planning system	Planning school	Scenario-based planning
Strategy?		Positioning school	
	Social process		Cultural school
			Learning school
			Power school

specialist knowledge, which entails the formal setting up of a planning system to cope with such complexity. And third, strategy formation is a fundamentally social process: it occurs in a social context in which there are relations of influence and power as well as social bonds among those involved. In this case, strategy is no longer seen as an individual accomplishment but as a collective endeavour.

Putting these two questions together (How is thinking related to action? Who sets strategy?) we obtain Table 15.1, in which the different perspectives on strategy are laid out.

The design school, game-theoretical approaches, and the cognitive school (which Mintzberg et al. (1998) include in the positioning school) are shown to share the same individualist assumptions with regard to who sets the strategy, and a representationalist approach. Likewise, the planning and positioning schools remain within a representationalist approach, while substituting a formal system for analysing and deciding strategy for the individual strategist(s). Here, whatever else strategy may be, it is above all else a systematic analysis of relevant information. Strategy, therefore, as an outcome of such a process, is seen as the commitment of substantial resources in a particular direction over the long term. Driven by already available information, strategy appears as a rational inference to be drawn from a mass of data, rather than as a creative synthesis; it is a measured continuation of past and present trends, not a bold step into the unknown future.

The entrepreneurial school, by privileging the decisive role of the entrepreneur in shaping strategy, is committed to an avowedly individualist conception of strategy formation while, at the same time, showing a much more experimental orientation to action. The entrepreneur does not so much analyse the environment as playfully interact with it. The world outside the firm is an occasion for creative action not for detached calculation. Scenario-based planning shares the same enactive approach with the entrepreneurial school while at the same time privileging the planning system for constructing scenarios for the future. It combines the open-endedness towards the world that is characteristic of the enactive approach with an emphasis on a systemic understanding of organizational agency—ultimately it is the system for making scenarios that produces strategies.

The constructionist view (which Mintzberg et al., 1998 include in the cognitive school) is possibly the best illustration of the enactivist approach. It is based on individualist assumptions, since it is the individual strategist who interprets his/her environment and acts on the basis of those interpretations. As Smircich and Stubbart (1985: 726) nicely put it: 'The world is essentially an ambiguous field of experience. There are no threats or opportunities out there in the environment, just material and symbolic records of action. But a strategist—determined to find meaning—makes relationships by bringing connections and patterns to action'.

Finally, the cultural, the learning schools, and the power are paradigmatic cases of both strategy-making-as-a-social-process and the enactive approach. Strategy-making is seen taking place within a social context, and this has led researchers to explore the contextual influences on strategy—typically those of power, social, learning, and culture. Here action is accorded a significant place in explaining strategy. Actors are not detached thinkers making their plans within a social vacuum; rather, they are beings-in-the-world, partaking in social activities, having locally situated knowledge, being connected to networks of influence and power, and mobilizing their political and cultural resources in order to get things done.

Strategy research has opened up over time from a representationalist-cum-individualist approach to include an enactive-cum-social-process approach. This has been a reflection of the growing awareness that strategy is a much more complex affair than its formulation by a single decision maker, or the outcome of detached rational planning. Instead, it has been increasingly realized that the formation of strategy is a primarily social process whose outcome should ideally be a novel one; that the future is not out there to be discovered but is rather invented; that strategy is not plucked from the tree of some already available strategies but is painstakingly developed to suit a firm's unique profile and circumstances. Such a widening of the agenda of strategy research, a view of which is very engagingly provided by Mintzberg et al. (1998), has also been reflected in the epistemology used: process explanations have increasingly become as prominent as conventional variance-model explanations (Mohr 1982). Methodologically, case studies and historical analyses have been especially popular in an attempt to capture the contextual dynamics of strategy formation (Malerba et al., 1999; Mintzberg and Waters 1982, 1985; Pettigrew 1985, 1992, 1997).

The Missing Element in Strategy Research:
A Theory of Creative Action

Although strategy formation as an object of study has been complexified, and such complexity has been reflected in the methodology used in relevant empirical studies, this has not been followed by an equally sophisticated attempt to reconceive the relation between strategy research and business-policy advice. In other words, when it comes to praxeology—How should knowledge about strategy be used?—representationalism prevails: there is a difficulty in translating those more contextually sensitive research findings into business-policy advice. This is amply illustrated in SM textbooks.

Johnson and Scholes's best-selling textbook (1997) is a good case in point. The authors offer the reader a comprehensive view of SM, including those perspectives that are more explanatory and descriptive in orientation (e.g. the power school, the cultural school, etc.). Acknowledging also the influence of context on strategy formation, they encourage managers to take into account the important issues of politics and culture when designing strategies. However, the bulk of the textbook is taken by the positioning and planning schools. When it comes to offering readers the necessary conceptual tools with which to think strategically, the authors tend to resort to industry analysis, generic strategies, and planning techniques. This is also manifested in the way even politics and culture are tackled. They are reduced to quasi-measurable concepts, not substantially different from those used for industry analysis. The representationalist approach is evident throughout the text—it is clearly manifested in the multitude of tables, checklists, and graphs. The organization and its environment are objects that need to be mapped by an independent cognizing subject (that is, the managerial elite) and on the basis of such mapping the strategy needs to be formulated.

Even when authors such as Johnson and Scholes are sensitive enough (as they clearly are) to appreciate the difference between strategy formation and strategy formulation, their analysis pays lip service to the former and places emphasis, instead, on the latter. What they seem to be saying is something like this: 'We know that realized strategies are always different from those intended, but in aiming to offer managers advice about how to design their strategies, we need to give them those tools that will enable them to do so.' However, these authors find it difficult to adopt any other than a representationalist position. Consequently, any references to the *unique* features of a firm's dynamic context tend to be downgraded, in so far as such references can only be expressed in a (necessarily generic) propositional language. Additionally, *creative action* is downgraded too, since strategic choice is seen to be the outcome of an overtly analytical process that seeks to force the organization to choose from the already existing menu of generic strategies.

The same difficulty is also evident in Mintzberg et al.'s account (1998) of the learning school. Since the essence of the learning school, according to the authors, is the emergence of strategy through experimentation, Mintzberg et al. are also keen to point out that continuous experimentation is not an end in itself, but needs to be balanced with a sense of direction. The key is, note the authors, 'to know what to change when. And that means balancing change with continuity' (ibid. 227). This is indeed the case, but how can one know 'what to change when'. How can one know 'when to cut off initiatives that venture beyond the [strategic] umbrella as opposed to when to enlarge the umbrella to recognise their benefits' (ibid.)? Such questions, to which Mintzberg et al. provide no answer, are especially pertinent, given that the authors criticize certain perspectives (such as the cultural school) for failing 'to let managers know when and how to go about challenging [successful strategies]' (ibid. 282) in order to develop their own.

The difficulty Mintzberg et al., and Johnson and Scholes, have with providing contextually sensitive business-policy advice stems from the lack of a theory of creative action (Joas 1996). Johnson and Scholes (and most authors of SM textbooks) are trapped within a representationalist theory of action, and thus unable to incorporate contextual uniqueness and creative choice into their generic policy advice, while Mintzberg et al., although explicitly espousing novelty as a constitutive feature of strategic action, have not developed it into a coherent theory of creative action.

A good illustration of the difficulties of a representationalist theory of action in conceiving of human action as anything else but instrumental application of propositions is Goold's reply (1992) to Mintzberg (1990*b*), regarding the latter's account of a Boston Consulting Group (BCG) report, (1975) especially the report's handling of the development of Honda's strategy for entering the American motorcycle market. Goold (1992: 169), a co-author of the report, points out that the report never attempted to answer historical questions such as 'How did this situation arise?', but only managerial questions such as 'What should we do?'. As Goold (ibid. 169–70) remarks, 'its purpose was to discern what lay behind and accounted for Honda's success, in a way that would help others to think through what strategies would be likely to work. [...] [The report tried] to discern patterns in Honda's strategic decisions and actions, and to use these patterns in identifying what works well and badly'.

How did the report achieve this? By mobilizing an array of concepts borrowed from the positioning school, especially pointing out Honda's dedication to low cost aided by its large-scale domestic production.

The basic philosophy of the Japanese manufacturers [says the report] is that high volumes per model provide the potential for high productivity as a result of using capital intensive and highly automated techniques. Their marketing strategies are, therefore, directed towards developing these high model volumes, hence the careful attention that we have observed them giving to growth and market share. (BCG 1975: 59)

Notice the rationalizing language of the BCG report. Honda's success in the American motorcycle market is explained by making use of concepts from the positioning school. But this is exactly where the problem lies. What the report says does make sense, but it does so by giving an *ex post facto* rationalizing account of events. Looking *back* at Honda's success, the BCG report reconstructs it in its own image, so to speak. It shows us the structure of an already built system, but tells us very little about *how* that system came to be built in the first place; it is silent on precisely those *action* questions which are most important for practitioners: How did it occur to Honda to follow the strategy it did? How did it happen? How did they do it, at that particular time and place? Why this strategy and not something else?

BCG's explanation of the Honda success leaves *action* out of the picture: we see nothing in the account provided by BCG, about Honda managers' *reasons* for doing what they did; no statement describing their *beliefs* and *desires* that led them to undertake the actions they did. BCG's account is a paradigmatic case in SM of what philosophers call 'extensional descriptions': any true description of behaviour will remain true whenever we substitute equivalent descriptions into it (Rosenberg 1988: 48). Indeed, one can easily imagine countless other managers in BCG's account being substituted for Honda's particular managers, without changing the content of the account provided. That those particular Honda managers, at that particular point in time, at that particular place, held those particular beliefs and desires, which led them to undertake that particular stream of actions, are of no consequence to BCG's explanation. Yet our common experience tells us, and philosophical analysis shows, that explaining human action without reference to non-substitutable beliefs and desires is profoundly flawed (Bohman 1991; Rosenberg 1988).

Goold dismisses *action* questions as irrelevant for managers, and that is why he describes, misleadingly, the learning school as advocating 'random experiments' (Goold 1992: 170). History is irrelevant, he is in effect saying; strategic action needs to be based on strong foundations consisting of 'extensional models' (Rosenberg 1988) derived from past experiences. For Goold (and for several others), to answer the managerial question 'What should we do now?' implies that a generic model should be built from *past* experiences, and this model should then be used by others in the *future*. Strategic action is seen as propositional in structure: If in a situation like Honda's, then do something similar to what Honda did; or, if you want to do what Honda did, try to create conditions similar to those of Honda's. On this view, managers should look for those (Cartesian) 'clear and distinct ideas' on the basis of which they may reliably base their actions. Successful action is derived from reliable, codified knowledge, not from an experimental orientation towards the world. The strategist should not let himself/herself be surprised by the world; instead, the world should fit into the strategist's categories—the latter have logical priority over the former. Taken to its logical extreme, such a position encourages imitation, not creativity—do what others did, or what is typically done, slightly adapted, perhaps, to your circumstances. Needless to say that such a mode of thinking cannot accommodate Porter's desiderata (1991) for a dynamic theory of strategy.

Conclusions

Searching for a dynamic theory of strategy has been something like searching for the Holy Grail in SM. It has increasingly been recognized that for a firm to create and sustain a competitive advantage it must position itself uniquely in its industry and develop its internal capabilities in such as way as to make it very difficult for its competitors to imitate it. Moreover, a firm must do these things continuously. To put it simply, the current orthodoxy in SM underlines the *uniqueness* of the firm, the *novelty* of its choices, and the *time-dependent* nature of its development (Hamel and Prahalad 1994; Kay 1995; Markides 1999; Porter 1991). All this may sound obvious to practitioners, but not necessarily to theorists!

As we hope to have shown in this paper, the economic models that have provided the bedrock for most of the research on business strategy have been unable adequately to account for endogenous change, for process and time, and for creative action. In so far as the neoclassical firm has had any theoretical reason to exist at all, it has been thought to be an entity possessing no internal complexity and without a history, since changes in its productive knowledge are attributed entirely to exogenous shifts in its production function. Focusing predominantly on explaining outcomes, economic models have tended to view the firm from 'outside': firms strive to optimally respond to environmental conditions or to organizational problems rather than creatively engage with them in real time (cf. Rumelt et al., 1991).

On this view, as the Honda illustration mentioned earlier shows, strategy exists as a theoretically validated set of prescriptions waiting to be discovered by particular firms. There is a set of generic strategies that has been deduced and validated from the study of firms' aggregate strategic behaviour in the past, which serves as a menu for a particular firm to choose from. Such a deductive mode of explanation has been linked with a closed-world ontology and an instrumental praxeology. Even when economic actors behave in new and unexpected ways, as for example in the case of Honda, the dominant tendency has been to explain their novel strategic choices in terms of the existing vocabulary of strategy theories (to be precise, in terms of the vocabulary of the positioning school). Novel outcomes are accounted for by extensional descriptions containing substitutable actors who apply timeless, generic, agency-free formulae.

As well as strategy research being largely dominated by a preference for outcome explanations, it has tended to cluster around a theory of action that privileges representationalism and individualism. Strategy has been conceptualized as the exercise of (mostly) individual cognition followed by implementation (Huff 1990). From that perspective, the purpose of strategy research has predominantly been the supplying of managers with increasingly sophisticated formal models capturing essential features of firms and their environments. Knowledge of such models has been thought to be propositional in structure and thus instrumentally applicable by practitioners.

In this chapter we have critiqued that view (which is best represented by the planning and cognitive schools) and argued that formal strategy models cannot offer contextually sensitive and time-sensitive advice, nor can they formally suggest novel ways of acting. Their analyses are heavily skewed towards past behaviours, while they incorporate the premiss that a firm needs to choose its strategy from a currently available menu of ideal-type strategies. Strategy, on that view, is discovered; it is not invented; it is more an inferential than a creative process.

The field of SM (and much of management studies, for that matter) has suffered from what Bergson (1946) and James (1909/96) called 'intellectualism'. Intellectualism is the reduction of human experience to a conceptual order. Why is this a problem? It is a problem for the reason that, as James (ibid.) notes, 'an immediate experience, as yet unnamed or classed, is a mere *that* that we undergo, a thing that asks, "*What* am I". When we name and class it, we say for the first time what it is, and all these whats are abstract names or concepts' (emphasis in the original). Using concepts is an efficient way of handling experience, since once we have classed the various parts of experience in concepts, we can treat them by the law of the class they belong to. However, the real problem intellectualism presents consists in the fact that when we start identifying experience with concepts, we tend to treat the latter as a substitute for the former and, thus, 'deny the very properties with which the things sensibly present themselves' (ibid. 218–19). To put it simply, reality is much more complex and rich than our concepts and theories allow for.

Social-scientific understanding aims at a level of generality which glosses over particularities, imperfections, uniqueness. Yet it is taking advantage of those particularities and imperfections that gives a company an edge over its competitors (Nelson 1991; Spender 1996). For these features of reality to be made sense of, the faculty of perceiving needs to be given higher priority over the faculty of conceiving. Whereas concepts class our experiences and thus obliterate differences, in perception we are attentive to qualitative differences. Action is always situational and it takes place in time. Practitioners necessarily act *in concreto*, no matter how much they have been informed *in abstracto* about certain regularities (Schon 1983; Tsoukas 1996, 1998a).

Remember the language of the BCG report (1975)? Honda's success in America was thought to stem from their emphasis on high volume, which led them to pursue market share, which was linked with high productivity, and so on. This is a prime example of intellectualism. The situated action of those particular Honda managers is described via a timeless, generic proposition that has been validated through the study of aggregates of firms in the past. Details, personalities, interpretations, timing, context—all these particularities do not seem to matter. They are mere appearances that can be glossed over in search of the essential forces that move companies—the Four Principles, the Seven Dilemmas, the Key Drivers. What is, however, missing from such intellectualist accounts is something which practitioners intuitively understand: uniqueness; an answer to the question 'Why them and not others?'. Countless companies have tried to enter foreign markets, but having codified such experiences would not necessarily have given the Honda managers concrete advice as to what to do when contemplating penetrating the American market. What made the difference was how *they read* the situation; their perceptiveness in seeing connections (Strawson 1992: ch. 2); their sense of unease; their boldness in undertaking action in the face of uncertainty about the consequences of their action. Such an understanding is not nomological, and such action is not propositional (Berlin 1996: 15–39).

In order to explain distinctiveness and singularity, and incorporate time and creative action into their theoretical accounts, strategy researchers need to engage in ethnographic and historical modes of research. They need to embrace process explanations, if they wish to do justice to potential novelty, to human agency, and to the situatedness of strategy-making. In process explanations it is possible to show the links between thought and action as they unfold in time, and to focus on the historicity of the social context (i.e. the cultural and political dynamics) surrounding strategy-making. It is also possible to avoid the dilemma of choice versus change mentioned in the introductory section, since in process explanations, change is all there is, and change cannot be comprehended without human agency (strategic choice).

There is a respectable tradition of qualitative research into strategy that is close to process explanations, but it has tended to be relatively atheoretical. As well as 'thick descriptions' of strategy-making, we also need theories of creative action in organizations. How new actions emerge and how they cohere to constitute a pattern (Mintzberg and Waters 1985); how redescription through the metaphorical use of language occurs (Rorty 1991) and how new descriptions are legitimated in particular contexts (Burgelman 1988); and how key actors' historically formed webs of beliefs influence strategic choice (Pettigrew 1985; Woiceshyn 1997) are important issues that such theories ought to address.

Process explanations, however, lack the generality of outcome explanations. They cannot offer practitioners propositional advice, transcending context and time. If actors are not substitutable and their actions are not interchangeable, business-policy advice cannot be algorithmic—it can at best draw attention to things that matter. But what process accounts lose in scope they gain in depth: by re-entering the world of practitioners hermeneutically, process accounts can connect with the concrete experiences of practitioners, thus inviting them to reflect on their circumstances in novel ways (Tsoukas 1998*a*: 56–7; Weick 1990: 7). The utility of process accounts lies not so much in the standard reactions they evoke as in their mode of use: they offer practitioners the chance to reflect on, and make links with, others' experiences, thus leading to potentially new forms of action. To paraphrase Weick (ibid.), good strategy-theorizing, like good strategies, invites practitioners to 'rewrite' their experiences in order to construct new strategies. From a process-cum-enactivist perspective, just as thought and action are intimately connected, so are strategy-theorizing and strategy-making.

References

Andrews, K. R. (1980), *The Concept of Corporate Strategy* (Homewood, Ill.: Irwin).

Ansoff, I. H. (1965), *Corporate Strategy* (London: Penguin).

—— (1987), 'The Emerging Paradigm of Strategic Behavior', *Strategic Management Journal*, 8: 501–15.

—— (1991), 'Critique of Henrry Mintzberg's "The Design School: Reconsidering the Basic Premises of Strategic Management" ', *Strategic Management Journal*, 12: 449–61.

Araujo, L., and Easton, G. (1996), 'Strategy: Where is the Pattern?', *Organization*, 3: 361–83.

Austin, J. L. (1962), *How to Do Things with Words* (Cambridge, Mass.: Harvard University Press).

Bergson, H. (1946), *The Creative Mind* (New York: Citadel).

Berlin, I. (1996), 'The Sense of Reality', in I. Berlin, *The Sense of Reality* (London: Pimlico), 1–39.

Besanko, D., Dranove, D., and Shansley, M. (1996), *Economics of Strategy* (New York: Wiley).

Bhaskar, R. (1978), *A Realist Theory of Science* (Hassocks: Harvester).

Bicchieri, C. (1993), *Rationality and Coordination* (Cambridge: Cambridge University Press).

Binmore, K. (1990), *Essays on the Foundations of Game Theory* (Oxford: Blackwell).

Bohman, J. (1991), *New Philosophy of Social Science* (Cambridge: Polity).

Boston Consulting Group (BCG) (1975), *Strategy Alternatives for the British Motorcycle Industry* (London: HMSO).

Boudon, R. (1981), *The Logic of Social Action* (London: Routledge & Kegan Paul).

Bowman, E. H. (1995), 'Strategic History: Through Different Mirrors', *Advances in Strategic Management*, 11A: 25–45.

Burgelman, R. A. (1988), 'Strategy Making as a Social Learning Process: The Case of Internal Corporate Venturing', *Interfaces*, 18: 74–85.

Calori, R. (1998), '*Essai*: Philosophizing on Strategic Management Models', *Organization Studies*, 19: 281–306.

Camerer, C. (1985), 'Redirecting Strategy Research in Business Policy and Strategy', *Strategic Management Journal*, 6: 1–15.

Chandler, A. (1990), *Strategy and Structure*, 1st edn. 1962 (Cambridge, Mass.: MIT Press).

—— (1992), 'Organizational Capabilities and the Economic History of the Industrial Enterprise', *Journal of Economic Perspectives* 6: 79–100.

Cohen, B. (1994), 'Newton and the Social Sciences, with Special Reference to Economics, or, the Case of the Missing Paradigm', in P. Mirowski (ed.), *Natural Images in Economic Thought* (Cambridge: Cambridge University Press), 55–90.

Cyert, R. M. and March, J. G. (1963), *A Behavioral Theory of the Firm* (Englewood Cliffs, NJ: Prentice Hall).

Demsetz, H. (1973), 'Industry Structure, Market Rivalry, and Public Policy', *Journal of Law and Economics*, 16: 1–9.

Descartes, R. (1968), *Discourse on Method and the Meditations* (London: Penguin).

Devlin, K. (1997), *Goodbye, Descartes* (New York: Wiley).

Donaldson, Lex (1995), *American Anti-Management Theories of Organizations* (Cambridge: Cambridge University Press).

Elster, Jon (1983), *Explaining Technical Change* (Cambridge: Cambridge University Press).

Gharajedaghi, J. and Ackoff, R. (1984), 'Mechanisms, Organisms, and Social Systems', *Strategic Management Journal*, 5: 289–300.

Ghemawat, P. (1991), *Commitment: The Dynamic of Strategy* (New York: Free Press).

Ghemawat, G. (1997), *Games Businesses Play* (Cambridge, Mass.: MIT Press).

Gilbert, D. R. Jr., Hartman, E., Mauriel, J. J., and Freeman, R. E. (1988), *A Logic for Strategy* (New York: Ballinger).

Goold, M. (1992), 'Design, Learning and Planning: A Further Observation on the Design School Debate', *Strategic Management Journal*, 13: 169–70.

Gopinath, C., and Hoffman, R. (1995), 'The Relevance of Strategy Research: Practitioner and Academic Viewpoints', *Journal of Management Studies*, 32: 575–94.

Haugeland, J. (1985), *Artificial Intelligence* (Cambridge, Mass.: MIT Press).

Hamel, G., and Prahalad, C. K. (1994), *Competing for the Future* (Boston, Mass.: Harvard Business School Press).

Hayek, F. (1948), 'Economics and knowledge', in F. Hayek, *Individualism and Economic Order* (London: Routledge).

Hedstrom, P., and Swedberg, R. (1998), *Social Mechanisms* (Cambridge: Cambridge University Press).

Heidegger, M. (1962), *Being and Time* (New York: Harper & Row).

Huff, A. S. (1990), (ed.), *Mapping Strategic Thought* (Chichester: Wiley).

Hutchins, E. (1993), 'Learning to Navigate', in S. Chaiklin and J. Lave (eds.) *Understanding Practice* (Cambridge: Cambridge University Press), 35–63.

James, W. (1909/96), *A Pluralistic Universe* (Lincoln, Nebr.: University of Nebraska Press).

Joas, H. (1996), *The Creativity of Action*, trans. J. Gaines and P. Keast (Cambridge: Polity).

Johnson, G., and Scholes, K. (1997), *Exploring Corporate Strategy* 4th edn. (London: Prentice Hall).

Kay, J. (1995), *Foundations of Corporate Success* (Oxford: Oxford University Press).

Knudsen, Christian (1993), 'Equilibrium, Perfect Rationality and the Problem of Self-reference in Economics', in U. Mäki, B. Gustafsson and C. Knudsen (eds.), *Rationality, Institutions and Economic Methodology* (London: Routledge), 133–70.

Knudsen, Christian (1996), 'The Competence Perspective: A Historical Review', in N. J. Foss and C. Knudsen (eds.), *Towards a Competence Theory of the Firm* (London: Routledge), 13–37.

Kreps, D. M. (1990), 'Corporate Culture and Economic Theory', in J. E. Alt and K. Shepsle (eds.), *Perspectives on Positive Political Economy* (Cambridge: Cambridge University Press), 90–143.

Kuhn, T. (1970), *The Structure of Scientific Revolutions* (Chicago, Ill.: University of Chicago Press).

Latsis, S. (1972), 'Situational Determinism in Economics', *British Journal for the Philosophy of Science*, 23: 207–45.

—— (1976), 'A research Programme in Economics', in S. Latsis (ed.), *Method and Appraisal in Economics* (Cambridge: Cambridge University Press), 1–42.

Lawson, T. (1997), *Economics and Reality* (London: Routledge).

Learned, E. P., Christensen, C. R., Andrews, K. R., and Gush, W. D. (1965), *Business Policy* (Homewood, Ill.: Richard D. Irwin).

Lindblom, C. E. (1968), *The Policy Making Process* (Englewood Cliffs, NJ: Prentice Hall).

McClelland, E. F. (1993), 'Rationality, Constitutions, and the Ethics of Rules', *Constitutional Political Economy*, 4: 173–210.

Machlup, F. (1955), 'The Problem of Verification in Economics', *Southern Economic Journal*, 21: 1–21.

MacIntyre, A. (1985), *After Virtue*, 2nd edn. (London: Duckworth).

Mahoney, J. (1993), 'Strategic Management and Determinism: Sustaining the Conversation', *Journal of Management Studies*, 30: 173–91.

Malerba, F., Nelson, R., Orsenigo, L., and Winter, S. (1999), ' "History-friendly" Models of Industry Evolution: The Computer Industry', *Industrial and Corporate Change*, 8: 33–40.

March, J. G. (1994), *A Primer on Decision Making* (New York: Free Press).

Markides, C. C. (1999), 'A Dynamic View of Strategy', *Sloan Management Review*, 40: 55–64.

Mintzberg, H. (1990*a*), 'Strategy Formation: Schools of Thought', in J. W. Fredrickson (ed.), *Perspectives on Strategic Management* (New York: Harper), 105–236.

—— (1990*b*), 'The Design School: Reconsidering the Basic Premises of Strategic Management', *Strategic Management Journal*, 11: 171–95.

—— and Waters, J. A. (1982), 'Tracking Strategy in an Entrepreneurial Firm', *Academy of Management Journal*, 25: 465–99.

—— and —— (1985), 'Of Strategies, Deliberate and Emergent', *Strategic Management Journal*, 6: 257–72.

—— Ahlstrand, B., and Lampel, J. (1998), *Strategy Safari* (London: Prentice Hall).

Mirowski, P. (1989), *More Heat than Light: Economics as Social Physics, Physics as Nature's Economics* (Cambridge: Cambridge University Press).

Moch, M., and Huff, A. S. (1983), 'Power Enactment through Language and Ritual', *Journal of Business Research*, 11: 293–316.

Mohr, L. (1982), *Explaining Organizational Behavior* (San Francisco Calif.: Jossey-Bass).

Nelson, R. (1991), 'Why Firms Differ, and How Does it Matter?', *Strategic Management Journal* 12: 61–74.

—— and Winter, S. (1982), *An Evolutionary Theory of Economic Change* (Cambridge, Mass. Harvard University Press, (Belknap)).

Penrose, E. T. (1955), 'Limits to the Growth and Size of Firms', *American Economic Review, Papers and Proceedings*, 45: 531–43.

—— (1959), *The Theory of the Growth of the Firm* (Oxford: Oxford University Press).

Pettigrew, A. (1985), *The Awakening Giant* (Oxford: Blackwell).

—— (1990), 'Longitudinal Field Research on Change: Theory and Practice', *Organization Science*, 1: 267–92.

—— (1992), 'The Character and Significance of Strategy Process Research', *Strategic Management Journal*, 13: 5–16.

—— (1997), 'What is a Processual Analysis?', *Scandinavian Journal of Management*, 13: 337–48.

Polanyi, M. (1962), *Personal Knowledge: Towards a Post-Critical Philosophy* (Chicago Ill.: University of Chicago Press).

—— (1975), 'Personal Knowledge', in M. Polanyi and H. Prosch, *Meaning* (Chicago, Ill: University of Chicago Press).

Popper, K. (1988), *The Open Universe* (London: Hutchinson).

Porter, M. E. (1980), *Competitive Strategy* (New York: Free Press).

—— (1991), 'Towards a Dynamic Theory of Strategy', *Strategic Management Journal*, 12: 95–117.

Quinn, J. B. (1980), *Strategies for Change* (Homewood, Ill: Irwin).

Reed, E. S. (1996), *The Necessity of Experience* (New Haven Conn.: Yale University Press).

Rorty, R. (1980), *Philosophy and the Mirror of Nature* (Oxford: Blackwell).

—— (1991), *Objectivity, Relativism and Truth* (Cambridge: Cambridge University Press).

Rosenberg, A. (1988), *Philosophy of Social Science* (Oxford: Clarendon).

Rumelt, R. P., Schendel, D., and Teece, D. J. (1991), 'Strategic Management and Economics', *Strategic Management Journal*, 12: 5–29.

—— (1994), 'Fundamental Issues in Strategy', in R. P. Rumelt, D. E. Schendel, and D. J. Teece (eds.), *Fundamental Issues in Strategy* (Boston, Mass.: Harvard Business School Press), 9–47.

Saloner, G. (1991), 'Modelling, Game Theory, and Strategic Management', *Strategic Management Journal*, 12: 5–29.

Samuelson, P. (1947), *Foundations of Economic Analysis* (Cambridge: Harvard University Press).

Schelling, T. (1960), *The Strategy of Conflict* (Cambridge: Harvard University Press).

Schendel, D. E., and Hofer, C. (1979), 'Theory Building and Theory Testing in Strategic Management', in D. E. Schendel and C. Hofer (eds.), *Strategic Management* (Boston, Mass.: Little, Brown), 382–94.

Scherer, F. M. (1970), *Industrial Market Structure and Economic Performance* (Chicago, Ill.: Rand-McNally).

Scherer, A. G., and Dowling, M. J. (1995), 'Towards a Reconciliation of the Theory-pluralism in Strategic Management—Incommensurability and the Constructivist Approach of the Erlangen School', *Advances in Strategic Management*, 12A: 195–247.

Schon, D. (1983), *The Reflective Practitioner* (London: Avebury).

Schwenk, C. R., and Dalton, D. R. (1991), 'The Changing Shape of Strategic Management Research', *Advances in Strategic Management*, 7: 277–300.

Selten, R. (1975), 'Reexamination of the Perfectness Concept for Equilibrium Points in Extensive Games', *International Journal of Game Theory*, 4: 25–35.

Selten, R. (1990), 'Bounded Rationality', *Journal of Institutional and Theoretical Economics*, 146: 649–58.

Shrivastava, P. (1987), 'Rigor and Practical Usefulness of Research in Strategic Management', *Strategic Management Journal*, 8: 77–92.

Simon, H. (1978), 'Rationality as Process and as Product of Thought', *American Economic Review, Papers and Proceedings* 68 (May), 1–16.

—— (1979), 'Rational Decision Making in Business Organizations', *American Economic Review*, 69: 493–513.

—— (1983), *Reason in Human Affairs* (Stanford, Calif.: Stanford University Press).

Singer, A. E. (1994), 'Strategy as Moral Philosophy', *Strategic Management Journal*, 15: 191–213.

Smircich, L., and Stubbart, C. (1985), 'Strategic Management in an Enacted World', *Academy of Management Review*, 10: 724–36.

Soros, G. (1987), *The Alchemy of Finance*, 2nd edn. (New York: Wiley).

Spender, J.-C. (1993), 'Some Frontier Activities around Strategy Theorizing', *Journal of Management Studies*, 30: 11–30.

—— (1996), 'Organizational Knowledge, Learning and Memory: Three Concepts in Search of a Theory', *Journal of Organizational Change Management*, 9: 63–78.

Stigler, G. J., and Becker, G. (1977), 'De gustibus non est disputandum', *American Economic Review*, 67: 76–90.

Strawson, P. F. (1992), *Analysis and Metaphysics* (Oxford: Oxford University Press).

Taylor, C. (1985), *Philosophy and the Human Sciences, ii* (Cambridge: Cambridge University Press).

—— (1993), 'To Follow a Rule . . .', in C. Calhoun, E. LiPuma, and M. Postone (eds.), *Bourdieu: Critical Perspectives* (Cambridge: Polity), 45–59.

Thomas, H., and Pruett, M. (1993), 'Editorial: Perspectives on Theory Building in Strategic Management', *Journal of Management Studies*, 30: 3–10.

Tirole, J. (1988), *The Theory of Industrial Organization* (Cambridge, Mass.: MIT Press).

Toulmin, S. (1990), *Cosmopolis* (Chicago Ill.: University of Chicago Press).

Tsoukas, H. (1994), 'Refining Common Sense: Types of Knowledge in Management Studies', *Journal of Management Studies*, 31: 761–80.

—— (1996), 'The Firm as a Distributed Knowledge System: A Constructionist Approach', *Strategic Management Journal*, 17 (special winter issue): 11–25.

—— (1998a), 'Forms of Knowledge and Forms of Life in Organized Contexts', in R. Chia (ed.), *In the Realm of Organization* (London: Routledge), 43–66.

—— (1998b), 'The Word and the World: A Critique of Representationalism in Management Research', *International Journal of Public Administration*, 21: 781–817.

Ullmann-Margalitt, E. (1977), *The Emergence of Norms* (Oxford: Clarendon).

Varela, F. J., Thompson, E., and Rosch, E. (1991), *The Embodied Mind* (Cambridge, Mass.: MIT Press).

Weick, K. (1990), 'Introduction: Cartographic Myths in Organizations', in A. S. Huff (ed.), *Mapping Strategic Thought* (Chichester: Wiley), 1–10.

Winograd, T., and Flores, F. (1987), *Understanding Computers and Cognition* (Reading, Mass.: Addison-Wesley).

Winter, S. (1988), 'On Coase, Competence and Corporation', *Journal of Law, Economics and Organizations* 4: 163–80.

Wittgenstein, L. (1958), *Philosophical Investigations* (Oxford: Blackwell).

Woiceshyn, J. (1997), 'The Role of Management in the Adoption of Technology: A Longitudinal Investigation', *Technology Studies*, 4: 62–99.

Zan, L. (1990), 'Looking for Theories in Strategy Studies', *Scandinavian Journal of Management*, 6: 89–108.

SIXTEEN

New Times, Fresh Challenges: Reflections on the Past and the Future of Organization Theory

Thought deals [...] solely with surfaces. It can name the thickness of reality, but it cannot fathom it, and its insufficiency here is essential and permanent, not temporary

(William James 1909/996: 250)

We are observing the birth of a science that is no longer limited to idealized and simplified situations but reflects the complexity of the real world, a science that views us and our creativity as part of a fundamental trend present at all levels of nature

(Ilya Prigogine 1996: 7)

As one would expect of all social scientific fields, organization theory bears the marks of its birth. Ever since Weber, OT has largely been concerned with the study of formal organizations. Organization, understood as the generic phenomenon of patterned interaction, has been approached from the perspective of how coordinated interaction is authoritatively achieved within formal organizations (Barnard 1968; March and Simon 1993; Thompson 1967). In the imagery of mainstream OT, organizations are places of 'imperative control' (or 'imperative coordination') (Weber 1947: 152, 324), that is, cohesive as well as enduring totalities that resist change, have a dominant

This chapter was first published in H. Tsoukas and C. Knudsen (eds.), *The Oxford Handbook of Organization Theory* (Oxford: Oxford University Press, 2003), 607–22. Reprinted by permission of Oxford University Press, Copyright (2003).

An earlier draft of this chapter was delivered as a keynote address at the Joint IFSAM–ASAC Conference, Organization Theory Division, 8–11 July 2000, Montreal.

culture and a hierarchical power structure that ensures conformity and control so that certain behavioural regularities will more probably occur than others (Bauman 1992: 60; Pfeffer 1997).

Following such imagery the key phenomena of interest have been the following two. First, how power and cognitive structures, having the attributes of being independent and logically prior to individual actors and of relative inflexibility, result in 'de-randomizing' the voluntary actions of agents so that individual human behaviour becomes *organizational* behaviour. In essence, this is the classic Hobbesian problem on a small scale: how order is created out of the actions of diverse actors. Second, how the hierarchy of power and knowledge, empirically manifested in organizational structure, is related to certain key variables for organizational performance, such as the environment, strategy, technology, and societal institutions (Donaldson 1996; Pfeffer 1997). In both instances formal organization is seen as something solid and enduring, and stands in a causal relation to both human agency and its environment. Moreover, humans are conceived in minimalist terms, ex-temporally and ex-spatially, as self-interested information processors following a consequential rationality.

We have learned a great deal from such a synoptic treatment of organization(s). We have been able to learn about different kinds of organizations operating in different environments as well as about the mechanisms through which control is exerted and uniformity of behaviour is generated. But there have been some problems. First, the structure of formal organizations is not something originating outside society but constructed from the symbolic 'raw materials' provided by society at a point in time. As such, structure must be thought of as incorporating (or reflecting) the socially recognized myths and metaphors of the society within which organizations operate. Society does not cause organizations to adopt a particular structure, any more than it causes individuals to adopt a particular culture—in both cases society is a supplier of raw materials, not a causal agent. Embeddedness, not causal interaction, is the mode of relating both organizations to their environments and intra-organizational phenomena to one another. The elaboration of this thesis has been the significant contribution of the institutionalist research programme (Powell and DiMaggio 1991; Scott 1995).

Second, in the imagery of mainstream OT action and interaction tend to be significantly underplayed. What is neglected is the process through which apparently 'solid' structures are constructed, maintained, and modified in the course of interaction. Weick's theory of organizing (1979) and the associated cognitivist research it has inspired have been an important corrective to the mainstream view. Structure has been shown to emerge in the mind, in the gradual reduction of equivocality surrounding human interaction. We encounter here a classic theme running through OT: structure versus process. Over time the debate has shifted from a single-minded preoccupation with structure (the organization as a 'solid' entity) to the examination of the processes through which structure is generated, although the more demanding task of investigating how structure and process interact has not been taken up as much as it might have been.

And third, it has been increasingly recognized that individuals within organizations are not mere self-interested information processors; they rather have tangible bonds, attachments, and affiliations to communities, they are emotional beings, and, yes, they have a body. This recognition has had some intriguing implications. Relatively recently a considerable amount of research has been directed towards exploring the 'communities of practice' and collectively held meaning systems that sustain individual action at work (Brown and Duguid 1991; Tsoukas 1998*a*), the emotional side of human beings that inescapably affects what they do and how they act (Fineman, 1993), and the organizational implications of gender and race (Gherardi 1995; Nkomo 1992).

I hope you can see the picture I am trying to paint: over time, OT has become more complex in its treatment of its object of study. Its initially rigid assumptions have been relaxed and real-life complexity has been let in (March and Olsen 1986: 28). In effect, it has been recognized that (a) organizational phenomena are embedded in, and derive their significance from, broader patterns of meaning and nexuses of activity; (b) the apparent solidity of organizations is the result of social processes at work; and (c) individuals are inherently social and bodily creatures. However, despite the significant conceptual progress that has been made, we are still captive to an intellectualist onto-epistemology that fails to recognize the inherent *sociality* of organizational phenomena—that organizations and organizational members are constitutively (not contingently) social entities. I shall have more to say about this later on.

The move towards incorporating greater complexity and, therefore, increasing OT's theoretical sophistication will be strengthened if it is also recognized that as well as being concerned with the study of formal organizations OT is par excellence the field that ought to be focusing on *organization* (Chia 1996; Tsoukas 2001). This is important partly because it licenses OT theorists to look around in the non-social realm for patterns of organization which might provide useful insights into social organization—notice, for example, the increasing popularity of notions such as 'complex adaptive systems' and 'dynamical chaotic systems' (Anderson 1999; Morel and Ramanujam 1999). But, more significantly, it is important because it enables us to understand the new network forms of organization and patterns of inter-organizational cooperation that are increasingly emblematic of late-modern knowledge economies (Castells 2000). And finally, focusing on organization enables us to get a clear picture of the dynamic processes through which organization emerges (Tsoukas and Chia 2002; Weick 1979).

What new patterns of social organization suggest is that it is possible for actors to be organized outside the bounds of 'imperative co-ordination' (Gulati et al. 2000; Hardy 1994; Nohria 1992). We need, therefore, new categories that are appropriate to the analysis of patterned interaction in an extra-organizational space in which there is no dominant culture, imperative control, or single legitimate authority (Bauman 1992: 61). If we shift our attention from the study of formal organizations to the study of *organization* we will be able to see authoritative coordination as a contingent empirical manifestation of the broader process of social coordination—authority is one way through which patterned interaction may be achieved; actors following abstract rules or subscribing to the same values are alternative ways of achieving patterned interaction.

More generally, formal organization should be seen as the quest for closure— for contingencies to be eliminated and for meaning to be definitively established so that consistently effective action, across time and space, may become possible—but such a closure is inescapably incomplete (Tsoukas 2001). As several ethnographic studies have shown, human action occurs in necessarily open-ended contexts, whose features cannot be fully anticipated (Hutchins 1993; Orr 1996). And human action qua human has the potential to be reflexive, thus leading to new distinctions and meanings. Thus, in so far as actors follow abstract rules, formal organization is an input into human action, while organization at large is an *outcome* of it—a pattern emerging from actors adapting to local contingencies and closely interrelating their actions with those of others (Tsoukas and Chia, 2002). Organization emerges as situated accommodations become heedfully interrelated in time (Weick and Roberts 1993).

The preceding view has several benefits, since it enables us to see more clearly certain hitherto unappreciated aspects of organization. First, new empirical phenomena such as the increasingly distributed character of contemporary corporations and the pervasive agreements and partnerships seen in certain industries can be accounted for. More generally, it makes it possible for us to expand our understanding of organization by focusing on patterns of coordination between actors (or what was earlier called 'patterned interaction') at several levels of analysis (coordination between individuals, coordination among governments, corporations and NGOs in all permutations, as well as forms of governance), and how they are produced. Second, it helps us enrich our notion of organization to include *self-organization*—immanently generated order. Whereas we have often tended to think of organization as being almost exclusively imposed from the outside, we are now able to see that organization is, partly at least, a self-generating pattern or, to use Hayek's term, (1982), a 'spontaneous order'—a collectively generated outcome as actors improvise to accommodate local contingencies and interweave their actions across space and time (Tsoukas 1996, 2001; Weick 1998).

Against Intellectualism: The Inherent Sociality of Organizational Phenomena

A main feature of mainstream OT has been the conceptualization of formal organization as an internal realm of purely 'organizational' operations and, ever since March and Simon (1993), of computations and programmes. In this, OT has followed similar developments in sociology and, especially, psychology. Just as the mind has been considered as an inner set of mental processes (Harre and Gillet 1994) and society as a collection of mechanisms for establishing and maintaining control (Bauman 1992), formal organization has been seen as a 'pure' mechanism for reducing uncertainty, for making decisions, and generating behavioural regularities. The epistemological strategy behind such an approach has been that of intellectualism (or representationalism) (Tsoukas 1998*b*).

Intellectualism, as James (1909/96: 217) perceptively noted long ago, is the turning of experience into a conceptual order, identifying a thing with a concept and a concept with a definition. Our thinking, on this view, aims to represent a pre-given object of study as closely as possible. An object of study is divided into regions of discrete elements, which are isomorphically represented by names (Varela et al. 1991: 147). Social-scientific analysis aims at finding out the most appropriate names (concepts) to fit the structure of the world. This is a metaphysical stance, which, as Wittgenstein (1958) clearly saw, requires getting 'in front of' everything, 'looking at' our experiences from outside and mirroring them in our concepts (Finch 1995: 33). Since the world consists of discrete elements, rather than complexes or contexts, the task of social scientific analysis, according to the intellectualist view, is to name those elements and find out the contingent connections between them (Chia 1996; Tsoukas 1994).

In OT (and in the rest of the social sciences) such an approach has had the following two implications. First, social phenomena in organizations are thought to merely consist of, or be the product of, interrelated individuals. And second, the relationship between social phenomena and individuals is seen as merely external—the properties definitive of individuals are only contingently linked to social phenomena (Schatzki 2000). The first implication signals the difficulty we have had as OT theorists in paying proper attention to the collective nature of organizations and considering them as something more than mere sites of individual action. The second implication signifies our difficulty in appreciating the irreducible sociality of actors; that the possession of mind and performance of action inherently (not contingently) require a social context, a nexus of practice (ibid. 94–5).

Both of the above difficulties can be overcome if we grasp the Wittgensteinian point that social practices and institutions incorporate particular self-interpretations, certain ways in which evaluative distinctions are enacted

(Taylor 1985*a*, 1985*b*). Without such distinctions a social institution would not be what it is, could not have the shape it has. Moreover, a social institution cannot be intelligible unless its constitutive distinctions are grasped (Winch 1958). Consider, for example, organizational decision-making. The typically Anglo-Saxon practice of making decisions manifests a certain self-understanding, a set of evaluative distinctions which are constitutive of 'decision making' (cf. Taylor 1985*b*: 32–5; Tsoukas 1998*b*: 787–8). These are typically bound up with clarity of expression, confrontation between different views, and impersonal analysis of the situation, with the view of getting 'to the heart' of the problem. Such distinctions, however, have no place in other societies, such as, for example, Japan, where the prevailing set of distinctions incorporates compromise, consensus, respect for seniority, and saving face (Dore 1973; Rosenberger 1992). The difference in what constitutes decision-making in both cases is not merely linguistic; more crucially, it is a difference in social reality. As Taylor (1985*b*: 33) observes, 'the realities here are practices; and these cannot be identified in abstraction from the language we use to describe them, or invoke them, or carry them out'.

If institutions and practices are what they are by virtue of the particular sets of distinctions that are incorporated in them, where do those distinctions get their meaning from? As Wittgenstein (1958) insightfully observed, the meaning of our signs and symbols comes from the uses we put them to. This happens in the context of *discursive practices*—intentional, normatively constrained sets of actions. According to Harre and Gillett (1994: 28–9), 'a discursive practice is the use of a sign system, for which there are norms of right and wrong use, and the signs concern or are directed at various things' (see also Bruner 1990: 17–19; Harre 1997: 175; MacIntyre 1985: 185–90). A crucial feature of discursive practices is that the meanings they embody are not just in the minds of the individuals involved but in the practices themselves; the meanings are the common property of the practice at hand—they are intersubjective (Bruner 1990: 12–13; Taylor 1985*b*: 36–40). This is ontologically important, for it shifts attention from the individual to the individual-embedded-in-practice. It is also epistemologically significant because since intersubjective meanings do not primarily reside in the minds of individuals, they cannot be known through the traditional methods of empiricist science (e.g. individual answers to questionnaires) but through the use of interpretative methods (Taylor 1985*b*: 40). Intersubjective meanings are more than just shared in the sense that each of us has them in our individual minds: they are part of a common reference world which is over and above, and is constitutive of, the individual mind (Bruner 1990: 12–15).

For example, if decision-making is seen as a discursive practice—as what people *do* when they take decisions, subject to standards of correctness—then what decision-making is, what it consists of, is not something the individuals involved define; decision-making has already been defined by the discourse in which individuals participate. The point here is that the condition for an individual to be a competent member of a discursive practice at all is to be taking for granted the meanings constitutive of the practice. This does not mean, of course, that the individual may not bring his/her own beliefs and attitudes to a particular decision-making process. What, however, he/she will not bring is what *constitutes* decision-making—that has already been defined in the discursive practice in which the individual participates (Taylor 1985*b*: 36).

Clearly, without intersubjective meanings there could not be collective forms of action at all, since individuals would be lacking a common language whereby to engage in a collective activity. The notion of intersubjective meanings enables us to conceive of a 'collective subject' without thinking of it as a contradiction in terms. This is especially important when it comes to organizations, since the latter are first and foremost *collective* actors. Yet the ontological individualism that has characterized OT has obscured the collective nature of organizations.

For example, March and Simon (1993: 2) have remarked that 'organizations are systems of co-ordinated action among individuals and groups whose preferences, information, interests, or knowledge differ'. Notice that, on such a view, in the beginning there was difference, conflict, even discord, which are then turned by the organization into cooperation. In the words of March and Simon (ibid.), 'organization theories describe the delicate conversion of conflict into co-operation'. This, however, is a limited view of what organizational life is about. The point of departure for individuals is not only difference but also similarity; conflict and cooperation. Prior to becoming members of a particular organization, individuals were members of other organizations; moreover, societal membership is prior to organizational membership. In so far as individuals are embedded in broader societal systems of meaning, they draw on them to carry out their tasks. And in so far as organizations similarly incorporate the self-understandings of the wider social system, their identity is always already partly defined. Organizations do not just convert conflict into cooperation; they may also convert cooperation into conflict—as, for example, when organizational members are asked to behave in ways that may not be congruent with some of the dominant societal self-understandings. A more rounded view of organizational life is possible when we discard ontological individualism and begin to appreciate that intersubjective meanings, manifested in discursive practices, are constitutive of individuals; and, at a higher level of analysis, that societal self-understandings are constitutive of organizations.

As argued earlier, the intellectualist approach leads to thinking of individuals as only *contingently* connected to social practices. A person's actions respond to events in his/her environment, the argument goes, but the fact that the person acts depends solely on the person's characteristics, especially his/her mental condition. At the individual level of analysis, the mind itself determines actions; at the collective level of analysis, the collective mind (culture) determines collective practices. But the mind is not a mere set of logical operations—whatever those operations are, they must *mean* something. Meanings are deeply implicated in how people act, and we can find out what those meanings are by looking at what people *do*. The mind therefore is inextricably linked to action—it is manifested in action (Bruner 1990; Harre and Gillett 1994; Weick and Roberts 1993). If this point had been fully grasped, a number of harmful dualisms encountered in OT could have been avoided. Consider the following examples.

(1) Hofstede's research on the impact of national culture on organizational structure and functioning is based on a conceptual dichotomy between 'values' and 'practices' (McSweeney 2002). 'Values', argues Hofstede (1991: 8), 'are broad tendencies to prefer certain states of affairs than others [...] they are not directly observed by outsiders'. Practices, on the other hand, are less fundamental and as such 'are visible to an outside observer' (ibid.). 'Their cultural meaning, however,' remarks Hofstede (ibid.), 'is invisible and lies precisely and only in the way these practices are interpreted by the insiders'. Notice that culture for Hofstede is something that only the privileged 'insiders' have access to, and are, therefore, capable of describing (this is an argument very similar to the psychologistic claim that only individuals have direct access to the content of their minds) (cf. Rorty 1991). What this view misses is that just as an individual needs a language in order to describe his/her mental content and that language necessarily needs to be public, so the insiders in a culture need to describe their values using some public language, and that renders their values public. The metaphysically private self assumed by Hofstede's view is unsustainable because it presupposes the existence of a private language, which, as Wittgenstein (1958) ingeniously showed, is impossible. A private language is an illusion, for such a language would need to establish the meaning of its signs independently of the truth it claims to report—which, since it is a private language, cannot be achieved. And if a private language is an illusion, so is a private subject, be it an individual mind or a collective mind. Whatever it is that values are, they are manifested in the practices people are engaged in; values and practices are not—cannot be—separate. As Finch (1995: 86), an interpreter of Wittgenstein, argues, 'the attempt to ground both self and objects in "in-itselfness" or "own being", in order to guarantee their reality, lies at the very heart of the ratio-mythic "duplication" which created the metaphysical age'.

(2) The currently popular split of organizational knowledge into 'tacit' and 'explicit' is another example of problematic distinctions stemming from an intellectualist epistemology. It is interesting to note that the intellectualist understanding of tacit and explicit knowledge is nowhere to be seen in the work of Polanyi (1962, 1975), who first introduced such a distinction, but has been added later by his interpreters in management studies. Thus, for Nonaka and Takeuchi (1995: 62–3) tacit and explicit knowledge are 'independent' and they 'interact with and interchange into each other in the creative activities of human beings' (ibid. 61). Indeed, the authors' model of organizational-knowledge creation is crucially based on the assumption that tacit and explicit knowledge are not only independent but also convertible to one another.

However, very sensibly, this is not what Polanyi had in mind when he introduced that distinction. For him, tacit and explicit knowledge are mutually constituted—they are not contingently linked. Tacit knowledge can be formalized and explicitly communicated *if* we focus our attention on it. And vice versa: explicit knowledge, no matter how explicit and codified it is, is *always* grounded on a tacit component. Tacit knowledge and explicit knowledge are two sides of the same coin—being mutually constituted, they cannot 'interact', nor can they be 'converted' into one another (Tsoukas 2003). As Cook and Brown (1999: 385) aptly remark, when we ride a bicycle, the explicit knowledge does not lie inside the tacit knowledge in a dormant form; it is rather generated in the context of riding with the aid of tacit knowledge.

Likewise [remark Cook and Brown] 'if you know explicitly which way to turn but cannot ride, there is no operation you can perform on the explicit knowledge that will turn it into the tacit knowledge necessary to riding. That tacit knowledge is acquired on its own; it is not made out of explicit knowledge. Prior to being generated, one form of knowledge does not lie hidden in the other. (ibid.)

If we persist in such a misunderstanding of tacit and explicit knowledge we risk hypostasizing tacit knowledge and treating it as if it were a version of explicit knowledge—a set of quasi-rules waiting to be discovered. However, in a social context, the crucial feature of tacit knowledge is that it provides the unarticulated background—a set of evaluative distinctions—of what is taken for granted, which is a necessary prerequisite for action. Such an unarticulated background is learned through actors' participation in a social practice, a form of life, and that is why the locus of an actor's tacit knowledge is not in his/her head but in the practice he/she is a member of. At both the individual and the collective levels of analysis, tacit knowledge is the process of instrumentalizing experiences—the lapse into unawareness of the manner in which tools, be they physical and/or intellectual, are used (Polanyi 1962: 59–65). There is no conversion of tacit knowledge to explicit, but a shift of attention from focal awareness to subsidiary awareness. Thus, more generally, if the above is accepted, it follows that viewing organizational phenomena as aggregates of contingently related elements leads to major distortions in our understanding of those phenomena, since we are prevented from seeing the *internal* relations holding between individuals and social practices as well as between articulated beliefs and unarticulated distinctions.

Explaining Organizational Action: From Causes to Reasons

The task of OT has traditionally been assumed to be the noticing of relevant regularities and their subsequent causal explanation through contingency models of the type 'If A, then B, in circumstances Z'. In a more elaborate form, contingency models take the following form: 'Given any organization X, if X wants to maximize its performance A and X believes that B is a means to attain A, under the circumstances, then X does B' (Rosenberg 1988: 25). Notice that this general statement connects beliefs and desires to actions. The question is: What is the nature of such a connection? Does it identify causes of action or does it reveal reasons for action? Or, as Rosenberg (ibid. 30) asks,

Does [a contingency model of explanation (CME)] underwrite our explanations of actions because it describes causal relations—that is lawlike connections—in virtue of which actions are determined by beliefs and desires? Or does [a CME] underwrite these explanations because it helps us identify the reasons that make a particular action justified, intelligible, rational, meaningful, or somehow significant to us?

The CME would describe a causal explanation if beliefs and desires could be objectively established; that is, if they could be defined independently of the explanandum (i.e. independently of action). But this cannot be done. An action such as an act of 'loyalty', for example, is identified in relation to a belief as to what constitutes 'loyalty', and incorporates a desire as to how to behave in a manner that is recognized by others as 'loyal' (Taylor 1985b: 23). In other words, in so far as human action is constituted by evaluative distinctions and, therefore, involves rule-following, the criteria of its intelligibility must be internal to that action (Harre 2004; Winch 1958: 89–91). What is even worse is that an actor's beliefs and desires cannot be straightforwardly inferred from his/her actions, for the actor may hold quite different second-order or context-dependent beliefs and desires. For example, as Popper (1979: 246) remarked, Kepler's desire in his mathematical work was to discover the harmony of the world order, although we regard his contribution today as a mathematical description of motion in a set of two-body planetary systems. More generally, action cannot be used as a guide to find out an actor's beliefs, unless we hold the actor's desires constant. And in order to use action as a guide for an actor's desires we need to hold his/her beliefs constant. As Rosenberg (1988: 33) remarks, 'any action can be the result of almost any belief, provided the agent has the appropriate desire'. It follows, therefore, that in explaining action our aim is to render it intelligible, to find out the reasons it happened, by moving into a 'hermeneutical circle' where we aim to show the coherence between actions, beliefs, and desires (Bohman 1991: 27; Rosenberg 1988: 34; Taylor 1985b: 23–4).

   It is because of the hermeneutical circle that we find it so difficult to identify causes in OT and, instead, our explanations cite reasons, thus often having a circular character (Rosenberg 1988; Strawson (1992); Taylor 1985a; Tsoukas, 1998b). Thus, a significant body of research has shown that organizations reproduce the beliefs and practices of the society in which they are embedded. Interacting with their environments, organizations do not confront independent entities, but rather engage in processes whereby organizations create opportunities for learning and action, and, in so doing, they shape the links with other organizations in their own image. Individual, as well as organizational, action is hardly ever purely instrumental; it is also a display at which actors look to find what they are. As March and Simon (1993: 16) perceptively noted, action is a purpose in itself. Desires are formed by experiencing choices. Goals lead to actions and actions lead to goals. Problems lead to solutions but, also, solutions create problems. Strategy follows structure, but the reverse is also true.

Should we worry about this circularity? Not necessarily, if our purpose is to *elucidate* the phenomena we deal with; that is, to bring out the relationships between actions, beliefs, and desires, and how they came to be established. If we conceive of theory as elucidation we would be quite happy to view our inquiry as an elaborate network of connected items, such that each concept could be understood by grasping its connections with other concepts (Strawson 1992: 19). The charge of circularity would not worry us, for, in the perceptive words of Strawson (ibid. 19–20), 'we might have moved in a wide, revealing, and illuminating circle'. [Strawson continues]:

This is not to say that the charge of circularity would lose its sting in every case. Some circles are too small and we move in them unawares, thinking we have established a revealing connection when we have not. But it would be a matter for judgement to say when the charge was damaging and when it was not. (ibid.)

Overcoming Harmful Dualisms

As said earlier, OT has traditionally been assumed to be the study of authoritative coordinated interaction. Our emphasis has largely been on how human behaviour is homogenized in organized contexts and how behavioural regularities come about. Hence the emphasis that has often been put on routines, programmes, schemata. What has been less explored is how change and novelty come about in organized contexts. Interestingly, just as 'structure' was taken to be separate from 'process', 'creativity' was thought to be separate from 'repetition'. It was further assumed that we could focus on 'repetition' or on 'creativity' but not simultaneously on both; we could study 'stability' and 'order' or 'change' and 'evolution', but not both. Moreover, even when creativity and change were the foci of study, they were approached as phenomena already accomplished not as ongoing processes (Chia 1999). Much of OT is, to use James's apt phrase (1909/96: 262), 'a post-mortem dissection'.

The reason for this synoptic approach is the intellectualist stance mentioned earlier, which compels us to transform the perceptual order into a conceptual order. The trouble with concepts synoptically employed is that while they shed light on particular aspects of reality, they obstruct our access to those other aspects that are not pointed at by the relevant concept. For example, 'routine' is an organizational phenomenon we can easily find evidence for. But by describing a particular behaviour as routine we fail to notice that, unlike machine behaviour, human behaviour is never completely routine, and that it always contains the possibility of novelty and change (Feldman 2000). Even the very experience of routine is sufficient to reshape it (Tsoukas and Chia 2002). As James (1909/96: 219) remarks, 'once you have conceived things as "independent", you must proceed to deny the possibility of any connexion whatever among them, because the notion of connexion is not contained in the definition of independence'. 'Stability' and 'change' are two independently defined phenomena, as are 'repetition' and 'creativity', and when we proceed on such intellectualist premises we are easily trapped into focusing on the one at the expense of the other, thus ignoring that *both* terms of each pair are part of the same reality (Wallerstein 1999: 166).

The implications of such an intellectualist epistemology are that we fail properly to understand 'change' and 'novelty' in their own terms, rather treating them as special cases of 'stability' and 'routine' (North 1996; Orlikowski 1996: 63; Tsoukas and Chia 2002; Weick 1998: 551). This failure is a challenge for us to develop more nuanced accounts of these phenomena and how they are interwoven in organizational life (Tsoukas and Chia, 2002). What is crucially missing from OT is, as Porter (1991) has pointed out with reference to strategic management, theories of creative action in organizations. This in turn calls for more work on how structure interacts with process over time, how reflexivity functions, and how context and contingencies influence action paths (Garud and Karnoe 2000). To paraphrase Wallerstein (1999: 166), OT ought to be the search for the narrow passage between the determined and the arbitrary, the general and the particular, closure and open-endedness.

If this point is accepted, then OT should not so much be concerned with the study of authoritatively coordinated interaction as the study of *patterned interaction*, of *chaosmos* (Edgar Morin's term, cited in Castoriadis 1987, 1991; Kofman 1996: ch. 5). Our ontology must be broad enough to accept that organizations have the features of a cosmos (a pattern) but also that, at their roots, they are chaos, a gaping void from which new patterns, a new cosmos, arises. Human imagination and interaction give rise to new forms, enable new practices to emerge. It is precisely the interdependence of chaos and cosmos that makes organizational life patterned yet indeterminate, and enables the human mind to account for it, although in an irremediably incomplete way (Tsoukas 2001).

Accepting the ontology of *chaosmos* implies that we must discard two of the foundational myths of our field; namely, that 'formal organizations are abstract systems' (Barnard 1968: 74; Thompson 1956/57)—sets of formal rules—and that our enquiry should be guided by the pursuit of the 'decontextualized ideal' (Toulmin 1990: 30–5)—the search for the abstract, the timeless, and the universal at the expense of the concrete, the temporal, and the local. Since organizations incorporate self-interpretations articulating evaluative distinctions, they do not have a fixed identity over time and space that might be captured in the same way that DNA captures the essence of genes. In the view suggested here, organizations do not have a certain 'inner' logic, a set of intrinsic properties; they rather are constitutively social all the way—discursive practices embedded within discursive practices. Perhaps our motto, if we need one, should be: Don't search for the logic of organizing; look for the discursive practices involved in organizing.

References

Anderson, P. (1999), 'Complexity Theory and Organization Science', *Organization Science*, 10: 216–32.

Barnard, C. (1968), *The Functions of the Executive* (Cambridge, Mass.: Harvard University Press).

Bauman, Z. (1992), 'Sociological Responses to Postmodernity', in Bauman, *Intimations of Postmodernity* (London: Routledge), 26–67.

Bohman, J. (1991), *New Philosophy of Social Science* (Cambridge: Polity).

Brown, J. S., and Duguid, P. (1991), 'Organizational Learning and Communities of Practice: Towards a Unified View of Working, Learning, and Innovation', *Organization Science*, 2: 40–57.

Bruner, J. (1990), *Acts of Meaning* (Cambridge, Mass.: Harvard University Press).

Castells, M. (2000), 'Materials for an Exploratory Theory of the Network Society, *British Journal of Sociology*, 51: 5–24.

Castoriadis, C. (1987), *The Imaginary Institution of Society* (Cambridge: Polity).

—— (1991), *Philosophy, Politics, Autonomy*, ed. and trans. D. A. Curtis (New York: Oxford University Press).

Chia, R. (1996), 'The Problem of Reflexivity in organizational Research: Towards a Postmodern Science of Organization', *Organization*, 3: 31–59.

—— (1999), A 'Rhizomic' Model of Organizational Change and Transformation: Perspective from a Metaphysics of Change', *British Journal of Management*, 10: 209–27.

Cook, S. D. N., and Brown, J. S. (1999), 'Bridging Epistemologies: The Generative Dance between Organizational Knowledge and Organizational Knowing', *Organization Science*, 10: 381–400.

Donaldson, L. (1996), *For Positivist Organization Theory*, (London: Sage).

Dore, R. (1973), *British Factory—Japanese Factory* (Berkeley, Calif.: University of California Press).

Feldman, M. (2000), 'Organizational Routines as a Source of Continuous Change', *Organization Science*, 11: 611–29.

Finch, H. L. (1995), *Wittgenstein*, (Rockport, Mass.: Element).

Fineman, S. (1993) (ed.), *Emotion in Organizations* (London: Sage).

Garud, R., and Karnoe, P. (2000), *Path Dependence and Creation* (Mahawa, NJ: Lawrence Erlbaum).

Gherardi, S. (1995), *Gender, Symbolism and Organizationl Cultures* (Thousand Oaks, Calif.: Sage).

Granovetter, M. (1992), 'Problems of Explanation in Economic Sociology', in N. Nohria, and R. G. Eccles (eds.), *Networks and Organizations* (Boston, Mass.: Harvard Business School Press), 25–56.

Gulati, R., Nohria, N., and Zaheer, A. (2000), 'Strategic Networks', *Strategic Management Journal*, 21: 203–15.

Hardy, C. (1994), 'Underorganized Interorganizational Domains: The Case of Refuge Systems', *Journal of Applied Behavioral Science*, 30: 278–96.

—— (1997), 'Forward to Aristotle: The Case for a Hybrid Ontology', *Journal for the Theory of Social Behaviour*, 27: 173–91.

Harré, R. (2004), 'Discursive Psychology and the Boundaries of Sense', *Organization Studies*, forthcoming.

—— and Gillett, G. (1994), *The Discursive Mind* (Thousand Oaks, Calif.: Sage).

Hayek, F. A. (1982), *Law, Legislation and Liberty* (London: Routledge & Kegan Paul).

Hofstede, G. (1991), *Cultures and Organizations* (London: HarperCollins).

Hutchins, E. (1993), 'Learning to navigate', in S. Chaiklin and J. Lave (eds.), *Understanding Practice* (Cambridge: Cambridge University Press), 35–63.

James, W. (1909/96), *A Pluralistic Universe*, (Lincoln Nebr.: University of Nebraska Press).

Joas, H. (1996), *The Creativity of Action*, trans. J. Gaines and P. Keast (Cambridge: Polity).

Kofman, M. (1996), *Edgar Morin* (London: Pluto).

MacIntyre, A. (1985), *After Virtue*, 2nd edn. (London: Duckworth).

McSweeney, B. (2002), 'Hofstede's Model of National Cultural Differences and their Consequences: A Triumph of Faith—a Failure of Analysis', *Human Relations*, 55: 89–118.

March, J. G., and Olsen, J. (1986), Garbage Can Models of Decision Making in Organizations', in J. March and R. Weissinger-Baylon (eds.), *Ambiguity and Command* (Marshfield, Mass.: Pitman), 11–35.

March, J. G., and Simon, H. A. (1993), *Organizations* 2nd edn. (Cambridge, Mass.: Blackwell).

Morel, B., and Ramanujam, R. (1999), 'Through the Looking Glass of Complexity: The Dynamics of Organizations as Adaptive and Evolving Systems', *Organization Science*, 10: 278–93.

Nkomo, S. (1992), 'The Emperor Has No Clothes: Rewriting "Race" in the Study of Organizations', *Academy of Management Review*, 17: 487–513.

Nohria, N. (1992), 'Introduction: Is a Network Perspective a Useful Way of Studying Organizations?', in N. Nohria, and R. G. Eccles (eds.), *Networks and Organizations* (Boston: Harvard Business School Press), 1–22.

Nonaka, I. and Takeuchi, H. (1995), *The Knowledge-creating Company* (New York: Oxford University Press).

North, D. (1996), 'Epilogue: Economic Performance Through Time', in L.J. Alston, T. Eggertsson, and D. North, (eds.), *Empirical Studies in Institutional Change* (Cambridge: Cambridge University Press), 342–55.

Orlikowski, W. J. (1996), 'Improvising Organizational Transformation Over Time: A Situated Change Perspective', *Information Systems Research*, 7: 63–92.

Orr, J. (1996), *Talking About Machines* (New York: ILR/Cornell University Press).

Pfeffer, J. (1997), *New Directions in Organization Theory* (New York: Oxford University Press).

Polanyi, M. (1962), *Personal Knowledge*, (Chicago, Ill.: University of Chicago Press).

—— (1975), 'Personal Knowledge'. in M. Polanyi and H. Prosch, *Meaning* (Chicago, Ill.: University of Chicago Press), 22–45.

Popper, K. R. (1979), *Objective Knowledge*, rev. edn. (Oxford: Clarendon).

Porter, M. E. (1991), 'Towards a Dynamic Theory of Strategy', *Strategic Management Journal*, 12: 95–117.

Powell, W. W., and DiMaggio, P. J. (1991), (eds.), *The New Institutionalism in Organizational Analysis* (Chicago, Ill.: University of Chicago Press).

Prigogine, I. (1996), *The End of Certainty* (New York: Free Press).

Rorty, R. (1980), *Philosophy and the Mirror of Nature* (Oxford: Blackwell).

—— (1991), *Objectivity, Relativism and Truth* (Cambridge: Cambridge University Press).

Rosenberg, A. (1988), *Philosophy of Social Science* (Oxford: Clarendon).

Rosenberger, N. R. (1992), *Japanese Sense of Self,* (Cambridge: Cambridge University Press).

Schatzki, T. R. (2000), 'Wittgenstein and the Social Context of an Individual Life', *History of the Human Sciences*, 13: 93–107.

Scott, R. W. (1995), *Institutions and Organizations* (Thousand Oaks, Calif.: Sage).

Strawson, P. F. (1992), *Analysis and Metaphysics* (Oxford: Oxford University Press).

—— (1956/7), 'On Building an Administrative Science', *Administrative Science Quarterly*, 1: 102–11.

—— (1967), *Organizations in Action* (New York: McGraw Hill).

Taylor, C. (1985*a*), *Human Agency and Language: Philosophical Papers, i* (Cambridge: Cambridge University Press).

—— (1985*b*), *Philosophy and the Human Sciences: Philosophical Papers, ii* (Cambridge: Cambridge University Press).

Toulmin, S. (1990), *Cosmopolis* (Chicago, Ill.: University of Chicago Press).

Tsoukas, H. (1994), 'Refining Common Sense: Types of Knowledge in Management Studies', *Journal of Management Studies*, 31: 761–80.

—— (1996), 'The Firm as a Distributed Knowledge System: A Constructionist Approach', *Strategic Management Journal*, 17 (special winter issue): 11–25.

—— (1998*a*). 'Forms of Knowledge and Forms of Life in Organized Contexts', in R. Chia (ed.), *In the Realm of Organization* (London: Routledge), 43–66.

—— (1998*b*), 'The Word and the World: A Critique of Representationalism in Management Research', *International Journal of Public Administration*, 21: 781–817.

—— (2001), 'Re-viewing Organization', *Human Relations*, 54 (special millennial issue): 7–12.

—— (2003), 'Do We Really Understand Tacit Knowledge?', in M. Easterby-Smith and M. A. Lyles (eds.), *Handbook of Organizational Learning and Knowledge* (Oxford: Blackwell), 410–27.

—— and Chia, R. (2002), 'On Organizational Becoming: Rethinking Organizational Change', *Organization Science*, 13: 567–82.

Varela, F. J., Thompson, E., and Rosch, E. (1991), *The Embodied Mind* (Cambridge, Mass.: MIT Press).

Wallerstein, I. (1999), 'Differentiation and Reconstruction in the Social Sciences', in I. Wallerstein, *The End of the World as we Know it* (Minneapolis, Minn.: University of Minnesota Press), 157–67.

Weber, M. (1947), *The Theory of Social and Economic Organization*, trans. A. M. Henderson and T. Parsons, ed. T. Parsons, (New York: Free Press).

Weick, K. (1979), *The Social Psychology of Organizing*, (New York: McGraw-Hill).

—— (1998), 'Improvisation as a Mindset for Organizational Analysis', *Organization Science*, 9: 399–405.

—— and Roberts, K. (1993), 'Collective Mind in Organizations: Heedful Interrelating on Flight Decks', *Administrative Science Quarterly*, 38: 357–81.

Wittgenstein, L. (1958), *Philosophical Investigations* (Oxford: Blackwell).

Winch, P. (1958), *The Idea of Social Science and its Relation to Philosophy* (London: Routledge & Kegan Paul).

INDEX

Morel, B. 380
Morgan, G. 100, 203, 237, 309, 323
  on change 200
  formism 302
  narratives 232, 235, 312
  qualitative approach 307, 312
  on social practice 106, 168
  on social systems 171, 172
  theory classification 299, 300, 301
Morin, E. 224
Moss, E. 99, 103
motion 187
motives 252
  reciprocal typification 73, 86
Mouzelis, N. 104, 105, 106
Mowday, R.T. 322, 328
Mulhall, S. 82
Mulkay, M. 237
multiplicative corroboration 300
Murphy, J.B. 212, 214
Mylonopoulos, N. 3, 19

Naisbitt, J. 13
Narayanan, V.K. 275
narrative approach 222, 230–56, 294
  collecting stories 234, 235
  context 247–8, 249, 256
  emplotment 246–7, 255
  narrating organizations 234–5
  narrative positions 249
  organizing as narration 234, 235
  purposes and motives 250–2, 256
  recursiveness 249–50, 252, 255, 256
  sequencing 246–7
  stock market crash 222
  storytelling organization 247
  and strategic management 315
  temporality 252–5, 256
narrative knowledge 70, 79–86, 87, 88
  and historical know-how 243
narratives
  and collective memory 84, 85, 86, 87
  complicating by 237
  and contextualism 307
  as inputs 83
  and organizational knowledge 131–2
  as repository of tacit knowledge 85–6, 87
  and rules 82
  subjunctivation of reality 290–1, 293
  utility of 83–4
nation building 266–7

Nelson, R. 95, 110, 111, 341, 349, 353, 354, 357, 370
Neustadt, R.E. 254, 255, 274, 275
Newtonian style 212, 213–16, 240, 348
Nkomo, S. 380
Nohria, N. 182, 183, 190, 381
noise 213
  and complexity 289
  and literature 286
  meaning from 285–7, 288, 293
  noisy organizations 280–94
  self-organization from 285–7
non-linearity 224, 236, 238, 239, 255
  and chaos theory 216, 217, 218
Nonaka, I. 120, 142, 143, 156, 385
  on knowledge creation 97, 117, 152
  on knowledge dependency 40
  Matsushita's Home Bakery 152–4, 155
  tacit knowledge 98, 99, 119, 151, 154, 158
Norris, C. 14
North, D. 184, 197, 389
novelty 104, 173, 211, 389
  and contextualism 305
  and information 283
  noise and 288
Nowotny, H. 328
Numagami, T. 332, 333

Oakeshott, M. 154, 155, 156
Obel, B. 70, 71, 241
objects of study and contingent existence 331
observing 322, 323, 333
  see also research
O'Connor, E.S. 235, 247, 248
Offe, C. 267
oil industry and trust 59
Olsen, J. 211, 236, 327, 380
O'Neil, O. 25, 26
Open University 174
order
  social 212
  and unpredictablity 211
O'Reilly, C. 266
organicism 301, 307–9
  and change 308
organization
  as emerging from change 186, 199
  and generalizing 124, 135
  and language communities 325–6
  in late modernity 41–52

Lightning Source UK Ltd.
Milton Keynes UK
25 June 2010

156093UK00002B/6/P